Conference on Empirical Methods in Natural Language Processing (EMNLP 2020)

Systems Demonstrations

Online
16 – 20 November 2020

ISBN: 978-1-7138-1980-6

EMNLP 2020

**The 2020 Conference on
Empirical Methods in Natural Language Processing**

Proceedings of Systems Demonstrations

November 16 – 20, 2020

Introduction

Welcome to the proceedings of the system demonstrations session. This volume contains the papers of the system demonstrations presented at the 2020 Conference on Empirical Methods in Natural Language Processing, which was held online, on November 16–20, 2020.

The system demonstrations session includes papers describing systems ranging from early research prototypes to mature production-ready software. We received 91 submissions, 10 of which were either invalid or withdrawn by the authors. Of the 81 valid submissions, 29 were selected for inclusion in the proceedings after review of three members of the program committee, achieving an overall acceptance rate of 36%.

We thank all authors for their submissions, and the 115 members of the program committee for their timely and thoughtful reviews.

David Schlangen and Qun Liu
EMNLP 2020 System Demonstration Co-Chairs

Organizers:

Qun Liu, Huawei Noah's Ark Lab, Hong Kong
David Schlangen, University of Potsdam, Germany

Program Committee:

Adrián Pastor López Monroy, Ahmed Abdelali, Alan Akbik, Ales Horak, Aljoscha Burchardt, Amy Siu, Andrea Varga, Anoop Kunchukuttan, Arushi Raghuvanshi, Barbora Hladka, Ben Hachey, Benjamin Marie, Carlos Escolano, Carlos Ramisch, Carolin Lawrence, Carsten Eickhoff, Changhan Wang, Changsong Liu, Chenchen Ding, Christos Christodoulopoulos, Clare Llewellyn, Danilo Croce, Deyi Xiong, Dezhao Song, Dian Yu, Diane Napolitano, Dimitris Galanis, Doug Downey, Eleftherios Avramidis, Eugene Kharitonov, Fabian David Schmidt, Falavigna Daniele, Fernando Alva-Manchego, Georgeta Bordea, German Rigau, Gianni Barlacchi, Guangyou Zhou, Hai Leong Chieu, Hao Li, Imed Zitouni, Irene Russo, Ivan Vladimir Meza Ruiz, Ivan Vulić, James Fan, Jenna Kanerva, John Arevalo, John Lee, Jonas Pfeiffer, Joseph P. Dexter, Juan-Manuel Torres-Moreno, Jun Araki, Jun Zhao, Koji Mineshima, Konstantinos Skianis, Leo Wanner, Leonhard Hennig, Liang-Chih Yu, Liang-Hsin Shen, Mamoru Komachi, Margot Mieskes, Marie-Jean Meurs, Marina Danilevsky, Marina Litvak, Masoud Rouhizadeh, Michael Stewart, Michal Shmueli-Scheuer, Ming Gong, Mo Yu, Montse Cuadros, Natalia Vanetik, Nicolas Rodolfo Fauceglia, Niloofar Safi Samghabadi, Oren Pereg, Pablo Ruiz Fabo, Pascual Martínez-Gómez, Patrick Ernst, Petya Osenova, Pierre Nugues, Pradipto Das, Preslav Nakov, Prokopis Prokopidis, Qiongkai Xu, Rui Wang, Sameer Singh, Sanuj Sharma, Saurav Sahay, Sebastin Santy, Seid Muhie Yimam, Shajith Ikbal, Siddharth Patwardhan, Stelios Piperidis, Stella Markantonatou, Sudipta Kar, Sunayana Sitaram, Sven Schmeier, Tae Yano, Taesun Moon, Valia Kordoni, vishwajeet kumar, Wei Lu, Wolfgang Maier, Xianpei Han, Xu Han, Youngsoo Jang, Yuanfeng Song, Yusuke Oda, Zeynep Akkalyoncu Yilmaz, Zhanming Jie, Zhe Zhao, Ziyue Wang

Table of Contents

OpenUE: An Open Toolkit of Universal Extraction from Text

Ningyu Zhang [1,2], **Shumin Deng** [1,2], **Zhen Bi** [1,2], **Haiyang Yu** [1,2], **Jiacheng Yang** [1,2],
Mosha Chen [3], **Fei Huang** [3], **Wei Zhang** [2,3], **Huajun Chen**[1,2] [*]

[1] Zhejiang University
[2] AZFT Joint Lab for Knowledge Engine
[3] Alibaba Group

{zhangningyu,231sm,21921233,yuhaiyang,21951039,huajunsir}@zju.edu.cn
{chenmosha.cms,f.huang,lantu.zw}@alibaba-inc.com

Abstract

Natural language processing covers a wide variety of tasks with token-level or sentence-level understandings. In this paper, we provide a simple insight that most tasks can be represented in a single universal extraction format. We introduce a prototype model and provide an open-source and extensible toolkit called OpenUE for various extraction tasks. OpenUE allows developers to train custom models to extract information from the text and supports quick model validation for researchers. Besides, OpenUE provides various functional modules to maintain sufficient modularity and extensibility. Except for the toolkit, we also deploy an online demo[1] with restful APIs to support real-time extraction without training and deploying. Additionally, the online system can extract information in various tasks, including relational triple extraction, slot & intent detection, event extraction, and so on. We release the source code, datasets, and pre-trained models to promote future researches in `http://github.com/zjunlp/openue`.

1 Introduction

A large number of natural language processing (NLP) tasks exist to analyze various aspects of human language. Most of them focus on token-level classification (e.g., named entity recognition, slot filling, and argument role classification) or sentence-level understanding (e.g., relation classification, intent detection, and event classification). Previous researchers usually use specifically designed neural network architectures for those tasks. Note that most of those tasks share similar encoder and decoder modules (Jiang et al., 2019). It is beneficial to achieve a unified model for all diverse information extraction tasks without task-specific architectures.

Intuitively, we rethink most of the previous tasks and find that most tasks fall in two categories: **token-oriented tasks**, where the goal is to predict labeled spans (e.g., named entities, slots, aspects) and **sentence-oriented tasks**, where the goal is to predict labels regarding the semantic understanding of sentences (e.g., relations, intents, sentiments). The commonality of these tasks inspires us whether there is a universal framework. Moreover, in the domain of efficient human annotation interfaces, it is already standard to use unified representations for a wide variety of NLP tasks. Taking the BRAT (Stenetorp et al., 2012) annotation as an example, this framework has a single unified format which consists of spans (e.g., the span of an entity), and labeled relations between the spans (e.g., "born-in" and "live-in").

Motivated by this, we formulate those tasks regarding both token and sentence as *universal extraction* and design a simple unified model. Our prototype model studies the possibility of bridging the gap between tasks with single architecture and providing future insight for unified natural language understanding. Furthermore, as there is a lack of practical and stable toolkit to support the implementation, deployment and evaluation of those tasks, we develop a toolkit which is a compliment for existing toolsets such as Spacy[2] for named entity recognition (NER), TagMe (Ferragina and Scaiella, 2010) for entity linking (EL), OpenKE (Han et al., 2018) for knowledge embedding, Stanford OpenIE (Angeli et al., 2015) for open information extraction, and OpenNER (Han et al., 2019) for relation extraction.

To be specific, we develop an open and extensible toolkit named "OpenUE". The toolkit prioritizes operational efficiency based on TensorFlow

---

[*] Corresponding author: C.Hua(huajunsir@zju.edu.cn)
[1] `http://openue.top`
[2] `https://spacy.io/`

Proceedings of the 2020 EMNLP (Systems Demonstrations), pages 1–8
November 16-20, 2020. ©2020 Association for Computational Linguistics

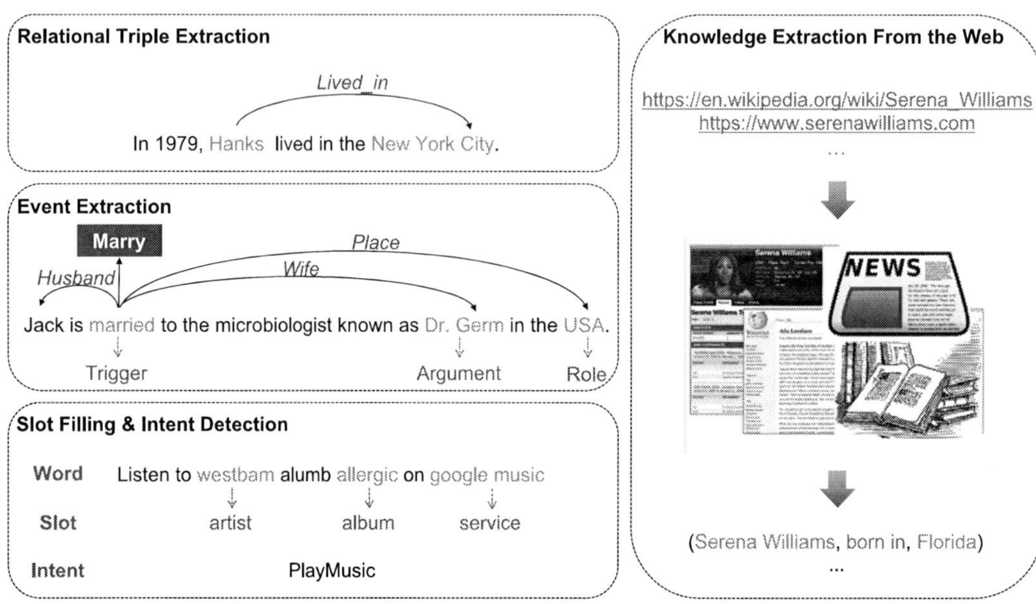

Figure 1: The examples of all application scenarios in OpenUE.

and Pytorch[3], which supports quick model training and validation. Besides, OpenUE is able to meet some individual requirements of incorporating new models with system encapsulation and model extensibility. OpenUE provides interfaces for developers aiming at custom models; thus, it is convenient to start up an extraction system based on OpenUE without writing tedious glue code and knowing too many technical details. We provide an online system to extract structured relational facts, slots as well as intents or events from the text with friendly interactive interfaces and fast reaction speed. We will provide maintenance to meet new requests, add new tasks, and fix bugs in the future. This toolkit may benefit both researchers and industry developers. We highlight our contributions as follows:

- We provide a simple prototype implementation of one single model to perform various NLP tasks.

- We provide an open and extensible toolkit to train, evaluate, and serve with multilingual support for universal extraction.

- We open-source our code and release dataset, as well as pre-trained models with open restful APIs for future researchers.

---

[3]Pytorch version is under development.

2 Application Scenarios

OpenUE is designed for various tasks, including relational triple extraction, slot filling, intent detection, event extraction, and knowledge extraction from the Web, etc. As shown in Figure 1, we give some examples of these application scenarios.

2.1 Relational Triple Extraction

Relational Triple Extraction is an essential task in Information Extraction (IE) for Natural Language Processing (NLP) and Knowledge Graph (KG) (Zhang et al., 2018b; Yu et al., 2017; Zhang et al., 2019; Huang et al., 2020; Nan et al., 2020; Zhang et al., 2020a; Ye et al., 2020; Zhang et al., 2020b), which is aimed at detecting a pair of entities along with their relations from unstructured text. For instance, there is a sentence *"Paris is known as the romantic capital of France."*, and in this example, an ideal relational triple extraction system should extract the relational triple ⟨*Paris, Capital_of, France*⟩, in which *Capital_of* is the relation between *Paris* and *France*. In this paper, we provide a simple implementation which firstly classifies relations with the sentence and then conduct sequence labeling to extract entities. The *relation first* approach is beneficial in the real-world setting as most of the sentences contain *NA* relations; therefore, openUE can filter out noisy candidates that do not have relations to improve computation efficacy.

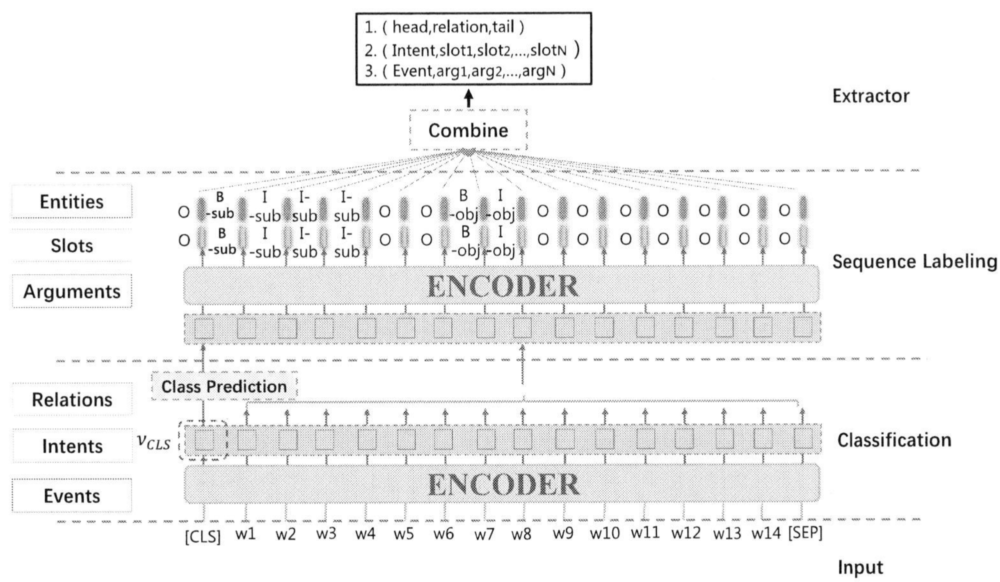

Figure 2: The architecture of OpenUE. Best view in color.

Moreover, we also provide a simple implementation of knowledge extraction from the Web. We implement crawler to obtain raw web pages and apply our approach to extract fact knowledge. Note that the recent knowledge graph is far from complete, while vast numbers of facts exist in web pages. OpenUE is suitable to serve as a schema-based never ended learner from the Web.

2.2 Event Extraction

Extracting events from natural language text is an essential yet challenging task for natural language understanding (Deng et al., 2020). When given a document, event extraction systems need to recognize event triggers with their specific types and their corresponding arguments with the roles. In real-world settings, classifying documents with specific event types and extracting arguments with role types is necessary. We integrate event extraction into OpenUE (without trigger identification).

2.3 Slot Filling and Intent Detection

Natural language understanding (NLU) is critical to the performance of goal-oriented spoken dialogue systems. NLU typically includes the intent detection and slot filling tasks, aiming to form a semantic parse for user utterances. For example, given an utterance from the user, the slot filling annotates the utterance on a word-level, indicating the slot type mentioned by a specific word such as

the slot *artist* mentioned by the word *westbam* as shown in Figure 1. At the same time, the intent detection works on the utterance-level to give intent label(s) to the whole sentence. As slot filling and intent detection rely on both token-level and sentence-level understanding, we integrate this task into OpenUE.

Note that the OpenUE can also be applied to more related tasks such as aspect-based sentiment analysis (Pontiki et al., 2016), semantic role labeling (Carreras and Màrquez, 2005), and so on.

3 Toolkit Design and Implementation

To implement a single prototype model for all tasks, we introduce our OpenUE approach, as Figure 2 shows. We design the prototype implementation with *separated sentence classification and sequence labeling modules* based the following three empirical observations: 1) joint optimization of sequence labeling and sentence classification requires labor-intensive hyper-parameters fine-tuning (Chen et al., 2019); 2) sentence classification first can filter out vast amounts of instances which can reduce computation for sequence labeling; 3) sentence labels with additional information (like a machine reading comprehension style) can provide more signals for sequence labeling (Li et al., 2019).

To design the toolkit, we build a unified underlying platform. OpenUE encapsulates various data processing and training strategies, which implies that developers can maximize the reuse of code to avoid redundant and unnecessary model implementations. We design OpenUE based on TensorFlow and PyTorch, enabling developers to train models on GPUs for operational efficiency. We introduce the model and design details in the following sections.

3.1 Tokenization

The tokenization module is designed for tokenizing input text into several tokens. In OpenUE, we implement both word-level tokenization and subword-level tokenization. These two kinds of tokenization can satisfy most tokenization demands; thus, developers can avoid spending too much time writing glue code for data processing. Developers can also build customer tokenizer by extending the `BasicTokenizer` class and implementing specific tokenization operations.

3.2 Classification

The classification module is designed for the sentence-level task. We adopt pre-trained language models as default instance encoders in OpenUE. For each sentence $x = \{w_1, w_2, \ldots, w_n\}$ in the training set, where $w_i \in x$ is the word token in sentence x, we first construct input sentence in the form: $\{[CLS], w_1, w_2, \ldots, w_n, [SEP]\}$. Then we leverage the output of [CLS] representation to encode the entire sentence information. We apply an MLP layer with a cross-entropy loss to perform sentence classification. In OpenUE, we have also implemented other common encoders such as XL-Net (Yang et al., 2019).

3.3 Sequence Labeling

The sequence labeling module is designed for the token-level task. We utilize the same encoder from the previous section to represent instance. We concatenate the output of the classification module (e.g., relations, event types or intents) with the raw sentence as input for sequence labeling. Specifically, take the relational triple extraction as an example, the input is $\{[CLS], relation, [SEP], w_1, w_2, ..., w_n\}$. To perform sequence labeling, we provide different kinds of implementations. Traditionally, when the hidden states of the words in the sentence are learned, it is convenient to apply the softmax function to obtain final logits. Moreover, we also provide sequence labeling implementations such as

CRF (Ye et al., 2009) to tag dependencies for each transition pattern between adjacent tags.

3.4 Extractor

To obtain final results, we implement an extractor module to combine the outputs of classification and sequence labeling. For entity and relation extraction, we utilize greedy methods to combine the final results. For other tasks such as slot filling and intent detection, we group those outputs as final predictions.

4 Experiment and Evaluation

In this section, we evaluate our toolkit OpenUE on several datasets in different tasks. The experimental results illustrate that our implementation with OpenUE can achieve comparable or even better performance compared to some state-of-the-art results.

4.1 Relational Triple Extraction

We carry out experiments on four datasets of relational triple extraction: NYT (Riedel et al., 2010), WebNLG (Gardent et al., 2017), SKE and ChMedIE. NYT dataset was originally produced by the distant supervision method. It consists of 1.18M sentences with 24 predefined relation types. WebNLG dataset was originally created for Natural Language Generation (NLG) tasks and adapted by (Zeng et al., 2018) for relational triple extraction task. It contains 246 predefined relation types. Different from the two previous English datasets, SKE is a Chinese dataset for information extraction, which is released in the 2019 Language and Intelligence Challenge[4]. SKE contains 50 relation types, and training texts exceed 200,000. We build our training set, development set, and test set by randomly selecting 50,000, 5,000, and 5,000 texts. ChMedIE is also a Chinese dataset for information extraction in the medical domain. We craw corpus from the Chinese health website[5] and build this dataset via distant supervision. It contains 4 relation types.

We compare our OpenUE with four baseliens. **Tagging** (Zheng et al., 2017) is an end-to-end method with a novel tagging scheme. **CopyR** (Zeng et al., 2018) is a Seq2Seq learning framework with a copy mechanism. **HRL** (Takanobu

---

[4] `http://lic2019.ccf.org.cn/kg`
[5] `http://www.39.net/`

4

Model	SNIPS-NLU			ATIS		
	Slot (F1)	Intent (Acc)	Overall (Acc)	Slot (F1)	Intent (Acc)	Overall (Acc)
CNN TriCRF	-	-	-	0.944	-	-
Joint Seq	0.873	0.969	0.732	0.942	0.926	0.807
Attention BiRNN	0.878	0.967	0.741	0.942	0.911	0.789
Slot-Gated Full Atten	0.888	0.970	0.755	0.948	0.936	0.822
Capsule-NLU	0.918	0.973	0.809	0.952	0.950	0.834
Joint-BERT	0.986	0.970	0.928	**0.975**	**0.961**	**0.882**
OpenUE	0.985	**0.988**	**0.930**	0.953	0.960	0.874

Table 1: Evaluation results of slot filling and intent detection on SNIPS-NLU and ATIS datasets.

Model	NYT	WebNLG	SKE	ChMedIE
Tagging	42.0	28.3	-	-
CopyR	58.7	37.1	-	-
HRL	68.3	66.0	-	-
CasRel	89.6	**91.8**	78.4	81.0
OpenUE	**89.9**	89.9	**79.3**	**81.2**

Table 2: Evaluation results of entity and relation extraction on NYT, WebNLG, SKE and ChMedIE datasets.

Model	ACE		DuEE	
	Type	Arg	Type	Arg
DMCNN	69.1	53.5	-	-
dbRNN	71.9	58.7	-	-
JMEE	73.7	60.3	80.2	79.5
OpenUE	**75.5**	**60.5**	**86.2**	**85.3**

Table 3: Evaluation results of event extraction extraction on ACE and DuEE datasets.

et al., 2019) addresses relation extraction by regarding related entities as the arguments of relation via hierarchical reinforcement learning. **CasRel** (Wei et al., 2019) provides a novel cascade binary tagging framework which models relations as functions that map subjects to objects in a sentence. From Table 2 we observe that OpenUE can archive comparable results with CasRel,

4.2 Event Extraction

We carry out experiments on two datasets of event extraction: ACE05 [6], DuEE. The ACE 2005 dataset annotates 33 event subtypes and 36 role classes, along with the NONE class and BIO annotation schema, we classify each sentence into 67 categories in event classification and 37 categories in argument extraction. DuEE is a Chinese dataset for event extraction, which is released in the 2020 Lan-

guage and Intelligence Challenge[7]. DuEE contains 65 event types and 121 argument roles.

We compare our OpenUE with three baseliens. **DMCNN** (Chen et al., 2015) uses dynamic multi-pooling to keep multiple events' information. **dbRNN** (Sha et al., 2018) adds dependency which bridges over Bi-LSTM for event extraction. **JMEE** (Liu et al., 2018) proposes an approach which jointly extract multiple event triggers and arguments by introducing syntactic shortcut arcs to enhance information flow and attention-based graph convolution networks to model graph information. From Table 3 we observe that OpenUE can archive comparable results with JMEE,

4.3 Slot Filling and Intent Detection

We conduct experiments on two benchmarks NLU datasets: SNIPS Natural Language Understanding benchmark[8] (SNIPS-NLU) and the Airline Travel Information Systems (ATIS) dataset (Tur et al., 2010). SNIPS-NLU dataset is collected from the Snips personal voice assistant. There are 72 slot labels and 7 intent types in the SNIPS dataset. ATIS dataset is a widely used dataset in NLU research, which includes audio recordings of people making flight reservations. There are 120 slot labels and 21 intent types in the ATIS dataset.

We compare OpenUE with six baselines as follows: **CNN TriCRF** (Xu and Sarikaya, 2013) introduces a Convolution Neural Network (CNN) based sequential labeling model for slot filling. **Joint Seq** (Hakkani-Tür et al., 2016) proposes a Recurrent Neural Network (RNN) for slot filling and utilizes the last hidden state of the RNN to pre-

---

[6] https://catalog.ldc.upenn.edu/ LDC2006T06

[7] https://aistudio.baidu.com/aistudio/ competition/detail/32

[8] https://github.com/snipsco/ nlu-benchmark/

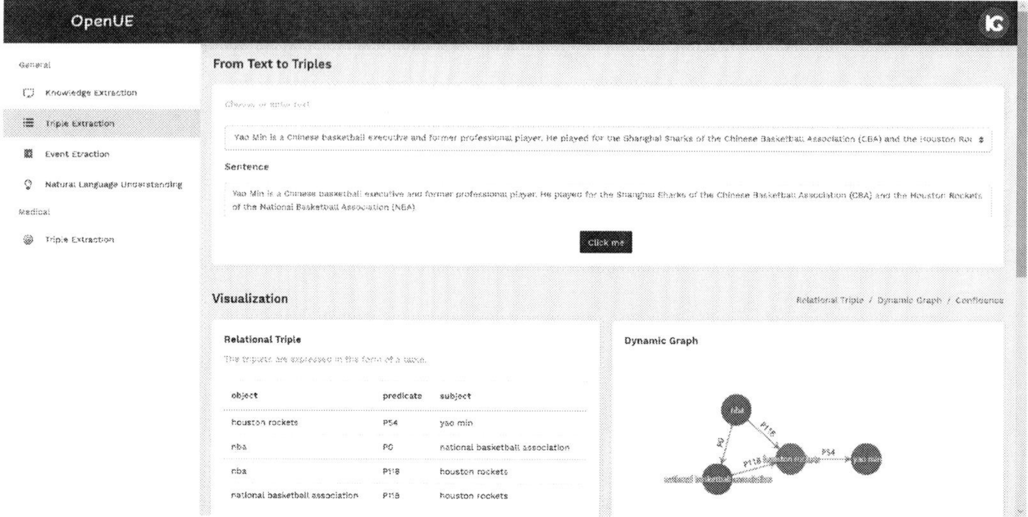

Figure 3: An example of the online system.

dict the utterance intent. **Attention BiRNN** (Liu and Lane, 2016) proposes a RNN based encoder-decoder model for joint intent detection and slot filling. **Slot-gated Full Atten** (Goo et al., 2018) proposes a slot gate that focuses on learning the relationship between intent and slot attention vectors in order to obtain better semantic frame results by the global optimization. **Capsule-NLU** (Zhang et al., 2018a) proposes a capsule-based neural network model that accomplishes slot filling and intent detection via a dynamic routing-by-agreement schema. **Joint-BERT** (Chen et al., 2019) adapts the standard BERT classification, and token classification pipeline to jointly model the slot and intent. From Table 1, we observe that OpenUE can archive comparable performance with Capsule-NLU.

In summary, we conclude that **there exist general architectures for diverse tasks and OpenUE can achieve comparable performance compared with baselines.**

5   Online System

Besides the toolkit, we also release an online system in `http://openue.top`. As shown in Figure 3, we train models in different scenarios with multi-lingual support (English and Chinese) and deploy the model for online access. The online system can be directly applied to extract structured facts, events, and slots & intents from plain text. We also visualize the graph of relational triples and the probabilities of sentence logits (e.g., relation probabilities) to help to analyze model performance.

Additionally, we deploy a schema-based never ended learner that can extract factual knowledge from the Web. Our system has already obtained millions of facts. More details can be shown in the `https://openue-docs.readthedocs.io/en/latest/`.

Moreover, we provide open restful APIs[9] for diverse tasks by OpenUE. More tasks, such as aspect-based sentiment analysis, semantic role labeling, and more domains, will be supported in the future.

6   Conclusion

We provide a simple insight that lots of NLP tasks can be represented in a single format. To this end, we provide a prototype model implementation of universal extraction and introduce an open and extensible toolkit, namely, OpenUE. We conduct extensive experiments which demonstrate that the models implemented by OpenUE are efficient, effective, and can achieve comparable performance compared to the state-of-the-art results. Furthermore, we also provide an online system with restful APIs for meeting real-time extraction without training and deploying. In the future, we plan to utilize the multitask learning or meta-learning algorithms to enhance extraction performance. We will provide long-term maintenance to fix bugs and meet new requests.

---

[9]`https://github.com/zjunlp/openue/blob/master/API.md`

Acknowledgments

We want to express gratitude to the anonymous reviewers for their hard work and kind comments, which will further improve our work in the future. This work is funded by NSFC91846204/SQ2018YFC000004/2018YFB1402800, Alibaba CangJingGe (Knowledge Engine) Research Plan.

References

Gabor Angeli, Melvin Jose Johnson Premkumar, and Christopher D Manning. 2015. Leveraging linguistic structure for open domain information extraction. In *Proceedings of the 53rd Annual Meeting of the Association for Computational Linguistics and the 7th International Joint Conference on Natural Language Processing (Volume 1: Long Papers)*, pages 344–354.

Xavier Carreras and Lluís Màrquez. 2005. Introduction to the conll-2005 shared task: Semantic role labeling. In *Proceedings of the ninth conference on computational natural language learning (CoNLL-2005)*, pages 152–164.

Qian Chen, Zhu Zhuo, and Wen Wang. 2019. Bert for joint intent classification and slot filling. *arXiv preprint arXiv:1902.10909*.

Yubo Chen, Liheng Xu, Kang Liu, Daojian Zeng, and Jun Zhao. 2015. Event extraction via dynamic multi-pooling convolutional neural networks. In *Proceedings of the 53rd Annual Meeting of the Association for Computational Linguistics and the 7th International Joint Conference on Natural Language Processing (Volume 1: Long Papers)*, pages 167–176.

Shumin Deng, Ningyu Zhang, Jiaojian Kang, Yichi Zhang, Wei Zhang, and Huajun Chen. 2020. Meta-learning with dynamic-memory-based prototypical network for few-shot event detection. In *Proceedings of the 13th International Conference on Web Search and Data Mining*, pages 151–159.

Paolo Ferragina and Ugo Scaiella. 2010. Tagme: on-the-fly annotation of short text fragments (by wikipedia entities). In *Proceedings of the 19th ACM international conference on Information and knowledge management*, pages 1625–1628.

Claire Gardent, Anastasia Shimorina, Shashi Narayan, and Laura Perez-Beltrachini. 2017. Creating training corpora for nlg micro-planning.

Chih-Wen Goo, Guang Gao, Yun-Kai Hsu, Chih-Li Huo, Tsung-Chieh Chen, Keng-Wei Hsu, and Yun-Nung Chen. 2018. Slot-gated modeling for joint slot filling and intent prediction. In *Proceedings of the 2018 Conference of the North American Chapter of the Association for Computational Linguistics: Human Language Technologies, Volume 2 (Short Papers)*, pages 753–757.

Dilek Hakkani-Tür, Gökhan Tür, Asli Celikyilmaz, Yun-Nung Chen, Jianfeng Gao, Li Deng, and Ye-Yi Wang. 2016. Multi-domain joint semantic frame parsing using bi-directional rnn-lstm. In *Interspeech*, pages 715–719.

Xu Han, Shulin Cao, Xin Lv, Yankai Lin, Zhiyuan Liu, Maosong Sun, and Juanzi Li. 2018. Openke: An open toolkit for knowledge embedding. In *Proceedings of the 2018 conference on empirical methods in natural language processing: system demonstrations*, pages 139–144.

Xu Han, Tianyu Gao, Yuan Yao, Demin Ye, Zhiyuan Liu, and Maosong Sun. 2019. Opennre: An open and extensible toolkit for neural relation extraction. *arXiv preprint arXiv:1909.13078*.

Luyang Huang, Lingfei Wu, and Lu Wang. 2020. Knowledge graph-augmented abstractive summarization with semantic-driven cloze reward. *ArXiv*, abs/2005.01159.

Zhengbao Jiang, Wei Xu, Jun Araki, and Graham Neubig. 2019. Generalizing natural language analysis through span-relation representations. *arXiv preprint arXiv:1911.03822*.

Xiaoya Li, Jingrong Feng, Yuxian Meng, Qinghong Han, Fei Wu, and Jiwei Li. 2019. A unified mrc framework for named entity recognition. *arXiv preprint arXiv:1910.11476*.

Bing Liu and Ian Lane. 2016. Attention-based recurrent neural network models for joint intent detection and slot filling. *arXiv preprint arXiv:1609.01454*.

Xiao Liu, Zhunchen Luo, and Heyan Huang. 2018. Jointly multiple events extraction via attention-based graph information aggregation. *arXiv preprint arXiv:1809.09078*.

Guoshun Nan, Zhijiang Guo, Ivan Sekulić, and Wei Lu. 2020. Reasoning with latent structure refinement for document-level relation extraction. In *In ACL*.

Maria Pontiki, Dimitrios Galanis, Haris Papageorgiou, Ion Androutsopoulos, Suresh Manandhar, Mohammad Al-Smadi, Mahmoud Al-Ayyoub, Yanyan Zhao, Bing Qin, Orphée De Clercq, et al. 2016. Semeval-2016 task 5: Aspect based sentiment analysis. In *10th International Workshop on Semantic Evaluation (SemEval 2016)*.

Sebastian Riedel, Limin Yao, and Andrew McCallum. 2010. Modeling relations and their mentions without labeled text. In *In KDD*, pages 148–163.

Lei Sha, Feng Qian, Baobao Chang, and Zhifang Sui. 2018. Jointly extracting event triggers and arguments by dependency-bridge rnn and tensor-based argument interaction. In *Thirty-Second AAAI Conference on Artificial Intelligence*.

Pontus Stenetorp, Sampo Pyysalo, Goran Topić, Tomoko Ohta, Sophia Ananiadou, and Jun'ichi Tsujii. 2012. Brat: a web-based tool for nlp-assisted text annotation. In *Proceedings of the Demonstrations at the 13th Conference of the European Chapter of the Association for Computational Linguistics*, pages 102–107.

Ryuichi Takanobu, Tianyang Zhang, Jiexi Liu, and Minlie Huang. 2019. A hierarchical framework for relation extraction with reinforcement learning. In *In AAAI*, volume 33, pages 7072–7079.

Gokhan Tur, Dilek Hakkani-Tür, and Larry Heck. 2010. What is left to be understood in atis? In *2010 IEEE Spoken Language Technology Workshop*, pages 19–24. IEEE.

Zhepei Wei, Yantao Jia, Yuan Tian, Mohammad Javad Hosseini, Mark Steedman, and Yi Chang. 2019. A novel cascade binary tagging framework for relational triple extraction. *arXiv preprint arXiv:1908.08672*.

Puyang Xu and Ruhi Sarikaya. 2013. Convolutional neural network based triangular crf for joint intent detection and slot filling. In *2013 ieee workshop on automatic speech recognition and understanding*, pages 78–83. IEEE.

Zhilin Yang, Zihang Dai, Yiming Yang, Jaime Carbonell, Russ R Salakhutdinov, and Quoc V Le. 2019. Xlnet: Generalized autoregressive pretraining for language understanding. In *Advances in neural information processing systems*, pages 5753–5763.

Hongbin Ye, Ningyu Zhang, Shumin Deng, Mosha Chen, Chuanqi Tan, Fei Huang, and Huajun Chen. 2020. Contrastive triple extraction with generative transformer. *arXiv preprint arXiv:2009.06207*.

Nan Ye, Wee S Lee, Hai L Chieu, and Dan Wu. 2009. Conditional random fields with high-order features for sequence labeling. In *Advances in neural information processing systems*, pages 2196–2204.

Mo Yu, Wenpeng Yin, Kazi Saidul Hasan, Cícero Nogueira dos Santos, Bing Xiang, and Bowen Zhou. 2017. Improved neural relation detection for knowledge base question answering. *ArXiv*, abs/1704.06194.

Xiangrong Zeng, Daojian Zeng, Shizhu He, Kang Liu, Jun Zhao, et al. 2018. Extracting relational facts by an end-to-end neural model with copy mechanism.

Chenwei Zhang, Yaliang Li, Nan Du, Wei Fan, and Philip S Yu. 2018a. Joint slot filling and intent detection via capsule neural networks. *arXiv preprint arXiv:1812.09471*.

Ningyu Zhang, Shumin Deng, Zhanlin Sun, Jiaoyan Chen, Wei Zhang, and Huajun Chen. 2020a. Relation adversarial network for low resource knowledge graph completion. In *Proceedings of The Web Conference 2020*, pages 1–12.

Ningyu Zhang, Shumin Deng, Zhanlin Sun, Guanying Wang, Xi Chen, Wei Zhang, and Huajun Chen. 2019. Long-tail relation extraction via knowledge graph embeddings and graph convolution networks. In *Proceedings of NAACL*.

Ningyu Zhang, Shumin Deng, Zhanling Sun, Xi Chen, Wei Zhang, and Huajun Chen. 2018b. Attention-based capsule networks with dynamic routing for relation extraction. In *Proceedings of EMNLP*.

Ningyu Zhang, Luoqiu Li, Shumin Deng, Haiyang Yu, Xu Cheng, Wei Zhang, and Huajun Chen. 2020b. Can fine-tuning pre-trained models lead to perfect nlp? a study of the generalizability of relation extraction. *arXiv preprint arXiv:2009.06206*.

Suncong Zheng, Yuexing Hao, Dongyuan Lu, Hongyun Bao, Jiaming Xu, Hongwei Hao, and Bo Xu. 2017. Joint entity and relation extraction based on a hybrid neural network. *Neurocomputing*, 257:59–66.

BERTweet: A pre-trained language model for English Tweets

Dat Quoc Nguyen[1], Thanh Vu[2,*] and Anh Tuan Nguyen[3,†]
[1]VinAI Research, Vietnam; [2]Oracle Digital Assistant, Oracle, Australia; [3]NVIDIA, USA
`v.datnq9@vinai.io; thanh.v.vu@oracle.com; tuananhn@nvidia.com`

Abstract

We present **BERTweet**, the *first* public large-scale pre-trained language model for English Tweets. Our BERTweet, having the same architecture as BERT$_{base}$ (Devlin et al., 2019), is trained using the RoBERTa pre-training procedure (Liu et al., 2019). Experiments show that BERTweet outperforms strong baselines RoBERTa$_{base}$ and XLM-R$_{base}$ (Conneau et al., 2020), producing better performance results than the previous state-of-the-art models on three Tweet NLP tasks: Part-of-speech tagging, Named-entity recognition and text classification. We release BERTweet under the MIT License to facilitate future research and applications on Tweet data. Our BERTweet is available at: `https://github.com/VinAIResearch/BERTweet`.

1 Introduction

The language model BERT (Devlin et al., 2019)—the Bidirectional Encoder Representations from Transformers (Vaswani et al., 2017)—and its variants have successfully helped produce new state-of-the-art performance results for various NLP tasks. Their success has largely covered the common English domains such as Wikipedia, news and books. For specific domains such as biomedical or scientific, we could retrain a domain-specific model using the BERTology architecture (Beltagy et al., 2019; Lee et al., 2019; Gururangan et al., 2020).

Twitter has been one of the most popular microblogging platforms where users can share real-time information related to all kinds of topics and events. The enormous and plentiful Tweet data has been proven to be a widely-used and real-time source of information in various important analytic tasks (Ghani et al., 2019). Note that the characteristics of Tweets are generally different from those of traditional written text such as Wikipedia and news articles, due to the typical short length of Tweets and frequent use of informal grammar as well as irregular vocabulary e.g. abbreviations, typographical errors and hashtags (Eisenstein, 2013; Han et al., 2013). Thus this might lead to a challenge in applying existing language models pre-trained on large-scale conventional text corpora with formal grammar and regular vocabulary to handle text analytic tasks on Tweet data. To the best of our knowledge, there is not an existing language model pre-trained on a large-scale corpus of English Tweets.

To fill the gap, we train the *first* large-scale language model for English Tweets using a 80GB corpus of 850M English Tweets. Our model uses the BERT$_{base}$ model configuration, trained based on the RoBERTa pre-training procedure (Liu et al., 2019). We evaluate our model and compare it with strong competitors, i.e. RoBERTa$_{base}$ and XLM-R$_{base}$ (Conneau et al., 2020), on three downstream Tweet NLP tasks: Part-of-speech (POS) tagging, Named-entity recognition (NER) and text classification. Experiments show that our model outperforms RoBERTa$_{base}$ and XLM-R$_{base}$ as well as the previous state-of-the-art (SOTA) models on all these tasks. Our contributions are as follows:

- We present the first large-scale pre-trained language model for English Tweets.

- Our model does better than its competitors RoBERTa$_{base}$ and XLM-R$_{base}$ and outperforms previous SOTA models on three downstream Tweet NLP tasks of POS tagging, NER and text classification, thus confirming the effectiveness of the large-scale and domain-specific language model pre-trained for English Tweets.

- We also provide the first set of experiments investigating whether a commonly used approach of applying lexical normalization dictionaries on Tweets (Han et al., 2012) would help im-

---

*Most of the work done when Thanh Vu was at the Australian e-Health Research Centre, CSIRO, Australia.

†Work done during internship at VinAI Research.

9

Proceedings of the 2020 EMNLP (Systems Demonstrations), pages 9–14
November 16-20, 2020. ©2020 Association for Computational Linguistics

prove the performance of the pre-trained language models on the downstream tasks.

- We publicly release our model under the name BERTweet which can be used with `fairseq` (Ott et al., 2019) and `transformers` (Wolf et al., 2019). We hope that BERTweet can serve as a strong baseline for future research and applications of Tweet analytic tasks.

2 BERTweet

In this section, we outline the architecture, and describe the pre-training data and optimization setup that we use for BERTweet.

Architecture

Our BERTweet uses the same architecture as $\text{BERT}_{\text{base}}$, which is trained with a masked language modeling objective (Devlin et al., 2019). BERTweet pre-training procedure is based on RoBERTa (Liu et al., 2019) which optimizes the BERT pre-training approach for more robust performance. Given the widespread usage of BERT and RoBERTa, we do not detail the architecture here. See Devlin et al. (2019) and Liu et al. (2019) for more details.

Pre-training data

We use an 80GB pre-training dataset of uncompressed texts, containing 850M Tweets (16B word tokens). Here, each Tweet consists of at least 10 and at most 64 word tokens. In particular, this dataset is a concatenation of two corpora:

- We first download the general Twitter Stream grabbed by the Archive Team,[1] containing 4TB of Tweet data streamed from 01/2012 to 08/2019 on Twitter. To identify English Tweets, we employ the language identification component of fastText (Joulin et al., 2017). We tokenize those English Tweets using "TweetTokenizer" from the NLTK toolkit (Bird et al., 2009) and use the `emoji` package to translate emotion icons into text strings (here, each icon is referred to as a word token).[2] We also normalize the Tweets by converting user mentions and web/url links into special tokens `@USER` and `HTTPURL`, respectively. We filter out retweeted Tweets and the ones shorter than 10 or longer than 64 word tokens. This pre-process results in the first corpus of 845M English Tweets.

- We also stream Tweets related to the COVID-19 pandemic, available from 01/2020 to 03/2020.[3] We apply the same data pre-process step as described above, thus resulting in the second corpus of 5M English Tweets.

We then apply `fastBPE` (Sennrich et al., 2016) to segment all 850M Tweets with subword units, using a vocabulary of 64K subword types. On average there are 25 subword tokens per Tweet.

Optimization

We utilize the RoBERTa implementation in the `fairseq` library (Ott et al., 2019). We set a maximum sequence length at 128, thus generating 850M × 25 / 128 ≈ 166M sequence blocks. Following Liu et al. (2019), we optimize the model using Adam (Kingma and Ba, 2014), and use a batch size of 7K across 8 V100 GPUs (32GB each) and a peak learning rate of 0.0004. We pre-train BERTweet for 40 epochs in about 4 weeks (here, we use the first 2 epochs for warming up the learning rate), equivalent to 166M × 40 / 7K ≈ 950K training steps.

3 Experimental setup

We evaluate and compare the performance of BERTweet with strong baselines on three downstream NLP tasks of POS tagging, NER and text classification, using benchmark Tweet datasets.

Downstream task datasets

For POS tagging, we use three datasets Ritter11-T-POS (Ritter et al., 2011), ARK-Twitter[4] (Gimpel et al., 2011; Owoputi et al., 2013) and TWEEBANK-V2[5] (Liu et al., 2018). For NER, we employ datasets from the WNUT16 NER shared task (Strauss et al., 2016) and the WNUT17 shared task on novel and emerging entity recognition (Derczynski et al., 2017). For text classification, we employ the 3-class sentiment analysis dataset from the SemEval2017 Task 4A (Rosenthal et al., 2017) and the 2-class irony detection dataset from the SemEval2018 Task 3A (Van Hee et al., 2018).

For Ritter11-T-POS, we employ a 70/15/15 training/validation/test pre-split available from Gui et al. (2017).[6] ARK-Twitter contains two

---

[1] `https://archive.org/details/twitterstream`

[2] `https://pypi.org/project/emoji`

[3] We collect Tweets containing at least one of 11 COVID-19 related keywords, e.g. covid19, coronavirus, sars-cov-2.

[4] `https://code.google.com/archive/p/ark-tweet-nlp/downloads` (twpos-data-v0.3.tgz)

[5] `https://github.com/Oneplus/Tweebank`

[6] `https://github.com/guitaowufeng/TPANN`

files `daily547.conll` and `oct27.conll` in which `oct27.conll` is further split into files `oct27.traindev` and `oct27.test`. Following Owoputi et al. (2013) and Gui et al. (2017), we employ `daily547.conll` as a test set. In addition, we use `oct27.traindev` and `oct27.test` as training and validation sets, respectively. For the TWEEBANK-V2, WNUT16 and WNUT17 datasets, we use their existing training/validation/test split. The SemEval2017-Task4A and SemEval2018-Task3A datasets are provided with training and test sets only (i.e. there is not a standard split for validation), thus we sample 10% of the training set for validation and use the remaining 90% for training.

We use a "soft" normalization strategy to all of the experimental datasets by translating word tokens of user mentions and web/url links into special tokens `@USER` and `HTTPURL`, respectively, and converting emotion icon tokens into corresponding strings. We also apply a "hard" strategy by further applying lexical normalization dictionaries (Aramaki, 2010; Liu et al., 2012; Han et al., 2012) to normalize word tokens in Tweets.

Fine-tuning

Following Devlin et al. (2019), for POS tagging and NER, we append a linear prediction layer on top of the last Transformer layer of BERTweet with regards to the first subword of each word token, while for text classification we append a linear prediction layer on top of the pooled output.

We employ the `transformers` library (Wolf et al., 2019) to independently fine-tune BERTweet for each task and each dataset in 30 training epochs. We use AdamW (Loshchilov and Hutter, 2019) with a fixed learning rate of 1.e-5 and a batch size of 32 (Liu et al., 2019). We compute the task performance after each training epoch on the validation set (here, we apply early stopping when no improvement is observed after 5 continuous epochs), and select the best model checkpoint to compute the performance score on the test set.

We repeat this fine-tuning process 5 times with different random seeds, i.e. 5 runs for each task and each dataset. We report each final test result as an average over the test scores from the 5 runs.

Baselines

Our main competitors are the pre-trained language models RoBERTa$_{base}$ (Liu et al., 2019) and XLM-R$_{base}$ (Conneau et al., 2020), which

Model	Ritter11		ARK		TB-v2	
	soft	hard	soft	hard	soft	hard
RoBERTa$_{large}$	91.7	91.5	93.7	93.2	94.9	94.6
XLM-R$_{large}$	92.6	92.1	94.2	93.8	95.5	95.1
RoBERTa$_{base}$	88.7	88.3	91.8	91.6	93.7	93.5
XLM-R$_{base}$	**90.4**	**90.3**	92.8	92.6	94.7	94.3
BERTweet	90.1	89.5	**94.1**	**93.4**	**95.2**	**94.7**
DCNN (Gui et al.)	89.9		–		–	
DCNN (Gui et al.)	91.2 [+a]		92.4 [+a+b]		–	
TPANN	90.9 [+a]		92.8 [+a+b]		–	
ARKtagger	90.4		93.2 [+b]		94.6 [+c]	
BiLSTM-CNN-CRF	–		–		92.5 [+c]	

Table 1: POS tagging accuracy results on the Ritter11-T-POS (Ritter11), ARK-Twitter (ARK) and TWEEBANK-V2 (TB-v2) test sets. Result of ARK-tagger (Owoputi et al., 2013) on Ritter11 is reported in the TPANN paper (Gui et al., 2017). Note that Ritter11 uses Twitter-specific POS tags for retweeted (RT), user-account, hashtag and url word tokens which can be tagged perfectly using some simple regular expressions. Therefore, we follow Gui et al. (2017) and Gui et al. (2018) to tag those words appropriately for all models. Results of ARKtagger and BiLSTM-CNN-CRF (Ma and Hovy, 2016) on TB-v2 are reported by Liu et al. (2018). Also note that "+a", "+b" and "+c" denote the additional use of extra training data, i.e. models trained on bigger training data. "+a": additional use of the POS annotated data from the English WSJ Penn treebank sections 00-24 (Marcus et al., 1993). "+b": the use of both training and validation sets for learning models. "+c": additional use of the POS annotated data from the UD_English-EWT training set (Silveira et al., 2014).

have the same architecture configuration as our BERTweet. In addition, we also evaluate the pretrained RoBERTa$_{large}$ and XLM-R$_{large}$ although it is not a fair comparison due to their significantly larger model configurations.

The pre-trained RoBERTa is a strong language model for English, learned from 160GB of texts covering books, Wikipedia, CommonCrawl news, CommonCrawl stories, and web text contents. XLM-R is a cross-lingual variant of RoBERTa, trained on a 2.5TB multilingual corpus which contains 301GB of English CommonCrawl texts.

We fine-tune RoBERTa and XLM-R using the same fine-tuning approach we use for BERTweet.

4 Experimental results

Main results

Tables 1, 2, 3 and 4 present our obtained scores for BERTweet and baselines regarding both "soft" and "hard" normalization strategies. We find that for

Model	WNUT16		WNUT17			
			entity		surface	
	soft	hard	soft	hard	soft	hard
RoBERTa$_{large}$	55.4	54.8	56.9	57.0	55.6	55.6
XLM-R$_{large}$	55.8	55.3	57.1	57.5	55.9	56.4
RoBERTa$_{base}$	49.7	49.2	52.2	52.0	51.2	51.0
XLM-R$_{base}$	49.9	49.4	53.5	53.0	51.9	51.6
BERTweet	**52.1**	**51.3**	**56.5**	**55.6**	**55.1**	**54.1**
CambridgeLTL	52.4 [+b]		–		–	
DATNet (Zhou et al.)	53.0 [+b]		42.3		–	
Aguilar et al. (2017)	–		41.9		40.2	

Rows under "Our results": RoBERTa$_{large}$, XLM-R$_{large}$, RoBERTa$_{base}$, XLM-R$_{base}$, BERTweet.

Table 2: F1 scores on the WNUT16 and WNUT17 test sets. CambridgeLTL result is reported by Limsopatham and Collier (2016). "entity" and "surface" denote the scores computed for the standard entity level and the surface level (Derczynski et al., 2017), respectively.

Model	AvgRec		F_1^{NP}		Accuracy	
	soft	hard	soft	hard	soft	hard
RoBERTa$_{large}$	72.5	72.2	72.0	71.8	70.7	71.3
XLM-R$_{large}$	71.7	71.7	71.1	70.9	70.7	70.6
RoBERTa$_{base}$	71.6	71.8	71.2	71.2	71.6	70.9
XLM-R$_{base}$	70.3	70.3	69.4	69.6	69.3	69.7
BERTweet	**73.2**	**72.8**	**72.8**	**72.5**	**71.7**	**72.0**
Cliche (2017)	68.1		68.5		65.8	
Baziotis et al. (2017)	68.1		67.7		65.1	

Rows under "Our results": RoBERTa$_{large}$, XLM-R$_{large}$, RoBERTa$_{base}$, XLM-R$_{base}$, BERTweet.

Table 3: Performance scores on the SemEval2017-Task4A test set. See Rosenthal et al. (2017) for the definitions of the AvgRec and F_1^{NP} metrics, in which AvgRec is the main ranking metric.

Model	F_1^{pos}		Accuracy	
	soft	hard	soft	hard
RoBERTa$_{large}$	73.2	71.9	76.5	75.1
XLM-R$_{large}$	70.8	69.7	74.2	73.2
RoBERTa$_{base}$	71.0	71.2	74.0	74.0
XLM-R$_{base}$	66.6	66.2	70.8	70.8
BERTweet	**74.6**	**74.3**	**78.2**	**78.2**
Wu et al. (2018)	70.5		73.5	
Baziotis et al. (2018)	67.2		73.2	

Rows under "Our results": RoBERTa$_{large}$, XLM-R$_{large}$, RoBERTa$_{base}$, XLM-R$_{base}$, BERTweet.

Table 4: Performance scores on the SemEval2018-Task3A test set. F_1^{pos}—the main ranking metric—denotes the F_1 score computed for the positive label.

each pre-trained language model the "soft" scores are generally higher than the corresponding "hard" scores, i.e. applying lexical normalization dictionaries to normalize word tokens in Tweets generally does not help improve the performance of the pre-trained language models on downstream tasks.

Our BERTweet outperforms its main competitors RoBERTa$_{base}$ and XLM-R$_{base}$ on all experimental datasets (with only one exception that XLM-R$_{base}$ does slightly better than BERTweet on Ritter11-T-POS). Compared to RoBERTa$_{large}$ and XLM-R$_{large}$ which use significantly larger model configurations, we find that they obtain better POS tagging and NER scores than BERTweet. However, BERTweet performs better than those large models on the two text classification datasets.

Tables 1, 2, 3 and 4 also compare our obtained scores with the previous highest reported results on the same test sets. Clearly, the pre-trained language models help achieve new SOTA results on all experimental datasets. Specifically, BERTweet improves the previous SOTA in the novel and emerging entity recognition by absolute 14+% on the WNUT17 dataset, and in text classification by 5% and 4% on the SemEval2017-Task4A and SemEval2018-Task3A test sets, respectively. Our results confirm the effectiveness of the large-scale BERTweet for Tweet NLP.

Discussion

Our results comparing the "soft" and "hard" normalization strategies with regards to the pre-trained language models confirm the previous view that lexical normalization on Tweets is a lossy translation task (Owoputi et al., 2013). We find that RoBERTa outperforms XLM-R on the text classification datasets. This finding is similar to what is found in the XLM-R paper (Conneau et al., 2020) where XLM-R obtains lower performance scores than RoBERTa for sequence classification tasks on traditional written English corpora.

We also recall that although RoBERTa and XLM-R use 160 / 80 = 2 times and 301 / 80 ≈ 3.75 times bigger English data than our BERTweet, respectively, BERTweet does better than its competitors RoBERTa$_{base}$ and XLM-R$_{base}$. Thus this confirms the effectiveness of a large-scale and domain-specific pre-trained language model for English Tweets. In future work, we will release a "large" version of BERTweet, which possibly performs better than RoBERTa$_{large}$ and XLM-R$_{large}$ on all three evaluation tasks.

5 Conclusion

We have presented the first large-scale language model BERTweet pre-trained for English Tweets. We demonstrate the usefulness of BERTweet by showing that BERTweet outperforms its baselines RoBERTa$_{base}$ and XLM-R$_{base}$ and helps produce better performances than the previous SOTA models for three downstream Tweet NLP tasks of POS tagging, NER, and text classification (i.e. sentiment analysis & irony detection).

As of September 2020, we have collected a corpus of about 23M "cased" COVID-19 English Tweets consisting of at least 10 and at most 64 word tokens. In addition, we also create an "uncased" version of this corpus. Then we continue pre-training from our pre-trained BERTweet on each of the "cased" and "uncased" corpora of 23M Tweets for 40 additional epochs, resulting in two BERTweet variants of pre-trained "cased" and "uncased" *BERTweet-COVID19* models, respectively. By publicly releasing BERTweet and its two variants, we hope that they can foster future research and applications of Tweet analytic tasks, such as identifying informative COVID-19 Tweets (Nguyen et al., 2020) or extracting COVID-19 events from Tweets (Zong et al., 2020).

References

Gustavo Aguilar, Suraj Maharjan, Adrian Pastor López-Monroy, and Thamar Solorio. 2017. A Multi-task Approach for Named Entity Recognition in Social Media Data. In *Proceedings of WNUT*, pages 148–153.

Eiji Aramaki. 2010. TYPO CORPUS. http://luululu.com/tweet/.

Christos Baziotis, Athanasiou Nikolaos, Pinelopi Papalampidi, Athanasia Kolovou, Georgios Paraskevopoulos, Nikolaos Ellinas, and Alexandros Potamianos. 2018. NTUA-SLP at SemEval-2018 task 3: Tracking ironic tweets using ensembles of word and character level attentive RNNs. In *Proceedings of SemEval*, pages 613–621.

Christos Baziotis, Nikos Pelekis, and Christos Doulkeridis. 2017. DataStories at SemEval-2017 task 4: Deep LSTM with attention for message-level and topic-based sentiment analysis. In *Proceedings of SemEval*, pages 747–754.

Iz Beltagy, Kyle Lo, and Arman Cohan. 2019. SciBERT: A pretrained language model for scientific text. In *Proceedings of EMNLP-IJCNLP*, pages 3615–3620.

Steven Bird, Ewan Klein, and Edward Loper, editors. 2009. *Natural language processing with Python*. O'Reilly.

Mathieu Cliche. 2017. BB_twtr at SemEval-2017 task 4: Twitter sentiment analysis with CNNs and LSTMs. In *Proceedings of SemEval*, pages 573–580.

Alexis Conneau, Kartikay Khandelwal, Naman Goyal, Vishrav Chaudhary, Guillaume Wenzek, Francisco Guzmán, Edouard Grave, Myle Ott, Luke Zettlemoyer, and Veselin Stoyanov. 2020. Unsupervised Cross-lingual Representation Learning at Scale. In *Proceedings of ACL*, page to appear.

Leon Derczynski, Eric Nichols, Marieke van Erp, and Nut Limsopatham. 2017. Results of the WNUT2017 Shared Task on Novel and Emerging Entity Recognition. In *Proceedings of WNUT*, pages 140–147.

Jacob Devlin, Ming-Wei Chang, Kenton Lee, and Kristina Toutanova. 2019. BERT: Pre-training of deep bidirectional transformers for language understanding. In *Proceedings of NAACL*, pages 4171–4186.

Jacob Eisenstein. 2013. What to do about bad language on the internet. In *Proceedings of NAACL-HLT*, pages 359–369.

Norjihan Abdul Ghani, Suraya Hamid, Ibrahim Abaker Targio Hashem, and Ejaz Ahmed. 2019. Social media big data analytics: A survey. *Comput. Hum. Behav.*, 101:417–428.

Kevin Gimpel, Nathan Schneider, Brendan O'Connor, Dipanjan Das, Daniel Mills, Jacob Eisenstein, Michael Heilman, Dani Yogatama, Jeffrey Flanigan, and Noah A. Smith. 2011. Part-of-Speech Tagging for Twitter: Annotation, Features, and Experiments. In *Proceedings of ACL-HLT*, pages 42–47.

Tao Gui, Qi Zhang, Jingjing Gong, Minlong Peng, Di Liang, Keyu Ding, and Xuanjing Huang. 2018. Transferring from Formal Newswire Domain with Hypernet for Twitter POS Tagging. In *Proceedings of EMNLP*, pages 2540–2549.

Tao Gui, Qi Zhang, Haoran Huang, Minlong Peng, and Xuanjing Huang. 2017. Part-of-Speech Tagging for Twitter with Adversarial Neural Networks. In *Proceedings of EMNLP*, pages 2411–2420.

Suchin Gururangan, Ana Marasović, Swabha Swayamdipta, Kyle Lo, Iz Beltagy, Doug Downey, and Noah A. Smith. 2020. Don't Stop Pretraining: Adapt Language Models to Domains and Tasks. In *Proceedings of ACL*, pages 8342–8360.

Bo Han, Paul Cook, and Timothy Baldwin. 2012. Automatically Constructing a Normalisation Dictionary for Microblogs. In *Proceedings of EMNLP-CoNLL*, pages 421–432.

Bo Han, Paul Cook, and Timothy Baldwin. 2013. Lexical Normalization for Social Media Text. *ACM Transactions on Intelligent Systems and Technology*, 4(1).

Armand Joulin, Edouard Grave, Piotr Bojanowski, and Tomas Mikolov. 2017. Bag of tricks for efficient text classification. In *Proceedings of EACL*, pages 427–431.

Diederik P. Kingma and Jimmy Ba. 2014. Adam: A Method for Stochastic Optimization. *arXiv preprint*, arXiv:1412.6980.

Jinhyuk Lee, Wonjin Yoon, Sungdong Kim, Donghyeon Kim, Sunkyu Kim, Chan Ho So, and Jaewoo Kang. 2019. BioBERT: a pre-trained biomedical language representation model for biomedical text mining. *Bioinformatics*, page btz682.

Nut Limsopatham and Nigel Collier. 2016. Bidirectional LSTM for Named Entity Recognition in Twitter Messages. In *Proceedings of WNUT*, pages 145–152.

Fei Liu, Fuliang Weng, and Xiao Jiang. 2012. A Broad-Coverage Normalization System for Social Media Language. In *Proceedings of ACL*, pages 1035–1044.

Yijia Liu, Yi Zhu, Wanxiang Che, Bing Qin, Nathan Schneider, and Noah A. Smith. 2018. Parsing Tweets into Universal Dependencies. In *Proceedings of NAACL-HLT*, pages 965–975.

Yinhan Liu, Myle Ott, Naman Goyal, Jingfei Du, Mandar Joshi, Danqi Chen, Omer Levy, Mike Lewis, Luke Zettlemoyer, and Veselin Stoyanov. 2019. RoBERTa: A Robustly Optimized BERT Pretraining Approach. *arXiv preprint*, arXiv:1907.11692.

Ilya Loshchilov and Frank Hutter. 2019. Decoupled Weight Decay Regularization. In *Proceedings of ICLR*.

Xuezhe Ma and Eduard Hovy. 2016. End-to-end sequence labeling via bi-directional LSTM-CNNs-CRF. In *Proceedings of ACL*, pages 1064–1074.

Mitchell P. Marcus, Beatrice Santorini, and Mary Ann Marcinkiewicz. 1993. Building a Large Annotated Corpus of English: The Penn Treebank. *Computational Linguistics*, 19(2):313–330.

Dat Quoc Nguyen, Thanh Vu, Afshin Rahimi, Mai Hoang Dao, Linh The Nguyen, and Long Doan. 2020. WNUT-2020 Task 2: Identification of Informative COVID-19 English Tweets. In *Proceedings of WNUT*.

Myle Ott, Sergey Edunov, Alexei Baevski, Angela Fan, Sam Gross, Nathan Ng, David Grangier, and Michael Auli. 2019. fairseq: A Fast, Extensible Toolkit for Sequence Modeling. In *Proceedings of NAACL-HLT 2019: Demonstrations*, pages 48–53.

Olutobi Owoputi, Brendan O'Connor, Chris Dyer, Kevin Gimpel, Nathan Schneider, and Noah A. Smith. 2013. Improved Part-of-Speech Tagging for Online Conversational Text with Word Clusters. In *Proceedings of NAACL-HLT*, pages 380–390.

Alan Ritter, Sam Clark, Mausam, and Oren Etzioni. 2011. Named Entity Recognition in Tweets: An Experimental Study. In *Proceedings of EMNLP*, pages 1524–1534.

Sara Rosenthal, Noura Farra, and Preslav Nakov. 2017. SemEval-2017 Task 4: Sentiment Analysis in Twitter. In *Proceedings of SemEval*, pages 502–518.

Rico Sennrich, Barry Haddow, and Alexandra Birch. 2016. Neural Machine Translation of Rare Words with Subword Units. In *Proceedings of ACL*, pages 1715–1725.

Natalia Silveira, Timothy Dozat, Marie-Catherine de Marneffe, Samuel Bowman, Miriam Connor, John Bauer, and Christopher D. Manning. 2014. A gold standard dependency corpus for English. In *Proceedings of LREC*.

Benjamin Strauss, Bethany Toma, Alan Ritter, Marie-Catherine de Marneffe, and Wei Xu. 2016. Results of the WNUT16 Named Entity Recognition Shared Task. In *Proceedings of WNUT*, pages 138–144.

Cynthia Van Hee, Els Lefever, and Véronique Hoste. 2018. SemEval-2018 Task 3: Irony Detection in English Tweets. In *Proceedings of SemEval*, pages 39–50.

Ashish Vaswani, Noam Shazeer, Niki Parmar, Jakob Uszkoreit, Llion Jones, Aidan N Gomez, Łukasz Kaiser, and Illia Polosukhin. 2017. Attention is All you Need. In *Advances in Neural Information Processing Systems 30*, pages 5998–6008.

Thomas Wolf, Lysandre Debut, Victor Sanh, Julien Chaumond, Clement Delangue, Anthony Moi, Pierric Cistac, Tim Rault, R'emi Louf, Morgan Funtowicz, and Jamie Brew. 2019. HuggingFace's Transformers: State-of-the-art Natural Language Processing. *arXiv preprint*, arXiv:1910.03771.

Chuhan Wu, Fangzhao Wu, Sixing Wu, Junxin Liu, Zhigang Yuan, and Yongfeng Huang. 2018. THU_NGN at SemEval-2018 task 3: Tweet irony detection with densely connected LSTM and multitask learning. In *Proceedings of SemEval*, pages 51–56.

Joey Tianyi Zhou, Hao Zhang, Di Jin, Hongyuan Zhu, Meng Fang, Rick Siow Mong Goh, and Kenneth Kwok. 2019. Dual Adversarial Neural Transfer for Low-Resource Named Entity Recognition. In *Proceedings of ACL*, pages 3461–3471.

Shi Zong, Ashutosh Baheti, Wei Xu, and Alan Ritter. 2020. Extracting COVID-19 Events from Twitter. *arXiv preprint*, arXiv:2006.02567.

NeuralQA: A Usable Library for Question Answering (Contextual Query Expansion + BERT) on Large Datasets

Victor Dibia

Cloudera Fast Forward Labs

vdibia@cloudera.com

Abstract

Existing tools for Question Answering (QA) have challenges that limit their use in practice. They can be complex to set up or integrate with existing infrastructure, do not offer configurable interactive interfaces, and do not cover the full set of subtasks that frequently comprise the QA pipeline (query expansion, retrieval, reading, and explanation/sensemaking). To help address these issues, we introduce NeuralQA - a usable library for QA on large datasets. NeuralQA integrates well with existing infrastructure (e.g., ElasticSearch instances and reader models trained with the HuggingFace Transformers API) and offers helpful defaults for QA subtasks. It introduces and implements contextual query expansion (CQE) using a masked language model (MLM) as well as relevant snippets ($RelSnip$) - a method for condensing large documents into smaller passages that can be speedily processed by a document reader model. Finally, it offers a flexible user interface to support workflows for research explorations (e.g., visualization of gradient-based explanations to support qualitative inspection of model behaviour) and large scale search deployment. Code and documentation for NeuralQA is available as open source on Github.

1 Introduction

The capability of providing *exact* answers to queries framed as natural language questions can significantly improve the user experience in many real world applications. Rather than sifting through lists of retrieved documents, automatic QA (also known as reading comprehension) systems can surface an exact answer to a query, thus reducing the cognitive burden associated with the standard search task. This capability is applicable in extending conventional information retrieval systems (search engines) and also for emergent use cases,

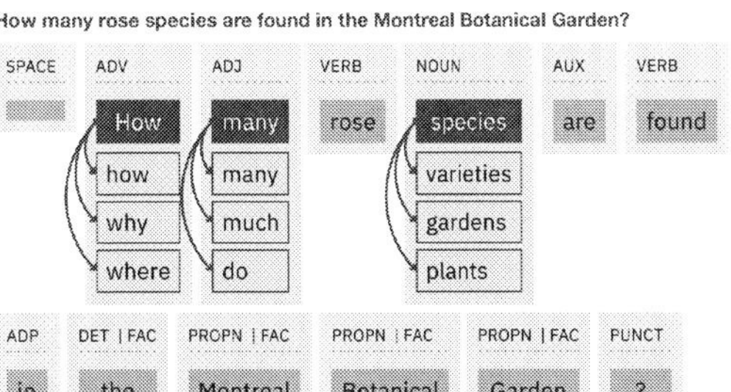

Figure 1: NeuralQA implements Contextual Query Expansion (CQE 3.2.1) using Masked Language Models (MLM) and offers a visualization to explain behaviour. A rule set is used to determine which tokens are *candidates* for expansion (solid blue box); each *candidate* is iteratively masked, and an MLM is used to identify expansion terms (blue outline box).

such as open domain conversational AI systems (Gao et al., 2018; Qu et al., 2019). For enterprises, QA systems that are both fast and precise can help unlock knowledge value in large unstructured document collections. Conventional methods for open domain QA (Yang et al., 2015, 2019) follow a two-stage implementation - (i) a **retriever** that returns a subset of relevant documents. Retrieval is typically based on sparse vector space models such as BM25 (Robertson and Zaragoza, 2009) and TF-IDF (Chen et al., 2017); (ii) a machine reading comprehension model (**reader**) that identifies spans from each document which contain the answer. While sparse representations are fast to compute, they rely on exact keyword match, and suffer from the *vocabulary mismatch* problem - scenarios where the vocabulary used to express a query is different from the vocabulary used to express the same concepts within the documents. To address these issues, recent studies have proposed neural ranking (Lee et al., 2018; Kratzwald et al., 2019) and retrieval methods (Karpukhin et al., 2020; Lee et al., 2019; Guu et al.,

Proceedings of the 2020 EMNLP (Systems Demonstrations), pages 15–22

November 16-20, 2020. ©2020 Association for Computational Linguistics

2020), which rely on dense representations.

However, while dense representations show significantly improved results, they introduce additional complexity and latency, which limits their practical application. For example, Guu et al. (2020) require a specialized MLM pretraining regime, as well as a supervised fine-tuning step, to obtain representations used in a retriever. Similarly Karpukhin et al. (2020) use dual encoders in learning a dense representation for queries and all documents in the target corpus. Each of these methods require additional infrastructure to compute dense representation vectors for all documents in the target corpus as well as implement efficient similarity search at run time. In addition, transformer-based architectures (Vaswani et al., 2017) used for dense representations are unable to process long sequences due to their self-attention operations which scale quadratically with sequence length. As a result, these models require that documents are indexed/stored in small paragraphs. For many use cases, meeting these requirements (rebuilding retriever indexes, training models to learn corpus specific representations, precomputing representations for all indexed documents) can be cost-intensive. These costs are hard to justify, given that simpler methods can yield comparable results (Lin, 2019; Weissenborn et al., 2017). Furthermore, as reader models are applied to domain-specific documents, they fail in counter-intuitive ways. It is thus valuable to offer visual interfaces that support debugging or sensemaking of results (e.g., explanations for *why* a set of documents were retrieved or *why* an answer span was selected from a document). While several libraries exist to explain NLP models, they do not integrate interfaces that help users make sense of both the query expansion, retriever and the reader tasks. Collectively, these challenges can hamper experimentation with QA systems and the integration of QA models into practitioner workflows.

In this work, we introduce NeuralQA to help address these limitations. Our contributions are summarized as follows:

- An easy to use, end-to-end library for implementing QA systems. It integrates methods for query expansion, document retrieval (ElasticSearch[1]), and document reading (QA models trained using the HuggingFace Transformers API (Wolf et al., 2019)). It also offers an

interactive user interface for sensemaking of results (retriever + reader). NeuralQA is open source and released under the MIT License.

- To address the vocabulary mismatch problem, NeuralQA introduces and implements a method for contextual query expansion (CQE), using a masked language model (MLM) fine-tuned on the target document corpus (see Fig 1). Early qualitative results show CQE can surface relevant additional query terms that help improve recall and require minimal changes for integration with existing retrieval infrastructure.

- In addition, we implement $RelSnip$, a simple method for extracting relevant snippets from retrieved passages before feeding it into a document reader. This, in turn, reduces the latency required to chunk and read lengthy documents. Importantly, these options offer the opportunity to improve latency and recall, with no changes to existing retriever infrastructure.

Overall, NeuralQA complements a line of end-to-end applications that improve QA system deployment (Akkalyoncu Yilmaz et al., 2019; Yang et al., 2019) and provide visual interfaces for understanding machine learning models (Wallace et al., 2019; Strobelt et al., 2018; Madsen, 2019; Dibia, 2020a,b).

2 The Question Answering Pipeline

There are several subtasks that frequently comprise the QA pipeline and are implemented in NeuralQA.

2.1 Document Retrieval

The first stage in the QA process focuses on retrieving a list of candidate passages, which are subsequently processed by a reader. Conventional approaches to QA apply representations from sparse vector space models (e.g., BM25, TF-IDF) in identifying the most relevant document candidates. For example, Chen et al. (2017) introduce an end-to-end system combining TF-IDF retrieval with a multi-layer RNN for document reading. This is further improved upon by Yang et al. (2019), who utilize BM25 for retrieval with a modern BERT transformer reader. However, sparse representations are keyword dependent, and suffer from the *vocabulary mismatch* problem in information retrieval (IR); given a query Q and a relevant document D, a sparse retrieval method may fail to retrieve D if D

---

[1]ElasticSearch https://www.elastic.co

uses a different vocabulary to refer to the same content in Q. Furthermore, given that QA queries are under-specified by definition (users are searching for unknown information), sparse representations may lack the contextual information needed to retrieve the most relevant documents. To address these issues, a set of related work has focused on methods for re-ranking retrieved documents to improve recall (Wang et al., 2018; Kratzwald et al., 2019). More recently, there have been efforts to learn representations of queries and documents useful for retrieval. Lee et al. (2019) introduce an inverse cloze task for pretraining encoders used to create static embeddings that are indexed and used for similarity retrieval during inference. Their work is further expanded by Guu et al. (2020) who introduce non-static representations that are learned simultaneous to reader fine-tuning. Finally, Karpukhin et al. (2020) use dual encoders for retrieval: one encoder that learns to map queries to a fixed dimension vector, and another that learns to map documents to a similar fixed-dimension vector (such that representations for similar query and documents are close).

2.2 Query Expansion

In addition to re-ranking and dense representation retrieval, query expansion methods have also been proposed to help address the vocabulary mismatch problem. They serve to identify additional relevant query terms, using a variety of sources - such as the target corpus, external dictionaries (e.g., WordNet), or historical queries. Existing research has explored how implicit information contained in queries can be leveraged in query expansion. For example, Lavrenko and Croft (2017); Lv and Zhai (2010) show how a relevance model (RM3) can be applied for query expansion and improve retrieval performance. More recently, (Lin, 2019) also show that the use of a well-tuned relevance model such as RM3 (Lavrenko and Croft, 2017; Abdul-Jaleel et al., 2004) results in performance at par with complex neural retrieval methods. Word embeddings have been explored as a potential method for query expansion, as well. In their work, Kuzi et al. (2016) train a word2vec (Mikolov et al., 2013) CBOW model on their search corpora and use embeddings to identify expansion terms that are either semantically related to the query as a whole or to its terms. Their results suggest that a combination of word2vec embeddings and a relevance model

(RM3) provide good results. However, while word embeddings trained on a target corpus are useful, they are static and do not take into consideration the context of the words in a specific query. In this work, we propose an extension to this direction of thought and explore how contextual embeddings produced by an MLM, such as BERT (Devlin et al., 2018), can be applied in generating query expansion terms.

2.2.1 Document Reading

Recent advances in pretrained neural language models, like BERT (Vaswani et al., 2017) and GPT (Radford et al., 2019), have enabled robust contextualized representation of natural language, which, in turn, have enabled significant performance increases on the QA task. Each QA model (reader) consists of a base representation and an output feedforward layer which produces two sets of scores: (i) scores for each input token that indicate the likelihood of an answer span starting at the token offset, and (ii) scores for each input token that indicate the likelihood of an answer span ending at the token offset.

3 NeuralQA System Architecture

In this section, we review the architecture for NeuralQA, as well as design decisions and supported workflows. The core modules for NeuralQA (Fig. 2) include a user interface, retriever, expander, and reader. Each of these modules are implemented as extensible python classes (to facilitate code reuse and incremental development), and are exposed as REST API endpoints that can be either consumed by 3rd party applications or interacted with via the NeuralQA user interface.

3.1 Retriever

The retriever supports the execution of queries on an existing ElasticSearch instance, using the industry standard BM25 scoring algorithm.

3.1.1 Condensing Passages with $RelSnip$

In practice, open corpus documents can be of arbitrary length (sometimes including thousands of tokens) and are frequently indexed for retrieval *as is*. On the other hand, document reader models have limits on the maximum number of tokens they can process in a single pass (e.g., BERT-based models can process a maximum of 512 tokens). Thus, retrieving large documents can incur latency costs, as a reader will have to first split the document into

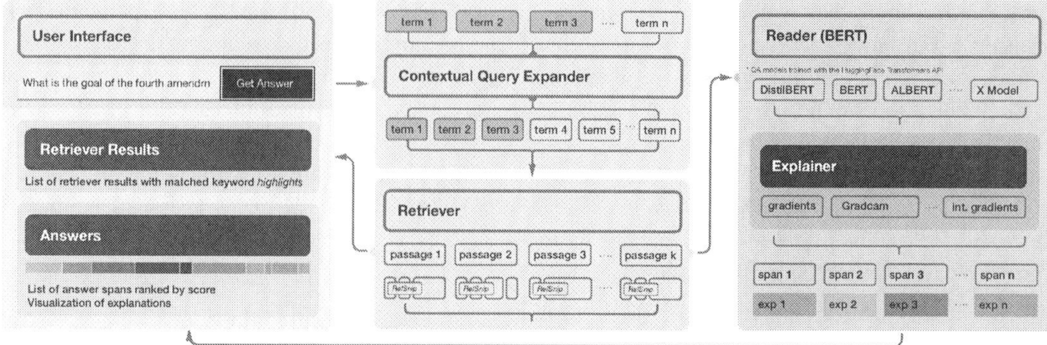

Figure 2: The NeuralQA Architecture is comprised of four primary modules. (a) User interface: enables user queries and visualizes results from the retriever and reader (b) Contextual Query Expander: offers options for generating query expansion terms using an MLM (c) Retriever: leverages the BM25 scoring algorithm in retrieving a list of candidate passages; it also optionally condenses lengthy documents to smaller passages via 3.1 $RelSnip$. (d) Document Reader: identifies answer spans within documents (where available) and provides explanations for each prediction.

manageable *chunks*, and then process each *chunk* individually. To address this issue, NeuralQA introduces $RelSnip$, a method for constructing smaller documents from lengthy documents. $RelSnip$ is implemented as follows: For each retrieved document, we apply a highlighter (Lucene Unified Highlighter), which breaks the document into fragments of size k_{frag} and uses the BM25 algorithm to score each fragment as if they were individual documents in the corpus. Next, we concatenate the top n fragments as a new document, which is then processed by the reader. $RelSnip$ relies on the simplifying assumption that fragments with higher match scores contain more relevant information. As an illustrative example, $RelSnip$ can yield a document of 400 tokens (depending on k_{frag} and n) from a document containing 10,000 tokens. In practice, this can translate to 25x increase in speed.

3.2 Expander

3.2.1 Contextual Query Expansion (CQE)

CQE relies on the assumption that an MLM which has been fine-tuned on the target document corpus contains implicit information (Petroni et al., 2019) on the target corpus. The goal is to exploit this information in identifying relevant query expansion terms. Ideally, we want to expand a query, such that expansion tokens serve to increase recall, while adding minimal noise and without significantly altering the semantics of the original query. We implement CQE as follows: First, we identify a set of expansion candidate tokens. For each token t_i in the query t_{query}, we use the SpaCy (Honnibal and Montani, 2017) library to infer its part of speech tag $t_{i_{pos}}$ and apply a filter f_{rule} to determine if it is added to a list of candidate tokens for expansion $t_{candidates}$. Next, we construct intermediate versions of the original query, in which each token in $t_{candidates}$ is masked, and an MLM (BERT) predicts the top n tokens that are contextually most likely to complete the query. These predicted tokens $t_{expansion}$ can then be added to the original query as expansion terms.

To minimize the chance of introducing spurious terms that are unrelated to the original query, we find that two quality control measures are useful. First, we leverage confidence scores returned by the MLM and only accept expansion tokens above a certain threshold (e.g., $k_{thresh} = 0.5$) where k_{thresh} is a hyperparameter. Secondly, we find that a conservative filter in selecting token expansion candidates can mitigate the introduction of spurious terms. Our filter rule f_{rule} currently only expands tokens that are either nouns or adjectives $t_{i_{pos}} \in (noun, adj)$ and are not named entities; tokens for other parts of speech are not expanded. Finally, the list of expansion terms are further cleaned by the removal of duplicate terms, punctuation, and stop words. Fig. 3 shows a qualitative comparison of query expansion terms suggested by a static word embedding and an MLM for a given query. The NeuralQA interface offers a user-in-the-loop visualization of CQE which highlights POS tags for each token to help the user make sense of expansion values. The user can then select expansion candidates for inclusion in retrieval.

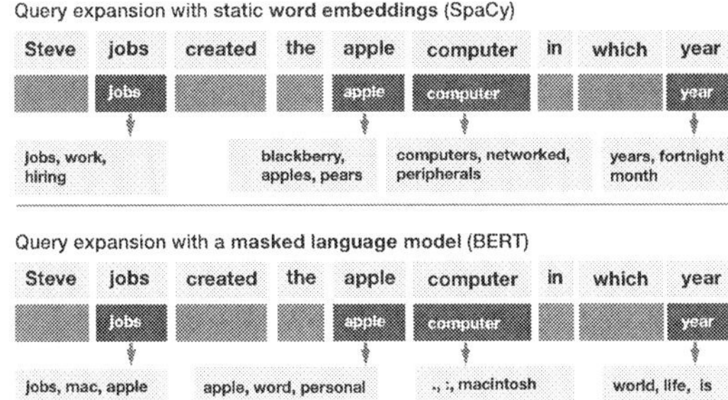

Figure 3: Examples of qualitative results from applying query expansion: (a) Query expansion using SpaCy word embeddings to identify the most similar words for each expansion candidate token. This approach yields terms with low relevance (e.g., terms related to work (jobs, hiring) and fruits (apple, blackberry, pears) are not relevant to the current query context) (b) Query expansion using an MLM (BERT). This approach yields terms that are absent in the original query (e.g., mac, macintosh, personal) but are, *in general*, relevant to the current query.

3.3 Reader

The reader module implements an interface for predicting answer spans, given a query and context documents. Underneath, it loads any QA model trained using the HuggingFace Transformers API (Wolf et al., 2019). Documents that exceed the maximum token size for the reader are automatically split into chunks with a configurable stride and answer spans provided for each chunk. All answers are then sorted, based on an associated score (start and end token softmax probabilities). Finally, each reader model provides a method that generates gradient-based explanations (Vanilla Gradients (Simonyan et al., 2013; Erhan et al., 2009; Baehrens et al., 2010)).

3.3.1 User Interface

The NeuralQA user interface (Fig. 4) seeks to aid the user in performing queries and in sensemaking of underlying model behaviour. As a first step, we provide a visualization of retrieved document highlights that indicate what portions of the retrieved document contributed to their relevance ranking. Next, following work done in AllenNLP Interpret(Wallace et al., 2019), we implement gradient-based explanations that help the user understand what sections of the input (question and passage) were most relevant to the choice of answer span. We do not use attention weights, as they have have been shown to be unfaithful explanations of model behaviour (Jain and Wallace, 2019; Ser-

rano and Smith, 2019) and not intuitive for end user sensemaking. We also implement a document and answer tagging scheme that indicates the source document from which an answer span is derived.

NeuralQA is scalable, as it is built on industry standard OSS tools that are designed for scale (ElasticSearch, HuggingFace Transformers API, FastAPI, Uvicorn asgi web server). We have tested deployments of NeuralQA on docker containers running on CPU machine clusters which rely on ElasticSearch clusters. The UI is responsive and optimized to work on desktop, as well as on mobile devices.

3.4 Configuration and Workflow

NeuralQA implements a command line interface for instantiating the library, and a declarative approach for specifying the parameters for each module. At run time, users can provide a command line argument specifying the location of a configuration YAML file[2]. If no configuration file is found in the provided location and in the current folder, NeuralQA will create a default configuration file that can be subsequently modified. As an illustrative example, users can configure properties of the user interface (views to show or hide, title and description of the page, etc.), retriever properties (a list of supported retriever indices), and reader properties (a list of supported models that are loaded into memory on application startup).

3.4.1 User Personas

NeuralQA is designed to support use cases and personas at various levels of complexities. We discuss two specific personas briefly below.

Data Scientists: Janice, a data scientist, has extensive experience applying a collection of machine learning models to financial data. Recently, she has started a new project, in which the deliverable includes a QA model that is skillful at answering factoid questions on financial data. As part of this work, Janice has successfully fine-tuned a set of transformer models on the QA task, but would like to better understand how the model behaves. More importantly, she would like to enable visual interaction with the model for her broader team. To achieve this, Janice hosts NeuralQA on an internal server accessible to her team. Via a configuration file, she can specify a set of trained models, as well as enable user selection of reader/retriever parameters. This workflow also extends to other user types

---

[2]A sample configuration file can be found on Github.

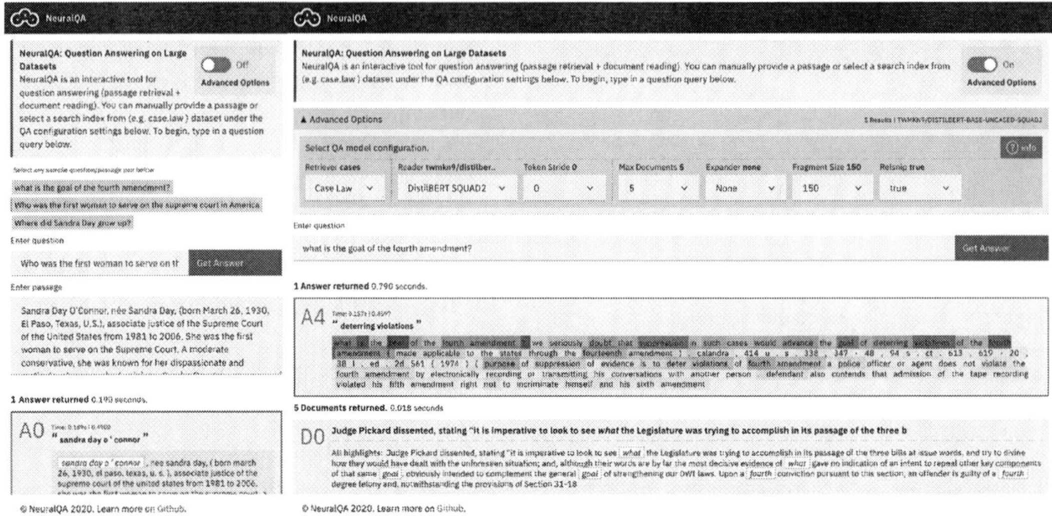

Figure 4: The NeuralQA UI. a.) Basic view (mobile) for closed domain QA, i.e., the user provides a question *and* passage. b.) Advanced options view (desktop mode) for open domain QA. The user can select the retriever (e.g., # of returned documents, toggle $RelSnip$, fragment size k_{frag}), set expander and reader parameters (BERT reader model, token stride size)). View also shows a list of returned documents (D0-D4) with highlights that match query terms; a list of answers (A0) with gradient-based explanation of which tokens impact the selected answer span.

(such as hobbyists, entry level data scientists, or researchers) who want an interface for qualitative inspection of custom reader models on custom document indices.

Engineering Teams: Candice manages the internal knowledge base service for her startup. They have an internal ElasticSearch instance for search, but would like to provide additional value via QA capabilities. To achieve this, Candice provisions a set of docker containers running instances for NeuralQA and then modifies the frontend of their current search application to make requests to the NeuralQA REST API and serve answer spans.

3.5 Related Work

QA systems that integrate deep learning models remain an active area of research and practice. For example, AllenNLP Interpret (Wallace et al., 2019) provides a demonstration interface and sample code for interpreting a set of AllenNLP models across multiple tasks. Similarly, Chakravarti et al. (2019) provide a gRPC-based orchestration flow for QA. However, while these projects provide a graphical user interface (GUI), their installation process is complex and requires specialized code to adapt them to existing infrastructure, such as retriever instances. Several open source projects also offer a programmatic interface for inference (e.g., HugginFace Pipelines), as well as joint retrieval paired with reading (e.g., Deepset Haystack). NeuralQA makes progress along these lines, by providing an extensible code base, a low-code declarative configuration interface, tools for query expansion and a visual interface for sensemaking of results. It supports a local research/development workflow (via the pip) package manager and scaled deployment via containerization (we provide a Dockerfile). We believe this ease of use can serve to remove barriers to experimentation for researchers, and accelerate the deployment of QA interfaces for experienced teams.

4 Conclusion

In this paper, we presented NeuralQA - a usable library for question answering on large datasets. NeuralQA is useful for developers interested in qualitatively exploring QA models for their custom datasets, as well as for enterprise teams seeking a flexible QA interface/API for their customers. NeuralQA is under active development, and roadmap features include support for a Solr retriever, additional model explanation methods and additional query expansion methods such as RM3 (Lavrenko and Croft, 2017). Future work will also explore empirical evaluation of our CQE and $RelSnip$ implementation to better understand their strengths and limitations.

Acknowledgments

The author thanks Melanie Beck, Andrew Reed, Chris Wallace, Grant Custer, Danielle Thorpe and other members of the Cloudera Fast Forward team for their valuable feedback.

References

Nasreen Abdul-Jaleel, James Allan, W Bruce Croft, Fernando Diaz, Leah Larkey, Xiaoyan Li, Mark D Smucker, and Courtney Wade. 2004. Umass at trec 2004: Novelty and hard. *Computer Science Department Faculty Publication Series*, page 189.

Zeynep Akkalyoncu Yilmaz, Shengjin Wang, Wei Yang, Haotian Zhang, and Jimmy Lin. 2019. Applying BERT to document retrieval with birch. In *Empirical Methods in Natural Language Processing (EMNLP-IJCNLP): System Demonstrations*, pages 19–24, Hong Kong, China. Association for Computational Linguistics.

David Baehrens, Timon Schroeter, Stefan Harmeling, Motoaki Kawanabe, Katja Hansen, and Klaus-Robert MÃžller. 2010. How to explain individual classification decisions. *Journal of Machine Learning Research*, 11(Jun):1803–1831.

Rishav Chakravarti, Cezar Pendus, Andrzej Sakrajda, Anthony Ferritto, Lin Pan, Michael Glass, Vittorio Castelli, J William Murdock, Radu Florian, Salim Roukos, and Avi Sil. 2019. CFO: A framework for building production NLP systems. In *EMNLP-IJCNLP 2019: System Demonstrations*, pages 31–36, Hong Kong, China. Association for Computational Linguistics.

Danqi Chen, Adam Fisch, Jason Weston, and Antoine Bordes. 2017. Reading wikipedia to answer open-domain questions. *ACL 2017*.

Jacob Devlin, Ming-Wei Chang, Kenton Lee, and Kristina Toutanova. 2018. Bert: Pre-training of deep bidirectional transformers for language understanding. *arXiv preprint arXiv:1810.04805*.

Victor Dibia. 2020a. Anomagram: An interactive visualization for training and evaluating autoencoders on the task of anomaly detection. *ArXiv*. https://github.com/victordibia/anomagram.

Victor Dibia. 2020b. Convnet playground: A learning tool for exploring representations learned by convolutional neural networks. *arXiv*. https://github.com/fastforwardlabs/convnetplayground.

Dumitru Erhan, Yoshua Bengio, Aaron Courville, and Pascal Vincent. 2009. Visualizing higher-layer features of a deep network. *University of Montreal*, 1341(3):1.

Jianfeng Gao, Michel Galley, and Lihong Li. 2018. Neural approaches to conversational ai. In *The 41st International ACM SIGIR Conference on Research & Development in Information Retrieval*, pages 1371–1374.

Kelvin Guu, Kenton Lee, Zora Tung, Panupong Pasupat, and Ming-Wei Chang. 2020. Realm: Retrieval-augmented language model pre-training. *arXiv preprint arXiv:2002.08909*.

Matthew Honnibal and Ines Montani. 2017. spaCy 2: Natural language understanding with Bloom embeddings, convolutional neural networks and incremental parsing. To appear.

Sarthak Jain and Byron C Wallace. 2019. Attention is not explanation. *NAACL 2019*.

Vladimir Karpukhin, Barlas Oğuz, Sewon Min, Ledell Wu, Sergey Edunov, Danqi Chen, and Wen-tau Yih. 2020. Dense passage retrieval for open-domain question answering. *arXiv preprint arXiv:2004.04906*.

Bernhard Kratzwald, Anna Eigenmann, and Stefan Feuerriegel. 2019. RankQA: Neural question answering with answer re-ranking. In *ACL*, pages 6076–6085, Florence, Italy. Association for Computational Linguistics.

Saar Kuzi, Anna Shtok, and Oren Kurland. 2016. Query expansion using word embeddings. In *Proceedings of the 25th ACM international on conference on information and knowledge management*, pages 1929–1932.

Victor Lavrenko and W Bruce Croft. 2017. Relevance-based language models. In *ACM SIGIR Forum*, volume 51, pages 260–267. ACM New York, NY, USA.

Jinhyuk Lee, Seongjun Yun, Hyunjae Kim, Miyoung Ko, and Jaewoo Kang. 2018. Ranking paragraphs for improving answer recall in open-domain question answering. In *Proceedings of the 2018 Conference on Empirical Methods in Natural Language Processing*, pages 565–569, Brussels, Belgium. Association for Computational Linguistics.

Kenton Lee, Ming-Wei Chang, and Kristina Toutanova. 2019. Latent retrieval for weakly supervised open domain question answering. *arXiv preprint arXiv:1906.00300*.

Jimmy Lin. 2019. The neural hype and comparisons against weak baselines. In *ACM SIGIR Forum*, volume 52, pages 40–51. ACM New York, NY, USA.

Yuanhua Lv and ChengXiang Zhai. 2010. Positional relevance model for pseudo-relevance feedback. In *Proceedings of the 33rd international ACM SIGIR conference on Research and development in information retrieval*, pages 579–586.

Andreas Madsen. 2019. Visualizing memorization in rnns. *Distill*. https://distill.pub/2019/memorization-in-rnns.

Tomas Mikolov, Ilya Sutskever, Kai Chen, Greg S Corrado, and Jeff Dean. 2013. Distributed representations of words and phrases and their compositionality. In *Advances in neural information processing systems*, pages 3111–3119.

Fabio Petroni, Tim Rocktäschel, Sebastian Riedel, Patrick Lewis, Anton Bakhtin, Yuxiang Wu, and Alexander Miller. 2019. Language models as knowledge bases? In *Proceedings of the 2019 Conference on Empirical Methods in Natural Language Processing and the 9th International Joint Conference on Natural Language Processing (EMNLP-IJCNLP)*, pages 2463–2473, Hong Kong, China. Association for Computational Linguistics.

Chen Qu, Liu Yang, Minghui Qiu, W Bruce Croft, Yongfeng Zhang, and Mohit Iyyer. 2019. Bert with history answer embedding for conversational question answering. In *Proceedings of the 42nd International ACM SIGIR Conference on Research and Development in Information Retrieval*, pages 1133–1136.

Alec Radford, Jeffrey Wu, Rewon Child, David Luan, Dario Amodei, and Ilya Sutskever. 2019. Language models are unsupervised multitask learners. *OpenAI Blog*, 1(8):9.

Stephen Robertson and Hugo Zaragoza. 2009. *The probabilistic relevance framework: BM25 and beyond*. Now Publishers Inc.

Sofia Serrano and Noah A. Smith. 2019. Is attention interpretable? In *Proceedings of the 57th Annual Meeting of the Association for Computational Linguistics*, pages 2931–2951, Florence, Italy. Association for Computational Linguistics.

Karen Simonyan, Andrea Vedaldi, and Andrew Zisserman. 2013. Deep inside convolutional networks: Visualising image classification models and saliency maps. *arXiv preprint arXiv:1312.6034*.

H. Strobelt, S. Gehrmann, M. Behrisch, A. Perer, H. Pfister, and A. M. Rush. 2018. Seq2Seq-Vis: A Visual Debugging Tool for Sequence-to-Sequence Models. *ArXiv e-prints*.

Ashish Vaswani, Noam Shazeer, Niki Parmar, Jakob Uszkoreit, Llion Jones, Aidan N Gomez, Łukasz Kaiser, and Illia Polosukhin. 2017. Attention is all you need. In *Advances in neural information processing systems*, pages 5998–6008.

Eric Wallace, Jens Tuyls, Junlin Wang, Sanjay Subramanian, Matt Gardner, and Sameer Singh. 2019. AllenNLP Interpret: A framework for explaining predictions of NLP models. In *Empirical Methods in Natural Language Processing*.

Shuohang Wang, Mo Yu, Xiaoxiao Guo, Zhiguo Wang, Tim Klinger, Wei Zhang, Shiyu Chang, Gerry Tesauro, Bowen Zhou, and Jing Jiang. 2018. R3: Reinforced ranker-reader for open-domain question answering. *Thirty-Second AAAI Conference on Artificial Intelligence*.

Dirk Weissenborn, Georg Wiese, and Laura Seiffe. 2017. Fastqa: A simple and efficient neural architecture for question answering. *CoRR*, abs/1703.04816.

Thomas Wolf, Lysandre Debut, Victor Sanh, Julien Chaumond, Clement Delangue, Anthony Moi, Pierric Cistac, Tim Rault, R'emi Louf, Morgan Funtowicz, and Jamie Brew. 2019. Huggingface's transformers: State-of-the-art natural language processing. *ArXiv*, abs/1910.03771.

Wei Yang, Yuqing Xie, Aileen Lin, Xingyu Li, Luchen Tan, Kun Xiong, Ming Li, and Jimmy Lin. 2019. End-to-end open-domain question answering with bertserini. *arXiv preprint arXiv:1902.01718*.

Yi Yang, Wen-tau Yih, and Christopher Meek. 2015. Wikiqa: A challenge dataset for open-domain question answering. In *Proceedings of the 2015 conference on empirical methods in natural language processing*, pages 2013–2018.

Wikipedia2Vec: An Efficient Toolkit for Learning and Visualizing the Embeddings of Words and Entities from Wikipedia

Ikuya Yamada[1,2]

ikuya@ousia.jp

Akari Asai[3]

akari@cs.washington.edu

Jin Sakuma[4]

jsakuma@tkl.iis.u-tokyo.ac.jp

Hiroyuki Shindo[5,2]

shindo@is.naist.jp

Hideaki Takeda[6]

takeda@nii.ac.jp

Yoshiyasu Takefuji[7]

takefuji@sfc.keio.ac.jp

Yuji Matsumoto[2]

matsu@is.naist.jp

[1]Studio Ousia [2]RIKEN AIP [3]University of Washington [4]The University of Tokyo
[5]Nara Institute of Science and Technology [6]National Institute of Informatics [7]Keio University

Abstract

The embeddings of entities in a large knowledge base (e.g., Wikipedia) are highly beneficial for solving various natural language tasks that involve real world knowledge. In this paper, we present Wikipedia2Vec, a Python-based open-source tool for learning the embeddings of words and entities from Wikipedia. The proposed tool enables users to learn the embeddings efficiently by issuing a single command with a Wikipedia dump file as an argument. We also introduce a web-based demonstration of our tool that allows users to visualize and explore the learned embeddings. In our experiments, our tool achieved a state-of-the-art result on the KORE entity related-ness dataset, and competitive results on various standard benchmark datasets. Furthermore, our tool has been used as a key component in various recent studies. We publicize the source code, demonstration, and the pretrained embeddings for 12 languages at `https://wikipedia2vec.github.io`.

1 Introduction

Entity embeddings, i.e., vector representations of entities in knowledge base (KB), have played a vital role in many recent models in natural language processing (NLP). These embeddings provide rich information (or *knowledge*) regarding entities available in KB using fixed continuous vectors. They have been shown to be beneficial not only for tasks directly related to entities (e.g., entity linking (Yamada et al., 2016; Ganea and Hofmann, 2017)) but also for general NLP tasks (e.g., text classification (Yamada and Shindo, 2019), question answering (Poerner et al., 2019)). Notably, recent studies have also shown that these embeddings can be used to enhance the performance of state-of-the-art contextualized word embeddings (i.e., BERT (Devlin et al., 2019)) on downstream tasks (Zhang et al., 2019; Peters et al., 2019; Poerner et al., 2019).

In this work, we present *Wikipedia2Vec*, a Python-based open source tool for learning the embeddings of words and entities easily and efficiently from Wikipedia. Due to its scale, availability in a variety of languages, and constantly evolving nature, Wikipedia is commonly used as a KB to learn entity embeddings. Our proposed tool jointly learns the embeddings of words and entities, and places semantically similar words and entities close to one another in the vector space. In particular, our tool implements the word-based skip-gram model (Mikolov et al., 2013a,b) to learn word embeddings, and its extensions proposed in Yamada et al. (2016) to learn entity embeddings. Wikipedia2Vec enables users to train embeddings by simply running a single command with a Wikipedia dump file as an input. We highly optimized our implementation, which makes our implementation of the skip-gram model faster than the well-established implementation available in gensim (Řehůřek and Sojka, 2010) and fastText (Bojanowski et al., 2017).

Experimental results demonstrated that our tool achieved enhanced quality compared to the existing tools on several standard benchmarks. Notably, our tool achieved a state-of-the-art result on the entity relatedness task based on the KORE dataset. Due to its effectiveness and efficiency, our tool has been successfully used in various downstream NLP tasks, including entity linking (Yamada et al., 2016; Eshel et al., 2017; Chen et al., 2019), named entity recognition (Sato et al., 2017; Lara-Clares and Garcia-Serrano, 2019), question answering (Yamada et al., 2018b; Poerner et al., 2019), knowledge graph completion (Shah et al., 2019), paraphrase detection (Duong et al., 2019), fake news detection (Singh et al., 2019), and text classification (Yamada and Shindo, 2019).

We also introduce a web-based demonstration of our tool that visualizes the embeddings by plotting them onto a two- or three-dimensional space

Proceedings of the 2020 EMNLP (Systems Demonstrations), pages 23–30
November 16-20, 2020. ©2020 Association for Computational Linguistics

using dimensionality reduction algorithms. The demonstration also allows users to explore the embeddings by querying similar words and entities.

The source code has been tested on Linux, Windows, and macOS, and released under the Apache License 2.0. We also release the pretrained embeddings for 12 languages (i.e., English, Arabic, Chinese, Dutch, French, German, Italian, Japanese, Polish, Portuguese, Russian, and Spanish).

The main contributions of this paper are summarized as follows:

- We present Wikipedia2Vec, a tool for learning the embeddings of words and entities easily and efficiently from Wikipedia.
- Our tool achieved a state-of-the-art result on the KORE entity relatedness dataset, and performed competitively on the various benchmark datasets.
- We present a web-based demonstration that allows users to explore the learned embeddings.
- We publicize the code, demonstration, and the pretrained embeddings for 12 languages at `https://wikipedia2vec.github.io`.

2   Related Work

Many studies have recently proposed methods to learn entity embeddings from a KB (Hu et al., 2015; Li et al., 2016; Tsai and Roth, 2016; Yamada et al., 2016, 2017, 2018a; Cao et al., 2017; Ganea and Hofmann, 2017). These embeddings are typically based on conventional word embedding models (e.g., skip-gram (Mikolov et al., 2013a)) trained with data retrieved from a KB. For example, Ristoski et al. (2018) proposed RDF2Vec, which learns entity embeddings using the skip-gram model with inputs generated by random walks over the large knowledge graphs such as Wikidata and DBpedia. Furthermore, a simple method that has been widely used in various studies (Yaghoobzadeh and Schutze, 2015; Yamada et al., 2017, 2018a; Al-Badrashiny et al., 2017; Suzuki et al., 2018) trains entity embeddings by replacing the entity annotations in an input corpus with the unique identifier of their referent entities, and feeding the corpus into a word embedding model (e.g., skip-gram). Two open-source tools, namely Wiki2Vec[1] and Wikipedia Entity Vectors,[2] have implemented this method. Our proposed tool is based on Yamada et al. (2016), which extends this idea by using

---

[1] `https://github.com/idio/wiki2vec`
[2] `https://github.com/singletongue/WikiEntVec`

```
$ wget https://dumps.wikimedia.org/enwiki/latest/
    enwiki-latest-pages-articles.xml.bz2
$ wikipedia2vec train enwiki-latest-pages-articles.
    xml.bz2 MODEL_FILE
```

Figure 1: Shell commands to train embeddings from the latest English Wikipedia dump.

```
>>> from wikipedia2vec import Wikipedia2Vec
>>> model = Wikipedia2Vec.load(MODEL_FILE)
>>> model.get_entity_vector("Scarlett_Johansson")
memmap([-0.1979,  0.3086, ..., ], dtype=float32)
>>> model.get_word_vector("tokyo")
memmap([ 0.0161, -0.0332, ..., ], dtype=float32)
>>> model.most_similar(model.get_entity("Python_(
    programming_language)"))[:3]
[(<Word python>, 0.7265),
 (<Entity Ruby (programming language)>, 0.6856),
 (<Entity Perl>, 0.6794)]
```

Figure 2: An example that uses the Wikipedia2Vec embeddings on a Python interactive shell.

neighboring entities connected by internal hyperlinks of Wikipedia as additional contexts to train the model. Note that we used the RDF2Vec and Wiki2Vec as baselines in our experiments, and achieved enhanced empirical performance over these tools on the KORE dataset. Additionally, there have been various relational embedding models proposed (Bordes et al., 2013; Wang et al., 2014; Lin et al., 2015) that aim to learn the entity representations that are particularly effective for knowledge graph completion tasks.

3   Overview

Wikipedia2Vec is an easy-to-use, optimized tool for learning embeddings from Wikipedia. This tool can be installed using the Python's `pip` tool (`pip install wikipedia2vec`). Embeddings can be learned easily by running the `wikipedia2vec train` command with a Wikipedia dump file[3] as an argument. Figure 1 shows the shell commands that download the latest English Wikipedia dump file and run training of the embeddings based on this dump using the default hyper-parameters.[4] Furthermore, users can easily use the learned embeddings. Figure 2 shows the example Python code that loads the learned embedding file, and obtains the embeddings of an entity *Scarlett Johansson* and a word *tokyo*, as well as the most similar words and entities of an entity *Python*.

---

[3] The dump file can be downloaded at Wikimedia Downloads: `https://dumps.wikimedia.org`
[4] The *train* command has many optional hyper-parameters that are described in detail in the documentation.

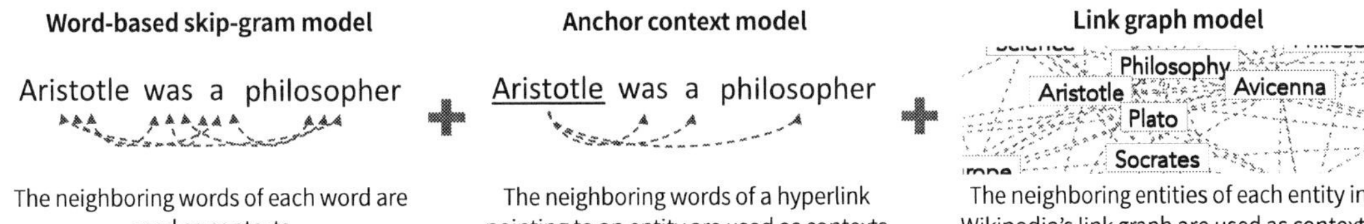

Figure 3: Wikipedia2Vec learns embeddings by jointly optimizing word-based skip-gram, anchor context, and link graph models.

3.1 Model

Wikipedia2Vec implements the conventional skip-gram model (Mikolov et al., 2013a,b) and its extensions proposed in Yamada et al. (2016) to map words and entities into the same d-dimensional vector space. The skip-gram model is a neural network model with a training objective to find embeddings that are useful for predicting context items (i.e., words or entities in this paper) given each item. The loss function of the model is defined as:

$$\mathcal{L}_s = -\sum_{o_i \in O} \sum_{o_c \in C_{o_i}} \log P(o_c|o_i), \quad (1)$$

where O is a set of all items (i.e., words or entities), C_o is the set of context items of o, and the conditional probability $\log P(o_c|o_i)$ is defined using the following softmax function:

$$P(o_c|o_i) = \frac{\exp(\mathbf{V}_{o_i}^\top \mathbf{U}_{o_c})}{\sum_{o \in O} \exp(\mathbf{V}_{o_i}^\top \mathbf{U}_o)}, \quad (2)$$

where $\mathbf{V}_o \in \mathbb{R}^d$ and $\mathbf{U}_o \in \mathbb{R}^d$ denote the embeddings of item o in embedding matrices $\mathbf{V}$ and $\mathbf{U}$, respectively.

Our tool learns the embeddings by jointly optimizing the three skip-gram-based sub-models described below (see also Figure 3). Note that the matrices $\mathbf{V}$ and $\mathbf{U}$ contain the embeddings of both words and entities.

Word-based Skip-gram Model Given each word in a Wikipedia page, this model learns word embeddings by predicting the neighboring words of the given word. Formally, given a sequence of words $w_1, w_2, ..., w_N$, the loss function of this model is defined as follows:

$$\mathcal{L}_w = -\sum_{i=1}^{N} \sum_{-c \leq j \leq c, j \neq 0} \log P(w_{i+j}|w_i), \quad (3)$$

where c is the size of the context words, and $P(w_{i+j}|w_i)$ is computed based on Eq.(2).

Anchor Context Model This model aims to place similar words and entities close to one another in the vector space using hyperlinks and their neighboring words in Wikipedia. From a given Wikipedia page, the model extracts the referent entity and surrounding words (i.e., previous and next c words) from each hyperlink in the page, and learns embeddings by predicting surrounding words given each entity. Consequently, the loss function of this model is defined as follows:

$$\mathcal{L}_a = -\sum_{(e_i,Q) \in A} \sum_{w_c \in Q} \log P(w_c|e_i), \quad (4)$$

where A denotes a set of all hyperlinks in Wikipedia, each containing a pair of a referent entity e_i and a set of surrounding words Q, and $P(w_c|e_i)$ is computed based on Eq.(2).

Link Graph Model This model aims to learn entity embeddings by predicting the neighboring entities of each entity in the Wikipedia's link graph– an undirected graph whose nodes are entities and the edges represent the presence of hyperlinks between the entities. We create an edge between a pair of entities if the page of one entity has a hyperlink to that of the other entity, or if both pages link to each other. The loss function of this model is defined as:

$$\mathcal{L}_e = -\sum_{e_i \in E} \sum_{e_o \in C_{e_i}} \log P(e_o|e_i), \quad (5)$$

where E is the set of all entities in the vocabulary, and C_e is the neighboring entities of entity e in the link graph, and $P(e_o|e_i)$ is computed by Eq.(2).

Finally, we define the loss function of our model by linearly combining the three loss functions described above:

$$\mathcal{L} = \mathcal{L}_w + \mathcal{L}_a + \mathcal{L}_e \quad (6)$$

The training is performed by minimizing this loss function using stochastic gradient descent. We use negative sampling (Mikolov et al., 2013b) to convert the softmax function (Eq.(2)) into computationally feasible ones. The resulting matrix V is used as the learned embeddings.

3.2 Automatic Generation of Hyperlinks

Because Wikipedia instructs its contributors to create a hyperlink only at the first occurrence of the entity name on a page, many entity names do not appear as hyperlinks. This is problematic for our anchor context model because it uses hyperlinks as a source to learn the embeddings.

To address this problem, our tool automatically generates hyperlinks using a mention-entity dictionary that maps entity names (e.g., "apple") to its possible referent entities (e.g., *Apple Inc.* or *Apple_(food)*) (see Section 4 for details). Our tool extracts all words and phrases from a Wikipedia page and converts each into a hyperlink to an entity if either the entity is referred to by a hyperlink on the same page, or there is only one referent entity associated with the name in the dictionary.

4 Implementation

Our tool is implemented in Python and most of its code is compiled into C++ using Cython (Behnel et al., 2011) to optimize the run-time performance.

As described in Section 3.1, our link graph and anchor context models are based on the hyperlinks in Wikipedia. Because Wikipedia contains numerous hyperlinks, it is challenging to use them efficiently. To address this, we introduce two optimized components–link graph matrix and mention-entity dictionary–that are used during training.

Link Graph Matrix During training, our link graph model needs to obtain numerous neighboring entities of an entity in a large link graph of Wikipedia. To reduce latency, this component stores the entire graph in the memory using the binary sparse matrix in the compressed sparse row (CSR) format, in which its rows and columns represent entities and its values represent the presence of hyperlinks between corresponding entity pairs. Because the size of this matrix is typically small, it can easily be stored on the memory.[5] Note that given a row index in the CSR matrix, the time complexity of obtaining its non-zero column indices (corresponding to the neighboring entities of the entity that corresponds to the row index) is $O(1)$.

Mention-entity Dictionary A mention-entity dictionary is used to generate hyperlinks described in Section 3.2. The dictionary maps entity names to their possible referent entities and is created based on the names and their referent entities obtained from all hyperlinks in Wikipedia. Our tool extracts all words and phrases from a Wikipedia page that are included in the dictionary containing a large number of entity names. To implement this in an efficient manner, we use the Aho–Corasick algorithm, which is an efficient string search algorithm using finite state machine constructed from all entity names. After detecting the words and phrases in the dictionary, our tool converts them to hyperlinks based on heuristics described in Section 3.2.

The embeddings are trained by simultaneously iterating over pages in Wikipedia and entities in the link graph in a random order. The texts and hyperlinks in each page are extracted using the mw-parserfromhell MediaWiki parser.[6] We do not use semi-structured data such as tables and infoboxes. We also generate hyperlinks using the mention-entity dictionary. We store the embeddings as a float matrix in a shared memory and update it using multiple processes. Linear algebraic operations required to learn embeddings are implemented using C functions in Basic Linear Algebra Subprograms (BLAS).

Additionally, our tool uses a tokenizer to detect words from a Wikipedia page. The following four tokenizers are currently implemented in our tool: (1) the multi-lingual ICU tokenizer[7] that implements the unicode text segmentation algorithm (Davis, 2019), (2) a simple rule-based tokenizer that splits the text using white space characters, (3) the Jieba tokenizer[8] for Chinese, and (4) the MeCab tokenizer[9] for Japanese and Korean.

5 Experiments

We conducted experiments to compare the quality and efficiency of our tool with those of the existing tools. To evaluate the quality of the entity embeddings, we used the KORE entity relatedness dataset (Hoffart et al., 2012). The dataset consists of 21 entities, and each entity has 20 related entities with scores assessed by humans. Following past work, we reported the Spearman's rank correlation co-

---

[5] The size of the matrix of English Wikipedia is less than 500 megabytes with our default hyper-parameter settings.

[6] `https://github.com/earwig/mwparserfromhell`

[7] `http://site.icu-project.org`

[8] `https://github.com/fxsjy/jieba`

[9] `https://taku910.github.io/mecab`

Name	Score
Ours	**0.71**
Ours (w/o link graph model)	0.61
Ours (w/o hyperlink generation)	0.69
RDF2Vec (Ristoski et al., 2018)	0.69
Wiki2vec	0.52

Table 1: The results of Wikipedia2Vec and the baseline entity embeddings on the KORE dataset.

efficient between the gold scores and the cosine similarity between the entity embeddings. We used two popular entity embedding tools, RDF2Vec (Ristoski et al., 2018) and Wiki2vec, as baselines.

We also evaluated the quality of the word embeddings by employing two standard tasks: (1) a word analogy task using the semantic subset (SEM) and syntactic subset (SYN) of the Google Word Analogy data set (Mikolov et al., 2013a), and (2) a word similarity task using two standard datasets, namely SimLex-999 (SL) (Hill et al., 2015) and WordSim-353 (WS) (Finkelstein et al., 2002). Following past work, we reported the accuracy for the word analogy task, and the Spearman's rank correlation coefficient between the gold scores and the cosine similarity between the word embeddings for the word similarity task. As baselines for these tasks, we used the skip-gram model (Mikolov et al., 2013a) implemented in the gensim library 3.6.0 (Řehůřek and Sojka, 2010) and the extended skip-gram model implemented in the fastText tool 0.1.0 (Bojanowski et al., 2017). We used WikiExtractor[10] to create the training corpus for baselines. To the extent possible, we used the same hyper-parameters to train our models and the baselines.[11]

We also reported the time required for training using our tool and the baseline word embedding tools. Note that the training of RDF2Vec and Wiki2vec tools are implemented using gensim.

We conducted experiments using Python 3.6 and OpenBLAS 0.3.3 installed on the c5d.9xlarge instance with 36 CPU cores deployed on Amazon Web Services. To train our models and the baseline word embedding models, we used the April 2018 version of the English Wikipedia dump.

5.1 Results

Table 1 shows the results of our models and the baseline entity embedding models of the KORE

	SEM	SYN	SL	WS	Time
Ours	**0.79**	0.68	**0.40**	0.71	276min
Ours (w/o link graph model)	0.77	0.67	0.39	0.70	170min
Ours (w/o hyperlink generation)	**0.79**	0.67	0.39	**0.72**	211min
Ours (word-based skip-gram)	0.75	0.67	0.36	0.70	154min
gensim (Řehůřek and Sojka, 2010)	0.75	0.67	0.37	0.70	197min
fastText (Bojanowski et al., 2017)	0.63	**0.70**	0.37	0.69	243min

Table 2: The results of Wikipedia2Vec and the baseline word embeddings on the word analogy and word similarity datasets.

dataset.[12] *w/o link graph model* and *w/o hyperlink generation* are the results of ablation studies disabling the link graph model and automatic generation of hyperlinks, respectively.

Our model successfully outperformed the RDF2Vec and Wiki2vec models and achieved a state-of-the-art result on the KORE dataset. The results also indicated that the link graph model and automatic generation of hyperlinks improved the performance of the KORE dataset.

Table 2 shows the results of our models with the baseline word embedding models on the word analogy and word similarity datasets. We also tested the performance of the word-based skip-gram model implemented in our tool by disabling the link graph and anchor context models.

Our model performed better than the baseline word embedding models on the SEM dataset, as well as on both word similarity datasets. This demonstrates that the semantic signals of entities provided by the link graph and anchor context models are beneficial for improving the quality of word embeddings. Additionally, the feature of the automatic generation of hyperlinks did not generally contribute to the performance on these datasets.

Our implementation of the word-based skip-gram model was substantially faster than gensim and fastText. Furthermore, the training time of our full model was comparable to that of the baseline word embedding models.

6 Interactive Demonstration

We developed a web-based interactive demonstration that enables users to explore the embeddings of words and entities learned by our proposed tool (see Figure 4). This demonstration enables users to visualize the embeddings onto a two- or three-dimensional space using three dimensionality reduction algorithms, namely t-distributed stochastic

---

[10] https://github.com/attardi/wikiextractor

[11] We used the following settings: $dim\_size = 500$, $window = 5$, $negative = 5$, $iteration = 5$

[12] We obtained the results of the RDF2Vec and Wiki2vec models from Ristoski et al. (2018).

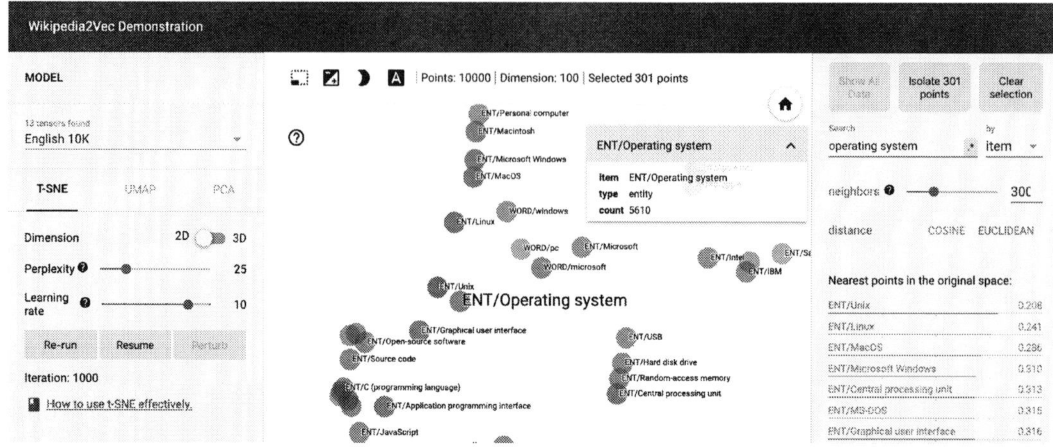

Figure 4: The screenshot of our web-based demonstration. Users can select the target embeddings (top left), configure the dimensionality reduction algorithm (bottom left), explore the visualized embeddings (center), and query similar words and entities based on an arbitrary word or an entity (right).

neighbor embedding (t-SNE) (Maaten and Hinton, 2008), uniform manifold approximation and projection (UMAP) (McInnes et al., 2018), and principal component analysis (PCA). Users can move around the visualized embedding space by dragging and zooming using the mouse. Moreover, the demonstration also allows users to explore the embeddings by querying similar items (words or entities) of an arbitrary item.

We used the pretrained embeddings of 12 languages released with this paper as the target embeddings. Furthermore, we also provided the English embeddings trained without the link graph model to allow users to qualitatively investigate how the link graph model affects the resulting embeddings.

Our demonstration is developed by extending the TensorFlow Embedding Projector.[13] The demonstration is available at `https://wikipedia2vec.github.io/demo`.

7   Use Cases

The embeddings learned using our proposed tool have already been used effectively in various recent studies. Poerner et al. (2019) have recently demonstrated that by combining BERT with the entity embeddings trained by our tool outperforms BERT and knowledge-enhanced contextualized word embeddings (i.e., ERNIE (Zhang et al., 2019)) on unsupervised question answering and relation classification tasks, without any computationally expensive additional pretraining of BERT. Yamada

et al. (2018b) developed a neural network-based question answering system based on our tool, and won a competition held by the NIPS 2017 conference. Sato et al. (2017), Chen et al. (2019), and Yamada and Shindo (2019) achieved state-of-the-art results on named entity recognition, entity linking, and text classification tasks, respectively, based on the embeddings learned by our tool. Furthermore, Papalampidi et al. (2019) proposed a neural network model of analyzing the plot structure of movies using the entity embeddings learned by our tool. Other examples include entity linking (Yamada et al., 2016; Eshel et al., 2017), named entity recognition (Lara-Clares and Garcia-Serrano, 2019), paraphrase detection (Duong et al., 2019), fake news detection (Singh et al., 2019), and knowledge graph completion (Shah et al., 2019).

8   Conclusions

In this paper, we present Wikipedia2Vec, an open-source tool for learning the embeddings of words and entities easily and efficiently from Wikipedia. Our experiments demonstrate the superiority of the proposed tool in terms of the quality of the embeddings and the efficiency of the training compared to the existing tools. Furthermore, our tool has been effectively used in many recent state-of-the-art models, which indicates the effectiveness of our tool on downstream tasks. We also introduce a web-based interactive demonstration that enables users to explore the learned embeddings. The source code and the pre-trained embeddings for 12 languages are released with this paper.

---

[13]`https://projector.tensorflow.org`

References

Mohamed Al-Badrashiny, Jason Bolton, Arun Tejasvi Chaganty, Kevin Clark, Craig Harman, Lifu Huang, Matthew Lamm, Jinhao Lei, Di Lu, Xiaoman Pan, and others. 2017. TinkerBell: Cross-lingual Cold-Start Knowledge Base Construction. In *Text Analysis Conference*.

Stefan Behnel, Robert Bradshaw, Craig Citro, Lisandro Dalcin, Dag Sverre Seljebotn, and Kurt Smith. 2011. Cython: The Best of Both Worlds. *Computing in Science & Engineering*, 13(2):31–39.

Piotr Bojanowski, Edouard Grave, Armand Joulin, and Tomas Mikolov. 2017. Enriching Word Vectors with Subword Information. *Transactions of the Association for Computational Linguistics*, 5:135–146.

Antoine Bordes, Nicolas Usunier, Alberto Garcia-Duran, Jason Weston, and Oksana Yakhnenko. 2013. Translating Embeddings for Modeling Multi-relational Data. In *Advances in Neural Information Processing Systems 26*, pages 2787–2795.

Yixin Cao, Lifu Huang, Heng Ji, Xu Chen, and Juanzi Li. 2017. Bridge Text and Knowledge by Learning Multi-Prototype Entity Mention Embedding. In *Proceedings of the 55th Annual Meeting of the Association for Computational Linguistics (Volume 1: Long Papers)*, pages 1623–1633.

Haotian Chen, Sahil Wadhwa, Xi David Li, and Andrej Zukov-Gregoric. 2019. YELM: End-to-End Contextualized Entity Linking. *arXiv preprint arXiv:1911.03834v1*.

Mark Davis. 2019. Unicode Text Segmentation. *Unicode Technical Reports*.

Jacob Devlin, Ming-Wei Chang, Kenton Lee, and Kristina Toutanova. 2019. BERT: Pre-training of Deep Bidirectional Transformers for Language Understanding. In *Proceedings of the 2019 Conference of the North American Chapter of the Association for Computational Linguistics: Human Language Technologies, Volume 1 (Long and Short Papers)*, pages 4171–4186.

Phuc H. Duong, Hien T. Nguyen, Hieu N. Duong, Khoa Ngo, and Dat Ngo. 2019. A Hybrid Approach to Paraphrase Detection. In *Proceedings of 2018 5th NAFOSTED Conference on Information and Computer Science*, pages 366–371.

Yotam Eshel, Noam Cohen, Kira Radinsky, Shaul Markovitch, Ikuya Yamada, and Omer Levy. 2017. Named Entity Disambiguation for Noisy Text. In *Proceedings of the 21st Conference on Computational Natural Language Learning*, pages 58–68.

Lev Finkelstein, Evgeniy Gabrilovich, Yossi Matias, Ehud Rivlin, Zach Solan, Gadi Wolfman, and Eytan Ruppin. 2002. Placing Search in Context: The Concept Revisited. *ACM Transactions on Information Systems*, 20(1):116–131.

Octavian-Eugen Ganea and Thomas Hofmann. 2017. Deep Joint Entity Disambiguation with Local Neural Attention. In *Proceedings of the 2017 Conference on Empirical Methods in Natural Language Processing*, pages 2619–2629.

Felix Hill, Roi Reichart, and Anna Korhonen. 2015. SimLex-999: Evaluating Semantic Models with Genuine Similarity Estimation. *Computational Linguistics*, 41(4):665–695.

Johannes Hoffart, Stephan Seufert, Dat Ba Nguyen, Martin Theobald, and Gerhard Weikum. 2012. KORE: Keyphrase Overlap Relatedness for Entity Disambiguation. In *Proceedings of the 21st ACM International Conference on Information and Knowledge Management*, pages 545–554.

Zhiting Hu, Poyao Huang, Yuntian Deng, Yingkai Gao, and Eric Xing. 2015. Entity Hierarchy Embedding. In *Proceedings of the 53rd Annual Meeting of the Association for Computational Linguistics and the 7th International Joint Conference on Natural Language Processing (Volume 1: Long Papers)*, pages 1292–1300.

Alicia Lara-Clares and Ana Garcia-Serrano. 2019. LSI2 UNED at eHealth-KD Challenge 2019: A Few-shot Learning Model for Knowledge Discovery from eHealth Documents. In *Proceedings of the Iberian Languages Evaluation Forum*.

Yuezhang Li, Ronghuo Zheng, Tian Tian, Zhiting Hu, Rahul Iyer, and Katia Sycara. 2016. Joint Embedding of Hierarchical Categories and Entities for Concept Categorization and Dataless Classification. In *Proceedings of the 26th International Conference on Computational Linguistics*, pages 2678–2688.

Yankai Lin, Zhiyuan Liu, Maosong Sun, Yang Liu, and Xuan Zhu. 2015. Learning Entity and Relation Embeddings for Knowledge Graph Completion. In *Proceedings of the 29th AAAI Conference on Artificial Intelligence*, pages 2181–2187.

Laurens van der Maaten and Geoffrey Hinton. 2008. Visualizing Data using t-SNE. *Journal of machine learning research*, 9(Nov):2579–2605.

Leland McInnes, John Healy, and James Melville. 2018. UMAP: Uniform Manifold Approximation and Projection for Dimension Reduction. *arXiv preprint arXiv:1802.03426v1*.

Tomas Mikolov, Greg Corrado, Kai Chen, and Jeffrey Dean. 2013a. Efficient Estimation of Word Representations in Vector Space. In *Proceedings of the 2013 International Conference on Learning Representations*, pages 1–12.

Tomas Mikolov, Ilya Sutskever, Kai Chen, Greg S. Corrado, and Jeff Dean. 2013b. Distributed Representations of Words and Phrases and their Compositionality. In *Advances in Neural Information Processing Systems 26*, pages 3111–3119.

Pinelopi Papalampidi, Frank Keller, and Mirella Lapata. 2019. Movie Plot Analysis via Turning Point Identification. In *Proceedings of the 2019 Conference on Empirical Methods in Natural Language Processing and the 9th International Joint Conference on Natural Language Processing*, pages 1707–1717.

Matthew E. Peters, Mark Neumann, Robert Logan, Roy Schwartz, Vidur Joshi, Sameer Singh, and Noah A. Smith. 2019. Knowledge Enhanced Contextual Word Representations. In *Proceedings of the 2019 Conference on Empirical Methods in Natural Language Processing and the 9th International Joint Conference on Natural Language Processing*, pages 43–54.

Nina Poerner, Ulli Waltinger, and Hinrich Schütze. 2019. BERT is Not a Knowledge Base (Yet): Factual Knowledge vs. Name-Based Reasoning in Unsupervised QA. *arXiv preprint arXiv:1911.03681v1*.

Radim Řehůřek and Petr Sojka. 2010. Software Framework for Topic Modelling with Large Corpora. In *LREC 2010 Workshop on New Challenges for NLP Frameworks*, pages 45–50.

Petar Ristoski, Jessica Rosati, Tommaso Di Noia, Renato De Leone, and Heiko Paulheim. 2018. RDF2Vec: RDF Graph Embeddings and Their Applications. *Semantic Web*, 10(4):721–752.

Motoki Sato, Hiroyuki Shindo, Ikuya Yamada, and Yuji Matsumoto. 2017. Segment-Level Neural Conditional Random Fields for Named Entity Recognition. In *Proceedings of the Eighth International Joint Conference on Natural Language Processing (Volume 2: Short Papers)*, pages 97–102.

Haseeb Shah, Johannes Villmow, Adrian Ulges, Ulrich Schwanecke, and Faisal Shafait. 2019. An Open-World Extension to Knowledge Graph Completion Models. *Proceedings of the AAAI Conference on Artificial Intelligence*, 33:3044–3051.

Iknoor Singh, Deepak P, and Anoop K. 2019. On the Coherence of Fake News Articles. *arXiv preprint arXiv:1906.11126v1*.

Masatoshi Suzuki, Koji Matsuda, Satoshi Sekine, Naoaki Okazaki, and Kentaro Inui. 2018. A Joint Neural Model for Fine-Grained Named Entity Classification of Wikipedia Articles. *IEICE Transactions on Information and Systems*, E101.D(1):73–81.

Chen-Tse Tsai and Dan Roth. 2016. Cross-lingual Wikification Using Multilingual Embeddings. In *Proceedings of the 2016 Conference of the North American Chapter of the Association for Computational Linguistics: Human Language Technologies*, pages 589–598.

Zhen Wang, Jianwen Zhang, Jianlin Feng, and Zheng Chen. 2014. Knowledge Graph and Text Jointly Embedding. In *Proceedings of the 2014 Conference on Empirical Methods in Natural Language Processing*, pages 1591–1601.

Yadollah Yaghoobzadeh and Hinrich Schutze. 2015. Corpus-level Fine-grained Entity Typing Using Contextual Information. In *Proceedings of the 2015 Conference on Empirical Methods in Natural Language Processing*, pages 715–725.

Ikuya Yamada and Hiroyuki Shindo. 2019. Neural Attentive Bag-of-Entities Model for Text Classification. In *Proceedings of the 23rd Conference on Computational Natural Language Learning*, pages 563–573.

Ikuya Yamada, Hiroyuki Shindo, Hideaki Takeda, and Yoshiyasu Takefuji. 2016. Joint Learning of the Embedding of Words and Entities for Named Entity Disambiguation. In *Proceedings of the 20th SIGNLL Conference on Computational Natural Language Learning*, pages 250–259.

Ikuya Yamada, Hiroyuki Shindo, Hideaki Takeda, and Yoshiyasu Takefuji. 2017. Learning Distributed Representations of Texts and Entities from Knowledge Base. *Transactions of the Association for Computational Linguistics*, 5:397–411.

Ikuya Yamada, Hiroyuki Shindo, and Yoshiyasu Takefuji. 2018a. Representation Learning of Entities and Documents from Knowledge Base Descriptions. In *Proceedings of the 27th International Conference on Computational Linguistics*, pages 190–201.

Ikuya Yamada, Ryuji Tamaki, Hiroyuki Shindo, and Yoshiyasu Takefuji. 2018b. Studio Ousia's Quiz Bowl Question Answering System. In *The NIPS '17 Competition: Building Intelligent Systems*, pages 181–194.

Zhengyan Zhang, Xu Han, Zhiyuan Liu, Xin Jiang, Maosong Sun, and Qun Liu. 2019. ERNIE: Enhanced Language Representation with Informative Entities. In *Proceedings of the 57th Annual Meeting of the Association for Computational Linguistics*, pages 1441–1451.

ARES: A Reading Comprehension Ensembling Service

Anthony Ferritto, Lin Pan, Rishav Chakravarti, Salim Roukos
Radu Florian, J. William Murdock, Avirup Sil[*]
IBM Research AI
Yorktown Heights, NY
aferritto@ibm.com
{panl, rchakravarti, roukos, raduf, murdockj, avi}@us.ibm.com

Abstract

We introduce ARES (A Reading Comprehension Ensembling Service): a novel Machine Reading Comprehension (MRC) demonstration system which utilizes an ensemble of models to increase F1 by 2.3 points. While many of the top leaderboard submissions in popular MRC benchmarks such as the Stanford Question Answering Dataset (SQuAD) and Natural Questions (NQ) use model ensembles, the accompanying papers do not publish their ensembling strategies. In this work, we detail and evaluate various ensembling strategies using the NQ dataset. ARES leverages the CFO (Chakravarti et al., 2019) and ReactJS distributed frameworks to provide a scalable interactive Question Answering experience that capitalizes on the agreement (or lack thereof) between models to improve the answer visualization experience.

1 Introduction

Machine Reading Comprension (MRC) involves computer systems that can take a question and some text and produce an answer to that question using the content in that text. This field has recently received considerable attention, yielding popular leaderboard challenges such as SQuAD (Rajpurkar et al., 2016, 2018) and NQ (Kwiatkowski et al., 2019).

Currently, the top submissions on both the SQuAD and NQ leaderboards combine multiple system outputs. These ensembled systems traditionally outperform single models by 1-4 F-measure. Unfortunately, many of the papers for these systems provide little to no information about the ensembling techniques they use.

In this work, we use GAAMA, a prototype question-answering system using the MRC techniques of (Pan et al., 2019), as our starting point and explore how to ensemble multiple MRC models from GAAMA[1]. We evaluate these techniques on the NQ short answer task. Using our ensemble of models, for each example (question, passage pair), we take the top predictions per system, group by span (answer extracted from the passage), normalize and aggregate the scores, take the mean score across systems for each span, and then take the highest scoring short and long answer spans as our final prediction. These improved ensembling techniques are applied to our MRC systems to produce stronger answers.

Whereas other systems such as (Chakravarti et al., 2019; Yang et al., 2019a) and Allen NLP's[2] make use of a single model, we are able to use multiple models to produce a stronger result. We further take advantage of the fact that both the individual model predictions and the ensembed predictions are returned to help increase explainability for the user. For the graphical interface we use a heatmap to show the level of (dis)agreement between the underlying models along with the "best ensemble" answer. An example of this can be seen in Figure 1.

More completely, our contributions include:

- A novel MRC demonstration system, which leverages multiple underlying MRC model predictions and ensembles them for the user.

- A system architecture that provides scalability to the system designer (by leveraging the cloud ready CFO[3] (Chakravarti et al., 2019) orchestration framework) and flexibility to add and remove models based on the desired latency versus accuracy trade-off.

---

[*]Corresponding author.

[1]ARES can use any MRC model.

[2]`https://demo.allennlp.org/reading-comprehension`

[3]`https://github.com/IBM/flow-compiler/`

Proceedings of the 2020 EMNLP (Systems Demonstrations), pages 31–37
November 16-20, 2020. ©2020 Association for Computational Linguistics

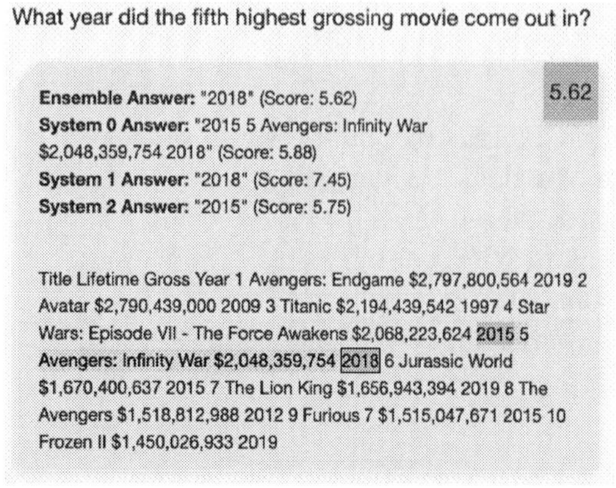

Figure 1: ARES client interface. The correct answer 2018 is boxed and the MRC system answers are highlighted based on a heatmap.

- A GUI with enhanced explainability that allows users to see the (dis)agreement of responses from individual models.

- An analysis of various ensembling strategies with experimental results on the challenging NQ dataset which show that diversity of models is better for ensembling than seed variation. We detail the process for selecting the "best-diverse" set.

2 Related Work

2.1 Ensembled MRC Systems

There have been multiple works creating systems utilizing MRC models. BERTserini (Yang et al., 2019a) is an end-to-end question answering system utilizing a BERT (Devlin et al., 2019) model. (Ma et al., 2019) creates an end-to-end dialogue tracking system featuring an XLNet (Yang et al., 2019b) model. (Qu et al., 2020) performs conversational question answering and utilizes separate ALBERT (Lan et al., 2019) encoders for the question and passage in addition to a BERT (Devlin et al., 2019) model. Allen NLP's MRC demo provides reading comprehension through the use of a variety of different model types. However, to the best of our knowledge we are the first to propose using an ensemble of MRC models to provide a MRC service.

There have likewise been multiple approaches to visualization of system results. BertSerini highlights the answer in the context. Allen NLP's demo allows using gradients to view the most important words in the passage. ARES allows for viewing the most important regions of the passage from the perspective of different models in addition to boxing in the ensembled answer as seen in Figure 1.

2.2 Ensembling Techniques

Many of the top recent MRC systems publish few details on their ensembling strategies. Systems such as (Devlin et al., 2019; Alberti et al., 2019; Liu et al., 2019; Wang et al., 2019; Lan et al., 2019; Group, 2017; Seo et al., 2016) report using ensembles of 5 to 18 models to gain 1.3 - 4 F1 points on tasks such as GLUE, SQuAD 1.0, and SQuAD 2.0; unfortunately most of these systems report little information on their ensembling techniques. (Liu et al., 2020) reports slightly more information: gaining 1.8 and 0.6 F1 points short answer (SA) and long answer (LA) respectively on the NQ dev set with an ensemble of three models with different hyperparameters.

We also consider work in the field of information retrieval (IR) as a way to aggregate multiple scores for the same span. Similar to the popular Comb-SUM and CombMNZ (Kurland and Culpepper, 2018; Wu, 2012) methods, considering the spans as the "documents", we use span-score weighted aggregation in our noisy-or aggregator. Futher, we additionally incorporate the use of rank-based scoring from Borda (Young, 1974) and RRF (Cormack et al., 2009) for our exponential sum approach (in addition to utilizing score for this approach). We finally consider a reciprocal rank sum aggregation strategy based on the ideas in RRF (Cormack et al., 2009). To our knowledge this is the first published application of IR methods for this purpose.

3 System Overview

We describe the architecture of the system and additionally provide an overview of the client (GUI) used in this demonstration. The system is composed of MRC and ensembling services which are orchestrated by CFO. The MRC services (in our case GAAMA) provide reading comprehension via a transformer model (Pan et al., 2019); multiple services utilizing different model architectures are run to extract answers for a given question and passage. After the MRC services extract their answers, they are all passed to ARES which ensembles the results. The ensembling algorithm used by ARES is detailed in Sections 4 and 5. Note that the MRC service only extracts short answers, therefore only those portions of our ensembling approach are used.

Both the ensembled and original answers are then returned to the caller, allowing the clients to display the final ensembled answers and the original answers they were generated from to the end user.

More completely, the system takes the following as input through a grpc (Talvar, 2016) interface: question, passage, minimum confidence score threshold δ, maximum number of answers N, maximum number of answers per model n, and number of models k. These inputs are sent from the client (we discuss our client below) and received by the CFO node which orchestrates the containers. The choice of k is bounded on how many GAAMA containers are deployed (e.g. if there are 3 then $k \in \{1, 2, 3\}$). By tweaking the parameter k, clients can opt for increased accuracy (higher k) or decreased latency (lower k) as when multiple models run on the same GPU the request latency increases. As depicted in Figure 2 (where there are 3 MRC models running), each of the k=2 GAAMA containers then receive the question and passage from CFO, returning at most n answers to CFO. These answers, together with their confidence scores, are then sent to the ensembler by CFO which produces at most N ensembled answers (each with confidence score at least δ) and returns them to CFO. Finally, both the answers of the k models and the ensembled answers predicted by ARES are returned by CFO to the caller.

The GUI client for our system is based on a ReactJS[4] web interface. A request is taken as input from the user and sent to the system where is is processed as described above. When an answer with sufficient confidence score is returned, it is displayed to the user as seen in Figure 1. Both the ensembled answer and the individual answers are shown together with their respective confidence scores. These answers are also shown in the context of the original passage. The ensembled answer is boxed in. For the individual answers a character heatmap is created representing how many of the candidate answers each character appears in. This heatmap is used to highlight the passage different different colors corresponding to the heatmap (characters not used in any answers are not highlighted). Both the boxing and highlighting of answers are done using MarkJS[5]. Note that while these visualizations only show the top answer for each MRC model, n answers per model are ensembled together. If

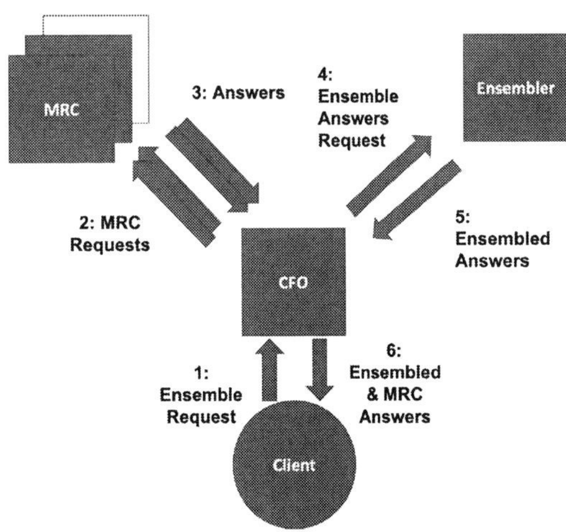

Figure 2: Architecture of the the ARES system. We use GAAMA as our MRC service.

an answer with sufficient confidence score is not returned, this is relayed to the user through the GUI.

4 Methods

We investigate a number of strategies for ensembling models on the NQ dataset. We use the NQ dataset as it is more realistic and challenging than SQuAD, as its questions were created by Google Search users prior to seeing the answer documents (so they do not suffer from observational bias). In order to formally compare approaches we partition the NQ dev set into "dev-train" and "dev-test" by taking the first three dev files for the "train" set and using the last two for the "test" set (the original dev set for NQ is partitioned into 5 files for distribution). This yields "train" and "test" sets of 4,653 and 3,177 examples respectively.

For each strategy considered we search for the best k-model ensemble over the "train" set and then evaluate on the "test" set. For these experiments we use $k = 4$ as this is the number of models that we can decode in the 24 hours (the limit for the NQ leaderboard). We begin by outlining our core strategy that underlies the approaches we have investigated.

Using this strategy we investigate a baseline approach of ensembling multiple versions of the same model trained with different seeds. We then investigate search strategies for choosing the best models from candidates trained with different hyperparameters, in addition to different normalization and aggregation strategies that are used on a set of candidates.

---

[4]https://reactjs.org/
[5]https://markjs.io/

4.1 Core Strategy

For each example processed by the k systems being ensembled, our system assigns a score to each long and short span according to the normalization and aggregation strategies (see below). Note that our system currently only predicts single short spans rather than sets, so we currently score each short span independently.

We use the top-20 candidate long and short answers (LA and SA respectively) for each system. We experimented with additional values, but empirically found 20 to provide an ideal accuracy versus latency trade-off given hardware resources. To combine systems we take the arithmetic mean of the scores for each long and short span predicted by at least one system. We have experimented with other approaches such as median, geometric mean, and harmonic mean; however these are omitted here as they resulted in much lower scores than arithmetic mean. For spans which are only predicted by some systems a score of zero is assigned (for the systems which do not predict the span) to penalize spans which are only predicted by some systems. The predicted long span is then the span with the greatest arithmetic mean. Similarly for short answers the predicted span is the one with the greatest arithmetic mean (it must also be in a non-null long answer span).

4.2 Seed Ensembles

We first examine the baseline approach of ensembling k versions of the same model trained with the same hyperparameters, only varying the seed between models. We use the model with the best hyperparameters based on (Pan et al., 2019) having the highest sum of short and long answer F1 scores on dev. This model is trained $k-1$ additional times with different seeds and then they are all ensembled using the core strategy.

4.3 Search Strategies

We consider two main strategies when searching for ensembles: exhaustive and greedy. These search over model candidates with different hyperparameters as described in (Pan et al., 2019). Note that we also considered a "simple greedy" approach where the k best models on dev were selected, however this underperformed other approaches by 1 - 2 F1 points.

In exhaustive search we consider all possible ensembles, whereas in greedy search we build the ensemble one model at a time by looking for which

model we can add to an i model ensemble to make the best $i + 1$ model ensemble.

4.3.1 Exhaustive Search (ES)

In the exhaustive search approach where we consider each of the $\binom{m}{k}$ ensembles of k candidates from our group of m models. We then use our core strategy for each ensemble to obtain short and long answer F1 scores for each ensemble. After searching all possible ensembles we return two ensembles: (i) the ensemble with the highest long answer F1 score and (ii) the ensemble with the highest short answer F1 score.

4.3.2 Greedy Search (GS)

We select the models by greedily building $1, 2, ..., k$ model ensembles optimizing for short or long answer F1 using our core strategy.

4.4 Normalization Strategies

We investigate two primary methods for normalizing the scores predicted for a span: not normalizing and logistic regression. We also investigated normalizing by dividing the scores for a span by the sum of all scores for the span, however we omit these results for brevity as they did not produce interesting results.

4.4.1 None

As a baseline we run experiments where the scores for a span are used as-is.

4.4.2 Logistic Regression

We also experiment with normalization using logistic regression where the scores from the top prediction for the "dev-train" examples is used to predict whether the example is correctly answered. In our experiments using the top example performed equally well to using the top 20 predictions per example to train on. We also experimented with using other features which did not improve performance. To ensure an appropriate regularization strength is used, we use the scikit-learn (Pedregosa et al., 2011) implementation of logistic regression with stratified 5-fold cross-validation to select the L2 regularization strength.

4.5 Aggregation Strategies

We consider a number of aggregation strategies to produce a single span score for each span predicted by a system for an example. These include the baseline approach of max as well as the exponentially decaying sum, reciprocal rank sum, and noisy-or methods influenced by IR. These approaches operate on a vector P of scores on which one of the above normalization strategies has been applied.

4.5.1 Max

For a vector P, $score = \max_{i=1}^{|P|} P_i$.

4.5.2 Exponential Sum (ExS)

Based on the ideas of (Young, 1974; Cormack et al., 2009), we sort P in descending order and take

$$score = \sum_{i=1}^{|P|} P_i * \beta^{i-1}$$

for some constant β (we use $\beta = 0.5$).

4.5.3 Reciprocal Rank Sum (RRS)

Based on the ideas of (Cormack et al., 2009), we sort P in descending order and take

$$score = \sum_{i=1}^{|P|} P_i * \frac{1}{i}$$

4.5.4 Noisy-Or (NO)

Based on the ideas of (Kurland and Culpepper, 2018; Wu, 2012), we take

$$score = 1 - \prod_{i=1}^{|P|}(1 - P_i)$$

5 Experiments and Results

We examine two types of ensembling experiments: (i) ensembling the same model trained with different seeds and (ii) ensembling different models. Ensembling the same model trained on different seeds attempts to smooth the variance to produce a stronger result. On the other hand ensembling different models attempts to find models that may not be the strongest individually but harmonize well to produce strong results. Throughout this section we will use $SA\ F1$ and $LA\ F1$ to denote the short and long answer performance on "dev-test". Similarly we will use N_S to indicate the number of models searched for an experiment and types SA and LA to indicate optimization for SA and LA F1 respectively.

5.1 Seed experiments

In Table 1 we find that there is a benefit to ensembling multiple versions of the same model trained with different seeds. Note that there is some data

# Models	$SA\ F1$	$LA\ F1$
1	56.1	67.1
4	**58.7**	**69.6**

Table 1: Ensembling the same model trained with different seeds.

Search	N_S	Type	$SA\ F1$	$LA\ F1$
-	-	-	58.7	69.6
ES	20	LA	59.6	70.5
ES	20	SA	59.6	70.0
GS	41	LA	**59.7**	**70.8**
GS	41	SA	59.1	69.8

Table 2: Comparison of Search Strategies. All experiments run without normalization using max aggregation. The first row is 4 seed ensemble from Table 1.

snooping ocuring here as the model is selected based on full dev performance (which is a superset of "dev-test"). RikiNet (Liu et al., 2020) and the 1 model performance reported above represent the top published NQ models at the time of writing this paper.

5.2 Main experiments

We investigate the different search strategies in Table 2. We find that the greedy approach performs best overall, with the greedy ensemble optimized for LA performance performing the best on both short and long answer F1. Note that the numbers seen here, particularly when optimizing greedily for long answer performance are higher than those observed for ensembling the same model with multiple seeds. We hypothesize the superior generalization of greedy is due to exhaustive search "overfitting". For the remainder of this paper we will focus on greedy search optimized for long answer to keep the number of experiments presented to a manageable level.

We investigate the impact of the IR inspired normalization strategies in Table 3. The max experiment is as-before run without normalization to greedily optimize for long answer F1. The other experiments here are normalized with logistic regression, as our experiments showed that not normalizing decreased performance. We find that using max aggregation results in the best short answer F1 whereas using normalized noisy-or aggregation results in the best long answer F1. Based on these results, we run a final experiment using unnormal-

Aggregator	$SA\ F1$	$LA\ F1$
Max	**59.7**	70.8
Exponential Sum	58.3	70.4
Reciprocal Rank Sum	57.3	70.7
Noisy-Or	57.3	**71.5**

Table 3: Comparison of IR inspired aggregation strategies. All experiments run with a greedy search strategy optimized exclusively for long answer F1 with logistic regression normalization (except max which is not normalized).

ized max for short answers and logistic regression normalized noisy-or works for long answers. We find that this approach produces the strongest performance for both short and long answers with 59.3 $SA\ F1$ and 71.5 $LA\ F1$. Consequently we use unnormalized max ensembling of GAAMA answers (as GAAMA works on short answers) from 4 models in ARES. These numbers translate to a full dev performance of 59.3 short answer F1 and 71.1 long answer F1, which represents an improvement of 2.3 short answer F1 and 4.0 long answer F1 over our best single model.

6 Ensemble Candidate Contributions

When doing manual error analysis on the NQ dev set, we do observe patterns suggesting that each of the ensemble components do bring different strengths over the single best model. For example, the Wikipedia article for *Salary Cap* contains multiple sentences related to the query *"when did the nfl adopt a salary cap"*:

> The new Collective Bargaining Agreement (CBA) formulated in 2011 had an initial salary cap of $120 million...The cap was first introduced for the 1994 season and was initially $34.6 million. Both the cap and...

The later sentence contains the correct answer, *1994*, since the question is asking for when the salary cap was initially adopted. One of our models A correctly makes this prediction whereas another one of our models B predicts *2011* from the earlier sentence. There are also cases where the correct answer span appears in the middle or later part of a paragraph and, though our model B predict the spans correctly, they assign a lower score (relative to its optimal threshold) than the model A. The position bias, therefore, appears to hurt the performance of the system in certain situations where location of the answer span relative to the paragraph is not a useful signal of correctness.

Finally, in our manual review we do see that the ensemble of these models performs better in the expected ways: (1) boosting scores when multiple models agree on an answer span even though no one model is extremely confident (2) reducing confidence when there is disagreement among models.

7 Conclusion

We introduce a novel concept for a MRC service, ARES, which uses an ensemble of models to respond to requests. This provides for multiple advantages over the traditional single model paradigm: improved F1, the ability to control the performance vs runtime tradeoff for each individual request, and improved explaiability of results by showing both candidate answers in addition to the final ensembled answer. We outline several ensembling approaches for question answering models investigated for use in ARES and compare their performance on the NQ challenge. Our findings show that ensembling unique models outperforms ensembling the same model trained with different seeds and provide further analysis to show how ensembling diverse models improves performance. We also show that using unnormalized max aggregation for short answers and logistic regression normalized noisy-or aggregation for long answers yields an F1 improvement of 2 to 4 points over single model performance on the NQ challenge.

References

Chris Alberti, Daniel Andor, Emily Pitler, Jacob Devlin, and Michael Collins. 2019. Synthetic QA corpora generation with roundtrip consistency. *CoRR*, abs/1906.05416.

Rishav Chakravarti, Cezar Pendus, Andrzej Sakrajda, Anthony Ferritto, Lin Pan, Michael Glass, Vittorio Castelli, J William Murdock, Radu Florian, Salim Roukos, and et al. 2019. Cfo: A framework for building production nlp systems. *Proceedings of the 2019 Conference on Empirical Methods in Natural Language Processing and the 9th International Joint Conference on Natural Language Processing (EMNLP-IJCNLP): System Demonstrations.*

Gordon V. Cormack, Charles L A Clarke, and Stefan Buettcher. 2009. Reciprocal rank fusion outperforms condorcet and individual rank learning methods. In *Proceedings of the 32Nd International ACM SIGIR Conference on Research and Development in Information Retrieval*, SIGIR '09, pages 758–759, New York, NY, USA. ACM.

Jacob Devlin, Ming-Wei Chang, Kenton Lee, and Kristina Toutanova. 2019. BERT: Pre-training of deep bidirectional transformers for language understanding. In *NAACL-HLT*.

Natural Language Computing Group. 2017. R-net: Machine reading comprehension with self-matching networks.

Oren Kurland and J. Culpepper. 2018. Fusion in information retrieval: Sigir 2018 half-day tutorial. pages 1383–1386.

Tom Kwiatkowski, Jennimaria Palomaki, Olivia Redfield, Michael Collins, Ankur Parikh, Chris Alberti, Danielle Epstein, Illia Polosukhin, Matthew Kelcey, Jacob Devlin, Kenton Lee, Kristina N. Toutanova, Llion Jones, Ming-Wei Chang, Andrew Dai, Jakob Uszkoreit, Quoc Le, and Slav Petrov. 2019. Natural Questions: a benchmark for question answering research. *TACL*.

Zhenzhong Lan, Mingda Chen, Sebastian Goodman, Kevin Gimpel, Piyush Sharma, and Radu Soricut. 2019. Albert: A lite bert for self-supervised learning of language representations.

Dayiheng Liu, Yeyun Gong, Jie Fu, Yu Yan, Jiusheng Chen, Daxin Jiang, Jiancheng Lv, and Nan Duan. 2020. Rikinet: Reading wikipedia pages for natural question answering.

Yinhan Liu, Myle Ott, Naman Goyal, Jingfei Du, Mandar Joshi, Danqi Chen, Omer Levy, Mike Lewis, Luke Zettlemoyer, and Veselin Stoyanov. 2019. RoBERTa: A robustly optimized BERT pretraining approach. *CoRR*, abs/1907.11692.

Yue Ma, Zengfeng Zeng, Dawei Zhu, Xuan Li, Yiying Yang, Xiaoyuan Yao, Kaijie Zhou, and Jianping Shen. 2019. An end-to-end dialogue state tracking system with machine reading comprehension and wide & deep classification.

Lin Pan, Rishav Chakravarti, Anthony Ferritto, Michael Glass, Alfio Gliozzo, Salim Roukos, Radu Florian, and Avirup Sil. 2019. Frustratingly easy natural question answering.

F. Pedregosa, G. Varoquaux, A. Gramfort, V. Michel, B. Thirion, O. Grisel, M. Blondel, P. Prettenhofer, R. Weiss, V. Dubourg, J. Vanderplas, A. Passos, D. Cournapeau, M. Brucher, M. Perrot, and E. Duchesnay. 2011. Scikit-learn: Machine learning in Python. *Journal of Machine Learning Research*, 12:2825–2830.

Chen Qu, Liu Yang, Cen Chen, Minghui Qiu, W. Bruce Croft, and Mohit Iyyer. 2020. Open-retrieval conversational question answering.

Pranav Rajpurkar, Robin Jia, and Percy Liang. 2018. Know what you don't know: Unanswerable questions for SQuAD. *arXiv preprint arXiv:1806.03822*.

Pranav Rajpurkar, Jian Zhang, Konstantin Lopyrev, and Percy Liang. 2016. SQuAD: 100,000+ questions for machine comprehension of text. *EMNLP*.

Min Joon Seo, Aniruddha Kembhavi, Ali Farhadi, and Hannaneh Hajishirzi. 2016. Bidirectional attention flow for machine comprehension. *CoRR*, abs/1611.01603.

Varun Talvar. 2016. grpc design and implementation. Talk by Varun Talwar, Product Manager at Google at Stanford, California [Accessed: 2019 06 20].

Alex Wang, Amanpreet Singh, Julian Michael, Felix Hill, Omer Levy, and Samuel R. Bowman. 2019. GLUE: A multi-task benchmark and analysis platform for natural language understanding. In *International Conference on Learning Representations*.

Shengli Wu. 2012. *Data Fusion in Information Retrieval*. Springer Publishing Company, Incorporated.

Wei Yang, Yuqing Xie, Aileen Lin, Xingyu Li, Luchen Tan, Kun Xiong, Ming Li, and Jimmy Lin. 2019a. End-to-end open-domain question answering with. *Proceedings of the 2019 Conference of the North*.

Zhilin Yang, Zihang Dai, Yiming Yang, Jaime G. Carbonell, Ruslan Salakhutdinov, and Quoc V. Le. 2019b. XLNet: Generalized autoregressive pretraining for language understanding. *CoRR*, abs/1906.08237.

H.P Young. 1974. An axiomatization of borda's rule. *Journal of Economic Theory*, 9(1):43 – 52.

 Transformers: State-of-the-Art Natural Language Processing

Thomas Wolf, Lysandre Debut, Victor Sanh, Julien Chaumond, Clement Delangue,
Anthony Moi, Pierric Cistac, Tim Rault, Rémi Louf, Morgan Funtowicz, Joe Davison,
Sam Shleifer, Patrick von Platen, Clara Ma, Yacine Jernite, Julien Plu, Canwen Xu,
Teven Le Scao, Sylvain Gugger, Mariama Drame, Quentin Lhoest, Alexander M. Rush

Hugging Face, Brooklyn, USA / `{first-name}@huggingface.co`

Abstract

Recent progress in natural language processing has been driven by advances in both model architecture and model pretraining. Transformer architectures have facilitated building higher-capacity models and pretraining has made it possible to effectively utilize this capacity for a wide variety of tasks. *Transformers* is an open-source library with the goal of opening up these advances to the wider machine learning community. The library consists of carefully engineered state-of-the art Transformer architectures under a unified API. Backing this library is a curated collection of pretrained models made by and available for the community. *Transformers* is designed to be extensible by researchers, simple for practitioners, and fast and robust in industrial deployments. The library is available at `https://github.com/huggingface/transformers`.

1 Introduction

The Transformer (Vaswani et al., 2017) has rapidly become the dominant architecture for natural language processing, surpassing alternative neural models such as convolutional and recurrent neural networks in performance for tasks in both natural language understanding and natural language generation. The architecture scales with training data and model size, facilitates efficient parallel training, and captures long-range sequence features.

Model pretraining (McCann et al., 2017; Howard and Ruder, 2018; Peters et al., 2018; Devlin et al., 2018) allows models to be trained on generic corpora and subsequently be easily adapted to specific tasks with strong performance. The Transformer architecture is particularly conducive to pretraining on large text corpora, leading to major gains in accuracy on downstream tasks including text classification (Yang et al., 2019), language understanding (Liu et al., 2019b; Wang et al., 2018, 2019), machine translation (Lample and Conneau, 2019a), coreference resolution (Joshi et al., 2019), commonsense inference (Bosselut et al., 2019), and summarization (Lewis et al., 2019) among others.

This advance leads to a wide range of practical challenges that must be addressed in order for these models to be widely utilized. The ubiquitous use of the Transformer calls for systems to train, analyze, scale, and augment the model on a variety of platforms. The architecture is used as a building block to design increasingly sophisticated extensions and precise experiments. The pervasive adoption of pretraining methods has led to the need to distribute, fine-tune, deploy, and compress the core pretrained models used by the community.

Transformers is a library dedicated to supporting Transformer-based architectures and facilitating the distribution of pretrained models. At the core of the libary is an implementation of the Transformer which is designed for both research and production. The philosophy is to support industrial-strength implementations of popular model variants that are easy to read, extend, and deploy. On this foundation, the library supports the distribution and usage of a wide-variety of pretrained models in a centralized model hub. This hub supports users to compare different models with the same minimal API and to experiment with shared models on a variety of different tasks.

Transformers is an ongoing effort maintained by the team of engineers and researchers at Hugging Face with support from a vibrant community of over 400 external contributors. The library is released under the Apache 2.0 license and is available on GitHub[1]. Detailed documentation and tutorials are available on Hugging Face's website[2].

---

[1] `https://github.com/huggingface/transformers`

[2] `https://huggingface.co/transformers/`

Proceedings of the 2020 EMNLP (Systems Demonstrations), pages 38–45
November 16-20, 2020. ©2020 Association for Computational Linguistics

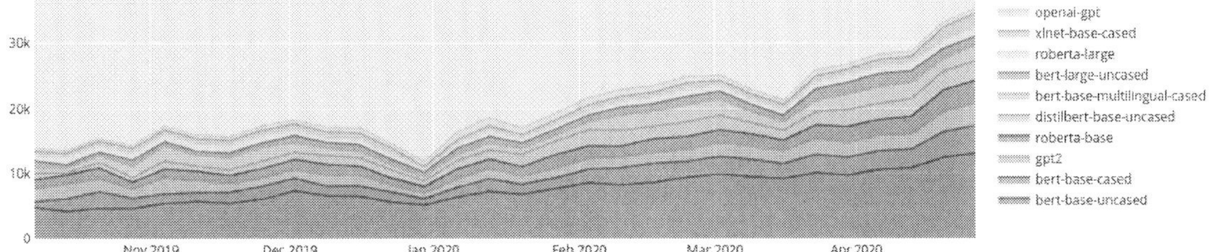

Figure 1: Average daily unique downloads of the most downloaded pretrained models, Oct. 2019 to May 2020.

2 Related Work

The NLP and ML communities have a strong culture of building open-source research tools. The structure of *Transformers* is inspired by the pioneering tensor2tensor library (Vaswani et al., 2018) and the original source code for BERT (Devlin et al., 2018), both from Google Research. The concept of providing easy caching for pretrained models stemmed from AllenNLP (Gardner et al., 2018). The library is also closely related to neural translation and language modeling systems, such as Fairseq (Ott et al., 2019), OpenNMT (Klein et al., 2017), Texar (Hu et al., 2018), Megatron-LM (Shoeybi et al., 2019), and Marian NMT (Junczys-Dowmunt et al., 2018). Building on these elements, *Transformers* adds extra user-facing features to allow for easy downloading, caching, and fine-tuning of the models as well as seamless transition to production. *Transformers* maintains some compatibility with these libraries, most directly including a tool for performing inference using models from Marian NMT and Google's BERT.

There is a long history of easy-to-use, user-facing libraries for general-purpose NLP. Two core libraries are NLTK (Loper and Bird, 2002) and Stanford CoreNLP (Manning et al., 2014), which collect a variety of different approaches to NLP in a single package. More recently, general-purpose, open-source libraries have focused primarily on machine learning for a variety of NLP tasks, these include Spacy (Honnibal and Montani, 2017), AllenNLP (Gardner et al., 2018), flair (Akbik et al., 2019), and Stanza (Qi et al., 2020). *Transformers* provides similar functionality as these libraries. Additionally, each of these libraries now uses the

Transformers library and model hub as a low-level framework.

Since *Transformers* provides a hub for NLP models, it is also related to popular model hubs including Torch Hub and TensorFlow Hub which collect framework-specific model parameters for easy use. Unlike these hubs, *Transformers* is domain-specific which allows the system to provide automatic support for model analysis, usage, deployment, benchmarking, and easy replicability.

3 Library Design

Transformers is designed to mirror the standard NLP machine learning model pipeline: process data, apply a model, and make predictions. Although the library includes tools facilitating training and development, in this technical report we focus on the core modeling specifications. For complete details about the features of the library refer to the documentation available on `https://huggingface.co/transformers/`.

Every model in the library is fully defined by three building blocks shown in the diagram in Figure 2: (a) a tokenizer, which converts raw text to sparse index encodings, (b) a transformer, which transforms sparse indices to contextual embeddings, and (c) a head, which uses contextual embeddings to make a task-specific prediction. Most user needs can be addressed with these three components.

Transformers Central to the library are carefully tested implementations of Transformer architecture variants which are widely used in NLP. The full list of currently implemented architectures is shown in Figure 2 (Left). While each of these architectures

Heads				
Name	Input	Output	Tasks	Ex. Datasets
Language Modeling	$x_{1:n-1}$	$x_n \in \mathcal{V}$	Generation	WikiText-103
Sequence Classification	$x_{1:N}$	$y \in \mathcal{C}$	Classification, Sentiment Analysis	GLUE, SST, MNLI
Question Answering	$x_{1:M}, x_{M:N}$	y span $[1:N]$	QA, Reading Comprehension	SQuAD, Natural Questions
Token Classification	$x_{1:N}$	$y_{1:N} \in \mathcal{C}^N$	NER, Tagging	OntoNotes, WNUT
Multiple Choice	$x_{1:N}, \mathcal{X}$	$y \in \mathcal{X}$	Text Selection	SWAG, ARC
Masked LM	$x_{1:N \backslash n}$	$x_n \in \mathcal{V}$	Pretraining	Wikitext, C4
Conditional Generation	$x_{1:N}$	$y_{1:M} \in \mathcal{V}^M$	Translation, Summarization	WMT, IWSLT, CNN/DM, XSum

Transformers	
Masked $[x_{1:N \backslash n} \Rightarrow x_n]$	
BERT	(Devlin et al., 2018)
RoBERTa	(Liu et al., 2019a)
Autoregressive $[x_{1:n-1} \Rightarrow x_n]$	
GPT / GPT-2	(Radford et al., 2019)
Trans-XL	(Dai et al., 2019)
XLNet	(Yang et al., 2019)
Seq-to-Seq $[\sim x_{1:N} \Rightarrow x_{1:N}]$	
BART	(Lewis et al., 2019)
T5	(Raffel et al., 2019)
MarianMT	(J.-Dowmunt et al., 2018)
Specialty: Multimodal	
MMBT	(Kiela et al., 2019)
Specialty: Long-Distance	
Reformer	(Kitaev et al., 2020)
Longformer	(Beltagy et al., 2020)
Specialty: Efficient	
ALBERT	(Lan et al., 2019)
Electra	(Clark et al., 2020)
DistilBERT	(Sanh et al., 2019)
Specialty: Multilingual	
XLM/RoBERTa	(Lample and Conneau, 2019b)

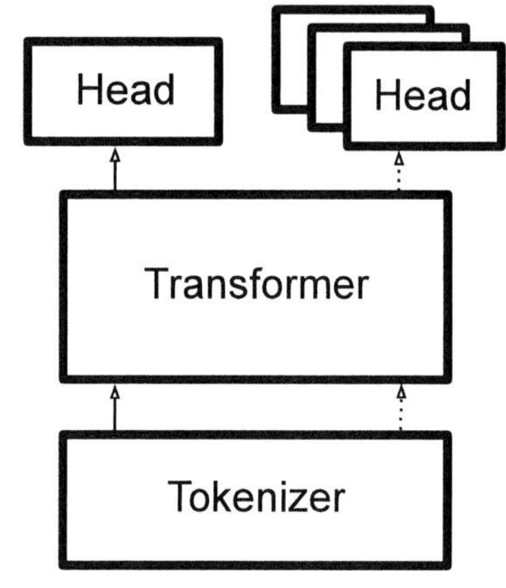

Tokenizers	
Name	Ex. Uses
Character-Level BPE	NMT, GPT
Byte-Level BPE	GPT-2
WordPiece	BERT
SentencePiece	XLNet
Unigram	LM
Character	Reformer
Custom	Bio-Chem

Figure 2: The *Transformers* library. **(Diagram-Right)** Each model is made up of a Tokenizer, Transformer, and Head. The model is pretrained with a fixed head and can then be further fine-tuned with alternate heads for different tasks. **(Bottom)** Each model uses a specific Tokenizer either implemented in Python or in Rust. These often differ in small details, but need to be in sync with pretraining. **(Left)** Transformer architectures specialized for different tasks, e.g. understanding versus generation, or for specific use-cases, e.g. speed, image+text. **(Top)** heads allow a Transformer to be used for different tasks. Here we assume the input token sequence is $x_{1:N}$ from a vocabulary $\mathcal{V}$, and y represents different possible outputs, possibly from a class set $\mathcal{C}$. Example datasets represent a small subset of example code distributed with the library.

shares the same multi-headed attention core, there are significant differences between them including positional representations, masking, padding, and the use of sequence-to-sequence design. Additionally, various models are built to target different applications of NLP such as understanding, generation, and conditional generation, plus specialized use cases such as fast inference or multi-lingual applications.

Practically, all models follow the same hierarchy of abstraction: a base class implements the model's computation graph from an encoding (projection on the embedding matrix) through the series of self-attention layers to the final encoder hidden states. The base class is specific to each model and closely follows the model's original implementation which gives users the flexibility to easily dissect the inner workings of each individual architecture. In most cases, each model is implemented in a single file to enable ease of extensibility.

Wherever possible, different architectures follow the same API allowing users to switch easily between different models. A set of `Auto` classes provides a unified API that enables very fast switching between models and even between frameworks. These classes automatically instantiate with the configuration specified by the user-specified pretrained model.

Tokenizers A critical NLP-specific aspect of the library is the implementations of the tokenizers necessary to use each model. Tokenizer classes (each inheriting from a common base class) can either be instantiated from a corresponding pretrained model or can be configured manually. These classes store the vocabulary token-to-index map for their corresponding model and handle the encoding and decoding of input sequences according to a model's specific tokenization process. The tokenizers implemented are shown in Figure 2 (Right). Users can easily modify tokenizer with interfaces to add additional token mappings, special tokens (such as classification or separation tokens), or otherwise resize the vocabulary.

Tokenizers can also implement additional useful features for the users. These range from token type indices in the case of sequence classification to maximum length sequence truncating taking into account the added model-specific special tokens (most pretrained Transformer models have a maximum sequence length).

For training on very large datasets, Python-based tokenization is often undesirably slow. In the most recent release, *Transformers* switched its implementation to use a highly-optimized tokenization library by default. This low-level library, available at `https://github.com/huggingface/tokenizers`, is written in Rust to speed up the tokenization procedure both during training and deployment.

Heads Each Transformer can be paired with one out of several ready-implemented heads with outputs amenable to common types of tasks. These heads are implemented as additional wrapper classes on top of the base class, adding a specific output layer, and optional loss function, on top of the Transformer's contextual embeddings. The full set of implemented heads are shown in Figure 2 (Top). These classes follow a similar naming pattern: `XXXForSequenceClassification` where `XXX` is the name of the model and can be used for adaptation (fine-tuning) or pretraining. Some heads, such as conditional generation, support extra functionality like sampling and beam search.

For pretrained models, we release the heads used to pretrain the model itself. For instance, for BERT we release the language modeling and next sentence prediction heads which allows easy for adaptation using the pretraining objectives. We also make it easy for users to utilize the same core Transformer parameters with a variety of other heads for finetuning. While each head can be used generally, the library also includes a collection of examples that show each head on real problems. These examples demonstrate how a pretrained model can be adapted with a given head to achieve state-of-the-art results on a large variety of NLP tasks.

4   Community Model Hub

Transformers aims to facilitate easy use and distribution of pretrained models. Inherently this is a community process; a single pretraining run facilitates fine-tuning on many specific tasks. The Model Hub makes it simple for any end-user to access a model for use with their own data. This hub now contains 2,097 user models, both pretrained and fine-tuned, from across the community. Figure 1 shows the increase and distribution of popular transformers over time. While core models like BERT and GPT-2 continue to be popular, other specialized models including DistilBERT (Sanh et al., 2019), which was developed for the library, are

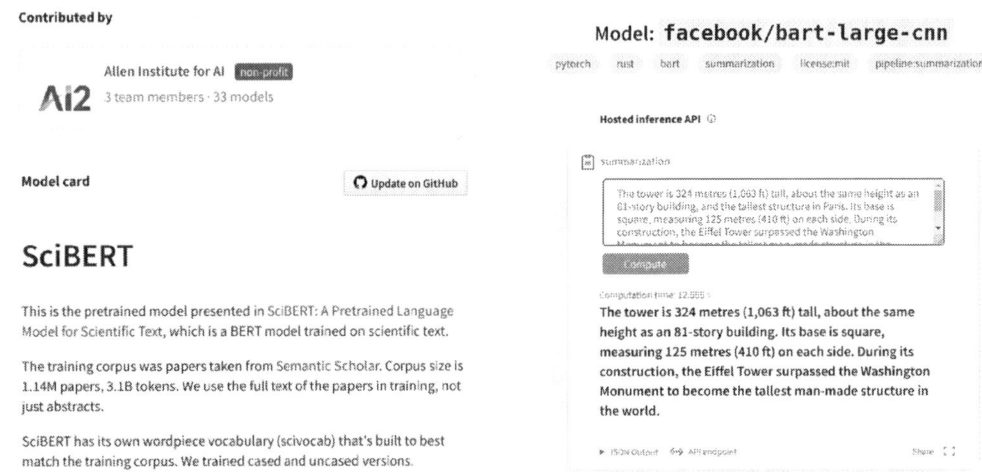

Figure 3: *Transformers* Model Hub. **(Left)** Example of a model page and model card for SciBERT (Beltagy et al., 2019), a pretrained model targeting extraction from scientific literature submitted by a community contributor. **(Right)** Example of an automatic inference widget for the pretrained BART (Lewis et al., 2019) model for summarization. Users can enter arbitrary text and a full version of the model is deployed on the fly to produce a summary.

now widely downloaded by the community.

The user interface of the Model Hub is designed to be simple and open to the community. To upload a model, any user can sign up for an account and use a command-line interface to produce an archive consisting a tokenizer, transformer, and head. This bundle may be a model trained through the library or converted from a checkpoint of other popular training tools. These models are then stored and given a canonical name which a user can use to download, cache, and run the model either for fine-tuning or inference in two lines of code. To load FlauBERT (Le et al., 2020), a BERT model pretrained on a French training corpus, the command is:

```
1  tknzr = AutoTokenizer.from_pretrained(
2      "flaubert/flaubert_base_uncased")
3  model = AutoModel.from_pretrained(
4      "flaubert/flaubert_base_uncased")
```

When a model is uploaded to the Model Hub, it is automatically given a landing page describing its core properties, architecture, and use cases. Additional model-specific metadata can be provided via a model card (Mitchell et al., 2018) that describes properties of its training, a citation to the work, datasets used during pretraining, and any caveats about known biases in the model and its predictions. An example model card is shown in Figure 3 (Left).

Since the Model Hub is specific to transformer-based models, we can target use cases that would be difficult for more general model collections. For example, because each uploaded model includes metadata concerning its structure, the model page can include live inference that allows users to experiment with output of models on a real data. Figure 3 (Right) shows an example of the model page with live inference. Additionally, model pages include links to other model-specific tools like benchmarking and visualizations. For example, model pages can link to exBERT (Hoover et al., 2019), a Transformer visualization library.

Community Case Studies The Model Hub highlights how *Transformers* is used by a variety of different community stakeholders. We summarize three specific observed use-cases in practice. We highlight specific systems developed by users with different goals following the architect, trainer, and end-user distinction of Strobelt et al. (2017):

Case 1: Model Architects AllenAI, a major NLP research lab, developed a new pretrained model for improved extraction from biomedical texts called SciBERT (Beltagy et al., 2019). They were able to train the model utilizing data from PubMed to produce a masked language model with state-of-the-art results on targeted text. They then used the Model Hub to distribute the model and promote it as part of their CORD - COVID-19 challenge, making it trivial for the community to use.

Case 2: Task Trainers Researchers at NYU were

interested in developing a test bed for the performance of *Transformers* on a variety of different semantic recognition tasks. Their framework Jiant (Pruksachatkun et al., 2020) allows them to experiment with different ways of pretraining models and comparing their outputs. They used the *Transformers* API as a generic front-end and performed fine-tuning on a variety of different models, leading to research on the structure of BERT (Tenney et al., 2019).

Case 3: Application Users Plot.ly, a company focused on user dashboards and analytics, was interested in deploying a model for automatic document summarization. They wanted an approach that scaled well and was simple to deploy, but had no need to train or fine-tune the model. They were able to search the Model Hub and find *DistilBART*, a pretrained and fine-tuned summarization model designed for accurate, fast inference. They were able to run and deploy the model directly from the hub with no required research or ML expertise.

5 Deployment

An increasingly important goal of *Transformers* is to make it easy to efficiently deploy model to production. Different users have different production needs, and deployment often requires solving significantly different challenges than training. The library therefore allows for several different strategies for production deployment.

One core propery of the libary is that models are available both in PyTorch and TensorFlow, and there is interoperability between both frameworks. A model trained in one of frameworks can be saved through standard serialization and be reloaded from the saved files in the other framework seamlessly. This makes it particularly easy to switch from one framework to the other one along the model lifetime (training, serving, etc.).

Each framework has deployment recommendations. For example, in PyTorch, models are compatible with TorchScript, an intermediate representation of a PyTorch model that can then be run either in Python in a more efficient way, or in a highperformance environment such as C++. Fine-tuned models can thus be exported to production-friendly environment, and run through TorchServing. TensorFlow includes several serving options within its ecosystem, and these can be used directly.

Transformers can also export models to intermediate neural network formats for further compila-

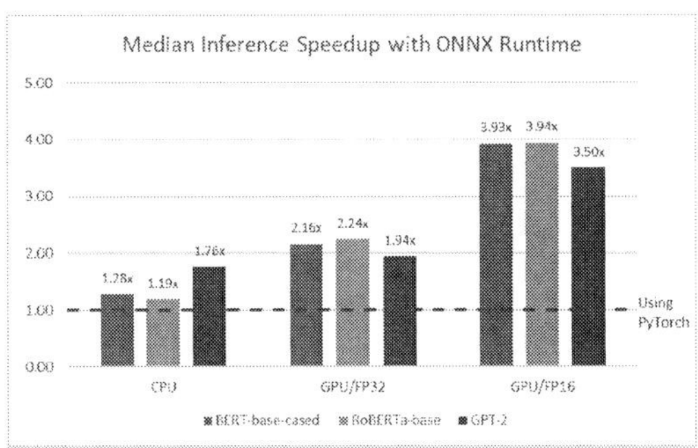

Figure 4: Experiments with *Transformers* inference in collaboration with ONNX.

tion. It supports converting models to the Open Neural Network Exchange format (ONNX) for deployment. Not only does this allow the model to be run in a standardized interoperable format, but also leads to significant speed-ups. Figure 4 shows experiments run in collaboration with the ONNX team to optimize BERT, RoBERTa, and GPT-2 from the *Transformers* library. Using this intermediate format, ONNX was able to achieve nearly a 4x speedup on this model. The team is also experimenting with other promising intermediate formats such as JAX/XLA (Bradbury et al., 2018) and TVM (Chen et al., 2018).

Finally, as Transformers become more widely used in all NLP applications, it is increasingly important to deploy to edge devices such as phones or home electronics. Models can use adapters to convert models to *CoreML* weights that are suitable to be embedded inside a iOS application, to enable on-the-edge machine learning. Code is also made available[3]. Similar methods can be used for Android devices.

6 Conclusion

As Transformer and pretraining play larger roles in NLP, it is important for these models to be accessible to researchers and end-users. *Transformers* is an open-source library and community designed to facilitate users to access large-scale pretrained models, to build and experiment on top of them, and to deploy them in downstream tasks with state-of-the-art performance. *Transformers* has gained significant organic traction since its release and is set up to continue to provide core infrastructure while helping to facilitate access to new models.

---

[3]`https://github.com/huggingface/swift-coreml-transformers`

References

a. PyTorch Hub. https://pytorch.org/hub/. Accessed: 2020-6-29.

b. TensorFlow hub. https://www.tensorflow.org/hub. Accessed: 2020-6-29.

Alan Akbik, Tanja Bergmann, Duncan Blythe, Kashif Rasul, Stefan Schweter, and Roland Vollgraf. 2019. Flair: An easy-to-use framework for state-of-the-art nlp. In *Proceedings of the 2019 Conference of the North American Chapter of the Association for Computational Linguistics (Demonstrations)*, pages 54–59. aclweb.org.

Iz Beltagy, Kyle Lo, and Arman Cohan. 2019. SciB-ERT: A pretrained language model for scientific text. In *Proceedings of the 2019 Conference on Empirical Methods in Natural Language Processing and the 9th International Joint Conference on Natural Language Processing (EMNLP-IJCNLP)*, pages 3615–3620.

Iz Beltagy, Matthew E Peters, and Arman Cohan. 2020. Longformer: The Long-Document transformer.

Antoine Bosselut, Hannah Rashkin, Maarten Sap, Chaitanya Malaviya, Asli Çelikyilmaz, and Yejin Choi. 2019. Comet: Commonsense transformers for automatic knowledge graph construction. In *ACL*.

James Bradbury, Roy Frostig, Peter Hawkins, Matthew James Johnson, Chris Leary, Dougal Maclaurin, and Skye Wanderman-Milne. 2018. JAX: composable transformations of Python+NumPy programs.

Tianqi Chen, Thierry Moreau, Ziheng Jiang, Lianmin Zheng, Eddie Yan, Haichen Shen, Meghan Cowan, Leyuan Wang, Yuwei Hu, Luis Ceze, et al. 2018. {TVM}: An automated end-to-end optimizing compiler for deep learning. In *13th {USENIX} Symposium on Operating Systems Design and Implementation ({OSDI} 18)*, pages 578–594.

Kevin Clark, Minh-Thang Luong, Quoc V Le, and Christopher D Manning. 2020. ELECTRA: Pre-training text encoders as discriminators rather than generators.

Zihang Dai, Zhilin Yang, Yiming Yang, Jaime Carbonell, Quoc V Le, and Ruslan Salakhutdinov. 2019. Transformer-XL: Attentive language models beyond a Fixed-Length context.

Jacob Devlin, Ming-Wei Chang, Kenton Lee, and Kristina Toutanova. 2018. BERT: Pre-training of deep bidirectional transformers for language understanding.

Matt Gardner, Joel Grus, Mark Neumann, Oyvind Tafjord, Pradeep Dasigi, Nelson Liu, Matthew Peters, Michael Schmitz, and Luke Zettlemoyer. 2018. AllenNLP: A deep semantic natural language processing platform.

Matthew Honnibal and Ines Montani. 2017. spacy 2: Natural language understanding with bloom embeddings, convolutional neural networks and incremental parsing. *To appear*, 7(1).

Benjamin Hoover, Hendrik Strobelt, and Sebastian Gehrmann. 2019. exBERT: A visual analysis tool to explore learned representations in transformers models.

Jeremy Howard and Sebastian Ruder. 2018. Universal language model fine-tuning for text classification. In *ACL*.

Zhiting Hu, Haoran Shi, Bowen Tan, Wentao Wang, Zichao Yang, Tiancheng Zhao, Junxian He, Lianhui Qin, Di Wang, Xuezhe Ma, Zhengzhong Liu, Xiaodan Liang, Wangrong Zhu, Devendra Singh Sachan, and Eric P Xing. 2018. Texar: A modularized, versatile, and extensible toolkit for text generation.

Mandar Joshi, Danqi Chen, Yinhan Liu, Daniel S Weld, Luke Zettlemoyer, and Omer Levy. 2019. Spanbert: Improving pre-training by representing and predicting spans. *arXiv preprint arXiv:1907.10529*.

Marcin Junczys-Dowmunt, Roman Grundkiewicz, Tomasz Dwojak, Hieu Hoang, Kenneth Heafield, Tom Neckermann, Frank Seide, Ulrich Germann, Alham Fikri Aji, Nikolay Bogoychev, André F T Martins, and Alexandra Birch. 2018. Marian: Fast neural machine translation in c++.

Douwe Kiela, Suvrat Bhooshan, Hamed Firooz, and Davide Testuggine. 2019. Supervised multimodal bitransformers for classifying images and text.

Nikita Kitaev, Łukasz Kaiser, and Anselm Levskaya. 2020. Reformer: The efficient transformer.

Guillaume Klein, Yoon Kim, Yuntian Deng, Jean Senellart, and Alexander Rush. 2017. OpenNMT: Opensource toolkit for neural machine translation. In *Proceedings of ACL 2017, System Demonstrations*, pages 67–72, Vancouver, Canada. Association for Computational Linguistics.

Guillaume Lample and Alexis Conneau. 2019a. Cross-lingual language model pretraining. In *NeurIPS*.

Guillaume Lample and Alexis Conneau. 2019b. Cross-lingual language model pretraining.

Zhenzhong Lan, Mingda Chen, Sebastian Goodman, Kevin Gimpel, Piyush Sharma, and Radu Soricut. 2019. ALBERT: A lite BERT for self-supervised learning of language representations.

Hang Le, Loïc Vial, Jibril Frej, Vincent Segonne, Maximin Coavoux, Benjamin Lecouteux, Alexandre Allauzen, Benoît Crabbé, Laurent Besacier, and Didier Schwab. 2020. Flaubert: Unsupervised language model pre-training for french. In *Proceedings of The 12th Language Resources and Evaluation Conference*, pages 2479–2490, Marseille, France. European Language Resources Association.

Mike Lewis, Yinhan Liu, Naman Goyal, Marjan Ghazvininejad, Abdelrahman Mohamed, Omer Levy, Ves Stoyanov, and Luke Zettlemoyer. 2019. BART: Denoising Sequence-to-Sequence pretraining for natural language generation, translation, and comprehension.

Yinhan Liu, Myle Ott, Naman Goyal, Jingfei Du, Mandar Joshi, Danqi Chen, Omer Levy, Mike Lewis, Luke Zettlemoyer, and Veselin Stoyanov. 2019a. RoBERTa: A robustly optimized BERT pretraining approach.

Yinhan Liu, Myle Ott, Naman Goyal, Jingfei Du, Mandar S. Joshi, Danqi Chen, Omer Levy, Mike Lewis, Luke S. Zettlemoyer, and Veselin Stoyanov. 2019b. Roberta: A robustly optimized bert pretraining approach. *ArXiv*, abs/1907.11692.

Edward Loper and Steven Bird. 2002. NLTK: The natural language toolkit.

Christopher D Manning, Mihai Surdeanu, John Bauer, Jenny Rose Finkel, Steven Bethard, and David McClosky. 2014. The stanford CoreNLP natural language processing toolkit. In *Proceedings of 52nd annual meeting of the association for computational linguistics: system demonstrations*, pages 55–60. aclweb.org.

Bryan McCann, James Bradbury, Caiming Xiong, and Richard Socher. 2017. Learned in translation: Contextualized word vectors. In I Guyon, U V Luxburg, S Bengio, H Wallach, R Fergus, S Vishwanathan, and R Garnett, editors, *Advances in Neural Information Processing Systems 30*, pages 6294–6305. Curran Associates, Inc.

Margaret Mitchell, Simone Wu, Andrew Zaldivar, Parker Barnes, Lucy Vasserman, Ben Hutchinson, Elena Spitzer, Inioluwa Deborah Raji, and Timnit Gebru. 2018. Model cards for model reporting.

Myle Ott, Sergey Edunov, Alexei Baevski, Angela Fan, Sam Gross, Nathan Ng, David Grangier, and Michael Auli. 2019. fairseq: A fast, extensible toolkit for sequence modeling.

Matthew E Peters, Mark Neumann, Mohit Iyyer, Matt Gardner, Christopher Clark, Kenton Lee, and Luke Zettlemoyer. 2018. Deep contextualized word representations.

Yada Pruksachatkun, Phil Yeres, Haokun Liu, Jason Phang, Phu Mon Htut, Alex Wang, Ian Tenney, and Samuel R Bowman. 2020. jiant: A software toolkit for research on general-purpose text understanding models. *arXiv preprint arXiv:2003.02249*.

Peng Qi, Yuhao Zhang, Yuhui Zhang, Jason Bolton, and Christopher D Manning. 2020. Stanza: A python natural language processing toolkit for many human languages.

Alec Radford, Jeffrey Wu, Rewon Child, David Luan, Dario Amodei, and Ilya Sutskever. 2019. Language models are unsupervised multitask learners. *OpenAI Blog*, 1(8):9.

Colin Raffel, Noam Shazeer, Adam Roberts, Katherine Lee, Sharan Narang, Michael Matena, Yanqi Zhou, Wei Li, and Peter J Liu. 2019. Exploring the limits of transfer learning with a unified Text-to-Text transformer.

Victor Sanh, Lysandre Debut, Julien Chaumond, and Thomas Wolf. 2019. DistilBERT, a distilled version of BERT: smaller, faster, cheaper and lighter.

Mohammad Shoeybi, Mostofa Patwary, Raul Puri, Patrick LeGresley, Jared Casper, and Bryan Catanzaro. 2019. Megatron-lm: Training multi-billion parameter language models using gpu model parallelism. *arXiv preprint arXiv:1909.08053*.

Hendrik Strobelt, Sebastian Gehrmann, Hanspeter Pfister, and Alexander M Rush. 2017. Lstmvis: A tool for visual analysis of hidden state dynamics in recurrent neural networks. *IEEE transactions on visualization and computer graphics*, 24(1):667–676.

Ian Tenney, Dipanjan Das, and Ellie Pavlick. 2019. Bert rediscovers the classical nlp pipeline. In *ACL*.

Ashish Vaswani, Samy Bengio, Eugene Brevdo, Francois Chollet, Aidan N. Gomez, Stephan Gouws, Llion Jones, Łukasz Kaiser, Nal Kalchbrenner, Niki Parmar, Ryan Sepassi, Noam Shazeer, and Jakob Uszkoreit. 2018. Tensor2tensor for neural machine translation. *CoRR*, abs/1803.07416.

Ashish Vaswani, Noam Shazeer, Niki Parmar, Jakob Uszkoreit, Llion Jones, Aidan N Gomez, Ł Ukasz Kaiser, and Illia Polosukhin. 2017. Attention is all you need. In I Guyon, U V Luxburg, S Bengio, H Wallach, R Fergus, S Vishwanathan, and R Garnett, editors, *Advances in Neural Information Processing Systems 30*, pages 5998–6008. Curran Associates, Inc.

Alex Wang, Yada Pruksachatkun, Nikita Nangia, Amanpreet Singh, Julian Michael, Felix Hill, Omer Levy, and Samuel R. Bowman. 2019. Superglue: A stickier benchmark for general-purpose language understanding systems. *ArXiv*, abs/1905.00537.

Alex Wang, Amanpreet Singh, Julian Michael, Felix Hill, Omer Levy, and Samuel R. Bowman. 2018. Glue: A multi-task benchmark and analysis platform for natural language understanding. In *ICLR*.

Zhilin Yang, Zihang Dai, Yiming Yang, Jaime G. Carbonell, Ruslan Salakhutdinov, and Quoc V. Le. 2019. Xlnet: Generalized autoregressive pretraining for language understanding. *ArXiv*, abs/1906.08237.

AdapterHub: A Framework for Adapting Transformers

Jonas Pfeiffer[*1], **Andreas Rücklé**[*1], **Clifton Poth**[*1],
Aishwarya Kamath[2], **Ivan Vulić**[4], **Sebastian Ruder**[5],
Kyunghyun Cho[2,3], **Iryna Gurevych**[1]
[1]Technical University of Darmstadt
[2]New York University   [3]CIFAR Associate Fellow
[4]University of Cambridge
[5]DeepMind
`AdapterHub.ml`

Abstract

The current modus operandi in NLP involves downloading and fine-tuning pre-trained models consisting of hundreds of millions, or even billions of parameters. Storing and sharing such large trained models is expensive, slow, and time-consuming, which impedes progress towards more general and versatile NLP methods that learn from and for many tasks. Adapters—small learnt bottleneck layers inserted within each layer of a pretrained model— ameliorate this issue by avoiding full fine-tuning of the entire model. However, sharing and integrating adapter layers is not straightforward. We propose AdapterHub, a framework that allows dynamic "stiching-in" of pre-trained adapters for different tasks and languages. The framework, built on top of the popular HuggingFace Transformers library, enables extremely easy and quick adaptations of state-of-the-art pre-trained models (e.g., BERT, RoBERTa, XLM-R) across tasks and languages. Downloading, sharing, and training adapters is as seamless as possible using minimal changes to the training scripts and a specialized infrastructure. Our framework enables scalable and easy access to sharing of task-specific models, particularly in low-resource scenarios. AdapterHub includes all recent adapter architectures and can be found at AdapterHub.ml.

1 Introduction

Recent advances in NLP leverage transformer-based language models (Vaswani et al., 2017), pre-trained on large amounts of text data (Devlin et al., 2019; Liu et al., 2019; Conneau et al., 2020). These models are fine-tuned on a target task and achieve state-of-the-art (SotA) performance for most natural language understanding tasks. Their performance has been shown to scale with their size (Kaplan et al., 2020) and recent models have reached billions of parameters (Raffel et al., 2019; Brown et al., 2020). While fine-tuning large pre-trained models on target task data can be done fairly efficiently (Howard and Ruder, 2018), training them for multiple tasks and sharing trained models is often prohibitive. This precludes research on more modular architectures (Shazeer et al., 2017), task composition (Andreas et al., 2016), and injecting biases and external information (e.g., world or linguistic knowledge) into large models (Lauscher et al., 2019; Wang et al., 2020).

Adapters (Houlsby et al., 2019) have been introduced as an alternative lightweight fine-tuning strategy that achieves on-par performance to full fine-tuning (Peters et al., 2019) on most tasks. They consist of a small set of additional newly initialized weights at every layer of the transformer. These weights are then trained during fine-tuning, while the pre-trained parameters of the large model are kept frozen/fixed. This enables efficient parameter sharing between tasks by training many task-specific and language-specific adapters for the same model, which can be exchanged and combined post-hoc. Adapters have recently achieved strong results in multi-task and cross-lingual transfer learning (Pfeiffer et al., 2020a,b).

However, reusing and sharing adapters is not straightforward. Adapters are rarely released individually; their architectures differ in subtle yet important ways, and they are model, task, and language dependent. To mitigate these issues and facilitate transfer learning with adapters in a range of settings, we propose AdapterHub, a framework that enables seamless training and sharing of adapters.

AdapterHub is built on top of the popular `transformers` framework by HuggingFace[1] (Wolf et al., 2020), which provides access to state-of-the-art pre-trained language models. We en-

---

*Equal contribution.

[1]https://github.com/huggingface/transformers

Proceedings of the 2020 EMNLP (Systems Demonstrations), pages 46–54
November 16-20, 2020. ©2020 Association for Computational Linguistics

hance `transformers` with adapter modules that can be combined with existing SotA models with minimal code edits. We additionally provide a website that enables quick and seamless upload, download, and sharing of pre-trained adapters. AdapterHub is available online at: AdapterHub.ml.

AdapterHub for the first time enables NLP researchers and practitioners to easily and efficiently share and obtain access to models that have been trained for particular tasks, domains, and languages. This opens up the possibility of building on and combining information from many more sources than was previously possible, and makes research such as intermediate task training (Pruksachatkun et al., 2020), composing information from many tasks (Pfeiffer et al., 2020a), and training models for very low-resource languages (Pfeiffer et al., 2020b) much more accessible.

Contributions. 1) We propose an easy-to-use and extensible adapter training and sharing framework for transformer-based models such as BERT, RoBERTa, and XLM(-R); 2) we incorporate it into the HuggingFace `transformers` framework, requiring as little as two additional lines of code to train adapters with existing scripts; 3) our framework automatically extracts the adapter weights, storing them separately to the pre-trained transformer model, requiring as little as 1Mb of storage; 4) we provide an open-source framework and website that allows the community to upload their adapter weights, making them easily accessible with only one additional line of code; 5) we incorporate adapter composition as well as adapter stacking out-of-the-box and pave the way for a wide range of other extensions in the future.

2   Adapters

While the predominant methodology for transfer learning is to fine-tune all weights of the pre-trained model, *adapters* have recently been introduced as an alternative approach, with applications in computer vision (Rebuffi et al., 2017) as well as the NLP domain (Houlsby et al., 2019; Bapna and Firat, 2019; Wang et al., 2020; Pfeiffer et al., 2020a,b).

2.1   Adapter Architecture

Adapters are neural modules with a small amount of additional newly introduced parameters Φ within a large pre-trained model with parameters Θ. The parameters Φ are learnt on a target task while keeping Θ fixed; Φ thus learn to encode task-specific representations in intermediate layers of the pre-trained model. Current work predominantly focuses on training adapters for each task separately (Houlsby et al., 2019; Bapna and Firat, 2019; Pfeiffer et al., 2020a,b), which enables parallel training and subsequent combination of the weights.

In NLP, adapters have been mainly used within deep transformer-based architectures (Vaswani et al., 2017). At each transformer layer l, a set of adapter parameters Φ_l is introduced. The placement and architecture of adapter parameters Φ within a pre-trained model is non-trivial and may impact their efficacy: Houlsby et al. (2019) experiment with different adapter architectures, empirically validating that a two-layer feed-forward neural network with a bottleneck works well. While this down- and up-projection has largely been agreed upon, the actual placement of adapters within each transformer block, as well as the introduction of new LayerNorms[2] (Ba et al., 2016) varies in the literature (Houlsby et al., 2019; Bapna and Firat, 2019; Stickland and Murray, 2019; Pfeiffer et al., 2020a). In order to support standard adapter architectures from the literature, as well as to enable easy extensibility, AdapterHub provides a configuration file where the architecture settings can be defined dynamically. We illustrate the different configuration possibilities in Figure 3, and describe them in more detail in §3.

2.2   Why Adapters?

Adapters provide numerous benefits over fully fine-tuning a model such as scalability, modularity, and composition. We now provide a few use-cases for adapters to illustrate their usefulness in practice.

Task-specific Layer-wise Representation Learning. Prior to the introduction of adapters, in order to achieve SotA performance on downstream tasks, the entire pre-trained transformer model needs to be fine-tuned (Peters et al., 2019). Adapters have been shown to work on-par with full fine-tuning, by adapting the representations at every layer. We present the results of fully fine-tuning the model compared to two different adapter architectures on the GLUE benchmark (Wang et al., 2018) in Table 1. The adapters of Houlsby et al. (2019, Figure 3c) and Pfeiffer et al. (2020a, Figure 3b) comprise two and one down- and up-projection

---

[2]Layer normalization learns to normalize the inputs across the features. This is usually done by introducing a new set of features for mean and variance.

	Full	**Pfeif.**	**Houl.**
RTE (Wang et al., 2018)	66.2	70.8	69.8
MRPC (Dolan and Brockett, 2005)	90.5	89.7	91.5
STS-B (Cer et al., 2017)	88.8	89.0	89.2
CoLA (Warstadt et al., 2019)	59.5	58.9	59.1
SST-2 (Socher et al., 2013)	92.6	92.2	92.8
QNLI (Rajpurkar et al., 2016)	91.3	91.3	91.2
MNLI (Williams et al., 2018)	84.1	84.1	84.1
QQP (Iyer et al., 2017)	91.4	90.5	90.8

Table 1: Mean development scores over 3 runs on GLUE (Wang et al., 2018) leveraging the BERT-Base pre-trained weights. We present the results with full fine-tuning (**Full**) and with the adapter architectures of Pfeiffer et al. (2020a, **Pfeif.**, Figure 3b) and Houlsby et al. (2019, **Houl.**, Figure 3c) both with bottleneck size 48. We show F1 for MRPC, Spearman rank correlation for STS-B, and accuracy for the rest. RTE is a combination of datasets (Dagan et al., 2005; Bar-Haim et al., 2006; Giampiccolo et al., 2007).

within each transformer layer, respectively. The former adapter thus has more capacity at the cost of training and inference speed. We find that for all settings, there is no large difference in terms of performance between the model architectures, verifying that training adapters is a suitable and lightweight alternative to full fine-tuning in order to achieve SotA performance on downstream tasks.

Small, Scalable, Shareable. Transformer-based models are very deep neural networks with millions or billions of weights and large storage requirements, e.g., around 2.2Gb of compressed storage space is needed for XLM-R Large (Conneau et al., 2020). Fully fine-tuning these models for each task separately requires storing a copy of the fine-tuned model for each task. This impedes both iterating and parallelizing training, particularly in storage-restricted environments.

Adapters mitigate this problem. Depending on the model size and the adapter bottleneck size, a single task requires as little as 0.9Mb storage space. We present the storage requirements in Table 2. This highlights that $> 99\%$ of the parameters required for each target task are fixed during training and can be shared across all models for inference. For instance, for the popular Bert-Base model with a size of 440Mb, storing 2 fully fine-tuned models amounts to the same storage space required by 125 models with adapters, when using a bottleneck size of 48 and adapters of Pfeiffer et al. (2020a). Moreover, when performing inference on a mobile device, adapters can be leveraged to save a significant amount of storage space, while supporting a large

| | **Base** | | **Large** | |
CRate	#Params	Size	#Params	Size
64	0.2M	0.9Mb	0.8M	3.2Mb
16	0.9M	3.5Mb	3.1M	13Mb
2	7.1M	28Mb	25.2M	97Mb

Table 2: Number of additional parameters and compressed storage space of the adapter of Pfeiffer et al. (2020a) in (Ro)BERT(a)-Base and Large transformer architectures. The adapter of Houlsby et al. (2019) requires roughly twice as much space. *CRate* refers to the adapter's compression rate: e.g., a. rate of 64 means that the adapter's bottleneck layer is 64 times smaller than the underlying model's hidden layer size.

number of target tasks. Additionally, due to the small-size of the adapter modules—which in many cases do not exceed the file size of an image—new tasks can be added on-the-fly. Overall, these factors make adapters a much more computationally—and ecologically (Strubell et al., 2019)—viable option compared to updating entire models (Rücklé et al., 2020). Easy access to fine-tuned models may also improve reproducibility as researchers will be able to easily rerun and evaluate trained models of previous work.

Modularity of Representations. Adapters learn to encode information of a task within designated parameters. Due to the encapsulated placement of adapters, wherein the surrounding parameters are fixed, at each layer an adapter is forced to learn an output representation compatible with the subsequent layer of the transformer model. This setting allows for modularity of components such that adapters can be stacked on top of each other, or replaced dynamically. In a recent example, Pfeiffer et al. (2020b) successfully combine adapters that have been independently trained for specific tasks and languages. This demonstrates that adapters are modular and that output representations of different adapters are compatible. As NLP tasks become more complex and require knowledge that is not directly accessible in a single monolithic pre-trained model (Ruder et al., 2019), adapters will provide NLP researchers and practitioners with many more sources of relevant information that can be easily combined in an efficient and modular way.

Non-Interfering Composition of Information. Sharing information across tasks has a long-standing history in machine learning (Ruder, 2017). Multi-task learning (MTL), which shares a set of parameters between tasks, has arguably received the most attention. However, MTL suffers from problems such as catastrophic forgetting where information learned during earlier stages of training is "overwritten" (de Masson d'Autume et al., 2019), catastrophic interference where the performance of a set of tasks deteriorates when adding new tasks (Hashimoto et al., 2017), and intricate task weighting for tasks with different distributions (Sanh et al., 2019).

The encapsulation of adapters forces them to learn output representations that are compatible across tasks. When training adapters on different downstream tasks, they store the respective information in their designated parameters. Multiple adapters can then be combined, e.g., with attention (Pfeiffer et al., 2020a). Because the respective adapters are trained separately, the necessity of sampling heuristics due to skewed data set sizes no longer arises. By separating knowledge extraction and composition, adapters mitigate the two most common pitfalls of multi-task learning, catastrophic forgetting and catastrophic interference.

Overcoming these problems together with the availability of readily available trained task-specific adapters enables researchers and practitioners to leverage information from specific tasks, domains, or languages that is often more relevant for a specific application—rather than more general pretrained counterparts. Recent work (Howard and Ruder, 2018; Phang et al., 2018; Pruksachatkun et al., 2020; Gururangan et al., 2020) has shown the benefits of such information, which was previously only available by fully fine-tuning a model on the data of interest prior to task-specific fine-tuning.

3 AdapterHub

AdapterHub consists of two core components: **1)** A library built on top of HuggingFace `transformers`, and **2)** a website that dynamically provides analysis and filtering of pre-trained adapters. AdapterHub provides tools for the entire life-cycle of adapters, illustrated in Figure 1 and discussed in what follows: ① introducing new adapter weights Φ into pre-trained transformer weights Θ; ② training adapter weights Φ on a downstream task (while keeping Θ frozen); ③ automatic extraction of the trained adapter weights Φ' and open-sourcing the adapters; ④ automatic visualization of the adapters with configuration filters; ⑤ on-the-fly downloading/caching the pre-trained adapter weights Φ' and stitching the adapter into the pre-

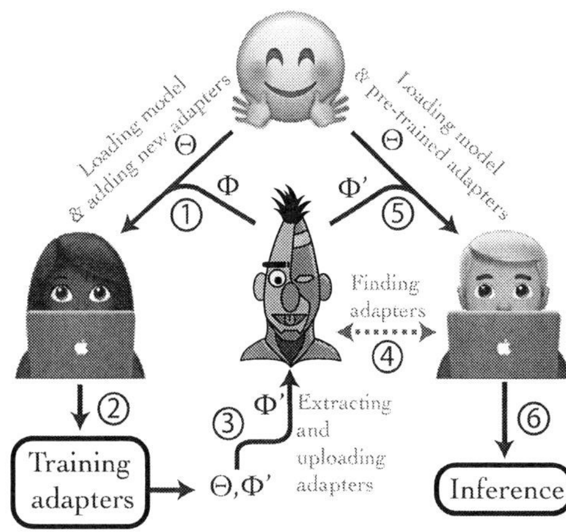

Figure 1: The AdapterHub Process graph. Adapters Φ are introduced into a pre-trained transformer Θ (step ①) and are trained (②). They can then be extracted and open-sourced (③) and visualized (④). Pre-trained adapters are downloaded on-the-fly (⑤) and stitched into a model that is used for inference (⑥).

trained transformer model Θ; ⑥ performing inference with the trained adapter transformer model.

① Adapters in Transformer Layers

We minimize the required changes to existing HuggingFace training scripts, resulting in only two additional lines of code. In Figure 2 we present the required code to add adapter weights (line 3) and freeze all the transformer weights Θ (line 4). In this example, the model is prepared to train a task adapter on the binary version of the Stanford Sentiment Treebank (SST; Socher et al., 2013) using the adapter architecture of Pfeiffer et al. (2020a). Similarly, language adapters can be added by setting the type parameter to `AdapterType.text_language`, and other adapter architectures can be chosen accordingly.

While we provide ready-made configuration files for well-known architectures in the current literature, adapters are dynamically configurable, which makes it possible to define a multitude of architectures. We illustrate the configurable components as dashed lines and objects in Figure 3. The configurable components are placements of new weights, residual connections as well as placements of LayerNorm layers (Ba et al., 2016).

The code changes within the HuggingFace `transformers` framework are realized through `MixIns`, which are inherited by the respective transformer classes. This minimizes the amount of code changes of our proposed extensions and en-

```
from transformers import AutoModelForSequenceClassification, AdapterType
model = AutoModelForSequenceClassification.from_pretrained("roberta-base")
model.add_adapter("sst-2", AdapterType.text_task, config="pfeiffer")
model.train_adapter(["sst-2"])
# Train model ...
model.save_adapter("adapters/text-task/sst-2/", "sst-2")
# Push link to zip file to AdapterHub ...
```

Figure 2: ① Adding new adapter weights Φ to pre-trained RoBERTa-Base weights Θ (line 3), and freezing Θ (line 4). ③ Extracting and storing the trained adapter weights Φ' (line 7).

capsulates adapters as designated classes. It further increases readability as adapters are clearly separated from the main `transformers` code base, which makes it easy to keep both repositories in sync as well as to extend AdapterHub.

② Training Adapters

Adapters are trained in the same manner as full fine-tuning of the model. The information is passed through the different layers of the transformer where additionally to the pre-trained weights at every layer the representations are additionally passed through the adapter parameters. However, in contrast to full fine-tuning, the pre-trained weights Θ are fixed and only the adapter weights Φ and the prediction head are trained. Because Θ is fixed, the adapter weights Φ are encapsuled within the transformer weights, forcing them to learn compatible representations across tasks.

③ Extracting and Open-Sourcing Adapters

When training adapters instead of full fine-tuning, it is no longer necessary to store checkpoints of the entire model. Instead, only the adapter weights Φ', as well as the prediction head need to be stored, as the base model's weights Θ remain the same. This is integrated automatically as soon as adapters are trained, which significantly reduces the required storage space during training and enables storing a large number of checkpoints simultaneously.

When adapter training has completed, the parameter file together with the corresponding adapter configuration file are zipped and uploaded to a public server. The user then enters the metadata (e.g., URL to weights, user info, description of training procedure, data set used, adapter architecture, GitHub handle, Twitter handle) into a designated YAML file and issues a pull request to the Adapter-Hub GitHub repository. When all automatic checks pass, the AdapterHub.ml website is automatically regenerated with the newly available adapter, which makes it possible for users to immediately find

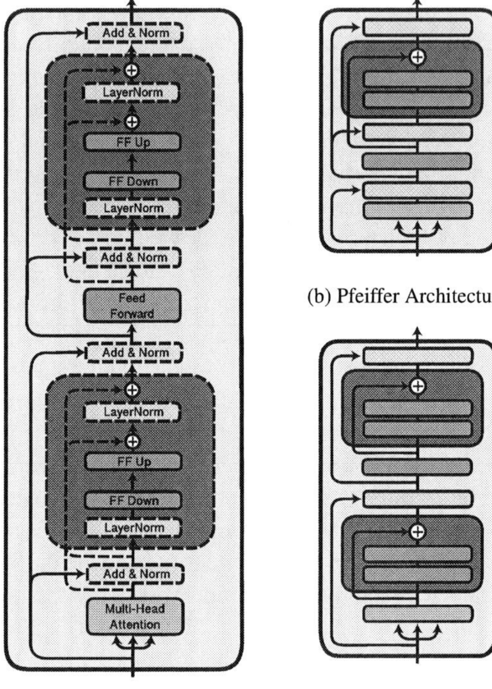

(a) Configuration Possibilities   (c) Houlsby Architecture

(b) Pfeiffer Architecture

Figure 3: Dynamic customization possibilities where dashed lines in (a) show the current configuration options. These options include the placements of new weights Φ (including down and up projections as well as new LayerNorms), residual connections, bottleneck sizes as well as activation functions. All new weights Φ are illustrated within the pink boxes, everything outside belongs to the pre-trained weights Θ. In addition, we provide pre-set configuration files for architectures in the literature. The resulting configurations for the architecture proposed by Pfeiffer et al. (2020a) and Houlsby et al. (2019) are illustrated in (b) and (c) respectively. We also provide a configuration file for the architecture proposed by Bapna and Firat (2019), not shown here.

and use these new weights described by the metadata. We hope that the ease of sharing pre-trained adapters will further facilitate and speed up new developments in transfer learning in NLP.

```
1 from transformers import AutoModelForSequenceClassification, AdapterType
2 model = AutoModelForSequenceClassification.from_pretrained("roberta-base")
3 model.load_adapter("sst-2", config="pfeiffer")
```

Figure 4: ⑤ After the correct adapter has been identified by the user on the explore page of AdapterHub.ml, they can load and stitch the pre-trained adapter weights Φ' into the transformer Θ (line 3).

④ Finding Pre-Trained Adapters

The website AdapterHub.ml provides a dynamic overview of the currently available pre-trained adapters. Due to the large number of tasks in many different languages as well as different transformer models, we provide an intuitively understandable hierarchical structure, as well as search options. This makes it easy for users to find adapters that are suitable for their use-case. Namely, Adapter-Hub's explore page is structured into three hierarchical levels. At the *first* level, adapters can be viewed by task or language. The *second* level allows for a more fine-grained distinction separating adapters into data sets of higher-level NLP tasks following a categorization similar to paperswith-code.com. For languages, the second level distinguishes the adapters by the language they were trained on. The *third* level separates adapters into individual datasets or domains such as SST for sentiment analysis or Wikipedia for Swahili.

When a specific dataset has been selected, the user can see the available pre-trained adapters for this setting. Adapters depend on the transformer model they were trained on and are otherwise *not* compatible.[3] The user selects the model architecture and certain hyper-parameters and is shown the compatible adapters. When selecting one of the adapters, the user is provided with additional information about the adapter, which is available in the metadata (see ③ again for more information).

⑤ Stitching-In Pre-Trained Adapters

Pre-trained adapters can be stitched into the large transformer model as easily as adding randomly initialized weights; this requires a single line of code, see Figure 4, line 3. When selecting an adapter on the website (see ④ again) the user is provided with sample code, which corresponds to the configuration necessary to include the specific weights.[4]

⑥ Inference with Adapters

Inference with a pre-trained model that relies on adapters is in line with the standard inference practice based on full fine-tuning. Similar to *training* adapters, during inference the active adapter name is passed into the model together with the text tokens. At every transformer layer the information is passed through the transformer layers and the corresponding adapter parameters.

The adapters can be used for inference in the designated task they were trained on. To this end, we provide an option to upload the prediction heads together with the adapter weights. In addition, they can be used for further research such as transferring the adapter to a new task, stacking multiple adapters, fusing the information from diverse adapters, or enriching AdapterHub with adapters for other modalities, among many other possible modes of usage and future directions.

4   Conclusion and Future Work

We have introduced AdapterHub, a novel easy-to-use framework that enables simple and effective transfer learning via training and community sharing of *adapters*. Adapters are small neural modules that can be stitched into large pre-trained transformer models to facilitate, simplify, and speed up transfer learning across a range of languages and tasks. AdapterHub is built on top of the commonly used HuggingFace `transformers`, and it requires only adding as little as two lines of code to existing training scripts. Using adapters in Adapter-Hub has numerous benefits such as improved reproducibility, much better efficiency compared to full fine-tuning, easy extensibility to new models and new tasks, and easy access to trained models.

With AdapterHub, we hope to provide a suitable and stable framework for the community to train, search, and use adapters. We plan to continuously improve the framework, extend the composition and modularity possibilities, and support other transformer models, even the ones yet to come.

---

[3]We plan to look into mapping adapters between different models as future work.

[4]When selecting an adapter based on a name, we allow for string matching as long as there is no ambiguity.

Acknowledgments

Jonas Pfeiffer is supported by the LOEWE initiative (Hesse, Germany) within the emergenCITY center. Andreas Rücklé is supported by the German Federal Ministry of Education and Research and the Hessen State Ministry for Higher Education, Research and the Arts within their joint support of the National Research Center for Applied Cybersecurity ATHENE, and by the German Research Foundation under grant EC 503/1-1 and GU 798/21-1. Aishwarya Kamath is supported in part by a DeepMind PhD Fellowship. The work of Ivan Vulić is supported by the ERC Consolidator Grant LEXICAL: Lexical Acquisition Across Languages (no 648909). Kyunghyun Cho is supported by Samsung Advanced Institute of Technology (Next Generation Deep Learning: from pattern recognition to AI) and Samsung Research (Improving Deep Learning using Latent Structure).

We would like to thank Isabel Pfeiffer for the illustrations.

References

Jacob Andreas, Marcus Rohrbach, Trevor Darrell, and Dan Klein. 2016. Learning to compose neural networks for question answering. In *NAACL HLT 2016, The 2016 Conference of the North American Chapter of the Association for Computational Linguistics: Human Language Technologies, San Diego California, USA, June 12-17, 2016*, pages 1545–1554.

Lei Jimmy Ba, Jamie Ryan Kiros, and Geoffrey E. Hinton. 2016. Layer normalization. *arXiv preprint*.

Ankur Bapna and Orhan Firat. 2019. Simple, scalable adaptation for neural machine translation. In *Proceedings of the 2019 Conference on Empirical Methods in Natural Language Processing and the 9th International Joint Conference on Natural Language Processing, EMNLP-IJCNLP 2019, Hong Kong, China, November 3-7, 2019*, pages 1538–1548.

Roy Bar-Haim, Ido Dagan, Bill Dolan, Lisa Ferro, Danilo Giampiccolo, Bernardo Magnini, and Idan Szpektor. 2006. The second pascal recognising textual entailment challenge. In *Proceedings of the PASCAL@ACL 2006*.

Tom B. Brown, Benjamin Mann, Nick Ryder, Melanie Subbiah, Jared Kaplan, Prafulla Dhariwal, Arvind Neelakantan, Pranav Shyam, Girish Sastry, Amanda Askell, Sandhini Agarwal, Ariel Herbert-Voss, Gretchen Krueger, Tom Henighan, Rewon Child, Aditya Ramesh, Daniel M. Ziegler, Jeffrey Wu, Clemens Winter, Christopher Hesse, Mark Chen, Eric Sigler, Mateusz Litwin, Scott Gray, Benjamin Chess, Jack Clark, Christopher Berner, Sam McCandlish, Alec Radford, Ilya Sutskever, and Dario Amodei. 2020. Language models are few-shot learners. *arXiv preprint*.

Daniel Cer, Mona Diab, Eneko Agirre, Iñigo Lopez-Gazpio, and Lucia Specia. 2017. SemEval-2017 task 1: Semantic textual similarity multilingual and crosslingual focused evaluation. In *Proceedings of SemEval-2017*.

Alexis Conneau, Kartikay Khandelwal, Naman Goyal, Vishrav Chaudhary, Guillaume Wenzek, Francisco Guzmán, Edouard Grave, Myle Ott, Luke Zettlemoyer, and Veselin Stoyanov. 2020. Unsupervised cross-lingual representation learning at scale. In *Proceedings of the 58th Conference of the Association for Computational Linguistics, ACL 2020, Virtual Conference, July 6-8, 2020*, pages 8440–8451.

Ido Dagan, Oren Glickman, and Bernardo Magnini. 2005. The PASCAL recognising textual entailment challenge. In *Machine Learning Challenges, Evaluating Predictive Uncertainty, Visual Object Classification and Recognizing Textual Entailment, First PASCAL Machine Learning Challenges Workshop, MLCW 2005, Southampton, UK, April 11-13, 2005, Revised Selected Papers*, pages 177–190.

Jacob Devlin, Ming-Wei Chang, Kenton Lee, and Kristina Toutanova. 2019. BERT: pre-training of deep bidirectional transformers for language understanding. In *Proceedings of the 2019 Conference of the North American Chapter of the Association for Computational Linguistics: Human Language Technologies, NAACL-HLT 2019, Minneapolis, MN, USA, June 2-7, 2019, Volume 1 (Long and Short Papers)*, pages 4171–4186.

William B. Dolan and Chris Brockett. 2005. Automatically constructing a corpus of sentential paraphrases. In *Proceedings of the Third International Workshop on Paraphrasing, IWP@IJCNLP 2005, Jeju Island, Korea, October 2005, 2005*.

Danilo Giampiccolo, Bernardo Magnini, Ido Dagan, and Bill Dolan. 2007. The third pascal recognizing textual entailment challenge. In *Proceedings of the PASCAL@ACL 2007*.

Suchin Gururangan, Ana Marasovic, Swabha Swayamdipta, Kyle Lo, Iz Beltagy, Doug Downey, and Noah A. Smith. 2020. Don't stop pretraining: Adapt language models to domains and tasks. In *Proceedings of the 58th Annual Meeting of the Association for Computational Linguistics, ACL 2020, Online, July 5-10, 2020*, pages 8342–8360.

Kazuma Hashimoto, Caiming Xiong, Yoshimasa Tsuruoka, and Richard Socher. 2017. A joint many-task model: Growing a neural network for multiple NLP tasks. In *Proceedings of the 2017 Conference on Empirical Methods in Natural Language Processing, EMNLP 2017, Copenhagen, Denmark, September 9-11, 2017*, pages 1923–1933.

Neil Houlsby, Andrei Giurgiu, Stanislaw Jastrzkeb-ski, Bruna Morrone, Quentin de Laroussilhe, Andrea Gesmundo, Mona Attariyan, and Sylvain Gelly. 2019. Parameter-efficient transfer learning for NLP. In *Proceedings of the 36th International Conference on Machine Learning, ICML 2019, 9-15 June 2019, Long Beach, California, USA*, pages 2790–2799.

Jeremy Howard and Sebastian Ruder. 2018. Universal Language Model Fine-tuning for Text Classification. In *Proceedings of the 56th Annual Meeting of the Association for Computational Linguistics, ACL 2018, Melbourne, Australia, July 15-20, 2018, Volume 1: Long Papers*, pages 328–339.

Shankar Iyer, Nikhil Dandekar, and Kornel Csernai. First quora dataset release: Question pairs [online]. 2017.

Jared Kaplan, Sam McCandlish, Tom Henighan, Tom B. Brown, Benjamin Chess, Rewon Child, Scott Gray, Alec Radford, Jeffrey Wu, and Dario Amodei. 2020. Scaling Laws for Neural Language Models. *arXiv preprint*.

Anne Lauscher, Ivan Vulić, Edoardo Maria Ponti, Anna Korhonen, and Goran Glavaš. 2019. Specializing unsupervised pretraining models for word-level semantic similarity. *arXiv preprint*.

Yinhan Liu, Myle Ott, Naman Goyal, Jingfei Du, Mandar Joshi, Danqi Chen, Omer Levy, Mike Lewis, Luke Zettlemoyer, and Veselin Stoyanov. 2019. Roberta: A robustly optimized bert pretraining approach. *arXiv preprint*.

Cyprien de Masson d'Autume, Sebastian Ruder, Lingpeng Kong, and Dani Yogatama. 2019. Episodic memory in lifelong language learning. In *Advances in Neural Information Processing Systems 32: Annual Conference on Neural Information Processing Systems 2019, NeurIPS 2019, 8-14 December 2019, Vancouver, BC, Canada*, pages 13122–13131.

Matthew E. Peters, Sebastian Ruder, and Noah A. Smith. 2019. To tune or not to tune? adapting pretrained representations to diverse tasks. In *Proceedings of the 4th Workshop on Representation Learning for NLP, RepL4NLP@ACL 2019, Florence, Italy, August 2, 2019*, pages 7–14.

Jonas Pfeiffer, Aishwarya Kamath, Andreas Rücklé, Kyunghyun Cho, and Iryna Gurevych. 2020a. AdapterFusion: Non-destructive task composition for transfer learning. *arXiv preprint*.

Jonas Pfeiffer, Ivan Vulić, Iryna Gurevych, and Sebastian Ruder. 2020b. MAD-X: An Adapter-based Framework for Multi-task Cross-lingual Transfer. In *Proceedings of the 2020 Conference on Empirical Methods in Natural Language Processing, EMNLP 2020, Virtual Conference*.

Jason Phang, Thibault Févry, and Samuel R Bowman. 2018. Sentence encoders on stilts: Supplementary training on intermediate labeled-data tasks. *arXiv preprint*.

Yada Pruksachatkun, Jason Phang, Haokun Liu, Phu Mon Htut, Xiaoyi Zhang, Richard Yuanzhe Pang, Clara Vania, Katharina Kann, and Samuel R. Bowman. 2020. Intermediate-task transfer learning with pretrained language models: When and why does it work? In *Proceedings of the 58th Annual Meeting of the Association for Computational Linguistics, ACL 2020, Online, July 5-10, 2020*, pages 5231–5247.

Colin Raffel, Noam Shazeer, Adam Roberts, Katherine Lee, Sharan Narang, Michael Matena, Yanqi Zhou, Wei Li, and Peter J. Liu. 2019. Exploring the Limits of Transfer Learning with a Unified Text-to-Text Transformer. *arXiv preprint*.

Pranav Rajpurkar, Jian Zhang, Konstantin Lopyrev, and Percy Liang. 2016. SQuAD: 100,000+ Questions for Machine Comprehension of Text. In *Proceedings of the 2016 Conference on Empirical Methods in Natural Language Processing, EMNLP 2016, Austin, Texas, USA, November 1-4, 2016*, pages 2383–2392.

Sylvestre-Alvise Rebuffi, Hakan Bilen, and Andrea Vedaldi. 2017. Learning multiple visual domains with residual adapters. In *Advances in Neural Information Processing Systems 30: Annual Conference on Neural Information Processing Systems 2017, 4-9 December 2017, Long Beach, CA, USA*, pages 506–516.

Andreas Rücklé, Gregor Geigle, Max Glockner, Tilman Beck, Jonas Pfeiffer, Nils Reimers, and Iryna Gurevych. 2020. AdapterDrop: On the Efficiency of Adapters in Transformers. *arXiv preprint*.

Sebastian Ruder. 2017. An Overview of Multi-Task Learning in Deep Neural Networks. *arXiv preprint*.

Sebastian Ruder, Matthew E Peters, Swabha Swayamdipta, and Thomas Wolf. 2019. Transfer learning in natural language processing. In *Proceedings of the 2019 Conference of the North American Chapter of the Association for Computational Linguistics: Human Language Technologies, NAACL-HLT 2019, Minneapolis, MN, USA, June 2-7, 2019, Tutorials*.

Victor Sanh, Thomas Wolf, and Sebastian Ruder. 2019. A hierarchical multi-task approach for learning embeddings from semantic tasks. In *The Thirty-Third AAAI Conference on Artificial Intelligence, AAAI 2019, The Thirty-First Innovative Applications of Artificial Intelligence Conference, IAAI 2019, The Ninth AAAI Symposium on Educational Advances in Artificial Intelligence, EAAI 2019, Honolulu, Hawaii, USA, January 27 - February 1, 2019*, pages 6949–6956.

Noam Shazeer, Azalia Mirhoseini, Krzysztof Maziarz, Andy Davis, Quoc V. Le, Geoffrey E. Hinton, and Jeff Dean. 2017. Outrageously large neural networks: The sparsely-gated mixture-of-experts layer.

In *5th International Conference on Learning Representations, ICLR 2017, Toulon, France, April 24-26, 2017, Conference Track Proceedings*.

Richard Socher, Alex Perelygin, Jean Wu, Jason Chuang, Christopher D. Manning, Andrew Y. Ng, and Christopher Potts. 2013. Recursive deep models for semantic compositionality over a sentiment treebank. In *Proceedings of the 2013 Conference on Empirical Methods in Natural Language Processing, EMNLP 2013, 18-21 October 2013, Grand Hyatt Seattle, Seattle, Washington, USA, A meeting of SIGDAT, a Special Interest Group of the ACL*, pages 1631–1642.

Asa Cooper Stickland and Iain Murray. 2019. BERT and pals: Projected attention layers for efficient adaptation in multi-task learning. In *Proceedings of the 36th International Conference on Machine Learning, ICML 2019, 9-15 June 2019, Long Beach, California, USA*, pages 5986–5995.

Emma Strubell, Ananya Ganesh, and Andrew McCallum. 2019. Energy and policy considerations for deep learning in NLP. In *Proceedings of the 57th Conference of the Association for Computational Linguistics, ACL 2019, Florence, Italy, July 28- August 2, 2019, Volume 1: Long Papers*, pages 3645–3650.

Ashish Vaswani, Noam Shazeer, Niki Parmar, Jakob Uszkoreit, Llion Jones, Aidan N. Gomez, Lukasz Kaiser, and Illia Polosukhin. 2017. Attention Is All You Need. In *Advances in Neural Information Processing Systems 30: Annual Conference on Neural Information Processing Systems 2017, 4-9 December 2017, Long Beach, CA, USA*, pages 5998–6008.

Alex Wang, Amanpreet Singh, Julian Michael, Felix Hill, Omer Levy, and Samuel R. Bowman. 2018. GLUE: A multi-task benchmark and analysis platform for natural language understanding. In *Proceedings of the Workshop: Analyzing and Interpreting Neural Networks for NLP, BlackboxNLP@EMNLP 2018, Brussels, Belgium, November 1, 2018*, pages 353–355.

Ruize Wang, Duyu Tang, Nan Duan, Zhongyu Wei, Xuanjing Huang, Jianshu Ji, Guihong Cao, Daxin Jiang, and Ming Zhou. 2020. K-adapter: Infusing knowledge into pre-trained models with adapters. *arXiv preprint*.

Alex Warstadt, Amanpreet Singh, and Samuel R. Bowman. 2019. Neural network acceptability judgments. *Transactions of the Association for Computational Linguistics*, 7:625–641.

Adina Williams, Nikita Nangia, and Samuel R. Bowman. 2018. A broad-coverage challenge corpus for sentence understanding through inference. In *Proceedings of the 2018 Conference of the North American Chapter of the Association for Computational Linguistics: Human Language Technologies, NAACL-HLT 2018, New Orleans, Louisiana, USA, June 1-6, 2018, Volume 1 (Long Papers)*, pages 1112–1122.

Thomas Wolf, Lysandre Debut, Victor Sanh, Julien Chaumond, Clement Delangue, Anthony Moi andArt Pierric Cistac, Tim Rault, Rémi Louf, Morgan Funtowicz, and Jamie Brew. 2020. HuggingFace's Transformers: State-of-the-art Natural Language Processing. In *Proceedings of the 2020 Conference on Empirical Methods in Natural Language Processing, EMNLP 2020, Virtual Conference, 2020 Proceedings of EMNLP: Systems Demonstrations*.

HUMAN: Hierarchical Universal Modular ANnotator

Moritz Wolf[1*], **Dana Ruiter**[12*], **Ashwin Geet D'Sa**[3*]
Liane Reiners[4], **Jan Alexandersson**[1], **Dietrich Klakow**[2]
[1]DFKI GmbH, [2]Spoken Language System Group, Saarland University
[3]Université de Lorraine, CNRS, Inria, LORIA
[4]Department of Communication, Johannes Gutenberg University Mainz
{moritz.wolf, jan.alexandersson}@dfki.de
{druiter, dietrich.klakow}@lsv.uni-saarland.de
ashwin-geet.dsa@loria.fr, liane.reiners@uni-mainz.de

Abstract

A lot of real-world phenomena are complex and cannot be captured by single task annotations. This causes a need for *subsequent* annotations, with interdependent questions and answers describing the nature of the subject at hand. Even in the case a phenomenon is easily captured by a single task, the high specialisation of most annotation tools can result in having to switch to another tool if the task only slightly changes. We introduce HUMAN, a novel web-based annotation tool that addresses the above problems by a) covering a variety of annotation tasks on both textual and image data, and b) the usage of an internal deterministic state machine, allowing the researcher to chain different annotation tasks in an interdependent manner. Further, the modular nature of the tool makes it easy to define new annotation tasks and integrate machine learning algorithms e.g., for active learning. HUMAN comes with an easy-to-use graphical user interface that simplifies the annotation task and management.

1 Introduction

Access to suitable annotated data constitutes a fundamental prerequisite for R&D of machine learning algorithms and models. The demand for new annotated data is growing as new data is collected or existing data is being re-annotated from a new perspective. In the area of natural language processing (NLP) alone, there is a large variety of tasks that require different types of annotations to be covered by a tool. This includes named-entity recognition or part-of-speech tagging, which require a tool to cover sequence labeling (Kiesel et al., 2017), co-reference and dependency parsing requiring relational annotations (Stenetorp et al., 2012; Eckart de Castilho et al., 2016; Shindo et al., 2018), or any

type of text classification task requiring document-level annotations (Nakayama et al., 2018).

Neves and Ševa (2019) find that enabling document-level classification is the top missing feature in a large number of reviewed annotation tools. At the same time, document-level annotation has been the most frequently sought-after annotation type according to a recent online survey (Tan, 2020). Another feature missing from about half of the reviewed tools is multi-label annotations.

Since most annotation tools cover only one or two annotation types, a change in the annotation task can easily require a change in the annotation tool itself. Commercial platforms such as Light-Tag[1] or Prodigy[2] cover a larger array of tasks to choose from. However, none of these are able to chain a mixture of different tasks (e.g., document-level classification followed by finer-grained sequence labeling) to be performed on a single annotation instance. One tool that comes close to achieving this, is Angrist[3], however, its lack of modularity makes it difficult to adapt to new annotation scenarios.

Hierarchical Universal Modular ANnotator (HUMAN) follows a highly modular concept, which makes it easy to adapt to a specific annotation scenario. It uses an internal deterministic state machine (DSM) to guide the annotator through the pre-defined annotation task(s). This usage of a DSM allows annotation tasks to be chained in any order needed and makes it easy to implement entirely new annotation tasks and custom features in the future. This **modular** nature is especially useful when single task annotations do not capture the reality of a problem or when several dependencies exist in the annotations. One example being hate speech corpora (Zampieri et al., 2019; Struß et al.,

---

* Equal contribution.

[1]https://www.lighttag.io
[2]https://prodi.gy/
[3]https://github.com/Tarlanc/angrist

Proceedings of the 2020 EMNLP (Systems Demonstrations), pages 55–61
November 16-20, 2020. ©2020 Association for Computational Linguistics

2019), where the target of hate is only supposed to be annotated if a comment has been previously annotated as hateful.

Further, HUMAN covers a variety of annotation tasks, including the often lacking multi-label annotations and document-level classification, but also sequence labeling on textual data as well as image labeling; a pursuit towards **universality**. An example involving both document-level annotation as well as sequence labeling is multi-lingual Named Entity Recognition (NER), where the annotator has to identify the language on the document level and then annotate the named entities on the sequence-level. Moreover, when the annotation need is single-task, the fact that many tasks are covered by HUMAN makes it easy to re-use previous installations of HUMAN for a new scenario, even if the task at hand changes.

Lastly, HUMAN makes the annotation of **hierarchical** data possible. That is, if an annotation instance is embedded in a context of previous content (e.g., comments in a forum) this context can be shown to the annotators.

The remainder of this paper is organized as follows. In Section 2, we explain the structure of HUMAN, starting with the architecture and followed by the internal deterministic state machine, annotation protocol, API, database, and graphical user interface. In Section 3, we demonstrate the application of HUMAN for a real-life use case. This is followed by a discussion (Section 4) and conclusion (Section 5).

2 System Description

The HUMAN annotation tool is primarily designed to run on a web server. As such its architecture follows a basic client-server model (Figure 1). Clients and servers exchange messages in a request–response pattern, where the client sends a request to which the server responds.

The **server**, consisting of the database and the API, serves the code for the client. The database (Section 2.4) is used for sending new annotation instances to the client or saving finished annotations which are sent by the client.

The **client** is controlled by a DSM (Section 2.1) to show an annotation task in the GUI (Section 2.5). For this it requests new content and sends finished annotations to the server when an annotation instance is completed. The annotators interact with the GUI to solve annotation tasks.

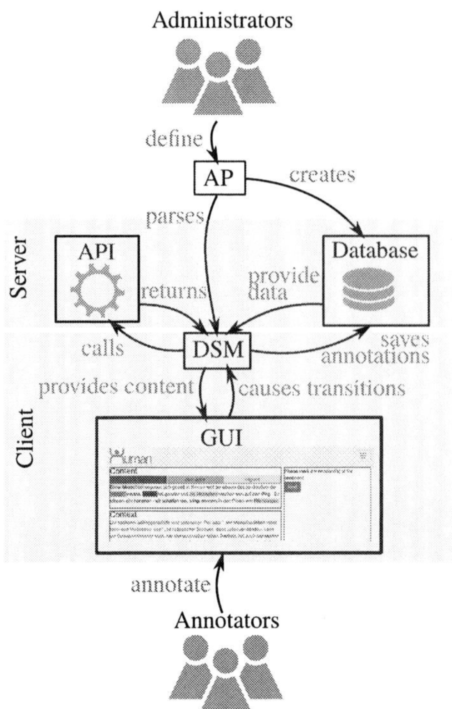

Figure 1: The basic structure behind HUMAN: Administrators define the annotation protocol (AP) which gets parsed to a DSM. The different components in client (GUI and DSM) and server (API and database) interact with each other. Annotators annotate using the GUI.

During **setup** of the HUMAN system, administrators design the *annotation protocol* (AP), which is a JSON-style definition of the annotation task(s) at hand. This is then used to generate both the database and the DSM. Further, it is possible for the administrator to write a custom API on the server and call its functions through the DSM (Section 2.3. Annotations can be given as arguments to these functions making it easy to realize active learning or similar tasks.

The server is implemented using Flask (Grinberg, 2018), a common web framework for Python. The client is written in Typescript and transpiled to JavaScript. The client was tested on Chrome/Chromium (v85.0) and Firefox (v80.0.1).

2.1 Deterministic State Machine

The back-bone of HUMAN is its deterministic state machine implemented using XState[4], a library for finite state machines and statecharts for JavaScript. It controls how each annotation instance is handled during the annotation process.

---

[4]`https://github.com/davidkpiano/xstate`

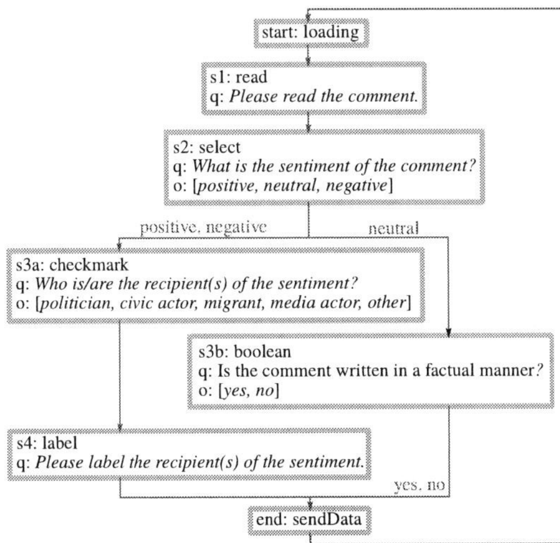

Figure 2: Visualization of a deterministic state machine as used by HUMAN.

The DSM (Figure 2) starts at a `start` state which assigns and loads an annotation instance to be presented to the annotator. It then passes through all of the **annotation states** (AS) that have been defined by the administrator. This allows for the definition of complex **transitions** between ASs, as the answer an annotator provided to a given question can influence to which subsequent AS the DSM will guide them. As such, it is easy to design a flow of questions presented to the annotator that contains sub-branches and even loops. While accounting for the transitions between ASs, the DSM can also accommodate different **actions**, such as saving annotations.

By default the DSM comes with three obligatory states:

- **start**: Assigns and loads an annotation instance to the annotator.

- **failure**: If any unexpected errors occur during annotation, the platform automatically generates an error message and displays it to the user. This state serves as a dead state.

- **end**: The end state passes the annotations collected to the `annotations` table in the data base.

All other states that handle the transitions between questions, need to be defined in the *Annotation Protocol* by the administrator when setting up the HUMAN server.

2.2 Annotation Protocol

The annotation protocol is the definition of the DSM, using a simplified JSON-style syntax. Within the AP, the project administrators define each annotation task, i.e., state, that should be passed by the DSM. Each state comes with at least two obligatory **fields**. These are the *transition* field, which describes to which state the DSM should move next, and the state *type*. Depending on the state type, there may be additional fields that further define the quality of a state. The predefined **state types** are:

- Functional States

  loading : This is usually used to define the type of the `start` state and loads a textual annotation instance.

  loadingFile : Analogous to `loading`, but used to load PDF files or images.

  callAPI : This state is for calling API functions (Section 2.3) on the server. It requires the `api_call` field.

- Annotation States: An annotation state requires at least the additional `question` field in which an instruction or question to be presented to the annotator is defined.

  - **read**: Shows the annotation instance to the annotator.
  - **select**: Shows a question and a number of options to choose from. Only one option may be selected by the annotator. It also requires the `options` field, which lists the options the annotator can choose from.
  - **checkmark**: Analogous to `select` but allows the choice of multiple options.
  - **label**: Prompts the annotator to highlight portions of a text and label it with previously chosen labels.
  - **boolean**: Used for yes-no questions.
  - **choosePage**: Allows the annotator to choose a page from a PDF to annotate.
  - **bbox**: Asks the annotator to set bounding boxes on an image. By writing a custom API call, users can connect models that pre-select parts of an image with bounding boxes.
  - **bboxLabel**: Analogous to `bbox`, but annotators are required to add a text label to each bounding box they place.

```
"s2": {
    "type": "select",
    "question": "What is the sentiment of the comment?",
    "options": ["positive", "neutral", "negative"],
    "transitions": [["positive"], ["s3"], ["save"],
                    ["neutral"], ["s3"], ["save"]],
                    ["negative"], ["end"]]
}
```

Figure 3: AP definition of a state of type `select`.

All of these annotation types can be chained after each other in a modular-fashion. State types `select`, and `checkmark` can be especially useful for document-level annotations, e.g., creating labels for text classification models. Additionally, `label` states can be used for sequence annotations such as part-of-speech or named entity tagging, or highlighting certain entities of interest in a text. States `choosePage`, `bbox` and `bboxLabel` can be applied to PDFs or images in which something should be selected. This is practical when creating data for tasks such as optical character recognition or object detection and labeling.

Actions Each state can be asked to perform different actions. While the `load` action is handled automatically by the `loading` type, the `save` action can be used in ASs and needs to be explicitly stated. When the `save` action is included in the state definition, then the answer provided by the annotator at this AS will be saved. Non-saving states might be useful to handle transitions in the DSM that are needed to design specific sub-branches, but are not needed during the further assessment of the data annotations.

Syntax The JSON-style AP syntax is simplistic and can best be explained by the example code in Figure 3, which is the description of a state named `s2` of type `select`. It asks the annotator about *the sentiment of the comment* and provides three options *positive, neutral, negative* to the annotator. If the annotator chooses *positive* or *neutral*, the answer will be saved and the DSM directs the annotator to another state named `s3`. If, however, the annotator chooses *negative*, they are redirected to the `end` state without saving.

We provide full documentation with instructions on how to define an AP using the defined syntax.[5]

Parsing Once the AP is defined, the `ap_parser` will parse it into `XState` compatible format. If any definitions in the AP are ambiguous

---

[5]https://github.com/uds-lsv/human/wiki

or undefined, an error message appears that helps the user resolve the problem.

Apart from creating the DSM, the parser also initializes the database instance.

2.3 API

We provide the possibility to define a custom API on the server. Functions of this API can be called via the DSM with the `callAPI` state or by adding a `callAPI` option to a state in the AP. The arguments can contain annotations and/or the current annotation instance. The reasoning behind this is to enable active learning or similar tasks and have direct access to any machine learning algorithm.

Example We want to train an optical character recognition algorithm and need to annotate pictures with bounding boxes around words. We want to show the predicted boxes of the algorithm to the annotator and let them correct them. For that we can write an API function to call the prediction function of our algorithm. In the AP we define a state `bbox` with the `callAPI` option and the name of our API function. When entering this state, the DSM will then call the API function with the current annotation instance (in this case a picture). The returned bounding boxes will then be displayed on the picture and corrected by the user.

2.4 Managing the Database

HUMAN uses an SQLite database with four different tables: `data`, `annotations`, `users`, and `options`.

Inputs Data can dynamically be input into the `data` table via the GUI. All inputs must be formatted as tab-separated CSV files consisting of the three columns `content`, `context`, `meta`. In `content`, the content of an instance to be annotated is placed, the `context` is for optional context information relevant for the annotator, and `meta` is an encoded JSON object containing any meta information that should be stored with an instance, but that should not be shown to the annotators (e.g., author of a comment, project internal ID of an instance or date of publication).

After uploading the tab-separated CSV file to the server, it will be checked for errors and then parsed into the `data` table of the database, ready to be distributed to annotators.

Outputs At any given time, collected annotations can be downloaded from the `annotations`

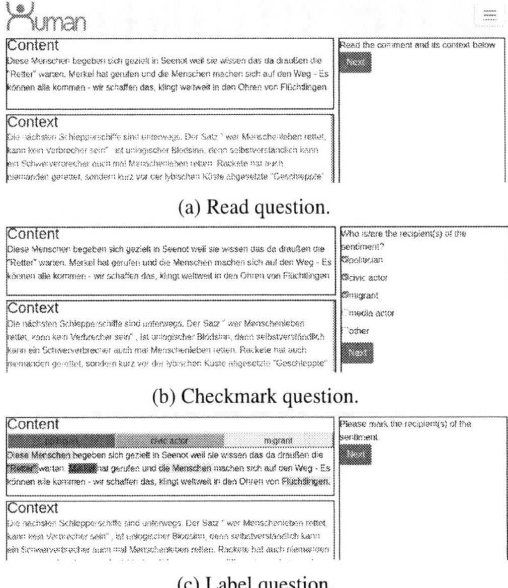

(a) Read question.

(b) Checkmark question.

(c) Label question.

Figure 4: The annotation page while passing through different annotation states.

table. It is returned as an Excel file. By default, the name of a column is tied to the name of the state in the DSM that generated the annotation contained. That is, a state named `s2` will by default write answers into column `s2`. The file also contains the unique instance ID and user ID to match each annotation with its corresponding annotation instance in `data` and annotator in `users`. It is also possible to separately extract each table of the database on the server as tab-separated CSV files.

Users Each annotator needs a user account to access the HUMAN server. User information such as username, e-mail, full name and the hashed password are stored in the `users` table. Further, the user type is stored, in order to separate annotator accounts from administrator accounts. While annotators only have access to the annotation page and their profile information, administrators also have access to the data upload and download page as well as the administrator console.

Options The `options` table contains information about the set-up of the tool, such as the number of annotators an annotation instance should be assigned to.

2.5 Graphical User Interface

The graphical user interface (GUI) makes the tool easy to use for annotators and administrators. On the **annotation page** (Figure 4), the left-hand side shows the current annotation instance, with content to be annotated on top and optional context information at the bottom. This makes it possible to perform hierarchical annotations, by showing an annotation instance together with the context it was originally embedded in. The right-hand side is dedicated to showing the questions one-by-one as annotators pass through the DSM.

The **administrator console** in the GUI allows the administrators to manage annotators and annotation settings. This includes activating users that have registered for an account, or deactivating users that should be removed, or changing the annotator's password when required. The administrator can check the total number of annotations made by the annotators. It is further possible to specify how many annotators are required per annotation instance. Data upload and download is done via the **data console** in the GUI and is also only available to administrators.

3   Use-Case

In the case of the interdisciplinary project M-PHASIS, where computer and communication scientists are collaborating to study online hate speech in user-generated content, an annotation tool was needed that can implement multiple facets of hate speech in the AP. Annotating in communication science means following a complex AP which consists of different theoretically deduced categories to answer previously defined research questions or hypotheses (Früh, 2017). Often there are multiple levels of analysis units which are hierarchical (Rössler, 2017), e.g., news articles with corresponding comments which can be also divided into various statements. Due to the analytical splitting of comments into different statements, it was crucial to have a tool that allows answering specific questions more than once for the same comment (*loops*).

Due to collaboration across disciplines it was necessary to combine the different types of select and label questions (Section 2.2). To study media content, communication scholars apply an empirical method called quantitative content analysis, by which they try to systematically categorize content and formal characteristics of messages (Früh, 2017). The computational linguists, on the other hand, also required sequence labels to identify specific entities in the texts, e.g., targets of hate speech.

For M-PHASIS there are different questions which depend on the type of text input: news articles (3 select questions, 1 label question, 1 boolean question) and comments. For comments, the questions vary according to type: moderating comment (1 select question) or user comment (10 label questions, up to 30 questions of another type). For the user comments, there are six different thematic blocks in the AP. Some questions must be answered for all comments, other (follow-up) questions must only be answered when certain conditions apply to the particular comment (*branching*). This includes, inter alia, the question of whether statements within a comment contain a positive or negative evaluation of a target or an action recommendation of how to deal with a target, for example when the adaption of a specific behavior is demanded or a threat of physical violence is expressed. Depending on the annotator's decision, follow-up questions are shown, e.g., regarding the characteristics of a negative evaluation. If required, the tool loops through a block of questions as many times as needed, for example when various evaluations of different targets are expressed in one comment.

The flexible structure of HUMAN allows one to change the extent of the tool in consideration of the actual content. This enables complex annotations when necessary, but also makes it possible to shorten the AP and therefore the time spent per annotation – something no other tool has been able to accomplish until now.

4 Discussion

HUMAN strongly follows its concept of modularity and allows for the design and implementation of complex annotation protocols. And while it is currently already able to handle a variety of tasks on textual data as well as PDFs and images, many tasks are still uncovered. Two examples here being relationship annotations or asking open answer questions. In order to truly reach *universality*, we envision that the modular nature of the code will invite anyone interested to add new and custom features and annotation types to this open-source tool.

5 Conclusion and Future Work

We have described HUMAN, a **modular** annotation tool that covers a variety of annotation tasks, ranging from document-level annotation over sequence labeling to image annotations. Its usage of a deterministic state machine, also accommodates different annotation tasks to be chained in such a way that annotation decisions of the annotator can be followed by different subsequent questions (branching) or the revisions of previous questions (loops). Its context and content fields make it possible to perform **hierarchical** annotations, i.e., annotating an instance together with the context it was embedded in.

This is, as far as we know, the only annotation tool capable of covering such complex annotation needs. This is of use not only for disciplines that require multi-task annotation protocols, but also for various single-task scenarios where users do not want change the tool every time they have a new annotation need with a slightly different task.

While HUMAN is already fully functional and has been used for a real-life annotation scenario, it is a work in progress. Possible new annotation tasks could be e.g., annotations of relationships as in Brat (Stenetorp et al., 2012), of wave signals, similar to Praat (Boersma and Weenink, 2001) or even videos as in NOVA (Heimerl et al., 2019).

In order to improve accessibility of the tool in the future, we plan to implement a drag-and-drop GUI for the creation of the AP, as well as a visualization of the internally generated DSM to improve debugging. Automatic calculation of statistics such as the inter annotator agreement and average time spent on an annotation instance are planned.

To further ease the database management, administrators should have direct insight on each annotation instance in the database, which can then be added, removed or edited in the GUI without the need of `SQLite` commands on the server.

The code[6] is published under a GPL-3 licence together with a Wiki with detailed instructions on how to setup the server and define an AP. It also explains how to write custom annotation states and API calls. Two functioning demos of the HUMAN annotation page on two different APs are published on our homepage[7].

Acknowledgments

The development of this tool is partially funded by ANR-DFG Project M-PHASIS (WI 4204/3-1). A special thanks for all the feedback to Thomas Kleinbauer, Christian Schemer, Laura Ascone, Angeliki Monnier, Irina Illina and Dominique Fohr.

---

[6]`https://github.com/uds-lsv/human`
[7]`http://human.lsv.uni-saarland.de/`

References

Paul Boersma and David Weenink. 2001. Praat, a system for doing phonetics by computer. *Glot International*, 5(9/10):341–345.

Richard Eckart de Castilho, Éva Mújdricza-Maydt, Seid Muhie Yimam, Silvana Hartmann, Iryna Gurevych, Anette Frank, and Chris Biemann. 2016. A web-based tool for the integrated annotation of semantic and syntactic structures. In *Proceedings of the Workshop on Language Technology Resources and Tools for Digital Humanities (LT4DH)*, pages 76–84, Osaka, Japan. The COLING 2016 Organizing Committee.

Werner Früh. 2017. *Inhaltsanalyse. Theorie und Praxis*. UVK, Konstanz.

Miguel Grinberg. 2018. *Flask web development: developing web applications with python*. " O'Reilly Media, Inc.".

Alexander Heimerl, Tobias Baur, Florian Lingenfelser, Johannes Wagner, and Elisabeth André. 2019. Nova - a tool for explainable cooperative machine learning. In *2019 8th International Conference on Affective Computing and Intelligent Interaction (ACII)*, pages 109–115.

Johannes Kiesel, Henning Wachsmuth, Khalid Al-Khatib, and Benno Stein. 2017. WAT-SL: A customizable web annotation tool for segment labeling. In *Proceedings of the Software Demonstrations of the 15th Conference of the European Chapter of the Association for Computational Linguistics*, pages 13–16, Valencia, Spain. Association for Computational Linguistics.

Hiroki Nakayama, Takahiro Kubo, Junya Kamura, Yasufumi Taniguchi, and Xu Liang. 2018. doccano: Text annotation tool for human. Software available from https://github.com/doccano/doccano.

Mariana Neves and Jurica Ševa. 2019. An extensive review of tools for manual annotation of documents. *Briefings in Bioinformatics*. Bbz130.

Patrick Rössler. 2017. *Inhaltsanalyse*. UVK, Konstanz.

Hiroyuki Shindo, Yohei Munesada, and Yuji Matsumoto. 2018. PDFAnno: a Web-based Linguistic Annotation Tool for PDF Documents. In *Proceedings of the Eleventh International Conference on Language Resources and Evaluation (LREC 2018)*, pages 1082–1086, Miyazaki, Japan. European Language Resources Association (ELRA).

Pontus Stenetorp, Sampo Pyysalo, Goran Topić, Tomoko Ohta, Sophia Ananiadou, and Jun'ichi Tsujii. 2012. brat: a web-based tool for NLP-assisted text annotation. In *Proceedings of the Demonstrations at the 13th Conference of the European Chapter of the Association for Computational Linguistics*, pages 102–107, Avignon, France. Association for Computational Linguistics.

Julia Maria Struß, Melanie Siegel, Josep Ruppenhofer, Michael Wiegand, and Manfred Klenner. 2019. Overview of germeval task 2, 2019 shared task on the identification of offensive language. In *Proceedings of the 15th Conference on Natural Language Processing (KONVENS 2019)*, pages 354–365, Erlangen, Germany. German Society for Computational Linguistics & Language Technology.

Liling Tan. 2020. A survey of nlp annotation platforms. https://github.com/alvations/annotate-questionnaire.

Marcos Zampieri, Shervin Malmasi, Preslav Nakov, Sara Rosenthal, Noura Farra, and Ritesh Kumar. 2019. Semeval-2019 task 6: Identifying and categorizing offensive language in social media (offenseval). In *Proceedings of the 13th International Workshop on Semantic Evaluation*, pages 75–86.

DeezyMatch: A Flexible Deep Learning Approach
to Fuzzy String Matching

Kasra Hosseini
The Alan Turing Institute

Federico Nanni
The Alan Turing Institute

Mariona Coll Ardanuy
The Alan Turing Institute

{khosseini,fnanni,mcollardanuy}@turing.ac.uk

Abstract

We present DeezyMatch, a free, open-source software library written in Python for fuzzy string matching and candidate ranking. Its *pair classifier* supports various deep neural network architectures for training new classifiers and for fine-tuning a pretrained model, which paves the way for transfer learning in fuzzy string matching. This approach is especially useful where only limited training examples are available. The learned DeezyMatch models can be used to generate rich vector representations from string inputs. The *candidate ranker* component in DeezyMatch uses these vector representations to find, for a given query, the best matching candidates in a knowledge base. It uses an adaptive searching algorithm applicable to large knowledge bases and query sets. We describe DeezyMatch's functionality, design and implementation, accompanied by a use case in toponym matching and candidate ranking in realistic noisy datasets.

1 Introduction

String matching is an integral component of many natural language processing (NLP) pipelines. One such application is in entity linking (EL), the task of mapping a mention (i.e., a string) to its corresponding entry in a knowledge base (KB). Most EL systems currently rely on a lookup table (Ferragina and Scaiella, 2010; Mendes et al., 2011; Raiman and Raiman, 2018; Sil et al., 2018)[1] or shallow string similarity approaches (e.g., based on n-gram overlaps as in McNamee et al. (2011b); Plu et al. (2016), or super-string matching, as in Moro et al.

(2014)) to narrow the entries of a KB down to a set of potential candidates the mention may refer to (i.e., aliases). While these choices allow fast run-time, they generally rely on the assumption that all surface forms of each entity are present as aliases in the KB. The performances of these systems degrade when dealing with domain-specific vocabulary (Munnelly and Lawless, 2018), local variations (Rovera et al., 2017), historical materials (Olieman et al., 2017; McDonough et al., 2019) and, in general, challenges that emerge when performing EL on non-standard documents.[2] This subtask of EL, often referred to as candidate ranking (and selection), is mostly ignored when designing downstream systems, even though its significant impact on downstream NLP pipelines has been shown previously (Quercini et al., 2010; Hachey et al., 2013).

In this paper, we present DeezyMatch, a new deep learning approach that strives to address advanced string matching and candidate ranking in a more comprehensive and integrated manner than existing tools. DeezyMatch is a free, open-source community software written in Python. It uses PyTorch (Paszke et al., 2019) to implement various state-of-the-art neural network architectures, and it has been tested on both CPU and GPU. One of the main features of DeezyMatch is its modular design and flexibility. We describe DeezyMatch's functionalities, design choices and technical implementation. We compare its performance in relation to other approaches on several realistic string matching scenarios, covering different languages, alphabets, and domains, and we evaluate the quality of the candidate ranker in a real-case setting. Thanks to its easy-to-use interface, DeezyMatch can be seamlessly integrated into existing EL systems. This allows DeezyMatch to be adopted out-

---

[1] See, for instance, DBpedia Lexicalization dataset used as a lookup table by DBpedia Spotlight: https://wiki.dbpedia.org/lexicalizations, or how Spacy currently retrieves candidates from a given KB: https://spacy.io/api/kb/#get_candidates.

[2] As opposed to Wikipedia or contemporary newspaper text, which are employed in widespread EL benchmarks, such as WikiDisamb30, CoNLL (YAGO), and AC KBP 2010.

62

Proceedings of the 2020 EMNLP (Systems Demonstrations), pages 62–69
November 16-20, 2020. ©2020 Association for Computational Linguistics

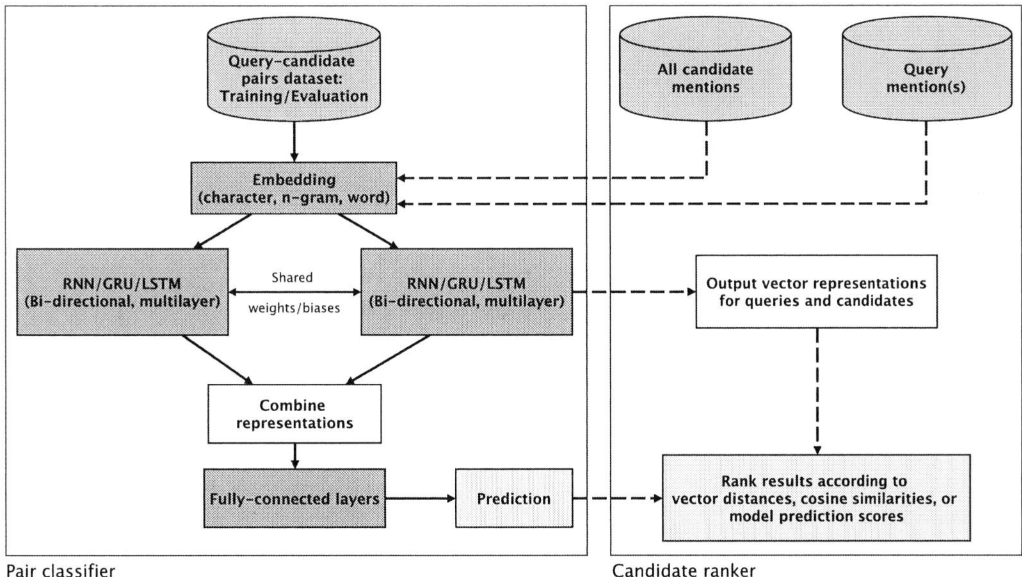

Figure 1: DeezyMatch architecture consists of two main components: *pair classifier* (left box) and *candidate ranker* (right box). The learnable parameters in *pair classifier* are highlighted in blue. During fine-tuning, any of these parameters can be frozen, that is, they will not be changed during fine-tuning. Various hyperparameters including the architecture of the neural network and tokenization can be changed by the user (see text). In *candidate ranker*, for each query and candidate pair, learned vector representations are first generated using a DeezyMatch model. These vectors are then used to rank candidates according to different metrics (e.g., L_2-norm distance, cosine similarity and prediction scores). The steps of *candidate ranker* are depicted by dashed lines in the figure.

side the NLP community, especially in Digital Humanities, where it could play a major role in addressing known issues concerning the EL systems and their adaptability to the non-standard nature of the datasets typically used in this field (Olieman et al., 2017).

DeezyMatch is released under MIT License. It is available via PyPI,[3] and its source codes are on GitHub.[4] We provide extensive documentation, including examples in Jupyter Notebooks, to enable the smooth adoption of all its components.

2   Description of the system

Fig. 1 shows the two main components of Deezy-Match: *pair classifier* and *candidate ranker*. Together they allow the training or fine-tuning of a query-candidate classifier and finding best matching candidates to a query from a KB.

2.1   Pair classifier

Inspired by the work of Santos et al. (2018a), DeezyMatch's pair-classifier component has at

its core a siamese deep neural network classifier. The network takes query-candidate pairs as inputs which can be further processed (e.g., lower-cased and normalized) and tokenized at different levels (character, n-gram and word). Such pairs are either possible referents of the same entity or not, which form the positive and negative examples for training and testing. The neural network architecture and its hyperparameters can be configured in the input file without requiring the user to modify the code. Currently, DeezyMatch supports Elman Recurrent neural network (RNN) (Elman, 1990), Long short-term memory (LSTM) (Hochreiter and Schmidhuber, 1997) and Gated Recurrent Unit (GRU) (Cho et al., 2014) architectures. The number of layers and directions (mono or bi-directional) in the recurrent units as well as the dimensions of hidden states and embedding layers can be changed in the input file. The two parallel recurrent layers in Fig. 1 share their weights and biases which helps the model to learn transformations regardless of the order of strings in an input pair.

During training, a dataset of string pairs is first read, preprocessed, tokenized, and they are converted into dense vectors (i.e., two embeddings per

---

[3]https://pypi.org/project/DeezyMatch
[4]https://github.com/Living-with-machines/DeezyMatch

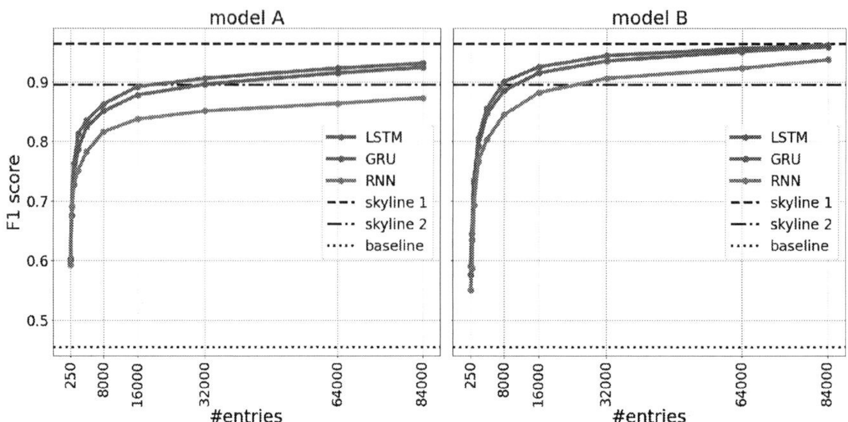

Figure 2: Impact of fine-tuning and freezing neural network layers on the performance of *pair classifier* as measured by F1-score. Three neural network architectures (LSTM, GRU and RNN) are fine-tuned and compared as a function of data instances (x-axis) used in fine-tuning. In model A, only the last layer (fully-connected layers in Fig. 1) is fine-tuned while in model B, both the recurrent units and the fully-connected layers are used. By adding more data instances in fine-tuning, the performance of all models improve logarithmically.

pair); the dimensionality of which can be specified in the input. The two embedding vectors of a string pair are then fed into two parallel recurrent units to generate vector representations (i.e., hidden states of the last units in each direction and layer). Next, the two vectors can be combined in different ways specified in the input, e.g., via concatenation, element-wise product, difference, or a combination of these. This aggregated representation is then given as input to a feed-forward network with one hidden layer and with Rectified Linear Unit (ReLU) as the activation function. The output layer has one unit with a sigmoid activation function for producing the final prediction. During training, the target and the predicted outputs are compared by the Binary Cross Entropy criterion. The dimensionality of the hidden layer and other hyperparameters (e.g., learning rate, number of epochs, batch size, early stopping and dropout probability) can all be tuned in the input file. DeezyMatch logs and outputs all standard evaluation metrics for binary classification (accuracy, precision, recall and F1) during training, evaluation and testing. Similar to Tam et al. (2019), it also calculates mean average precision (MAP), which evaluates the quality of candidate ranks per query. After a training is finished, DeezyMatch can be used to plot loss and evaluation metrics at each epoch for model selection. The outputs of each epoch can be also visualized during training via TensorBoard (Abadi et al., 2016).

2.1.1 Transfer learning

In addition to training a model from scratch, Deezy-Match supports fine-tuning a pretrained model; this way, an already trained model on a large dataset can be fine-tuned to a new domain. This transfer learning approach helps especially where only limited training examples are available. Any learnable parameters (as highlighted by blue boxes in Fig. 1) can be "frozen" during fine-tuning, and the fine-tuning can be done on a specified number of training instances by the user.

Fig. 2 shows the results of two sets of models fine-tuned progressively on more training instances. In model A, both embedding and recurrent units are frozen (i.e., their parameters are not updated during fine-tuning), and in model B, only the embedding layer is frozen. The baseline, skyline 1 and 2 are trained on *WG:en*, *OCR* and *WG:en+OCR*, respectively. Refer to Section 3.1.1 for details on these datasets. The performance of these models is then assessed on the *OCR* test set. To show the impact of fine-tuning and choice of architecture on the model performance, we trained various models starting with the baseline model and included more training instances from the training set of *OCR*. In this experiment, only ≈8K data points were needed to improve the performance of all models from ≈0.45 (baseline) to ≈0.82. In model B, by using around 20% of the data points (≈16K), the performance of GRU and LSTM architectures improve to ≈0.92 which highlights the importance of fine-tuning in scenarios with limited training datasets. When including all the data points, all models, except RNN in model A, pass skyline-2, and two of them reach the performance of skyline-1 ($\approx$0.964). It is worth noting that model B shows better performance compared to model A in fine-tuning. The improved performance can be attributed to the more unfrozen parameters during fine-tuning, which increases the learning capacity.

2.2 Candidate Ranker

The trained pair-classifiers in Section 2.1 predict if an input string pair is a good match or not by providing not only the label (True/False) but also the confidence of the model on each label. The same models can then be used for the task of candidate ranking. First, a trained DeezyMatch model is used to generate vector representations for all known variations of entity names in a KB (i.e. "all candidate mentions" in Fig. 1). These vector representations are extracted from the recurrent units for each direction and layer. This step is done only once for a given model and KB. The vectors (e.g. forward/backward vectors in a bi-directional recurrent network) are then assembled to form one file containing all the vector representations for unique candidate mentions. Next, given a query (i.e. a mention of an entity as a string), the same DeezyMatch model generates its vector representation similar to the previous step. At the final stage, the query vectors are compared with candidate vectors using a metric specified by the user. The choices of this metric are the DeezyMatch prediction scores, L_2-norm distances (as implemented in the *faiss* library of Johnson et al. (2019)) or cosine similarities between the query and candidate vectors. Based on the selected method and for a given query, DeezyMatch ranks the results and outputs the best matching candidates (the number of which can be specified by the user).

An advantage of the proposed method is that vector representations for the KB are computed only once (for a given trained model). For all subsequent queries, only the query vectors are generated and compared to the KB vectors. This significantly reduces the computation time compared to more traditional methods (e.g. Levenshtein distance) in which one query is compared to n possible variations of all potential candidates in each run.

When the selected ranking metric is L_2-norm distance or cosine similarity, the above procedure can be done efficiently using generated matrices (i.e., assembled vector representations) and available linear algebra packages. However, model inference on large datasets can be prohibitively expensive. In DeezyMatch, we developed an adaptive method to avoid the search of whole KB for a given query. We start with the query vector and find a set of "close" candidate vectors as measured by the L_2-norm distance (i.e., two vectors are similar when the distance is low). We then perform model inference only on these candidates. If the number of desired candidates (specified by the user) is reached, DeezyMatch goes to the next query mention. Otherwise, it expands the search space by a user-specified search size and repeats the model inference on new instances. This procedure continues until the number of desired candidates is reached or all candidates in the KB are tested. In our experiments in Section 3.1.2, this adaptive procedure significantly reduces the computation time of similarity search in large datasets.

2.3 DeezyMatch interface

DeezyMatch is available as a Python library and can be used as a stand-alone command-line tool or as a module in existing Python NLP pipelines. As an example, the training and inference steps described in Section 2.1 can be executed by:

```python
from DeezyMatch import train
from DeezyMatch import inference

# train a new model
train(input_file_path,
      dataset_train_path,
      model_name)
# model inference
inference(input_file_path,
          dataset_inference_path,
          pretrained_model_path)
```

Other functionalities, such as fine-tuning and candidate ranking, have similar easy-to-use interfaces. Consult DeezyMatch's GitHub page for additional information and examples.

3 Comparison with existing systems

The majority of readily available EL tools rely on a lookup table or on shallow string similarity approaches to select an initial set of candidates, followed by a disambiguation step. TagMe! (Ferragina and Scaiella, 2010), for instance, a well established EL baseline, performs candidate selection through perfect matches between mentions and a list of alias surface forms derived from Wikipedia, as also discussed by Hasibi et al. (2016).

Alternatives to perfect matches involve the adoption of edit-distance techniques, such as Levensthein distance (see, for example, its adoption in McNamee et al. (2011a); Moreno et al. (2017)). While there are many implementations of such approaches readily available, these methods suffer from poor scalability (i.e., time complexity, as we discuss in our experiments in Section 3.1.1). Due to this, some EL pipelines (e.g., Greenfield et al. (2016)) have incorporated such techniques only when no exact matching entry can be retrieved.

More recently, researchers have developed deep learning solutions for candidate selection. Le and Titov (2019) framed it as a distance learning task with a noise detector in their EL system, in which the linkage between mentions that are not necessarily in the KB is learned from lists of positive candidates (the top matching candidates) and negative candidates (randomly sampled from the KB). Tam et al. (2019) have recently presented STANCE, a model for computing the similarity of two strings by encoding the characters of each of them, aligning the encodings using Sinkhorn Iteration, and scoring the alignment with a convolutional neural network. The associated repository[5] offers codes for reproducing the experiments in the paper. Unfortunately, their implementation is not directly comparable with DeezyMatch, as it was not designed to be integrated directly into an EL pipeline.

The work closest to ours, which has directly inspired our initial development, is by Santos et al. (2018a). The authors presented a recurrent neural network architecture to encode pairs of toponyms followed by a multi-layer perceptron to determine if they are matching. The authors accompanied their work with a repository to reproduce the results presented in the paper.[6] However, the user has little control over the model architecture, including its hyperparameters and processing steps. Moreover, the authors do not offer a method for either loading a trained model and applying it to new data or for candidate ranking.

Building upon this previous work, we present an easy to use library that *(a)* relies on deep neural networks for fuzzy string matching and candidate ranking beyond surface similarities; *(b)* is significantly faster than edit-distance approaches; and *(c)* can be seamlessly integrated into existing EL pipelines with a single Python command.

3.1 Performance

We test DeezyMatch in the context of geographical candidate selection, the task of identifying potential entities that can be referred to by a toponym (i.e., a place name). This can be understood as the middle step between named entity recognition (in this case, toponym recognition) and the downstream task of EL (in this case, toponym resolution). See Coll Ardanuy et al. (2020) for a detailed description of the datasets and KBs, experimental settings, and analysis of the results reported in Sections 3.1.1 and 3.1.2. Evaluation of the impact of transfer learning and domain adaptation (as described in Section 2.1.1) on candidate ranking will be the subject of future work.

3.1.1 Pair classifier

We compare our method to Santos et al. (2018a) and normalized Levenshtein Damerau edit distance (henceforth *LevDam*)[7] on three datasets of positive and negative string pairs. The datasets against which we compare the three methods are *Santos* ($\sim$4.3M toponym pairs in different alphabets derived from GeoNames[8] and introduced in Santos et al. (2018b)); *WG:en* ($\sim$670K toponym pairs derived from the English version of WikiGazetteer; see Coll Ardanuy et al. (2019)); and *OCR* ($\sim$93K named entity pairs derived from OCR'd text aligned to its human correction).

All datasets are balanced and contain an equal number of positive and negative pairs per query. In all cases, negative examples have been constructed carefully to capture both trivial and challenging transformations. Table 1 reports the F-Score of the three methods on the three datasets. Both for *LevDam* and *DeezyMatch*, we have left out 10% of each dataset for testing, whereas for Santos et al. (2018a), we show an F-Score obtained through twofold cross validation (the setting allowed by the implementation). The DeezyMatch models used in the experiments have similar architecture and hyperparameters.[9]

3.1.2 Candidate ranker

We evaluate the performance of DeezyMatch's *candidate ranker* in a real-case toponym resolution application by assessing the quality of ranked candidates and its computation time on three datasets:

---

[5]https://github.com/iesl/stance
[6]https://github.com/ruipds/Toponym-Matching
[7]https://pypi.org/project/pyxDamerauLevenshtein
[8]https://www.geonames.org
[9]Refer to the *DeezyMatch Models* section in Coll Ardanuy et al. (2020) for the choice of hyperparameters.

	Santos	WG:en	OCR
LevDam	0.70	0.74	0.76
Santos et al. (2018a)	0.82	0.92	0.95
DeezyMatch	0.89	0.94	0.95

Table 1: DeezyMatch's *pair-classifier* performance as measured by F-score compared with other methods.

	P@1	MAP@10	MAP@20	T/q
ArgM:exact	0.69	-	-	-
ArgM:LD	0.78	0.72	0.70	9s
ArgM:DM	0.78	0.76	0.74	0.3s
WOTR:exact	0.86	-	-	-
WOTR:LD	0.92	0.84	0.80	31.6s
WOTR:DM	0.93	0.90	0.87	0.7s
FMP:exact	0.77	-	-	-
FMP:LD	0.92	0.82	0.76	14.1s
FMP:DM	0.85	0.82	0.78	0.7s

Table 2: DeezyMatch (*DM*) *candidate ranker* performance on three datasets compared to two other methods: LevDam (*LD*) and *exact*. *T/q* indicates 'Time per query' on CPU.

(1) *ArgManuscrita (ArgM)*, a toponym-resolved dataset in Spanish created from a seventeenth-century travelogue and composed of 799 toponyms (of which 200 are unique after lower-casing); (2) *WOTR*, an OCR-corrected dataset of letters and reports in English from 1860s, of which we used its test set. It contains 1,479 toponyms manually annotated with their resolved coordinates (of which 584 unique toponyms, after lower-casing); and (3) *BNA-FMP*, a dataset of digitized nineteenth-century newspaper articles in English with 1,248 toponyms already recognized and resolved to their correct geographic coordinates (of which 509 unique toponyms, after lower-casing), containing several toponyms with OCR errors, such as *'DORSETSIIIRR'* for *'Dorsetshire'*.

As KBs, we used the English version of WikiGazetteer (with 2,455,966 candidate mentions) for *WOTR* and *BNA-FMP*; and the Spanish version of WikiGazetteer combined with the *HGIS de las Indias* gazetteer (Stangl, 2018) (with 556,985 candidate mentions) for *ArgManuscrita*. We considered that a retrieved candidate mention correctly matched a query if it could refer to an entity in our KB within 10 km of the coordinates in the gold standard.[10] In Table 2, we compare DeezyMatch with two baselines: *exact* selects the exact-matching candidate from the KB, which is the most common approach in EL systems, and *LevDam* ranks candidates according to the normalized Levenshtein-Damerau edit distance, traditionally considered a strong baseline. The advantage of using Deezy-Match is stressed both in terms of mean average precision (at 10 and 20 candidates) and especially by its reduced computation time in comparison with LevDam.[11]

4 Conclusions

We presented DeezyMatch, a new user-friendly Python library for fuzzy string matching and candidate ranking, based on deep neural network architectures. DeezyMatch can be seamlessly integrated into existing EL pipelines. Its flexibility allows the user to easily fine-tune a pretrained model or to adapt the model architecture to the specificity of a real-case scenario. We compared its design, implementation and functionalities with other approaches. In the future, we plan to support self-attention and state-of-the-art pretrained character-based models, integrate learning to rank functionalities in the candidate selection process and to release a zoo of models trained on large datasets which can be fine-tuned further in other downstream NLP tasks.

DeezyMatch was designed with flexibility in mind, and we encourage the community to further extend its implementation for addressing other related tasks, such as record linkage, transliteration and data integration.

Acknowledgments

We thank Katherine McDonough and the anonymous reviewers for their careful and constructive reviews. This work was supported by Living with Machines (AHRC grant AH/S01179X/1) and The Alan Turing Institute (EPSRC grant EP/N510129/1).

---

[10]Due to a lack of a true gold standard of coordinates for locations, allowing an error distance is common practice in evaluating toponym resolution systems (DeLozier et al., 2015; Roller et al., 2012; Speriosu and Baldridge, 2013). Additionally, due to this, we skip toponyms if no correct match has been found by all the tested methods.

[11]Here, we do not take into account the time spent on training the model and generating the candidate vectors, as this is done offline only once and can be reused for all following candidate ranking tasks that use the same model and gazetteer. Training a model on a dataset with $\approx$670K pairs (including preprocessing) takes 28m on GPU and 54m on CPU, while generating and combining candidate vectors takes 39m on GPU and 204m on CPU.

References

Martin Abadi, Paul Barham, Jianmin Chen, Zhifeng Chen, Andy Davis, Jeffrey Dean, Matthieu Devin, Sanjay Ghemawat, Geoffrey Irving, Michael Isard, Manjunath Kudlur, Josh Levenberg, Rajat Monga, Sherry Moore, Derek G. Murray, Benoit Steiner, Paul Tucker, Vijay Vasudevan, Pete Warden, Martin Wicke, Yuan Yu, and Xiaoqiang Zheng. 2016. Tensorflow: A system for large-scale machine learning. In *12th USENIX Symposium on Operating Systems Design and Implementation (OSDI 16)*, pages 265–283.

Kyunghyun Cho, Bart van Merriënboer, Caglar Gulcehre, Dzmitry Bahdanau, Fethi Bougares, Holger Schwenk, and Yoshua Bengio. 2014. Learning phrase representations using RNN encoder–decoder for statistical machine translation. In *Proceedings of the 2014 Conference on Empirical Methods in Natural Language Processing (EMNLP)*, pages 1724–1734, Doha, Qatar. Association for Computational Linguistics.

Mariona Coll Ardanuy, Kasra Hosseini, Katherine McDonough, Amrey Krause, Daniel van Strien, and Federico Nanni. 2020. Deezymatch: A deep learning approach to geographical candidate selection through toponym matching. In *SIGSPATIAL: Poster Paper*.

Mariona Coll Ardanuy, Katherine McDonough, Amrey Krause, Daniel CS Wilson, Kasra Hosseini, and Daniel van Strien. 2019. Resolving places, past and present: toponym resolution in historical british newspapers using multiple resources. In *Proc. of GIR*.

Grant DeLozier, Jason Baldridge, and Loretta London. 2015. Gazetteer-independent toponym resolution using geographic word profiles. In *Proc. of AAAI*.

Jeffrey L Elman. 1990. Finding structure in time. *Cognitive science*, 14(2):179–211.

Paolo Ferragina and Ugo Scaiella. 2010. Tagme: on-the-fly annotation of short text fragments (by wikipedia entities). In *Proceedings of the 19th ACM international conference on Information and knowledge management*, pages 1625–1628.

Kara Greenfield, Rajmonda S Caceres, Michael Coury, Kelly Geyer, Youngjune Gwon, Jason Matterer, Alyssa C Mensch, Cem Safak Sahin, and Olga Simek. 2016. A reverse approach to named entity extraction and linking in microposts. In *# Microposts*, pages 67–69.

Ben Hachey, Will Radford, Joel Nothman, Matthew Honnibal, and James R Curran. 2013. Evaluating entity linking with wikipedia. *Artificial intelligence*.

Faegheh Hasibi, Krisztian Balog, and Svein Erik Bratsberg. 2016. On the reproducibility of the tagme entity linking system. In *European Conference on Information Retrieval*, pages 436–449. Springer.

Sepp Hochreiter and Jürgen Schmidhuber. 1997. Long short-term memory. *Neural Comput.*, 9(8):1735–1780.

Jeff Johnson, Matthijs Douze, and Herve Jegou. 2019. Billion-scale similarity search with gpus. *IEEE Transactions on Big Data*.

Phong Le and Ivan Titov. 2019. Distant learning for entity linking with automatic noise detection. In *Proceedings of the 57th Annual Meeting of the Association for Computational Linguistics*, pages 4081–4090, Florence, Italy. Association for Computational Linguistics.

Katherine McDonough, Ludovic Moncla, and Matje van de Camp. 2019. Named entity recognition goes to old regime france: geographic text analysis for early modern french corpora. *International Journal of Geographical Information Science*, 33(12):2498–2522.

Paul McNamee, James Mayfield, Dawn Lawrie, Douglas Oard, and David Doermann. 2011a. Cross-language entity linking. In *Proceedings of 5th International Joint Conference on Natural Language Processing*, pages 255–263, Chiang Mai, Thailand. Asian Federation of Natural Language Processing.

Paul McNamee, James Mayfield, Dawn Lawrie, Douglas W Oard, and David Doermann. 2011b. Cross-language entity linking. In *Proceedings of 5th International Joint Conference on Natural Language Processing*, pages 255–263.

Pablo N Mendes, Max Jakob, Andrés García-Silva, and Christian Bizer. 2011. Dbpedia spotlight: shedding light on the web of documents. In *Proceedings of the 7th international conference on semantic systems*, pages 1–8.

Jose G Moreno, Romaric Besançon, Romain Beaumont, Eva D'hondt, Anne-Laure Ligozat, Sophie Rosset, Xavier Tannier, and Brigitte Grau. 2017. Combining word and entity embeddings for entity linking. In *European Semantic Web Conference*, pages 337–352. Springer.

Andrea Moro, Alessandro Raganato, and Roberto Navigli. 2014. Entity linking meets word sense disambiguation: a unified approach. *Transactions of the Association for Computational Linguistics*, 2:231–244.

Gary Munnelly and Séamus Lawless. 2018. Investigating entity linking in early english legal documents. In *Proceedings of the 18th ACM/IEEE on Joint Conference on Digital Libraries*, pages 59–68.

Alex Olieman, Kaspar Beelen, Milan van Lange, Jaap Kamps, and Maarten Marx. 2017. Good applications for crummy entity linkers? the case of corpus selection in digital humanities. In *Proceedings of the 13th International Conference on Semantic Systems*, pages 81–88.

Adam Paszke, Sam Gross, Francisco Massa, Adam Lerer, James Bradbury, Gregory Chanan, Trevor Killeen, Zeming Lin, Natalia Gimelshein, Luca Antiga, Alban Desmaison, Andreas Kopf, Edward Yang, Zachary DeVito, Martin Raison, Alykhan Tejani, Sasank Chilamkurthy, Benoit Steiner, Lu Fang, Junjie Bai, and Soumith Chintala. 2019. Pytorch: An imperative style, high-performance deep learning library. In *Advances in Neural Information Processing Systems 32*, pages 8024–8035. Curran Associates, Inc.

Julien Plu, Giuseppe Rizzo, and Raphaël Troncy. 2016. Enhancing entity linking by combining ner models. In *Semantic Web Evaluation Challenge*, pages 17–32. Springer.

Gianluca Quercini, Hanan Samet, Jagan Sankaranarayanan, and Michael D Lieberman. 2010. Determining the spatial reader scopes of news sources using local lexicons. In *Proc. of SIGSPATIAL*.

Jonathan Raphael Raiman and Olivier Michel Raiman. 2018. Deeptype: multilingual entity linking by neural type system evolution. In *Thirty-Second AAAI Conference on Artificial Intelligence*.

Stephen Roller, Michael Speriosu, Sarat Rallapalli, Benjamin Wing, and Jason Baldridge. 2012. Supervised text-based geolocation using language models on an adaptive grid. In *Proc. of EMNLP*.

Marco Rovera, Federico Nanni, Simone Paolo Ponzetto, and Anna Goy. 2017. Domain-specific named entity disambiguation in historical memoirs. *CLiC-it 2017 11-12 December 2017, Rome*, page 287.

Rui Santos, Patricia Murrieta-Flores, Pável Calado, and Bruno Martins. 2018a. Toponym matching through deep neural networks. *International Journal of Geographical Information Science*.

Rui Santos, Patricia Murrieta-Flores, and Bruno Martins. 2018b. Learning to combine multiple string similarity metrics for effective toponym matching. *International journal of digital earth*.

Avirup Sil, Gourab Kundu, Radu Florian, and Wael Hamza. 2018. Neural cross-lingual entity linking. In *Thirty-Second AAAI Conference on Artificial Intelligence*.

Michael Speriosu and Jason Baldridge. 2013. Text-driven toponym resolution using indirect supervision. In *Proceedings of the 51st Annual Meeting of the Association for Computational Linguistics (Volume 1: Long Papers)*, pages 1466–1476, Sofia, Bulgaria. Association for Computational Linguistics.

Werner Stangl. 2018. 'the empire strikes back'?: Hgis de las indias and the postcolonial death star. *IJHAC*.

Derek Tam, Nicholas Monath, Ari Kobren, Aaron Traylor, Rajarshi Das, and Andrew McCallum. 2019. Optimal transport-based alignment of learned character representations for string similarity. *arXiv preprint arXiv:1907.10165*.

COSATA: A Constraint Satisfaction Solver and Interpreted Language for Semi-Structured Tables of Sentences

Peter A. Jansen

School of Information, University of Arizona, Tucson, AZ, USA

`pajansen@email.arizona.edu`

Abstract

This work presents COSATA, an intuitive constraint satisfaction solver and interpreted language for knowledge bases of semi-structured tables expressed as text. The stand-alone COSATA solver allows easily expressing complex compositional "inference patterns" for how knowledge from different tables tends to connect to support inference and explanation construction in question answering and other downstream tasks, while including advanced declarative features and the ability to operate over multiple representations of text (words, lemmas, or part-of-speech tags). COSATA also includes a hybrid imperative/declarative interpreted language for expressing simple models through minimally-specified simulations grounded in constraint patterns, helping bridge the gap between question answering, question explanation, and model simulation. The solver and interpreter are released as open source.[1]

1 Introduction

Performing inference for complex question answering typically requires combining multiple facts from a knowledge base to arrive at a correct answer, where this set of facts can then be used to generate detailed human-readable explanations for the reasoning behind those answers. Combining multiple facts to perform natural language inference is extremely challenging, with contemporary methods generally unable to reliably combine more than two facts together. This is a significant limitation, as even elementary science questions require an average of six (and, as many as 16) atomic facts to answer and explain (Jansen et al., 2018; Xie et al., 2020) – particularly when those explanations include detailed world knowledge. For example,

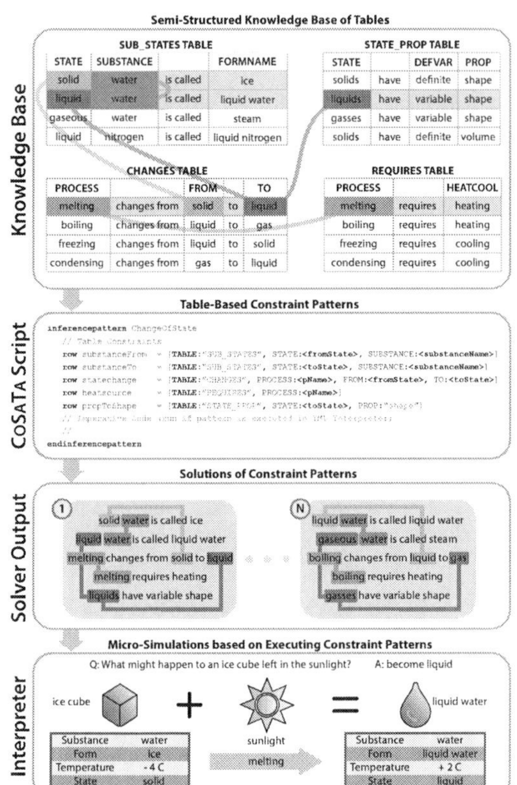

Figure 1: An overview of the proposed system. A semi-structured knowledge base of tables *(top)* serves as input to the COSATA scripting language for expressing multi-hop inference patterns as constraints over table rows. A stand-alone constraint solver and full interpreter are provided.

explaining the common process of *an ice cube melting in sunlight* (see Figure 1) can require a large number of facts, especially when those facts are expressed at a fine level of granularity.

Compositional (or *"multi-hop"*) inference solving methods tend to exist on a formality continuum. At one end of the continuum, logical or declarative methods (e.g. Lenat et al., 1990; Forbus, 2019) model a knowledge base as a set of assertions, and inference as sets of axioms and combinatorial rules

---

[1] Demo: `https://youtu.be/t93Acsz7LyE`

Proceedings of the 2020 EMNLP (Systems Demonstrations), pages 70–76
November 16-20, 2020. ©2020 Association for Computational Linguistics

acting on those assertions. While logical methods provide provably correct inference and detailed explanations, these methods tend to be brittle in practice (MacCartney and Manning, 2007). At the other end of the formality continuum are inference methods that use unstructured text as knowledge (modeled at the level of the word (Fried et al., 2015), sentence (Valentino et al., 2020), or paragraph (Yang et al., 2018)), which is typically combined using connectivity (e.g. Jansen et al., 2017), embedding (e.g. Tu et al., 2020), or other features. Due to the difficulty of combining free text (Jansen, 2018), these methods typically reach peak performance when combining only a small number of facts together – typically two or three.

A middle-ground exists between these two extremes, where semi-structured knowledge bases of text (such as tables) are used to support multi-hop inference (e.g. Sun et al., 2016). This approach offers many practical benefits, such as ease of knowledge base creation (over logical decomposition methods), and providing structure to help infer when combining facts is appropriate (versus free text methods). In spite of these benefits, it is often still challenging to implement inference models that compose (or "hop" between) facts expressed in tables of language data in practice, and practitioners tend to resort to using complex models (such as integer linear programming (e.g. TableILP; Khashabi et al., 2016)) that significantly increase development time and limit interpretability, maintainability, and reuse.

This work presents an easy-to-use scripting language paired with an open source solver and interpreter designed to make compositional inference over semi-structured knowledge bases of tables easy, particularly when those tables express knowledge as lightly structured sentences. The contributions of this work are:

1. The COSATA SOLVER, a stand-alone solver for Constraint Satisfaction over Tables of text. The COSATA language allows easily expressing large multi-hop *"inference patterns"* that describe how facts typically connect across tables in a knowledge base to express a larger compositional solution. The optimized multi-threaded solver supports advanced features for dealing with text, including enumerative variable span detection, and robustness to surface form variations with patterns that can match words, lemmas, or parts-of-speech.

2. The COSATA INTERPRETER, a hybrid imperative/declarative interpreted language for modeling simple inferences through minimally-specified simulations grounded in constraint patterns.

2   Language Description

The COSATA language includes declarative features for performing *constraint satisfaction over tables*, and imperative features for expressing and executing models. The fundamental unit is the *pattern*, analogous to a *class* in object oriented programming, which (at a minimum) contains a declarative constraint pattern of table rows. The declarative features are sufficient for easily expressing variablized compositional patterns over collections of table rows, and the output of the stand-alone constraint satisfaction solver (e.g. solutions in JSON format) can serve as input to further processing.

The language also supports a suite of imperative features for expressing and executing models. In this paradigm, each pattern is considered a process that, if executed, imparts some change upon a small model of the world (such as *an object warming from heat transfer*) by executing a *pattern code block*. Agents, physical objects, and environments in the model are represented as *objects*, here sets of property-value pairs. A *control script* imports a library of patterns, initializes objects, and executes a small subset of patterns in a particular order to create a simulation. A *state space* keeps a log of each object, it's properties, the patterns executed, and their resulting changes, to form a detailed and human-readable record of a simulation performed to arrive at a particular inference.

2.1   Declarative: Constraints over tables

Table Row Constraints: Each pattern contains one or more *table row constraints*, which collect interconnected sets of facts (table rows) from one or more tables based on satisfying constraints on the content of those facts. Each table row constraint requires: (a) a *name* for the row, (b) a *table* where rows are drawn from, and (c) a list of *variablized constraint expressions* that specific cells (columns) in a given row must satisfy in order for the entire constraint pattern to be valid. An example pattern with 8 table row constraints surrounding *Changes of State of Matter* is shown in Figure 2.

Constraint Expressions: Constraint expressions for table cells can be expressed as mixtures of

```
// Constraint Pattern: Changing States of Matter
inferencepattern changeStateOfMatter
  // Plain text description
  description = "A substance changing its state of matter"

  // Row definitions
  // e.g. solid/liquid/gas is a kind of state of matter
  row som1 = [TABLE:"KINDOF", HYPONYM:<SOM1>, HYPERNYM:"state of matter"]
  row som2 = [TABLE:"KINDOF", HYPONYM:<SOM2>, HYPERNYM:"state of matter"]

  // e.g. melting/boiling/freezing is a kind of change of state
  row cos  = [TABLE:"KINDOF", HYPONYM:<ChangeOfState>, HYPERNYM:"change of state"]

  // e.g. state of matter is a property of a substance
  row somprop = [TABLE:"PROP-GENERIC", PROPERTY:"state of matter", OBJECT:<obj>]

  // e.g. a boiling point is a kind of phase transition point
  row point = [TABLE:"KINDOF", HYPONYM:<PhaseTransitionPoint>, HYPERNYM:"phase transition point"]

  // e.g. melting means (matter; a substance) changes from a solid to a liquid by increasing heat energy
  row change = [TABLE:"CHANGE", PROCESSNAME:<ChangeOfState>, PROPERTY:"state of matter", OBJECT:<obj>, FROM:<SOM1>, INTO:<SOM2>,
      BY_THROUGH_HOW:<incDec> + "heat energy"]

  // e.g. melting occurs when the temperature of a substance is increased above the substance's melting point, and below it's
  //      boiling point
  row thresh = [TABLE:"CONDITION-VEC", EVENT:<ChangeOfState>, OBJECT:<obj>, INCREASE_DECREASE:<tempDir>, ABOVE_BELOW1:
      <aboveBelow>, VALUE1:<PhaseTransitionPoint>, ABOVE_BELOW2:<*aboveBelow2>, VALUE2:<*PhaseTransitionPoint2>]

  // e.g. heating means the (temperature; heat energy) of an (object; substance) is increased
  row heatcool = [TABLE:"CHANGE-VEC-PROP", PROCESS_NAME:<heatingOrCooling>, PROPERTY:"heat energy", INCREASE_DECREASE:<incDec>]

endinferencepattern
```

(a) An example listing for a constraint satisfaction pattern that collects 8 facts surrounding Changes of State of Matter.

Row Name	Table Row
som1	a <solid> is a kind of "state of matter"
som2	a <liquid> is a kind of "state of matter"
cos	<melting> is a kind of "change of state"
somprop	"state of matter" is a property of a <substance>
point	a <melting point> is a kind of "phase transition point"
change	<melting> means the "state of matter" of <substance> changes from a <solid> into a <liquid> by <increasing> "heat energy"
thresh	<melting> occurs when the temperature of a <substance> is <increased> <above> the substance 's <melting point>
heatcool	<heating> means the "heat energy" of a substance is <increased>

(b) An example enumerated solution of the above constraint pattern.

Constraint Variable Name	Value
<aboveBelow>	above
<aboveBelow2>	not populated
<ChangeOfState>	melt
<heatingOrCooling>	heat
<incDec>	increase
<obj>	substance
<PhaseTransitionPoint>	melt point
<PhaseTransitionPoint2>	not populated
<SOM1>	solid
<SOM2>	liquid
<tempDir>	increase

(c) The variable values from this solution.

Figure 2: *(Top)* An example constraint satisfaction pattern expressed in the CoSaTa. *(Bottom)* One of several solutions provided by the CoSaTa solver when evaluating this pattern with a semi-structured knowledge base of tables.

strings (words, lemmas, or part-of-speech tags) and variables. Elements can be combined with simple boolean operations, as well as advanced booleans (e.g. optional elements, enumerative *AND*s that automatically determine variable spans). Example constraint expressions are shown in Table 1.

Inheritance and Composite Patterns: Similar to object oriented programming, patterns can contain their own table row constraints, and/or inherit their table row constraints from one or more other patterns. This enables software engineering practices like problem decomposition into objects to be applied to constraint patterns. For example, the *ChangeOfStateWithSubstanceFromTo* pattern in Table 4 inherits table row constraints from three other patterns: one that describes the general concept of changes of state, another that describes the idea of a substance having a particular melting or boiling point, and a final pattern describing the substance being in it's changed state. Because of this decomposition, these smaller generic patterns are available for reuse in other patterns.

2.2 Imperative: Executable Micro-Models

Objects: Objects are expressed as lists of property-value pairs that can be added, modified, or executed against. For example, an object named *ice cube* might have properties *location:fridge* and *temperature:-4C*.

Pattern Code Block: Each pattern can contain an imperative code block that, if executed, typically imparts changes to the objects or knowledge base suggestive of a particular process having taken place. For example, a *heatTransfer* pattern might have rows that match on any two objects that are touching, while its code block could decrease the temperature of the warmer object, and increase the temperature of the cooler object. Similarly, the code block in Figure 4 changes the state of matter of an object (for example from a solid to a liquid).

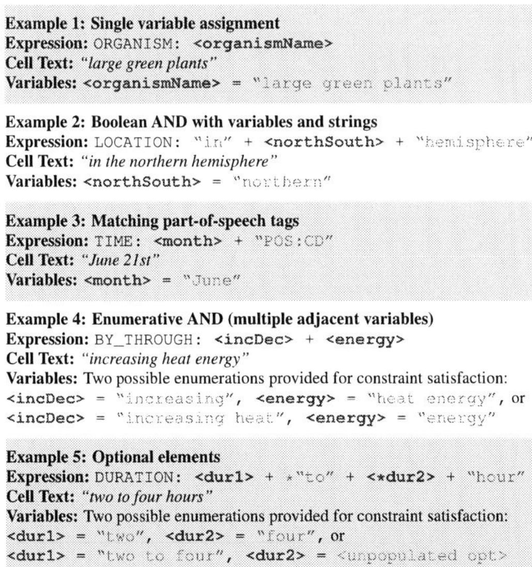

Table 1: Example constraint expressions for a given table cell, evaluated against example cell text.

Requirements Specification: Code typically requires certain preconditions to be satisfied for execution to be valid, such as *heatTransfer* requiring two objects that have non-empty *temperature* properties. Patterns have specific functions for verifying that preconditions are met, as well as levels of preconditions (required, or recommended).

Model Control Script: Models take the form of small, easily-composed control scripts that import a library of patterns, initialize the objects required for a model, then sequentially execute a series of patterns that impart changes on those objects. For example, the control script in Figure 3 initializes three objects: an *ice cube*, *freezer*, and *outside environment*. The ice cube begins in the *freezer*, and is then moved to the *outside environment*. *Heat transfer* happens between the *ice cube* and *outside environment* until the *ice cube* meets the conditions for a *Change of State*. The *Change of State* then happens, in this case melting, changing the ice cube's *state of matter* property from *solid* to *liquid*.

3 Solver and Interpreter

Both the constraint satisfaction solver and interpreter are implemented in Scala, with Stanford CoreNLP (Manning et al., 2014) used to provide tokenization, lemmatization, and part-of-speech tags for the knowledge base of tables. The solver pipeline first creates shortlists of rows that may potentially satisfy individual table row constraints for

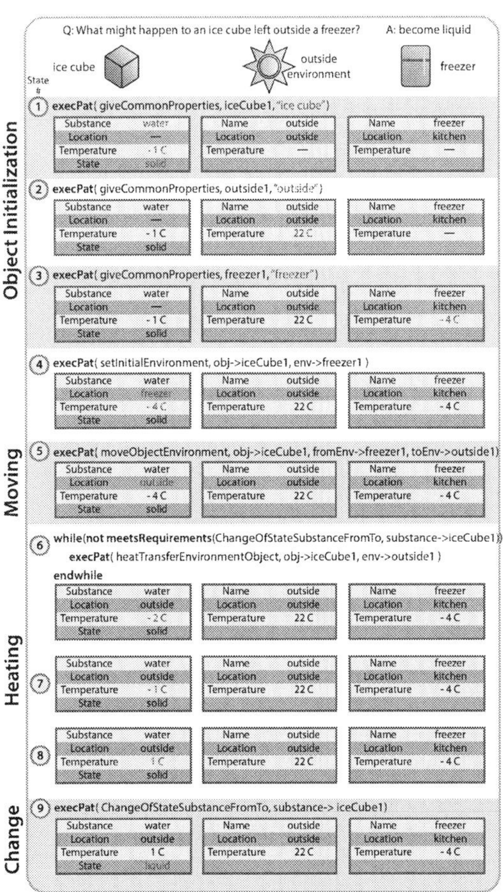

Figure 3: An example micro-model control script *(numbered states and instructions)* with three objects *(ice cube, outside environment, freezer)*, and the resulting state space changes *(red highlights)*. This control script simulates the result of leaving an ice cube outside of a freezer. The full script and CoSATA interpreter output is provided in the distribution.

each pattern, then implements a backtrack search (e.g. Davis et al., 1962) to exhaustively find all combinations of table rows that meet the constraints for a given pattern (each unique collection of table rows that satisfies a given pattern is termed a *solution* of that pattern).[2] While some powerful declarative features (such as enumerative ANDs with automatic variable span detection) are expensive to evaluate, nearly all stages of evaluation are multi-threaded for speed, and rely heavily on precomputed look-up tables for evaluating constraint expressions. In practice, the patterns presented in Section 4 below are typically evaluated in between several seconds to a few minutes each.

---

[2]Constraint satisfaction solvers are typically formulated to efficiently find a single solution that satisfies the constraints. In contrast, the solver presented in this work finds all possible solutions that can then be used for downstream processing.

```
inferencepattern ChangeOfStateWithSubstanceFromTo
  patterndescription = "Change the state of a substance from " + COS.<SOM1> + " to " + COS.<SOM2>

  // Requirements: This pattern acts on a single object (sub1), that is a kind of substance, and should have a state of matter.
  require instance sub1 = [KINDOF:"substance"]
  shouldhave (sub1."state of matter" != "")

  // Composite requirements: This pattern inherits rows from 3 other patterns
  infpat COS = changeStateOfMatter              // Change of state (fundamentals, requirements, etc.)
  infpat fromSOM = substanceInSOMWithPhaseTransitionPoint // A substance, and its melting/boiling/freezing point
  infpat toSOM = substanceInSOM                 // A substance, in a particular state of matter
  rowequiv COS.som1 = fromSOM.subSOM.som  // To be valid, COS.som1 and fromSOM.subSOM.som should be the same fact.
  rowequiv COS.som2 = toSOM.som           // To be valid, COS.som2 and toSOM.som should be the same fact.

  instmap sub1 = COS.substance1           // The substance in this pattern refers to the same substance in the
  instmap sub1 = fromSOM.substance        // changeStateOfMatter (COS), substanceInSOMWithPhaseTransitionPoint (fromSOM),
  instmap sub1 = toSOM.substance          // and substanceInSom (toSOM) patterns.

  // Additional constraints
  // Combined patterns must be talking about the same (melting/boiling/freezing) point, and same material, to be valid.
  musthaveoromit(COS.<PhaseTransitionPoint> == fromSOM.<PhaseTransitionPoint>)
  musthaveoromit(fromSOM.<materialName> == toSOM.<materialName>)
  // The substance object (sub1) should be in state of matter <SOM1>, and have changed temperature above/below <pointTemp>.
  musthave(sub1."state of matter" == COS.<SOM1>)
  musthave(sub1."temperature" CHANGE [direction:COS.<tempDir> threshold:fromSOM.<pointTemp>])

  // Row definitions: All rows in this pattern are inherited from COS, fromSOM, and toSOM.

  // Code: Run the imperative code below if a given enumeration of this pattern is executed.
  // If the object (sub1) recently changed temperature above/below <pointTemp>, and is in state of matter <SOM1>
  if ((sub1."temperature" CHANGE [direction:COS.<tempDir> threshold:fromSOM.<pointTemp>]) && (sub1."state of matter" == COS.
      <SOM1>)) then
    // Set the object (sub1)'s new state of matter to be <SOM2>
    sub1."state of matter" = COS.<SOM2>
    // Add a human-readable explanation to the state space describing what this inference pattern did.
    addExplanationText("Substance (" + sub1."name" + ") made of (" + sub1."material" + ") is within the temperature range to
        change from a (" + COS.<SOM1> + ") to a (" + COS.<SOM2> + ").")
  endif

endinferencepattern
```

Inference Pattern: *ChangeOfStateWithSubstanceFromTo*	

Inherited Pattern 1: COS:changeStateOfMatter

Row Name	Table Row
som1	a <solid> is a kind of "state of matter"
som2	a <liquid> is a kind of "state of matter"
cos	<melting> is a kind of "change of state"
somprop	"state of matter" is a property of a <substance>
point	a <melting point> is a kind of "phase transition point"
change	<melting> means the "state of matter" of <substance> changes from a <solid> into a <liquid> by <increasing> "heat energy"
thresh	<melting> occurs when the temperature of a <substance> is <increased> <above> the substance 's <melting point>
heatcool	<heating> means the "heat energy" of a substance is <increased>

Inherited Pattern 2: fromSOM:substanceInSOMWithPhaseTransitionPoint

Row Name	Table Row
somHasPoint	a <solid> has a <melting point>
point1	the <melting point> of <water> is <0.0> <C>

fromSOM.subSOM:substanceInSOM (nested)

Row Name	Table Row
som	a <solid> is a kind of "state of matter"
propSomTemp	the <water> is in the <solid> state, called <ice>, for temperatures below 0.0 C

Inherited Pattern 3: toSOM:substanceInSOM

Row Name	Table Row
som	a <liquid> is a kind of "state of matter"
propSomTemp	the <water> is in the <liquid> state, called <water>, for temperatures between 0.0 C and 100.0 C

Figure 4: *(Top)* An example composite pattern that (i) inherits row constraints from three other simpler patterns, and (ii) includes imperative code that effects the change described by the constraint satisfaction pattern. *(Bottom)* One example solution of this pattern, *melting ice into liquid water*. All other combinations of state changes (*e.g. freezing, boiling*) for all substances described in the knowledge base of semi-structured tables are also enumerated, but not shown here for space.

4   Example Solutions

Here the feasibility of generating constraint patterns (for downstream processing) or executable patterns (for modeling) is empirically demonstrated in the context of generating detailed multi-hop explanations to standardized elementary and middle school science exam questions drawn from the AI2 Aristo Reasoning Challenge (Clark et al., 2018).

4.1   Explanation Regeneration

The explanation regeneration task (Jansen and Ustalov, 2019) requires models to reconstruct large multi-fact gold explanations by selecting a set of interconnected facts from a knowledge base that match gold explanations provided in an explanation corpus. The task is very challenging, and current state-of-the-art models (e.g. Das et al., 2019) achieve nearly all of their performance by evaluat-

# Solutions Combined	Avg. Ceiling Accuracy	Avg. Extra Facts @ Ceiling
Automatically Converted Patterns Only (N=353)		
1	56.0%	7.8
2	67.5%	11.2
3	70.8%	12.6
Automatic and Manually Curated Patterns (N=385)		
1	58.3%	5.9
2	72.3%	7.7
3	78.0%	8.5

Table 2: Ceiling performance of the converted explanatory patterns from the WorldTree V2 corpus evaluated using CoSATA on the explanation regeneration task.

ing facts independently rather than jointly.

The Worldtree V2 corpus (Xie et al., 2020) includes detailed multi-fact explanations for 4,400 standardized science exam questions grounded in a knowledge base of 63 tables and approximately 10k table rows, as well as a set of 353 semi-automatically authored collections of facts surrounding specific subtopics, such as *changes of state*, *inherited characteristics*, or *seasonal changes in daylight*. Here, those 353 inference patterns were converted to the CoSATA constraint language using a prototype automatic converter, and all solutions to each pattern were enumerated with the CoSATA solver. 42 of the automatically converted patterns were selected based on frequency of use for manual curation, where they were further abstracted, decomposed, and debugged. Ceiling performance on the explanation regeneration task was calculated for a shortlist of ranked solutions, in terms of both single solutions, and combinations of up to 3 solutions, with results shown in Table 2. Performance is evaluated in terms of accuracy (proportion of gold rows included in the explanation) and the average number of "extra" facts included in the solutions but not included in the gold explanation. The results show that the pattern solutions enumerated by CoSATA have a ceiling performance of regenerating up to 58% of gold explanations when using a single solution, and up to 78% when combining up to three solutions. This empirically demonstrates the potential utility of using CoSATA patterns as input to downstream inference models that are able to accurately select which patterns to combine to generate an explanation. The inference patterns in this experiment and their solutions are included as examples in the distribution.

4.2 Micro-models and Interpreter

Constructing micro-models from scratch requires (i) authoring a knowledge base of semi-structured

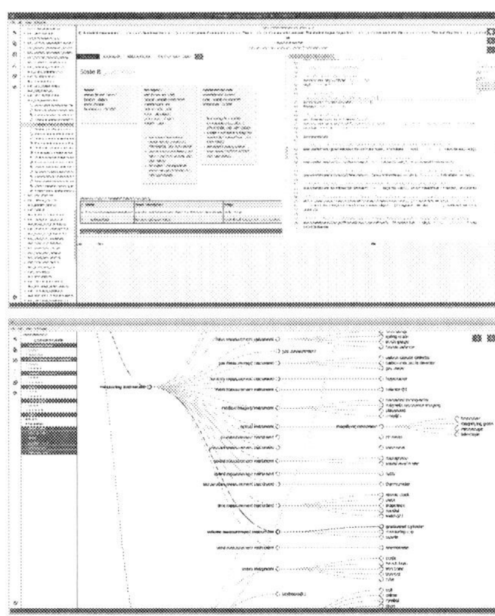

Figure 5: Screenshots of the prototype IDE. *(Top)* The debugger/editor for micro-model control scripts. *(Bottom)* The visual taxonomy editor, a component of the table editor.

tables, (ii) authoring patterns that reference those tables (such as those in Figures 2 and 4), and (iii) constructing micro-model control scripts (such as the example in Figure 3) that describe, in a short series of steps, how processes interact with objects and agents to reach a given outcome.

To demonstrate this workflow, a series of 23 patterns including imperative code were authored for topics in *heat transfer* and *changes of state*, as well as a supporting semi-structured knowledge base containing several hundred facts across 21 tables including *taxonomic relations*, *locations of common objects*, *processes causing discrete changes*, and *physical properties of substances*. To support this effort, a prototype IDE called *Procession* (shown in Figure 5) was implemented using ELECTRON that integrates a table-editor (including D3-based visual taxonomy editor), MONACO-based code editor, and side-to-side debugger/editor for micro-model control scripts that enables fast debug cycles. These example imperative patterns and the resulting interpreter output of the control scripts are included as examples in the distribution.

5 Conclusion

CoSATA is an open-source constraint satisfaction solver for easily expressing and evaluating multi-fact compositional patterns in semi-structured tables of text, paired with an interpreted language that allows expressing micro-models. The tool, source, examples, and documentation are available at `http://www.github.com/clulab/cosata/` .

Acknowledgments

Thanks to Sebastian Thiem, who assisted in conducting the ceiling test of the WorldTree V2 patterns, and to Peter Clark for thoughtful discussions. The prototype IDE was developed in part under contract by Soft Design SRL. This work supported in part by the National Science Foundation (NSF Award #1815948, "Explainable Natural Language Inference", to PJ).

References

Peter Clark, Isaac Cowhey, Oren Etzioni, Tushar Khot, Ashish Sabharwal, Carissa Schoenick, and Oyvind Tafjord. 2018. Think you have solved question answering? try arc, the ai2 reasoning challenge. *arXiv preprint arXiv:1803.05457*.

Rajarshi Das, Ameya Godbole, Manzil Zaheer, Shehzaad Dhuliawala, and Andrew McCallum. 2019. Chains-of-reasoning at textgraphs 2019 shared task: Reasoning over chains of facts for explainable multi-hop inference. In *Proceedings of the Thirteenth Workshop on Graph-Based Methods for Natural Language Processing (TextGraphs-13)*, pages 101–117.

Martin Davis, George Logemann, and Donald Loveland. 1962. A machine program for theorem-proving. *Communications of the ACM*, 5(7):394–397.

Kenneth D Forbus. 2019. *Qualitative representations: How people reason and learn about the continuous world*.

Daniel Fried, Peter Jansen, Gustave Hahn-Powell, Mihai Surdeanu, and Peter Clark. 2015. Higher-order lexical semantic models for non-factoid answer reranking. *Transactions of the Association for Computational Linguistics*, 3:197–210.

Peter Jansen. 2018. Multi-hop inference for sentence-level textgraphs: How challenging is meaningfully combining information for science question answering? In *Proceedings of the Twelfth Workshop on Graph-Based Methods for Natural Language Processing (TextGraphs-12)*, pages 12–17.

Peter Jansen, Rebecca Sharp, Mihai Surdeanu, and Peter Clark. 2017. Framing QA as building and ranking intersentence answer justifications. *Computational Linguistics*, 43(2):407–449.

Peter Jansen and Dmitry Ustalov. 2019. Textgraphs 2019 shared task on multi-hop inference for explanation regeneration. In *Proceedings of the Thirteenth Workshop on Graph-Based Methods for Natural Language Processing (TextGraphs-13)*, pages 63–77.

Peter Jansen, Elizabeth Wainwright, Steven Marmorstein, and Clayton Morrison. 2018. WorldTree: A corpus of explanation graphs for elementary science questions supporting multi-hop inference. In *Proceedings of the Eleventh International Conference on Language Resources and Evaluation (LREC-2018)*, Miyazaki, Japan. European Languages Resources Association (ELRA).

Daniel Khashabi, Tushar Khot, Ashish Sabharwal, Peter Clark, Oren Etzioni, and Dan Roth. 2016. Question answering via integer programming over semi-structured knowledge. In *Proceedings of the Twenty-Fifth International Joint Conference on Artificial Intelligence*, pages 1145–1152.

Douglas B Lenat, Ramanathan V. Guha, Karen Pittman, Dexter Pratt, and Mary Shepherd. 1990. Cyc: toward programs with common sense. *Communications of the ACM*, 33(8):30–49.

Bill MacCartney and Christopher D Manning. 2007. Natural logic for textual inference. In *Proceedings of the ACL-PASCAL Workshop on Textual Entailment and Paraphrasing*, pages 193–200.

Christopher D Manning, Mihai Surdeanu, John Bauer, Jenny Rose Finkel, Steven Bethard, and David McClosky. 2014. The stanford corenlp natural language processing toolkit. In *Proceedings of 52nd annual meeting of the association for computational linguistics: system demonstrations*, pages 55–60.

Huan Sun, Hao Ma, Xiaodong He, Wen-tau Yih, Yu Su, and Xifeng Yan. 2016. Table cell search for question answering. In *Proceedings of the 25th International Conference on World Wide Web*, pages 771–782.

Ming Tu, Kevin Huang, and Guangtao Wang. 2020. Select, answer and explain: Interpretable multi-hop reading comprehension over multiple documents. In *Proceedings of the Thirty-Fourth AAAI Conference on Artificial Intelligence*.

Marco Valentino, Mokanarangan Thayaparan, and André Freitas. 2020. Unification-based reconstruction of explanations for science questions. *arXiv preprint arXiv:2004.00061*.

Zhengnan Xie, Sebastian Thiem, Jaycie Martin, Elizabeth Wainwright, Steven Marmorstein, and Peter Jansen. 2020. Worldtree v2: A corpus of science-domain structured explanations and inference patterns supporting multi-hop inference. In *Proceedings of The 12th Language Resources and Evaluation Conference*, pages 5456–5473.

Zhilin Yang, Peng Qi, Saizheng Zhang, Yoshua Bengio, William Cohen, Ruslan Salakhutdinov, and Christopher D Manning. 2018. Hotpotqa: A dataset for diverse, explainable multi-hop question answering. In *Proceedings of the 2018 Conference on Empirical Methods in Natural Language Processing*, pages 2369–2380.

InVeRo: Making Semantic Role Labeling Accessible
with Intelligible Verbs and Roles

Simone Conia[1], **Fabrizio Brignone**[2], **Davide Zanfardino**[2], and **Roberto Navigli**[1]

[1]Sapienza NLP Group, Department of Computer Science, Sapienza University of Rome
[2]Babelscape, Italy
`lastname@di.uniroma1.it`, `lastname@babelscape.com`

Abstract

Semantic Role Labeling (SRL) is deeply dependent on complex linguistic resources and sophisticated neural models, which makes the task difficult to approach for non-experts. To address this issue we present a new platform named Intelligible Verbs and Roles (InVeRo). This platform provides access to a new verb resource, VerbAtlas, and a state-of-the-art pretrained implementation of a neural, span-based architecture for SRL. Both the resource and the system provide human-readable verb sense and semantic role information, with an easy to use Web interface and RESTful APIs available at `http://nlp.uniroma1.it/invero`.

1 Introduction

Since its introduction (Gildea and Jurafsky, 2002), Semantic Role Labeling (SRL) has been recognized as a key task to enable Natural Language Understanding in that it aims at explicitly answering the "Who did What to Whom, When and Where?" question by identifying and labeling the predicate-argument structure of a sentence, namely, the actors that take part in the scenario outlined by a predicate. In fact, SRL has already proven to be useful in a wide range of downstream tasks, including Question Answering (Shen and Lapata, 2007; He et al., 2015), Information Extraction (Christensen et al., 2011), Situation Recognition (Yatskar et al., 2016), Machine Translation (Marcheggiani et al., 2018), and Opinion Role Labeling (Zhang et al., 2019).

Unfortunately, the integration of SRL knowledge into downstream applications has often been hampered and slowed down by the intrinsic complexity of the task itself (Navigli, 2018). Indeed, SRL is strongly intertwined with elaborate linguistic theories, as identifying and labeling predicate-argument relations requires well-defined predicate sense and semantic role inventories such as the popular PropBank (Palmer et al., 2005), VerbNet

(Kipper-Schuler, 2005), or FrameNet (Baker et al., 1998). The linguistic intricacies of such resources may, however, dishearten and turn away new practitioners. Regardless of which linguistic resource is used in the task, to further complicate the situation SRL has been usually divided into four subtasks – predicate identification, predicate sense disambiguation, argument identification and argument classification – but, to the best of our knowledge, recent state-of-the-art systems do not address all these four subtasks simultaneously without relying on external systems (Swayamdipta et al., 2017; He et al., 2018; Strubell et al., 2018; He et al., 2019). Therefore, obtaining predicate sense and semantic role annotations necessitates the tedious orchestration of multiple automatic systems, which in its turn further complicates the use of SRL in practice and in semantics-first approaches to NLP more generally.

In this paper, we present InVeRo (Intelligibile Verbs and Roles), an online platform designed to tackle the aforementioned issues and make Semantic Role Labeling accessible to a broad audience. InVeRo brings together resources and tools to perform human-readable SRL, and it accomplishes this by using the intelligible verb senses and semantic roles of a recently proposed resource named VerbAtlas (Di Fabio et al., 2019) and exploiting them to annotate sentences with high performance. In more detail, the InVeRo platform includes:

- a Resource API to obtain linguistic information about the verb senses and semantic roles in VerbAtlas.

- a Model API to effortlessly annotate sentences using a state-of-the-art end-to-end pretrained model for span-based SRL.

- a Web interface where users can easily query linguistic information and automatically an-

Proceedings of the 2020 EMNLP (Systems Demonstrations), pages 77–84
November 16-20, 2020. ©2020 Association for Computational Linguistics

notate sentences on-the-go without having to write a single line of code.

Notably, InVeRo also takes advantage of PropBank to get the best of both worlds, and provides annotations according to both resources, enabling comparability and fostering integration.

2 The InVeRo Platform

The InVeRo platform aims at making SRL more approachable to a wider audience, not only in order to promote advances in the area of SRL itself, but also to encourage the integration of semantics into other fields of NLP. The two main barriers to this objective are the complexity of i) the linguistic resources used in SRL which are, however, indispensable for the definition of the task itself, and ii) the complexity of the recently proposed techniques.

Section 2.1 explains how InVeRo takes advantage of the intelligible verb senses and semantic roles of VerbAtlas to gently introduce non-expert users to SRL, while Section 2.2 details how the InVeRo model for SRL can make semantic role annotations accessible to everyone.

2.1 Intelligible Verb Senses and Roles

One of the most contentious points of discussion in SRL is how to formalize predicate-argument structures, that is, the semantic roles that actors can play in a scenario defined by a predicate. Prop-Bank (Palmer et al., 2005), one of the most popular predicate-argument structure inventories, uses an enumerative approach where each predicate sense has a possibly different roleset, e.g., for the predicate *make*, the sense *make.01* (as in "making a product") bears the semantic roles ARG0 (creator), ARG1 (creation), ARG2 (created from) and ARG3 (beneficiary), whereas *make.02* (as in "cause to be") bears only ARG0 (impeller) and ARG1 (impelled). This exhaustive approach, however, requires an expert linguist to tell which roles share similar semantics across senses (e.g., ARG0 is an agent in both *make.01* and *make.02*) and which do not (e.g., ARG1 is a product in *make.01* but a result in *make.02*).

On the other hand, VerbAtlas (Di Fabio et al., 2019), a recently proposed predicate-argument structure inventory, in contrast to the enumerative approach of PropBank and the thousands of frame-specific roles of FrameNet, adopts a small set of explicit and intelligible semantic roles (AGENT, PRODUCT, RESULT, DESTINATION, ..., THEME) inspired by VerbNet (Kipper-Schuler, 2005). As a result, in

VerbAtlas, whenever two predicate senses can bear the same semantic role, the semantics of this role is coherent across the two predicate senses by definition, resulting in readable labels for non-expert users. VerbAtlas also clusters predicate senses into so-called frames (COOK, DRINK, HIT, etc.) inspired by FrameNet (Baker et al., 1998), with the idea that senses sharing similar semantic behavior lie in the same frame. For non-expert users, this organization has the added advantage of explicitly linking predicate senses that are otherwise unrelated, like *make.01* and *create.01* in PropBank which, instead, are part of the same frame MOUNT-ASSEMBLE-PRODUCE in VerbAtlas and, therefore, also share the same semantic roles. In a bid to make SRL more accessible, the InVeRo platform adopts the intelligible verb senses and semantic roles of VerbAtlas.

2.2 An All-in-One Solution for SRL

As already mentioned in Section 1, the traditional SRL pipeline consists of four main steps: predicate identification, predicate sense disambiguation, argument identification and argument classification. While some of the above steps are considered easier than others, each of them features distinct peculiarities, which has driven recent works to focus on improving only specific aspects of the entire SRL pipeline. Instead, little attention has been paid to systems that can tackle all the above-mentioned steps at the same time. As a result, anyone wishing to take advantage of SRL annotations in another NLP task has to choose, mix and match multiple automatic systems in order to obtain sentences fully annotated with predicate sense and semantic role labels. Understandably, this has been a major deterrent for the integration of semantics into downstream applications.

As part of the InVeRo platform, not only do we introduce an all-in-one model that addresses the complete SRL pipeline with a single forward pass, but we also make this model available through a Web interface to let everyone label sentences with SRL annotations without the need to install any software. In other words, a user only has to provide a raw text sentence; the InVeRo all-in-one model for SRL takes care of the rest, making the predicate sense and role labeling process accessible and effortless.

Model Design. The InVeRo all-in-one system for SRL is based on the ideas put forward by He et al. (2018) in that, unlike other works that used word-level BIO tagging schemes to label arguments (He et al., 2017; Strubell et al., 2018; Tan et al., 2018), it directly models span-level features. In particular, we follow He et al. (2018) by letting the neural model learn span-level representations from the word-level representations of the span start and span end words, while also adding a span-length specific trainable embedding. More formally, the span representation $\mathbf{s}_{ij}$ from word i to word j is obtained as follows:

$$\mathbf{s}_{ij} = \mathbf{W}^s(\mathbf{e}_i^w \oplus \mathbf{e}_j^w \oplus \mathbf{e}_{j-i}^l) + \mathbf{b}^s$$

where $\mathbf{e}_i^w$ and $\mathbf{e}_j^w$ are the word representations of start and end of the span, $\mathbf{e}_{j-i}^l$ is the span length embedding, and $\oplus$ is the concatenation operation.

However, our approach features a few key differences that set the InVeRo model apart from the aforementioned works. First, it creates contextualized word representations from the inner states of BERT (`bert-base-cased`), a recent language model trained on massive amounts of textual data (Devlin et al., 2018). Differently from the recent work of Shi and Lin (2019), our model takes advantage of the topmost four layers of BERT and directly builds a word representation from its subword representations, similarly to Bevilacqua and Navigli (2020). More formally, given the BERT representations $\mathbf{h}_{ij}^k$ at layer k of the m_i subwords w_{ij} in word w_i, with $1 \leq j \leq m_i$:

$$\mathbf{c}_{ij} = \mathbf{h}_{ij}^{-1} \oplus \mathbf{h}_{ij}^{-2} \oplus \mathbf{h}_{ij}^{-3} \oplus \mathbf{h}_{ij}^{-4}$$
$$\mathbf{c}'_{ij} = \mathrm{ReLU}(\mathbf{W}^c \mathbf{c}_{ij} + \mathbf{b}^c)$$
$$\mathbf{e}_i^w = \frac{1}{m_i} \sum_j \mathbf{c}'_{ij}$$

Second, in contrast to other span-based SRL systems, our model integrates predicate disambiguation as an additional objective in a multitask fashion (Caruana, 1997). Third, our model is trained to jointly learn to label sentences with both VerbAtlas and PropBank so as to exploit the complementary knowledge of the two resources, and, at the same time, provide a means to directly compare the predicate sense and semantic role labels of two different inventories for the same input sentences.[1]

Comparison with previous systems. Over the years, several SRL systems have been developed and made available as prepackaged downloads, e.g. SENNA[2], or as online demos, e.g., AllenNLP's SRL demo[3]. However, recent BERT-based online systems, such as AllenNLP's SRL demo, do not perform predicate sense disambiguation (in addition to predicate identification, argument identification and argument classification), which is a crucial step in SRL, especially when considering that the PropBank roles ARG0, ARG1, through ARG5 become meaningful only if they are associated with a PropBank predicate sense (see Section 2.1).

Results. Thanks to the use of contextualized word representations from BERT, the joint exploitation of two complementary linguistic resources for SRL, and the introduction of a predicate sense disambiguation layer, our model achieves 84.0% in F_1 score in the standard argument identification and classification test split of the CoNLL-2012 dataset (Pradhan et al., 2012), significantly outperforming the previous state of the art among end-to-end models, currently represented by Strubell et al. (2018) with a 0.6% absolute improvement in F_1 score[4] (84.0% against 83.4%). We note that this measure does not take into account the performance on predicate sense disambiguation, where our system achieves 86.1% in F_1 score, which is a significant absolute improvement (+5.7%) over the most-frequent-sense strategy (86.1% against 80.4%).

3 The InVeRo APIs

To foster the integration of semantics into a wider range of applications, the InVeRo platform introduces a set of RESTful APIs[5] that offer i) easy-to-use abstractions to query resource-specific information in VerbAtlas (Section 3.1), and ii) out-of-the-box predicate and semantic role annotations from a state-of-the-art pretrained model (Section 3.2).

3.1 Resource API

The Resource API provides a RESTful interface to easily link predicate-level information, e.g., predicate lemmas and/or predicate senses, to VerbAtlas-specific features, e.g., frames and semantic roles. In particular:

---

[1] We used the PropBank-to-VerbAtlas mappings available at `http://verbatlas.org/download` to remap CoNLL-2012.

[2] `https://ronan.collobert.com/senna`
[3] `https://demo.allennlp.org/semantic-role-labeling`
[4] Score computed with the official CoNLL-2005 script.
[5] `http://nlp.uniroma1.it/invero/api-documentation`

- the `/predicate` endpoint exposes functionalities to obtain frame-level information starting from a predicate lemma or a synset from WordNet 3.0 (Fellbaum et al., 1998) or BabelNet 4.0 (Navigli and Ponzetto, 2012);

- the `/frame` endpoint exposes functionalities to retrieve, for a given frame, its Predicate Argument Structure, and the WordNet/BabelNet synsets belonging to this frame.

Also included is a manually-curated PropBank-to-VerbAtlas alignment to remap existing corpora like the CoNLL-2009 and CoNLL-2012 datasets. In particular:

- the `/align/sense` endpoint returns, for a given PropBank predicate sense, its corresponding VerbAtlas frame, i.e., the VerbAtlas frame that generalizes the given PropBank predicate sense;

- the `/align/roles` endpoint returns, for a given PropBank predicate sense, e.g., *aim.01*, the alignment of each role in the PropBank argument structure of the given predicate sense to a VerbAtlas role, e.g., ARG0 → AGENT, ARG1 → THEME, and so on.

The online documentation provides an overview of the accepted parameters at the endpoints available in the Resource API.

3.2 Model API

To encourage the integration of SRL into downstream applications, the Model API offers a simple solution for out-of-the-box role labeling by providing an interface to a full end-to-end state-of-the-art pretrained model. Unlike most currently available models which focus on specific aspects of the entire SRL task, our solution jointly addresses in a single forward pass the whole traditional SRL pipeline, namely, i) predicate identification, ii) predicate sense disambiguation, iii) argument identification, and iv) argument classification. Furthermore, our model is fully self-contained as it does not require any of the additional linguistic information, from lemmatization to part-of-speech tags and syntactic parse trees, that are usually exploited by many systems. Our Model API is:

- **Easy to use:** an end user avoids the struggle of mixing and matching a set of automatic systems where each system independently addresses a different part of the SRL pipeline;

- **Fully self-contained:** the only input to the underlying model is a raw text sentence, dropping any dependency on external preprocessing tools;

- **State-of-the-Art:** the underlying model carries out SRL with high performances on the standard CoNLL-2012 benchmark dataset.

Usage. The Model API exposes a single endpoint named `/model/` which accepts `GET` requests with a single parameter named `sentence` containing the raw text sentence to label with semantic role annotations. The Model API returns a `JSON` response that contains, for each predicate it identifies in the sentence, the semantic role that each argument plays with respect to the identified predicate. For example, the response for the sentence *"Eliminating the income tax will benefit peasants"* contains:

```
[{
  "tokenIndex": 0,
  ...
}, {
  "tokenIndex": 5,
  "verbatlas": {
    "frameName": "HELP_HEAL_CARE_CURE",
    "roles": [
        {"role": "agent", "score": 0.89, "span": [0, 4]},
        {"role": "beneficiary", "score": 1., "span": [6, 7]}
    ]
  },
  "propbank": {
    "frameName": "benefit.01",
    "roles": [
        {"role": "ARG0", "score": 0.97, "span": [0, 4]},
        {"role": "ARG1", "score": 1.00, "span": [6, 7]}
    ]
  },
}]
```

Our Model API also supports the more popular PropBank predicate sense and semantic role labels so as to provide a direct comparison with VerbAtlas and promote synergistic approaches that exploit both inventories to advance SRL.

4   The InVeRo User Interface

Like many other linguistic resources in SRL, VerbAtlas may be daunting for inexperienced practitioners who may still face difficulties in finding their way with the formalisms defined in a linguistic resource for SRL. On top of the previously described APIs (Section 3) and in an effort to make VerbAtlas easier to interact with, the InVeRo platform includes a public-facing Web interface that provides a user-friendly environment to explore not only the functionalities offered by the resource, but

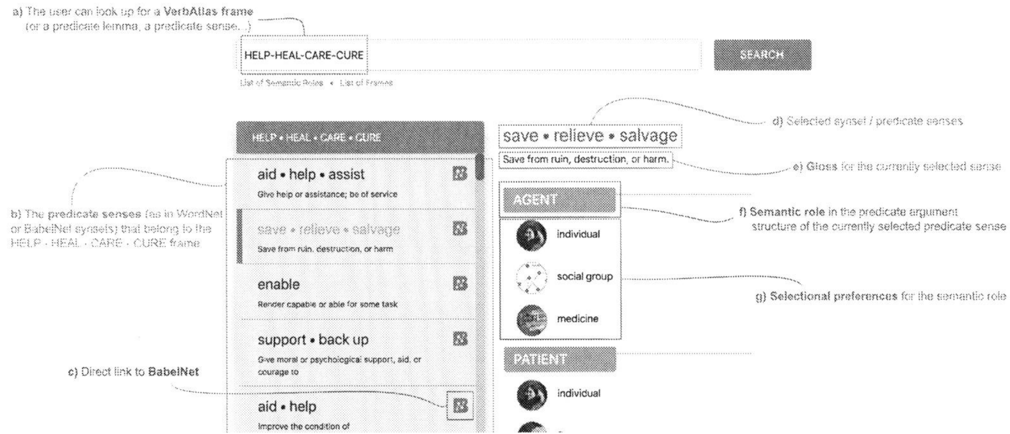

Figure 1: A look at the online interface when a user searches for resource-specific information about VerbAtlas. The user can a) search for a frame name, as in the Figure, or an individual predicate. The interface displays b) all the predicates belonging to the same frame, with each predicate c) directly linked to BabelNet. The right side displays the d) selected predicate with e) its WordNet gloss, f) the semantic roles of its predicate-argument structure, and g) the selectional preferences of each role.

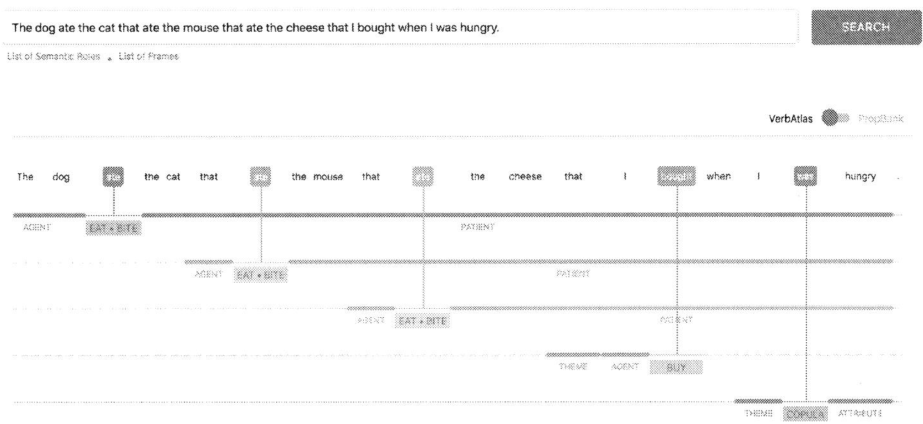

Figure 2: A look at the online interface when a user inserts a sentence in the search bar. The system uses a pretrained model to display all the information of all the steps of a traditional SRL pipeline: predicate identification, predicate sense disambiguation, argument identification and argument classification.

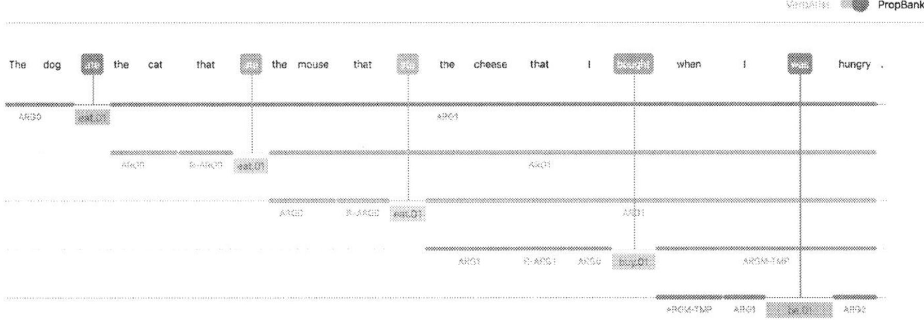

Figure 3: The interface can seamlessly switch between VerbAtlas and PropBank labels with a single click (the switch button at the top-right). Here we show the same sentence as in Figure 2 but labeled with PropBank predicates and roles, which enables comparison across the two annotation styles.

also to understand visually how an SRL system annotates a sentence in a live interactive demo. The Web interface mirrors the functionalities of both the Resource API and the Model API in a minimal unified view, letting users perform resource-specific queries or annotate sentences wherever they are without writing a single line of code.

Resource interface. Figure 1 shows the Web interface when a user inserts the name of a VerbAtlas frame in the search bar. Notice that, since the interface makes use of the Resource API, a user can also search for other resource-specific information such as individual predicates. Particular attention has been given to the visualization of a VerbAtlas frame (Figure 1, left side) which displays all the predicate senses that share similar semantic behavior. Each predicate sense is also conveniently linked to BabelNet 4.0 (Navigli and Ponzetto, 2012), a multilingual knowledge graph where users can find more information such as hypernyms, hyponyms, and semantically related concepts. Equally important is the visualization of a VerbAtlas predicate-argument structure (Figure 1, right side) which displays all the semantic roles that the currently selected predicate/frame can bear in a sentence.

Model interface. Figure 2 shows, instead, the online model interface when a user inserts a sentence with its corresponding predicate sense and semantic role labels from VerbAtlas. Notice how the user can quickly switch between the VerbAtlas and the PropBank predicate sense and semantic role annotations with just a single click, so that the two annotation styles can easily be compared one with the other (Figures 2 and 3). To the best of our knowledge, this is the first online demo where a neural model helps users visualize all the four steps of the traditional SRL pipeline for two different linguistic resources for SRL, VerbAtlas and PropBank, at the same time.

5 Conclusion and Future Work

Semantic Role Labeling is deeply dependent on complex linguistic resources and elaborate neural models: the combination of these two factors has made Semantic Role Labeling (SRL) difficult to approach for experts from other fields who are interested in exploring its integration into downstream applications. In this paper, we aim at ameliorating both of the issues by presenting the InVeRo platform. InVeRo features easy-to-use RESTful APIs to effortlessy query VerbAtlas, a recently introduced linguistic resource for SRL, and to transparently use a pretrained state-of-the-art end-to-end system for the recent VerbAtlas-style and the more traditional PropBank-style approaches to SRL. Notably, the InVeRo system is fully self-contained as it tackles all the steps of the traditional SRL pipeline – predicate identification, predicate sense disambiguation, argument identification, and argument classification – and it does not require external tools such as lemmatizers, part-of-speech taggers or syntactic tree parsers: users just have to provide a raw text sentence to obtain its corresponding predicate and argument labels. Moreover, the InVeRo platform includes an online Web interface which repackages the APIs in a user-friendly environment. Thanks to this interface, users can easily obtain human-readable linguistic information about VerbAtlas, but also annotate entire sentences on-the-go without the need to install any software.

InVeRo is a growing platform: in the future, we plan to enhance our Model API by adding, alongside the already available state-of-the-art span-based model, the state-of-the-art dependency-based model of Conia and Navigli (2020a), so that users can easily switch between the two approaches and choose the one that best suits their needs. Thanks to BabelNet and recent advances in cross-lingual techniques for tasks where semantics is crucial (Barba et al., 2020; Blloshmi et al., 2020; Conia and Navigli, 2020b; Pasini, 2020; Scarlini et al., 2020), we also plan to provide support for multiple languages to enable SRL integration into multilingual and cross-lingual settings. We believe that the InVeRo platform can make SRL more accessible to the research community, and we look forward to the development of semantics-first approaches in an ever wider range of NLP applications.

Acknowledgments

The authors gratefully acknowledge the support of the ERC Consolidator Grant MOUSSE No. 726487 under the European Union's Horizon 2020 research and innovation programme.

This work was supported in part by the MIUR under grant "Dipartimenti di eccellenza 2018-2022" of the Department of Computer Science of Sapienza University.

References

Collin F. Baker, Charles J. Fillmore, and John B. Lowe. 1998. The Berkeley FrameNet Project. In *36th Annual Meeting of the Association for Computational Linguistics and 17th International Conference on Computational Linguistics, COLING-ACL '98, August 10-14, 1998, Université de Montréal, Montréal, Quebec, Canada. Proceedings of the Conference*, pages 86–90.

Edoardo Barba, Luigi Procopio, Niccolò Campolungo, Tommaso Pasini, and Roberto Navigli. 2020. MuLaN: Multilingual Label propagatioN for word sense disambiguation. In *Proceedings of the Twenty-Ninth International Joint Conference on Artificial Intelligence, IJCAI 2020*, pages 3837–3844.

Michele Bevilacqua and Roberto Navigli. 2020. Breaking through the 80% glass ceiling: Raising the state of the art in Word Sense Disambiguation by incorporating knowledge graph information. In *Proceedings of the 58th Annual Meeting of the Association for Computational Linguistics*, pages 2854–2864, Online.

Rexhina Blloshmi, Rocco Tripodi, and Roberto Navigli. 2020. XL-AMR: Enabling Cross-Lingual AMR parsing with transfer learning techniques. In *Proceedings of the 2020 Conference on Empirical Methods in Natural Language Processing, EMNLP 2020*.

Rich Caruana. 1997. Multitask learning. *Mach. Learn.*, 28(1):41–75.

Janara Christensen, Mausam, Stephen Soderland, and Oren Etzioni. 2011. An analysis of open information extraction based on semantic role labeling. In *Proceedings of the 6th International Conference on Knowledge Capture (K-CAP 2011), June 26-29, 2011, Banff, Alberta, Canada*, pages 113–120.

Simone Conia and Roberto Navigli. 2020a. Bridging the gap in multilingual Semantic Role Labeling: A language agnostic approach. In *Proceedings of the 28th International Conference on Computational Linguistics, COLING 2020*.

Simone Conia and Roberto Navigli. 2020b. Conception: Multilingually-enhanced, human-readable concept vector representations. In *Proceedings of the 28th International Conference on Computational Linguistics, COLING 2020*.

Jacob Devlin, Ming-Wei Chang, Kenton Lee, and Kristina Toutanova. 2018. BERT: pre-training of deep bidirectional transformers for language understanding. *arXiv preprint arXiv:1810.04805*.

Andrea Di Fabio, Simone Conia, and Roberto Navigli. 2019. VerbAtlas: A novel large-scale verbal semantic resource and its application to Semantic Role Labeling. In *Proceedings of the 2019 Conference on Empirical Methods in Natural Language Processing and the 9th International Joint Conference on Natural Language Processing, EMNLP-IJCNLP 2019, Hong Kong, China, November 3-7, 2019*, pages 627–637.

Christiane Fellbaum et al. 1998. *WordNet: An electronic database*. MIT Press, Cambridge, MA.

Daniel Gildea and Daniel Jurafsky. 2002. Automatic labeling of semantic roles. *Comput. Linguistics*, 28(3):245–288.

Luheng He, Kenton Lee, Omer Levy, and Luke Zettlemoyer. 2018. Jointly predicting predicates and arguments in neural semantic role labeling. In *Proceedings of the 56th Annual Meeting of the Association for Computational Linguistics, ACL 2018, Melbourne, Australia, July 15-20, 2018, Volume 2: Short Papers*, pages 364–369.

Luheng He, Kenton Lee, Mike Lewis, and Luke Zettlemoyer. 2017. Deep semantic role labeling: What works and what's next. In *Proceedings of the 55th Annual Meeting of the Association for Computational Linguistics, ACL 2017, Vancouver, Canada, July 30 - August 4, Volume 1: Long Papers*, pages 473–483.

Luheng He, Mike Lewis, and Luke Zettlemoyer. 2015. Question-answer driven semantic role labeling: Using natural language to annotate natural language. In *Proceedings of the 2015 Conference on Empirical Methods in Natural Language Processing, EMNLP 2015, Lisbon, Portugal, September 17-21, 2015*, pages 643–653.

Shexia He, Zuchao Li, and Hai Zhao. 2019. Syntax-aware multilingual semantic role labeling. In *Proceedings of the 2019 Conference on Empirical Methods in Natural Language Processing and the 9th International Joint Conference on Natural Language Processing, EMNLP-IJCNLP 2019, Hong Kong, China, November 3-7, 2019*, pages 5349–5358.

Karin Kipper-Schuler. 2005. *VerbNet: A broad-coverage, comprehensive verb lexicon*. University of Pensylvania.

Diego Marcheggiani, Jasmijn Bastings, and Ivan Titov. 2018. Exploiting semantics in neural machine translation with graph convolutional networks. In *Proceedings of the 2018 Conference of the North American Chapter of the Association for Computational Linguistics: Human Language Technologies, NAACL-HLT, New Orleans, Louisiana, USA, June 1-6, 2018, Volume 2 (Short Papers)*, pages 486–492.

Roberto Navigli. 2018. Natural Language Understanding: Instructions for (present and future) use. In *Proc. of IJCAI 2018*, pages 5697–5702.

Roberto Navigli and Simone Paolo Ponzetto. 2012. Babelnet: The automatic construction, evaluation and application of a wide-coverage multilingual semantic network. *Artif. Intell.*, 193:217–250.

Martha Palmer, Paul R. Kingsbury, and Daniel Gildea. 2005. The Proposition Bank: An annotated corpus of semantic roles. *Comput. Linguistics*, 31(1):71–106.

Tommaso Pasini. 2020. The knowledge acquisition bottleneck problem in multilingual Word Sense Disambiguation. In *Proceedings of the Twenty-Ninth International Joint Conference on Artificial Intelligence, IJCAI 2020*, pages 4936–4942.

Sameer Pradhan, Alessandro Moschitti, Nianwen Xue, Olga Uryupina, and Yuchen Zhang. 2012. CoNLL-2012 Shared Task: Modeling Multilingual Unrestricted Coreference in OntoNotes. In *Joint Conference on EMNLP and CoNLL - Shared Task*, CoNLL 2012, pages 1–40, Stroudsburg, PA, USA.

Bianca Scarlini, Tommaso Pasini, and Roberto Navigli. 2020. With more contexts comes better performance: Contextualized sense embeddings for all-round Word Sense Disambiguation. In *Proceedings of the 2020 Conference on Empirical Methods in Natural Language Processing, EMNLP 2020*.

Dan Shen and Mirella Lapata. 2007. Using semantic roles to improve question answering. In *EMNLP-CoNLL 2007, Proceedings of the 2007 Joint Conference on Empirical Methods in Natural Language Processing and Computational Natural Language Learning, June 28-30, 2007, Prague, Czech Republic*, pages 12–21.

Peng Shi and Jimmy Lin. 2019. Simple BERT models for relation extraction and semantic role labeling. *arXiv preprint arXiv:1904.05255*, abs/1904.05255.

Emma Strubell, Patrick Verga, Daniel Andor, David Weiss, and Andrew McCallum. 2018. Linguistically-informed self-attention for semantic role labeling. In *Proceedings of the 2018 Conference on Empirical Methods in Natural Language Processing, Brussels, Belgium, October 31 - November 4, 2018*, pages 5027–5038.

Swabha Swayamdipta, Sam Thomson, Chris Dyer, and Noah A. Smith. 2017. Frame-semantic parsing with softmax-margin segmental RNNs and a syntactic scaffold. *arXiv preprint arXiv:1706.09528*, abs/1706.09528.

Zhixing Tan, Mingxuan Wang, Jun Xie, Yidong Chen, and Xiaodong Shi. 2018. Deep semantic role labeling with self-attention. In *Proceedings of the Thirty-Second AAAI Conference on Artificial Intelligence, (AAAI-18), the 30th innovative Applications of Artificial Intelligence (IAAI-18), and the 8th AAAI Symposium on Educational Advances in Artificial Intelligence (EAAI-18), New Orleans, Louisiana, USA, February 2-7, 2018*, pages 4929–4936.

Mark Yatskar, Luke S. Zettlemoyer, and Ali Farhadi. 2016. Situation recognition: Visual semantic role labeling for image understanding. In *2016 IEEE Conference on Computer Vision and Pattern Recognition, CVPR 2016, Las Vegas, NV, USA, June 27-30, 2016*, pages 5534–5542.

Meishan Zhang, Peili Liang, and Guohong Fu. 2019. Enhancing opinion role labeling with semantic-aware word representations from semantic role labeling. In *Proceedings of the 2019 Conference of the North American Chapter of the Association for Computational Linguistics: Human Language Technologies, NAACL-HLT 2019, Minneapolis, MN, USA, June 2-7, 2019, Volume 1 (Long and Short Papers)*, pages 641–646.

Youling: an AI-Assisted Lyrics Creation System

Rongsheng Zhang[1]*, **Xiaoxi Mao**[1]†*, **Le Li**[1], **Lin Jiang**[1],
Lin Chen[1], **Zhiwei Hu**[1], **Yadong Xi**[1], **Changjie Fan**[1], **Minlie Huang**[2]
[1] Fuxi AI Lab, NetEase Inc., Hangzhou, China
[2] Department of Computer Science and Technology, Institute for Artifical Intelligence, State Key
Lab of Intelligent Technology and Systems, Beijing National Research Center for
Information Science and Technology, Tsinghua University, Beijing, China.
{zhangrongsheng, maoxiaoxi, lile, jianglin02}@corp.netease.com,
aihuang@tsinghua.edu.cn

Abstract

Recently, a variety of neural models have been proposed for lyrics generation. However, most previous work completes the generation process in a single pass with little human intervention. We believe that lyrics creation is a creative process with human intelligence centered. AI should play a role as an assistant in the lyrics creation process, where human interactions are crucial for high-quality creation. This paper demonstrates *Youling*, an AI-assisted lyrics creation system, designed to collaborate with music creators. In the lyrics generation process, *Youling* supports traditional one pass full-text generation mode as well as an interactive generation mode, which allows users to select the satisfactory sentences from generated candidates conditioned on preceding context. The system also provides a revision module which enables users to revise undesired sentences or words of lyrics repeatedly. Besides, *Youling* allows users to use multifaceted attributes to control the content and format of generated lyrics. The demo video of the system is available at https://youtu.be/DFeNpHk0pm4.

1 Introduction

Lyrics Generation has been a prevalent task in Natural Language Generation (NLG), due to the easy availability of training data and the value of the application. However, despite the popularity of lyrics generation, there still lacks a comprehensive lyrics creation assistant system for music creators. Previous researches (Castro and Attarian, 2018; Saeed et al., 2019; Lu et al., 2019; Manjavacas et al., 2019; Watanabe et al., 2018; Potash et al., 2018; Fan et al., 2019; Li et al., 2020) and systems (Potash et al., 2015; Lee et al., 2019; Shen et al., 2019), are mostly model-oriented, utilizing

neural networks including GAN, RNN-based or Transformer-based (Vaswani et al., 2017) sequence to sequence (Seq2Seq) models for sentence-wise lyrics generation. They complete the lyrics generation process in a single pass with specific keywords or content controlling attributes as input, involving little human intervention. However, we believe the lyrics creation process should be human intelligence centered, and AI systems shall serve as assistants, providing inspiration and embellishing the wording of lyrics.

Therefore, we demonstrate *Youling*, an AI-assisted lyrics creation system, which is designed to collaborate with music creators, help them efficiently create and polish draft lyrics. To fulfill the goal, *Youling* supports interactive lyrics generation, in addition to the traditional one pass full-text generation. Interactive lyrics generation allows users to carefully choose desirable sentences from generated candidates conditioned on preceding context line by line. Preceding context can be either pre-generated, written by users, or a mix. *Youling* also has a revision module, which supports users to revise any unsatisfied sentences or words of draft lyrics repeatedly.

To ensure the controllability of generated lyrics, *Youling* supports multifaceted controlling attributes to guide the model to generate lyrics. These controlling attributes can be divided into two categories, content controlling attributes and format controlling attributes. Content controlling attributes include the lyrics' text style, the emotion or sentiment expressed in the lyrics, the theme described in the lyrics, and the keywords expected to appear in the lyrics. Format controlling attributes include the acrostic characters(letters), the rhymes of the lyrics, the number of sentences, and the number of words per sentence.

To ensure the quality and relevance of generated lyrics with controlling attributes, we implement

---

85

Proceedings of the 2020 EMNLP (Systems Demonstrations), pages 85–91
November 16-20, 2020. ©2020 Association for Computational Linguistics

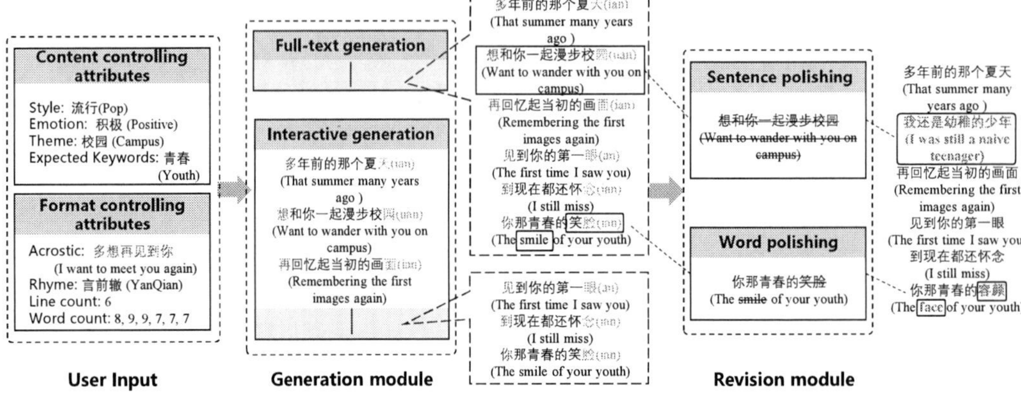

Figure 1: Architecture of *Youling*. The system supports multifaceted controlling attributes in user input to control the content and format of lyrics. The generation module provides two modes for draft lyrics creation: full-text generation and interactive generation. The former generates a full lyrics while the latter generates following sentences conditioned on the preceding context. Besides, a revision module is introduced to polish undesirable sentences or words.

Youling basing on a GPT-2 (Radford et al., 2019) based language model with 210M parameters, pre-trained on around 30 gigabytes of Chinese books corpus. We further finetune *Youling* on a corpus of 300K lyrics collected online.

The contributions of the *Youling* system are summarized as follows:

1. *Youling* provides multiple modes to assist users in lyrics creation. It supports both the traditional one pass full-text generation and the interactive lyrics generation. It also provides a revision module for users to revise undesirable sentences or words of draft lyrics repeatedly.

2. To the best of our knowledge, *Youling* supports the largest variety of content controlling attributes and format controlling attributes to date.

3. *Youling* is implemented on top of GPT-2 model to ensure the quality and relevance of generated lyrics with controlling attributes.

We believe that *Youling* [1] can assist music creators in lyrics creation and inspire other developers to make practical solutions for real-world problems. The 2-minute demonstration video can be available at https://youtu.be/DFeNpHk0pm4.

---

[1] Our system is available at https://yl.fuxi.netease.com/, visitors can log in with the public account (*youlingtest@163.com*) and password (*youling666*).

2 Architecture

The framework of *Youling* is shown in Figure 1. The system mainly contains three parts: **user input**, **generation module** and **revision module**. We will describe them in detail in the following subsections.

2.1 User Input

The input includes a wide variety of controlling attributes provided by users. They can be divided into two categories: content controlling attributes and format controlling attributes. Content controlling attributes consist of the lyrics' text style, the emotion expressed in the lyrics, the theme described in the lyrics, and the keywords expected to appear in the lyrics. Our system supports four kinds of text styles, including Pop, Hip-hop, Chinese Neo-traditional and Folk; three kinds of emotion (positive, negative, and neutral); 14 kinds of themes such as college life, unrequited love, reminiscence, friendship, and so on. Format controlling attributes consist of the acrostic characters (letters), the rhymes of the lyrics, the number of lines of lyrics, and the number of words per line. Users can choose rhyme from 13 Chinese traditional rhyming groups (十三辙).

2.2 Generation Module

Once users have prepared the controlling attributes, the generation module can generate lyrics in full-text generation mode or interactive generation mode. Below we will explain in detail how we implement the lyrics generation conditioned on so many controlling attributes.

2.2.1 Full-Text Generation

Model and Pre-training: We use a Transformer-based sequence to sequence model for the generation of lyrics. To ensure the performance, we use a pre-trained language model based on GPT-2 to initialize the weights of the Transformer encoder and decoder. Our encoder uses a unidirectional self-attention similar to GPT-2; in addition, GPT-2 has only one self-attention block per layer, so the two self-attention blocks in each decoder layer share the same weights. For saving memory, the encoder and decoder share the same weights (Zheng et al., 2020). Our pre-trained language model has 16 layers, 1,024 hidden dimensions, 16 self-attention heads, and 210 million parameters. It is pre-trained on around 30 gigabytes of Chinese Internet novels collected online, which is tokenized with Chinese character. The vocabulary size is 11,400 and the context size is 512.

Training: Here we describe how we train the sequence to sequence model. We collected 300K lyrics from the Internet as training data, including 60M tokens in total. To achieve controllable generation, we need to annotate the style and mood tags corresponding to each song's lyrics and extract the keywords in the lyrics. The style tags corresponding to the lyrics were also obtained as we crawled the lyrics, so no additional processing is required. To get emotion labels, we used a ternary emotion classifier to classify emotion for each song's lyrics. The emotion classifier was trained on 20k labeled data and achieved 80% accuracy on the validation set. To get the keywords contained in each song's lyrics, we extracted all the nouns, verbs, and adjectives in the lyrics.

After the pre-processing described above, we have the style tags, emotion tags, and keyword lists corresponding to each song's lyrics and can start building the training data. The encoder input is a concatenation of the style tag, emotion tag and keywords corresponding to the song lyrics with the *[SEP]* special character. Since there are too many keywords extracted from a song's lyrics, we augment training examples by sampling different numbers of keywords multiple times. This approach is to allow the model to better generalize to the number of keywords. To construct the decoder output, we use a special token *[SEP]* to concatenate every line in a song lyrics, where the last character of

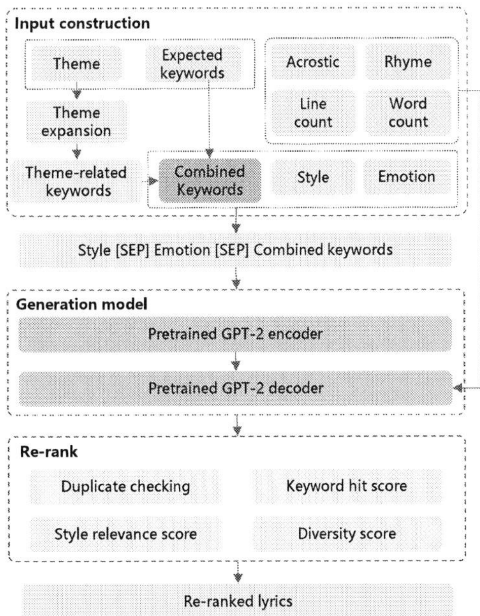

Figure 2: The inference process of full-text generation.

each line is placed at the beginning for rhyming control. Finally, we append a special token *[EOS]* to the end of the decoder output. Kindly note that the constraints on format attributes, as well as the theme tag, are imposed during inference, so they will not be included in the training phase.

Inference: Here we introduce the inference process, as shown in Figure 2. Under full-text generation mode, the source sequence is a concatenation of the user-entered style tag, emotion tag, and keywords. The keywords include the expected keywords, as well as keywords related to the theme selected by the user. The keywords related to different themes are obtained through offline computation. We calculated PMI (Pointwise Mutual Information) for all word pairs in the lyrics corpus after removing low-frequency words. The PMI of word pair w_i, w_j is calculated as

$$\mathrm{PMI}(w_i, w_j) = \log \frac{p(w_i, w_j)}{p(w_i) * p(w_j)}, \qquad (1)$$

where $p(w_i)$ and $p(w_i, w_j)$ are the word frequency and co-occurrence frequency. We keep all word pairs with PMI above a specific threshold, which gives us the lists of keywords corresponding to specific themes. At inference time, we randomly sample the keywords list corresponding to the theme selected by the user to get the input keywords, which are then concatenated with user-entered keywords, style tag, and emotion tag to form the final source sequence.

Format control in decoding: We describe the details of format control in decoding. To keep the number of lines and words per line in accordance to the user's requirements, we record the number of lines and words of the generated lyrics at every decoding step and adjust the logits of *[SEP]* and *[EOS]* in the decoder output accordingly. To achieve rhyming control, we always generate the last character of a line first and then generate the rest from left to right. We adjust the training examples accordingly, as mentioned before. To achieve the acrostic control, we simply amplify the corresponding logit in the decoder output to a very large value when generating the acrostic character of each line of lyrics.

Re-rank: We adopt the top-k sampling method at decoding to generate candidate results. Then we re-rank the candidates according to four rules. (1) Duplicate checking: Due to the strong copy ability of Transformer (Lioutas and Drozdyuk, 2019), the generated lyrics may contain original pieces of text in the training corpus, which will introduce copyright issues. To avoid that, we remove any candidate result containing three or more lines overlapping with the training corpus. (2) Keyword hit (kh) score: For each candidate, we compute the keyword hit score as $S_{kh} = n/n_{max}$, where n is the number of keywords appearing in the current candidate, n_{max} is the number of of keywords in the one with the most hits in all candidates. (3) Style relevance (sr) score: This score measures how well each candidate matches its target style $style_t$. To compute the score, we train a style classifier g on the collected lyrics corpus, and take the classification probability of the target style of the generated lyrics as $S_{sm} = g(style_t|lyric)$. (4) Diversity (div) score: As mentioned before, the Transformer model is likely to copy original lyrics in the training data. Besides, repetition is also common in lyrics; thus, the learned model may constantly generate repeated pieces of text. Sometimes repetition is good, but too much repetition needs to be avoided. We count the number of repeated sentences in each candidate and calculate the diversity score as $S_{div} = 1 - n_{rep}/n_{tot}$, where n_{rep} and n_{tot} denotes the number of repeated sentences and all sentences respectively. The final ranking score of each candidate is computed as

$$S_{rank} = \lambda_1 S_{kh} + \lambda_2 S_{sm} + \lambda_3 S_{div}, \quad (2)$$

where λ_1, λ_2, λ_3 are weights and default to 1.0.

2.2.2 Interactive Generation

For the interactive generation, we use the same model used for full-text generation. The differences exist at decoding. The first difference is that under the interactive generation mode, generation is conditioned on both the encoder input and the preceding context. In other words, the interactive generation can be formulated as

$$s_{i+1}, ..., s_{i+k} = \text{Model}(X, s_0, s_1, ..., s_i), \quad (3)$$

where the s_i means the i-th line of the lyrics text Y, and k is the number of lines to be generated. In comparison the full-text generation is just formulated as $Y = \text{Model}(X)$. The second difference is that the interactive generation mode generates only a few lines $s_{i+1}, .., s_{i+k}$ rather than the full lyrics Y. Hence, under the interactive generation mode, the preceding context must be provided, which can either be pre-generated by *Youling*, written by the user, or a mix of them.

For the example of interactive generation in Figure 1, the system generates the following three lines *"The first time I saw you [SEP] I still miss [SEP] The smile of your youth"* based on the user input and the preceding context *"That summer many years ago [SEP] Want to wander with you on campus [SEP] Remembering the first images again"*.

2.3 Revision Module

The revision module provides useful features allowing users to further polish draft lyrics at the sentence or word level. The framework of the revision module is shown in Figure 3.

The model of revision module follows the same sequence to sequence framework used in the full-text generation model, initialized with weights of the same pre-trained language model.

To build training examples for the model, we simply randomly replace a sentence or a word of lyrics in the training corpus with a special token *[MASK]*. The result is concatenated with the corresponding style tag as the final source sequence, with the form *"Style [SEP] Masked Lyrics."* The sentence or word replaced becomes the target sequence. We use an example to illustrate this idea, given the lyrics *"The snow glows white on the mountain tonight [SEP] Not a footprint to be seen [SEP] A kingdom of isolation [SEP] And it looks like I'm the queen ..."*, we replace the sentence *"Not*

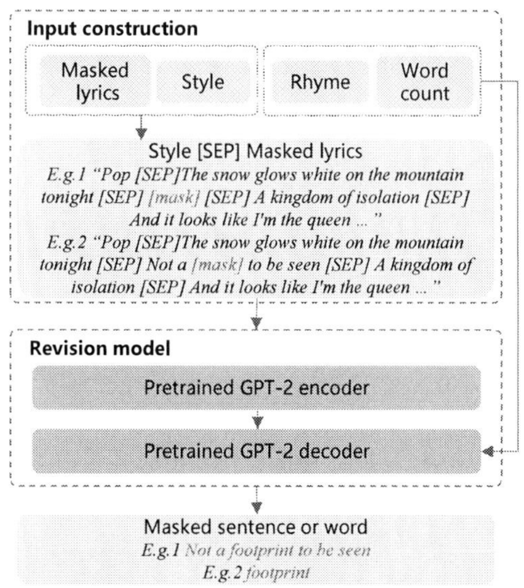

Figure 3: The process of the revision module polishing lyrics.

a footprint to be seen" or the word "*footprint*" with the masking token *[MASK]*, and take the masked contents as the target sequence, as shown in Figure 3. Note that we don't treat word-level and sentence-level replacement differently, so the revision is executed with the same model.

3 Demonstration

In this section, we demonstrate how *Youling* assists music creators to create lyrics conveniently.

First, we show how to generate draft lyrics based on multifaceted controlling attributes. Users are asked to specify the controlling attributes, as shown in Figure 4. After the controlling attributes have been prepared, we use the full-text generation mode to generate the draft lyrics, as shown in Figure 5(a).

After the draft lyrics are generated, we use the interactive generation mode to generate the following lines. Note that in real cases, users can directly write lyrics or modify pre-generated lyrics in the input box and generate the following lines with interactive generation mode. Here we use the unchanged generated draft lyrics for convenience of demonstration.

After completing the draft lyrics by carefully choosing the final line from generated candidates, we can further polish the undesired parts of the generated lyrics. Here we replace a flawed sentence with the best suggestion made by the revision module under sentence level, as seen in Figure 6(a).

Figure 4: A case of the input page. Users can set content and format controlling attributes.

However, we are still not completely satisfied with the last word in the previous suggested sentence. We switch to word level and replace the last word with an appropriate word suggested by the revision model, as shown in Figure 6(b).

As described above, users can repeatedly revise the lyrics until desirable results are obtained. To facilitate the process, *Youling* provides version control so that users can create lyrics with peace of mind.

4 Conclusion

In this paper, we demonstrate *Youling*, an AI-assisted lyrics creation system. *Youling* can accept multifaceted controlling attributes to control the content and format of generated lyrics. In the lyrics generation process, *Youling* supports traditional one pass full-text generation mode as well as an interactive generation mode. Besides, the system also provides a revision module which enables users to revise the undesirable sentences or words of lyrics repeatedly. We hope our system can assist music creators in lyrics creation and inspire other developers to make better solutions for NLG applications.

(a) Full-text generation   (b) Interactive generation

Figure 5: Examples of the two generation modes. (a) Full-text generation: this mode will generates three full-text candidates for users to choose. (b) Interactive generation: the mode generates following three sentences conditioned on the preceding context.

(a) Sentence polishing

(b) Word polishing

Figure 6: Examples of revision module polishing sentences and words in lyrics. Users can select undesirable sentences or words, then ask the system to generate candidates for selected contents conditioned on the context.

References

Pablo Samuel Castro and Maria Attarian. 2018. Combining learned lyrical structures and vocabulary for improved lyric generation. *arXiv preprint arXiv:1811.04651*.

Haoshen Fan, Jie Wang, Bojin Zhuang, Shaojun Wang, and Jing Xiao. 2019. A hierarchical attention based seq2seq model for chinese lyrics generation. In *Pacific Rim International Conference on Artificial Intelligence*, pages 279–288. Springer.

Hsin-Pei Lee, Jhih-Sheng Fang, and Wei-Yun Ma. 2019. iComposer: An automatic songwriting system for Chinese popular music. In *Proceedings of the 2019 Conference of the North American Chapter of the Association for Computational Linguistics (Demonstrations)*, pages 84–88, Minneapolis, Minnesota. Association for Computational Linguistics.

Piji Li, Haisong Zhang, Xiaojiang Liu, and Shuming Shi. 2020. Rigid formats controlled text generation. *arXiv preprint arXiv:2004.08022*.

Vasileios Lioutas and Andriy Drozdyuk. 2019. Copy this sentence. *arXiv preprint arXiv:1905.09856*.

Xu Lu, Jie Wang, Bojin Zhuang, Shaojun Wang, and Jing Xiao. 2019. A syllable-structured, contextually-based conditionally generation of chinese lyrics. *arXiv preprint arXiv:1906.09322*.

Enrique Manjavacas, Mike Kestemont, and Folgert Karsdorp. 2019. Generation of hip-hop lyrics with hierarchical modeling and conditional templates. In *Proceedings of the 12th International Conference on Natural Language Generation*, pages 301–310.

Peter Potash, Alexey Romanov, and Anna Rumshisky. 2015. GhostWriter: Using an LSTM for automatic rap lyric generation. In *Proceedings of the 2015 Conference on Empirical Methods in Natural Language Processing*, pages 1919–1924, Lisbon, Portugal. Association for Computational Linguistics.

Peter Potash, Alexey Romanov, and Anna Rumshisky. 2018. Evaluating creative language generation: The case of rap lyric ghostwriting. pages 29–38.

Alec Radford, Karthik Narasimhan, Tim Salimans, and Ilya Sutskever. Improving language understanding by generative pre-training.

Alec Radford, Jeffrey Wu, Rewon Child, David Luan, Dario Amodei, and Ilya Sutskever. 2019. Language models are unsupervised multitask learners. *OpenAI Blog*, 1(8).

Asir Saeed, Suzana Ilić, and Eva Zangerle. 2019. Creative gans for generating poems, lyrics, and metaphors. *arXiv preprint arXiv:1909.09534*.

Liang-Hsin Shen, Pei-Lun Tai, Chao-Chung Wu, and Shou-De Lin. 2019. Controlling sequence-to-sequence models - a demonstration on neural-based acrostic generator. In *Proceedings of the 2019 Conference on Empirical Methods in Natural Language Processing and the 9th International Joint Conference on Natural Language Processing (EMNLP-IJCNLP): System Demonstrations*, pages 43–48, Hong Kong, China. Association for Computational Linguistics.

Ashish Vaswani, Noam Shazeer, Niki Parmar, Jakob Uszkoreit, Llion Jones, Aidan N Gomez, Łukasz Kaiser, and Illia Polosukhin. 2017. Attention is all you need. In *Advances in neural information processing systems*, pages 5998–6008.

Kento Watanabe, Yuichiroh Matsubayashi, Satoru Fukayama, Masataka Goto, Kentaro Inui, and Tomoyasu Nakano. 2018. A melody-conditioned lyrics language model. In *Proceedings of the 2018 Conference of the North American Chapter of the Association for Computational Linguistics: Human Language Technologies, Volume 1 (Long Papers)*, pages 163–172, New Orleans, Louisiana. Association for Computational Linguistics.

Yinhe Zheng, Rongsheng Zhang, Xiaoxi Mao, and Minlie Huang. 2020. A pre-training based personalized dialogue generation model with persona-sparse data. In *Proceedings of AAAI*.

A Technical Question Answering System with Transfer Learning

Wenhao Yu[†], Lingfei Wu[‡], Yu Deng[‡], Ruchi Mahindru[‡],
Qingkai Zeng[†], Sinem Guven[‡], Meng Jiang[†]
†University of Notre Dame, Notre Dame, IN, USA
‡IBM Thomas J. Watson Research Center, Yorktown Heights, NY, USA
†{wyu1, qzeng, mjiang2}@nd.edu
‡{wuli, dengy, rmahindr, sguven}@us.ibm.com

Abstract

In recent years, the need for community technical question-answering sites has increased significantly. However, it is often expensive for human experts to provide timely and helpful responses on those forums. We develop TransTQA, which is a novel system that offers automatic responses by retrieving proper answers based on correctly answered similar questions in the past. TransTQA is built upon a siamese ALBERT network, which enables it to respond quickly and accurately. Furthermore, TransTQA adopts a standard deep transfer learning strategy to improve its capability of supporting multiple technical domains.

1 Introduction

Technical community (e.g., StackOverflow) is the most active and compelling open forum community for question answering (CQA) that has played an important role for technicians sharing and spreading professional knowledge (Srba and Bielikova, 2016). Recently, many technology companies have been developing and actively maintaining their own technical support forums (e.g., IBM Developer-Works) where users/consumers can post technical issues to seek advice and solutions from peers and experts. Technology companies are investing in training their employees with professional communication skills and technical knowledge to effectively respond to users' questions. However, it is often expensive to provide timely and helpful responses on these forums. Statistics show that at least 30% questions do not hold an accepted answer on StackOverflow and AskUbuntu. First, the users/peers often have limited domain-specific knowledge to describe their issues or accurately answer complex questions in appropriate technical terminology. Second, it is common for such forum threads to become multi-turn asynchronous

interactions, such that the users/peers give additional information, forming a series of discussions, which is time-consuming for experts to track such ongoing interactions. Therefore, building an intelligent system to automatically respond to new questions with useful information or a solution is in high demand. In scenarios where the automatic response does not address a user's technical issue, human experts can further intervene such discussions. A straightforward approach is to properly match potential candidate answers to the new question, since many questions have recurred, allowing for new questions to be answered using the historically accepted answers.

The Information Retrieval (IR) and Natural Language Processing (NLP) communities have witnessed the growing dominance of retrieval approaches based on neural networks over the last decade (Abbasiyantaeb and Momtazi, 2020). Recent advances of pre-training language models (e.g., BERT) achieved superior performance on the retrieval Question Answering (QA) task (Reimers and Gurevych, 2019; Chang et al., 2020). Several BERT based QA systems in the general domain have been deployed for real-world applications (Yang et al., 2019; Yilmaz et al., 2019). In these approaches, BERT first concatenates a QA pair as [CLS, Q, SEP, A, SEP], then passes the concatenation to the transformer network (Devlin et al., 2019). This setup is time-consuming and resource intensive for retrieval task because of too many possible combinations. Finding the pair of the highest similarity in a collection of 10,000 sentences requires 49,995,000 inference computations in BERT. On a modern V100 GPU, it requires around 60 hours. Furthermore, while different technical communities have different focuses, there is still substantial overlap in the abilities of intelligent systems required to answer questions across multiple technical domains. To the best of our

Proceedings of the 2020 EMNLP (Systems Demonstrations), pages 92–99
November 16-20, 2020. ©2020 Association for Computational Linguistics

knowledge, there is no existing system that uses transfer learning to address technical QA tasks.

We develop a novel system called TransTQA (in short for "**trans**fer learning for **t**echnical **q**uestion **a**nswering"). Our system leverages accepted questions and answers (tagged by human users) for answering similar technical questions. The system consists of two modes: evaluation mode and usage mode. The evaluation mode demonstrates retrieved answers by four different transfer learning strategies. The usage mode displays three highest ranked answers retrieved from the database of answer candidates. We employ the latest algorithm ALBERT (Lan et al., 2020) with a siamese network, to make our system efficient and accurate. First, an ALBERT has 18x fewer parameters than BERT-large with the same configuration. A siamese network has two separate ALBERT encoders to generate question and answer embeddings, and applies a similarity measure at the top layer. The similarity measuring process can perform efficiently on modern hardware, allowing our system to be used for real-time usage. Second, our system demonstrates superior accuracy compared to traditional LSTM based QA systems (Rücklé and Gurevych, 2017; Loginova and Neumann, 2018). Third, we adopt a standard deep transfer learning technique, so our system is able to work on different technical domains. Experiments show our proposed system is both time efficient and memory efficient.

We have provide the following links for readers to easily access our (1) demo video and (2) source code (3) website for research purpose.

(1) Video: `https://vimeo.com/431118548`
(2) Code: `https://github.com/wyu97/TTQA`
(The website URL may change, please go to the above github page to view real-time updates.)

2   Related Work

Question Answering   Question answering is a long-standing challenge in NLP. Several QA benchmarks have been introduced over the past decade, such as answer selection (Yang et al., 2015) and reading comprehension (Rajpurkar et al., 2016). As an increasing number of researchers are focusing on the above tasks, the role of retrieval has been gradually overlooked. In real-world scenarios, however, it is less practical to assume people are given a small set of candidate answers or a golden passage. The large database of answers to previous questions should be properly utilized for answering

new questions. So we focus on retrieval QA in the task formulation and model architecture.

Retrieval Question Answering   Retrieval Question Answering (a.k.a Answer Retrieval) finds the most similar answer between multiple candidate answers for a given question (Abbasiyantaeb and Momtazi, 2020). Recently, several researchers have proposed different deep neural models in text-based QA that compare two segments of texts and produces a similarity score. Both document-level (Chen et al., 2017; Seo et al., 2018, 2019; Wu et al., 2018) and sentence-level (Ahmad et al., 2019; Yu et al., 2020) retrieval has been studied on many public datasets such as SQuAD (Rajpurkar et al., 2016) and NQ (Kwiatkowski et al., 2019).

Transfer Learning for QA   Transfer learning studies how to transfer knowledge from a source domain to a target domain (Pan and Yang, 2009; Jiang et al., 2016). Recent advances of deep transfer learning technologies have achieved great success in various NLP tasks (Ruder et al., 2019). Several research work in this domain greatly enrich the application and technology of transfer learning on question answering from different perspectives (Min et al., 2017; Golub et al., 2017; Deng et al., 2018; Wang et al., 2019; Castelli et al., 2020). Although transfer learning has been successfully applied to various QA applications, its applicability to technical QA has yet to be investigated.

Question Answering System   Early neural based QA systems (Kato et al., 2017; Loginova and Neumann, 2018; Chen et al., 2019) are often based on QALSTM models (Tan et al., 2016) with self-attention mechanism (Lin et al., 2017) in order to visualize and illuminate the inner workings of a specific LSTM. As recent advances of Transformer (Vaswani et al., 2017) and BERT (Devlin et al., 2019) achieved superior performance on many NLP tasks in general domains, Transformer-based QA systems (Ma et al., 2019) and fine-tuned BERT QA systems (Yang et al., 2019; Yilmaz et al., 2019) have been deployed to better retrieve answers.

3   Proposed System

3.1   System Configuration

Our system is configured with ALBERT model according to the specified arguments that defines the model architecture. The backbone of the ALBERT

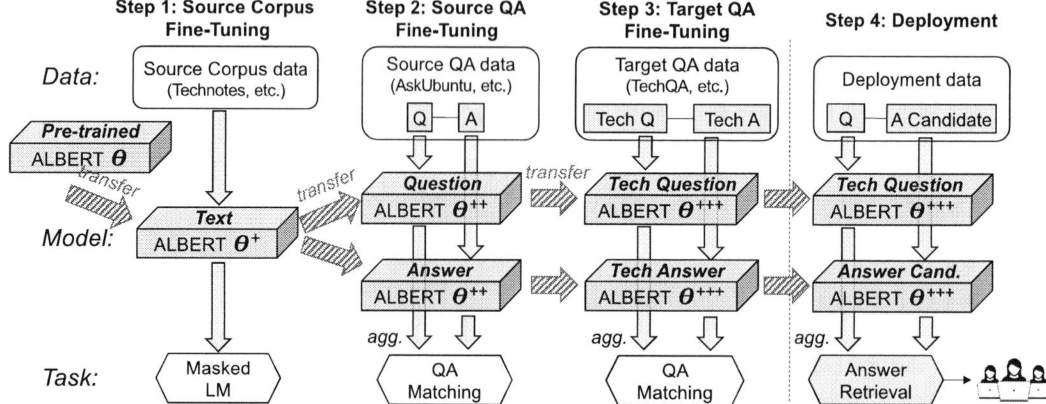

Figure 1: High level architecture of our proposed TransTQA system. First, the pre-trained ALBERT model is fine tuned with unstructured source technical corpus with masked language model (MLM) task, i.e., $\theta \rightarrow \theta^+$. Second, a siamese ALBERT takes fine tuned ALBERT and fine tunes with source technical QA, i.e., $\theta^+ \rightarrow \theta^{++}$. Third, the siamese ALBERT further fine tunes with target QA, i.e., $\theta^{++} \rightarrow \theta^{+++}$. Our deployed system takes θ^{+++}. Given a query, our system first calculates similarity scores between the query and each candidate answer, then ranks all scores from highest to lowest. Finally, the system returns top-3 ranked answers.

architecture is similar to BERT in that it also uses a Transformer encoder. In order to allow reproducability, we integrate Huggingface Transformer (Wolf et al., 2019) into the system construction. Huggingface is an open-source toolkit containing more than 10 popular pre-training language model implementations (e.g., BERT, XLNet). Therefore, when reproducing the system with other data, only the model name would need to be adjusted (e.g., BERT-Large, XLNet-Base) according to the training resources without manually adjust the specified model configurations. Different pre-training language models can be found at HuggingFace[1]. For instance, the configurations of our siamese-ALBERT are automatically taken as default settings inclduing *vocabulary*, *embedding size* etc.

3.2 Siamese ALBERT

The central challenge of retrieving a proper answer lies in the complex and versatile semantic relations observed between questions and responses. Unlike several factoid QA scenarios (Rajpurkar et al., 2016; Kwiatkowski et al., 2019), linguistic similarities between such non-factoid QA might be non-indicative. Since ALBERT makes use of Transformer network (Vaswani et al., 2017), it benefits from multi-head attention mechanism, allowing the model to jointly attend to information from different representation subspaces at different positions.

3.2.1 Siamese Encoder

First, the ALBERT tokenizer split original words into smaller subwords and characters. After tokenization, two special tokens (i.e. [CLS] and [SEP]) are added to the tokenized sequence. Besides, the tokenizer also generates "Mask IDs", which is used to indicate which elements in the sequence are tokens and which are padding elements.

Second, Two ALBERT encoders generate contextualized representations of each tokenized element in an input question Q and a candidate answer A, which are denoted by $\text{ALBERT}_\Theta(Q)[X] \in \mathbb{R}^d$ and $\text{ALBERT}_\Theta(A)[X] \in \mathbb{R}^d$, where d is the dimension of word embedding. In order to produce a single vector of question embedding $\mathbf{h}_Q$ and answer embedding $\mathbf{h}_A$ from the input question and answer. We apply mean pooling to the representations of all tokens:

$$\mathbf{h}_Q = \text{MEAN}(\{\text{ALBERT}_\Theta(Q)[X]|X \in Q\}), \quad (1)$$
$$\mathbf{h}_A = \text{MEAN}(\{\text{ALBERT}_\Theta(A)[X]|X \in A\}). \quad (2)$$

3.2.2 Matching Layer

The scoring function F is factorized as an inner product between question embedding $\mathbf{h}_Q$ and answer embedding $\mathbf{h}_A$. This is similar to using feed forward networks to project queries and responses into a common space where the relevance is computed by cosine distance (Huang et al., 2013).

$$F(\mathbf{h}_Q, \mathbf{h}_A) = \frac{\mathbf{h}_Q}{||\mathbf{h}_Q||_2} \cdot \frac{\mathbf{h}_A}{||\mathbf{h}_A||_2}. \quad (3)$$

---

[1] https://huggingface.co/models

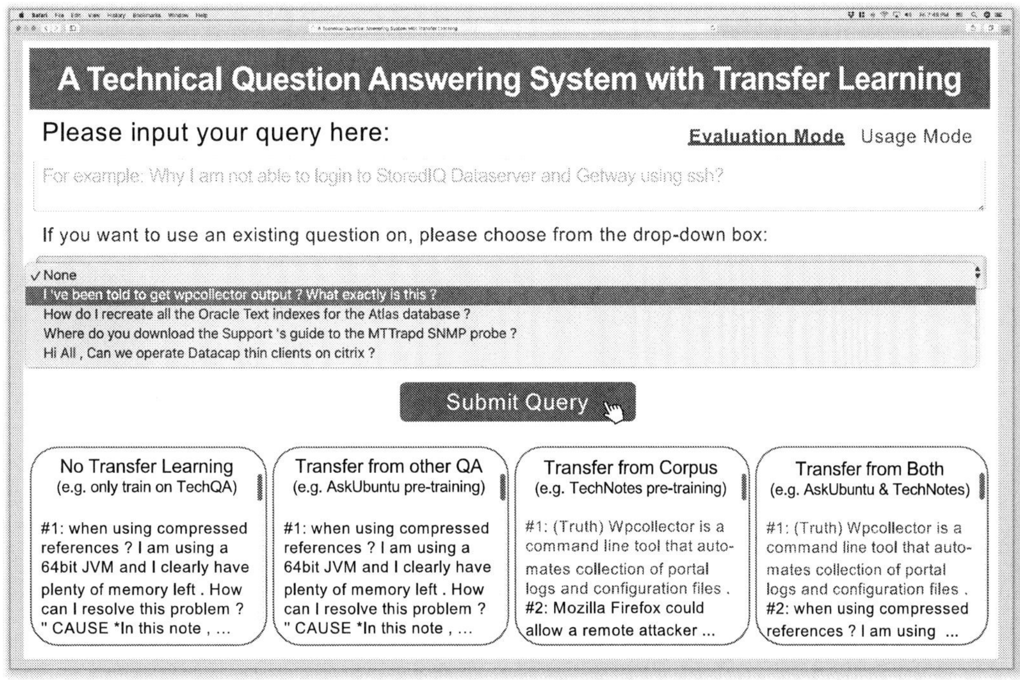

Figure 2: A screenshot of our system. User can either submit their query or choose a query from a pre-defined set. Our system will return top-3 recommended answers retrieved from the existing database.

3.2.3 Optimization

The goal of response selection is to model $P(A|Q)$, which is used to rank possible responses A given an input question Q. This probability distribution can be written as:

$$P(A|Q) = \frac{P(Q,A)}{\sum_k P(Q,A_k)} \quad (4)$$

For efficiency and simplicity, we adopt multiple negatives ranking loss in the training, which takes the responses of other examples in a training batch of stochastic gradient descent as negative responses (Henderson et al., 2017). Specifically, for a batch of size K, there will be K input questions $\mathcal{Q}_{batch} = (X_1, \cdots, X_K)$ and their corresponding responses $\mathcal{A}_{batch} = (A_1, \cdots, A_K)$. Every reply A_j is effectively treated as a negative candidate for Q_i if $i \neq j$. The $K-1$ negative examples for each Q are different at each pass through the data due to shuffling in stochastic gradient descent. So, the goal of training is to minimize the approximated mean negative log probability of the data. Formally,

$$\mathcal{L}(\mathcal{Q}_{batch}, \mathcal{A}_{batch}, \Theta) = -\frac{1}{K} \sum_{i=1}^{K} \log P(A_i|Q_i)$$
$$= -\frac{1}{K} \sum_{i=1}^{K} \left[F(\mathbf{h}_{Q_i}, \mathbf{h}_{A_i}) - \log \sum_{k=1}^{K} e^{F(\mathbf{h}_{Q_i}, \mathbf{h}_{A_k})} \right] \quad (5)$$

3.3 Transfer: Three-step Fine Tuning

The transfer learning strategy used in our system consists of a three-step fine tuning process. First, the pre-trained ALBERT model is fine tuned with unstructured source technical corpus with masked language model (MLM) task, i.e., $\theta \to \theta^+$. Second, a siamese ALBERT takes fine tuned ALBERT and fine tunes with source technical QA, i.e., $\theta^+ \to \theta^{++}$. Third, the siamese ALBERT further fine tunes with target QA, i.e., $\theta^{++} \to \theta^{+++}$.

3.3.1 Fine Tuning on Source Corpus

Though ALBERT has demonstrated state-of-the-art performances in many NLP tasks, directly applying ALBERT to technical domain tasks suffers from certain limitations. Since ALBERT is pre-trained on datasets only containing general domain corpora (e.g., Wikipedia, BookCorpus), many technical terminology are not well represented in the model. In order to make ALBERT equipped with technical domain knowledge, we first fine tune the pre-trained ALBERT on technical corpus (e.g., solution documents, user manuals and forum posts etc). We adopt the classic masked language model (MLM) pre-training task that learns to predict randomly masked tokens in the input sequence. MLM

Table 1: Performance on TechQA and StackUnix. Transferring knowledge from both source QA (e.g., AskUbuntu) and technical corpora (e.g., IBM Technotes) demonstrates the best performance.

Methods		Source QA	Source Corpus	TechQA				StackUnix			
				MRR	R@1	R@5	R@10	MRR	R@1	R@5	R@10
SASE (LSTM)	M1	-	-	23.45	14.65	33.12	36.31	31.22	24.37	38.71	45.88
	M2	✔	-	26.19	17.20	35.03	42.68	34.03	27.24	40.01	45.16
	M3	-	✔	30.85	20.38	40.13	52.23	35.26	25.45	43.73	53.05
	M4	✔	✔	__36.31__	__25.48__	__48.41__	__56.05__	__38.69__	__29.30__	__46.24__	__55.20__
ALBERT	M1	-	-	36.52	25.00	50.63	56.25	40.55	31.89	50.18	56.99
	M2	✔	-	__45.11__	__34.38__	56.88	64.38	42.61	34.05	50.89	55.56
	M3	-	✔	41.61	29.38	55.00	63.13	46.27	35.12	58.06	67.03
	M4	✔	✔	44.13	31.88	__60.00__	__70.63__	__50.04__	__38.35__	__63.08__	__71.32__

is the primary pre-training task used in BERT and ALBERT (Devlin et al., 2019; Lan et al., 2020).

3.3.2 Fine Tuning on Source QA

Compared to evolved technical communities (e.g., StackOverflow, AskUbuntu), many emerging technical forums have limited size of existing QA pairs. To address the lack of knowledge caused by data shortage, we further fine tuned the ALBERT using source technical QA data to facilitate the ALBERT to better represent questions and responses in the latent space. For instance, since Ubuntu is a operating system built upon the Unix/Linux, many questions on AskUbuntu and StackUnix are related and share common technical knowledge.

3.3.3 Fine Tuning on Target QA

After fine tuning on unstructured technical corpora and source technical QA, a straightforward way to transfer these knowledge is to keep the same model architecture and directly initialize the weights of the target model with the weights of the models fine tuned on the source technical QA, and then we train on the target model with the target technical QA dataset (e.g., TECHQA, StackUnix).

4 Front End and User Interface

Our system consists of two different modes: evaluation mode and usage mode. First, the usage mode allows users to select an existing question from the drop-down box or ask a question themselves. Then, the system returns three retrieved responses with highest probabilities from the database to the user. Second, the evaluation mode retrieves responses through different transfer learning settings, which can be used to compare different model performance. Overall, the QA front end service was

Table 2: Comparison with existing retrieval QA system on number of parameters and average inference time. The siamese-ALBERT in our TransTQA system has the least parameters and fastest inference time.

Methods	#Parameters	Inference time
BERT-Rerank (Nogueira et al., 2019)	170M	62.67s
BERT-Serini (Yang et al., 2019)	170M	0.55s
Siamese-ALBERT (Ours TransTQA)	__10M__	__0.13s__

implemented in Python with Flask web framework. It is fully configurable and allows multiple candidate ranking services to be used at the same time.

4.1 Usage Mode

To begin with, the system receives a question from the user via a text field input. The question is filtered by length: too long ($>$512) or empty questions are discarded. Then, the question is tokenized, padded and concatenated with special tokens. Given the tokenized query, the response retrieval reduces to encoding a new question in a encoding step to the question embedding, and then ranks all candidate answers based on the inner product with the query embedding. Since embeddings of candidate answers can be pre-computed, the usage mode is able to make quick response.

4.2 Evaluation Mode

In evaluation mode, when the system receives a query, the system retrieves responses from four different settings: (1) M1: no transfer learning; (2) M2: transfer knowledge from source corpus

Table 3: Case study of real user queries.

Case Study of Evaluation Mode
User Query: Hi All, Can we operate Datacap thin clients on citrixs ?
Ground Truth Answer: Remote users that access Datacap over a WAN can use Taskmaster Web-based thin clients , or FastDoc Capture operating in offline mode .
M1-Rank1: The upgrade must be initiated by using the attached script , which gives the non-root user (who originally installed this Jazz for Service Management instance) the correct permissions for the upgrade process .   **M2-Rank1:** WAS recently renamed WAS for Developers (WAS4D) to WAS ILAN . In response to this change , RAD 9.6 now packages WAS ILAN available in the RAD_WS_9.6_WASTE_9.0.zip file . It has the same capabilities and updates that RAD users expect .   **M3-Rank1:** You must install the 5.0.0.8 or later fix pack to upgrade to 6.0.0.0 or later . The 5.0.0.8 fix pack contains a required fix to allow the larger sized firmware image to fit .   **M4-Rank1:** Remote users that access Datacap over a WAN can use Taskmaster Web-based thin clients , or FastDoc Capture operating in offline mode .
Case Study of Usage Mode
User Query: Where do you download the Support 's guide to the MTTrapd SNMP probe ?
Ground Truth Answer: The attached Support 's guide to the SNMP probe provides details on how best to configure the probe , troubleshoot issues and how to use third party products to test the probes behaviour .
M4-Rank1: The attached Support 's guide to the SNMP probe provides details on how best to configure the probe , troubleshoot issues and how to use third party products to test the probes behaviour .   **M4-Rank2:** Supported methods are GUI and silent configuration . Also , silent configuration fully works both on UNIX and Windows platforms only at level 7.1.1.0.4 . Before this maintenance level there were issues and limitations with Managing Server and Transaction Tracking integration . Support Command Line configuration for J2EE DC will possibly be added in some future patch via Request For Enhancement .   **M4-Rank3:** This probe is written to support Nokia Network Functions Manager for Packet release 17.3 .

(e.g., Technotes); (3) M3: transfer knowledge from source QA (e.g., AskUbuntu); (4) M4: transfer learning from both (2) and (3). The retrieved responses are presented in four blocks corresponding with four different settings. In case the question was present in the dataset, because we know which one is the correct answer, we mark its text with a "Truth" tag and highlight in blue for a quicker performance assessment by the user.

5 System Evaluation

5.1 Experimental Settings

We conduct experiments on three technical datasets: TechQA (Castelli et al., 2020), StackUnix and an IBM internal dataset. Details about datasets are in Appendix **??**. We compare retrieval performance with SASE (Lin et al., 2017), which is a LSTM-based method adopted in previous QA systems (Loginova and Neumann, 2018; Rücklé and Gurevych, 2017). Implementation details can be found in Appendix **??**. We also compare inference time and memory consumption with two BERT-based QA systems: BERT-Rerank (Nogueira et al., 2019) and BERT-Serini (Yang et al., 2019).

5.2 Experimental Results

Comparisons with traditional QA systems As shown in Table 1, our TransTQA outperforms traditional QA system built upon LSTM-based models.

Effectiveness of knowledge transfer As shown in Table 1, knowledge transfer from source corpus and source QA are crucial for our task. We observe that fine tuning on both source corpus (e.g., Technotes) and source QA (e.g., AskUbuntu) makes superior performance than only fine tuning on either source domain corpus or source QA.

Time and memory efficiency As shown in Table 2, the siamese ALBERT is much faster than BERT-Rerank and BERT-Serini during the inference time. This is because all the answer embeddings stored in the database are pre-computed. So, given an unseen query, we only need to rank the answer based on its inner product with the query embedding.

5.3 Case Study

We show two real use cases in Table 3. Evaluation Mode returns top ranked answer retrieved by different transfer learning settings (M1 to M4). Usage Mode returns top ranked answer retrieved by M4. M4-Rank1 gives the correct answer.

6 Conclusions

We developed TransTQA, which is a novel system that offers automatic response by retrieving proper answers based on correctly answered similar questions. TransTQA was built upon a siamese ALBERT network, which enables it to respond to questions quickly and accurately. Furthermore, TransTQA adopted transfer learning to improve its performance on multiple tech domain QA.

Acknowledgements

This work is supported by National Science Foundation IIS-1849816.

References

Zahra Abbasiyantaeb and Saeedeh Momtazi. 2020. Text-based question answering from information retrieval and deep neural network perspectives: A survey. *arXiv preprint arXiv:2002.06612*.

Amin Ahmad, Noah Constant, Yinfei Yang, and Daniel Cer. 2019. Reqa: An evaluation for end-to-end answer retrieval models. In *Proceedings of Workshop on Machine Reading for Question Answering*.

Vittorio Castelli, Rishav Chakravarti, Saswati Dana, Anthony Ferritto, Radu Florian, Martin Franz, Dinesh Garg, Dinesh Khandelwal, Scott McCarley, Mike McCawley, et al. 2020. The techqa dataset. *Proceedings of the 58th Annual Meeting of the Association for Computational Linguistics (ACL)*.

Wei-Cheng Chang, Felix X Yu, Yin-Wen Chang, Yiming Yang, and Sanjiv Kumar. 2020. Pre-training tasks for embedding-based large-scale retrieval. *In Proceedings of 8th International Conference for Learning Representation (ICLR)*.

Danqi Chen, Adam Fisch, Jason Weston, and Antoine Bordes. 2017. Reading wikipedia to answer open-domain questions. In *Proceedings of the 55th Annual Meeting of the Association for Computational Linguistics (Volume 1: Long Papers)*.

Yu Chen, Lingfei Wu, and Mohammed J Zaki. 2019. Bidirectional attentive memory networks for question answering over knowledge bases. In *Proceedings of the 2019 Conference of the North American Chapter of the Association for Computational Linguistics: Human Language Technologies, Volume 1 (Long and Short Papers*, pages 2913–2923.

Yang Deng, Ying Shen, Min Yang, Yaliang Li, Nan Du, Wei Fan, and Kai Lei. 2018. Knowledge as a bridge: Improving cross-domain answer selection with external knowledge. In *Proceedings of the 27th international conference on computational linguistics*, pages 3295–3305.

Jacob Devlin, Ming-Wei Chang, Kenton Lee, and Kristina Toutanova. 2019. Bert: Pre-training of deep bidirectional transformers for language understanding. In *Proceedings of the 2019 Conference of the North American Chapter of the Association for Computational Linguistics: Human Language Technologies, Volume 1 (Long and Short Papers)*.

David Golub, Po-Sen Huang, Xiaodong He, and Li Deng. 2017. Two-stage synthesis networks for transfer learning in machine comprehension. In *Proceedings of the 2017 Conference on Empirical Methods in Natural Language Processing*.

Matthew Henderson, Rami Al-Rfou, Brian Strope, Yunhsuan Sung, László Lukács, Ruiqi Guo, Sanjiv Kumar, Balint Miklos, and Ray Kurzweil. 2017. Efficient natural language response suggestion for smart reply. *arXiv preprint arXiv:1705.00652*.

Po-Sen Huang, Xiaodong He, Jianfeng Gao, Li Deng, Alex Acero, and Larry Heck. 2013. Learning deep structured semantic models for web search using clickthrough data. In *Proceedings of the 22nd ACM international conference on Information & Knowledge Management*, pages 2333–2338.

Meng Jiang, Peng Cui, Nicholas Jing Yuan, Xing Xie, and Shiqiang Yang. 2016. Little is much: Bridging cross-platform behaviors through overlapped crowds. In *AAAI*, pages 13–19. Citeseer.

Sosuke Kato, Riku Togashi, Hideyuki Maeda, Sumio Fujita, and Tetsuya Sakai. 2017. Lstm vs. bm25 for open-domain qa: A hands-on comparison of effectiveness and efficiency. In *Proceedings of the 40th International ACM SIGIR Conference on Research and Development in Information Retrieval*, pages 1309–1312.

Tom Kwiatkowski, Jennimaria Palomaki, Olivia Redfield, Michael Collins, Ankur Parikh, Chris Alberti, Danielle Epstein, Illia Polosukhin, Jacob Devlin, Kenton Lee, et al. 2019. Natural questions: a benchmark for question answering research. *Transactions of the Association for Computational Linguistics*.

Zhenzhong Lan, Mingda Chen, Sebastian Goodman, Kevin Gimpel, Piyush Sharma, and Radu Soricut. 2020. Albert: A lite bert for self-supervised learning of language representations. *International Conference for Learning Representation (ICLR)*.

Zhouhan Lin, Minwei Feng, Cicero Nogueira dos Santos, Mo Yu, Bing Xiang, Bowen Zhou, and Yoshua Bengio. 2017. A structured self-attentive sentence embedding. *In Proceedings of 5th International Conference for Learning Representation (ICLR)*.

Ekaterina Loginova and Günter Neumann. 2018. An interactive web-interface for visualizing the inner workings of the question answering lstm. In *Proceedings of the 2018 Conference on Empirical Methods in Natural Language Processing: System Demonstrations*, pages 30–35.

Xiaofei Ma, Peng Xu, Zhiguo Wang, Ramesh Nallapati, and Bing Xiang. 2019. Universal text representation from bert: An empirical study. *arXiv preprint arXiv:1910.07973*.

Sewon Min, Minjoon Seo, and Hannaneh Hajishirzi. 2017. Question answering through transfer learning from large fine-grained supervision data. In *Proceedings of the 55th Annual Meeting of the Association for Computational Linguistics (Volume 2: Short Papers)*, pages 510–517.

Rodrigo Nogueira, , and Kyunghyun Cho. 2019. Passage re-ranking with bert. *arXiv preprint arXiv:1901.04085*.

Sinno Jialin Pan and Qiang Yang. 2009. A survey on transfer learning. *IEEE Transactions on knowledge and data engineering*, 22(10):1345–1359.

Pranav Rajpurkar, Jian Zhang, Konstantin Lopyrev, and Percy Liang. 2016. Squad: 100,000+ questions for machine comprehension of text. In *Proceedings of the 2016 Conference on Empirical Methods in Natural Language Processing*, pages 2383–2392.

Nils Reimers and Iryna Gurevych. 2019. Sentence-bert: Sentence embeddings using siamese bert-networks. In *Proceedings of the 2019 Conference on Empirical Methods in Natural Language Processing and the 9th International Joint Conference on Natural Language Processing (EMNLP-IJCNLP)*.

Andreas Rücklé and Iryna Gurevych. 2017. End-to-end non-factoid question answering with an interactive visualization of neural attention weights. In *Proceedings of ACL 2017, System Demonstrations*.

Sebastian Ruder, Matthew E Peters, Swabha Swayamdipta, and Thomas Wolf. 2019. Transfer learning in natural language processing. In *Proceedings of the 2019 Conference of the North American Chapter of the Association for Computational Linguistics: Tutorials*, pages 15–18.

Minjoon Seo, Tom Kwiatkowski, Ankur Parikh, Ali Farhadi, and Hannaneh Hajishirzi. 2018. Phrase-indexed question answering: A new challenge for scalable document comprehension. In *Proceedings of the 2018 Conference on Empirical Methods in Natural Language Processing*.

Minjoon Seo, Jinhyuk Lee, Tom Kwiatkowski, Ankur Parikh, Ali Farhadi, and Hannaneh Hajishirzi. 2019. Real-time open-domain question answering with dense-sparse phrase index. In *Proceedings of the 57th Annual Meeting of the Association for Computational Linguistics*.

Ivan Srba and Maria Bielikova. 2016. A comprehensive survey and classification of approaches for community question answering. *ACM Transactions on the Web (TWEB)*, 10(3):1–63.

Ming Tan, Cicero Dos Santos, Bing Xiang, and Bowen Zhou. 2016. Improved representation learning for question answer matching. In *Proceedings of the 54th Annual Meeting of the Association for Computational Linguistics (Volume 1: Long Papers)*, pages 464–473.

Ashish Vaswani, Noam Shazeer, Niki Parmar, Jakob Uszkoreit, Llion Jones, Aidan N Gomez, Łukasz Kaiser, and Illia Polosukhin. 2017. Attention is all you need. In *Advances in neural information processing systems (NeurIPS)*.

Huazheng Wang, Zhe Gan, Xiaodong Liu, Jingjing Liu, Jianfeng Gao, and Hongning Wang. 2019. Adversarial domain adaptation for machine reading comprehension. In *Proceedings of Empirical Methods in Natural Language Processing and the 9th International Joint Conference on Natural Language Processing (EMNLP-IJCNLP)*.

Thomas Wolf, Lysandre Debut, Victor Sanh, Julien Chaumond, Clement Delangue, Anthony Moi, Pierric Cistac, Tim Rault, Rémi Louf, Morgan Funtowicz, et al. 2019. Transformers: State-of-the-art natural language processing. *arXiv preprint arXiv:1910.03771*.

Lingfei Wu, Ian EH Yen, Kun Xu, Fangli Xu, Avinash Balakrishnan, Pin-Yu Chen, Pradeep Ravikumar, and Michael J Witbrock. 2018. Word mover's embedding: From word2vec to document embedding. In *Proceedings of the 2018 Conference on Empirical Methods in Natural Language Processing (EMNLP)*.

Wei Yang, Yuqing Xie, Aileen Lin, Xingyu Li, Luchen Tan, Kun Xiong, Ming Li, and Jimmy Lin. 2019. End-to-end open-domain question answering with bertserini. In *Proceedings of the 2019 Conference of the North American Chapter of the Association for Computational Linguistics (Demonstrations)*.

Yi Yang, Wen-tau Yih, and Christopher Meek. 2015. Wikiqa: A challenge dataset for open-domain question answering. In *Proceedings of the 2015 conference on empirical methods in natural language processing*, pages 2013–2018.

Zeynep Akkalyoncu Yilmaz, Shengjin Wang, Wei Yang, Haotian Zhang, and Jimmy Lin. 2019. Applying bert to document retrieval with birch. In *Proceedings of Empirical Methods in Natural Language Processing and the 9th International Joint Conference on Natural Language Processing (EMNLP-IJCNLP): System Demonstrations*.

Wenhao Yu, Lingfei Wu, Qingkai Zeng, Yu Deng, Shu Tao, and Meng Jiang. 2020. Crossing variational autoencoders for answer retrieval. *Proceedings of the 58th Annual Meeting of the Association for Computational Linguistics (ACL)*.

ENTYFI: A System for Fine-grained Entity Typing in Fictional Texts

Cuong Xuan Chu   **Simon Razniewski**   **Gerhard Weikum**

Max Planck Institute for Informatics
Saarbrücken, Germany
`{cxchu, srazniew, weikum}@mpi-inf.mpg.de`

Abstract

Fiction and fantasy are archetypes of long-tail domains that lack suitable NLP methodologies and tools. We present ENTYFI, a web-based system for fine-grained typing of entity mentions in fictional texts. It builds on 205 automatically induced high-quality type systems for popular fictional domains, and provides recommendations towards reference type systems for given input texts. Users can exploit the richness and diversity of these reference type systems for fine-grained supervised typing, in addition, they can choose among and combine four other typing modules: pre-trained real-world models, unsupervised dependency-based typing, knowledge base lookups, and constraint-based candidate consolidation. The demonstrator is available at `https://d5demos.mpi-inf.mpg.de/entyfi`.

1 Introduction

Motivation and Problem. Entity types are a core building block of current knowledge bases (KBs) and valuable for many natural language processing tasks, such as coreference resolution, relation extraction and question answering (Lee et al., 2006; Carlson et al., 2010; Recasens et al., 2013). Context-based entity typing, the task of assigning semantic types for mentions of entities in textual contexts (e.g., `musician`, `politician`, `location` or `battle`) therefore has become an important NLP task. While traditional methods often use coarse-grained classes, such as `person`, `location`, `organization` and `misc`, as targets, recent methods try to classify entities into finer-grained types, from hundreds to thousands of them, yet all limited to variants of the real world, like from Wikipedia or news (Lee et al., 2006; Ling and Weld, 2012; Corro et al., 2015; Choi et al., 2018).

Entity type information plays an even more important role in literary texts from fictional domains.

Fiction and fantasy are core parts of human culture, spanning from traditional folks and myths into books, movies, TV series and games. People have created sophisticated fictional universes such as the Marvel Universe, DC Comics, Middle Earth or Harry Potter. These universes include entities, social structures, and events that are completely different from the real world. Appropriate entity typing for these universes is a prerequisite for several end-user applications. For example, a Game of Thrones fan may want to query for House Stark members who are Faceless Men or which character is both a Warg and a Greenseer. On the other hand, an analyst may want to compare social structures between different mythologies or formations of different civilizations.

State-of-the-art methods for entity typing mostly use supervised models trained on Wikipedia content, and only focus on news and similar real-world texts. Due to low coverage of Wikipedia on fictional domains, these methods are thus not sufficient for literary texts. For example, for the following sentence from *Lord of the Rings*:

"After Melkor's defeat in the First Age, Sauron became the second Dark Lord and strove to conquer Arda by creating the Rings"

state-of-the-art entity typing methods only return few coarse types for entities, such as `person` for SAURON and MELKOR or `location` for FIRST AGE and ARDA. Moreover, existing methods typically produce predictions for each individual mention, so that different mentions of the same entity may be assigned incompatible types, e.g., ARDA may be predicted as `person` and `location` in different contexts.

Contribution. The prototype system presented in this demo paper, ENTYFI (fine-grained ENtity TYping on FIctional texts, see Chu et al. (2020) for full details) overcomes the outlined limitations.

Proceedings of the 2020 EMNLP (Systems Demonstrations), pages 100–106
November 16-20, 2020. ©2020 Association for Computational Linguistics

ENTYFI supports long input texts from any kind of literature, as well as texts from standard domains (e.g., news). With the sample text above, ENTYFI is able to predict more specific and meaningful types for entity mentions:

MELKOR: `Ainur, Villain`	FIRST AGE: `Eras, Time`
SAURON: `Maiar, Villain`	DARK LORD: `Ainur, Title`
RINGS: `Jewelry, Magic Things`	ARDA: `Location`

To address the lack of reference types, ENTYFI leverages the content of fan communities on Wikia.com, from which 205 reference type systems are induced. Given an input text, ENTYFI then retrieves the most relevant reference type systems and uses them as typing targets. By combining supervised typing method with unsupervised pattern extraction and knowledge base lookups, suitable type candidates are identified. To resolve inconsistencies among candidates, ENTYFI utilizes an integer linear programming (ILP) based consolidation stage.

Outline. The following section describes the architecture of ENTYFI with the approach underlying its main components. The demonstration is illustrated afterwards through its graphical user interface. Our demonstration system is available at: `https://d5demos.mpi-inf.mpg.de/entyfi`. We also provide a screencast video demonstrating our system, at: `https://youtu.be/g_ESaONagFQ`.

2 System Overview

ENTYFI comprises five steps: type system construction, reference universe ranking, mention detection, mention typing and type consolidation. Figure 1 shows an overview of the ENTYFI architecture.

2.1 Type System Construction

To counter the low coverage of entities and relevant types in Wikipedia for fictional domains, we make use of an alternative semi-structured resource, Wikia[1].

Wikia. Wikia is a large fiction community portal, includes over 385,000 individual universes. It covers a wide range of universes in fiction and fantasy, from old folks and myths like *Greek Mythology, Egyptian Mythology* to recent stories like *Harry Potter, The Lord of the Rings*. It also contains popular movies, TV series (e.g. *Game of Thrones,*

---

[1] https://wikia.com

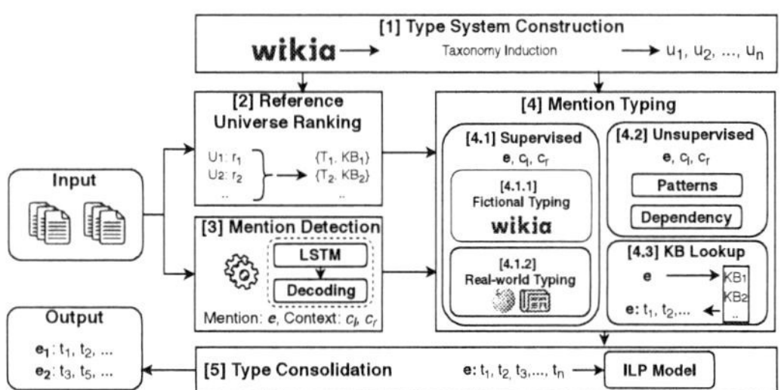

Figure 1: Overview of the architecture of ENTYFI (Chu et al., 2020).

Breaking Bad) and video games (e.g. *League of Legends, Pokemon*).

Each universe in Wikia is organized similarly to Wikipedia, such that they contain entities and categories that can be used to distill reference type systems. We adopt techniques from the TiFi system (Chu et al., 2019) to clean and structure Wikia categories. We remove noisy categories (e.g. metacategories) by using a dictionary-based method. To ensure connectedness of taxonomies, we integrate the category networks with WordNet (WN) by linking the categories to the most similar WN synsets. The similarity is computed between the context of the category (e.g., description, super/sub categories) and the gloss of the WN synset (Chu et al., 2019). Resulting type systems typically contain between 700 to 10,000 types per universe.

2.2 Reference Universe Ranking

Given an input text, the goal of this step is to find the most relevant universes among the reference universes. Each reference universe is represented by its entities and entity type system. We compute the cosine similarity between the TF-IDF vectors of the input and each universe. The top-ranked reference universes and their type systems are then used for mention typing (section 2.4).

2.3 Mention Detection

To detect entity mentions in the input text, we rely on a BIOES tagging scheme. Inspired by He et al. (2017) from the field of semantic role labeling, we design a BiLSTM network with embeddings and POS tags as input, highway connections between layers to avoid vanishing gradients (Zhang et al., 2016), and recurrent dropout to avoid over-fitting (Gal and Ghahramani, 2016). The output is then put into a decoding step by using dynamic programming to select the tag sequence with maximum score that satisfies the BIOES constraints. The decoding step does not add more complexity to the training.

2.4 Mention Typing

We produce type candidates for mentions by using a combination of supervised, unsupervised and lookup approaches.

Supervised Fiction Types. Given an entity mention and its textual context, we approach typing as multiclass classification problem. The mention representation is the average of all embeddings of tokens in the mention. The context representation is a combination of left and right context around the mention. The contexts are encoded by using BiLSTM models (Graves, 2012) and then put into attention layer to learn the weight factors (Shimaoka et al., 2017). Mention and context representations are concatenated and passed to the final logistic regression layer with cross entropy loss function to predict the type candidates.

Target Classes. There are two kinds of target classes: (i) general types - 7 disjunct high-level WordNet types that we manually chose, mirroring existing coarse typing systems: `living_thing`, `location`, `organization`, `object`, `time`, `event`, `substance`, (ii) top-performing types - types from reference type systems. Due to a large number of types as well as insufficient training data, predicting all types in the type systems is not effective. Therefore, for each reference universe, we predict those types for which, on withheld test data, at least 0.8 F1-score was achieved. This results in an average of 75 types per reference universe.

Supervised Real-world Types. Although fictional universes contain fantasy contents, many of them reflect our real-world, for instance, *House of Cards*, a satire of American politics. Even fictional stories like *Game of Thrones* or *Lord of the Rings* contain types presented in real world, such as `King` or `Battle`. To leverage this overlap, we incorporate the Wikipedia- and news-trained typing model from Choi et al. (2018), which is able to predict up to 10,331 real-world types.

Unsupervised Typing. Along with supervised technique, we use a pattern-based method to extract type candidates which appear explicitly in contexts for mentions. We use 36 manually crafted Hearst-style patterns for type extraction (Seitner et al., 2016). Moreover, from dependency parsing, a noun phrase can be considered as a type candidate if there exists a *noun compound modifier (nn)* between the noun phrase and the given mention. In the case of candidate types appearing in the mention itself, we extract the head word of the mention and consider it as a candidate if it appears as a noun in WordNet. For example, given the text *Queen Cersei was the twentieth ruler of the Seven Kingdoms*, `queen` and `kingdom` are type candidates for the mentions CERSEI and SEVEN KINGDOMS, respectively.

KB Lookup. Using top-ranked universes from section 2.2 as basis for the lookup, we map entity mentions to entities in reference universes by using lexical matching. The types of entities in corresponding type systems then become type candidates for the given mentions.

2.5 Type Consolidation

Using multiple universes as reference and typing in long texts may produce incompatibilities in predictions. For example, SARUMAN, a wizard in Lord of the Rings can be predicted as a white walker using the model learnt from Game of Thrones. To resolve possible inconsistencies, we rely on a consolidation step that uses an integer linear programming (ILP) model. The model captures several constraints, including disjointness, hierarchical coherence, cardinality limit and soft correlations (Chu et al., 2020).

ILP Model. Given an entity mention *e* with a list of type candidates with corresponding weights, a decision variable T_i is defined for each type candidate t_i. $T_i = 1$ if *e* belongs to t_i, otherwise, $T_i = 0$. With the constraints mentioned above, the objective function is:

maximize

$$\alpha \sum_i T_i * w_i + (1 - \alpha) \sum_{i,j} T_i * T_j * v_{ij}$$

subject to

$$T_i + T_j \leq 1 \quad \forall (t_i, t_j) \in D$$
$$T_i - T_j \leq 0 \quad \forall (t_i, t_j) \in H$$
$$\sum_i T_i \leq \delta$$

where w_i is the weight of the type candidate t_i, α is a hyper parameter, v_{ij} is Pearson correlation coefficient between a type pair (t_i, t_j), D is the set of disjoint type pairs, H is the set of (transitive) hyponym pairs (t_i, t_j) - t_i is the (transitive) hyponym of t_j, and δ is the threshold for the cardinality limit.

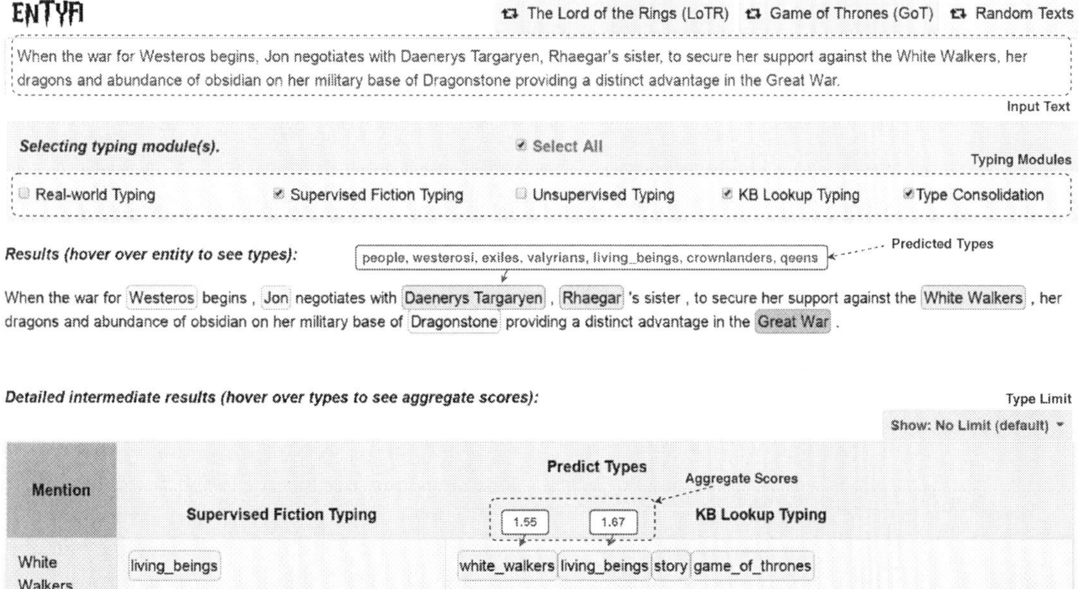

Figure 2: ENTYFI Web interface.

3 Web Interface

The ENTYFI system is deployed online at `https://d5demos.mpi-inf.mpg.de/entyfi`. A screencast video, which demonstrates ENTYFI, is also uploaded at `https://youtu.be/g_ESaONagFQ`.

Input. The web interface allows users to enter a text as input. To give a better experience, we provide various sample texts from three different sources: Wikia, books and fan fiction[2]. With each source, users can try with either texts from Lord of the Rings and Game of Thrones or random texts, as well as some cross-overs between different universes written by fans.

Output. Given an input text, users can choose different typing modules to run. The output is the input text marked by entity mentions and their predicted types. The system also shows the predicted types with their aggregate scores and the typing modules from which the types are extracted. Figure 2 shows an example input and output of the ENTYFI system.

Typing module selector. ENTYFI includes several typing modules, among which users can choose. If only the real-world typing module is chosen, the system runs typing on the text immediately, using one of the existing typing models which are able to predict up to 112 real-world types

(Shimaoka et al., 2017) or 10,331 types (Choi et al., 2018). *Note:* If the later model is selected to run the real-world typing, it requires more time to load the pre-trained embeddings (Pennington et al., 2014).

On the other hand, if supervised fiction typing or KB lookup typing are chosen, the system computes the similarity between the given text and reference universes from the database. With the default option, the type system of the most related universe is being used as targets for typing, while with the alternative case, users can choose different universes and use their type systems as targets. Users are also able to decide whether the consolidation step is executed or not.

Exploration of reference universes. ENTYFI builds on 205 automatically induced high-quality type systems for popular fictional domains. Along with top 5 most relevant universes showing up with similarity scores, users can also choose other universes in the database. For a better overview, with each universe, we provide a short description about the universe and a hyperlink to its Wikia source. Figure 3 show an example of reference universes presented in the demonstration.

Logs. To help users understand how the system works inside, we provide a log box that shows which step is running at the backend, step by step, along with timing information (Figure 4).

---

[2]https://www.fanfiction.net/

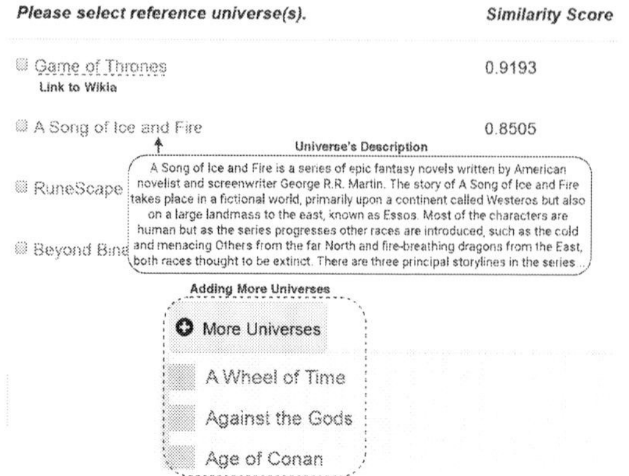

Figure 3: ENTYFI Reference Universes.

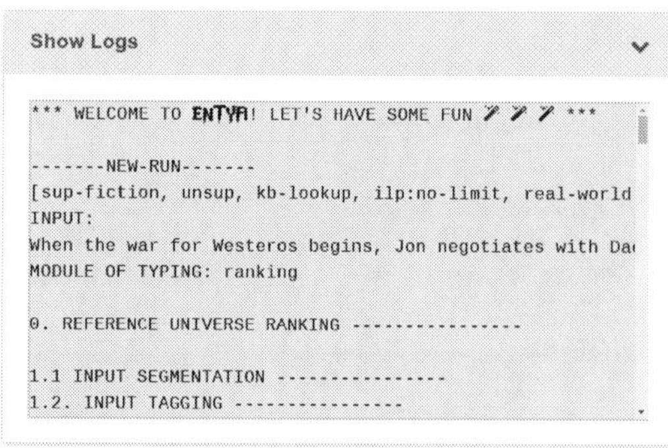

Figure 4: ENTYFI Logs.

4 Demonstration Experience

A common use of entity typing is as building block of more comprehensive NLP pipelines that perform tasks such as entity linking, relation extraction or question answering. We envision that ENTYFI could strengthen such pipelines considerably (see also extrinsic evaluation in (Chu et al., 2020)). Yet to illustrate its workings in isolation, in the following, we present a direct expert end-user application of entity typing in fictional texts.

Suppose a literature analyst is doing research on a collection of unfamiliar short stories from fanfiction.net. Their goal is to understand the setting of each story, to answer questions such as what the stories are about (e.g. politics or supernatural), what types of characters the authors create, finding all instances of a type or a combination of types (e.g. female elves) or to do further analysis like if female elves are more frequent than male elves and if there are patterns regarding where female villains appear mostly. Due to time constraints, the analyst cannot read all of stories manually. Instead of that, they can run ENTYFI on each story to extract the entity type system automatically. For instance, to analyze the story *Time Can't Heal Wounds Like These*[3], the analyst would paste the introduction of the story into the web interface of ENTYFI.

"Elladan and Elrohir are captured along with their mother, and in the pits below the unforgiving Redhorn one twin finds his final resting place. In a series of devastating events Imladris loose one of its princes and its lady. But everything is not over yet, and those left behind must lean to cope and fight on."

---

[3]*https://www.fanfiction.net/s/13484688/1/Time-Can-t-Heal-Wounds-Like-These*

Since they have no prior knowledge on the setting, they could let ENTYFI propose related universes for typing. After computing the similarity between the input and the reference universes from the database, ENTYFI would then propose *The Lord of the Rings, Vampires Diaries, Kid Icarus, Twin Peaks* and *Crossfire* as top 5 reference universes, respectively. The analyst may consider *The Lord of the Rings* and *Vampires Diaries*, top 2 in ranking, of particular interest, and in addition, select the universe *Forgotten Realms*, because that is influential in their literary domain. The analyst would then run ENTYFI with default settings, and get a list of entities with their predicted types as results. They could then see that ELLADAN and ELROHIR are recognized as `living thing, elves, hybrid people` and `characters`, while REDHORN as `living thing, villains, servants of morgoth`, and IMLADRIS as `location, kingdoms, landforms` and `elven cities`.

They could then decide to rerun the analysis with reference universes *The Lord of the Rings* and *Vampires Diaries* but without running type consolidation. By ignoring this module, the number of predicted types for each entity increases. Especially, ELLADAN & EHROHIR now are classified as `living thing, elves, characters`, but also `location` and `organization`. Similarly, REDHORN belongs to both `living thing` and `places`, while IMLADRIS is both a `kingdom` and a `devastating event`. Apparently, these incompatibilities in predictions appear when the system does not run type consolidation.

The analyst may wonder how the system performs when no reference universe is being used. By only selecting the real-world typing module (Choi et al., 2018), the predicted types for EL-

Mention	Settings		
	Default (Ref. universes + all modules)	Default without type consolidation	Only real-world typing
Elladan & Elrohir	men, hybrid peoples, elves of rivendell, real world, elves, characters, living thing, antagonists, supernatural, species, etc.	organization, men, the silmarillion characters, hybrid peoples, elves of rivendell, elves, characters, living thing, location, antagonists, vampire diaries characters, supernatural, etc.	athlete, god, character, body part, arm, person, goddess, companion, brother, child
Redhorn	creatures, villains, servants of morgoth, real world, minions of angmar, servants of sauron, species, living thing, characters, witches, supernatural, one	creatures, villains, evil, death, deaths in battle, servants of morgoth, minions of angmar, servants of sauron, characters, witches, places, arda, races, living thing, organization, etc.	city, god, tribe, county, holiday, body part, society, product, mountain, act
Imladris	kingdoms, location, realms, landforms, places, elven cities, eriador, elven realms, mordor, etc.	kingdoms, location, realms, arda, landforms, places, continents, organization, elven cities, etc.	city, writing, setting, castle, clan, location, character, eleven, etc.

Table 1: Results of ENTYFI on different settings.

LADAN & ELROHIR would change to `athlete, god, body part, arm, etc.` REDHORN now becomes a `city, god, tribe` and even an `act`, while IMLADRIS is a `city, writing, setting` and `castle`. The results show not only incompatible predictions, but also that the existing typing model in the real world domain lacks coverage on fictional domains. By using a database of fictional universes as reference, ENTYFI is able to fill these gaps, predict fictional types in a fine-grained level and remove incompatibilities in the final results. From this interaction, the literature analyst could conclude that the story is much related to *The Lord of the Rings*, which might help them to draw parallels and direct further manual investigations. Table 1 shows the result of this demonstration experience in details.

5 Related Work

Earliest approaches for entity typing are based on manually designed patterns (e.g., Hearst patterns (Hearst, 1992)) to extract explicit type candidates in given texts. These pattern-based approaches can achieve good precision, but their recall is low, and they are difficult to scale up.

Traditional named-entity recognition methods used both rule-based and supervised techniques to recognize and assign entity mentions into few coarse classes like `person`, `location` and `organization` (Sang and De Meulder, 2003; Finkel et al., 2005; Collobert et al., 2011; Lample et al., 2016). Recently, fine-grained named-entity recognition and typing are getting more attention (Ling and Weld, 2012; Corro et al., 2015; Shimaoka et al., 2017; Choi et al., 2018). Ling and Weld (2012) use a classic linear classifier to classify the mentions into a set of 112 types. At much larger scale, FINET (Corro et al., 2015) uses 16k types from the WordNet taxonomy as the targets for entity typing. FINET is a combination of pattern-based, mention-based and verb-based extractors to extract both explicit and implicit type candidates for the mentions from the contexts.

With the development of deep learning, many neural methods have been proposed (Dong et al., 2015; Shimaoka et al., 2017; Choi et al., 2018; Xu et al., 2018). Shimaoka et al. (2017) propose a neural network with LSTM and attention mechanisms to encode representations of a mention's contexts. Recently, Choi et al. (2018) use distant supervision to collect a training dataset which includes over 10k types. The model is trained with a multi-task objective function that aims to classify entity mentions into three levels: general (9 types), fine-grained (112 types) and ultra-fine (10201 types).

While most existing methods focus on entity mentions with single contexts (e.g. a sentence), ENTYFI attempts to work on long texts (e.g., a chapter of a book). By proposing a combination of supervised and unsupervised approaches, with a following consolidation step, ENTYFI is able to predict types for entity mentions based on different contexts, without producing incompatibilities in predictions.

Many web demo systems for entity typing have been built, such as Stanford NER[4], displaCy NER[5] and AllenNLP[6]. However, these systems all predict only a few coarse and real world types (4-16 types). ENTYFI is the first attempt to entity typing at a fine-grained level for fictional texts. In a related problem, the richness of Wikia has been utilized for entity linking and question answering (Gao and Cucerzan, 2017; Maqsud et al., 2014).

6 Conclusion

We have presented ENTYFI, an illustrative demonstration system for domain-specific and long-tail typing. We hope ENTYFI will prove useful both to language and cultural research, and to NLP researchers interested in understanding the challenges and opportunities in long-tail typing.

---

[4] http://nlp.stanford.edu:8080/ner/
[5] https://explosion.ai/demos/display-ent
[6] https://demo.allennlp.org/named-entity-recognition

References

Andrew Carlson, Justin Betteridge, Richard C Wang, Estevam R Hruschka Jr, and Tom M Mitchell. 2010. Coupled semi-supervised learning for information extraction. In *WSDM*.

Eunsol Choi, Omer Levy, Yejin Choi, and Luke Zettlemoyer. 2018. Ultra-fine entity typing. In *ACL*.

Cuong Xuan Chu, Simon Razniewski, and Gerhard Weikum. 2019. TiFi: Taxonomy induction for fictional domains. In *The Web Conference*.

Cuong Xuan Chu, Simon Razniewski, and Gerhard Weikum. 2020. ENTYFI: Entity typing in fictional texts. In *WSDM*.

Ronan Collobert, Jason Weston, Léon Bottou, Michael Karlen, Koray Kavukcuoglu, and Pavel Kuksa. 2011. Natural language processing (almost) from scratch. In *JMLR*.

Luciano del Corro, Abdalghani Abujabal, Rainer Gemulla, and Gerhard Weikum. 2015. Finet: Context-aware fine-grained named entity typing. In *ACL*.

Li Dong, Furu Wei, Hong Sun, Ming Zhou, and Ke Xu. 2015. A hybrid neural model for type classification of entity mentions. In *IJCAI*.

Jenny Rose Finkel, Trond Grenager, and Christopher Manning. 2005. Incorporating non-local information into information extraction systems by gibbs sampling. In *ACL*.

Yarin Gal and Zoubin Ghahramani. 2016. A theoretically grounded application of dropout in recurrent neural networks. In *NIPS*.

Ning Gao and Silviu Cucerzan. 2017. Entity linking to one thousand knowledge bases. In *ECIR*.

Alex Graves. 2012. Supervised sequence labelling. In *Supervised sequence labelling with recurrent neural networks*.

Luheng He, Kenton Lee, Mike Lewis, and Luke Zettlemoyer. 2017. Deep semantic role labeling: What works and what's next. In *ACL*.

Marti A Hearst. 1992. Automatic acquisition of hyponyms from large text corpora. In *COLING*.

Guillaume Lample, Miguel Ballesteros, Sandeep Subramanian, Kazuya Kawakami, and Chris Dyer. 2016. Neural architectures for named entity recognition. In *NAACL HLT*.

Changki Lee, Yi-Gyu Hwang, Hyo-Jung Oh, Soojong Lim, Jeong Heo, Chung-Hee Lee, Hyeon-Jin Kim, Ji-Hyun Wang, and Myung-Gil Jang. 2006. Fine-grained named entity recognition using conditional random fields for question answering. In *Asia Information Retrieval Symposium*.

Xiao Ling and Daniel S Weld. 2012. Fine-grained entity recognition. In *AAAI*.

Umar Maqsud, Sebastian Arnold, Michael Hülfenhaus, and Alan Akbik. 2014. Nerdle: Topic-specific question answering using wikia seeds. In *COLING*.

Jeffrey Pennington, Richard Socher, and Christopher Manning. 2014. Glove: Global vectors for word representation. In *EMNLP*.

Marta Recasens, Marie-Catherine de Marneffe, and Christopher Potts. 2013. The life and death of discourse entities: Identifying singleton mentions. In *NAACL*.

Erik F Sang and Fien De Meulder. 2003. Introduction to the CoNLL-2003 shared task: Language-independent named entity recognition. *arXiv*.

Julian Seitner, Christian Bizer, Kai Eckert, Stefano Faralli, Robert Meusel, Heiko Paulheim, and Simone Paolo Ponzetto. 2016. A large database of hypernymy relations extracted from the web. In *LREC*.

Sonse Shimaoka, Pontus Stenetorp, Kentaro Inui, and Sebastian Riedel. 2017. Neural architectures for fine-grained entity type classification. In *EACL*.

Bo Xu, Zheng Luo, Luyang Huang, Bin Liang, Yanghua Xiao, Deqing Yang, and Wei Wang. 2018. Metic: Multi-instance entity typing from corpus. In *CIKM*.

Yu Zhang, Guoguo Chen, Dong Yu, Kaisheng Yaco, Sanjeev Khudanpur, and James Glass. 2016. Highway long short-term memory rnns for distant speech recognition. In *ICASSP*.

The Language Interpretability Tool: Extensible, Interactive Visualizations and Analysis for NLP Models

Ian Tenney,[*] James Wexler,[*] Jasmijn Bastings, Tolga Bolukbasi,
Andy Coenen, Sebastian Gehrmann, Ellen Jiang, Mahima Pushkarna,
Carey Radebaugh, Emily Reif, Ann Yuan
Google Research
`{iftenney, jwexler}@google.com`

Abstract

We present the Language Interpretability Tool (LIT), an open-source platform for visualization and understanding of NLP models. We focus on core questions about model behavior: Why did my model make this prediction? When does it perform poorly? What happens under a controlled change in the input? LIT integrates local explanations, aggregate analysis, and counterfactual generation into a streamlined, browser-based interface to enable rapid exploration and error analysis. We include case studies for a diverse set of workflows, including exploring counterfactuals for sentiment analysis, measuring gender bias in coreference systems, and exploring local behavior in text generation. LIT supports a wide range of models—including classification, seq2seq, and structured prediction—and is highly extensible through a declarative, framework-agnostic API. LIT is under active development, with code and full documentation available at `https://github.com/pair-code/lit`.[1]

1 Introduction

Advances in modeling have brought unprecedented performance on many NLP tasks (e.g. Wang et al., 2019), but many questions remain about the behavior of these models under domain shift (Blitzer and Pereira, 2007) and adversarial settings (Jia and Liang, 2017), and for their tendencies to behave according to social biases (Bolukbasi et al., 2016; Caliskan et al., 2017) or shallow heuristics (e.g. McCoy et al., 2019; Poliak et al., 2018). For any new model, one might want to know: What kind of examples does my model perform poorly on? Why did my model make this prediction? And critically, does my model behave consistently if

---

[*] Equal contribution.

[1] A video walkthrough is available at `https://youtu.be/j0OfBWFUqIE`.

I change things like textual style, verb tense, or pronoun gender? Despite the recent explosion of work on model understanding and evaluation (e.g. Belinkov et al., 2020; Linzen et al., 2019; Ribeiro et al., 2020), there is no "silver bullet" for analysis. Practitioners must often experiment with many techniques, looking at local explanations, aggregate metrics, and counterfactual variations of the input to build a full understanding of model behavior.

Existing tools can assist with this process, but many come with limitations: offline tools such as TFMA (Mewald, 2019) can provide only aggregate metrics, interactive frontends (e.g. Wallace et al., 2019) may focus on single-datapoint explanation, and more integrated tools (e.g. Wexler et al., 2020; Mothilal et al., 2020; Strobelt et al., 2018) often work with only a narrow range of models. Switching between tools or adapting a new method from research code can take days of work, distracting from the real task of error analysis. An ideal workflow would be seamless and interactive: users should see the data, what the model does with it, and why, so they can quickly test hypotheses and build understanding.

With this in mind, we introduce the Language Interpretability Tool (LIT), a toolkit and browser-based user interface (UI) for NLP model understanding. LIT supports local explanations—including salience maps, attention, and rich visualizations of model predictions—as well as aggregate analysis—including metrics, embedding spaces, and flexible slicing—and allows users to seamlessly hop between them to test local hypotheses and validate them over a dataset. LIT provides first-class support for counterfactual generation: new datapoints can be added on the fly, and their effect on the model visualized immediately. Side-by-side comparison allows for two models, or two datapoints, to be visualized simultaneously.

We recognize that research workflows are con-

Proceedings of the 2020 EMNLP (Systems Demonstrations), pages 107–118
November 16-20, 2020. ©2020 Association for Computational Linguistics

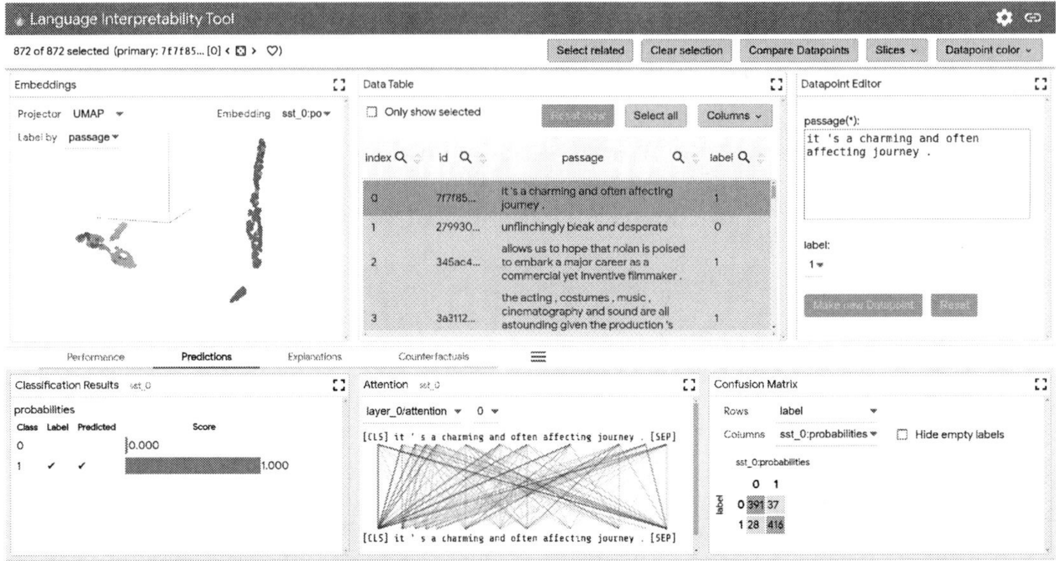

Figure 1: The LIT UI, showing a fine-tuned BERT (Devlin et al., 2019) model on the Stanford Sentiment Treebank (Socher et al., 2013) development set. The top half shows a selection toolbar, and, left-to-right: the embedding projector, the data table, and the datapoint editor. Tabs present different modules in the bottom half; the view above shows classifier predictions, an attention visualization, and a confusion matrix.

stantly evolving, and designed LIT along the following principles:

- **Flexible:** Support a wide range of NLP tasks, including classification, seq2seq, language modeling, and structured prediction.

- **Extensible:** Designed for experimentation, and can be reconfigured and extended for novel workflows.

- **Modular:** Components are self-contained, portable, and simple to implement.

- **Framework agnostic:** Works with any model that can run from Python —including TensorFlow (Abadi et al., 2015), PyTorch (Paszke et al., 2019), or remote models on a server.

- **Easy to use:** Low barrier to entry, with only a small amount of code needed to add models and data (Section 4.3), and an easy path to access sophisticated functionality.

2 User Interface and Functionality

LIT has a browser-based UI comprised of modules (Figure 1) which contain controls and visualizations for specific tasks (Table 1). At the most basic level, LIT works as a simple demo server: one can enter text, press a button, and see the model's predictions. But by loading an evaluation set, allowing dynamic datapoint generation, and an array of interactive visualizations, metrics, and modules that respond to user input, LIT supports a much richer set of user journeys:

J1 - Explore the dataset. Users can interactively explore datasets using different criteria across modules like the data table and the embeddings module (similar to Smilkov et al. (2016)), in which a PCA or UMAP (McInnes et al., 2018) projection can be rotated, zoomed, and panned to explore clusters and global structures (Figure 1-top left).

J2 - Find interesting datapoints. Users can identify interesting datapoints for analysis, cycle through them, and save selections for future use. For example, users can select off-diagonal groups from a confusion matrix, examine outlying clusters in embedding space, or select a range based on scalar values (Figure 4 (a)).

J3 - Explain local behavior. Users can deep-dive into model behavior on selected individual datapoints using a variety of modules depending on the model task and type. For instance, users can compare explanations from salience maps, including local gradients (Li et al., 2016) and LIME (Ribeiro et al., 2016), or look for patterns in attention heads (Figure 1-bottom).

Module	Description
Attention	Displays an attention visualization for each layer and head.
Confusion Matrix	A customizable confusion matrix for single model or multi-model comparison.
Counterfactual Generator	Creates counterfactuals for selected datapoint(s) using a variety of techniques.
Data Table	A tabular view of the data, with sorting, searching, and filtering support.
Datapoint Editor	Editable details of a selected datapoint.
Embeddings	Visualizes dataset by layer-wise embeddings, projected down to 3 dimensions.
Metrics Table	Displays metrics such as accuracy or BLEU score, on the whole dataset and slices.
Predictions	Displays model predictions, including classification, text generation, language model probabilities, and a graph visualization for structured prediction tasks.
Salience Maps	Shows heatmaps for token-based feature attribution for a selected datapoint using techniques like local gradients and LIME.
Scalar Plot	Displays a jitter plot organizing datapoints by model output scores, metrics or other scalar values.

Table 1: Built-in modules in the Language Interpretability Tool.

J4 - Generate new datapoints. Users can create new datapoints based on datapoints of interest either manually through edits, or with a range of automatic counterfactual generators, such as backtranslation (Bannard and Callison-Burch, 2005), nearest-neighbor retrieval (Andoni and Indyk, 2006), word substitutions ("great $\rightarrow$ terrible"), or adversarial attacks like HotFlip (Ebrahimi et al., 2018) (Figure A.1). Datapoint provenance is tracked to facilitate easy comparison.

J5 - Compare side-by-side. Users can interactively compare two or more models on the same data, or a single model on two datapoints simultaneously. Visualizations automatically "replicate" for a side-by-side view.

J6 - Compute metrics. LIT calculates and displays metrics for the whole dataset, the current selection, as well as on manual or automatically-generated slices (Figure 3 (c)) to easily find patterns in model performance.

LIT's interface allows these user journeys to be explored interactively. Selecting a dataset and model(s) will automatically show compatible modules in a multi-pane layout (Figure 1). A tabbed bottom panel groups modules by workflow and functionality, while the top panel shows persistent modules for dataset exploration.

These modules respond dynamically to user interactions. If a selection is made in the embedding projector, for example, the metrics table will respond automatically and compute scores on the selected datapoints. Global controls make it easy to

page through examples, enter a comparison mode, or save the selection as a named "slice". In this way, the user can quickly explore multiple workflows using different combinations of modules.

A brief video demonstration of the LIT UI is available at `https://youtu.be/j0OfBWFUqIE`.

3 Case Studies

Sentiment analysis. How well does a sentiment classifier handle negation? We load the development set of the Stanford Sentiment Treebank (SST; Socher et al., 2013), and use the search function in LIT's data table (**J1, J2**) to find the 56 datapoints containing the word "not". Looking at the Metrics Table (**J6**), we find that surprisingly, our BERT model (Devlin et al., 2019) gets 100% of these correct! But we might want to know if this is truly robust. With LIT, we can select individual datapoints and look for explanations (**J3**). For example, take the negative review, "*It's not the ultimate depression-era gangster movie.*". As shown in Figure 2, salience maps suggest that "not" and "ultimate" are important to the prediction.

We can verify this by creating modified inputs, using LIT's datapoint editor (**J4**). Removing "not" gets a strongly positive prediction from "*It's the ultimate depression-era gangster movie.*", while replacing "ultimate" to get "*It's not the worst depression-era gangster movie.*" elicits a mildly positive score from our model.

Gender bias in coreference. Does a system encode gendered associations, which might lead to incorrect predictions? We load a coreference model

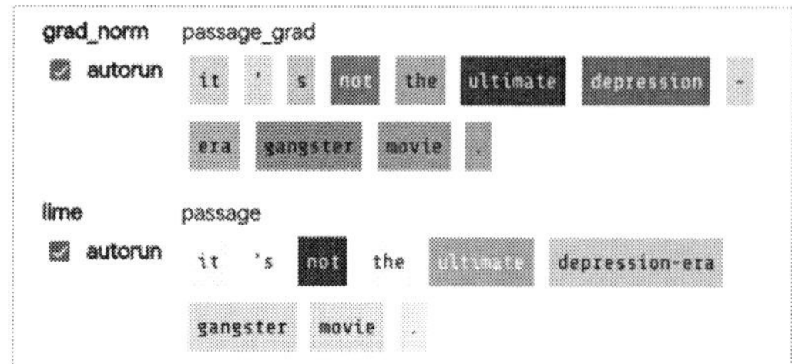

Figure 2: Salience maps on *"It's not the ultimate depression-era gangster movie."*, suggesting that "not" and "ultimate" are important to the model's prediction.

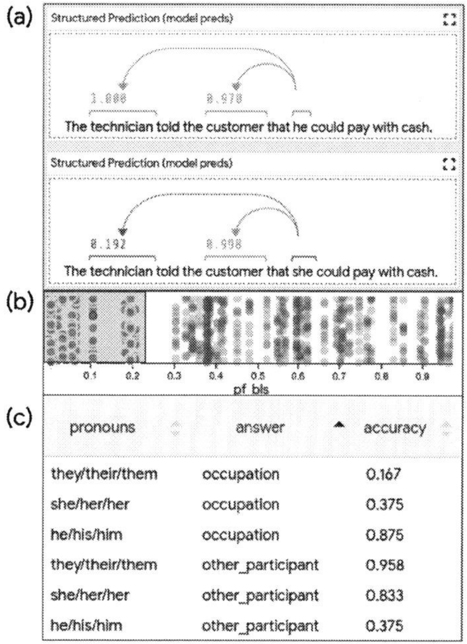

Figure 3: Exploring a coreference model on the Winogender dataset.

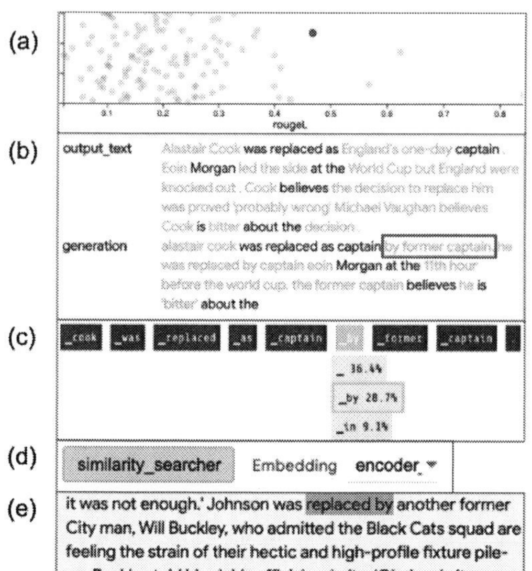

Figure 4: Investigating a local generation error, from selection of an interesting example to finding relevant training datapoints that led to an error.

trained on OntoNotes (Hovy et al., 2006), and load the Winogender (Rudinger et al., 2018) dataset into LIT for evaluation. Each Winogender example has a pronoun and two candidate referents, one a occupation term like ("technician") and one an "other participant" (like "customer"). Our model predicts coreference probabilities for each candidate. We can explore the model's sensitivity to pronouns by comparing two examples side-by-side (see Figure 3 (a).) We can see how commonly the model makes similar errors by paging through the dataset (**J1**), or by selecting specific slices of interest. For example, we can use the scalar plot module (**J2**) (Figure 3 (b)) to select datapoints where the occupation term is associated with a high proportion of male or female workers, according to the U.S. Bureau of

Labor Statistics (BLS; Caliskan et al., 2017).

In the Metrics Table (**J6**), we can slice this selection by pronoun type and by the true referent. On the set of male-dominated occupations ($< 25\%$ female by BLS), we see the model performs well when the ground-truth agrees with the stereotype - e.g. when the answer is the occupation term, male pronouns are correctly resolved 83% of the time, compared to female pronouns only 37.5% of the time (Figure 3 (c)).

Debugging text generation. Does the training data explain a particular error in text generation? We analyze a T5 (Raffel et al., 2019) model on the CNN-DM summarization task (Hermann et al., 2015), and loosely follow the steps of Strobelt et al. (2018). LIT's scalar plot module (**J2**) allows us to look at per-example ROUGE scores, and quickly select an example with middling performance (Figure 4 (a)). We find the generated text (Figure 4 (b)) contains an erroneous constituent: *"alastair cook was replaced as captain by former captain ...".* We can dig deeper, using LIT's language modeling module (Figure 4 (c)) to see that the token "by" is predicted with high probability (28.7%).

To find out how T5 arrived at this prediction, we utilize the "similarity searcher" component through the counterfactual generator tab (Figure 4 (d)). This performs a fast approximate nearest-neighbor lookup (Andoni and Indyk, 2006) from a pre-built index over the training corpus, using embeddings from the T5 decoder. With one click, we can retrieve 25 nearest neighbors and add them to the LIT UI for inspection (as in Figure A.1). We see that the words "captain" and "former" appear 34 and 16 times in these examples–along with 3 occurrences of "replaced by" (Figure 4 (e))–suggesting a strong prior toward our erroneous phrase.

4 System design and components

The LIT UI is written in TypeScript, and communicates with a Python backend that hosts models, datasets, counterfactual generators, and other interpretation components. LIT is agnostic to modeling frameworks; data is exchanged using NumPy arrays and JSON, and components are integrated through a declarative "spec" system (Section 4.4) that minimizes cross-dependencies and encourages modularity. A more detailed design schematic is given in the Appendix, Figure A.2.

4.1 Frontend

The browser-based UI is a single-page web app, built with lit-element[2] and MobX[3]. A shared framework of "service" objects tracks interaction state, such as the active model, dataset, and selection, and coordinates a set of otherwise-independent modules which provide controls and visualizations.

4.2 Backend

The Python backend serves models, data, and interpretation components. The server is stateless, but includes a caching layer for model predictions, which frees components from needing to store intermediate results and allows interactive use of large models like BERT (Devlin et al., 2019) and GPT-2 (Radford et al., 2019). Component types include:

- **Models** which implement a `predict()` function, `input_spec()`, and `output_spec()`.

- **Datasets** which load data from any source and expose an `.examples` field and a `spec()`.

- **Interpreters** are called on a model and a set of datapoints, and return output—such as a salience map—that may also depend on the model's predictions.

- **Generators** are interpreters that return new input datapoints from source datapoints.

- **Metrics** are interpreters which return aggregate scores for a list of inputs.

These components are designed to be self-contained and interact through minimalist APIs, with most exposing only one or two methods plus spec information. They communicate through standard Python and NumPy types, making LIT compatible with most common modeling frameworks, including TensorFlow (Abadi et al., 2015) and Py-Torch (Paszke et al., 2019). Components are also portable, and can easily be used in a notebook or standalone script. For example:

```
dataset = SSTData(...)
model = SentimentModel(...)
lime = lime_explainer.LIME()
lime.run([dataset.examples[0]],
         model, dataset)
```

will run the LIME (Ribeiro et al., 2016) component and return a list of tokens and their importance to the model prediction.

4.3 Running with your own model

LIT is built as a Python library, and its typical use is to create a short `demo.py` script that loads models and data and passes them to the `lit.Server` class:

```
models = {'foo': FooModel(...),
          'bar': BarModel(...)}
datasets = {'baz': BazDataset(...)}
server = lit.Server(models, datasets)
server.serve()
```

A full example script is included in the Appendix (Figure A.3). The same server can host several models and datasets for side-by-side comparison, and can also interact with remotely-hosted models.

4.4 Extensibility: the `spec()` system

NLP models come in many shapes, with inputs that may involve multiple text segments, additional categorical features, scalars, and more, and output modalities that include classification, regression, text generation, and span labeling. Models may have multiple heads of different types, and may also return additional values like gradients, embeddings, or attention maps. Rather than enumerate all variations, LIT describes each model and dataset with an extensible system of semantic types.

For example, a dataset class for textual entailment (Dagan et al., 2006; Bowman et al., 2015) might have `spec()`, describing available fields:

- **premise:** `TextSegment()`
- **hypothesis:** `TextSegment()`
- **label:** `MulticlassLabel(vocab=...)`

A model for the same task would have an `input_spec()` to describe required inputs:

- **premise:** `TextSegment()`
- **hypothesis:** `TextSegment()`

As well as an `output_spec()` to describe its predictions:

- **probas:** `MulticlassPreds(`
      `vocab=..., parent="label")`

Other LIT components can read this spec, and infer how to operate on the data. For example, the `MulticlassMetrics` component searches for `MulticlassPreds` fields (which contain probabilities), uses the `vocab` annotation to decode to string labels, and evaluates these against the input field described by `parent`. Frontend modules can detect these fields, and automatically display: for example, the embedding projector will appear if `Embeddings` are available.

New types can be easily defined: a `SpanLabels` class might represent the output of a named entity recognition model, and custom components can be added to interpret it.

5 Related Work

A number of tools exist for interactive analysis of trained ML models. Many are general-purpose, such as the What-If Tool (Wexler et al., 2020), Captum (Kokhlikyan et al., 2019), Manifold (Zhang et al., 2018), or InterpretML (Nori et al., 2019), while others focus on specific applications like fairness, including FairVis (Cabrera et al., 2019) and FairSight (Ahn and Lin, 2019). And some provide rich support for counterfactual analysis, either within-dataset (What-If Tool) or dynamically generated as in DiCE (Mothilal et al., 2020).

For NLP, a number of tools exist for specific model classes, such as RNNs (Strobelt et al., 2017), Transformers (Hoover et al., 2020; Vig and Belinkov, 2019), or text generation (Strobelt et al., 2018). More generally, AllenNLP Interpret (Wallace et al., 2019) introduces a modular framework for interpretability components, focused on single-datapoint explanations and integrated tightly with the AllenNLP (Gardner et al., 2017) framework.

While many components exist in other tools, LIT aims to integrate local explanations, aggregate analysis, and counterfactual generation into a single tool. In this, it is most similar to Errudite (Wu et al., 2019), which provides an integrated UI for NLP error analysis, including a custom DSL for text transformations and the ability to evaluate over a corpus. However, LIT is explicitly designed for flexibility: we support a broad range of workflows and provide a modular design for extension with new tasks, visualizations, and generation techniques.

Limitations LIT is an evaluation tool, and as such is not directly useful for training-time monitoring. As LIT is built to be interactive, it does not scale to large datasets as well as offline tools such as TFMA (Mewald, 2019). (Currently, the LIT UI can handle about 10,000 examples at once.) Because LIT is framework-agnostic, it does not have the deep model integration of tools such as AllenNLP Interpret (Wallace et al., 2019) or Captum (Kokhlikyan et al., 2019). This makes many things simpler and more portable, but also requires more code for techniques like integrated gradients (Sundararajan et al., 2017) that need to directly manipulate parts of the model.

6 Conclusion and Roadmap

LIT provides an integrated UI and a suite of components for visualizing and exploring the behavior of NLP models. It enables interactive analysis both at the single-datapoint level and over a whole dataset, with first-class support for counterfactual generation and evaluation. LIT supports a diverse range of workflows, from explaining individual predictions to disaggregated analysis to probing for bias through counterfactuals. LIT also supports a range of model types and techniques out of the box, and is designed for extensibility through simple, framework-agnostic APIs.

LIT is under active development by a small team. Planned upcoming additions include new counterfactual generation plug-ins, additional metrics and visualizations for sequence and structured output types, and a greater ability to customize the UI for different applications.

LIT is open-source under an Apache 2.0 license, and we welcome contributions from the community at `https://github.com/pair-code/lit`.

Acknowledgments

We thank Slav Petrov, Martin Wattenberg, Fernanda Viegas, Kellie Webster, Emily Pitler, Dipanjan Das, Leslie Lai, Kristen Olson, and other members of PAIR and the Language team at Google Research for many productive discussions during development. We also thank our anonymous reviewers for their helpful feedback, and Pere Lluis, Luke Gessler, and Kevin Robinson for their contributions to the open-source code.

References

Martín Abadi, Ashish Agarwal, Paul Barham, Eugene Brevdo, Zhifeng Chen, Craig Citro, Greg S. Corrado, Andy Davis, Jeffrey Dean, Matthieu Devin, Sanjay Ghemawat, Ian Goodfellow, Andrew Harp, Geoffrey Irving, Michael Isard, Yangqing Jia, Rafal Jozefowicz, Lukasz Kaiser, Manjunath Kudlur, Josh Levenberg, Dandelion Mané, Rajat Monga, Sherry Moore, Derek Murray, Chris Olah, Mike Schuster, Jonathon Shlens, Benoit Steiner, Ilya Sutskever, Kunal Talwar, Paul Tucker, Vincent Vanhoucke, Vijay Vasudevan, Fernanda Viégas, Oriol Vinyals, Pete Warden, Martin Wattenberg, Martin Wicke, Yuan Yu, and Xiaoqiang Zheng. 2015. TensorFlow: Large-scale machine learning on heterogeneous systems. Software available from tensorflow.org.

Yongsu Ahn and Yu-Ru Lin. 2019. Fairsight: Visual analytics for fairness in decision making. *IEEE Transactions on Visualization and Computer Graphics*, page 1–1.

Alexandr Andoni and Piotr Indyk. 2006. Near-optimal hashing algorithms for approximate nearest neighbor in high dimensions. In *2006 47th annual IEEE symposium on foundations of computer science (FOCS'06)*, pages 459–468. IEEE.

Colin Bannard and Chris Callison-Burch. 2005. Paraphrasing with bilingual parallel corpora. In *Proceedings of the 43rd Annual Meeting of the Association for Computational Linguistics (ACL'05)*, pages 597–604, Ann Arbor, Michigan. Association for Computational Linguistics.

Yonatan Belinkov, Sebastian Gehrmann, and Ellie Pavlick. 2020. Interpretability and analysis in neural NLP. In *Proceedings of the 58th Annual Meeting of the Association for Computational Linguistics: Tutorial Abstracts*, pages 1–5, Online. Association for Computational Linguistics.

John Blitzer and Fernando Pereira. 2007. Domain adaptation of natural language processing systems. *University of Pennsylvania*, pages 1–106.

Tolga Bolukbasi, Kai-Wei Chang, James Y Zou, Venkatesh Saligrama, and Adam T Kalai. 2016. Man is to computer programmer as woman is to homemaker? debiasing word embeddings. In *Advances in Neural Information Processing Systems 29*, pages 4349–4357.

Samuel R. Bowman, Gabor Angeli, Christopher Potts, and Christopher D. Manning. 2015. A large annotated corpus for learning natural language inference. In *Proceedings of the 2015 Conference on Empirical Methods in Natural Language Processing*, pages 632–642, Lisbon, Portugal. Association for Computational Linguistics.

Ángel Alexander Cabrera, Will Epperson, Fred Hohman, Minsuk Kahng, Jamie Morgenstern, and Duen Horng Chau. 2019. Fairvis: Visual analytics for discovering intersectional bias in machine learning. In *2019 IEEE Conference on Visual Analytics Science and Technology (VAST)*, pages 46–56. IEEE.

Aylin Caliskan, Joanna J. Bryson, and Arvind Narayanan. 2017. Semantics derived automatically from language corpora contain human-like biases. *Science*, 356(6334):183–186.

Ido Dagan, Oren Glickman, and Bernardo Magnini. 2006. The pascal recognising textual entailment challenge. In *Machine Learning Challenges. Evaluating Predictive Uncertainty, Visual Object Classification, and Recognising Tectual Entailment*, pages 177–190, Berlin, Heidelberg. Springer Berlin Heidelberg.

Jacob Devlin, Ming-Wei Chang, Kenton Lee, and Kristina Toutanova. 2019. BERT: Pre-training of deep bidirectional transformers for language understanding. In *Proceedings of the 2019 Conference of the North American Chapter of the Association for Computational Linguistics: Human Language Technologies, Volume 1 (Long and Short Papers)*, pages 4171–4186, Minneapolis, Minnesota. Association for Computational Linguistics.

Javid Ebrahimi, Anyi Rao, Daniel Lowd, and Dejing Dou. 2018. HotFlip: White-box adversarial examples for text classification. In *Proceedings of the 56th Annual Meeting of the Association for Computational Linguistics (Volume 2: Short Papers)*, pages 31–36, Melbourne, Australia. Association for Computational Linguistics.

Matt Gardner, Joel Grus, Mark Neumann, Oyvind Tafjord, Pradeep Dasigi, Nelson F. Liu, Matthew Peters, Michael Schmitz, and Luke S. Zettlemoyer. 2017. AllenNLP: A deep semantic natural language processing platform.

Karl Moritz Hermann, Tomas Kocisky, Edward Grefenstette, Lasse Espeholt, Will Kay, Mustafa Suleyman, and Phil Blunsom. 2015. Teaching machines to read and comprehend. In *Advances in Neural Information Processing Systems 28*, pages 1693–1701.

Benjamin Hoover, Hendrik Strobelt, and Sebastian Gehrmann. 2020. exBERT: A visual analysis tool to explore learned representations in Transformer models. In *Proceedings of the 58th Annual Meeting of the Association for Computational Linguistics: System Demonstrations*, pages 187–196, Online. Association for Computational Linguistics.

Eduard Hovy, Mitchell Marcus, Martha Palmer, Lance Ramshaw, and Ralph Weischedel. 2006. Ontonotes: The 90% solution. In *Proceedings of the Human Language Technology Conference of the NAACL, Companion Volume: Short Papers*, NAACL-Short '06, pages 57–60, Stroudsburg, PA, USA. Association for Computational Linguistics.

Robin Jia and Percy Liang. 2017. Adversarial examples for evaluating reading comprehension systems. In *Proceedings of the 2017 Conference on Empirical Methods in Natural Language Processing*, pages 2021–2031, Copenhagen, Denmark. Association for Computational Linguistics.

Narine Kokhlikyan, Vivek Miglani, Miguel Martin, Edward Wang, Jonathan Reynolds, Alexander Melnikov, Natalia Lunova, and Orion Reblitz-Richardson. 2019. Pytorch captum. `https://github.com/pytorch/captum`.

Jiwei Li, Xinlei Chen, Eduard Hovy, and Dan Jurafsky. 2016. Visualizing and understanding neural models in NLP. In *Proceedings of the 2016 Conference of the North American Chapter of the Association for Computational Linguistics: Human Language Technologies*, pages 681–691, San Diego, California. Association for Computational Linguistics.

Tal Linzen, Grzegorz Chrupała, Yonatan Belinkov, and Dieuwke Hupkes, editors. 2019. *Proceedings of the 2019 ACL Workshop BlackboxNLP: Analyzing and Interpreting Neural Networks for NLP*. Association for Computational Linguistics, Florence, Italy.

Tom McCoy, Ellie Pavlick, and Tal Linzen. 2019. Right for the wrong reasons: Diagnosing syntactic heuristics in natural language inference. In *Proceedings of the 57th Annual Meeting of the Association for Computational Linguistics*, pages 3428–3448, Florence, Italy. Association for Computational Linguistics.

Leland McInnes, John Healy, and James Melville. 2018. Umap: Uniform manifold approximation and projection for dimension reduction. *arXiv preprint arXiv:1802.03426*.

Clemens Mewald. 2019. Introducing tensorflow model analysis: Scaleable, sliced, and full-pass metrics. `https://blog.tensorflow.org/2018/03/introducing-tensorflow-model-analysis.html`.

Ramaravind K Mothilal, Amit Sharma, and Chenhao Tan. 2020. Explaining machine learning classifiers through diverse counterfactual explanations. In *Proceedings of the 2020 Conference on Fairness, Accountability, and Transparency*, pages 607–617.

Harsha Nori, Samuel Jenkins, Paul Koch, and Rich Caruana. 2019. InterpretML: A unified framework for machine learning interpretability. *arXiv preprint arXiv:1909.09223*.

Adam Paszke, Sam Gross, Francisco Massa, Adam Lerer, James Bradbury, Gregory Chanan, Trevor Killeen, Zeming Lin, Natalia Gimelshein, Luca Antiga, Alban Desmaison, Andreas Kopf, Edward Yang, Zachary DeVito, Martin Raison, Alykhan Tejani, Sasank Chilamkurthy, Benoit Steiner, Lu Fang, Junjie Bai, and Soumith Chintala. 2019. Pytorch: An imperative style, high-performance deep learning library. In *Advances in Neural Information Processing Systems 32*, pages 8024–8035.

Adam Poliak, Jason Naradowsky, Aparajita Haldar, Rachel Rudinger, and Benjamin Van Durme. 2018. Hypothesis only baselines in natural language inference. In *Proceedings of the Seventh Joint Conference on Lexical and Computational Semantics*, pages 180–191, New Orleans, Louisiana. Association for Computational Linguistics.

Alec Radford, Jeffrey Wu, Rewon Child, David Luan, Dario Amodei, and Ilya Sutskever. 2019. Language models are unsupervised multi-task learners. `https://blog.openai.com/better-language-models`.

Colin Raffel, Noam Shazeer, Adam Roberts, Katherine Lee, Sharan Narang, Michael Matena, Yanqi Zhou, Wei Li, and Peter J. Liu. 2019. Exploring the limits of transfer learning with a unified text-to-text transformer. *arXiv e-prints*.

Marco Ribeiro, Sameer Singh, and Carlos Guestrin. 2016. "why should I trust you?": Explaining the predictions of any classifier. In *Proceedings of the 2016 Conference of the North American Chapter of the Association for Computational Linguistics: Demonstrations*, pages 97–101, San Diego, California. Association for Computational Linguistics.

Marco Tulio Ribeiro, Tongshuang Wu, Carlos Guestrin, and Sameer Singh. 2020. Beyond accuracy: Behavioral testing of NLP models with CheckList. In *Proceedings of the 58th Annual Meeting of the Association for Computational Linguistics*, pages 4902–4912, Online. Association for Computational Linguistics.

Rachel Rudinger, Jason Naradowsky, Brian Leonard, and Benjamin Van Durme. 2018. Gender bias in coreference resolution. In *Proceedings of the 2018 Conference of the North American Chapter of the Association for Computational Linguistics: Human Language Technologies, Volume 2 (Short Papers)*, pages 8–14, New Orleans, Louisiana. Association for Computational Linguistics.

Daniel Smilkov, Nikhil Thorat, Charles Nicholson, Emily Reif, Fernanda B Viégas, and Martin Wattenberg. 2016. Embedding projector: Interactive visualization and interpretation of embeddings. In *NIPS*

2016 Workshop on Interpretable Machine Learning in Complex Systems.

Richard Socher, Alex Perelygin, Jean Wu, Jason Chuang, Christopher D. Manning, Andrew Ng, and Christopher Potts. 2013. Recursive deep models for semantic compositionality over a sentiment treebank. In *Proceedings of the 2013 Conference on Empirical Methods in Natural Language Processing*, pages 1631–1642, Seattle, Washington, USA. Association for Computational Linguistics.

Hendrik Strobelt, Sebastian Gehrmann, Michael Behrisch, Adam Perer, Hanspeter Pfister, and Alexander M Rush. 2018. Seq2seq-vis: A visual debugging tool for sequence-to-sequence models. *IEEE transactions on visualization and computer graphics*, 25(1):353–363.

Hendrik Strobelt, Sebastian Gehrmann, Hanspeter Pfister, and Alexander M Rush. 2017. LSTMvis: A tool for visual analysis of hidden state dynamics in recurrent neural networks. *IEEE transactions on visualization and computer graphics*, 24(1):667–676.

Mukund Sundararajan, Ankur Taly, and Qiqi Yan. 2017. Axiomatic attribution for deep networks. In *Proceedings of the 34th International Conference on Machine Learning*, volume 70, pages 3319–3328. PMLR.

Jesse Vig and Yonatan Belinkov. 2019. Analyzing the structure of attention in a transformer language model. In *Proceedings of the 2019 ACL Workshop BlackboxNLP: Analyzing and Interpreting Neural Networks for NLP*, pages 63–76, Florence, Italy. Association for Computational Linguistics.

Eric Wallace, Jens Tuyls, Junlin Wang, Sanjay Subramanian, Matt Gardner, and Sameer Singh. 2019. AllenNLP interpret: A framework for explaining predictions of NLP models. In *Proceedings of the 2019 Conference on Empirical Methods in Natural Language Processing and the 9th International Joint Conference on Natural Language Processing (EMNLP-IJCNLP): System Demonstrations*, pages 7–12, Hong Kong, China. Association for Computational Linguistics.

Alex Wang, Amanpreet Singh, Julian Michael, Felix Hill, Omer Levy, and Samuel R. Bowman. 2019. GLUE: A multi-task benchmark and analysis platform for natural language understanding. In *International Conference on Learning Representations*.

J. Wexler, M. Pushkarna, T. Bolukbasi, M. Wattenberg, F. Viégas, and J. Wilson. 2020. The what-if tool: Interactive probing of machine learning models. *IEEE Transactions on Visualization and Computer Graphics*, 26(1):56–65.

Adina Williams, Nikita Nangia, and Samuel Bowman. 2018. A broad-coverage challenge corpus for sentence understanding through inference. In *Proceedings of the 2018 Conference of the North American Chapter of the Association for Computational Linguistics: Human Language Technologies, Volume 1 (Long Papers)*, pages 1112–1122. Association for Computational Linguistics.

Tongshuang Wu, Marco Tulio Ribeiro, Jeffrey Heer, and Daniel Weld. 2019. Errudite: Scalable, reproducible, and testable error analysis. In *Proceedings of the 57th Annual Meeting of the Association for Computational Linguistics*, pages 747–763, Florence, Italy. Association for Computational Linguistics.

Jiawei Zhang, Yang Wang, Piero Molino, Lezhi Li, and David Ebert. 2018. Manifold: A model-agnostic framework for interpretation and diagnosis of machine learning models. *IEEE Transactions on Visualization and Computer Graphics*, PP:1–1.

A Appendices

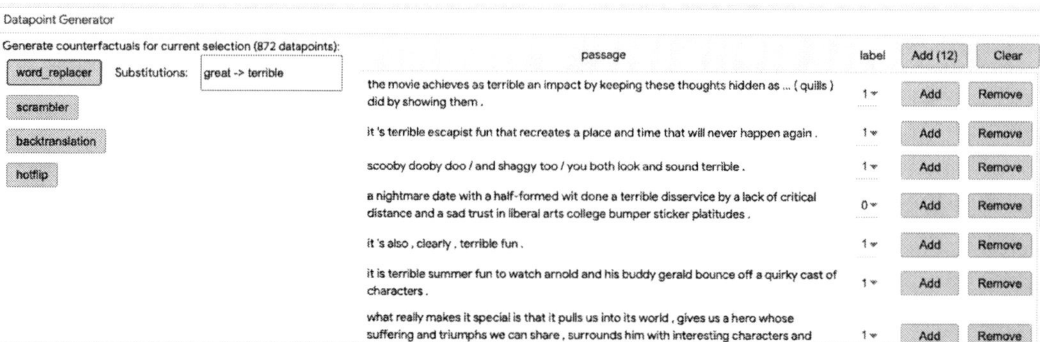

Figure A.1: The counterfactual generator module, showing a set of generated datapoints in the staging area. The labels can be maually edited before adding these to the dataset. In this example, the counterfactuals were created using the word replacer, replacing the word "great" with "terrible" in each passage.

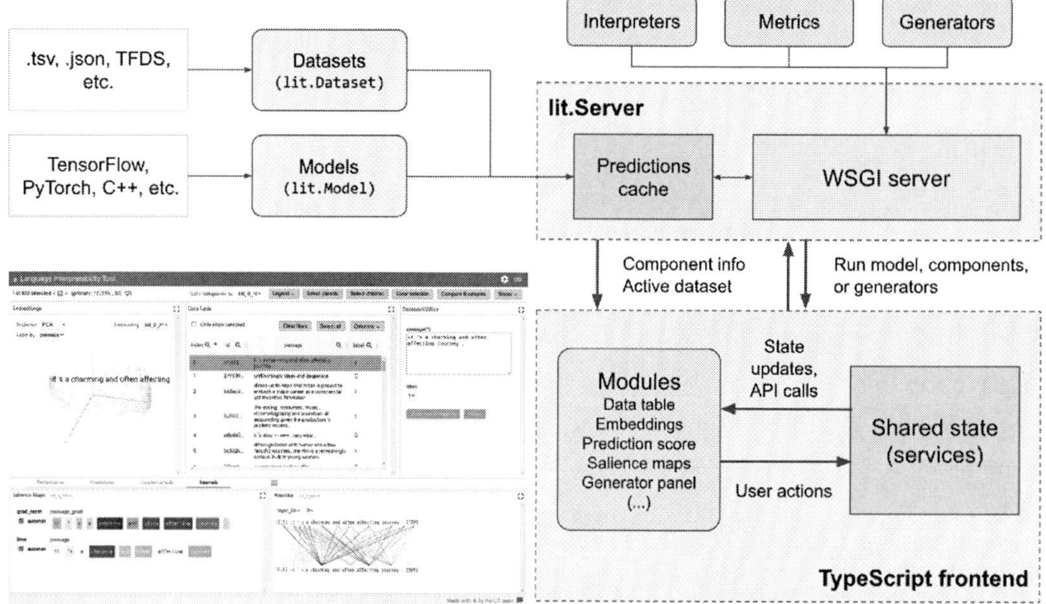

Figure A.2: Overview of LIT system architecture. The backend manages models, datasets, metrics, generators, and interpretation components, as well as a caching layer to speed up interactive use. The frontend is a TypeScript single-page app consisting of independent modules (webcomponents built with lit-element) which interact with shared "services" that manage interaction state. The backend can be extended by passing components to the `lit.Server` class in the demo script (Section 4.3 and Figure A.3), while the frontend can be extended by importing new components in a single file, `layout.ts`, which both lists available modules and specifies their position in the UI (Figure 1).

```python
NLI_LABELS = ['entailment', 'neutral', 'contradiction']

class MultiNLIData(lit.Dataset):
  """Loader for MultiNLI dataset."""

  def __init__(self, path):
    # Read the eval set from a .tsv file
    df = pandas.read_csv(path, sep='\t')
    # Store as a list of dicts, conforming to self.spec()
    self._examples = [{
      'premise': row['sentence1'],
      'hypothesis': row['sentence2'],
      'label': row['gold_label'],
      'genre': row['genre'],
    } for _, row in df.iterrows()]

  def spec(self):
    return {
      'premise': lit_types.TextSegment(),
      'hypothesis': lit_types.TextSegment(),
      'label': lit_types.Label(vocab=NLI_LABELS),
      # We can include additional fields, which don't have to be used by the model.
      'genre': lit_types.Label(),
    }


class MyNLIModel(lit.Model):
  """Wrapper for a Natural Language Inference model."""

  def __init__(self, model_path, **kw):
    # Load the model into memory so we're ready for interactive use.
    self._model = _load_my_model(model_path, **kw)

  ##
  # LIT API implementations
  def predict(self, inputs: List[Input]) -> Iterable[Preds]:
    """Predict on a single minibatch of examples."""
    examples = [self._model.convert_dict_input(d) for d in inputs]  # any custom preprocessing
    return self._model.predict_examples(examples)  # returns a dict for each input

  def input_spec(self):
    """Describe the inputs to the model."""
    return {
        'premise': lit_types.TextSegment(),
        'hypothesis': lit_types.TextSegment(),
    }

  def output_spec(self):
    """Describe the model outputs."""
    return {
      # The 'parent' keyword tells LIT where to look for gold labels when computing metrics.
      'probas': lit_types.MulticlassPreds(vocab=NLI_LABELS, parent='label'),
      # This model returns two different embeddings, but you can easily add more.
      'output_embs': lit_types.Embeddings(),
      'mean_word_embs':  lit_types.Embeddings(),
      # In LIT, we treat tokens as another model output. There can be more than one,
      # and the 'align' field describes which input segment they correspond to.
      'premise_tokens': lit_types.Tokens(align='premise'),
      'hypothesis_tokens': lit_types.Tokens(align='hypothesis'),
      # Gradients are also returned by the model; 'align' here references a Tokens field.
      'premise_grad': lit_types.TokenGradients(align='premise_tokens'),
      'hypothesis_grad': lit_types.TokenGradients(align='hypothesis_tokens'),
      # Similarly, attention references a token field, but here we want the model's full "internal"
      # tokenization, which might be something like: [START] foo bar baz [SEP] spam eggs [END]
      'tokens': lit_types.Tokens(),
      'attention_layer0': lit_types.AttentionHeads(align=['tokens', 'tokens']),
      'attention_layer1': lit_types.AttentionHeads(align=['tokens', 'tokens']),
      'attention_layer2': lit_types.AttentionHeads(align=['tokens', 'tokens']),
      # ...and so on. Since the spec is just a dictionary of dataclasses, you can populate it
      # in a loop if you have many similar fields.
    }


def main(_):
  datasets = {
      'mnli_matched': MultiNLIData('/path/to/dev_matched.tsv'),
      'mnli_mismatched': MultiNLIData('/path/to/dev_mismatched.tsv'),
  }

  models = {
      'model_foo': MyNLIModel('/path/to/model/foo/files'),
      'model_bar': MyNLIModel('/path/to/model/bar/files'),
  }

  lit_demo = lit.Server(models, datasets, port=4321)
  lit_demo.serve()

if __name__ == '__main__':
  main()
```

Figure A.3: Example demo script to run LIT with two NLI models and the MultiNLI (Williams et al., 2018) development sets. The actual model can be implemented in TensorFlow, PyTorch, C++, a REST API, or anything that can be wrapped in a Python class: to work with LIT, users needs only to define the spec fields and implement a `predict()` function which returns a dict of NumPy arrays for each input datapoint. The dataset loader is even simpler; a complete implementation is given above to read from a TSV file, but libraries like TensorFlow Datasets can also be used.

117

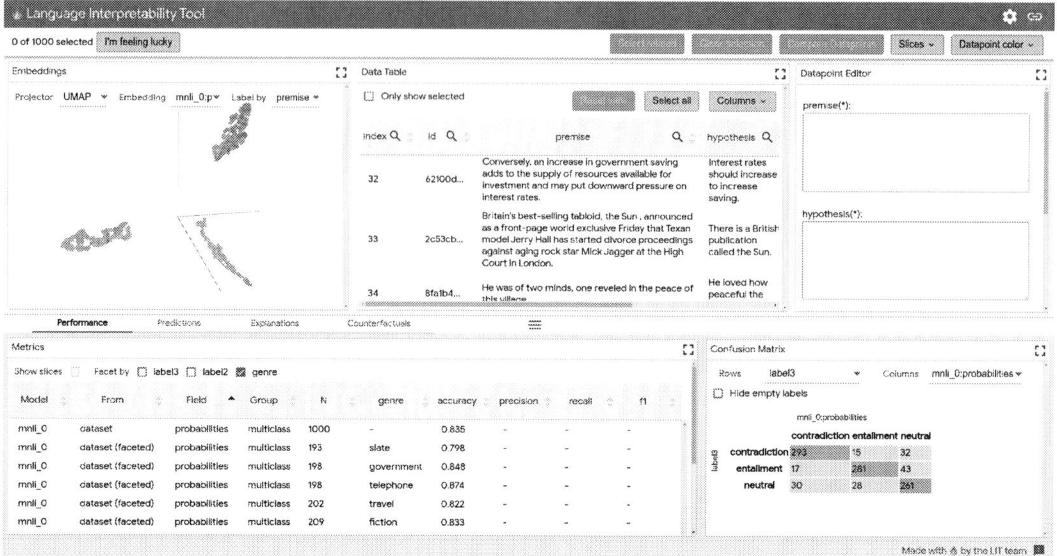

Figure A.4: Full UI screenshot, showing a BERT (Devlin et al., 2019) model on a sample from the "matched" split of the MultiNLI (Williams et al., 2018) development set. The embedding projector (top left) shows three clusters, corresponding to the output layer of the model, and colored by the true label. On the bottom, the metrics table shows accuracy scores faceted by genre, and a confusion matrix shows the model predictions against the gold labels.

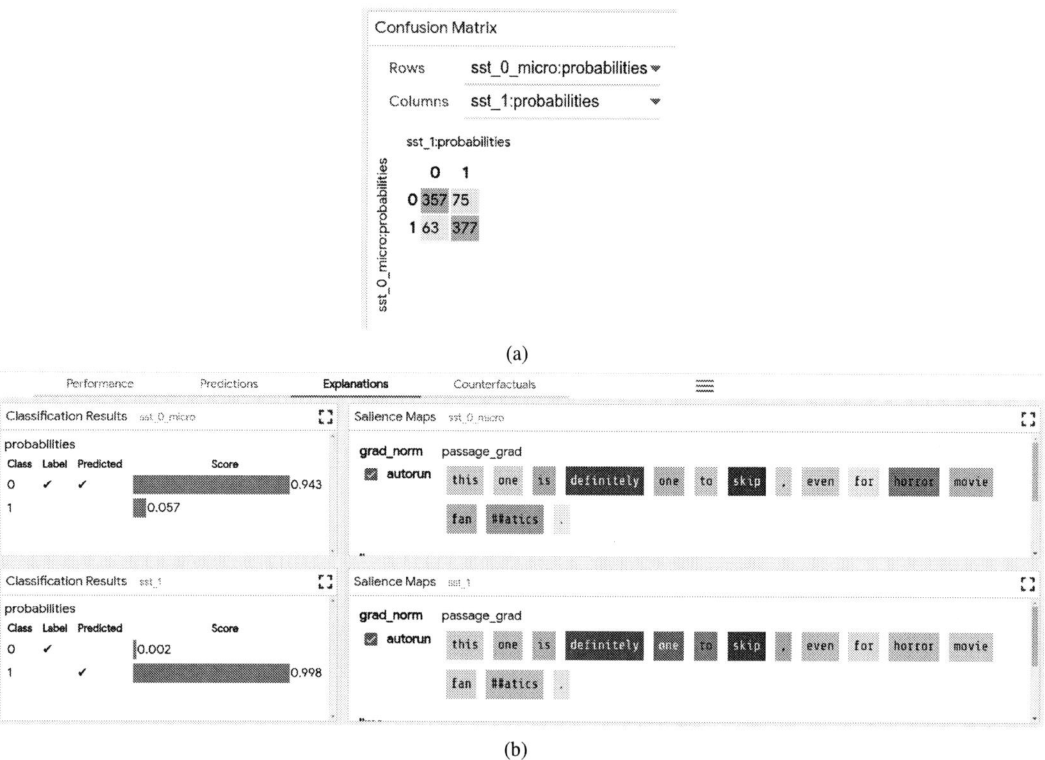

(a)

(b)

Figure A.5: Confusion matrix (a) and side-by-side comparison of predictions and salience maps (b) on two sentiment classifiers. In model comparison mode, the confusion matrix can compare two models, and clicking an off-diagonal cell with select examples where the two models make different predictions. In (b) we see one such example, where the model in the second row ("sst_1") predicts incorrectly, even though gradient-based salience show both models focusing on the same tokens.

TextAttack: A Framework for Adversarial Attacks, Data Augmentation, and Adversarial Training in NLP

John X. Morris[1], Eli Lifland[1], Jin Yong Yoo[1], Jake Grigsby[1], Di Jin[2], Yanjun Qi[1]

[1] Department of Computer Science, University of Virginia
[2] Computer Science and Artificial Intelligence Laboratory, MIT
{jm8wx, yq2h}@virginia.edu

Abstract

While there has been substantial research using adversarial attacks to analyze NLP models, each attack is implemented in its own code repository. It remains challenging to develop NLP attacks and utilize them to improve model performance. This paper introduces TextAttack, a Python framework for adversarial attacks, data augmentation, and adversarial training in NLP. TextAttack builds attacks from four components: a goal function, a set of constraints, a transformation, and a search method. TextAttack's modular design enables researchers to easily construct attacks from combinations of novel and existing components. TextAttack provides implementations of 16 adversarial attacks from the literature and supports a variety of models and datasets, including BERT and other transformers, and all GLUE tasks. TextAttack also includes data augmentation and adversarial training modules for using components of adversarial attacks to improve model accuracy and robustness. TextAttack is democratizing NLP: anyone can try data augmentation and adversarial training on any model or dataset, with just a few lines of code. Code and tutorials are available at https://github.com/QData/TextAttack.

1 Introduction

Over the last few years, there has been growing interest in investigating the adversarial robustness of NLP models, including new methods for generating adversarial examples and better approaches to defending against these adversaries (Alzantot et al., 2018; Jin et al., 2019; Kuleshov et al., 2018; Li et al., 2019; Gao et al., 2018; Wang et al., 2019; Ebrahimi et al., 2017; Zang et al., 2020; Pruthi et al., 2019). It is difficult to compare these attacks directly and fairly, since they are often evaluated on different data samples and victim models. Re-

Original
Perfect performance by the actor → Positive (99%)

Adversarial
Spotless performance by the actor → Negative (100%)

Figure 1: Adversarial example generated using Jin et al. (2019)'s TextFooler for a BERT-based sentiment classifier. Swapping out "perfect" with synonym "spotless" completely changes the model's prediction, even though the underlying meaning of the text has not changed.

implementing previous work as a baseline is often time-consuming and error-prone due to a lack of source code, and precisely replicating results is complicated by small details left out of the publication. These barriers make benchmark comparisons hard to trust and severely hinder the development of this field.

To encourage the development of the adversarial robustness field, we introduce TextAttack, a Python framework for adversarial attacks, data augmentation, and adversarial training in NLP.

To unify adversarial attack methods into one system, we decompose NLP attacks into four components: a goal function, a set of constraints, a transformation, and a search method. The attack attempts to perturb an input text such that the model output fulfills the goal function (i.e., indicating whether the attack is successful) and the perturbation adheres to the set of constraints (e.g., grammar constraint, semantic similarity constraint). A search method is used to find a sequence of transformations that produce a successful adversarial example.

This modular design enables us to easily assemble attacks from the literature while reusing components that are shared across attacks. TextAttack provides clean, readable implementations of 16 adversarial attacks from the literature. For the first time, these attacks can be benchmarked, compared, and analyzed in a standardized setting.

119

Proceedings of the 2020 EMNLP (Systems Demonstrations), pages 119–126
November 16-20, 2020. ©2020 Association for Computational Linguistics

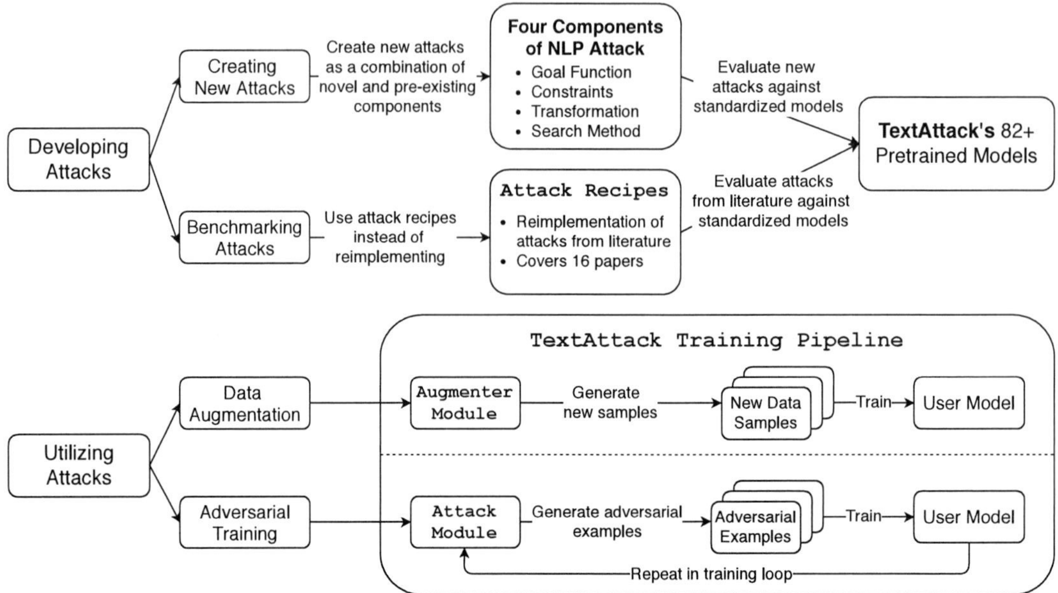

Figure 2: Main features of TextAttack.

TextAttack's design also allows researchers to easily construct new attacks from combinations of novel and existing components. In just a few lines of code, the same search method, transformation and constraints used in Jin et al. (2019)'s TextFooler can be modified to attack a translation model with the goal of changing every word in the output.

TextAttack is directly integrated with HuggingFace's transformers and nlp libraries. This allows users to test attacks on models and datasets. TextAttack provides dozens of pre-trained models (LSTM, CNN, and various transformer-based models) on a variety of popular datasets. Currently TextAttack supports a multitude of tasks including summarization, machine translation, and all nine tasks from the GLUE benchmark. TextAttack also allows users to provide their own models and datasets.

Ultimately, the goal of studying adversarial attacks is to improve model performance and robustness. To that end, TextAttack provides easy-to-use tools for data augmentation and adversarial training. TextAttack's Augmenter class uses a transformation and a set of constraints to produce new samples for data augmentation. Attack recipes are re-used in a training loop that allows models to train on adversarial examples. These tools make it easier to train accurate and robust models.

Uses for TextAttack include[1]:

- Benchmarking and comparing NLP attacks from previous works on standardized models & datasets.
- Fast development of NLP attack methods by re-using abundant available modules.
- Performing ablation studies on individual components of proposed attacks and data augmentation methods.
- Training a model (CNN, LSTM, BERT, RoBERTa, etc.) on an augmented dataset.
- Adversarial training with attacks from the literature to improve a model's robustness.

2 The TextAttack Framework

TextAttack aims to implement attacks which, given an NLP model, find a perturbation of an input sequence that satisfies the attack's goal and adheres to certain linguistic constraints. In this way, attacking an NLP model can be framed as a combinatorial search problem. The attacker must search within all potential transformations to find a sequence of transformations that generate a successful adversarial example.

Each attack can be constructed from four components:

1. A task-specific **goal function** that determines whether the attack is successful in terms of the model outputs.
   Examples: untargeted classification, targeted classification, non-overlapping output, minimum BLEU score.

---

[1]All can be done in < 5 lines of code. See A.1.

2. A set of **constraints** that determine if a perturbation is valid with respect to the original input.

    Examples: maximum word embedding distance, part-of-speech consistency, grammar checker, minimum sentence encoding cosine similarity.

3. A **transformation** that, given an input, generates a set of potential perturbations.

    Examples: word embedding word swap, thesaurus word swap, homoglyph character substitution.

4. A **search method** that successively queries the model and selects promising perturbations from a set of transformations.

    Examples: greedy with word importance ranking, beam search, genetic algorithm.

See A.2 for a full explanation of each goal function, constraint, transformation, and search method that's built-in to `TextAttack`.

3 Developing NLP Attacks with `TextAttack`

`TextAttack` is available as a Python package installed from PyPI, or via direct download from GitHub. `TextAttack` is also available for use through our demo web app, displayed in Figure 3.

Python users can test attacks by creating and manipulating `Attack` objects. The command-line API offers `textattack attack`, which allows users to specify attacks from their four components or from a single attack recipe and test them on different models and datasets.

`TextAttack` supports several different output formats for attack results:

- Printing results to stdout.
- Printing to a text file or CSV.
- Printing attack results to an HTML table.
- Writing a table of attack results to a visualization server, like Visdom or Weights & Biases.

3.1 Benchmarking Existing Attacks with Attack Recipes

`TextAttack`'s modular design allows us to implement many different attacks from past work in a shared framework, often by adding only one or two new components. Table 1 categorizes 16 attacks based on their goal functions, constraints, transformations and search methods.

All of these attacks are implemented as "attack recipes" in `TextAttack` and can be benchmarked with just a single command. See A.3

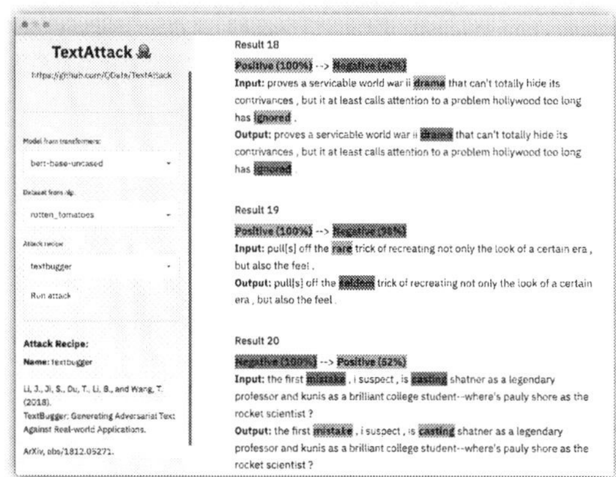

Figure 3: Screenshot of `TextAttack`'s web interface running the TextBugger black-box attack (Li et al., 2019).

for a comparison between papers' reported attack results and the results achieved by running `TextAttack`.

3.2 Creating New Attacks by Combining Novel and Existing Components

As is clear from Table 1, many components are shared between NLP attacks. New attacks often reuse components from past work, adding one or two novel pieces. `TextAttack` allows researchers to focus on the generation of new components rather than replicating past results. For example, Jin et al. (2019) introduced `TextFooler` as a method for attacking classification and entailment models. If a researcher wished to experiment with applying `TextFooler`'s search method, transformations, and constraints to attack translation models, all they need is to implement a translation goal function in `TextAttack`. They would then be able to plug in this goal function to create a novel attack that could be used to analyze translation models.

3.3 Evaluating Attacks on `TextAttack`'s Pre-Trained Models

As of the date of this submission, `TextAttack` provides users with 82 pre-trained models, including word-level LSTM, word-level CNN, BERT, and other transformer based models pre-trained on various datasets provided by HuggingFace nlp. Since `TextAttack` is integrated with the nlp library, it can automatically load the test or validation data set for the corresponding pre-trained model. While the literature has mainly focused on classification and entailment, `TextAttack`'s pretrained models enable research on the robustness of models across all GLUE tasks.

Attack Recipe	Goal Function	Constraints	Transformation	Search Method
`bae` (Garg and Ramakrishnan, 2020)	Untargeted Classification	USE sentence encoding cosine similarity	BERT Masked Token Prediction	Greedy-WIR
`bert-attack` (Li et al., 2020)	Untargeted Classification	USE sentence encoding cosine similarity, Maximum number of words perturbed	BERT Masked Token Prediction (with subword expansion)	Greedy-WIR
`deepwordbug` (Gao et al., 2018)	{Untargeted, Targeted} Classification	Levenshtein edit distance	{Character Insertion, Character Deletion, Neighboring Character Swap, Character Substitution}*	Greedy-WIR
`alzantot`, `fast-alzantot` (Alzantot et al., 2018; Jia et al., 2019)	Untargeted {Classification, Entailment}	Percentage of words perturbed, Language Model perplexity, Word embedding distance	Counter-fitted word embedding swap	Genetic Algorithm
`iga` (Wang et al., 2019)	Untargeted {Classification, Entailment}	Percentage of words perturbed, Word embedding distance	Counter-fitted word embedding swap	Genetic Algorithm
`input-reduction` (Feng et al., 2018)	Input Reduction		Word deletion	Greedy-WIR
`kuleshov` (Kuleshov et al., 2018)	Untargeted Classification	Thought vector encoding cosine similarity, Language model similarity probability	Counter-fitted word embedding swap	Greedy word swap
`hotflip` (word swap) (Ebrahimi et al., 2017)	Untargeted Classification	Word Embedding Cosine Similarity, Part-of-speech match, Number of words perturbed	Gradient-Based Word Swap	Beam search
`morpheus` (Tan et al., 2020)	Minimum BLEU Score		Inflection Word Swap	Greedy search
`pruthi` (Pruthi et al., 2019)	Untargeted Classification	Minimum word length, Maximum number of words perturbed	{Neighboring Character Swap, Character Deletion, Character Insertion, Keyboard-Based Character Swap}*	Greedy search
`pso` (Zang et al., 2020)	Untargeted Classification		HowNet Word Swap	Particle Swarm Optimization
`pwws` (Ren et al., 2019)	Untargeted Classification		WordNet-based synonym swap	Greedy-WIR (saliency)
`seq2sick` (black-box) (Cheng et al., 2018)	Non-overlapping output		Counter-fitted word embedding swap	Greedy-WIR
`textbugger` (black-box) (Li et al., 2019)	Untargeted Classification	USE sentence encoding cosine similarity	{Character Insertion, Character Deletion, Neighboring Character Swap, Character Substitution}*	Greedy-WIR
`textfooler` (Jin et al., 2019)	Untargeted {Classification, Entailment}	Word Embedding Distance, Part-of-speech match, USE sentence encoding cosine similarity	Counter-fitted word embedding swap	Greedy-WIR

Table 1: `TextAttack` attack recipes categorized within our framework: search method, transformation, goal function, constraints. All attack recipes include an additional constraint which disallows the replacement of stopwords. Greedy search with Word Importance Ranking is abbreviated as Greedy-WIR.
indicates a combination of multiple transformations

4 Utilizing `TextAttack` to Improve NLP Models

4.1 Evaluating Robustness of Custom Models

`TextAttack` is model-agnostic - meaning it can run attacks on models implemented in any deep learning framework. Model objects must be able to take a string (or list of strings) and return an output that can be processed by the goal function. For example, machine translation models take a list of strings as input and produce a list of strings as output. Classification and entailment models return an array of scores. As long as the user's model meets this specification, the model is fit to use with `TextAttack`.

4.2 Model Training

`TextAttack` users can train standard LSTM, CNN, and transformer based models, or a user-customized model on any dataset from the `nlp` library using the `textattack train` command. Just like pre-trained models, user-trained models are compatible with commands like `textattack attack` and `textattack eval`.

4.3 Data Augmentation

While searching for adversarial examples, `TextAttack`'s transformations generate perturbations of the input text, and apply constraints to verify their validity. These tools can be reused to dramatically expand the training dataset by introducing perturbed versions of existing samples. The `textattack augment` command gives users access to a number of pre-packaged recipes for augmenting their dataset. This is a stand-alone feature that can be used with any model or training framework. When using `TextAttack`'s models and training pipeline, `textattack train --augment` automatically expands the dataset before training begins. Users can specify the fraction of each input that should be modified and how many additional versions of each example to create. This makes it easy to use existing augmentation recipes on different models and datasets, and is a great way to benchmark new techniques.

Figure 4 shows empirical results we obtained using `TextAttack`'s augmentation. Augmentation with `TextAttack` immediately improves the performance of a `WordCNN` model on small datasets.

4.4 Adversarial Training

With `textattack train --attack`, attack recipes can be used to create new training

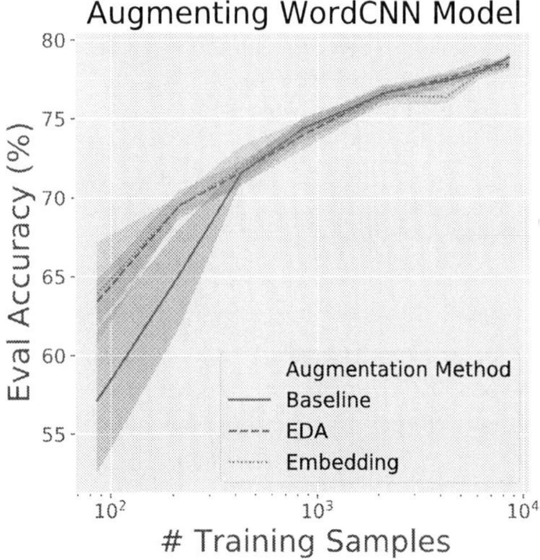

Figure 4: Performance of the built-in `WordCNN` model on the `rotten_tomatoes` dataset with increasing training set size. Data augmentation recipes like `EasyDataAugmenter` (EDA, (Wei and Zou, 2019)) and `Embedding` are most helpful when working with very few samples. Shaded regions represent 95% confidence intervals over $N = 5$ runs.

sets of adversarial examples. After training for a number of epochs on the clean training set, the attack generates an adversarial version of each input. This perturbed version of the dataset is substituted for the original, and is periodically regenerated according to the model's current weaknesses. The resulting model can be significantly more robust against the attack used during training. Table 2 shows the accuracy of a standard LSTM classifier with and without adversarial training against different attack recipes implemented in `TextAttack`.

5 `TextAttack` Under the Hood

`TextAttack` is optimized under-the-hood to make implementing and running adversarial attacks simple and fast.

AttackedText. A common problem with implementations of NLP attacks is that the original text is discarded after tokenization; thus, the transformation is performed on the tokenized version of the text. This causes issues with capitalization and word segmentation. Sometimes attacks swap a piece of a word for a complete word (for example, transforming ``aren't" into ``aren'too").

To solve this problem, `TextAttack` stores each input as a `AttackedText` object which contains the original text and helper methods for transforming the text while retaining tokenization. Instead of strings or tensors,

Trained Against	Attacked By					
	−	`deepwordbug`	`textfooler`	`pruthi`	`hotflip`	`bae`
baseline (early stopping)	**77.30%**	23.46%	2.23%	59.01%	64.57%	25.51%
`deepwordbug` (20 epochs)	76.38%	**35.07%**	4.78%	57.08%	65.06%	27.63%
`deepwordbug` (75 epochs)	73.16%	**44.74%**	13.42%	58.28%	66.87%	32.77%
`textfooler` (20 epochs)	61.85%	40.09%	**29.63%**	52.60%	55.75%	39.36%

Table 2: The default LSTM model trained on 3k samples from the `sst2` dataset. The baseline uses early stopping on a clean training set. `deepwordbug` and `textfooler` attacks are used for adversarial training. 'Accuracy Under Attack' on the eval set is reported for several different attack types.

classes in `TextAttack` operate primarily on `AttackedText` objects. When words are added, swapped, or deleted, an `AttackedText` can maintain proper punctuation and capitalization. The `AttackedText` also contains implementations for common linguistic functions like splitting text into words, splitting text into sentences, and part-of-speech tagging.

Caching. Search methods frequently encounter the same input at different points in the search. In these cases, it is wise to pre-store values to avoid unnecessary computation. For each input examined during the attack, `TextAttack` caches its model output, as well as the whether or not it passed all of the constraints. For some search methods, this memoization can save a significant amount of time.[2]

6 Related Work

We draw inspiration from the `Transformers` library (Wolf et al., 2019) as an example of a well-designed Natural Language Processing library. Some of `TextAttack`'s models and tokenizers are implemented using `Transformers`.

`cleverhans` (Papernot et al., 2018) is a library for constructing adversarial examples for computer vision models. Like `cleverhans`, we aim to provide methods that generate adversarial examples across a variety of models and datasets. In some sense, `TextAttack` strives to be a solution like `cleverhans` for the NLP community. Like `cleverhans`, attacks in `TextAttack` all implement a base `Attack` class. However, while `cleverhans` implements many disparate attacks in separate modules, `TextAttack` builds attacks from a library of shared components.

There are some existing open-source libraries related to adversarial examples in NLP. `Trickster` proposes a method for attacking NLP models based on graph search, but lacks the ability to ensure that generated examples satisfy a given constraint (Kulynych et al., 2018). `TEAPOT` is a library for evaluating adversarial perturbations on text, but only supports the application of ngram-based comparisons for evaluating attacks on machine translation models (Michel et al., 2019). Most recently, `AllenNLP Interpret` includes functionality for running adversarial attacks on NLP models, but is intended only for the purpose of interpretability, and only supports attacks via input-reduction or greedy gradient-based word swap (Wallace et al., 2019). `TextAttack` has a broader scope than any of these libraries: it is designed to be extendable to any NLP attack.

7 Conclusion

We presented `TextAttack`, an open-source framework for testing the robustness of NLP models. `TextAttack` defines an attack in four modules: a goal function, a list of constraints, a transformation, and a search method. This allows us to compose attacks from previous work from these modules and compare them in a shared environment. These attacks can be reused for data augmentation and adversarial training. As new attacks are developed, we will add their components to `TextAttack`. We hope `TextAttack` helps lower the barrier to entry for research into robustness and data augmentation in NLP.[3]

8 Acknowledgements

The authors would like to thank everyone who has contributed to make `TextAttack` a reality: Hanyu Liu, Kevin Ivey, Bill Zhang, and Alan Zheng, to name a few. Thanks to the IGA creators (Wang et al., 2019) for contributing an implementation of their algorithm to our framework. Thanks to the folks at HuggingFace for creating such easy-to-use software; without them, `TextAttack` would not be what it is today.

---

[2]Caching alone speeds up the genetic algorithm of Alzantot et al. (2018) by a factor of 5.

References

Abhaya Agarwal and Alon Lavie. 2008. Meteor, m-bleu and m-ter: Evaluation metrics for high-correlation with human rankings of machine translation output. In *WMT@ACL*.

Moustafa Alzantot, Yash Sharma, Ahmed Elgohary, Bo-Jhang Ho, Mani B. Srivastava, and Kai-Wei Chang. 2018. Generating natural language adversarial examples. *ArXiv*, abs/1804.07998.

Daniel Matthew Cer, Yinfei Yang, Sheng yi Kong, Nan Hua, Nicole Limtiaco, Rhomni St. John, Noah Constant, Mario Guajardo-Cespedes, Steve Yuan, Chris Tar, Yun-Hsuan Sung, Brian Strope, and Ray Kurzweil. 2018. Universal sentence encoder. *ArXiv*, abs/1803.11175.

Minhao Cheng, Jinfeng Yi, Pin-Yu Chen, Huan Zhang, and Cho-Jui Hsieh. 2018. Seq2sick: Evaluating the robustness of sequence-to-sequence models with adversarial examples.

Alexis Conneau, Douwe Kiela, Holger Schwenk, Loïc Barrault, and Antoine Bordes. 2017. Supervised learning of universal sentence representations from natural language inference data. In *EMNLP*.

Zhendong Dong, Qiang Dong, and Changling Hao. 2006. Hownet and the computation of meaning.

Javid Ebrahimi, Anyi Rao, Daniel Lowd, and Dejing Dou. 2017. Hotflip: White-box adversarial examples for text classification. In *ACL*.

Shi Feng, Eric Wallace, Alvin Grissom II, Mohit Iyyer, Pedro Rodriguez, and Jordan Boyd-Graber. 2018. Pathologies of neural models make interpretations difficult.

Ji Gao, Jack Lanchantin, Mary Lou Soffa, and Yanjun Qi. 2018. Black-box generation of adversarial text sequences to evade deep learning classifiers. *2018 IEEE Security and Privacy Workshops (SPW)*, pages 50–56.

Siddhant Garg and Goutham Ramakrishnan. 2020. Bae: Bert-based adversarial examples for text classification.

Ari Holtzman, Jan Buys, Maxwell Forbes, Antoine Bosselut, David Golub, and Yejin Choi. 2018. Learning to write with cooperative discriminators. In *Proceedings of the 56th Annual Meeting of the Association for Computational Linguistics (Volume 1: Long Papers)*, pages 1638–1649, Melbourne, Australia. Association for Computational Linguistics.

Robin Jia and Percy Liang. 2017. Adversarial examples for evaluating reading comprehension systems. In *Proceedings of the 2017 Conference on Empirical Methods in Natural Language Processing*, pages 2021–2031, Copenhagen, Denmark. Association for Computational Linguistics.

Robin Jia, Aditi Raghunathan, Kerem Göksel, and Percy Liang. 2019. Certified robustness to adversarial word substitutions. In *EMNLP/IJCNLP*.

Di Jin, Zhijing Jin, Joey Tianyi Zhou, and Peter Szolovits. 2019. Is bert really robust? natural language attack on text classification and entailment. *ArXiv*, abs/1907.11932.

Rafal Józefowicz, Oriol Vinyals, Mike Schuster, Noam Shazeer, and Yonghui Wu. 2016. Exploring the limits of language modeling. *ArXiv*, abs/1602.02410.

James Kennedy and Russell Eberhart. 1995. Particle swarm optimization. In *Proceedings of ICNN'95 - International Conference on Neural Networks*, volume 4, pages 1942–1948. IEEE.

Ryan Kiros, Yukun Zhu, Ruslan Salakhutdinov, Richard S. Zemel, Raquel Urtasun, Antonio Torralba, and Sanja Fidler. 2015. Skip-thought vectors. *ArXiv*, abs/1506.06726.

Volodymyr Kuleshov, Shantanu Thakoor, Tingfung Lau, and Stefano Ermon. 2018. Adversarial examples for natural language classification problems.

Bogdan Kulynych, Jamie Hayes, Nikita Samarin, and Carmela Troncoso. 2018. Evading classifiers in discrete domains with provable optimality guarantees. *CoRR*, abs/1810.10939.

Jinfeng Li, Shouling Ji, Tianyu Du, Bo Li, and Ting Wang. 2019. Textbugger: Generating adversarial text against real-world applications. *ArXiv*, abs/1812.05271.

Linyang Li, Ruotian Ma, Qipeng Guo, Xiangyang Xue, and Xipeng Qiu. 2020. Bert-attack: Adversarial attack against bert using bert.

Paul Michel, Xian Li, Graham Neubig, and Juan Miguel Pino. 2019. On evaluation of adversarial perturbations for sequence-to-sequence models. *CoRR*, abs/1903.06620.

George Armitage Miller, Richard Beckwith, Christiane Fellbaum, Derek Gross, and Katherine J. Miller. 1990. Introduction to wordnet: An on-line lexical database. *International Journal of Lexicography*, 3:235–244.

Nikola Mrkšić, Diarmuid O Séaghdha, Blaise Thomson, Milica Gašić, Lina Rojas-Barahona, Pei-Hao Su, David Vandyke, Tsung-Hsien Wen, and Steve Young. 2016. Counter-fitting word vectors to linguistic constraints. *arXiv preprint arXiv:1603.00892*.

Daniel Naber et al. 2003. *A rule-based style and grammar checker*. Citeseer.

Nicolas Papernot, Fartash Faghri, Nicholas Carlini, Ian Goodfellow, Reuben Feinman, Alexey Kurakin, Cihang Xie, Yash Sharma, Tom Brown, Aurko Roy,

Alexander Matyasko, Vahid Behzadan, Karen Hambardzumyan, Zhishuai Zhang, Yi-Lin Juang, Zhi Li, Ryan Sheatsley, Abhibhav Garg, Jonathan Uesato, Willi Gierke, Yinpeng Dong, David Berthelot, Paul Hendricks, Jonas Rauber, and Rujun Long. 2018. Technical report on the cleverhans v2.1.0 adversarial examples library. *arXiv preprint arXiv:1610.00768*.

Kishore Papineni, Salim Roukos, Todd Ward, and Wei-Jing Zhu. 2001. Bleu: a method for automatic evaluation of machine translation. In *ACL*.

Maja Popovic. 2015. chrf: character n-gram f-score for automatic mt evaluation. In *WMT@EMNLP*.

Danish Pruthi, Bhuwan Dhingra, and Zachary C. Lipton. 2019. Combating adversarial misspellings with robust word recognition.

Alec Radford, Jeff Wu, Rewon Child, David Luan, Dario Amodei, and Ilya Sutskever. 2019. Language models are unsupervised multitask learners.

Nils Reimers and Iryna Gurevych. 2019. Sentence-bert: Sentence embeddings using siamese bert-networks. In *Proceedings of the 2019 Conference on Empirical Methods in Natural Language Processing*. Association for Computational Linguistics.

Shuhuai Ren, Yihe Deng, Kun He, and Wanxiang Che. 2019. Generating natural language adversarial examples through probability weighted word saliency. In *Proceedings of the 57th Annual Meeting of the Association for Computational Linguistics*, pages 1085–1097, Florence, Italy. Association for Computational Linguistics.

Samson Tan, Shafiq Joty, Min-Yen Kan, and Richard Socher. 2020. It's morphin' time! Combating linguistic discrimination with inflectional perturbations. In *Proceedings of the 58th Annual Meeting of the Association for Computational Linguistics*, pages 2920–2935, Online. Association for Computational Linguistics.

Eric Wallace, Jens Tuyls, Junlin Wang, Sanjay Subramanian, Matthew Gardner, and Sameer Singh. 2019. Allennlp interpret: A framework for explaining predictions of nlp models. *ArXiv*, abs/1909.09251.

Xiaosen Wang, Hao Jin, and Kun He. 2019. Natural language adversarial attacks and defenses in word level.

Jason W. Wei and Kai Zou. 2019. EDA: easy data augmentation techniques for boosting performance on text classification tasks. *CoRR*, abs/1901.11196.

Thomas Wolf, Lysandre Debut, Victor Sanh, Julien Chaumond, Clement Delangue, Anthony Moi, Pierric Cistac, Tim Rault, R'emi Louf, Morgan Funtowicz, and Jamie Brew. 2019. Transformers: State-of-the-art natural language processing.

Yuan Zang, Fanchao Qi, Chenghao Yang, Zhiyuan Liu, Meng Zhang, Qun Liu, and Maosong Sun. 2020. Word-level textual adversarial attacking as combinatorial optimization. In *Proceedings of the 58th Annual Meeting of the Association for Computational Linguistics*, pages 6066–6080, Online. Association for Computational Linguistics.

Tianyi Zhang*, Varsha Kishore*, Felix Wu*, Kilian Q. Weinberger, and Yoav Artzi. 2020. Bertscore: Evaluating text generation with bert. In *International Conference on Learning Representations*.

Easy, Reproducible and Quality-Controlled Data Collection
with CROWDAQ

Qiang Ning♠   Hao Wu♣   Pradeep Dasigi♠   Dheeru Dua◇   Matt Gardner♠
Robert L. Logan IV◇   Ana Marasović♠   Zhen Nie♣
♠Allen Institute for AI   ◇University of California, Irvine   ♣Hooray Data Co., Ltd
{qiangn,pradeepd,mattg,anam}@allenai.org
{haowu,zhennie}@hooray.ai
{ddua,rlogan}@uci.edu

Abstract

High-quality and large-scale data are key to success for AI systems. However, large-scale data annotation efforts are often confronted with a set of common challenges: (1) designing a user-friendly annotation interface; (2) training enough annotators efficiently; and (3) reproducibility. To address these problems, we introduce CROWDAQ,[1] an open-source platform that standardizes the data collection pipeline with customizable user-interface components, automated annotator qualification, and saved pipelines in a re-usable format. We show that CROWDAQ simplifies data annotation significantly on a diverse set of data collection use cases and we hope it will be a convenient tool for the community.

1 Introduction

Data is the foundation of training and evaluating AI systems. Efficient data collection is thus important for advancing research and building time-sensitive applications.[2] Data collection projects typically require many annotators working independently to achieve sufficient scale, either in dataset size or collection time. To work with multiple annotators, data requesters (i.e., AI researchers and engineers) usually need to design a user-friendly annotation interface and a quality control mechanism. However, this involves a lot of overhead: we often spend most of the time resolving frontend bugs and manually checking or communicating with individual annotators to filter out those who are unqualified, instead of focusing on core research questions.

Another issue that has recently gained more attention is reproducibility. Dodge et al. (2019) and Pineau (2020) provide suggestions for *system* reproducibility, and Bender and Friedman (2018) and

Gebru et al. (2018) propose "data statements" and "datasheets for datasets" for *data collection* reproducibility. However, due to irreproducible human interventions in training and selecting annotators and the potential difficulty in replicating the annotation interfaces, it is often difficult to reuse or extend an existing data collection project.

We introduce CROWDAQ, an open-source data annotation platform for NLP research designed to minimize overhead and improve reproducibility. It has the following contributions. First, CROWDAQ standardizes the design of data collection pipelines, and separates that from software implementation. This standardization allows requesters to design data collection pipelines *declaratively* without being worried about many engineering details, which is key to solving the aforementioned problems (Sec. 2).

Second, CROWDAQ automates qualification control via multiple-choice exams. We also provide detailed reports on these exams so that requesters know how well annotators are doing and can adjust bad exam questions if needed (Sec. 2).

Third, CROWDAQ carefully defines a suite of pre-built UI components that one can use to compose complex annotation user-interfaces (UIs) for a wide variety of NLP tasks without expertise in HTML/CSS/JavaScript (Sec. 3). For non-experts on frontend design, CROWDAQ can greatly improve efficiency in developing these projects.

Fourth, a dataset collected via CROWDAQ can be more easily reproduced or extended by *future data requesters*, because they can simply copy the pipeline and pay for additional annotations, or treat existing pipeline as a starting point for new projects.

In addition, CROWDAQ has also integrated many useful features: requesters can conveniently monitor the progress of annotation jobs, whether they are paying annotators fairly, and the agreement

---

[1]Crowdsourcing with Automated Qualifcation; https://www.crowdaq.com/

[2]This holds not only for collecting static data annotations, but also for collecting human judgments of system outputs.

Proceedings of the 2020 EMNLP (Systems Demonstrations), pages 127–134
November 16-20, 2020. ©2020 Association for Computational Linguistics

level of different annotators on CROWDAQ. Finally, Sec. 4 shows how to use CROWDAQ and Amazon Mechanical Turk (MTurk)[3] to collect data for an example project. More use cases can be found in our documentation.

2 Standardized Data Collection Pipeline

A data collection project with multiple annotators generally includes some or all of the following: (1) Task definition, which describes what should be annotated. (2) Examples, which enhances annotators' understanding of the task. (3) Qualification, which tests annotators' understanding of the task and only those qualified can continue; this step is very important for reducing unqualified annotators. (4) Main annotation process, where qualified annotators work on the task. CROWDAQ provides easy-to-use functionality for each of these components of the data collection pipeline, which we expand next.

INSTRUCTION A Markdown document that defines a task and instructs annotators how to complete the task. It supports various formatting options, including images and videos.

TUTORIAL Additional training material provided in the form of multiple-choice questions with provided answers that workers can use to gauge their understanding of the INSTRUCTION. CROWDAQ received many messages from real annotators saying that TUTORIALS are quite helpful for learning tasks.

EXAM A collection of multiple-choice questions similar to TUTORIAL, but for which answers are not provided to participants. EXAM is used to test whether an annotator understands the instructions sufficiently to provide useful annotations. Participants will only have a finite number of opportunities specified by the requesters to work on an EXAM, and each time they will see a random subset of all the exam questions. After finishing an EXAM, participants are informed of how many mistakes they have made and whether they have passed, but they do not receive feedback on individual questions. Therefore, data requesters should try to design better INSTRUCTIONS and TUTORIALS instead of using EXAM to teach annotators.

We restrict TUTORIALS and EXAMS to always be in a multiple-choice format, irrespective of the

[3]https://www.mturk.com/

original task format, because it is natural for humans to learn and to be tested in a discriminative setting.[4] An important benefit of using multiple-choice questions is that their evaluation can be automated easily, minimizing the effort a requester spends on manual inspections. Another convenient feature of CROWDAQ is that it displays useful statistics to requesters, such as the distribution of scores in each exam and which questions annotators often make mistakes on, which can highlight areas of improvement in the INSTRUCTION and TUTORIAL. Below is the JSON syntax to specify TUTORIALS/EXAMS (see Fig. 3 and Fig. 4 in the appendix).

```
"question_set": [
  {
      "type": "multiple-choice",
      "question_id": ...,
      "context": [{
          "type": "text",
          "text": "As of Tuesday, 144 of the state's
              then-294 deaths involved nursing
              homes or longterm care facilities."
      }],
      "question": {
          "question_text": "In \"294 deaths\", what
              should you label as the quantity?",
          "options": {"A": "294", "B": "294 deaths"}
      },
      "answer": "A",
      "explanation": {
          "A": "Correct",
          "B": "In our definition, the quantity
              should be \"294\"."
      }
  },
  ...
]
```

TASK For example, if we are doing sentence-level sentiment analysis, then a TASK is to display a specific sentence and require the annotator to provide a label for its sentiment. A collection of TASKS are bundled into a TASK SET that we can launch as a group. Unlike TUTORIALS and EXAMS where we only need to handle multiple-choice questions in CROWDAQ's implementation, a major challenge for TASK is how to meet different requirements for annotation UI from different datasets in a single framework, which we discuss next.

3 Customizable Annotation Interface

It is time-consuming for non-experts on the frontend to design annotation UIs for various datasets. At present, requesters can only reuse the UIs of very similar tasks and still, they often need to make modifications with additional tests and debugging. CROWDAQ comes with a variety of built-in

[4]E.g., we can always test one's understanding of a concept by multiple-choice questions like *Do you think something is correct?* or *Choose the correct option(s) from below.*

resources for easily creating UIs, which we will explain using an example dataset collection project centered around confirmed COVID-19 cases and deaths mentioned in news snippets.

3.1 Concepts

The design of CROWDAQ's annotation UI is built on some key concepts. First, every TASK is associated with `contexts`—a list of objects of any type: `text`, `html`, `image`, `audio`, or `video`. It will be visible to the annotators during the entire annotation process before moving to the next TASK, so a requester can use `contexts` to show any useful information to the annotators. Below is an example of showing notes and a target news snippet (see Fig. 5 in the appendix for visualization). CROWDAQ is integrated with online editors that can auto-complete, give error messages, and quickly preview any changes.

```
"contexts": [
    {
        "label": "Note",
        "type": "html",
        "html": "<p>Remember to ...</p>",
        "id": "note"
    },
    {
        "type": "text",
        "label": "The snippet was from an article
            published on 2020-05-20 10:30:00",
        "text": "As of Tuesday, 144 of the state's
            then-294 deaths involved nursing homes
            or longterm care facilities.",
        "id": "snippet"
    }
],
```

Second, each TASK may have multiple `annotations`. Although the number of dataset formats can be arbitrary, we observe that the most basic formats fall into the following categories: multiple-choice, span selection, and free text generation. For instance, to emulate the data collection process used for the CoNLL-2003 shared task on named entity recognition (Tjong Kim Sang and De Meulder, 2003), one could use a combination of a span selection (for selecting a named entity) and a multiple-choice question (selecting whether it is a person, location, etc.); for the process used for natural language inference in SNLI (Bowman et al., 2015), one could use an input box (for writing a hypothesis) and a multiple-choice question (for selecting whether the hypothesis entails or contradicts the premise); for reading comprehension tasks in the question-answering (QA) format, one could use an input box (for writing a question) and a multiple-choice question (for yes/no answers; Clark et al. (2019)), a span selection (for span-based answers; Rajpurkar et al. (2016)), or another input box (for free text answers; Kočiský et al. (2018)).

These `annotation` types are built in CROWDAQ,[5] which requesters can easily use to compose complex UIs. For our example project, we would like the annotator to select a quantity from the "snippet" object in the `contexts`, and then tell us whether it is relevant to COVID-19 (see below for how to build it and Fig. 6 in the appendix for visualization).

```
"annotations": [
    {
        "type": "span-from-text",
        "from_context": "snippet",
        "prompt": "Select one quantity from below.",
        "id": "quantity",
    },
    {
        "type": "multiple-choice",
        "prompt": "Is this quantity related to
            COVID-19?",
        "options":{
            "A": "Relevant",
            "B": "Not relevant"
        }
        "id": "relevance"
    }
]
```

Third, a collection of `annotations` can form an `annotation group` and a TASK can have multiple of them. For complex TASKS, this kind of semantic hierarchy can provide a big picture for both the requesters and annotators. We are also able to provide very useful features for `annotation groups`. For example, we can put the `annotations` object above into an `annotation group`, and require 1-3 responses in this group. Below is its syntax, and Fig. 7 in the appendix shows the result.

```
"annotation_groups": [
    {
        "annotations": [
            {"id": "quantity", ...},
            {"id": "relevance", ...}
        ],
        "id": "quantity_extraction_typing",
        "title": "COVID-19 Quantities",
        "repeated": true, "min": 1, "max": 3
    }
],
```

3.2 Conditions

Requesters often need to collect some `annotations` only when certain `conditions` are satisfied. For instance, only if a quantity is related to COVID-19 will we continue to ask the type of it. These `conditions` are important because by construction, annotators will not make mistakes such as answering a question that should not be enabled at all.

As a natural choice, CROWDAQ has implemented `conditions` that take as input val-

---

ues of multiple-choice `annotations`. The field `conditions` can be applied to any `annotation`, which will be enabled only when the conditions are satisfied. Below we add a multiple-choice question asking for the type of a quantity *only if* the annotator has chosen option "A: Relevant" in the question whose ID is "relevance" (see Fig. 8 in the appendix).

```
"annotations": [
    {"id": "quantity", ...},
    {"id": "relevance", ...},
    {
      "id": "typing",
      "type": "multiple-choice",
      "prompt": "What type is it?",
      "options":{
        "A": "Number of Deaths",
        "B": "Number of confirmed cases",
        "C": "Number of hospitalized",
        ...
      },
      "conditions":[
        {
            "id": "relevance",
            "op": "eq",
            "value": "A"
        }
      ]
    }
],
```

CROWDAQ actually supports any boolean logic composed by "AND," "OR," and "NOT." Below is an example of $\neg(Q1 = A \lor Q2 = B)$.

```
"conditions": [
    {
      "op": "not", "arg": {
      "op": "or", "args":[
        {"id": "Q1","op": "eq","value": "A"},
        {"id": "Q2","op": "eq","value": "B"}
      ]
      }
    }
]
```

3.3 Constraints

An important quality control mechanism is to implement constraints for an annotator's work such that only if the constraints are satisfied will the annotator be able to submit the instance (and get paid). An implicit constraint in CROWDAQ is that all `annotations` should be finished except for those explicitly specified as "optional."

For things that are repeated, CROWDAQ allows the requester to specify the min/max number of repetitions. This corresponds to scenarios where, for instance, we know there is at least 1 quantity (min=1) in a news snippet or we want to have exactly two named entities selected for relation extraction (min=max=2). We have already shown usages of this when introducing `annotation group`, but the same also applies to text span selectors.

CROWDAQ also allows requesters to specify a regular expression constraint. For instance, in our COVID-19 example, when the annotator selects a text span as a quantity, we want to make sure that the span selection does not violate some obvious rules. To achieve this, we define `constraints` as a list of requirements and all of them must be satisfied; if any one of them is violated, the annotator will receive an error message specified by the `description` field and also not able to submit the work.

In addition, users can specify their own constraint functions via an API. Please refer to our documentation for more details.

```
"annotations":[
    {
      "id": "quantity",
      ...,
      "constraints": [
        {
          "description": "The quantity should
              only start with digits or
              letters.",
          "regex": "^[\\w\\d].*$",
          "type": "regex"
        },
        {
          "description": "The quantity should
              only end with digits, letters, or
              %.",
          "regex": "^.*[\\w\\d%]$",
          "type": "regex"
        },
        {
          "description": "The length of your
              selection should be within 1 and
              30.",
          "regex": "^.{1,30}$",
          "type": "regex"
        }
      ]
    },
    ...
]
```

3.4 Extensibility

As we cannot anticipate every possible UI requirement, we have designed CROWDAQ to be extensible. In addition to a suite of built-in `annotation` types, `conditions`, and `constraints`, users can write their own components and contribute to CROWDAQ easily. All these components are separate Vue.js[6] components and one only needs to follow some input/output specifications to extend CROWDAQ.

4 Usage

We have already deployed CROWDAQ at `https://www.crowdaq.com` with load balancing, backend cluster, relational database, failure recovery, and user authentication. Data requesters can simply register and enjoy the convenience it provides. For users who need to deploy CROWDAQ, we provide a Docker compose configuration so that they can bring up a cluster with all the features with one

---

[6]`https://vuejs.org/`

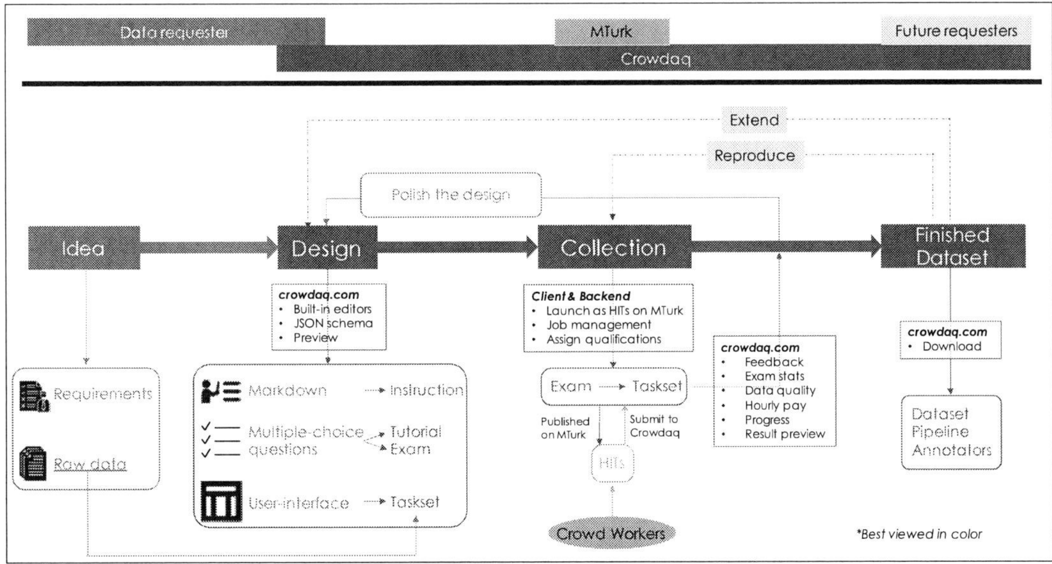

Figure 1: Data collection using CROWDAQ and MTurk. Note that this is a general workflow and one can use only part of it, or use it to build even more advanced workflows.

single command. Users will need to have their own domain name and HTTPS certificate in that case in order to use CROWDAQ with MTurk.

Figure 1 shows how a requester collects data using CROWDAQ and MTurk. The steps are: (1) identify the requirements of an application and find the raw data that one wants to annotate; (2) design the data collection pipeline using the built-in editors on CROWDAQ's website, including the Markdown INSTRUCTION, TUTORIAL, EXAM, and INTERFACE; (3) launch the EXAM and TASK SET onto MTurk and get crowd annotators to work on them; (4) if the quality and size of the data have reached one's requirement, publish the dataset. We have color-coded those components in Fig. 1 to show the responsibilities of the data requester, CROWDAQ, MTurk, and future requesters who want to reproduce or extend this dataset. We can see that CROWDAQ significantly reduces the effort a data requester needs to put in implementing all those features.

We have described how to write INSTRUCTIONS, TUTORIALS, and EXAMS (Sec. 2) and how to design the annotation UI (Sec. 3). Suppose we have provided 20 EXAM questions for the COVID-19 project. Before launching the EXAM, we need to configure the sample size of the EXAM, the passing score, and total number of chances (e.g., every time a participant will see a random subset of 10 questions, and to pass it, one must get a score higher than 80% within 3 chances). This can be done using the web interface of CROWDAQ (see Fig. 10 in the appendix).

It is also very easy to launch the EXAM to MTurk. CROWDAQ comes with a client package that one can run from a local computer (Fig. 11 in the appendix). The backend of CROWDAQ will do the job management, assign qualifications, and provide some handy analysis of how well participants are doing on the exam, including the score distribution of participants and analysis on each individual questions (Fig. 12).

The semantic difference between EXAMS and TASK SETS is handled by the backend of CROWDAQ. From MTurk's perspective, EXAMS and TASK SETS are both EXTERNALQUESTIONS.[7] Therefore, the same client package shown in Fig. 11 can also be used to launch a TASK SET to MTurk. CROWDAQ's backend will receive the annotations submitted by crowd workers; the website will show the annotation progress and average time spent on each TASK, and also provide quick preview of each individual annotations. If the data requester finds that the quality of annotations is not acceptable, the requester can go back and polish the design.

When data collection is finished, the requester can download the annotation pipeline and list of annotators from CROWDAQ, and get information about the process such as the average time spent

---

[7]EXTERNALQUESTION is a type of HITs on MTurk.

by workers on the task (and thus their average pay rate). Future requesters can then use the pipeline as the starting point for their projects, if desired, e.g., using the same EXAM, to get similarly-qualified workers on their follow-up project.

Although Fig. 1 shows a complete pipeline of using CROWDAQ and MTurk, CROWDAQ is implemented in such a way that data requesters have the flexibility to use only part of it. For instance, one can only use INSTRUCTION to host and render Markdown files, only use EXAM to test annotators, or only use TASK SET to quickly build annotation UIs. One can also create even more advanced workflows, e.g., using multiple EXAMS and filtering annotators sequentially (e.g., Gated Instruction; Liu et al., 2016), creating a second TASK SET to validate previous annotations, or splitting a single target dataset into multiple components, each of which has its own EXAM and TASK SET. In addition, data collection with in-house annotators can be done on CROWDAQ directly, instead of via MTurk. For instance, data requesters can conveniently create a contrast set (Gardner et al., 2020) on CROWDAQ by themselves.

We have put more use cases into the appendix, including DROP (Dua et al., 2019), MATRES (Ning et al., 2018), TORQUE (Ning et al., 2020), VQA-E (Li et al., 2018), and two ongoing projects.

5   Related Work

Crowdsourcing Platforms   The most commonly used platform at present is MTurk, and the features CROWDAQ provides are overall complementary to it. CROWDAQ provides integration with MTurk, but it also allows for in-house annotators and any platform that provides crowdsourcing service. Other crowdsourcing platforms, e.g., CrowdFlower/FigureEight,[8] Hive,[9] and Labelbox,[10] also have automated qualification control as CROWDAQ, but they do not separate the format of an exam from the format of a main task; therefore it is impossible to use its built-in qualification control for non-multiple-choice tasks like question-answering. In addition, CROWDAQ provides huge flexibility in annotation UIs as compared to these platforms. Last but not least, CROWDAQ is open-source and can be used, contributed to, extended, and deployed freely.

Customizable UI   To the best of our knowledge, existing works on customizable annotation UI, e.g., MMAX2[11] (Müller and Strube, 2006), PALinkA (Orăsan, 2003), and BRAT[12] (Stenetorp et al., 2012), were mainly designed for in-house annotators on classic NLP tasks, and their adaptability and extensibility are limited.

AMTI   is a command line interface for interacting with MTurk,[13] while CROWDAQ is a website providing one-stop solution including instructions, qualification tests, customizable interfaces, and job management on MTurk. AMTI also addresses the reproducibility issue by allowing HIT definitions to be tracked in version control, while CROWDAQ addresses by standardizing the workflow and automated qualification control.

Sprout   by Bragg and Weld (2018) is a *meta-framework* similar to the proposed workflow. They focus on *teaching* crowd workers, while CROWDAQ spends most of engineering effort to allow requesters specify the workflow *declaratively* without being a frontend or backend expert.

6   Conclusion

Efficient data collection at scale is important for advancing research and building applications in NLP. Existing workflows typically require multiple annotators, which introduces overhead in building annotation UIs and training and filtering annotators. CROWDAQ is an open-source online platform aimed to reduce this overhead and improve reproducibility via customizable UI components, automated qualification control, and easy-to-reproduce pipelines. The rapid modeling improvements seen in the last few years need a commensurate improvement in our data collection processes, and we believe that CROWDAQ is well-situated to aid in easy, reproducible data collection research.

References

Emily M. Bender and Batya Friedman. 2018. Data statements for natural language processing: Toward mitigating system bias and enabling better science. *Transactions of the Association for Computational Linguistics*, 6.

Samuel Bowman, Gabor Angeli, Christopher Potts, and Christopher D Manning. 2015. A large an-

---

⁸https://www.figure-eight.com/
⁹https://thehive.ai/
¹⁰https://labelbox.com/

¹¹http://mmax2.net/
¹²https://brat.nlplab.org/about.html
¹³https://github.com/allenai/amti

notated corpus for learning natural language inference. In *Proceedings of the Conference on Empirical Methods in Natural Language Processing (EMNLP)*, pages 632–642.

Jonathan Bragg and Daniel S Weld. 2018. Sprout: Crowd-powered task design for crowdsourcing. In *Proceedings of the 31st Annual ACM Symposium on User Interface Software and Technology*, pages 165–176.

Noam Chomsky and David W Lightfoot. 2002. *Syntactic structures*. Walter de Gruyter.

Christopher Clark, Kenton Lee, Ming-Wei Chang, Tom Kwiatkowski, Michael Collins, and Kristina Toutanova. 2019. BoolQ: Exploring the surprising difficulty of natural yes/no questions. In *Proceedings of the Conference of the North American Chapter of the Association for Computational Linguistics (NAACL)*, pages 2924–2936.

Jesse Dodge, Suchin Gururangan, Dallas Card, Roy Schwartz, and Noah A. Smith. 2019. Show your work: Improved reporting of experimental results. In *Proceedings of the Conference on Empirical Methods in Natural Language Processing (EMNLP)*, pages 2185–2194.

Dheeru Dua, Yizhong Wang, Pradeep Dasigi, Gabriel Stanovsky, Sameer Singh, and Matt Gardner. 2019. DROP: A reading comprehension benchmark requiring discrete reasoning over paragraphs. In *Proceedings of the Conference of the North American Chapter of the Association for Computational Linguistics (NAACL)*.

Matt Gardner, Yoav Artzi, Victoria Basmova, Jonathan Berant, Ben Bogin, Sihao Chen, Pradeep Dasigi, Dheeru Dua, Yanai Elazar, Ananth Gottumukkala, Nitish Gupta, Hanna Hajishirzi, Gabriel Ilharco, Daniel Khashabi, Kevin Lin, Jiangming Liu, Nelson F. Liu, Phoebe Mulcaire, Qiang Ning, Sameer Singh, Noah A. Smith, Sanjay Subramanian, Reut Tsarfaty, Eric Wallace, A. Zhang, and Ben Zhou. 2020. Evaluating NLP models via contrast sets. In *Proceedings of the Conference on Empirical Methods in Natural Language Processing (EMNLP)*.

Timnit Gebru, Jamie Morgenstern, Briana Vecchione, Jennifer Wortman Vaughan, Hanna M. Wallach, Hal Daumé, and Kate Crawford. 2018. Datasheets for datasets. In *Proceedings of the 5th Workshop on Fairness, Accountability, and Transparency in Machine Learning*.

Tomáš Kočiský, Jonathan Schwarz, Phil Blunsom, Chris Dyer, Karl Moritz Hermann, Gábor Melis, and Edward Grefenstette. 2018. The narrativeqa reading comprehension challenge. *Transactions of the Association for Computational Linguistics (TACL)*, 6:317–328.

Qing Li, Qingyi Tao, Shafiq R. Joty, Jianfei Cai, and Jiebo Luo. 2018. VQA-E: Explaining, Elaborating, and Enhancing Your Answers for Visual Questions. In *ECCV*.

Angli Liu, Stephen Soderland, Jonathan Bragg, Christopher H Lin, Xiao Ling, and Daniel S Weld. 2016. Effective crowd annotation for relation extraction. In *Proceedings of the Conference of the North American Chapter of the Association for Computational Linguistics (NAACL)*, pages 897–906.

Christoph Müller and Michael Strube. 2006. Multi-level annotation of linguistic data with mmax2. *Corpus technology and language pedagogy: New resources, new tools, new methods*, 3:197–214.

Qiang Ning, Hao Wu, Rujun Han, Nanyun Peng, Matt Gardner, and Dan Roth. 2020. TORQUE: A reading comprehension dataset of temporal ordering questions. In *Proceedings of the Conference on Empirical Methods in Natural Language Processing (EMNLP)*.

Qiang Ning, Hao Wu, and Dan Roth. 2018. A multi-axis annotation scheme for event temporal relations. In *Proceedings of the Annual Meeting of the Association for Computational Linguistics (ACL)*, pages 1318–1328. Association for Computational Linguistics.

Constantin Orăsan. 2003. PALinkA: A highly customisable tool for discourse annotation. In *Proceedings of the Fourth SIGdial Workshop of Discourse and Dialogue*, pages 39–43.

Joelle Pineau. 2020. The Machine Learning Reproducibility Checklist. `https://www.cs.mcgill.ca/~jpineau/ReproducibilityChecklist.pdf`.

Pranav Rajpurkar, Jian Zhang, Konstantin Lopyrev, and Percy Liang. 2016. SQuAD: 100,000+ questions for machine comprehension of text. In *Proceedings of the Conference on Empirical Methods in Natural Language Processing (EMNLP)*, pages 2383–2392.

Pontus Stenetorp, Sampo Pyysalo, Goran Topić, Tomoko Ohta, Sophia Ananiadou, and Jun'ichi Tsujii. 2012. Brat: A web-based tool for nlp-assisted text annotation. In *Proceedings of the Conference of the European Chapter of the Association for Computational Linguistics (EACL)*.

Carson T Schütze. 2016. *The empirical base of linguistics: Grammaticality judgments and linguistic methodology*. Language Science Press.

Erik F Tjong Kim Sang and Fien De Meulder. 2003. Introduction to the conll-2003 shared task: Language-independent named entity recognition. In *Proceedings of the Conference of the North American Chapter of the Association for Computational Linguistics (NAACL)*.

Naushad UzZaman, Hector Llorens, James Allen, Leon Derczynski, Marc Verhagen, and James Pustejovsky.

2013. SemEval-2013 Task 1: TEMPEVAL-3: Evaluating time expressions, events, and temporal relations. *Proceedings of the Joint Conference on Lexical and Computational Semantics (*SEM)*, 2:1–9.

`SciSight`: Combining faceted navigation and research group detection for COVID-19 exploratory scientific search

Tom Hope[♣,♡]   Jason Portenoy[♣,♥]*   Kishore Vasan[♥]*   Jonathan Borchardt[♣]*

Eric Horvitz[♠]   Daniel S. Weld[♣,♡]   Marti A. Hearst[◇]   Jevin West[♥]

[♣]Allen Institute for Artificial Intelligence
[♡]Paul G. Allen School for Computer Science & Engineering, University of Washington
[♥]Information School, University of Washington
[♠]Microsoft Research   [◇]University of California, Berkeley
{tomh,jasonp,jonathanb}@allenai.org   {kishorev,jevinw}@uw.edu

Abstract

The COVID-19 pandemic has sparked unprecedented mobilization of scientists, generating a deluge of papers that makes it hard for researchers to keep track and explore new directions. Search engines are designed for targeted queries, not for discovery of connections across a corpus. In this paper, we present **SciSight, a system for exploratory search** of COVID-19 research integrating two key capabilities: first, exploring associations between biomedical facets automatically extracted from papers (e.g., genes, drugs, diseases, patient outcomes); second, combining textual and network information to search and visualize *groups* of researchers and their ties. SciSight[1] has so far served over $15K$ users with over $42K$ page views and 13% returns.

1 Introduction

Scientists worldwide are racing against the growing number of COVID-19 infections, to understand and treat the disease (Apuzzo and Kirkpatrick, 2020). However, a very different kind of exponential growth has been plaguing researchers – the flurry of papers published every year, at a rate that continues to increase (Williamson and Minter, 2019). At the time of this writing, the COVID-19 Open Research Dataset (CORD-19) (Wang et al., 2020a) includes over 130,000 publications of potential relevance, both historical and cutting-edge.

To boost scientific discovery over this corpus, we propose SciSight, a working prototype system for **exploratory search of the COVID-19 literature**. Unlike many tools (see Section 2), we shift the focus from searching over lists of papers or authors, to navigating **networks of biomedical concepts and research groups** – for example, exploring links between COVID-19 and other diseases, or labs working on treatments. While search engines are a powerful tool for finding documents, they are mostly geared toward targeted search, when researchers know what they are looking for – less useful for exploring connections that are not obvious from reading individual papers (Bales et al., 2009; White and Roth, 2009).

Building exploratory interfaces in science is difficult not only due to the complexities of scientific content, but also because of social undercurrents that have tremendous effects on the construction of knowledge (Wagner and Leydesdorff, 2005; Pan et al., 2012; West et al., 2013) (as reflected, for example, in biased citation patterns (King et al., 2017)). Silos of knowledge throughout the literature (Vilhena et al., 2014)[2] can hinder research advancement and cross-fertilization across groups and fields that is crucial for driving innovation (Hope et al., 2017; Kittur et al., 2019), ultimately impacting human lives (Loevinsohn et al., 2015). These problems are acute when it comes to the COVID-19 pandemic, with new information rapidly emerging and urgently needed.

We aim to incorporate the social structure into an intuitive design interface, to help researchers **make connections to other groups and ideas in the literature** by traversing across networks of concepts and groups of scientists – helping users discover **who is working on what, and where?**

We identify groups by clustering the co-authorship graph, and extract topics and entities from the group's papers. Each group is represented using textual and network information: the group's salient authors (*who*), the topics they

---

* Equal contribution.
[1]http://scisight.apps.allenai.org/

[2]So Long to the Silos, Nature Biotech, https://www.nature.com/articles/nbt.3544

Proceedings of the 2020 EMNLP (Systems Demonstrations), pages 135–143
November 16-20, 2020. ©2020 Association for Computational Linguistics

work on (*what*) and their affiliations (*where*). We build meta-edges capturing topical affinity between groups using a language model fine-tuned for semantic similarity, and present approaches for searching for groups with queries consisting of authors, topics and affiliations. Each selected query automatically suggests new queries to try, to support exploration (Kairam et al., 2015).

In summary, our main contributions:

- A working prototype for exploratory search and visualization of COVID-19 scientific literature and collaboration networks, based on a fusion of automatically extracted textual information (topics, entities) and co-authorship network information.

- User interviews with experts suggest that SciSight can help complement standard search and help discover new directions.

2 Related work

The field of bibliometric visualization goes back decades (Borgman and Furner, 2002), with a large body of work. Visualizations of the scientific literature can take many shapes and forms, with the aim of depicting the connections between fields, topics, authors, and, most commonly, papers (Bales et al., 2020). While much research has been done in this field over the years, actual tools that are readily available primarily focus on visualization of citation-based graphs between *individual* authors, papers or topics (Van Eck and Waltman, 2010; Synnestvedt et al., 2005; Persson et al., 2009). While this rich information could in theory be useful, in practice it often renders the visualization inscrutable, especially for real-world networks comprising many authors. This problem is especially acute when the goal is to enable discovery of new areas with unfamiliar authors.

Recently, such tools have been applied to COVID-19 papers, such as journal networks and heat maps of frequently occurring terms (Haghani et al., 2020). However, many tools require training before being able to be used, and state of the art bibliometric mapping is currently considered "complex and unwieldy" (Bales et al., 2020), potentially because the typical user "does not *immediately* comprehend a map and (as a result) is not enticed into using it" (Buter et al., 2006).

COVID-19 tools. In response to COVID-19, many tools for exploring the relevant literature have been released. The great majority featured paper search interfaces, with lists of titles and abstracts being the main focus. Many of the COVID-19 tools we reviewed included standard faceted search functionality (Yee et al., 2003; Hearst, 2006; Tunkelang, 2009), enabling users to filter papers according to various facets. In a search tool from Microsoft Azure (Microsoft, 2020), for example, users can filter search results by various facets (such as by authors or gene mentions extracted automatically from texts). Similar services were made available by IBM Watson (IBM, 2020), Elsevier (Elsevier, 2020) and the National Institutes of Health (NIH, 2020).

Currently a small number of tools focus on concept associations. One tool (Tu et al., 2020) feeds a COVID-19 knowledge graph (KG) from (Wang et al., 2020b) into Kibana[3], an external product for creating dashboards with complex heat maps of term frequencies in documents, including a specialized query language for users with sufficient familiarity with Kibana. A tool from (Bras et al., 2020) shows clusters of high-level topics extracted with Latent Dirichlet Allocation (LDA) (Blei et al., 2003) (visualized with word clouds).

In this paper, we integrate textual information from papers and the network of author collaborations, allowing users to drill down from research groups to papers to associations between entities in one system, with a custom interface aimed to help users "comprehend the map" (Bales et al., 2020; Buter et al., 2006) intuitively.

3 SciSight: system overview

In this section we present an overview of our prototype and its distinct components. We motivate each by discussing researcher needs. We illustrate SciSight's features and potential with the following illustrative example:

Marc is a researcher interested in exploring Chloroquine, an anti-malarial drug that has been surrounded with controversies in the context of COVID-19 (Touret and de Lamballerie, 2020). In particular, Marc wants to find connections between Chloroquine and other drugs and diseases, and to understand how these entities are interconnected in order to explore other candidate drugs and potential side-effects. Marc is familiar with the field and its main papers, but the amount of re-

---

[3]https://www.elastic.co/kibana

lated work is overwhelming with a litany of drugs and diseases. Complicating things further, knowing that Chloroquine is not a new medication, Marc wants to examine connections across years of research, not just recent work.

3.1 Collocation explorer

Users of SciSight can search for a term/concept of interest, or get suggestions based on important COVID-19 topics. Searching for a term displays a network of top related terms mined from the corpus, based on term collocation counts across the corpus (co-appearance in the same sentence). Entities are displayed in a customized chord diagram (Lee et al., 2015) layout[4], with edge width corresponding to collocation frequency. As seen in Figure 1a, interrelations between all terms are shown (not just with the query), presenting the user with more potential connections to explore (users can also control the number of entities shown). Clicking an edge between two entities displays a list of papers containing both terms.

Continuing our example, Marc can search for Chloroquine and see its network of associations, such as a potential connection to liver damage, or its connection to other drugs such as the anti-viral drug Ribavirin. Marc can navigate the graph by clicking nodes to further explore new associations (e.g., clicking liver damage to potentially discover more related drugs and diseases). Navigation is known to help facilitate exploration (Kairam et al., 2015), such as when users do not have a pinpointed query in mind (White and Roth, 2009).

Entity extraction and selection To extract entities we use S2ORC-BERT (Lo et al., 2020), a new language model pre-trained on a large corpus of scientific papers. This model is fine-tuned[5] on two separate biomedical named entity recognition (NER) tasks (BC5CDR (Li et al., 2016) and JNLPBA (Kim et al., 2004)), enabling us to extract spans of text corresponding to *proteins, genes, cells, drugs, and diseases* from across the corpus. We extract entities only from titles and abstracts of papers to reduce noise and focus on the more salient entities in each paper. We show only entities collocated at least twice with other enti-

---

[4] SciSight is implemented with React, server-side Crossfilter, DC.js, D3.js, and Varnish.

[5] `https://github.com/allenai/scibert/blob/master/scripts/exp.py`.

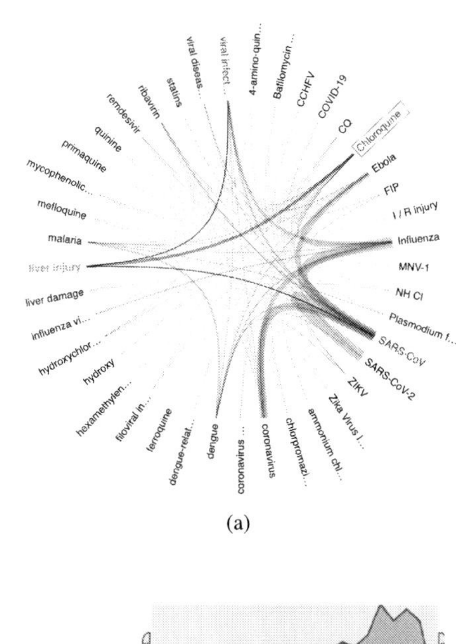

(a)

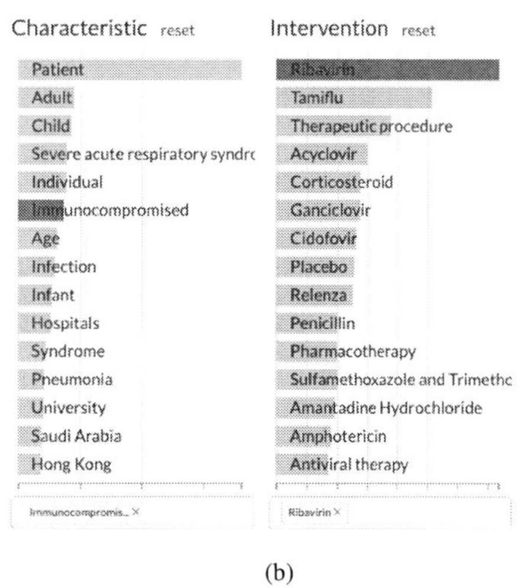

(b)

Figure 1: (a) **Collocation explorer**: corpus-wide associations between biomedical entities, such as drugs and conditions. Highlighted in the figure is the edge between Chloroquine and liver injury. (b) **Exploratory search** of connections between patient characteristics and interventions. Papers working with immunocomprimised patients and Ribavirin would be listed below the facet feature. The time graph above shows the number of papers per year with these criteria.

ties. Our choice of entities is the result of an initial round of interviews with biomedical experts, identifying these concepts as fundamental to the study of the virus. Participants with a more clinical orientation expressed interest in viewing associations between drugs and diseases, while users from a biology background wished to focus on proteins, genes and cells. When asked whether they would prefer to have all types of entities in one view, participants responded with a preference for separate graphs to avoid clutter and reduce cognitive effort.

3.2 Faceted exploratory search

Similarly to other tools, we incorporate a faceted search tool into SciSight. Our focus is on exploration of topics and associations, with relevant papers displayed below the facets for users wishing to dig deeper after refining their search – rather than being featured front and center. When searching for a topic or an author, new suggestions to help refine the search are presented based on top co-mentions with the initial query to help prevent fixation on an initial topic and boost associative exploration (Kairam et al., 2015). In our prototype for this feature we aimed at providing one compact set of facets that can cater to a wide range of interests but still be sufficiently granular. Based on formative interviews and a review of biomedical concept taxonomies, we converged on three widely-used topical facets in biomedicine, that capture characteristics of patients or the problem, interventions, and outcomes (Schardt et al., 2007) (see Figure 1b), extracted automatically from biomedical abstracts with the distant supervision model in (Wallace et al., 2016). In addition, CORD-19 metadata facets are available, such as journal, affiliation and author. The number of relevant publications is shown over time, possibly revealing trends for specific facets. Users can adjust the time range to update the papers and facets displayed.

Having spotted a potential connection to Ribavirin, Marc searches for it under the intervention facet to find out about related patient populations and outcomes, and to see how often it has been mentioned over time (see Figure 1b). A characteristic that pops-up and catches Marc's attention is immunocompromised patients, as he recalls a colleague discussing the risk of treating such populations. He finds peaks of interest around some points in time, and drilling down to papers from around 2016 finds a paper with the following conclusion: "No consensus was found regarding the use of oral versus inhaled RBV... such heterogeneity demonstrates the need for further studies ... in immunocompromised hosts." Marc realizes his knowledge of this domain is lacking, and decides to zoom out and find out what groups and labs are working on immunity and viral diseases, perhaps also discovering some familiar collaborators.

3.3 Network of science

In the course of formative interviews with domain experts, participants expressed the need to see what other groups are doing in order to keep track, explore new fields and potentially collaborate. We build a visualization of groups and their ties and integrate this social graph with exploratory faceted search over topics, authors and affiliations. We design our tool with the following components.

3.3.1 Author groups

To identify groups of researchers, we start by constructing a co-authorship network in which links between authors represent collaboration on a paper, weighted by the number of papers. We then employ an overlapping community detection algorithm based on ego-splitting (Epasto et al., 2017) so that authors can belong to multiple clusters (groups). We relax the assumption typically made in co-authorship analysis that authors belong to one group alone – in reality, researchers can "wear many hats" and belong to different groups depending on what they work on and with whom.

As shown in Figure 2, we represent groups with "cards" (Bota et al., 2016) of salient authors, affiliations and topics (with information from Microsoft Academic Graph (MAG) (Sinha et al., 2015)). Cards are color-coded to reflect relevance to the user's initial query – aiming to strike a balance between the relevance and diversity of the results shown. Users may select how many groups to view, zoom in/out, click a group to see a list of its topics, authors and papers.

To explore groups recently active in this space we select authors with at least one paper in CORD-19 since the year 2017. We focus on the giant connected component of this network (111,236 author nodes, 951,072 edges; smaller components typically represented disambiguation errors), and run the community detection algorithm. We observe a small number of "super clusters", large communities with hundreds of authors not densely linked, a

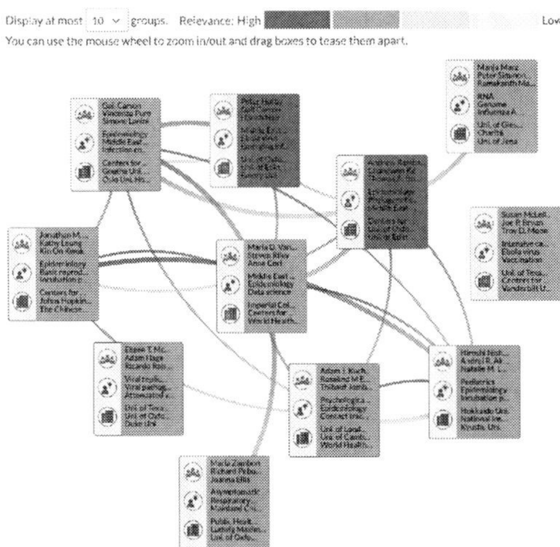

Figure 2:
Visualizing the network of groups with group "cards". Each card has three icons denoting the top three authors, topics and affiliations, respectively. Card color indicates relevance to the search query. Green edges capture social affinity (shared authors), and purple edges capture topical affinity.

well-known characteristic of community structure in real-world networks (Leskovec et al., 2009). We thus apply the clustering algorithm again within clusters with more than 120 authors to break them down further into denser groups. This results in 6,475 clusters. There are 5276 authors belonging to two groups; 6657 are in more than one cluster, and 1381 in more than two clusters.

We display a mix of textual and social information: the most salient authors (*who*), affiliations (*where*) and topics (*what*). We rank topics by their TF-IDF scores within a cluster, and authors and affiliations by relative frequency in a group. Users can also dig deeper into groups with two further levels of resolution. First, when hovering over a group with the cursor, users are shown a tooltip box with the top 5 authors, affiliations and topics, with full names shown. Secondly, upon clicking a group we show full ranked lists of these entities, in addition to the group's papers ranked by recency (with title, abstract, journal and authors, including a hyperlink to read the full paper).

3.3.2 Group links

We construct two types of links between groups. The first type (shown as purple edges) represents topical affinity across groups – the interests they have in common based on publishing on similar topics. The second type of link (shown as green edges) captures social affinity between groups, meaning groups with many shared author relationships. By providing both kinds of links, the tool implicitly suggests potential collaborations or connections, particularly when a social connection does not currently exist alongside a topical one.

Cluster Relationships To find topical affinity between clusters we embed topic surface forms with a language model trained to capture semantic similarity[6]. With each topic represented with its embedding, we get a vector representation of groups with a simple TF-IDF weighted average of embeddings, and compute cosine similarity.

Finding Bridges As a test case for demonstrating our framework's ability to find gaps and similarities across groups of researchers, we identify "bridges" between groups, potentially signifying structural holes (Burt, 2004) in the author network. We examine groups that work on *data science* (MAG topic), a highly interdisciplinary field connecting researchers from multiple domains. We discover *Derek AT Cummings*, a prominent biologist and epidemiologist with appointments at two different universities. We find him to be a sole shared author between two different clusters: one focusing on areas tied with virology and medical microbiology, while the other more associated with computational epidemiology. The former group has 15 authors, and the latter has 35.

Similarity Evaluation In a preliminary experiment, we selected 30 random clusters and computed topical affinities to other clusters. For each group we randomly sample one cluster out of the top 3 closely related clusters, and another cluster from the bottom 50% of farthest clusters (for network construction as shown to users, we only create links between top-most similar groups). We randomize the results and give them to a biomedical data analyst for annotation. We find that overall, we are able to correctly find pairs of research groups that work in similar areas with a 80% precision. In future work we plan to collect validation data enabling to measure both precision and recall.

3.3.3 Exploratory search for groups

Users can search topics, affiliations, or authors. We rank topics based on global TF-IDF scores. As in standard faceted search, queries across facets

---

[6]RoBERTa-large-STS-SNLI(Liu et al., 2019) `github.com/UKPLab/sentence-transformers`

are conjunctive (e.g., gene sequencing AND Harvard), and queries within facets are disjunctive (e.g., gene sequencing OR bioassays). Each query consists of one or more choices for each facets. A selection automatically suggests new facets that are frequently associated with the original query, suggesting more groups and topics to explore.

The problem of finding relevant communities to a query has been explored to a certain extent under the rubric of *community search* (Sozio and Gionis, 2010; Fang et al., 2020), in which given a graph $\mathcal{G}$ and a set of query nodes in the graph, the objective is to find a subgraph of $\mathcal{G}$ that contains the query nodes and is also densely connected. The problem of community search in *heterogeneous* networks has only recently been explored (Fang et al., 2020), and only for one query node. In addition, in our setting we aim to retrieve high-relevance groups, with ranked topics, authors and affiliations. We propose to retrieve relevant results for a user's query with two simple approaches. In the first, we compute the overlap between query facets q and the top-K salient facets f for each group, and rank groups by normalized overlap size $\frac{|\{q:q\in f\}|}{|f|}$. In the second approach, we compute weighted PageRank scores (Xing and Ghorbani, 2004) over a graph with meta-nodes representing groups, and meta-edges as described earlier in this section. We do so separately for both types of edges: one for topical affinity, and the other for social proximity. At query time, we compute the average of these scores and the facet overlap score.

4 Informal user studies and findings

We conduct preliminary user studies with four researchers and one practitioner. **P1** is a research scientist in virology, whose work also studies the Zika virus; **P2** is a postdoctoral fellow in the area of virology, working on viral infections and human antibody responses, and **P3** is a postdoctoral fellow and MD working primarily in Oncology. **P4** is a medical professional and PharmD. **P5** is a researcher working on viral diseases and proteins.

Discovering unknown associations. Based on interest in a the CR3022 antibody , **P2** searched for it with SciSight's collocation feature, finding "very relevant associations" and also "two potentially surprising and interesting publications. I'm going to look into those papers." **P1** searched for cells linked to a type of cytopathic effect and found Calu-3 (a human lung cancer cell line),

which led to "spotting an interferon with relevant and interesting studies, very useful." **P4** discovered a link between broad-spectrum antivirals and MERS, providing a "new and strongly relevant idea". **P5** was able to find associations considered new and interesting between the TNF inflammatory cytokine and ERK1/2, a type of protein kinase (relevant to **P5**'s interest in cytokine profiles).

Finding new groups and directions. **P1** gave an example of a group (lab) using assays to identify which proteins antibodies bind to in order to to neutralize HIV, and connecting to other groups working on serum utilization for SARS to potentially collaborate. When searching for groups tied with a prominent scientist, **P2** found a group associated with the scientist with recent work (Yuan et al., 2020) revealing a new direction regarding SARS-CoV-2 epitopes. **P2** also found a group in China with shared focus on epitopes but no social ties, revealing "new perspectives that I would not have found otherwise" on virus evolution.

Limitations: more information and features. **P1, P4** suggested that user-inputted concepts be combined with existing concepts/terms on-the-fly, and that edges could be removed by the user. **P3** and **P4** suggested ranking associations by "measures of novelty" to allow users to focus on emergent knowledge. Participants mentioned a diverse range of other entities to explore, e.g., patient weight, metabolic speed, drug dosages, vaccines, mutation mechanisms, and various techniques.

5 Conclusion

In this paper we presented SciSight, an evolving system for scientific literature search and exploration. We demonstrate SciSight's use on a large corpus of papers related to the COVID-19 pandemic and previous coronaviruses. We use state-of-the-art scientific language models to extract entities such as proteins, drugs and diseases, and an overlapping community detection approach for identifying groups of researchers. To visualize groups we display group "cards" with a novel link scheme capturing topical and social affinities between communities, designed to identify socially disjoint groups working on similar topics. Preliminary user interviews suggest that SciSight can help complement standard search and may pave new research directions. In future work, we plan to conduct extensive studies to validate SciSight and better understand its potential and limitations.

References

Matt Apuzzo and David D. Kirkpatrick. 2020. Covid-19 changed how the world does science, together. https://www.nytimes.com/2020/04/01/world/europe/coronavirus-science-research-cooperation.html.

Michael E Bales, David R Kaufman, and Stephen B Johnson. 2009. Evaluation of a prototype search and visualization system for exploring scientific communities. In *AMIA Annual Symposium Proceedings*, volume 2009, page 24. American Medical Informatics Association.

Michael E Bales, Drew N Wright, Peter R Oxley, and Terrie R Wheeler. 2020. Bibliometric visualization and analysis software: State of the art, workflows, and best practices.

David M Blei, Andrew Y Ng, and Michael I Jordan. 2003. Latent dirichlet allocation. *Journal of machine Learning research*, 3(Jan):993–1022.

Christine L Borgman and Jonathan Furner. 2002. Scholarly communication and bibliometrics. *Annual review of information science and technology*, 36(1):2–72.

Horatiu Bota, Ke Zhou, and Joemon M Jose. 2016. Playing your cards right: The effect of entity cards on search behaviour and workload. In *Proceedings of the 2016 ACM on Conference on Human Information Interaction and Retrieval*, pages 131–140.

Pierre Le Bras, Azimeh Gharavi, David A. Robb, Ana F. Vidal, Stefano Padilla, and Mike J. Chantler. 2020. Visualising covid-19 research.

Ronald S Burt. 2004. Structural holes and good ideas. *American journal of sociology*, 110(2):349–399.

RK Buter, ECM Noyons, M Van Mackelenbergh, and T Laine. 2006. Combining concept maps and bibliometric maps: First explorations. *Scientometrics*, 66(2):377–387.

Elsevier. 2020. Elsevier coronavirus research repository. https://coronavirus.1science.com/search. Last accessed 2020-05-12.

Alessandro Epasto, Silvio Lattanzi, and Renato Paes Leme. 2017. Ego-splitting framework: From non-overlapping to overlapping clusters. In *Proceedings of the 23rd ACM SIGKDD International Conference on Knowledge Discovery and Data Mining*, pages 145–154.

Yixiang Fang, Yixing Yang, Wenjie Zhang, Xuemin Lin, and Xin Cao. 2020. Effective and efficient community search over large heterogeneous information networks. *Proceedings of the VLDB Endowment*, 13(6):854–867.

Milad Haghani, Michiel CJ Bliemer, Floris Goerlandt, and Jie Li. 2020. The scientific literature on coronaviruses, covid-19 and its associated safety-related research dimensions: A scientometric analysis and scoping review. *Safety Science*.

Marti A Hearst. 2006. Clustering versus faceted categories for information exploration. *Communications of the ACM*, 49(4):59–61.

Tom Hope, Joel Chan, Aniket Kittur, and Dafna Shahaf. 2017. Accelerating innovation through analogy mining. In *Proceedings of the 23rd ACM SIGKDD International Conference on Knowledge Discovery and Data Mining*, pages 235–243.

IBM. 2020. Watson insights for medical literature — covid-19 navigator. https://covid-19-navigator.mybluemix.net/search. Last accessed 2020-05-12.

Sanjay Kairam, Nathalie Henry Riche, Steven Drucker, Roland Fernandez, and Jeffrey Heer. 2015. Refinery: Visual exploration of large, heterogeneous networks through associative browsing. In *Computer graphics forum*, volume 34, pages 301–310. Wiley Online Library.

Jin-Dong Kim, Tomoko Ohta, Yoshimasa Tsuruoka, Yuka Tateisi, and Nigel Collier. 2004. Introduction to the bio-entity recognition task at jnlpba. In *Proceedings of the international joint workshop on natural language processing in biomedicine and its applications*, pages 70–75. Citeseer.

Molly M King, Carl T Bergstrom, Shelley J Correll, Jennifer Jacquet, and Jevin D West. 2017. Men set their own cites high: Gender and self-citation across fields and over time. *Socius*, 3:2378023117738903.

Aniket Kittur, Lixiu Yu, Tom Hope, Joel Chan, Hila Lifshitz-Assaf, Karni Gilon, Felicia Ng, Robert E Kraut, and Dafna Shahaf. 2019. Scaling up analogical innovation with crowds and ai. *Proceedings of the National Academy of Sciences*, 116(6):1870–1877.

Sukwon Lee, Sung-Hee Kim, Ya-Hsin Hung, Heidi Lam, Youn-ah Kang, and Ji Soo Yi. 2015. How do people make sense of unfamiliar visualizations?: A grounded model of novice's information visualization sensemaking. *IEEE transactions on visualization and computer graphics*, 22(1):499–508.

Jure Leskovec, Kevin J Lang, Anirban Dasgupta, and Michael W Mahoney. 2009. Community structure in large networks: Natural cluster sizes and the absence of large well-defined clusters. *Internet Mathematics*, 6(1):29–123.

Jiao Li, Yueping Sun, Robin J Johnson, Daniela Sciaky, Chih-Hsuan Wei, Robert Leaman, Allan Peter Davis, Carolyn J Mattingly, Thomas C Wiegers, and Zhiyong Lu. 2016. Biocreative v cdr task corpus: a resource for chemical disease relation extraction. *Database*, 2016.

Yinhan Liu, Myle Ott, Naman Goyal, Jingfei Du, Mandar Joshi, Danqi Chen, Omer Levy, Mike Lewis, Luke Zettlemoyer, and Veselin Stoyanov. 2019. Roberta: A robustly optimized bert pretraining approach. *arXiv preprint arXiv:1907.11692*.

Kyle Lo, Lucy Lu Wang, Mark Neumann, Rodney Kinney, and Daniel S. Weld. 2020. S2ORC: The Semantic Scholar Open Research Corpus. In *Proceedings of ACL*.

Michael Loevinsohn, Lyla Mehta, Katie Cuming, Alan Nicol, Oliver Cumming, and Jeroen HJ Ensink. 2015. The cost of a knowledge silo: a systematic re-review of water, sanitation and hygiene interventions. *Health policy and planning*, 30(5):660–674.

Microsoft. 2020. Azure cognitive search - covid-19 search demo. `https://covid19search.azurewebsites.net/`. Last accessed 2020-05-12.

NIH. 2020. Nih litcovid. `https://www.ncbi.nlm.nih.gov/research/coronavirus/`. Last accessed 2020-05-12.

Raj Kumar Pan, Kimmo Kaski, and Santo Fortunato. 2012. World citation and collaboration networks: uncovering the role of geography in science. *Scientific reports*, 2:902.

Olle Persson, Rickard Danell, and J Wiborg Schneider. 2009. How to use bibexcel for various types of bibliometric analysis. *Celebrating scholarly communication studies: A Festschrift for Olle Persson at his 60th Birthday*.

Connie Schardt, Martha B Adams, Thomas Owens, Sheri Keitz, and Paul Fontelo. 2007. Utilization of the pico framework to improve searching pubmed for clinical questions. *BMC medical informatics and decision making*, 7(1):16.

Arnab Sinha, Zhihong Shen, Yang Song, Hao Ma, Darrin Eide, Bo-June Hsu, and Kuansan Wang. 2015. An overview of microsoft academic service (mas) and applications. In *Proceedings of the 24th international conference on world wide web*, pages 243–246.

Mauro Sozio and Aristides Gionis. 2010. The community-search problem and how to plan a successful cocktail party. In *Proceedings of the 16th ACM SIGKDD international conference on Knowledge discovery and data mining*, pages 939–948.

Marie B Synnestvedt, Chaomei Chen, and John H Holmes. 2005. Citespace ii: visualization and knowledge discovery in bibliographic databases. In *AMIA Annual Symposium Proceedings*. American Medical Informatics Association.

Franck Touret and Xavier de Lamballerie. 2020. Of chloroquine and covid-19. *Antiviral Research*, page 104762.

Jingxuan Tu, Marc Verhagen, Brent Cochran, and James Pustejovsky. 2020. Exploration and discovery of the covid-19 literature through semantic visualization. *arXiv preprint arXiv:2007.01800*.

Daniel Tunkelang. 2009. *Faceted search*, volume 5. Morgan & Claypool Publishers.

Nees Van Eck and Ludo Waltman. 2010. Software survey: Vosviewer, a computer program for bibliometric mapping. *Scientometrics*.

Daril A Vilhena, Jacob G Foster, Martin Rosvall, Jevin D West, James Evans, and Carl T Bergstrom. 2014. Finding cultural holes: How structure and culture diverge in networks of scholarly communication. *Sociological Science*, 1:221.

Caroline S Wagner and Loet Leydesdorff. 2005. Network structure, self-organization, and the growth of international collaboration in science. *Research policy*, 34(10):1608–1618.

Byron C Wallace, Joël Kuiper, Aakash Sharma, Mingxi Zhu, and Iain J Marshall. 2016. Extracting pico sentences from clinical trial reports using supervised distant supervision. *The Journal of Machine Learning Research*. Available from `drevidence.com`.

Lucy Lu Wang, Kyle Lo, Yoganand Chandrasekhar, Russell Reas, Jiangjiang Yang, Darrin Eide, Kathryn Funk, Rodney Kinney, Ziyang Liu, William Merrill, et al. 2020a. Cord-19: The covid-19 open research dataset. *arXiv preprint arXiv:2004.10706*.

Qingyun Wang, Xuan Wang, Manling Li, Heng Ji, and Jiawei Han. 2020b. Knowledge extraction to assist scientific discovery from corona virus literature. `http://blender.cs.illinois.edu/covid19/`. Last accessed 2020-05-12.

Jevin D West, Jennifer Jacquet, Molly M King, Shelley J Correll, and Carl T Bergstrom. 2013. The role of gender in scholarly authorship. *PloS one*, 8(7).

Ryen W White and Resa A Roth. 2009. Exploratory search: Beyond the query-response paradigm. *Synthesis lectures on information concepts, retrieval, and services*, 1(1):1–98.

Peace Ossom Williamson and Christian IJ Minter. 2019. Exploring pubmed as a reliable resource for scholarly communications services. *Journal of the Medical Library Association: JMLA*, 107(1):16.

Wenpu Xing and Ali Ghorbani. 2004. Weighted pagerank algorithm. In *Proceedings. Second Annual Conference on Communication Networks and Services Research, 2004.*, pages 305–314. IEEE.

Ka-Ping Yee, Kirsten Swearingen, Kevin Li, and Marti Hearst. 2003. Faceted metadata for image search and browsing. In *Proceedings of the SIGCHI conference on Human factors in computing systems*, pages 401–408.

Meng Yuan, Nicholas C Wu, Xueyong Zhu, Chang-Chun D Lee, Ray TY So, Huibin Lv, Chris KP Mok, and Ian A Wilson. 2020. A highly conserved cryptic epitope in the receptor binding domains of sars-cov-2 and sars-cov. *Science*, 368(6491):630–633.

SIMULEVAL : An Evaluation Toolkit
for Simultaneous Translation

Xutai Ma [1,2], Mohammad Javad Dousti[1], Changhan Wang[1], Jiatao Gu[1], Juan Pino[1]

[1]Facebook AI
[2]Johns Hopkins University

xutai_ma@jhu.edu
{juancarabina,dousti,changhan,jgu}@fb.com

Abstract

Simultaneous translation on both text and speech focuses on a real-time and low-latency scenario where the model starts translating before reading the complete source input. Evaluating simultaneous translation models is more complex than offline models because the latency is another factor to consider in addition to translation quality. The research community, despite its growing focus on novel modeling approaches to simultaneous translation, currently lacks a universal evaluation procedure. Therefore, we present SIMULEVAL, an easy-to-use and general evaluation toolkit for both simultaneous text and speech translation. A server-client scheme is introduced to create a simultaneous translation scenario, where the server sends source input and receives predictions for evaluation and the client executes customized policies. Given a policy, it automatically performs simultaneous decoding and collectively reports several popular latency metrics. We also adapt latency metrics from text simultaneous translation to the speech task. Additionally, SIMULEVAL is equipped with a visualization interface to provide better understanding of the simultaneous decoding process of a system. SIMULEVAL has already been extensively used for the IWSLT 2020 shared task on simultaneous speech translation. Code will be released upon publication. [1]

1 Introduction

Simultaneous translation, the task of generating translations before reading the entire text or speech source input, has become an increasingly popular topic for both text and speech translation (Grissom II et al., 2014; Cho and Esipova, 2016; Gu et al., 2017; Alinejad et al., 2018; Arivazhagan et al., 2019; Zheng et al., 2019; Ma et al., 2020; Ren et al., 2020). Simultaneous models are typically evaluated from quality and latency perspective. Note that the term *latency* is overloaded and sometimes refers to the actual system speed. In this paper, *latency* refers to the simultaneous ability, which is how much partial source information is needed to start the translation process.

While the translation quality is usually measured by BLEU (Papineni et al., 2002; Post, 2018), a wide variety of latency measurements have been introduced, such as Average Proportion (AP) (Cho and Esipova, 2016), Continues Wait Length (CW) (Gu et al., 2017), Average Lagging (AL) (Ma et al., 2019), Differentiable Average Lagging (DAL) (Cherry and Foster, 2019), and so on. Unfortunately, the latency evaluation processes across different works are not consistent: 1) the latency metric definitions are not precise enough with respect to text segmentation; 2) the definitions are also not precise enough with respect to the speech segmentation, for example some models are evaluated on speech segments (Ren et al., 2020) while others are evaluated on time duration (Ansari et al., 2020); 3) little prior work has released implementations of the decoding process and latency measurement. The lack of clarity and consistency of the latency evaluation process makes it challenging to compare different works and prevents tracking the scientific progress of this field.

In order to provide researchers in the community with a standard, open and easy-to-use method to evaluate simultaneous speech and text translation systems, we introduce SIMULEVAL, an open source evaluation toolkit which automatically simulates a real-time scenario and evaluates both latency

---

[1]The code is available at https://github.com/facebookresearch/SimulEval

Proceedings of the 2020 EMNLP (Systems Demonstrations), pages 144–150
November 16-20, 2020. ©2020 Association for Computational Linguistics

and translation quality. The design of this toolkit follows a server-client scheme, which has the advantage of creating a fully simultaneous translation environment and is suitable for shared tasks such as the IWSLT 2020 shared task on simultaneous speech translation[2] or the 1st Workshop on Automatic Simultaneous Translation at ACL 2020[3]. The server provides source input (text or audio) upon request from the client, receives predictions from the client and returns different evaluation metrics when the translation process is complete. The client contains two components, an agent and a state, where the former executes the system's policy and the latter keeps track of information necessary to execute the policy as well as generating a translation. SIMULEVAL has built-in support for quality metrics such as BLEU (Papineni et al., 2002; Post, 2018), TER (Snover et al., 2006) and METEOR (Banerjee and Lavie, 2005), and latency metrics such as AP, AL and DAL. It also support customized evaluation functions. While all latency metrics have been defined for text translation, we discuss issues and solutions when adapting them to the task of simultaneous speech translation. Additionally, SIMULEVAL users can define their own customized metrics. SIMULEVAL also provides an interface to visualize the policy of the agent. An interactive visualization interface is implemented to illustrate the simultaneous decoding process. The initial version of SIMULEVAL was used to evaluate submissions from the first shared task on simultaneous speech translation at IWSLT 2020 (Ansari et al., 2020).

In the remainder of the paper, we first formally define the task of simultaneous translation. Next, latency metrics and their adaptation to the speech task are introduced. After that, we provide a high-level overview of the client-server design of SIMULEVAL. Finally, usage instructions and a case study are provided before concluding.

2 Task Formalization

An evaluation corpus for a translation task contains one or several instances, each of which consists of a source sequence $X = [x_1, ..., x_{|X|}]$ and a reference sequence $Y^* = [y_1^*, ..., y_{|Y|}^*]$. The system to be evaluated takes X as input, and generates $Y = [y_1, ..., y_{|Y|}]$. We denote the elements of the X, Y and Y^* segments. For text translation, each x_j is an individual word while for speech translation, x_j is a raw audio segment of duration T_j. In the simultaneous translation task, a system starts generating a hypothesis with partial input only. Then it either reads a new source segment, or writes a new target segment. Assuming $X_{1:j} = [x_1, ..., x_j], j < |X|$ has been read when generating y_i, we define the delay of y_i as

$$d_i = \begin{cases} j, & \text{when input is text} \\ \sum_{k=1}^{j} T_k, & \text{when input is speech} \end{cases} \quad (1)$$

Similar to an offline model, the quality is measured by comparing the hypothesis Y to the reference Y^* after the translation process is complete. On the other hand, the latency measurement involves considering partial hypotheses. The latency metrics are calculated from a function which takes a sequence of delays $D = [d_1, ..., d_{|Y|}]$ as input.

3 Latency Evaluation

3.1 Existing Text Latency Metrics

First, we review three latency metrics previously introduced for the text translation task.

Average Proportion (AP) (Cho and Esipova, 2016), defined in Eq. (2), measures the average of proportion of source input read when generating a target prediction.

$$\text{AP} = \frac{1}{|X||Y|} \sum_{i=1}^{|Y|} d_i \quad (2)$$

Despite AP's simplicity, several concerns have been raised. Specifically, AP is not length invariant, i.e. the value of the metric depends on the input and output lengths. For instance, AP for a wait-3 model (Ma et al., 2019) is 0.72 when $|X| = |Y| = 10$ but 0.52 when $|X| = |Y| = 100$. Moreover, AP is not evenly distributed on the $[0, 1]$ interval, i.e., values below 0.5 represent models that have lower latency than an ideal policy, and an improvement of 0.1 from 0.7 to 0.6 is much more difficult to obtain than the same absolute improvement from 0.9 to 0.8 (Ma et al., 2019).

Average Lagging (AL) first defines an ideal policy, which is equivalent to a wait-0 policy that has the same prediction as the system to be evaluated. Ma et al. (2019) define AL as

$$\text{AL} = \frac{1}{\tau(|X|)} \sum_{i=1}^{\tau(|X|)} d_i - \frac{(i-1)}{\gamma} \quad (3)$$

where $\tau(|\boldsymbol{X}|) = \min\{i|d_i = |\boldsymbol{X}|\}$ is the index of the target token when the policy first reaches the end of the source sentence and $\gamma = |\boldsymbol{Y}|/|\boldsymbol{X}|$. $(i-1)/\gamma$ term is the ideal policy for the system to compare with. AL has good properties such as being length-invariant and intuitive. Its value directly describes the lagging behind the ideal policy.

Differentiable Average Lagging (DAL) introduces a minimum delay of $1/\gamma$ after each operation. Unlike AL, it considers the tokens when $i > \tau(|\boldsymbol{X}|)$ (Cherry and Foster, 2019). It is defined in Eq. (4):

$$\text{DAL} = \frac{1}{|\boldsymbol{Y}|} \sum_{i=1}^{|\boldsymbol{Y}|} d_i' - \frac{i-1}{\gamma}, \quad (4)$$

where

$$d_i' = \begin{cases} d_i & i = 0 \\ \max(d_i, d_{i-1}' + \gamma) & i > 0 \end{cases}. \quad (5)$$

A minimum delay prevent DAL recovering from lagging once it has been incurred.

3.2 Adapting Metrics to the Speech Task

In this section, we adapt the three latency metrics introduced in Section 3.1 to the simultaneous speech translation task.

Average Proportion is straightforward to adapt to the speech task and as follows:

$$\text{AP}_{\text{speech}} = \frac{1}{|\boldsymbol{Y}| \sum_{j=1}^{|\boldsymbol{X}|} T_j} \sum_{i=1}^{|\boldsymbol{Y}|} d_i \quad (6)$$

Average Lagging is adapted as follows:

$$\text{AL}_{\text{speech}} = \frac{1}{\tau'(|\boldsymbol{X}|)} \sum_{i=1}^{\tau'(|\boldsymbol{X}|)} d_i - d_i^*, \quad (7)$$

where $\tau'(|\boldsymbol{X}|) = \min\{i|d_i = \sum_{j=1}^{|\boldsymbol{X}|} T_j\}$ and d_i^* are the delays of an ideal policy, of which the straightforward adaption is $d_i^* = (i-1) \times \sum_{j=1}^{|\boldsymbol{X}|} T_j /|\boldsymbol{Y}|$. However such adaptation is not robust for models that tend to stop hypothesis generation too early and generate translations that are too short. This is more likely to happen in simultaneous speech translation where a model can generate the end of sentence token too early, for example when there is a long pause even though the entire source input has not been consumed. Fig. 1

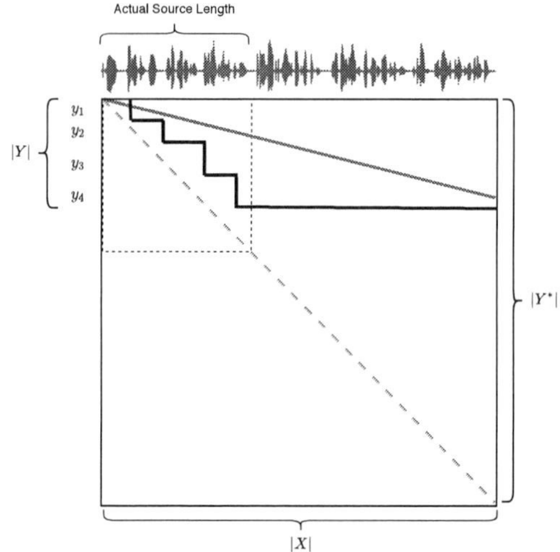

Figure 1: An example of original AL failed on early stop translation. Red (solid straight) line shows the ideal policy in (Ma et al., 2019). Green (dotted straight) line depicts the modified ideal policy in this paper. Black (solid zigzag) line demonstrates the alignment between source and target.

illustrate this phenomenon. The red line in Fig. 1 corresponds to the ideal policy defined in (Ma et al., 2019). We can see that when the model stops generating the translation, the lagging behind the ideal policy is negative. This is because the model stops reading any input after completing hypothesis generation. This kind of model can obtain relatively good latency-quality trade-offs as measured by AL (and BLEU), which does not reflect the reality. We thus define

$$d_i^* = (i-1) \cdot \sum_{j=1}^{|\boldsymbol{X}|} T_j /|\boldsymbol{Y}^*| \quad (8)$$

to prevent this issue, i.e., it is assumed that the ideal policy generates the reference rather than the system hypothesis. The newly defined ideal policy is represented by the green line in Fig. 1.

Differentiable Average Lagging for the speech task still uses Eq. (4) and Eq. (5) with a new γ defined as

$$\gamma_{\text{speech}} = |\boldsymbol{Y}|/ \sum_{j=1}^{|\boldsymbol{X}|} T_j \quad (9)$$

4 Architecture

SIMULEVAL simulates a real-time scenario by setting up a server and a client. The server and client

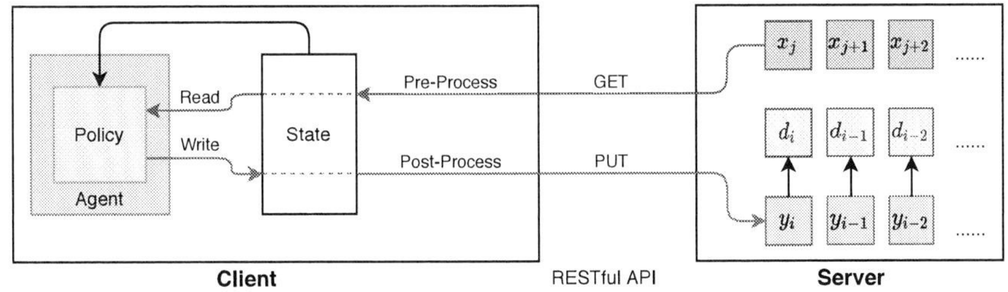

Figure 2: The architecture of SIMULEVAL. The client executes the policy and the server operates the evaluation.

can be run separately or jointly, and are connected through RESTful APIs. An overview is shown in Fig. 2.

4.1 Server

The server has primarily four functions. First, read source and reference files. Second, send source segments to the client upon a READ action. Third, receive predicted segments from the client upon a WRITE action, and record the corresponding delays. Fourth, run the evaluation on instances.

The evaluation process by the server on one instance is shown in Algorithm 1. Note that in line 18 in Algorithm 1, the server only runs sentence-level metrics. The server will collect Y, D and T for every instance in the evaluation corpus, and calculate corpus-level metrics after all hypotheses are complete.

Algorithm 1 Server side algorithm

    Input: $X = [x_1, ..., x_{|X|}], Y^* = [y_1^*, ..., y_{|Y^*|}^*]$
    Input: $Y = [], D = []$
    Input: $i = 0, j = 0, y_0 = \text{BOS}, d_0 = 0$
1: **while** $y_i \neq \text{EOS}$ **do**
2:     $r = \text{await\_request\_from\_client}()$
3:     **if** r.action $==$ READ **then**
4:         **if** $j < |X|$ **then**
5:             $j = j + 1$
6:             $\text{send\_segment\_to\_client}(x_j)$
7:         **else**
8:             $\text{send\_segment\_to\_client}(\text{EOS})$
9:     **else**
10:         $i = i + 1$
11:         $y_i = r.\text{segment}$
12:         $Y = Y + [y_i]$
13:         **if** data type is speech **then**
14:             $d_i = d_{i-1} + T_j$
15:         **else**
16:             $d_i = j$
17:         $D = D + [d_i]$
18: **return** $\text{evaluate}(Y, Y^*, D, T)$

4.2 Client

The client contains two components — an agent and a state. The agent is a user-defined class that

operates the policy and generates hypotheses for simultaneous translation, the latter provides functions such as pre-processing, post-processing and memorizing context. The purpose of this design is to make the user free from complicated setups, and focus on the policy. The client side algorithm is shown in Algorithm 2.

Algorithm 2 Client side algorithm

    Input: $X = [], i = 0, j = 0, y_0 = \text{BOS}, \text{State, Agent}$
1: **while** $y_i \neq \text{EOS}$ **do**
2:     $\text{action} = \text{Agent.policy(State)}$
3:     **if** action $==$ READ **then**
4:         $x = \text{request\_segment\_from\_server}()$
5:         **if** x is not EOS **then**
6:             $j = j + 1$
7:             $x_j = \text{State.preprocess}(x)$
8:             $\text{States.update\_source}(x_j)$
9:             continue
10:     $i = i + 1$
11:     $y_i = \text{Agent.predict(State)}$
12:     $y_i = \text{State.postprocess}(y_i)$
13:     $\text{States.update\_target}(y_i)$
14:     $\text{send\_segment\_to\_server}(y_i)$

---

5 Usage Instructions

5.1 User-Defined Agent

A user-defined agent class is required for evaluation, along with the user's model specific arguments. The user is able to add customized arguments and initialize the model. Two functions must be defined in order to successfully run online decoding. The first one is "policy", which takes the state as input and returns a decision on whether to perform a *read* or *write* action. The other function is "predict" which will be called when the "policy" returns a *write* action and return a new target prediction given the state. An example of a text wait-k model is shown below.

```python
from simuleval.agents import TextAgent
from simuleval import READ_ACTION, WRITE_ACTION,
↪    DEFAULT_EOS
# User defined model code
from user_library import init_model


class WaitKTextAgent(TextAgent):
    def __init__(self, args):
        super().__init__(args)
        # Initialization
        self.waitk = args.waitk
        self.model = init_model(args.model)

    @staticmethod
    def add_args(parser):
        # Customized arguments
        parser.add_argument(
            "--waitk", type=int,
            help="Lagging between source and
↪    target")
        parser.add_argument(
            "--model", help="model specifics")

    def preprocess(self, state):
        # preprocess code
        return state

    def postprocess(self, state):
        # postprocess code
        return state

    def policy(self, state):
        # Make a decision here
        if (
            len(state.source) - len(state.target)
            < self.waitk
            and not state.finish_read()
        ):
            return READ
        else:
            return WRITE

    def predict(self, state):
        # Predict a token here
        # Called when self.policy() returns
↪    WRITE_ACTION
        return model.predict(state)
```

Listing 1: An example of user defined agent class for a text wait-k model.

Additionally, the user can define pre-processing or post-processing methods to handle different types of input. For example, for a speech translation model, the pre-processing method can be a feature extraction function that converts speech samples to filterbank features while for text translation, the pre-processing can be tokenization or subword splitting. Post-processing can implement functions such as merging subwords and detokenization.

5.2 User-Defined Client

A typical user will only need to implement an agent and will rely on the out-of-the-box client implementation of Algorithm 2. However, sometimes, a user may want to customize the client, for example if they want to use a different programming language than Python or make the implementation of Algorithm 2 more efficient. In that case, they can take advantage of the RESTful APIs between the client and the server described in Table 1. Users can easily plug in these APIs into their own client implementations.

5.3 Evaluation

With a well-defined agent class, SIMULE-VAL is able to start the evaluation automatically. Assuming the agent class is stored in `text_waitk_agent.py`, the evaluation can be run in one single command or separate commands:

```
simuleval \
  --output $OUT_DIR \
  --source $SOURCE \
  --reference $TARGET \
  --agent text_waitk_agent.py \
  --waitk 3 \
  --model $MODEL_PARAMS
```

Listing 2: Evaluation command (joint)

```
simuleval server \
  --output $OUT_DIR \
  --port 5000 \
  --source $SOURCE \
  --reference $TARGET &

simuleval client \
  --port 5000 \
  --agent text_waitk_agent.py \
  --waitk 3 \
  --model $MODEL_PARAMS
```

Listing 3: Evaluation command (Separate)

After all hypotheses are generated, the intermediate results and corpus level evaluation metrics will be saved in the output directory. SIMULEVAL also supports resuming an evaluation if the process has been interrupted.

5.4 Visualization

SIMULEVAL provides a web user interface (UI) for visualizing the online decoding process. Fig. 3 shows an interactive example on simultaneous speech translation. A user can move the cursor to find the corresponding translation at a certain point. The visualization server can be simply started by

```
simuleval server --visual --log-dir $OUT_DIR
```

The default port is 7777 and the web UI can be accessed at `http://ip-of-server:7777`.

5.5 Case Study: IWSLT 2020

In order to avoid inconsistencies in how latency metrics are computed and to ensure fair comparisons between results presented in research papers, we encourage the research community to use SIMULEVAL when reporting latency in the future.

Function	Endpoint	Params	Response / Body
Get next source segment x_j	/src	{sent_id: sent_idx}	x_j (text)
Get next T_j ms speech segment x_j	/src	{sent_id: sent_idx, segment_size: T_j}	x_j (samples)
Send a predicted y_i	/hypo	{sent_id: sent_idx}	y_i

Table 1: A subset of the RESTful APIs for the SIMULEVAL server.

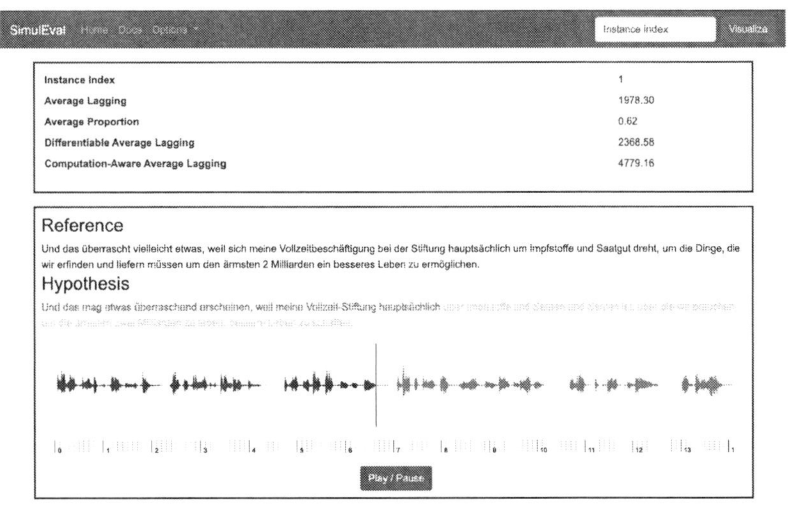

Figure 3: Visualization interface of SIMULEVAL.

In addition, an earlier version of SIMULEVAL was used in the context of the first simultaneous speech translation shared task at IWSLT (Ansari et al., 2020), where it is of paramount importance to have the same evaluation conditions for all submissions. In order to preserve the integrity of the evaluation process, the test set, including the source side, could not be released to participants. This motivated the client-server design, where participants defined their own agent file and submitted their system in a Docker (Merkel, 2014) environment. The organizers of the task were then able to run SIMULEVAL and score each submission in a consistent way, even for systems implemented in different frameworks.

6 Conclusion

In this paper, we introduced SIMULEVAL, a general and easy-to-use evaluation toolkit for simultaneous speech and text translation. It simulates a real-time scenario with a server-client scheme and automatically evaluates simultaneous translation given a user-defined agent, both for text and speech. Furthermore, it provides a visualization interface for the user to track the online decoding process. We introduced example use cases of the toolkit and showed that its general design allows evaluation on different frameworks. We encourage future research on simultaneous speech and text translation to make use of this toolkit in order to obtain an accurate and standard comparison of the latency between different systems.

References

Ashkan Alinejad, Maryam Siahbani, and Anoop Sarkar. 2018. Prediction improves simultaneous neural machine translation. In *Proceedings of the 2018 Conference on Empirical Methods in Natural Language Processing*, pages 3022–3027.

Ebrahim Ansari, amittai axelrod, Nguyen Bach, Ondřej Bojar, Roldano Cattoni, Fahim Dalvi, Nadir Durrani, Marcello Federico, Christian Federmann, Jiatao Gu, Fei Huang, Kevin Knight, Xutai Ma, Ajay Nagesh, Matteo Negri, Jan Niehues, Juan Pino, Elizabeth Salesky, Xing Shi, Sebastian Stüker, Marco Turchi, Alexander Waibel, and Changhan Wang. 2020. FINDINGS OF THE IWSLT 2020 EVALUATION CAMPAIGN. In *Proceedings of the 17th International Conference on Spoken Language Translation*, pages 1–34, Online. Association for Computational Linguistics.

Naveen Arivazhagan, Colin Cherry, Wolfgang Macherey, Chung-Cheng Chiu, Semih Yavuz, Ruoming Pang, Wei Li, and Colin Raffel. 2019. Monotonic infinite lookback attention for simultaneous machine translation. In *Proceedings of the*

57th Annual Meeting of the Association for Computational Linguistics, pages 1313–1323, Florence, Italy. Association for Computational Linguistics.

Satanjeev Banerjee and Alon Lavie. 2005. Meteor: An automatic metric for mt evaluation with improved correlation with human judgments. In *Proceedings of the acl workshop on intrinsic and extrinsic evaluation measures for machine translation and/or summarization*, pages 65–72.

Colin Cherry and George Foster. 2019. Thinking slow about latency evaluation for simultaneous machine translation. *arXiv preprint arXiv:1906.00048*.

Kyunghyun Cho and Masha Esipova. 2016. Can neural machine translation do simultaneous translation? *arXiv preprint arXiv:1606.02012*.

Alvin Grissom II, He He, Jordan Boyd-Graber, John Morgan, and Hal Daumé III. 2014. Don't until the final verb wait: Reinforcement learning for simultaneous machine translation. In *Proceedings of the 2014 Conference on empirical methods in natural language processing (EMNLP)*, pages 1342–1352.

Jiatao Gu, Graham Neubig, Kyunghyun Cho, and Victor OK Li. 2017. Learning to translate in real-time with neural machine translation. In *15th Conference of the European Chapter of the Association for Computational Linguistics, EACL 2017*, pages 1053–1062. Association for Computational Linguistics (ACL).

Mingbo Ma, Liang Huang, Hao Xiong, Renjie Zheng, Kaibo Liu, Baigong Zheng, Chuanqiang Zhang, Zhongjun He, Hairong Liu, Xing Li, Hua Wu, and Haifeng Wang. 2019. STACL: Simultaneous translation with implicit anticipation and controllable latency using prefix-to-prefix framework. In *Proceedings of the 57th Annual Meeting of the Association for Computational Linguistics*, pages 3025–3036, Florence, Italy. Association for Computational Linguistics.

Xutai Ma, Juan Miguel Pino, James Cross, Liezl Puzon, and Jiatao Gu. 2020. Monotonic multihead attention. In *International Conference on Learning Representations*.

Dirk Merkel. 2014. Docker: lightweight linux containers for consistent development and deployment. *Linux journal*, 2014(239):2.

Kishore Papineni, Salim Roukos, Todd Ward, and Wei-Jing Zhu. 2002. Bleu: a method for automatic evaluation of machine translation. In *Proceedings of the 40th annual meeting on association for computational linguistics*, pages 311–318. Association for Computational Linguistics.

Matt Post. 2018. A call for clarity in reporting BLEU scores. In *Proceedings of the Third Conference on Machine Translation: Research Papers*, pages 186–191, Belgium, Brussels. Association for Computational Linguistics.

Yi Ren, Jinglin Liu, Xu Tan, Chen Zhang, Tao QIN, Zhou Zhao, and Tie-Yan Liu. 2020. SimulSpeech: End-to-end simultaneous speech to text translation. In *Proceedings of the 58th Annual Meeting of the Association for Computational Linguistics*, pages 3787–3796, Online. Association for Computational Linguistics.

Matthew Snover, Bonnie Dorr, Richard Schwartz, Linnea Micciulla, and John Makhoul. 2006. A study of translation edit rate with targeted human annotation. In *Proceedings of association for machine translation in the Americas*, volume 200. Cambridge, MA.

Baigong Zheng, Renjie Zheng, Mingbo Ma, and Liang Huang. 2019. Simultaneous translation with flexible policy via restricted imitation learning. In *Proceedings of the 57th Annual Meeting of the Association for Computational Linguistics*, pages 5816–5822, Florence, Italy. Association for Computational Linguistics.

Agent Assist through Conversation Analysis

Kshitij P. Fadnis[1], Nathaniel Mills[1], Jatin Ganhotra[1], Haggai Roitman[2*], Gaurav Pandey[1],
Doron Cohen[1], Yosi Mass[1], Shai Erera[1], Chulaka Gunasekara[1], Danish Contractor[1],
Siva Sankalp Patel[1], Q. Vera Liao[1], Sachindra Joshi[1], Luis A. Lastras[1], David Konopnicki[1]

[1]IBM Research, [2]eBay Research
{kpfadnis, wnm3, jatinganhotra, lastrasl}@us.ibm.com
{hroitman}@ebay.com, {doronc, yosimass, shaie, davidko}@il.ibm.com
{siva.sankalp.patel, chulaka.gunasekara, vera.liao}@ibm.com
{gpandey1, dcontrac, jsachind}@in.ibm.com,

Abstract

Customer support agents play a crucial role as an interface between an organization and its end-users. We propose **CAIRAA: Conversational Approach to Information Retrieval for Agent Assistance**, to reduce the cognitive workload of support agents who engage with users through conversation systems. CAIRAA monitors an evolving conversation and recommends both responses and URLs of documents the agent can use in replies to their client. We combine traditional information retrieval (IR) approaches with more recent Deep Learning (DL) models to ensure high accuracy and efficient run-time performance in the deployed system. Here, we describe the CAIRAA system and demonstrate its effectiveness in a pilot study via a short video[1].

1 Introduction

Customer care conversation systems have been used in a variety of domains, including technical support, reservation systems, and banking applications (Acomb et al., 2007). The majority of such systems provide a dashboard to customer support agents, so that they can interact with multiple end-users in parallel. The support agents use such dashboards to perform diverse tasks to address user requests, such as question-answering, conversational search, document passage extraction and transactions. When identifying the responses to user queries, the support agents either, (1) rely on their own domain knowledge and articulate such knowledge to be sent to the users or, (2) manually extract the keywords from the conversation and use search functions provided in their dashboards to identify the relevant knowledge contained in documents, and send URLs for these documents. The

---

Dialogue

A:	Hello. Thank you for contacting Help@IBM. How may I help you?
U:	Hi yes. I cannot connect to ibm connections cloud in ios
U:	yesterday my phone asked for the pw out of the blue and I clicked cancel bec on the road and now I have no connection to server
A:	No worries. First you will need to create a 16 digit password for for ibm connections cloud `https://w3.ibm.com/help/#/article/ios_create_16char_pass` then you will need to open on the iphone settings-accounts and passwords-ibm connections cloud click on your email address and in the password field enter this 16 digit password.
U:	I have that pw. Can I use my old one or better to create a new one?
A:	Please always try the existing password first. If it doesn't work, then create a new password.
U:	Worked. ;) Thanks

Table 1: Sample dialog from Help@IBM where Agent (**A**) utterance includes a URL to the User (**U**) query.

continuous process of identifying knowledge and responding becomes an immense cognitive workload for the customer support agents.

Although automated conversation systems have improved immensely in the last decade with advances in natural language processing, machine learning and dialog management (Wen et al. (2016); Li et al. (2016); Li et al. (2017)), these systems still fail to satisfy the sophisticated customer's needs in real-life scenarios. This leads to frustration (Weisz et al., 2019) and less engagement (Vtyurina et al., 2017). Therefore, having an empathetic human agent in-the-loop supported by efficient and accurate content retrieval, allows better coverage of customer needs and reduces customer frustration.

With CAIRAA, we propose and showcase a system that provides real-time assistance to the support agents and alleviates their cognitive workload. Our system provides two forms of real-time rec-

---

* Work done when author was at IBM Research
[1]`https://youtu.be/EeqMLLBWhxQ`

Proceedings of the 2020 EMNLP (Systems Demonstrations), pages 151–157
November 16-20, 2020. ©2020 Association for Computational Linguistics

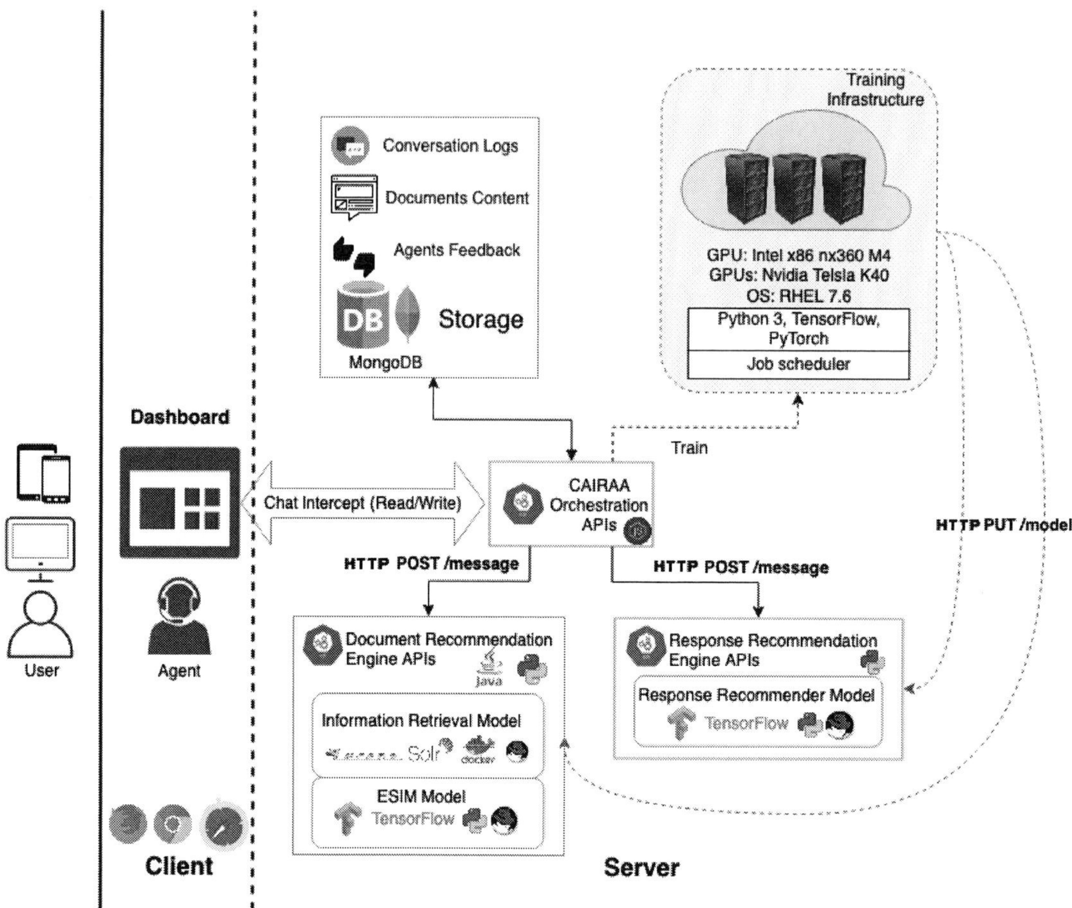

Figure 1: **CAIRAA System Architecture**: (a) Agent Dashboard - a web application (b) Orchestrator APIs - server side communications, controls data and process flow (c) Document Recommendation Engine - retrieves and recommends documents relevant to conversational context (d) Response Recommendation Engine - recommends agent responses based on conversational context (f) Storage - retains document content, conversation and system logs, agents feedback and activity (g) Training infrastructure - a dedicated cluster for deep learning models training (In development)

ommendations to the support agents: (1) URLs of the documents that contain information to resolve user issues, and (2) natural language responses that the agent can use to respond to their customer's queries. The operation of CAIRAA is illustrated in Table 1 with a sample conversation between a user and a support agent. In the example, the utterances made by the support agents are prefixed by **A** and the utterances made by the user are prefixed by **U**. The natural language utterances that CAIRAA predicted for the support agent are shown in different font (`monospace`) while the URLs of the related documents predicted by CAIRAA are shown in blue. In the following sections we describe the different components of our system and their implementation details.

2 System

The architecture of CAIRAA is illustrated in Figure 1. It consists of an Agent-dashboard that is used by customer-support agents to interact with customers (users). The agent is assisted by recommendations from two engines - Document Recommendation Engine and the Response Recommendation Engine. As their names suggest, these engines provide real-time recommendations for *documents* that could be relevant during the chat, as well as, *responses* to the agent. Figure 1 also depicts components for data storage as well as model training.

2.1 Web Content Extraction

Given a collection of human-to-human conversation logs, we extract the mentions of URLs (documents) from these conversations. We use Selenium[2] to render static as well as dynamic web-content. With our primary focus on text content, additional cleaning processes that filters selected HTML content (e.g., menus, search bars, side bars, headers and footers) and only preserves text content, along with embedded procedural and multimedia content references is implemented. The processed content is exported in two formats. a) markdown and b) formatted text.

2.2 Document Recommendation Engine

Given a set of conversational logs along with documents mentioned in those conversations, we train the Document Recommendation Engine using a pipeline consisting of an information-retrieval model followed by a deep-learning model to recommend URLs relevant to an evolving conversation. This Document Recommendation Engine is trained with the objective of predicting the most relevant web content for the conversation at hand. Once trained, this is provided as a real-time service to the agent dashboard to recommend the appropriate URLs to support agents while they converse.

2.2.1 Information Retrieval model

The Information Retrieval (IR) model is implemented using an Apache Lucene index, employed with English language analyzer and default BM25 similarity. Documents in the index are represented using two fields, (1) web page content, (2) document's representation augmented with the text of all historic conversations that link to it.

For a given (dialog) query d, matching documents are retrieved using four different ranking steps, which are combined using a cascade approach (Wang et al., 2011). Following (Van Gysel et al., 2016), we obtain an initial pool of candidate documents using a lexical query aggregation approach. To this end, each utterance $t_i \in d$ is represented as a separate weighted query-clause, having its weight assigned relatively to its sequence position in the dialog (Van Gysel et al., 2016). Various sub-queries are then combined using a single disjunctive query. The second ranker evaluates each document y obtained by the first ranker against an expanded query (applying relevance model (Lavrenko and Croft, 2001)). The third ranker applies a manifold-ranking approach (Xu et al., 2011), aiming to score content-similar doc-

uments (measured by Bhattacharyya language-model based similarity) with similar scores.

The last ranker in the cascade treats the dialog query d as a verbose query and applies the *Fixed-Point* (FP) method (Paik and Oard, 2014) for weighting its words. Yet, compared to "traditional" verbose queries, dialogs are further segmented into distinct utterances. Using this approach, we implement an *utterance-biased* extension for enhanced word-weighting. To this end, we first score the various utterances based on the initial FP weights of words they contain and their relative position. We then propagate utterance scores back to their associated words.

2.2.2 Deep Learning Model

We use the *Enhanced Sequential Inference Model* (ESIM) proposed by Chen et al. (2017) with the same goal as the IR model but it uses dense vectors to represent conversation-contexts and documents. The objective is to predict the relevant URL given the dialog history (context). The multi-turn dialog history is concatenated together to form the context of length m, represented as $C = (c_1, c_2, ..., c_i, ..., c_m)$, where c_i is the ith word in context. Given a web page content U as $U = (r_1, r_2, ..., r_j, ..., r_n)$, where r_j is the jth word in web page content, the web page is selected using the conditional probability $P(y = 1|C, U)$, which shows the confidence of selecting the web page U given context C.

We observe that the IR model is much faster than the neural ESIM model, but the ESIM model provides improved performance in comparison. We combine the ESIM model with the IR model using a re-ranking of latter's candidate pool, which provides a combination of both ranker models. For example, the IR model returns the top-k relevant web pages ($k = 20$) and then the ESIM model is used to re-rank them and show a subset to the agent based on their confidence scores. We refer to this two-stage pipeline as a *hybrid* approach, which combines the best of both worlds and deliver near real-time experience with better performance.

2.2.3 Rating and Confidence Estimation

In addition to providing a ranked list of webpages, the Document Recommendation Engine provides a rating and confidence estimate for each recommended web content, allowing to better guide the agent to the best solutions. The rating and confidence per each single recommended content URL

---

[2]http://www.seleniumhq.org

is estimated using a novel *query performance prediction* (QPP) model (Roitman et al., 2019), trained over a multitude of features obtained from the conversation context and recommended content analysis.

Besides, at every step of the conversation, a crucial decision that the Document Recommendation Engine has to make is to decide whether or not to present the recommendations to the agent. In case of a low confidence, the human agent may ask for further clarifications from the end-user. Such a decision is taken by training another confidence estimation model that considers the confidence of each individual recommended URL. Here, the system further exploits the interaction between the recommendations made by the IR and ESIM models, with the observation that higher agreement (measured by ranking-similarity) usually translates to higher overall confidence (Roitman and Kurland, 2019). We assessed the quality of our confidence estimation model by measuring its *accuracy* and *log-loss* per each task. For a single recommended URL, the model is trained to classify it as relevant or not. For a top-k recommended URLs list, the model is trained to determine whether it contains at least one relevant URL.

2.3 Response Recommendation Engine

As mentioned above, an agent is also shown recommended responses based on how other agents have responded to similar conversation contexts in the pasts. Thus, given the current dialog input context $C = (c_1, c_2, ..c_i..c_m)$, CAIRAA generates recommendations using a combination of *generative* as well as *retrieval* based methods.

2.3.1 Multi-task training

We use a hierarchical encoder (Serban et al., 2016) to encode conversation contexts. Specifically, the encoder first encodes each conversation turn and generates *turn-level* representations for the dialog. A secondary encoder then generates the overall context representation using the turn-level encodings.

We utilize this context encoding to generate response recommendations in three ways: (1) Using a vanilla decoder (Serban et al., 2016) (2) Using a decoder that additionally validates whether a subsequence at each time-step is likely to be relevant. (3) Using the encoded representations in a Siamese dual-encoder (Lowe et al., 2017) that also encodes the responses.

Vanilla Decoder: The decoder is initialized using the context encoding. The decoder generates the response autoregressively, that is, the token at each time-step is generated conditioned on the previous tokens of the response. The decoder is trained to minimize the log-perplexity of each word in the gold response.

Decoder with sub-sequence validation: When trained on actual conversation logs, vanilla decoders often resort to generic responses or responses that are irrelevant to the context. Hence, to enforce relevance, we enhance the decoder with a classifier for each time-step of decoding. At each time-step, the classifier predicts the relevance of the response so-far for the given conversational context. The classifier is trained to predict a relevance of 1 for a prefix of the gold response and 0 for a prefix of any other randomly sampled response at each time-step of decoding. Simultaneously, the decoder is also trained to minimize the word loss, that is, log-perplexity of each word in the gold response. For any response r, the relevance loss can be written as follows:

$$loss_r(r) = - \sum_{t=1}^{T} \log p(y_t | w_1, \ldots, w_t), \quad (1)$$

where $y_t = 1$ for the gold response and 0 for the randomly sampled response.

During inference, the token at each time-step is generated so as to maximize the sum of log-probability of the token and the log-relevance of the resultant partial response.

Siamese Dual-Encoder: Finally, the context encoding is also fed to a Siamese network. To train the Siamese network, we randomly sample $k - 1$ negative responses for each conversation context. The negative responses as well as the gold response are fed to a recurrent encoder (bidirectional LSTM) to generate the corresponding response embeddings. The context embedding as well as the corresponding response embeddings are fed to a 1-in-k classifier, where the k labels correspond to the k responses. The classifier is trained to predict the class-label that corresponds to the gold response. If the gold response r has label ℓ, the Siamese loss can be computed as follows:

$$loss_s(r) = - \log p(\ell | r_1, \ldots, r_k). \quad (2)$$

Multi-task training Objective: The final loss is the sum of the loss for each of the above models. The model is trained until the loss on an independent validation set stops decreasing.

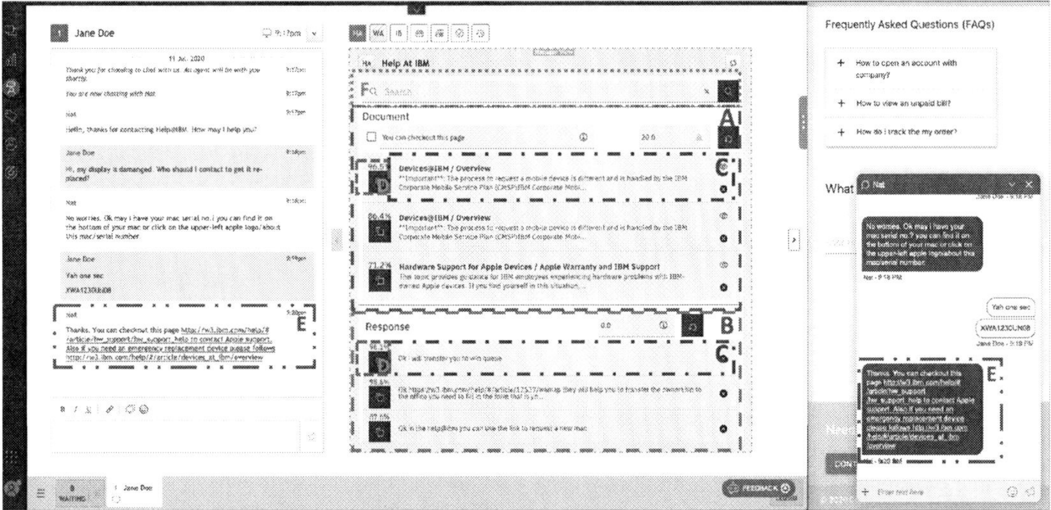

Figure 2: **CAIRAA In Action**; (A & B) Document and Response recommendations panel respectively; (C) Top Recommendation; (D) Confidence score of the recommendation and a button to copy URLs/responses into agent's chat with the end-user; (E) Agent's response; (F) Full-text search bar for agents to perform manual search.

2.3.2 Retrieval-based model

In order to build a retrieval based model, we encode the dialog contexts using the pre-trained Universal Sentence Encoder (USE) (Cer et al., 2018) as well as the context encoder trained using multi-task objective discussed above. For each encoder, we create an annoy index[3] which stores the context embeddings and the corresponding responses from the training data.

In order to return a response recommendation, a given dialog context is encoded either using USE or the context encoder. We fetch the responses of the k-nearest neighbours in the annoy index.

2.3.3 Scoring the responses

Before the retrieved and generated responses are presented to the user, they are scored from 0 to 1. We use a voting-based scoring mechanism, where each response votes for all the other responses (generated as well as retrieved). To achieve this, we encode each response using the pre-trained USE. The score of a response is the mean of the inner-product between the corresponding embedding and all the other response embeddings. Since USE embeddings are normalized, these inner products range between 0 and 1. Finally, the responses are sorted based on their scores and presented to the user.

---

[3] https://github.com/spotify/annoy

3 Deployment Details

Once the recommendation engines are trained, CAIRAA is tasked with the live operation of the agent dashboard. CAIRAA adopts optimized user interface design to deliver precise information with minimal agent interactions. Prioritizing scalability, each operational component is intentionally designed to be modular and stateless.

3.1 Agent Dashboard

The Agent dashboard (Figure 2) is an interactive web application that is integrated with customer support applications (e.g., LivePerson). Implemented using Javascript/ HTML5, it comprises of a chat interceptor; document and response recommendations panels; a full-text search; and a feedback facility runnable in an ES6 compliant browser. Chat interceptor monitors customer support applications (e.g., LivePerson) for conversation updates. Both document and response recommendations panels in their minimalist design limits information overload, where the former shows the title and a short description of the web content and the latter displays the recommended utterance. The agent interactivity with recommendations is limited to copy, view and reject. A full-text search allows the expert agents to perform simple keyword searches based on their domain knowledge.

While we have automated the agent assistance for recommending documents and responses, we have retained the support agent in the loop to provide final edits and control over what is presented to the end-user. This allows a support agent to adjust the tone of responses, and to include documents outside recommended ones in their responses. Our framework captures these responses and their embedded recommendations for future retraining / retesting so that the system can self learn and automatically adjust to support agent activities.

4 Conclusion and Future Work

By providing real-time assistance to agents to support their clients, we leverage the speed and accuracy of automated recommendation engines while retaining the agents' expertise. Learning from conversation logs, CAIRAA promotes more uniform support by keeping all agents aware of the latest information to address current end-user needs. Combining traditional information retrieval approaches with modern deep learning models ensures high accuracy and efficient run-time performance in our deployed system.

References

Kate Acomb, Jonathan Bloom, Krishna Dayanidhi, Phillip Hunter, Peter Krogh, Esther Levin, and Roberto Pieraccini. 2007. Technical support dialog systems: issues, problems, and solutions. In Proceedings of the Workshop on Bridging the Gap: Academic and Industrial Research in Dialog Technologies, pages 25–31. Association for Computational Linguistics.

Daniel Cer, Yinfei Yang, Sheng-yi Kong, Nan Hua, Nicole Limtiaco, Rhomni St. John, Noah Constant, Mario Guajardo-Cespedes, Steve Yuan, Chris Tar, Yun-Hsuan Sung, Brian Strope, and Ray Kurzweil. 2018. Universal sentence encoder. CoRR, abs/1803.11175.

Qian Chen, Xiaodan Zhu, Zhen-Hua Ling, Si Wei, Hui Jiang, and Diana Inkpen. 2017. Enhanced lstm for natural language inference. In Proceedings of the 55th Annual Meeting of the Association for Computational Linguistics (Volume 1: Long Papers), volume 1, pages 1657–1668.

Victor Lavrenko and W. Bruce Croft. 2001. Relevance based language models. In Proceedings of the 24th Annual International ACM SIGIR Conference on Research and Development in Information Retrieval, SIGIR '01, page 120–127, New York, NY, USA. Association for Computing Machinery.

Jiwei Li, Will Monroe, Alan Ritter, Michel Galley, Jianfeng Gao, and Dan Jurafsky. 2016. Deep reinforcement learning for dialogue generation. arXiv preprint arXiv:1606.01541.

Jiwei Li, Will Monroe, Tianlin Shi, Sébastien Jean, Alan Ritter, and Dan Jurafsky. 2017. Adversarial learning for neural dialogue generation. arXiv preprint arXiv:1701.06547.

Ryan Thomas Lowe, Nissan Pow, Iulian Vlad Serban, Laurent Charlin, Chia-Wei Liu, and Joelle Pineau. 2017. Training end-to-end dialogue systems with the ubuntu dialogue corpus. Dialogue & Discourse, 8(1):31–65.

Jiaul H. Paik and Douglas W. Oard. 2014. A fixed-point method for weighting terms in verbose informational queries. In Proceedings of the 23rd ACM International Conference on Conference on Information and Knowledge Management, CIKM '14, page 131–140, New York, NY, USA. Association for Computing Machinery.

Haggai Roitman, Shai Erera, and Guy Feigenblat. 2019. A study of query performance prediction for answer quality determination. In Proceedings of the 2019 ACM SIGIR International Conference on Theory of Information Retrieval, ICTIR '19, page 43–46, New York, NY, USA. Association for Computing Machinery.

Haggai Roitman and Oren Kurland. 2019. Query performance prediction for pseudo-feedback-based retrieval. In Proceedings of the 42nd International ACM SIGIR Conference on Research and Development in Information Retrieval, SIGIR'19, page 1261–1264, New York, NY, USA. Association for Computing Machinery.

Iulian V Serban, Alessandro Sordoni, Yoshua Bengio, Aaron Courville, and Joelle Pineau. 2016. Building end-to-end dialogue systems using generative hierarchical neural network models. In Thirtieth AAAI Conference on Artificial Intelligence.

Christophe Van Gysel, Evangelos Kanoulas, and Maarten de Rijke. 2016. Lexical query modeling in session search. In Proceedings of the 2016 ACM International Conference on the Theory of Information Retrieval, ICTIR '16, page 69–72, New York, NY, USA. Association for Computing Machinery.

Alexandra Vtyurina, Denis Savenkov, Eugene Agichtein, and Charles L. A. Clarke. 2017. Exploring conversational search with humans, assistants, and wizards. In Proceedings of the 2017 CHI Conference Extended Abstracts on Human Factors in Computing Systems, CHI EA '17, page 2187–2193, New York, NY, USA. Association for Computing Machinery.

Lidan Wang, Jimmy Lin, and Donald Metzler. 2011. A cascade ranking model for efficient ranked retrieval. In Proceedings of the 34th International ACM SIGIR Conference on Research and Development in Information Retrieval, SIGIR '11, page 105–114, New York, NY, USA. Association for Computing Machinery.

Justin D Weisz, Mohit Jain, Narendra Nath Joshi, James Johnson, and Ingrid Lange. 2019. Bigbluebot: teaching strategies for successful human-agent interactions. In *Proceedings of the 24th International Conference on Intelligent User Interfaces*, pages 448–459.

Tsung-Hsien Wen, David Vandyke, Nikola Mrksic, Milica Gasic, Lina M Rojas-Barahona, Pei-Hao Su, Stefan Ultes, and Steve Young. 2016. A network-based end-to-end trainable task-oriented dialogue system. *arXiv preprint arXiv:1604.04562*.

Bin Xu, Jiajun Bu, Chun Chen, Deng Cai, Xiaofei He, Wei Liu, and Jiebo Luo. 2011. Efficient manifold ranking for image retrieval. In *Proceedings of the 34th International ACM SIGIR Conference on Research and Development in Information Retrieval*, SIGIR '11, page 525–534, New York, NY, USA. Association for Computing Machinery.

NeuSpell: A Neural Spelling Correction Toolkit

Sai Muralidhar Jayanthi, Danish Pruthi, Graham Neubig
Language Technologies Institute
Carnegie Mellon University
`{sjayanth, ddanish, gneubig}@cs.cmu.edu`

Abstract

We introduce NeuSpell, an open-source toolkit for spelling correction in English. Our toolkit comprises ten different models, and benchmarks them on naturally occurring misspellings from multiple sources. We find that many systems do not adequately leverage the context around the misspelt token. To remedy this, (i) we train neural models using spelling errors in context, synthetically constructed by reverse engineering isolated misspellings; and (ii) use contextual representations. By training on our synthetic examples, correction rates improve by 9% (absolute) compared to the case when models are trained on randomly sampled character perturbations. Using richer contextual representations boosts the correction rate by another 3%. Our toolkit enables practitioners to use our proposed and existing spelling correction systems, both via a unified command line, as well as a web interface. Among many potential applications, we demonstrate the utility of our spell-checkers in combating adversarial misspellings. The toolkit can be accessed at neuspell.github.io.[1]

1 Introduction

Spelling mistakes constitute the largest share of errors in written text (Wilbur et al., 2006; Flor and Futagi, 2012). Therefore, spell checkers are ubiquitous, forming an integral part of many applications including search engines, productivity and collaboration tools, messaging platforms, etc. However, many well performing spelling correction systems are developed by corporations, trained on massive proprietary user data. In contrast, many freely available off-the-shelf correctors such as Enchant (Thomas, 2010), GNU Aspell (Atkinson, 2019), and JamSpell (Ozinov, 2019), do not effectively use the context of the misspelled word.

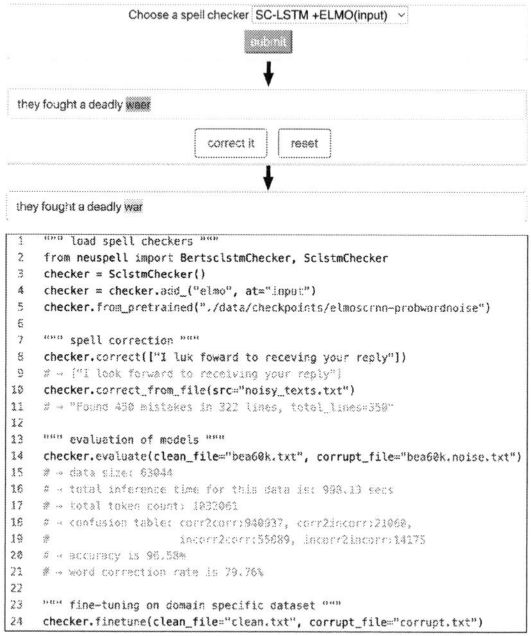


```python
1   """ load spell checkers """
2   from neuspell import BertsclstmChecker, SclstmChecker
3   checker = SclstmChecker()
4   checker = checker.add_("elmo", at="input")
5   checker.from_pretrained("./data/checkpoints/elmoscrnn-probwordnoise")
6
7   """ spell correction """
8   checker.correct(["I luk foward to receving your reply"])
9   # → ["I look forward to receiving your reply"]
10  checker.correct_from_file(src="noisy_texts.txt")
11  # → "Found 450 mistakes in 322 lines, total_lines=350"
12
13  """ evaluation of models """
14  checker.evaluate(clean_file="bea60k.txt", corrupt_file="bea60k.noise.txt")
15  # → data size: 63044
16  # → total inference time for this data is: 998.13 secs
17  # → total token count: 1032061
18  # → confusion table: corr2corr:940937, corr2incorr:21060,
19  #                    incorr2corr:55689, incorr2incorr:14175
20  # → accuracy is 96.58%
21  # → word correction rate is 79.76%
22
23  """ fine-tuning on domain specific dataset """
24  checker.finetune(clean_file="clean.txt", corrupt_file="corrupt.txt")
```

Figure 1: Our toolkit's web and command line interface for spelling correction.

For instance, they fail to disambiguate _thought_ to _taught_ or _thought_ based on the context: "Who thaught you calculus?" versus "I never thought I would be awarded the fellowship."

In this paper, we describe our spelling correction toolkit, which comprises of several neural models that accurately capture context around the misspellings. To train our neural spell correctors, we first curate synthetic training data for spelling correction _in context_, using several text noising strategies. These strategies use a lookup table for word-level noising, and a context-based character-level confusion dictionary for character-level noising. To populate this lookup table and confusion matrix, we harvest isolated misspelling-correction pairs from various publicly available sources.

---

[1] Code and pretrained models are available at: https://github.com/neuspell/neuspell

Proceedings of the 2020 EMNLP (Systems Demonstrations), pages 158–164
November 16-20, 2020. ©2020 Association for Computational Linguistics

Further, we investigate effective ways to incorporate contextual information: we experiment with contextual representations from pretrained models such as ELMo (Peters et al., 2018) and BERT (Devlin et al., 2018) and compare their efficacies with existing neural architectural choices (§ 5.1).

Lastly, several recent studies have shown that many state-of-the-art neural models developed for a variety of Natural Language Processing (NLP) tasks easily break in the presence of natural or synthetic spelling errors (Belinkov and Bisk, 2017; Ebrahimi et al., 2017; Pruthi et al., 2019). We determine the usefulness of our toolkit as a countermeasure against character-level adversarial attacks (§ 5.2). We find that our models are better defenses to adversarial attacks than previously proposed spell checkers. We believe that our toolkit would encourage practitioners to incorporate spelling correction systems in other NLP applications.

Model	Correction Rates	Time per sentence (milliseconds)
ASPELL (Atkinson, 2019)	48.7	7.3*
JAMSPELL (Ozinov, 2019)	68.9	**2.6***
CHAR-CNN-LSTM (Kim et al., 2015)	75.8	4.2
SC-LSTM (Sakaguchi et al., 2016)	76.7	**2.8**
CHAR-LSTM-LSTM (Li et al., 2018)	77.3	6.4
BERT (Devlin et al., 2018)	79.1	7.1
SC-LSTM		
+ELMO (input)	**79.8**	15.8
+ELMO (output)	78.5	16.3
+BERT (input)	77.0	6.7
+BERT (output)	76.0	7.2

Table 1: Performance of different correctors in the NeuSpell toolkit on the BEA-60K dataset with real-world spelling mistakes. * indicates evaluation on a CPU (for others we use a GeForce RTX 2080 Ti GPU).

2 Models in NeuSpell

Our toolkit offers ten different spelling correction models, which include: (i) two off-the-shelf non-neural models, (ii) four published neural models for spelling correction, (iii) four of our extensions. The details of first six systems are following:

- GNU Aspell (Atkinson, 2019): It uses a combination of metaphone phonetic algorithm,[2] Ispell's near miss strategy,[3] and a weighted edit distance metric to score candidate words.

- JamSpell (Ozinov, 2019): It uses a variant of the SymSpell algorithm,[4] and a 3-gram language model to prune word-level corrections.

- SC-LSTM (Sakaguchi et al., 2016): It corrects misspelt words using semi-character representations, fed through a bi-LSTM network. The semi-character representations are a concatenation of one-hot embeddings for the (i) first, (ii) last, and (iii) bag of internal characters.

- CHAR-LSTM-LSTM (Li et al., 2018): The model builds word representations by passing its individual characters to a bi-LSTM. These representations are further fed to another bi-LSTM trained to predict the correction.

- CHAR-CNN-LSTM (Kim et al., 2015): Similar to the previous model, this model builds word-level representations from individual characters using a convolutional network.

- BERT (Devlin et al., 2018): The model uses a pre-trained transformer network. We average the sub-word representations to obtain the word representations, which are further fed to a classifier to predict its correction.

To better capture the context around a misspelt token, we extend the SC-LSTM model by augmenting it with deep contextual representations from pre-trained ELMo and BERT. Since the best point to integrate such embeddings might vary by task (Peters et al., 2018), we append them either to semi-character embeddings before feeding them to the biLSTM or to the biLSTM's output. Currently, our toolkit provides four such trained models: ELMo/BERT tied at input/output with a semi-character based bi-LSTM model.

Implementation Details Neural models in NeuSpell are trained by posing spelling correction as a sequence labeling task, where a correct word is marked as itself and a misspelt token is labeled as its correction. Out-of-vocabulary labels are marked as UNK. For each word in the input text sequence, models are trained to output a probability distribution over a finite vocabulary using a softmax layer.

We set the hidden size of the bi-LSTM network in all models to 512 and use $\{50,100,100,100\}$ sized convolution filters with lengths $\{2,3,4,5\}$ respectively in CNNs. We use a dropout of 0.4 on the bi-LSTM's outputs and train the models using cross-entropy loss. We use the BertAdam[5] optimizer for models with a BERT component and the

---

[2] http://aspell.net/metaphone/
[3] https://en.wikipedia.org/wiki/Ispell
[4] https://github.com/wolfgarbe/SymSpell

[5] github.com/cedrickchee/pytorch-pretrained-BERT

Adam (Kingma and Ba, 2014) optimizer for the remainder. These optimizers are used with default parameter settings. We use a batch size of 32 examples, and train with a patience of 3 epochs.

During inference, we first replace UNK predictions with their corresponding input words and then evaluate the results. We evaluate models for accuracy (percentage of correct words among all words) and word correction rate (percentage of misspelt tokens corrected). We use AllenNLP[6] and Huggingface[7] libraries to use ELMo and BERT respectively. All neural models in our toolkit are implemented using the Pytorch library (Paszke et al., 2017), and are compatible to run on both CPU and GPU environments. Performance of different models are presented in Table 1.

3 Synthetic Training Datasets

Due to scarcity of available parallel data for spelling correction, we noise sentences to generate misspelt-correct sentence pairs. We use 1.6M sentences from the one billion word benchmark (Chelba et al., 2013) dataset as our clean corpus. Using different noising strategies from existing literature, we noise ~20% of the tokens in the clean corpus by injecting spelling mistakes in each sentence. Below, we briefly describe these strategies.

RANDOM: Following Sakaguchi et al. (2016), this noising strategy involves four character-level operations: permute, delete, insert and replace. We manipulate only the internal characters of a word. The permute operation jumbles a pair of consecutive characters, delete operation randomly deletes one of the characters, insert operation randomly inserts an alphabet and replace operation swaps a character with a randomly selected alphabet. For every word in the clean corpus, we select one of the four operations with 0.1 probability each. We do not modify words of length three or smaller.

WORD: Inspired from Belinkov and Bisk (2017), we swap a word with its noised counterpart from a pre-built lookup table. We collect 109K misspeltcorrect word pairs for 17K popular English words from a variety of public sources.[8]

For every word in the clean corpus, we replace it by a random misspelling (with a probability of 0.3)

sampled from all the misspellings associated with that word in the lookup table. Words not present in the lookup table are left as is.

PROB: Recently, Piktus et al. (2019) released a corpus of 20M correct-misspelt word pairs, generated from logs of a search engine.[9] We use this corpus to construct a character-level confusion dictionary where the keys are ⟨character, context⟩ pairs and the values are a list of potential character replacements with their frequencies. This dictionary is subsequently used to sample character-level errors in a given context. We use a context of 3 characters, and backoff to 2, 1, and 0 characters. Notably, due to the large number of unedited characters in the corpus, the most probable replacement will often be the same as the source character.

PROB+WORD: For this strategy, we simply concatenate the training data obtained from both WORD and PROB strategies.

4 Evaluation Benchmarks

Natural misspellings in context Many publicly available spell-checkers correctors evaluate on isolated misspellings (Atkinson, 2019; Mitton; Norvig, 2016). Whereas, we evaluate our systems using misspellings in context, by using publicly available datasets for the task of Grammatical Error Correction (GEC). Since the GEC datasets are annotated for various types of grammatical mistakes, we only sample errors of SPELL type.

Among the GEC datasets in BEA-2019 shared task[10], the Write & Improve (W&I) dataset along with the LOCNESS dataset are a collection of texts in English (mainly essays) written by language learners with varying proficiency levels (Bryant et al., 2019; Granger, 1998). The First Certificate in English (FCE) dataset is another collection of essays in English written by non-native learners taking a language assessment exam (Yannakoudakis et al., 2011) and the Lang-8 dataset is a collection of English texts from Lang-8 online language learning website (Mizumoto et al., 2011; Tajiri et al., 2012). We combine data from these four sources to create the BEA-60K test set with nearly 70K spelling mistakes (6.8% of all tokens) in 63044 sentences.

The JHU FLuency-Extended GUG Corpus (JFLEG) dataset (Napoles et al., 2017) is another

---

[6]allennlp.org/elmo
[7]huggingface.co/transformers/model_doc/bert.html
[8]https://en.wikipedia.org/, dcs.bbk.ac.uk, norvig.com, corpus.mml.cam.ac.uk/efcamdat

[9]https://github.com/facebookresearch/moe
[10]www.cl.cam.ac.uk/research/nl/bea2019st/

Spelling correction systems in NeuSpell (Word-Level Accuracy / Correction Rate)

	Synthetic		Natural		Ambiguous	
	WORD-TEST	PROB-TEST	BEA-60K	JFLEG	BEA-4660	BEA-322
ASPELL (Atkinson, 2019)	43.6 / 16.9	47.4 / 27.5	68.0 / 48.7	73.1 / 55.6	68.5 / 10.1	61.1 / 18.9
JAMSPELL (Ozinov, 2019)	90.6 / 55.6	93.5 / 68.5	97.2 / 68.9	98.3 / 74.5	**98.5** / 72.9	**96.7** / 52.3
CHAR-CNN-LSTM (Kim et al., 2015)	97.0 / 88.0	96.5 / 84.1	96.2 / 75.8	97.6 / 80.1	97.5 / 82.7	94.5 / 57.3
SC-LSTM (Sakaguchi et al., 2016)	97.6 / 90.5	96.6 / 84.8	96.0 / 76.7	97.6 / 81.1	97.3 / 86.6	94.9 / 65.9
CHAR-LSTM-LSTM (Li et al., 2018)	98.0 / 91.1	97.1 / 86.6	96.5 / 77.3	97.6 / 81.6	97.8 / 84.0	95.4 / 63.2
BERT (Devlin et al., 2018)	**98.9 / 95.3**	**98.2 / 91.5**	93.4 / 79.1	**97.9 / 85.0**	98.4 / **92.5**	96.0 / **72.1**
SC-LSTM						
+ELMO (input)	98.5 / 94.0	97.6 / 89.1	96.5 / **79.8**	97.8 / **85.0**	98.2 / 91.9	96.1 / 69.7
+ELMO (output)	97.9 / 91.4	97.0 / 86.1	**98.0** / 78.5	96.4 / 76.7	97.9 / 88.1	95.2 / 63.2
+BERT (input)	98.7 / 94.3	97.9 / 89.5	96.2 / 77.0	97.8 / 83.9	98.4 / 90.2	96.0 / 67.8
+BERT (output)	98.1 / 92.3	97.2 / 86.9	95.9 / 76.0	97.6 / 81.0	97.8 / 88.1	95.1 / 67.2

Table 2: Performance of different models in NeuSpell on natural, synthetic, and ambiguous test sets. All models are trained using PROB+WORD noising strategy.

collection of essays written by English learners with different first languages. This dataset contains 2K spelling mistakes (6.1% of all tokens) in 1601 sentences. We use the BEA-60K and JFLEG datasets only for the purposes of evaluation, and do not use them in training process.

Synthetic misspellings in context From the two noising strategies described in §3, we additionally create two test sets: WORD-TEST and PROB-TEST. Each of these test sets contain around 1.2M spelling mistakes (19.5% of all tokens) in 273K sentences.

Ambiguous misspellings in context Besides the natural and synthetic test sets, we create a challenge set of ambiguous spelling mistakes, *which require additional context to unambiguously correct them*. For instance, the word whitch can be corrected to "witch" or "which" depending upon the context. Simliarly, for the word begger, both "bigger" or "beggar" can be appropriate corrections. To create this challenge set, we select all such misspellings which are either 1-edit distance away from two (or more) legitimate dictionary words, or have the same phonetic encoding as two (or more) dictionary words. Using these two criteria, we sometimes end up with inflections of the same word, hence we use a stemmer and lemmatizer from the NLTK library to weed those out. Finally, we manually prune down the list to 322 sentences, with one ambiguous mistake per sentence. We refer to this set as BEA-322.

We also create another larger test set where we artificially misspell two different words in sentences to their common ambiguous misspelling. This process results in a set with 4660 misspellings in 4660 sentences, and is thus referred as BEA-4660. Notably, for both these ambiguous test sets, a spelling correction system that doesn't use any context information can at best correct 50% of the mistakes.

5 Results and Discussion

5.1 Spelling Correction

We evaluate the 10 spelling correction systems in NeuSpell across 6 different datasets (see Table 2). Among the spelling correction systems, all the neural models in the toolkit are trained using synthetic training dataset, using the PROB+WORD synthetic data. We use the recommended configurations for Aspell and Jamspell, but do not fine-tune them on our synthetic dataset. In all our experiments, vocabulary of neural models is restricted to the top 100K frequent words of the clean corpus.

We observe that although off-the-shelf checker Jamspell leverages context, it is often inadequate. We see that models comprising of deep contextual representations consistently outperform other existing neural models for the spelling correction task. We also note that the BERT model performs consistently well across all our benchmarks. For the ambiguous BEA-322 test set, we manually evaluated corrections from Grammarly—a professional paid service for assistive writing.[11] We found that our best model for this set, i.e. BERT, outperforms corrections from Grammarly (72.1% vs 71.4%) We attribute the success of our toolkit's well performing models to (i) better representations of the context, from large pre-trained models; (ii) swap invariant semi-character representations; and (iii) training models with synthetic data consisting of noise patterns from real-world misspellings. We follow up these results with an ablation study to understand the role of each noising strategy (Ta-

---

[11]Retrieved on July 13, 2020 .

Sentiment Analysis (1-char attack / 2-char attack)						
Defenses	**No Attack**	**Swap**	**Drop**	**Add**	**Key**	**All**
Word-Level Models						
SC-LSTM (Pruthi et al., 2019)	79.3	**78.6 / 78.5**	69.1 / 65.3	65.0 / 59.2	69.6 / 65.6	63.2 / 52.4
SC-LSTM+ELMO(input) (F)	**79.6**	77.9 / 77.2	**72.2 / 69.2**	**65.5 / 62.0**	**71.1 / 68.3**	**64.0 / 58.0**
Char-Level Models						
SC-LSTM (Pruthi et al., 2019)	70.3	65.8 / 62.9	58.3 / 54.2	**54.0 / 44.2**	**58.8** / 52.4	**51.6** / 39.8
SC-LSTM+ELMO(input) (F)	**70.9**	**67.0 / 64.6**	**61.2 / 58.4**	53.0 / 43.0	58.1 / **53.3**	51.5 / **41.0**
Word+Char Models						
SC-LSTM (Pruthi et al., 2019)	80.1	79.0 / 78.7	69.5 / 65.7	64.0 / **59.0**	66.0 / 62.0	61.5 / **56.5**
SC-LSTM+ELMO(input) (F)	**80.6**	**79.4 / 78.8**	**73.1 / 69.8**	**66.0** / 58.0	**72.2 / 68.7**	**64.0** / 54.5

Table 3: We evaluate spelling correction systems in NeuSpell against adversarial misspellings.

ble 4).[12] For each of the 5 models evaluated, we observe that models trained with PROB noise outperform those trained with WORD or RANDOM noises. Across all the models, we further observe that using PROB+WORD strategy improves correction rates by at least 10% in comparison to RANDOM noising.

Spelling Correction (Word-Level Accuracy / Correction Rate)			
Model	Train	Natural test sets	
	Noise	BEA-60K	JFLEG
CHAR-CNN-LSTM	RANDOM	95.9 / 66.6	97.4 / 69.3
(Kim et al., 2015)	WORD	95.9 / 70.2	97.4 / 74.5
	PROB	96.1 / 71.4	97.4 / 77.3
	PROB+WORD	96.2 / 75.5	97.4 / 79.2
SC-LSTM	RANDOM	96.1 / 64.2	97.4 / 66.2
(Sakaguchi et al., 2016)	WORD	95.4 / 68.3	97.4 / 73.7
	PROB	95.7 / 71.9	97.2 / 75.9
	PROB+WORD	95.9 / 76.0	97.6 / 80.3
CHAR-LSTM-LSTM	RANDOM	96.2 / 67.1	97.6 / 70.2
(Li et al., 2018)	WORD	96.0 / 69.8	97.5 / 74.6
	PROB	96.3 / 73.5	97.4 / 78.2
	PROB+WORD	96.3 / 76.4	97.5 / 80.2
BERT	RANDOM	**96.9** / 66.3	**98.2** / 74.4
(Devlin et al., 2018)	WORD	95.3 / 61.1	97.3 / 70.4
	PROB	96.2 / 73.8	97.8/ 80.5
	PROB+WORD	96.1 / 77.1	97.8 / 82.4
SC-LSTM	RANDOM	**96.9** / 69.1	97.8 / 73.3
+ELMO (input)	WORD	96.0 / 70.5	97.5 / 75.6
	PROB	96.8 / 77.0	97.7 / 80.9
	PROB+WORD	96.5 / **79.2**	97.8 / **83.2**

Table 4: Evaluation of models on the natural test sets when trained using synthetic datasets curated using different noising strategies.

5.2 Defense against Adversarial Mispellings

Many recent studies have demonstrated the susceptibility of neural models under word- and character-level attacks (Alzantot et al., 2018; Belinkov and Bisk, 2017; Piktus et al., 2019; Pruthi et al., 2019). To combat adversarial misspellings, Pruthi et al. (2019) find spell checkers to be a viable defense.

Therefore, we also evaluate spell checkers in our toolkit against adversarial misspellings.

We follow the same experimental setup as Pruthi et al. (2019) for the sentiment classification task under different adversarial attacks. We finetune SC-LSTM+ELMO(input) model on movie reviews data from the Stanford Sentiment Treebank (SST) (Socher et al., 2013), using the same noising strategy as in (Pruthi et al., 2019). As we observe from Table 3, our corrector from NeuSpell toolkit (SC-LSTM+ELMO(input)(F)) outperforms the spelling corrections models proposed in (Pruthi et al., 2019) in most cases.

6 Conclusion

In this paper, we describe NeuSpell, a spelling correction toolkit, comprising ten different models. Unlike popular open-source spell checkers, our models accurately capture the context around the misspelt words. We also supplement models in our toolkit with a unified command line, and a web interface. The toolkit is open-sourced, free for public use, and available at `https://github.com/neuspell/neuspell`. A demo of the trained spelling correction models can be accessed at `https://neuspell.github.io/`.

Acknowledgements

The authors thank Punit Singh Koura for insightful discussions and participation during the initial phase of the project.

References

Moustafa Alzantot, Yash Sharma, Ahmed Elgohary, Bo-Jhang Ho, Mani Srivastava, and Kai-Wei Chang. 2018. Generating natural language adversarial examples. In *Proceedings of the 2018 Conference on Empirical Methods in Natural Language Processing,*

---

[12]To fairly compare across different noise types, in this experiment we include only 50% of samples from each of PROB and WORD noises to construct the PROB+WORD noise set.

pages 2890–2896, Brussels, Belgium. Association for Computational Linguistics.

Kevin Atkinson. 2019. Gnu aspell.

Yonatan Belinkov and Yonatan Bisk. 2017. Synthetic and natural noise both break neural machine translation.

Christopher Bryant, Mariano Felice, Øistein E. Andersen, and Ted Briscoe. 2019. The BEA-2019 shared task on grammatical error correction. In *Proceedings of the Fourteenth Workshop on Innovative Use of NLP for Building Educational Applications*, pages 52–75, Florence, Italy. Association for Computational Linguistics.

Ciprian Chelba, Tomas Mikolov, Mike Schuster, Qi Ge, Thorsten Brants, Phillipp Koehn, and Tony Robinson. 2013. One billion word benchmark for measuring progress in statistical language modeling.

Jacob Devlin, Ming-Wei Chang, Kenton Lee, and Kristina Toutanova. 2018. Bert: Pre-training of deep bidirectional transformers for language understanding.

Javid Ebrahimi, Anyi Rao, Daniel Lowd, and Dejing Dou. 2017. Hotflip: White-box adversarial examples for text classification.

Michael Flor and Yoko Futagi. 2012. On using context for automatic correction of non-word misspellings in student essays. In *Proceedings of the Seventh Workshop on Building Educational Applications Using NLP*, pages 105–115, Montréal, Canada. Association for Computational Linguistics.

Sylviane Granger. 1998. The computerized learner corpus: a versatile new source of data for sla research.

Yoon Kim, Yacine Jernite, David Sontag, and Alexander M. Rush. 2015. Character-aware neural language models.

Diederik P. Kingma and Jimmy Ba. 2014. Adam: A method for stochastic optimization.

Hao Li, Yang Wang, Xinyu Liu, Zhichao Sheng, and Si Wei. 2018. Spelling error correction using a nested rnn model and pseudo training data.

Roger Mitton. Corpora of misspellings.

Tomoya Mizumoto, Mamoru Komachi, Masaaki Nagata, and Yuji Matsumoto. 2011. Mining revision log of language learning SNS for automated Japanese error correction of second language learners. In *Proceedings of 5th International Joint Conference on Natural Language Processing*, pages 147–155, Chiang Mai, Thailand. Asian Federation of Natural Language Processing.

Courtney Napoles, Keisuke Sakaguchi, and Joel Tetreault. 2017. JFLEG: A fluency corpus and benchmark for grammatical error correction. In *Proceedings of the 15th Conference of the European Chapter of the Association for Computational Linguistics: Volume 2, Short Papers*, pages 229–234, Valencia, Spain. Association for Computational Linguistics.

Peter Norvig. 2016. Spelling correction system.

Filipp Ozinov. 2019. Jamspell.

Adam Paszke, Sam Gross, Soumith Chintala, Gregory Chanan, Edward Yang, Zachary DeVito, Zeming Lin, Alban Desmaison, Luca Antiga, and Adam Lerer. 2017. Automatic differentiation in pytorch. In *NIPS-W*.

Matthew Peters, Mark Neumann, Mohit Iyyer, Matt Gardner, Christopher Clark, Kenton Lee, and Luke Zettlemoyer. 2018. Deep contextualized word representations. *Proceedings of the 2018 Conference of the North American Chapter of the Association for Computational Linguistics: Human Language Technologies, Volume 1 (Long Papers)*.

Aleksandra Piktus, Necati Bora Edizel, Piotr Bojanowski, Edouard Grave, Rui Ferreira, and Fabrizio Silvestri. 2019. Misspelling oblivious word embeddings. *Proceedings of the 2019 Conference of the North*.

Danish Pruthi, Bhuwan Dhingra, and Zachary C. Lipton. 2019. Combating adversarial misspellings with robust word recognition. *Proceedings of the 57th Annual Meeting of the Association for Computational Linguistics*.

Keisuke Sakaguchi, Kevin Duh, Matt Post, and Benjamin Van Durme. 2016. Robsut wrod reocginiton via semi-character recurrent neural network.

Richard Socher, Alex Perelygin, Jean Wu, Jason Chuang, Christopher D. Manning, Andrew Ng, and Christopher Potts. 2013. Recursive deep models for semantic compositionality over a sentiment treebank. In *Proceedings of the 2013 Conference on Empirical Methods in Natural Language Processing*, pages 1631–1642, Seattle, Washington, USA. Association for Computational Linguistics.

Toshikazu Tajiri, Mamoru Komachi, and Yuji Matsumoto. 2012. Tense and aspect error correction for ESL learners using global context. In *Proceedings of the 50th Annual Meeting of the Association for Computational Linguistics (Volume 2: Short Papers)*, pages 198–202, Jeju Island, Korea. Association for Computational Linguistics.

Reuben Thomas. 2010. Enchant.

W. John Wilbur, Won Kim, and Natalie Xie. 2006. Spelling correction in the pubmed search engine. *Inf. Retr.*, 9(5):543–564.

Helen Yannakoudakis, Ted Briscoe, and Ben Medlock. 2011. A new dataset and method for automatically grading ESOL texts. In *Proceedings of the 49th Annual Meeting of the Association for Computational*

Linguistics: Human Language Technologies, pages 180–189, Portland, Oregon, USA. Association for Computational Linguistics.

LibKGE
A knowledge graph embedding library for reproducible research

Samuel Broscheit, Daniel Ruffinelli, Adrian Kochsiek, Patrick Betz, Rainer Gemulla
Data and Web Science Group
University of Mannheim, Germany
`broscheit, daniel, adrian@informatik.uni-mannheim.de,`
`pbetz@mail.uni-mannheim.de,`
`rgemulla@uni-mannheim.de`

Abstract

LIBKGE[1] is an open-source PyTorch-based library for training, hyperparameter optimization, and evaluation of knowledge graph embedding models for link prediction. The key goals of LIBKGE are to enable *reproducible research*, to provide a framework for comprehensive experimental studies, and to facilitate analyzing the contributions of *individual components* of training methods, model architectures, and evaluation methods. LIBKGE is highly configurable and every experiment can be fully reproduced with a *single configuration file*. Individual components are decoupled to the extent possible so that they can be mixed and matched with each other. Implementations in LIBKGE aim to be as efficient as possible without leaving the scope of Python/Numpy/PyTorch. A comprehensive logging mechanism and tooling facilitates in-depth analysis. LIBKGE provides implementations of common knowledge graph embedding models and training methods, and new ones can be easily added. A comparative study (Ruffinelli et al., 2020) showed that LIBKGE reaches competitive to state-of-the-art performance for many models with a modest amount of automatic hyperparameter tuning.

1 Introduction

Knowledge graphs (KG) (Hayes-Roth, 1983) encode real-world facts as structured data. A knowledge graph can be represented as a set of (subject, relation, object)-triples, where the subject and object entities correspond to vertices, and relations to labeled edges in a graph.

KG embedding (KGE) models represent the KG's entities and relations as dense vectors, termed embeddings. KGE models compute a score based on these embeddings and are trained with the objective of predicting high scores for true triples and

low scores for false triples. Link prediction is the task of predicting edges missing in the KG (Nickel et al., 2015). Some uses of KGE models are: enhancing the knowledge representation in language models (Peters et al., 2019), drug discovery in biomedical KGs (Mohamed et al., 2019), as part of recommender systems (Wang et al., 2017), or for visual relationship detection (Baier et al., 2017).

KGE models for link prediction have seen a heightened interest in recent years. Many components of the KGE pipeline—i.e., KGE models, training methods, evaluation techniques, and hyperparameter optimization—have been studied in the literature, as well as the whole pipeline itself (Nickel et al., 2016; Wang et al., 2017; Ali et al., 2020). Ruffinelli et al. (2020) argued that it is difficult to reach a conclusion about the impact of each component based on the original publications. For example, multiple components may have been changed simultaneously without performing an ablation study, baselines may not have been trained with state-of-the-art methods, or the hyperparameter space may not have been sufficiently explored.

LIBKGE is an open-source KGE library for reproducible research. It aims to facilitate meaningful experimental comparisons of all components of the KGE pipeline. To this end, LIBKGE is faithful to the following principles:

Modularization and extensibility. LIBKGE is cleanly modularized. Individual components can be mixed and matched with each other, and new components can be easily added.

Configurability and reproducibility. In LIBKGE an experiment is entirely defined by a *single* configuration file with well-documented configuration options for *every* component. When an experiment is started, its current configuration is stored alongside the model to enable reproducibility and analysis.

---

[1] `https://github.com/uma-pi1/kge`

Proceedings of the 2020 EMNLP (Systems Demonstrations), pages 165–174
November 16-20, 2020. ©2020 Association for Computational Linguistics

Profiling and analysis. LIBKGE performs *extensive logging* during experiments and monitors performance metrics such as runtime, memory usage, training loss, and evaluation metrics. Additionally, specific monitoring of any part of the KGE pipeline can be added via a hook system. The logging is done in both human-readable form and in a machine-readable format.

Ease of use. LIBKGE is designed to support the workflow of researchers by convenient tooling and easy usage with single line commands. Each training job or hyperparameter search job can be interrupted and resumed at any time. For *tuning of hyperparameters*, LIBKGE supports grid search, quasi-random search and Bayesian Optimization. All implementations stay in the realm of Python/PyTorch/Numpy and aim to be as efficient as possible.

LIBKGE supports the needs of researchers who want to investigate new components or improvements of the KGE pipeline. The strengths of LIBKGE enabled a comprehensive study that provided new insights about training KGE models (Ruffinelli et al., 2020). For an overview about usage, pretrained models, and detailed documentation, please refer to LIBKGE's project page. In this paper, we discuss the key principles of LIBKGE.

2 Modularization and extensibility

LIBKGE is highly modularized, which allows to mix and match training methods, models, and evaluation methods (see Figure 1). The modularization allows for simple and clean ways to extend the framework with new features that will be available for every model.

For example, LIBKGE decouples the *RelationalScorer* (the KGE scoring function) and *KgeEmbedder* (the way embeddings are obtained) as depicted in Figure 1. In other frameworks, the embedder function is hardcoded to the equivalent of LIBKGE's *LookupEmbedder*, in which embeddings are explicitly stored for each entity. Due to LIBKGE's decoupling, the embedder type can be freely specified independently of the scoring function, which enables users to train a KGE model with other types of embedders. For example, the embedding function could be an encoder that computes an entity or relation embedding from textual descriptions or pixels of an image (Pezeshkpour et al., 2018; Broscheit et al., 2020, inter alia).

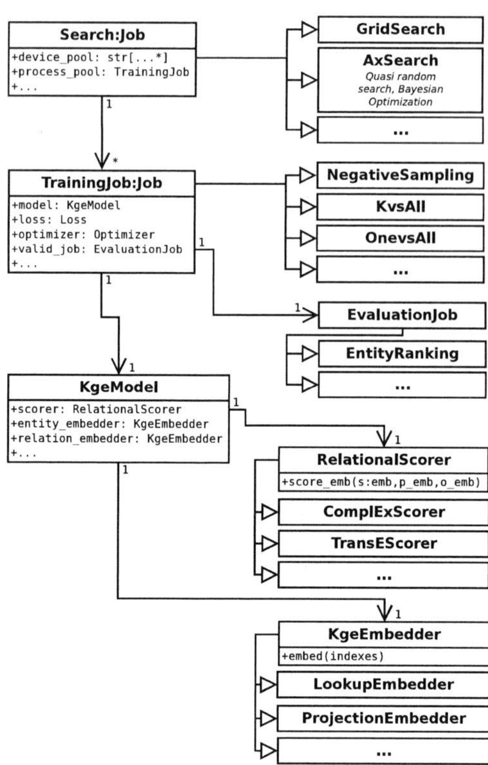

Figure 1: A brief overview of LIBKGE's architecture.

3 Configurability and reproducibility

Reproducibility is important, which means that configuration is important. To enable reproducibility, it is key that the entire configuration of each experiment be persistently stored and accessible. While this sounds almost obvious, the crux is how this can be achieved. Typically, source code can and will change. Therefore, to make an experiment in a certain setting reproducible, the configuration for an experiment has to be decoupled from the code as much as possible.

In LIBKGE *all* settings are always retrieved from a configuration object that is initialized from configuration files and is used by all components of the pipeline. This leads to comprehensive configuration files that fully *document* an experiment and make it reproducible as well.

To make this comprehensive configurability feasible—while also remaining modular—LIBKGE includes a lightweight `import` functionality for configuration files. In Figure 2, we show an (almost) minimal configuration for an experiment for training a *ComplEx* KGE model (Trouillon et al., 2016). The main configuration file

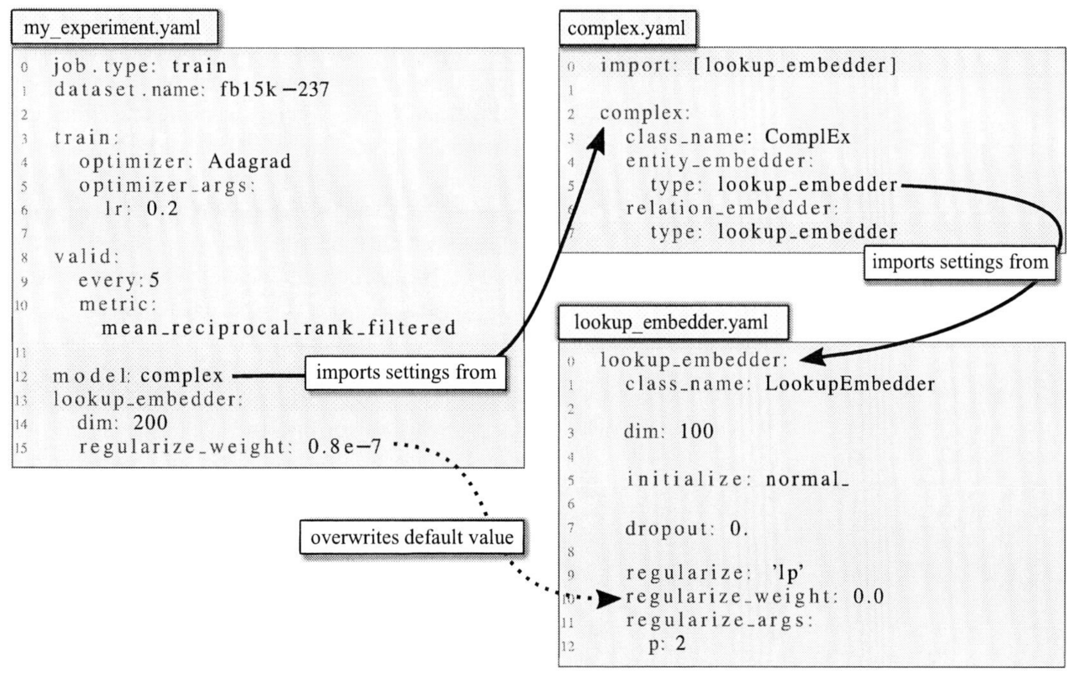

Figure 2: A minimal configuration `my_experiment.yaml` that defines 10 out of ≈ 100 configurable settings. *All* settings from the main configuration file `my_experiment.yaml` and from the imported configurations are merged and stored in one combined file. No default settings are defined in the code.

`my_experiment.yaml` in Figure 2 will automatically import the model-specific configuration `complex.yaml`, which in turn imports the configuration `lookup_embedder.yaml`. The latter defines the default configurations of the *LookupEmbedder* for entities and relations, which associates every entity and relation identifier with its respective embedding. All configurations are merged into a single configuration object. During merging, the settings in the main configuration file always have precedence over the settings from imported files. The resulting single configuration will be automatically saved in the experiment directory along with the checkpoints and the log files.

As an example of how configurability also helps modularization, we come back to the example of switching the *LookupEmbedder* with an encoder that computes entity embeddings from string tokens. For this purpose, one may implement a *TokenPoolEmbedder*. The simple changes to the configuration that uses the new embedder type are demonstrated in Figure 3 (see line 12).

It is worth noting that while the default settings in LIBKGE's main configuration file reflect

```
0   token_pool_embedder:
1       class_name: TokenPoolEmbedder
2       dim: 100
```

```
0   import: [token_pool_embedder]
1   job.type: train
2   dataset.name: fb15k-237
3
4   train:
5       optimizer: Adagrad
6       optimizer_args.lr: 0.2
7
8   model: complex
9   complex:
10      class_name: ComplEx
11      entity_embedder:
12          type: token_pool_embedder
13      relation_embedder:
14          type: lookup_embedder
```

Figure 3: Example of using a token-based embedder.

the currently known best practices, LIBKGE also includes—and makes configurable—some settings that might not be considered *best* practice, e.g., different tie breaking schemes for ranking evaluations (Sun et al., 2020). Therefore, with regards to configurability, the goal is not only that the frame-

```yaml
job.type: search
search:
  type: ax
  device_pool: [cuda:0, cuda:1]
  num_workers: 4

dataset.name: wnrr

model: complex

train:
  optimizer: Adagrad
  type: negative_sampling

valid.metric:
    mean_reciprocal_rank_filtered

ax_search:
  num_trials: 30
  # remaining trials after random
  # search are Bayesian Optimization
  num_sobol_trials: 10
  parameters:
    - name: train.batch_size
      type: choice
      values: [256, 512, 1024]
      is_ordered: True
    - name: train.optimizer_args.lr
      type: range
      bounds: [0.001, 1.0]
      log_scale: True
    - name: negative_sampling.num.s
      type: range
      bounds: [16, 8192]
    - name: negative_sampling.num.o
      type: range
      bounds: [16, 8192]
```

Figure 4: An example for a hyperparameter optimization job. This configurations first runs 10 trials of a quasi-random search followed by 10 trials of Bayesian Optimization (see `ax_search.num_trials` and `ax_search.num_sobol_trials`). By setting the keys `search.device_pool` and `search.num_workers` in lines 3 and 4 the execution of the trials is parallelized to run 4 parallel trials distributed over two GPU devices.

work reflects best practices, but also reflects popular practices that might influence ongoing research.

4 Hyperparameter optimization

Hyperparameter optimization is crucial in empirically investigating the impact of individual components of the KGE pipeline. LIBKGE offers manual search, grid search, random search, and Bayesian Optimization; the latter two provided by the hyperparameter optimization framework Ax.[2] In this context, LIBKGE further benefits from its configurability because everything can be treated

[2] https://ax.dev/

as a hyperparameter, even the choice of model, score function, or embedder. The example in Figure 4 shows a simple hyperparameter search with an initial quasi-random search, and a subsequent Bayesian Optimization phase over the learning rate, batch size and negative samples for the *ComplEx* model. The trials during the quasi-random search are independent, which can be exploited by parallelizing their runs over multiple devices. In this way, a comprehensive search over a large space of hyperparameters can be sped up significantly (also shown in the example; for more details, please refer to the documentation).

5 Profiling and metadata analysis

LIBKGE provides extensive options for profiling, debugging, and analyzing the KGE pipeline. While most frameworks print the current training loss and some frameworks also record the validation metrics, LIBKGE aims to make every moving part of the pipeline observable. Per default, LIBKGE records during training things such as runtimes, training loss and penalties (e.g., from the entity and relation embedders), relevant meta data such as the PyTorch version and the current commit hash, and dependencies between various jobs. We show an example logging output during training one epoch in Appendix B. For more fine-grained logging, LIBKGE also can log at the batch level.

During evaluation, the framework records many variations of the evaluation metrics, such as grouping relations by relation type, relation frequency, head or tail. Additionally, users can extract and add information by adding their custom function to one of multiple hooks that are executed before and after all relevant calls in the framework. In this way, users can interact with all components of the pipeline, without risking divergence from LIBKGE's master branch.

Finally, LIBKGE provides convenience methods to export (subsets of) the logged meta data into plain CSV files.

6 Comparison to other KGE Projects

In this section, we compare LIBKGE to other open source software (OSS) that provides functionality around training and evaluating KGE models for link prediction. The assessments are a snaphot taken at the end of May 2020. All model-specific comparisons have been evaluated w.r.t. the *ComplEx* model, which is supported by all projects.

	KGE project	Implementation language(s)	Configurable keys	Logging train/eval	Hyperparam. Optimization Grid	Rnd	BO	Resume	Active
Framework	LIBKGE (Ours)	PyTorch	91	17/414	x	x	x	x	668
	PyKeen	PyTorch	61	2/27		x	x		575
	Ampligraph	TF 1.x	20	0/8	x	x			286
	OpenKE	PyTorch/C++	19	1/30					22
	SK-libkge	TF 1.x	14	5/7	x				24
Large Scale	GraphVite	C++/PyTorch	34	2/5					14
	DGL-KE	PyTorch/MxNET	15	10/6				x	134
	PyTorch-BG	PyTorch	52	12/8				x	102
Paper Code	KBC	PyTorch	10	4/12					2
	Hyperb. KGE	TF 2.x/PyTorch	20	6/5					12/19
	ConvE	PyTorch	15	5/36				x	2
	RotatE	PyTorch	28	3/5					3

Table 1: Comparing LIBKGE and other OSS that provide functionality around training KGE models for link prediction. All assessments have been made at the end of May 2020. *Frameworks* denotes focus on fostering KGE research with modularization, extensibility and coverage of relevant models and training methods. *Large Scale* denotes focus on extremely large-scale graphs, with support of training in multi-node or multi-gpu mode, or both. *Paper Code* denotes projects published alongside a KGE model's publications. *Configurable keys* are the number of possible options for training a single *ComplEx* model, i.e. not counting options for hyperparameter search. *Logging* denotes the number of metadata keys that are logged per epoch for training and evaluation in a machine readable format for later analysis. *Hyperparameter optimization* shows if the project supports grid search, random search and Bayesian Optimization. *Resume* denotes the feature to resume hyperparameter search or training from checkpoints at any time. *Active* is the amount of commits to the master branch in the last 12 months.

In Table 1, we provide an overview of other KGE projects (full references in Appendix C) and compare them w.r.t. configurability and ease of use. We mainly included projects that could be considered as a basis for a researcher's experiments because they are active, functional, and cover at least a few of the most common models. All projects can be extended with models, losses, or training methods. Large-scale projects and paper code projects—in comparison to more holistic frameworks—typically have a more narrow scope, e.g., they often do not feature hyperparameter optimization. Large-scale projects are typically tailored towards parallelizing training methods and models.

The focus on configurability and reproducibility in LIBKGE is reflected by the large amount of configurable keys. For example, in contrast to other projects, LIBKGE does not tie the regularization weights of the entity and relation embedder to be the same. For entity ranking evaluation, only LIBKGE and PyKeen transparently implement different tie breaking schemes for equally ranked entities. This is important, because evaluation under different tie breaking schemes can result in differences of $\approx .40$ MRR in some models and can lead to misleading conclusions, as shown by Sun et al. (2020). OpenKE, for example, only supports the problematic tie breaking scheme named *TOP* by Sun et al. (2020). LIBKGE and PyKeen are the only frameworks that provide machine-readable logging. Only LIBKGE offers resuming from a checkpoint for training and hyperparameter search. LIBKGE, Ampligraph, and PyKeen are the most active projects in terms of amount of commits during the past 12 months.

Efficiency In Table 2, we show a comparison of KGE frameworks in terms of time for one full training epoch. The configuration setting was chosen such that it was supported by all frameworks, and also facilitates to demonstrate behaviour under varying load. We translate the configurations faithfully to each framework, ensuring that total number of embedding *parameters* per batch are the same for each framework. Most projects, including LIBKGE, can handle small numbers of negative samples efficiently, but LIBKGE seems to scale

Project	Parallel batch construction	Number of negative samples per triple					
		64		1024		16384	
		ran-dom	pseudo negative	ran-dom	pseudo negative	ran-dom	pseudo negative
LIBKGE (Ours)	x	9 s	13 s	14 s	19 s	74 s	113 s
PyKeen	x	10 s	-	64 s	-	930 s	-
Ampligraph		21 s	-	190 s	-	OOM	-
OpenKE	x	7 s	7 s	59 s	63 s	OOM	OOM
SK-libkge		99 s	-	1210 s	-	OOT	-
GraphVite (*)		54 s	-	58 s	-	82 s	-

Table 2: Runtime comparison between frameworks. The runtime is the time per epoch in seconds (averaged over 5 epochs executed on the same machine). The configuration is fixed to be similar for all frameworks (details in Appendix A). For negative samples, we show runtimes for *random*, i.e., sampling triples without checking if they are contained in the KG, and for *pseudo-negative*, which avoids sampling triples contained in the KG. The column *parallel batch construction* indicates whether the code in the training loop for generating the batches is parallelized; if yes, then we set the number of workers to 4. OOM stands for out-of-memory. OOT is short for out-of-time; we stopped the run when the first epoch did not finish within 30 minutes. (*) Graphvite is optimized for multi-gpu training with large batch sizes, therefore the chosen settings might not be optimal.

	MRR	HITS@10
LIBKGE (Ours)	0.35	0.54
PyKeen	-	0.44
Ampligraph	0.32	0.50
OpenKE	-	0.43
GraphVite	0.27	0.45

Table 3: The *reported* best performances (on the project's homepage or the related publication as of May 2020) for *ComplEx* on FB15K-237 for each project. The performances have been obtained with different amount of effort for hyperparameter optimization and should not be compared directly. Reported ranking metrics: Mean Reciprocal Rank (MRR) and HITS@10.

better to higher numbers of negative samples. A large number of negative samples becomes important when large KGs with millions of entities are embedded. Although the runtimes are purely anecdotal and should be taken with a grain of salt, they do show that LIBKGE can provide competitive runtime performance. Currently, LIBKGE only supports single-node single-gpu training. It nevertheless fares well when compared to GraphVite, one of the large-scale frameworks that dispatches some routines into C/C++. LIBKGE also has optimized versions of negative sampling for large graphs, which enables it to train *ComplEx* on Wikidata-5m (Wang et al., 2019), a large KG with 5M entities.

Predictive performance. In Table 3, we collected the reported performances for *ComplEx* on the dataset FB15K-237 (Toutanova and Chen, 2015). The numbers are not comparable due to different amount of effort to find a good configuration[3], but they reflect the performance that the framework authors achieved in their experiments. The results show that with LIBKGE's architecture and hyperparameter optimization a state-of-the-art result can be achieved. For more results obtained with LIBKGE and an in-depth analysis of the impact of hyperparameters on model performance we refer to the study by Ruffinelli et al. (2020).

7 Conclusions

In this work, we presented LIBKGE, a configurable, modular, and efficient framework for reproducible research on knowledge graph embedding models. We briefly described the internal structure of the framework and how it facilitates LIBKGE's goals. The framework is efficient and yields state-of-the-art performance. We hope that LIBKGE is a helpful ingredient to gain new insights into knowledge graph embeddings, and that a lively community gathers around this project to improve and extend it further.

---

[3]We did not attempt to use our best configuration with other frameworks because they only partly support the settings, e.g., they do not offer dropout or independent regularization for entity and relation embeddings.

References

Mehdi Ali, Max Berrendorf, Charles Tapley Hoyt, Laurent Vermue, Mikhail Galkin, Sahand Sharifzadeh, Asja Fischer, Volker Tresp, and Jens Lehmann. 2020. Bringing light into the dark: A large-scale evaluation of knowledge graph embedding models under a unified framework. *arXiv preprint arXiv:2006.13365*.

Stephan Baier, Yunpu Ma, and Volker Tresp. 2017. Improving visual relationship detection using semantic modeling of scene descriptions. In *Proceedings of the 16th International Semantic Web Conference (ISWC)*.

Antoine Bordes, Nicolas Usunier, Alberto García-Durán, Jason Weston, and Oksana Yakhnenko. 2013. Translating embeddings for modeling multi-relational data. In *Advances in Neural Information Processing Systems 26: 27th Annual Conference on Neural Information Processing Systems 2013. Proceedings of a meeting held December 5-8, 2013, Lake Tahoe, Nevada, United States*, pages 2787–2795.

Samuel Broscheit, Kiril Gashteovski, Yanjie Wang, and Rainer Gemulla. 2020. Can we predict new facts with open knowledge graph embeddings? A benchmark for open link prediction. In *Proceedings of the 58th Annual Meeting of the Association for Computational Linguistics*, pages 2296–2308, Online. Association for Computational Linguistics.

Ines Chami, Adva Wolf, Da-Cheng Juan, Frederic Sala, Sujith Ravi, and Christopher Ré. 2020. Low-dimensional hyperbolic knowledge graph embeddings. *Annual Meeting of the Association for Computational Linguistics*.

Luca Costabello, Sumit Pai, Chan Le Van, Rory McGrath, Nicholas McCarthy, and Pedro Tabacof. 2019. AmpliGraph: a library for representation learning on knowledge graphs.

Tim Dettmers, Pasquale Minervini, Pontus Stenetorp, and Sebastian Riedel. 2018. Convolutional 2d knowledge graph embeddings. In *Proceedings of the Thirty-Second AAAI Conference on Artificial Intelligence, (AAAI-18), the 30th innovative Applications of Artificial Intelligence (IAAI-18), and the 8th AAAI Symposium on Educational Advances in Artificial Intelligence (EAAI-18), New Orleans, Louisiana, USA, February 2-7, 2018*, pages 1811–1818.

Xu Han, Shulin Cao, Xin Lv, Yankai Lin, Zhiyuan Liu, Maosong Sun, and Juanzi Li. 2018. OpenKE: An open toolkit for knowledge embedding. In *Proceedings of the 2018 Conference on Empirical Methods in Natural Language Processing (EMNLP)*.

Frederick Hayes-Roth. 1983. *Building expert systems*, volume 1 of *Advanced book program*. Addison-Wesley.

Timothée Lacroix, Nicolas Usunier, and Guillaume Obozinski. 2018. Canonical tensor decomposition for knowledge base completion. In *Proceedings of the 35th International Conference on Machine Learning, ICML 2018, Stockholmsmässan, Stockholm, Sweden, July 10-15, 2018*, pages 2869–2878.

Adam Lerer, Ledell Wu, Jiajun Shen, Timothee Lacroix, Luca Wehrstedt, Abhijit Bose, and Alex Peysakhovich. 2019. PyTorch-BigGraph: A Large-scale Graph Embedding System. In *Proceedings of the 2nd SysML Conference*, Palo Alto, CA, USA.

Sameh K. Mohamed, Aayah Nounu, and Vít Nováček. 2019. Drug target discovery using knowledge graph embeddings. In *Proceedings of the 34th ACM/SIGAPP Symposium on Applied Computing*, SAC 19, page 1118, New York, NY, USA. Association for Computing Machinery.

Maximilian Nickel, Kevin Murphy, Volker Tresp, and Evgeniy Gabrilovich. 2015. A review of relational machine learning for knowledge graphs. *Proceedings of the IEEE*.

Maximilian Nickel, Kevin Murphy, Volker Tresp, and Evgeniy Gabrilovich. 2016. A review of relational machine learning for knowledge graphs. *Proceedings of the IEEE*, 104(1):11–33.

Matthew E. Peters, Mark Neumann, Robert Logan, Roy Schwartz, Vidur Joshi, Sameer Singh, and Noah A. Smith. 2019. Knowledge enhanced contextual word representations. In *Proceedings of the 2019 Conference on Empirical Methods in Natural Language Processing and the 9th International Joint Conference on Natural Language Processing (EMNLP-IJCNLP)*, pages 43–54, Hong Kong, China. Association for Computational Linguistics.

Pouya Pezeshkpour, Liyan Chen, and Sameer Singh. 2018. Embedding multimodal relational data for knowledge base completion. In *Proceedings of the 2018 Conference on Empirical Methods in Natural Language Processing*, pages 3208–3218, Brussels, Belgium. Association for Computational Linguistics.

Daniel Ruffinelli, Samuel Broscheit, and Rainer Gemulla. 2020. You CAN teach an old dog new tricks! on training knowledge graph embeddings. In *8th International Conference on Learning Representations, ICLR 2020, Addis Ababa, Ethiopia, April 26-30, 2020*.

Zhiqing Sun, Zhi-Hong Deng, Jian-Yun Nie, and Jian Tang. 2019. RotatE: Knowledge graph embedding by relational rotation in complex space. In *Proceedings of the 7th International Conference on Learning Representations (ICLR)*.

Zhiqing Sun, Shikhar Vashishth, Soumya Sanyal, Partha Talukdar, and Yiming Yang. 2020. A re-evaluation of knowledge graph completion methods. In *Proceedings of the 58th Annual Meeting of the*

Association for Computational Linguistics, pages 5516–5522, Online. Association for Computational Linguistics.

Kristina Toutanova and Danqi Chen. 2015. Observed versus latent features for knowledge base and text inference. In *Proceedings of the 3rd Workshop on Continuous Vector Space Models and their Compositionality*, pages 57–66, Beijing, China. Association for Computational Linguistics.

Théo Trouillon, Johannes Welbl, Sebastian Riedel, Éric Gaussier, and Guillaume Bouchard. 2016. Complex embeddings for simple link prediction. In *Proceedings of the 33nd International Conference on Machine Learning, ICML 2016, New York City, NY, USA, June 19-24, 2016*, pages 2071–2080.

Quan Wang, Zhendong Mao, Bin Wang, and Li Guo. 2017. Knowledge graph embedding: A survey of approaches and applications. *IEEE Transactions on Knowledge and Data Engineering*.

Xiaozhi Wang, Tianyu Gao, Zhaocheng Zhu, Zhiyuan Liu, Juanzi Li, and Jian Tang. 2019. Kepler: A unified model for knowledge embedding and pre-trained language representation.

Da Zheng, Xiang Song, Chao Ma, Zeyuan Tan, Zi-Hao Ye, J. Dong, Hao Xiong, Zheng Zhang, and G. Karypis. 2020. Dgl-ke: Training knowledge graph embeddings at scale. *Proceedings of the 43rd International ACM SIGIR Conference on Research and Development in Information Retrieval*.

Zhaocheng Zhu, Shizhen Xu, Meng Qu, and Jian Tang. 2019. Graphvite: A high-performance cpu-gpu hybrid system for node embedding. In *The World Wide Web Conference*, pages 2494–2504. ACM.

A   Runtime comparison experiment

The configuration was as follows: Dataset FB15K (Bordes et al., 2013), batch size 512, model *ComplEx*, effective parameter embedding size per entity/relation 128, optimizer Adagrad, negative sampling with negative log likelihood loss or sigmoid loss, no regularization. The hardware was a 8-core Intel Xeon E5-1630m v4.0, TitanXP GPU, dataset on SSD.

B Logging

```
{
    "entry_id":"84d75bf2-c3fe-4c6f-ac5e-001e1edb85de,
    "event":"job_created",
    "folder":/home/USER/kge/local/experiments/20200705-215353-toy-complex-train,
    "git_head":7fad132,
    "hostname":USER-Workstation,
    "job":"eval",
    "job_id":683d00bf-520d-4919-937e-d9b634c11d2e,
    "parent_job_id":dc960211-9cbe-4ba1-ad62-7ffd41d2017e,
    "timestamp":1593978837.304522,
    "torch_version":1.5.0,
    "username":"USER"
}{
    "entry_id":418889f0-728b-486f-9977-48795f6ed5fa,
    "event":"job_created",
    "folder":/home/USER/kge/local/experiments/20200705-215353-toy-complex-train,
    "git_head":7fad132,
    "hostname":USER-Workstation,
    "job":"train",
    "job_id":dc960211-9cbe-4ba1-ad62-7ffd41d2017e,
    "timestamp":1593978837.4033182,
    "torch_version":1.5.0,
    "username":"USER"
}{
    "avg_cost":1.06542689547832,
    "avg_loss":1.0650610147438764,
    "avg_penalties":{
        complex.entity_embedder.L2_penalty:0.00031927969330354246,
        complex.relation_embedder.L2_penalty:4.6601041140093004e-05
    },
    "avg_penalty":0.0003658807344436354,
    "backward_time":0.0765678882598877,
    "batches":20,
    "entry_id":4b07adfa-3e2b-42f4-a994-2b4f02e1b3f4,
    "epoch":1,
    "epoch_time":1.161754846572876,
    "event":"epoch_completed",
    "forward_time":0.7509596347808838,
    "job":"train",
    "job_id":dc960211-9cbe-4ba1-ad62-7ffd41d2017e,
    "lr":[ 0.2 ],
    "optimizer_time":0.015013933181762695,
    "other_time":0.2690012454986572,
    "prepare_time":0.05021214485168457,
    "scope":"epoch",
    "size":1949,
    "split":"train",
    "timestamp":1593978838.5940151,
    "type":"KvsAll"
}
```

Figure 5: Example for training logging output for one epoch. Evaluation logging output is too verbose to add an example here. Please see `https://github.com/uma-pi1/kge/blob/master/docs/examples/train_and_valid_trace_after_one_epoch.yaml` for an example for the output after one epoch of training and evaluation.

C   Related projects

KGE project	URL	Reference
LIBKGE (Ours)	https://github.com/uma-pi1/kge	Ruffinelli et al. (2020)
PyKeen	https://github.com/pykeen/pykeen	Ali et al. (2020)
Ampligraph	https://github.com/Accenture/AmpliGraph	Costabello et al. (2019)
OpenKE	https://github.com/thunlp/OpenKE	Han et al. (2018)
GraphVite	https://github.com/DeepGraphLearning/graphvite	Zhu et al. (2019)
DGL-KE	https://github.com/awslabs/dgl-ke	Zheng et al. (2020)
Pytorch-Biggraph	https://github.com/facebookresearch/PyTorch-BigGraph	Lerer et al. (2019)
SK-libkge	https://github.com/samehkamaleldin/libkge	
KBC	https://github.com/facebookresearch/kbc	Lacroix et al. (2018)
Hyperbolic KGE	https://github.com/tensorflow/neural-structured-learning/tree/master/research/kg_hyp_emb	Chami et al. (2020)
ConvE	https://github.com/TimDettmers/ConvE	Dettmers et al. (2018)
RotatE	https://github.com/DeepGraphLearning/KnowledgeGraphEmbedding	Sun et al. (2019)

Table 4: Overview of related work

WantWords: An Open-source Online Reverse Dictionary System

Fanchao Qi[1,2*], **Lei Zhang**[2*†], **Yanhui Yang**[2†], **Zhiyuan Liu**[1,2,3], **Maosong Sun**[1,2,3]

[1]Department of Computer Science and Technology, Tsinghua University
[2]Institute for Artificial Intelligence, Tsinghua University
Beijing National Research Center for Information Science and Technology
[3]Beijing Academy of Artificial Intelligence
`qfc17@mails.tsinghua.edu.cn, zhanglei9003@gmail.com`
`flutter0696@gmail.com, {liuzy,sms}@tsinghua.edu.cn`

Abstract

A reverse dictionary takes descriptions of words as input and outputs words semantically matching the input descriptions. Reverse dictionaries have great practical value such as solving the tip-of-the-tongue problem and helping new language learners. There have been some online reverse dictionary systems, but they support English reverse dictionary queries only and their performance is far from perfect. In this paper, we present a new open-source online reverse dictionary system named WantWords (`https://wantwords.thunlp.org/`). It not only significantly outperforms other reverse dictionary systems on English reverse dictionary performance, but also supports Chinese and English-Chinese as well as Chinese-English cross-lingual reverse dictionary queries for the first time. Moreover, it has user-friendly front-end design which can help users find the words they need quickly and easily. All the code and data are available at `https://github.com/thunlp/WantWords`.

1 Introduction

Opposite to a regular (forward) dictionary that provides definitions for query words, a *reverse dictionary* (Sierra, 2000) returns words semantically matching the query descriptions. In Figure 1, for example, a regular dictionary tells you the definition of "expressway" is "a wide road that allows traffic to travel fast", while a reverse dictionary outputs "expressway" and other semantically similar words like "freeway" which match the query description "a road where cars go very quickly without stopping" you input.

Reverse dictionaries are useful in practical applications. First and foremost, they can effectively solve the *tip-of-the-tongue* problem (Brown and

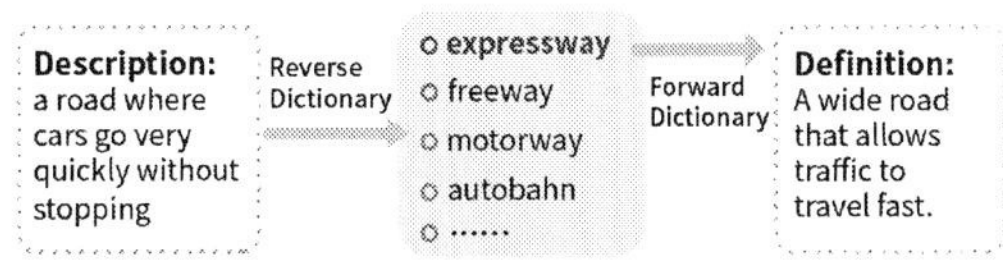

Figure 1: An example illustrating what a regular (forward) dictionary and a reverse dictionary are.

McNeill, 1966), namely the phenomenon of failing to retrieve a word from memory. Many people frequently suffer the problem, especially those who write a lot such as writers, researchers and students. With the help of reverse dictionaries, people can quickly and easily find the words that they need but temporarily forget.

In addition, reverse dictionaries are helpful to new language learners who grasp a limited number of words. They will know and learn some new words that have the meanings they want to express by using a reverse dictionary. Also, reverse dictionaries can help word selection (or word dictionary) anomia patients, people who can recognize and describe an object but fail to name it due to neurological disorder (Benson, 1979).

Currently, there are mainly two online reverse dictionaries, namely OneLook[1] and ReverseDictionary.[2] Their performance is far from perfect. Further, both of them are closed-source and only support English reverse dictionary queries.

To solve these problems, we design and develop a new online reverse dictionary system named WantWords, which is totally open-source. WantWords is mainly based on our proposed multi-channel reverse dictionary model (Zhang et al., 2020), which achieves state-of-the-art performance on an English benchmark dataset. Our system uses an improved version of the multi-channel reverse dictionary model and incorporates some

---

*Indicates equal contribution
†Work done during internship at Tsinghua University

[1]`https://onelook.com/thesaurus/`
[2]`https://reversedictionary.org/`

Proceedings of the 2020 EMNLP (Systems Demonstrations), pages 175–181
November 16-20, 2020. ©2020 Association for Computational Linguistics

engineering tricks to handle extreme cases. Evaluation results show that with these improvements, our system achieves higher performance. Besides, our system supports Chinese reverse dictionary queries and Chinese-English as well as English-Chinese cross-lingual reverse dictionary queries, all of which are realized for the first time. Finally, our system is very user-friendly. It includes multiple filters and sort methods, and can automatically cluster the candidate words, all of which help users find the target words as quickly as possible.

2 Related Work

There are mainly two methods for reverse dictionary building. The first one is based on sentence matching (Bilac et al., 2004; Zock and Bilac, 2004; Méndez et al., 2013; Shaw et al., 2013). Its main idea is to return the words whose dictionary definitions are most similar to the query description. Although effective in some cases, this method cannot cope with the problem that human-written query descriptions might differ widely from dictionary definitions.

The second method uses a neural language model (NLM) to encode the query description into a vector in the word embedding space, and returns the words with the closest embeddings to the vector of the query description (Hill et al., 2016; Morinaga and Yamaguchi, 2018; Kartsaklis et al., 2018; Hedderich et al., 2019; Pilehvar, 2019). Performance of this method depends largely on the quality of word embeddings. Unfortunately, according to Zipf's law (Zipf, 1949), many words are low-frequency and usually have poor embeddings.

To tackle this issue of the NLM-based method, we proposed a multi-channel reverse dictionary model (Zhang et al., 2020). This model is composed of a sentence encoder, more specifically, a bi-directional LSTM (BiLSTM) (Hochreiter and Schmidhuber, 1997) with attention (Bahdanau et al., 2015), and four characteristic predictors. The four predictors are used to predict the part-of-speech, morphemes, word category and sememes[3] of the target word according to the query description, respectively. The incorporation of the characteristic predictors can help find the target words with poor embeddings and exclude wrong words with similar embeddings to the target words, such

---

[3] A sememe is defined as the minimum semantic units of human languages (Bloomfield, 1926). The meaning of a word can be expressed by several sememes.

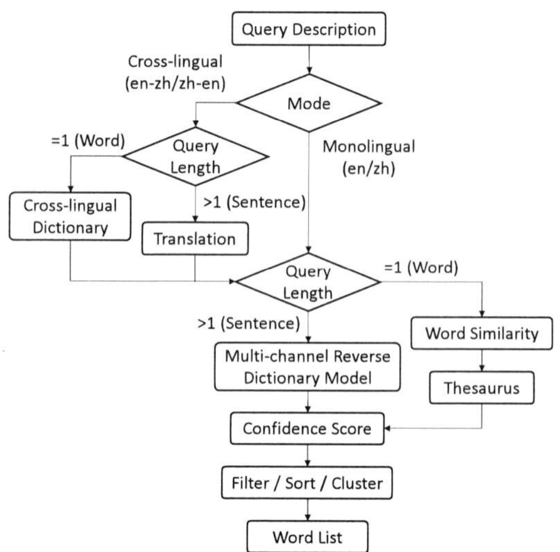

Figure 2: Workflow of WantWords.

as antonyms. Experimental results have demonstrated that our multi-channel reverse dictionary model achieves state-of-the-art performance. In WantWords, we employ an improved version of it that yields better results.

3 System Architecture

In this section, we describe the system architecture of WantWords. We first give an overview of its workflow, then we detail the improved multi-channel reverse dictionary model, and finally we introduce its front-end design.

3.1 Overall Workflow

The workflow of WantWords is illustrated in Figure 2. There are two reverse dictionary modes, namely monolingual and cross-lingual modes. In the monolingual mode, if the query description is longer than one word, it will be fed into the multi-channel reverse dictionary model directly, which calculates a confidence score for each candidate word in the vocabulary; if the query description is just a word, the confidence score of each candidate word is mostly based on the cosine similarity between the embeddings of the query word and candidate word.

In the cross-lingual mode, where the query descriptions are in the *source* language and the target words are in the *target* language, if the query description is longer than one word, it will be translated into the target language first and then processed in the monolingual mode of the target language; if the query description is just a word, cross-lingual dictionaries will be consulted for the target-language definitions of the query word, and then the definitions are fed into the multi-channel reverse dictionary model to calculate candidate words' confidence scores.

After obtaining confidence scores, all candidate words in the vocabulary will be sorted by descending confidence scores and listed as system output. The words in the query description are excluded since they are unlikely to be the target word. Different filters, other sort methods and clustering may be further employed to adjust the final results.

3.2 Multi-channel Reverse Dictionary Model

The multi-channel reverse dictionary model (MRDM) is the core module of our system. We use an improved version of MRDM that employs BERT (Devlin et al., 2019) rather than BiLSTM as the sentence encoder. Figure 3 illustrates the model.

For a given query description, MRDM calculates a confidence score for each candidate word in the vocabulary. The confidence score is composed of five parts:

(1) The first part is word score. To obtain it, the input query description is first encoded into a sentence vector by BERT, then the sentence vector is mapped into the space of word embeddings by a single-layer perceptron, and finally word score is the dot product of the mapped sentence vector and the candidate word's embedding.

(2) The second part is part-of-speech (PoS) score, which is based on the prediction for the PoS of the target word. MRDM first calculates a prediction score for each PoS tag by feeding the sentence vector into a single-layer perceptron, and then a candidate word's PoS score is the sum of the prediction scores of all its PoS tags.

(3) The third part is category score, which is related to the category of the target word and can be obtained in a similar way to PoS score.

(4) The fourth part is morpheme score, which is supposed to capture the morphemes of the target word. Each token of the input query description corresponds to a hidden state as the output of BERT. MRDM first feeds each hidden state into a single-layer perceptron to obtain a local morpheme prediction score, then does max-pooling over all the local morpheme prediction scores to obtain a prediction score for each morpheme, and finally a candidate word's morpheme score is the sum of the prediction scores of all its morphemes.

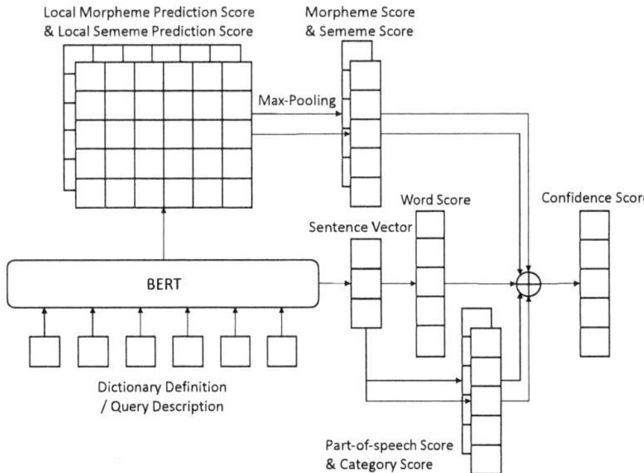

Figure 3: Revised version of the multi-channel reverse dictionary model.

(5) The fifth part is sememe score, which is based on the prediction for the sememes of the target word. Sememe score can be calculated in a similar way to morpheme score.

We use the official pre-trained BERT models for both English and Chinese.[4] As for fine-tuning (training) for English, we use the dictionary definition dataset created by Hill et al. (2016), which contains about $100,000$ words and $900,000$ word-definition pairs extracted from five dictionaries. For fine-tuning (training) for Chinese, we build a large-scale dictionary definition dataset based on the dataset created by Zhang et al. (2020). It contains $137,174$ words and $270,549$ word-definition pairs, where the definitions are extracted from several authoritative Chinese dictionaries including *Modern Chinese Dictionary*, *Xinhua Dictionary* and *Chinese Idiom Dictionary* as well as an open-source dictionary dataset.[5]

MRDM requires some other resources, and we simply follow the settings in Zhang et al. (2020). Specifically, for English, we use Morfessor (Virpioja et al., 2013) to segment words into morphemes, WordNet (Miller, 1995) to obtain PoS and word category information, and OpenHowNet[6] (Qi et al., 2019) to obtain sememe information. As for Chinese, we simply use Chinese characters as morphemes. We utilize the PoS tags in *Modern Chinese Dictionary*. In addition, we use HIT-IR Tongyici Cilin[7] and OpenHowNet to obtain word category and sememe information, respectively.

---

[4] https://github.com/google-research/bert

[5] https://github.com/pwxcoo/chinese-xinhua

[6] https://github.com/thunlp/OpenHowNet

[7] https://github.com/yaleimeng/Final_word_Similarity/tree/master/cilin

Figure 4: Front-end design of `WantWords` in the English monolingual mode.

3.3 One-word Query in the Monolingual Mode

In the monolingual reverse dictionary mode, in the case where the query description is a single word, we simply use word embedding similarity to calculate the confidence scores of candidate words in the vocabulary, rather than feed the query word into MRDM. We also take the synonyms into consideration and double the confidence score of a candidate word if it is a synonym of the query word. We use WordNet and HIT-IR Tongyici Cilin as English and Chinese thesauri, respectively.

3.4 The Cross-lingual Mode

In the cross-lingual mode, a query description longer than one word is first translated into the target language using Baidu Translation API[8], and then the translated query description is processed in the same procedure as the monolingual mode.

As for a one-word query description, we do not utilize machine translation because existing translation APIs cannot return all the possible translation results, especially for polysemous query words, which may impairs system performance. Instead, we consult cross-lingual dictionaries for definitions in the target language of the query word, and feed all the definitions into the target-language MRDM. Specifically, we use *StarDict* and *LangDao* English-Chinese Dictionaries in the

English-Chinese mode and *LangDao*, *CEDICT*, and *MDBG* Chinese-English dictionaries in the Chinese-English mode. We concatenate multiple dictionary definitions before feeding into MRDM.

3.5 Front-end Design

The front-end design of `WantWords` is simple and user-friendly, as shown in Figure 4. After inputting a query description in the textbox in the center of the system web page and clicking the "Search" button, one hundred candidate words will be listed in descending order of confidence scores. The words with confidence scores higher than a threshold have a background color whose shade is proportional to the confidence score.

A tool bar will appear below the textbox. Users can filter the candidate words by different filters in the tool bar. Specifically, for English candidate words, there are PoS, word length, initial and wildcard pattern filters; for Chinese candidate words, there are word length, total stroke number, wildcard pattern, pinyin initials, PoS and rhyme filters. These filters can help users find the word they need as quickly as possible.

In the tool bar, users can also change the sort method of the candidate words. Users can sort the English candidate words in regular or reverse alphabetical order and by word length, and Chinese candidate words in regular or reverse pinyin alphabetical order and by total stroke number. Besides,

---

[8]https://fanyi-api.baidu.com/

`WantWords` supports dividing candidate words into six clusters, where we use k-means clustering algorithm in the word embedding space. The sort methods and clustering are also beneficial to quickly finding the target word.

Considering the cases where users, especially new language learners, do not know rather than forget a word, our system provides definitions for candidate words. Users can click a candidate word to invoke a floating window that displays the PoS and definition of the word. The displayed definitions of English and Chinese words are from Word-Net and the open-source Chinese dictionary dataset respectively, both of which are freely available.

Finally, our system has quick feedback channels to collect real-world data. Due to the lack of human-written description data, existing reverse dictionary systems can only utilize dictionary definitions in training. However, dictionary definitions are usually different from human-written descriptions, which affects the performance of reverse dictionaries. Therefore, we design some feedback channels to collect users' feedback, aiming to use it to improve our system. Specifically, users can choose between "Matched Well" and "Not Matched" in the floating window of a candidate word to give their opinions about the candidate word. In addition, users can directly propose appropriate words matching the query description.

4 Evaluation

In this section, we evaluate the reverse dictionary performance of `WantWords`. We conduct both monolingual (English and Chinese) and cross-lingual (English-Chinese and Chinese-English) reverse dictionary evaluations.

4.1 Datasets

In the evaluation of English monolingual reverse dictionary performance, we use two test sets including (1) **Definition** set, which contains 500 pairs of words and WordNet definitions that are randomly selected and have been excluded from the training set; and (2) **Description** set, which comprises 200 pairs of words and human-written descriptions and is a benchmark dataset created by Hill et al. (2016).

As for Chinese, we use three test sets: (1) **Definition** set, which contains 2, 000 pairs of words and dictionary definitions that are selected at random and do not exist in the training set; (2) **Description** set, which is composed of 200 word-description

pairs given by Chinese native speakers and is built by Zhang et al. (2020); and (3) **Question** set, which collects 272 real-world Chinese exam question-answers of writing the right word given a description from the Internet and is also created by Zhang et al. (2020).

To evaluate cross-lingual reverse dictionary performance, we build two test sets based on the two monolingual Description sets. We manually translate the word of each word-description pair in the English Description sets into Chinese to obtain the **English-Chinese Description** set, which is composed of 200 pairs of English descriptions and Chinese words. In a similar way, we construct the **Chinese-English Description** set, which contains 200 pairs of Chinese descriptions and English words.

4.2 Baseline Methods

We choose two existing online reverse dictionary systems, namely OneLook and ReverseDictionary, and two reverse dictionary models, namely original MRDM and BERT, as baseline methods.

OneLook and ReverseDictionary can only support English monolingual reverse dictionary queries. MRDM, as mentioned before, is the current state-of-the-art reverse dictionary model (Zhang et al., 2020) and mainly differs from `WantWords` in the sentence encoder (BiLSTM vs BERT) and engineering tricks (e.g., special processing for one-word queries) to handle one-word queries. As for BERT, it does not have extra characteristic predictors and engineering tricks as compared to `WantWords`. MRDM and BERT are trained with the same training sets as `WantWords` to respond English and Chinese reverse dictionary queries, respectively. They can also support cross-lingual reverse dictionary queries processed with the same procedure as the cross-lingual mode of `WantWords`.

4.3 Evaluation Metrics

Following previous work (Hill et al., 2016; Zhang et al., 2020), we use four evaluation metrics: the median rank of the target words in the final word lists (lower better) and the accuracy that the target words appear in top 1/10/100 (acc@1/10/100, higher better). Every experiment is run five times, and we report the average results. We also conduct Student's t-test to measure the significance of performance difference.

Model	En_Definition		En_Description		Zh_Definition		Zh_Description		Zh_Question	
OneLook	–	–	6	.33/.54/.76	–	–	–	–	–	–
ReverseDictionary	–	–	4	.30/.64/.80	–	–	–	–	–	–
MRDM	53	.08/.29/.59	3	.31/.65/.88	8	.21/.51/.76	4	.27/.60/.85	1	.50/.79/.91
BERT	34	.09/.34/.61	2	.33/.76/.93	13	.13/.45/.72	5	.23/.62/.86	1	.49/.79/.91
WantWords	**19**	**.10/.38/.72**	2	**.36/.75/.92**	7	**.22/.54/.77**	2	**.37/.74/.91**	0	**.60/.82/.93**

Table 1: Evaluation results of English and Chinese monolingual reverse dictionaries (median rank and acc@1/10/100). The boldfaced results denote significant dominance, and the underlined results indicate insignificant difference, where the statistical significance threshold of p-value is 0.05. The same is true for Table 2.

Model	en-zh		zh-en	
MRDM	40	.12/.31/.63	8	.20/.52/.76
BERT	**16**	.14/.40/.75	7	.21/.54/.76
WantWords	19	.14/.38/.76	8	.22/.53/**.78**

Table 2: Evaluation results of cross-lingual reverse dictionaries (median rank and acc@1/10/100).

4.4 Evaluation Results

The monolingual reverse dictionary evaluation results of WantWords and baseline methods are shown in Table 1. OneLook and ReverseDictionary have stored all the WordNet definitions, and we cannot exclude the word-definition pairs in the Definition set from their databases. Therefore, they can be evaluated on the Description set only.

We observe that WantWords basically performs better than all the baseline methods on all the five test sets. On the English benchmark test set Description, WantWords completely outperforms the two existing online systems and achieves new state-of-the-art performance. On the three Chinese test sets, WantWords also yields significantly better results than the two baseline methods.

Table 2 shows the cross-lingual reverse dictionary evaluation results of WantWords and two baseline methods. We find that the performance of three models is similar and much poorer than that on corresponding monolingual datasets. We conjecture that the unsatisfying translation quality seriously affects final performance, based on our observation that translations of some query descriptions are inaccurate and even ungrammatical.

4.5 Case Study

Table 3 shows two English reverse dictionary cases, where the query descriptions and output word lists of three reverse dictionary systems are displayed. In the first case, WantWords finds 8 correct words among top 10 while the other two systems finds none among top 15. In the second case, OneLook and WantWords use the PoS filter to retain verbs only. After filtering, the target word "receive" is

System	Results
Query: a road where cars go very quickly without stopping	
Onelook	station stationing stations pass passed stump stumped stumping stumps shoulder turnout flash run turn turned
ReverseDictionary	run garage scoot tipple rush direct shoulder flash tollbooth interchange resort hie drive station cessation
WantWords	**superhighway autobahn beltway motorway freeway highway** gridlock pothole **expressway thruway** dragstrip
Query: when somebody gives something to you and afterwards you have it	
Onelook	~~can~~ lie ~~form~~ catch ~~else greyhound retribution~~ employ ~~tire snap order~~ find assure ~~employed face starter bolt~~ reach
ReverseDictionary	have satisfaction lose claim deposit guess license repent change ration misappropriate charge carry leave remember
WantWords	~~gift pawning gifting loaning beneficiary payment buying giving giver how cash bonus~~ refund purchase **receive**

Table 3: Two English reverse dictionary cases. The boldfaced words are correct answers while the words struck through are filtered out by PoS filter (verb).

ranked top 3 in the word list of WantWords while OneLook still cannot find any correct words among top 6. ReverseDictionary has no filter and none of correct words appear among top 15.

5 Conclusion and Future work

In this paper, we present WantWords, an online reverse dictionary system, which achieves state-of-the-art performance on an English reverse dictionary benchmark dataset. Besides, it supports Chinese and English-Chinese as well as Chinese-English cross-lingual reverse dictionary queries for the first time. In the future, we will try to incorporate multi-word expressions and idioms in the system. Also, we will work on improving cross-lingual reverse dictionary performance by bilingual word embeddings or multilingual BERT.

Acknowledgements

This work is supported by the Major Program of the National Social Science Fund of China (No. 18ZDA238), the National Key Research and Development Program of China (No. 2020AAA0105200 and 2018YFB1004503), the National Natural Science Foundation of China (NSFC, No. 61732008), the NExT++ project from the National Research Foundation, Prime Minister's Office, Singapore under its IRC@Singapore Funding Initiative, and Beijing Academy of Artificial Intelligence (BAAI).

References

Dzmitry Bahdanau, Kyunghyun Cho, and Yoshua Bengio. 2015. Neural machine translation by jointly learning to align and translate. In *Proceedings of ICLR*.

D Frank Benson. 1979. Neurologic correlates of anomia. In *Studies in Neurolinguistics*, pages 293–328. Elsevier.

Slaven Bilac, Wataru Watanabe, Taiichi Hashimoto, Takenobu Tokunaga, and Hozumi Tanaka. 2004. Dictionary search based on the target word description. In *Proceedings of NLP*.

Leonard Bloomfield. 1926. A set of postulates for the science of language. *Language*, 2(3):153–164.

Roger Brown and David McNeill. 1966. The "tip of the tongue" phenomenon. *Journal of Verbal Learning and Verbal Behavior*, 5(4):325–337.

Jacob Devlin, Ming-Wei Chang, Kenton Lee, and Kristina Toutanova. 2019. Bert: Pre-training of deep bidirectional transformers for language understanding. In *Proceedings of NAACL-HLT*.

Michael A Hedderich, Andrew Yates, Dietrich Klakow, and Gerard de Melo. 2019. Using multi-sense vector embeddings for reverse dictionaries. In *Proceedings of IWCS*.

Felix Hill, Kyunghyun Cho, Anna Korhonen, and Yoshua Bengio. 2016. Learning to understand phrases by embedding the dictionary. *TACL*, 4:17–30.

Sepp Hochreiter and Jürgen Schmidhuber. 1997. Long short-term memory. *Neural Computation*, 9(8):1735–1780.

Dimitri Kartsaklis, Mohammad Taher Pilehvar, and Nigel Collier. 2018. Mapping text to knowledge graph entities using multi-sense lstms. In *Proceedings of EMNLP*.

Oscar Méndez, Hiram Calvo, and Marco A. Moreno-Armendáriz. 2013. A reverse dictionary based on semantic analysis using wordnet. In *Proceedings of MICAI*.

George A Miller. 1995. Wordnet: a lexical database for english. *Communications of the ACM*, 38(11):39–41.

Yuya Morinaga and Kazunori Yamaguchi. 2018. Improvement of reverse dictionary by tuning word vectors and category inference. In *Proceedings of ICIST*.

Mohammad Taher Pilehvar. 2019. On the importance of distinguishing word meaning representations: A case study on reverse dictionary mapping. In *Proceedings of NAACL-HLT*.

Fanchao Qi, Chenghao Yang, Zhiyuan Liu, Qiang Dong, Maosong Sun, and Zhendong Dong. 2019. Openhownet: An open sememe-based lexical knowledge base. *arXiv preprint arXiv:1901.09957*.

Ryan Shaw, Anindya Datta, Debra E. VanderMeer, and Kaushik Dutta. 2013. Building a scalable database-driven reverse dictionary. *TKDE*, 25:528–540.

Gerardo Sierra. 2000. The onomasiological dictionary: a gap in lexicography. In *Proceedings of the Ninth Euralex International Congress*.

Sami Virpioja, Peter Smit, Stig Arne Grönroos, and Mikko Kurimo. 2013. Morfessor 2.0: Python implementation and extensions for morfessor baseline. *Aalto University Publication*.

Lei Zhang, Fanchao Qi, Zhiyuan Liu, Yasheng Wang, Qun Liu, and Maosong Sun. 2020. Multi-channel reverse dictionary model. In *Proceedings of AAAI*.

George Kingsley Zipf. 1949. Human behavior and the principle of least effort. *SERBIULA (sistema Librum 2.0)*.

Michael Zock and Slaven Bilac. 2004. Word lookup on the basis of associations: from an idea to a roadmap. In *Proceedings of the Workshop on Enhancing and Using Electronic Dictionaries*.

BENNERD: A Neural Named Entity Linking System for COVID-19

Mohammad Golam Sohrab[†,*], Khoa N. A. Duong[†,*], Makoto Miwa[†,‡]
, Goran Topić[†], Masami Ikeda[†], and Hiroya Takamura[†]
[†]Artificial Intelligence Research Center (AIRC)
National Institute of Advanced Industrial Science and Technology (AIST), Japan
[‡]Toyota Technological Institute, Japan
{sohrab.mohammad, khoa.duong, goran.topic}@aist.go.jp,
{ikeda-masami, takamura.hiroya}@aist.go.jp,
makoto-miwa@toyota-ti.ac.jp

Abstract

We present a biomedical entity linking (EL) system BENNERD that detects named entities in text and links them to the unified medical language system (UMLS) knowledge base (KB) entries to facilitate the corona virus disease 2019 (COVID-19) research. BENNERD mainly covers biomedical domain, especially new entity types (e.g., coronavirus, viral proteins, immune responses) by addressing CORD-NER dataset. It includes several NLP tools to process biomedical texts including tokenization, flat and nested entity recognition, and candidate generation and ranking for EL that have been pre-trained using the CORD-NER corpus. To the best of our knowledge, this is the first attempt that addresses NER and EL on COVID-19-related entities, such as COVID-19 virus, potential vaccines, and spreading mechanism, that may benefit research on COVID-19. We release an online system to enable real-time entity annotation with linking for end users. We also release the manually annotated test set and CORD-NERD dataset for leveraging EL task. The BENNERD system is available at https://aistairc.github.io/BENNERD/.

1 Introduction

In response to the coronavirus disease 2019 (COVID-19) for global research community to apply recent advances in natural language processing (NLP), COVID-19 Open Research Dataset (CORD-19)[1] is an emerging research challenge with a resource of over 181,000 scholarly articles that are related to the infectious disease COVID-19 caused by severe acute respiratory syndrome coronavirus 2 (SARS-CoV-2). To facilitate COVID-19 studies, since NER is considered a fundamental step

in text mining system, Xuan et al. (2020b) created CORD-NER dataset with comprehensive NE annotations. The annotations are based on distant or weak supervision. The dataset includes 29,500 documents from the CORD-19 corpus. The CORD-NER dataset gives a shed on NER, but they do not address linking task which is important to address COVID-19 research. For example, in the example sentence in Figure 1, the mention SARS-CoV-2 needs to be disambiguated. Since the term SARS-CoV-2 in this sentence refers to a virus, it should be linked to an entry of a virus in the knowledge base, not to an entry of 'SARS-CoV-2 vaccination', which corresponds to therapeutic or preventive procedure to prevent a disease.

We present a BERT-based Exhaustive Neural Named Entity Recognition and Disambiguation (BENNERD) system. The system is composed of four models: **NER model** (Sohrab and Miwa, 2018) that enumerates all possible spans as potential entity mentions and classifies them into entity types, **masked language model** BERT (Devlin et al., 2019), **candidate generation model** to find a list of candidate entities in the unified medical language system (UMLS) knowledge base (KB) for entity linking (EL) and **candidate ranking model** to disambiguate the entity for concept indexing. The BENNERD system provides a web interface to facilitate the process of text annotation and its disambiguation without any training for end users. In addition, we introduce CORD-NERD (COVID-19 Open Research Dataset for Named Entity Recognition and Disambiguation) dataset an extended version of CORD-NER as for leveraging EL task.

2 System Description

The main objective of this work is to address recent pandemic of COVID-19 research. To facilitate COVID-19 studies, we introduce the BEN-

---

*Both authors contributed equally.
[1]https://www.kaggle.com/
allen-institute-for-ai/
CORD-19-research-challenge

Proceedings of the 2020 EMNLP (Systems Demonstrations), pages 182–188
November 16-20, 2020. ©2020 Association for Computational Linguistics

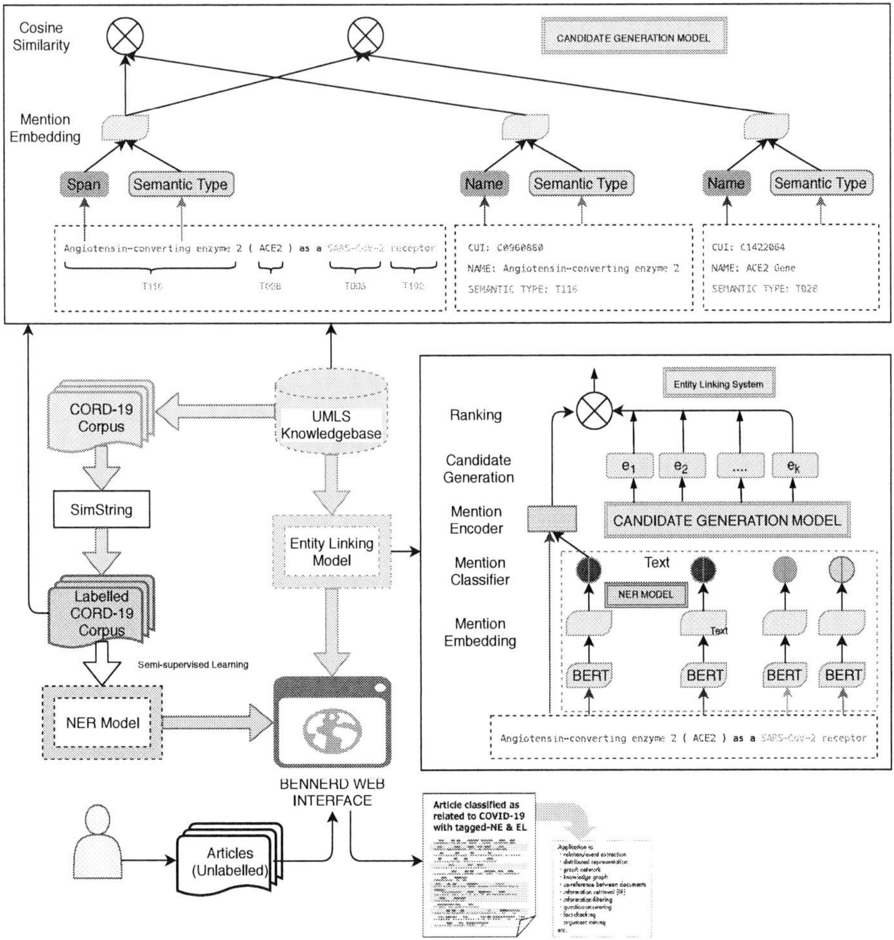

Figure 1: Workflow of BENNERD System

NERD system that finds nested named entities and links them to a UMLS knowledge base (KB). BENNERD mainly comprises two platforms: a web interface and a back-end server. The overall workflow of the BENNERD system is illustrated in Figure 1.

2.1 BENNERD Web Interface

The user interface of our BENNERD system is a web application with input panel, load a sample tab, annotation tab, gear box tab, and .TXT and .ANN tabs. Figure 2 shows an users' input interface of BENNERD. For a given text from users or loading a sample text from a sample list, the annotation tab will show the annotations with the text based on best NER- and EL-based training model. Figure 3 shows an example of text annotation based on the BENNERD's NER model. Different colors represent different entity types and, when the cursor floats over a coloured box representing an entity

above text, the corresponding concept unique identifier (CUI) on the UMLS is shown. Figure 3 also shows an example where entity mention SARS-CoV-2 links to its corresponding CUI. Users can save the machine readable text in txt format and annotation files in the ann format where the ann annotation file provides standoff annotation output in brat (Stenetorp et al., 2012)[2] format.

2.1.1 Data Flow of Web Interface

We provide a quick inside look of our BENNERD web interface (BWI). The data flow of BWI is presented as follows:

Server-side initialization (a) The BWI configuration, concept embeddings, and NER and EL models are loaded (b) GENIA sentence splitter and BERT basic tokenizer instances are initialized (c)

---

[2]https://brat.nlplab.org

Figure 2: BENNERD Users' Input Interface

Figure 3: Entity Annotation and Linking with BEN-
NERD

Concept embeddings are indexed by Faiss (Johnson
et al., 2019)

When a text is submitted (a) The text is split
into sentences and tokens (b) Token and sentence
standoffs are identified (c) NER model is run on tokenized sentences (d) EL model is run on the result
(e) The identified token spans are translated into
text standoffs (f) The identified concepts' names
are looked up in the UMLS database (g) A brat
document is created (h) The brat document is translated into JSON, and sent to the client side (i) The
brat visualizer renders the document

2.2 BENNERD Back-end

The BENNERD back-end implements a pipeline
of tools (e.g., NER, EL), following the data flow
described in Section 2.1.1. This section provides
implementation details of our back-end modules
for NER and EL.

2.2.1 Neural Named Entity Recognition

We build the mention detection, a.k.a NER, based
on the BERT model (Devlin et al., 2019). The layer
receives subword sequences and assigns contextual
representations to the subwords via BERT. We denote a sentence by $S = (x_1, ..., x_n)$, where x_i is
the i-th word, and x_i consists of s_i subwords. This
layer assigns a vector $v_{i,j}$ to the j-th subword of the
i-th word. Then, we generate the vector embedding
v_i for each word x_i by computing the unweighted
average of its subword embeddings $v_{i,j}$. We generate mention candidates based on the same idea
as the span-based model (Lee et al., 2017; Sohrab
and Miwa, 2018; Sohrab et al., 2019a,b), in which
all continuous word sequences are generated given
a maximal size L_x (span width). The representation $x_{b,e} \in R^{d_x}$ for the span from the b-th word to
the e-th word in a sentence is calculated from the
embeddings of the first word, the last word, and
the weighted average of all words in the span as
follows:

$$x_{b,e} = \left[v_b; \sum_{i=b}^{e} \alpha_{b,e,i} v_i; v_e \right], \qquad (1)$$

where $\alpha_{b,e,i}$ denotes the attention value of the i-th
word in a span from the b-th word to the e-th word,
and $[\ ;\ ]$ denotes concatenation.

2.2.2 Entity Linking

In our EL component, for every mention span $x_{b,e}$
of a concept in a document, we are supposed to
identify its ID in the target KB.[3] Let us call the ID
a concept unique identifier (CUI). The input is all
predicted mention spans $M = \{m_1, m_2, \dots, m_n\}$,
where m_i denotes the i-th mention and n denotes
the total number of predicted mentions. The list of
entity mentions $\{m_i\}_{i=1,\dots,n}$ needs to be mapped
to a list of corresponding CUIs $\{c_i\}_{i=1,\dots,n}$. We
decompose EL into two subtasks: candidate generation and candidate ranking.

Candidate Generation To find a list of candidate entities in KB to link with a given mention,
we build a candidate generation layer adapting a
dual-encoders model (Gillick et al., 2019). Instead
of normalizing entity definition to disambiguate
entities, we simply normalize the semantic types in
both mention and entity sides from UMLS.

The representation of a mention m in a document
by the semantic type t_m, can be denoted as:

$$v_m = [w_m; t_m], \qquad (2)$$

where $t_m \in R^{d_{t_m}}$ is the mention type embedding.
For the entity (concept) side with semantic type
information, the representation a_e, and its entity
type embedding $t_e \in R^{d_{t_e}}$ can be computed as:

$$v_e = [a_e; t_e]. \qquad (3)$$

---

[3]We used the UMLS KB in the experiments.

We use cosine similarity to compute the similarity score between a mention m and an entity e and feed it into a linear layer (LL) to transform the score into an unbounded logit as:

$$\text{sim}(m, e) = \cos(\boldsymbol{v}_m, \boldsymbol{v}_e), \qquad (4)$$
$$\text{score}(m, e) = \text{LL}(\text{sim}(m, e)). \qquad (5)$$

We employ the in-batch random negatives technique as described in the previous work (Gillick et al., 2019). For evaluating the performance of the model during training, we use the in-batch recall@1 metric (Gillick et al., 2019) on the development set to track and save the best model.

We calculate the embedding of each detected mention from the mention detection layer and each of all entities in KB and then using an approximate nearest neighbor search algorithm in Faiss (Johnson et al., 2019) to retrieve the top k entities as candidates for the ranking layer.

Candidate Ranking The cosine similarity score in the candidate generation is insufficient to disambiguate the entities in which the correct entity should be assigned the highest score which is comparable from the k candidate entities. We employed a fully-connected neural network model to aim at ranking the entity candidate list to select the best entity linked to the mention. Given a mention m and a set of candidate entities $\{e_1, e_2, ..., e_k\}$, we concatenate the embedding of m in Equation (2) with the embedding of each entity e_i in Equation (3) to form a vector $\boldsymbol{v}_{m,e_i}$. Then the vector $\boldsymbol{v}_{m,e_i}$ is fed into a LL to compute the ranking score:

$$\text{score}(m, e_i) = \text{LL}(\boldsymbol{v}_{m,e_i}). \qquad (6)$$

The model is then trained using a softmax loss to maximize the score of the correct entity compared with other incorrect entities retrieved from the trained candidate generation model.

3 Experimental Settings

In this section, we evaluate our toolkit on CORD-NER and CORD-NERD datasets.

3.1 CORD-NER Dataset

We carry out our experiments on CORD-NER, a distant or weak supervision-based large-scale dataset that includes 29,500 documents, 2,533,485 sentences, and 10,388,642 mentions. In our experiment, CORD-NER covers 63 fine-grained entity types[4]. CORD-NER mainly supports four sources including 18 biomedical entity types[5], 18 general entity types[6], knowledge base entity types, and nine[7] seed-guided new entity types. We split the CORD-NER dataset into three subsets: train, development, and test, which respectively contain 20,000, 4,500, and 5,000 documents.

3.2 CORD-NERD Dataset

CORD-NER dataset comprises only NER task. To solve the EL task, we expand this dataset by leveraging a CUI for each mention in the CORD-NER dataset, we call this CORD-NERD dataset. We use the most recent UMLS version 2020AA release that includes coronavirus-related concepts. To create CORD-NERD dataset, we use a dictionary matching approach based on exact match using UMLS KB. CORD-NERD includes 10,470,248 mentions, among which 6,794,126 and 3,676,122 mentions are respectively present and absent in the UMLS. Therefore, the entity coverage ratio of CORD-NERD over the UMLS is 64.89%. We annotate the entity mentions that are not found in the UMLS with CUI_LESS. To evaluate the EL performances on CORD-NERD, 302,166 mentions are assigned for 5,000 test set, we call this UMLS-based test set. The train and development sets of CORD-NERD dataset, we simply calls UMLS-based train- and UMLS-based dev-set respectively. Besides, we assigned a biologist to annotate 1,000 random sentences based on chemical, disease, and gene types to create a manually annotated test set. This test set includes 311 disease mentions for the NER task and 946 mentions[8] with their corresponding CUIs for the EL task.

3.3 Data Prepossessing

Each text and the corresponding annotation file are processed by BERT's basic tokenizer. After tokenization, each text and its corresponding annotation file was directly passed to the deep neural approach for mention detection and classification.

---

[4]In the original CORD-NER paper (Xuan et al., 2020b), the authors reported 75 fine-grained entity types, but we found only 63 types.

[5]https://uofi.app.box.com/s/
k8pw7d5kozzpoum2jwfaqdaeyloij93x/file/
637866394186

[6]https://spacy.io/api/annotation#
named-entities

[7]Coronavirus, Viral Protein, Livestock, Wildlife, Evolution, Physical Science, Substrate, Material, Immune Response

[8]Among them, 38, 311, and 597 mentions are of chemical, disease, and gene entity types respectively.

Model	Gene			Chemical			Disease		
	P	**R**	**F**	**P**	**R**	**F**	**P**	**R**	**F (%)**
SciSpacy(BIONLP13CG)	91.48	82.06	86.51	64.66	39.81	49.28	8.11	2.75	4.11
SciSpacy(BC5CDR)	-	-	-	86.97	51.86	64.69	80.31	59.65	68.46
CORD-NER System	82.14	74.68	72.23	82.93	75.22	78.89	75.73	68.42	71.89

Table 1: Performance comparison of baseline systems on three biomedical entity types in CORD-NER corpus.

Model	Development set			Test set		
	P	**R**	**F**	**P**	**R**	**F (%)**
BENNERD + ClinicalCovid BERT (CCB)	**84.62**	86.43	**85.52**	82.83	**83.23**	**83.03**
BENNERD + SciBERT	84.03	**87.05**	85.51	82.16	**83.81**	82.98
BENNERD + Covid BERT Base	78.31	66.80	72.10	77.44	66.80	71.73

Table 2: NER Performances using different pre-trained BERT models.

Model	Gene			Chemical			Disease		
	P	**R**	**F**	**P**	**R**	**F**	**P**	**R**	**F (%)**
BENNERD + CCB	76.07	74.83	75.45	83.55	84.60	84.07	84.85	84.99	84.92

Table 3: Performance comparison of BENNERD on three major biomedical entity types in CORD-NER corpus. CCB denotes ClinicalCovid BERT.

Model	**P**	**R**	**F (%)**
SciSpacy(BC5CDR)	36.01	**56.27**	43.91
BENNERD	**49.16**	47.27	**48.20**

Table 4: Performance comparison of BENNERD with pre-trained SciSpacy over the disease entity types on the manually annotated test set.

4 Results

4.1 NER Performances on Baseline Model

Table 1 shows the performance of SciSpacy on CORD-NER dataset. In this table, the results are based on randomly picked 1,000 manually annotated sentences as the test set.

4.2 NER Performances on BENNERD Model

Table 2 shows the performance comparison of our BENNERD with different pre-trained BERT models based on our test set. Since the manually annotated CORD-NER test set is not publicly available, we cannot directly compare our system performance. Instead, in Table 3, we show the performance of gene, chemical, and disease based on our UMLS-based test set. Besides, in Table 4, we also show the NER performances comparison of BENNERD with BC5CDR corpus-based SciSpacy model on the manually annotated disease entities.

4.3 Candidate Ranking Performance

As we are the first to perform EL task on CORD-19 dataset, we present different scenarios to evaluate our candidate ranking performance. The results of EL are depicted in Table 5. In this table, we evaluate our candidate ranking performances based on two experiment settings. In setting1, we train the CUIs based on manually annotated MedMention (Murty et al., 2018) dataset. In setting2, the BENNERD model is trained on automatically annotated CORD-NERD dataset. Table 5 also shows that our BENNERD model with setting2 is outperformed in compare to setting1 in every cases in terms of accuracy@(1, 10, 20, 30, 40, 50). Table 6 shows the EL performance on the manually annotated test set. In this table, it also shows that our system with setting2 is outperformed in compare to setting1. Besides, we also evaluate the manually annotated test set simply with string matching approach where the results of the top 10, 20, 30, 40 or 50 predictions for a gold candidate are unchanged.

4.4 Performances on COVID-19 Entity Types

Finally, in Table 7, we show the performance of nine new entity types discussed in Section 3.1 related to COVID-19 studies, which may benefit research on COVID-19 virus, spreading mechanism, and potential vaccines.

Model	UMLS-based Test set					
	A@1	A@10	A@20	A@30	A@40	A@50 (%)
BENNERD + NER's Pred. + Setting1	27.61	44.56	49.74	51.88	53.08	54.19
BENNERD + Gold NEs + Setting1	29.78	48.33	53.89	56.22	57.53	58.74
BENNERD + NER's TP + Setting1	30.31	48.91	54.60	56.95	58.27	59.49
BENNERD + NER's Pred. + Setting2	47.46	64.32	67.70	69.87	71.12	72.07
BENNERD + Gold NEs + Setting2	50.73	69.31	73.10	75.58	77.03	78.13
BENNERD + NER's TP + Setting2	53.90	73.06	76.90	79.36	80.79	81.87

Table 5: EL performance on test set. We report Accuracy@n, where $n = 1, 10, 20, 30, 40, 50$. Accuracy@1, gold candidate was ranked highest. Accuracy@{10, 20, 30, 40, 50} indicates, gold candidate was in top 10, 20, 30, 40 or in 50 predictions of the ranker. Pred., NEs, and TP refers to predictions, named entities, and true positive respectively. Setting1 and 2 denotes model is trained on MEDMention and CORD-NERD datasets respectively.

Model	Manually Annotated Test set					
	A@1	A@10	A@20	A@30	A@40	A@50 (%)
BENNERD + Setting1	24.27	42.95	47.07	48.81	50.00	50.92
BENNERD + Setting2	31.84	50.25	54.53	56.87	58.39	60.12
BENNERD + String Matching	30.21	41.00	41.00	41.00	41.00	41.00

Table 6: EL performance on our manually annotated test set.

Model	UMLS-based Test set		
	P	R	F (%)
Coronovirus	98.46	98.94	98.70
Viral Protein	89.39	91.09	90.23
Livestock	96.67	97.26	96.96
Wildlife	98.43	97.56	97.99
Evolution	97.16	98.46	97.80
Physical Science	96.80	93.08	94.90
Substrate	95.99	98.46	97.21
Material	94.80	90.46	92.58
Immune Response	97.29	99.42	98.35

Table 7: Performances on nine types of COVID-19

5   Related Work

To facilitate the biomedical text mining research on COVID-19, recently a few works have reported to address text mining tasks. Xuan et al. (2020b) created CORD-NER dataset with distant or weak supervision and reported first NER performances on different NER models. Motivated by this work, we presented a first web-based toolkit that addresses both NER and EL. In addition, we also extend the CORD-NER dataset to solve EL task.

Xuan et al. (2020a) created EvidenceMiner system that retrieves sentence-level textual evidence from CORD-NER dataset. Tonia et al. (2020) developed an NLP pipeline to extract drug and vaccine information about SARS-CoV-2 and other viruses to help biomedical experts to easily track the latest scientific publications. To the best of our knowledge, this work is our first effort to solve both NER and EL models in a pipeline manner.

6   Conclusion

We presented the BENNERD system for entity linking, hoping that we can bring insights for the COVID-19 studies on making scientific discoveries. To the best of our knowledge, BENNERD represents the first web-based workflow of NER and EL for NLP research that addresses CORD-19 dataset that leads to create CORD-NERD dataset to facilitate COVID-19 work. The online system is available for meeting real-time extraction for end users. The BENNERD system is continually evolving; we will continue to improve the system as well as to implement new functions such as relation extraction to further facilitate COVID-19 research. We refer to visit https://aistairc.github.io/BENNERD/ to know more about BENNERD and CORD-NERD.

Acknowledgments

We thank the anonymous reviewers for their valuable comments. This work is based on results obtained from a project commissioned by the Public/Private R&D Investment Strategic Expansion PrograM (PRISM).

References

Jacob Devlin, Ming-Wei Chang, Kenton Lee, and Kristina Toutanova. 2019. BERT: Pre-training of deep bidirectional transformers for language understanding. In *Proceedings of the 2019 Conference of the North American Chapter of the Association for Computational Linguistics: Human Language Technologies, Volume 1 (Long and Short Papers)*, pages 4171–4186.

Daniel Gillick, Sayali Kulkarni, Larry Lansing, Alessandro Presta, Jason Baldridge, Eugene Ie, and Diego Garcia-Olano. 2019. Learning dense representations for entity retrieval. In *Proceedings of the 23rd Conference on Computational Natural Language Learning (CoNLL)*, pages 528–537, Hong Kong, China. Association for Computational Linguistics.

J. Johnson, M. Douze, and H. Jégou. 2019. Billion-scale similarity search with GPUs. *IEEE Transactions on Big Data*.

Kenton Lee, Luheng He, Mike Lewis, and Luke Zettlemoyer. 2017. End-to-end neural coreference resolution. In *Proceedings of the 2017 Conference on Empirical Methods in Natural Language Processing*, pages 188–197, Copenhagen, Denmark. Association for Computational Linguistics.

Shikhar Murty, Patrick Verga, Luke Vilnis, Irena Radovanovic, and Andrew McCallum. 2018. Hierarchical losses and new resources for fine-grained entity typing and linking. In *Proceedings of the 56th Annual Meeting of the Association for Computational Linguistics (Volume 1: Long Papers)*, pages 97–109.

Mohammad Golam Sohrab and Makoto Miwa. 2018. Deep exhaustive model for nested named entity recognition. In *Proceedings of the 2018 Conference on Empirical Methods in Natural Language Processing*, pages 2843–2849, Brussels, Belgium. Association for Computational Linguistics.

Mohammad Golam Sohrab, Minh Thang Pham, Makoto Miwa, and Hiroya Takamura. 2019a. A neural pipeline approach for the pharmaconer shared task using contextual exhaustive models. In *Proceedings of The 5th Workshop on BioNLP Open Shared Tasks*, pages 47–55.

Mohammad Golam Sohrab, Pham Minh Thang, and Makoto Miwa. 2019b. A generic neural exhaustive approach for entity recognition and sensitive span detect. In *Proceedings of the Iberian Languages Evaluation Forum (IberLEF 2019)*, pages 735–743, Span. IberLEF 2019.

Pontus Stenetorp, Sampo Pyysalo, Goran Topić, Tomoko Ohta, Sophia Ananiadou, and Jun'ichi Tsujii. 2012. brat: a web-based tool for NLP-assisted text annotation. In *Proceedings of the Demonstrations at the 13th Conference of the European Chapter of the Association for Computational Linguistics*, pages 102–107, Avignon, France. Association for Computational Linguistics.

Korves Tonia, Peterson Matthew, Garay Christopher, Read Tom, Chang Wenling, Bartlett Marta, Quattrochi Lauren, and Hirschman Lynette. 2020. Nlp for extracting covid-19 drug and vaccine information from scientific literature. In *Proceedings of the 28th Conference on Intelligent Systems for Moleculer Biology*.

Wang Xuan, Liu Weili, Chauhan Aabhas, Guan Yingjun, and Han Jiawei. 2020a. Automatic textual evidence mining in COVID-19 literature. *2020 Intelligent Systems for Molecular Biology (ISMB'20)*.

Wang Xuan, Song Xiangchen, Li Bangzheng, Guan Yingjun, and Han Jiawei. 2020b. Comprehensive named entity recognition on CORD-19 with distant or weak supervision. *2020 Intelligent Systems for Molecular Biology (ISMB'20)*.

RoFT: A Tool for Evaluating Human Detection of Machine-Generated Text

Liam Dugan*,   Daphne Ippolito*,   Arun Kirubarajan*,   Chris Callison-Burch

University of Pennsylvania

{ldugan, daphnei, kiruba, ccb}@seas.upenn.edu

Abstract

In recent years, large neural networks for natural language generation (NLG) have made leaps and bounds in their ability to generate fluent text. However, the tasks of evaluating quality differences between NLG systems and understanding how humans perceive the generated text remain both crucial and difficult. In this system demonstration, we present Real or Fake Text (RoFT), a website that tackles both of these challenges by inviting users to try their hand at detecting machine-generated text in a variety of domains. We introduce a novel evaluation task based on detecting the boundary at which a text passage that starts off human-written transitions to being machine-generated. We show preliminary results of using RoFT to evaluate detection of machine-generated news articles.

1 Introduction

Despite considerable advancements in building natural language generation (NLG) systems that can output extremely fluent English text, there is still not very much understanding of how humans perceive machine-generated text. Such an understanding is crucial for the evaluation of the improvements in NLG systems and for the analysis of the societal ramifications of machine-generated text as it becomes increasingly easy to produce.

When evaluating NLG systems, it is considered standard practice to ask evaluators to rate generated text on criteria such as fluency, naturalness, or relevance to a prompt on a Likert scale (van der Lee et al., 2019). Preference studies, where a rater is shown two generated excerpts and asked which one they prefer, are also common. Some recent work has focused on the detection problem: how capable humans are at distinguishing textual excerpts gen-

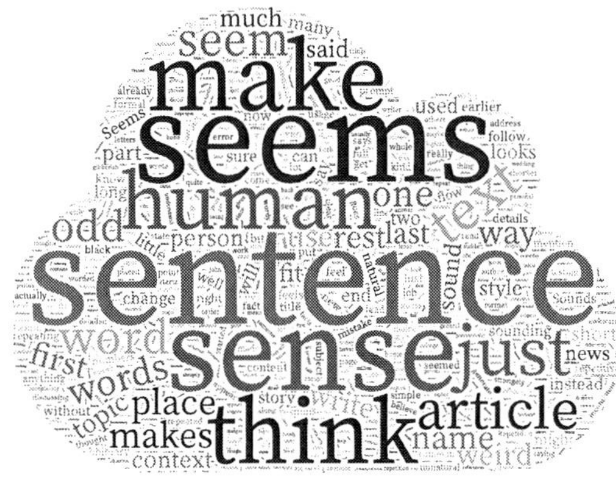

Figure 1: A word cloud of common words that annotators used to describe why they thought sentences were machine-generated.

erated by a system from those written by another human (Ippolito et al., 2020; Zellers et al., 2019).

However, due to the prohibitive cost of running human evaluation studies, most prior work in this area has been rather limited in scope. For example, analyses usually show results on only a single category of text (news articles, stories, webtext, etc.). This could be problematic since different domains have different levels of named entities, world facts, narrative coherence, and other properties that impact the success of NLG systems. In addition, most papers only evaluate on a very limited selection of decoding strategy hyperparameters. Holtzman et al. (2019) and Ippolito et al. (2020) both show that the decoding strategy chosen at inference time can have a significant impact on the quality of generated text.

In this work, we introduce the Real or Fake Text (RoFT) system, a novel application for simultaneously collecting quality annotations of machine-generated text while allowing the public to assess and improve their skill at detecting machine-generated text.

*Authors listed alphabetically contributed equally.

189

Proceedings of the 2020 EMNLP (Systems Demonstrations), pages 189–196
November 16-20, 2020. ©2020 Association for Computational Linguistics

In RoFT, we propose to use the task of detecting when text is machine-generated as a quality criterion for comparing NLG systems. Following Ippolito et al. (2020), we make the counterintuitive assumption that the *worse* annotators are at detecting that text is machine-generated, the *better* we can say that the NLG system is at generating text.

In RoFT's detection task, annotators are shown a passage of text one sentence at a time. The first several sentences are from a real human-written text source and the next several sentences are a machine-generated continuation. The user's goal is to guess where the boundary is. When they think that a sentence is machine-generated, they are asked to give an explanation for their choice. Afterwards the true boundary is revealed.

In the remainder of this paper, we discuss why we think this task is interesting from a research perspective and describe the technical details behind our implementation. We show preliminary results that showcase the types of analyses that are possible with the collected data, and finally we discuss plans for future work.

The RoFT website is located at `http://www.roft.io/`. The source code is available under an MIT License at `https://github.com/kirubarajan/roft`.

2   Research Motivations

The purpose behind RoFT is to collect annotations on the scale needed to probe the quality of text generated under a variety of NLG conditions and systems. In this section, we describe three research questions we aim to answer using RoFT data.

2.1   Length Threshold for Detection

State-of-the-art generative models tend to produce text that is locally fluent but lacking in long-term structure or coherence. Intuition suggests that fluent NLG systems ought to produce text that is high quality for long durations (measured in number of sentences). As such, we are interested in using the the boundary detection task—whether annotators can detect the boundary between human-written text and a machine-generated continuation—as a comparison method for NLG systems. We hypothesize that for better quality systems, the generated text will be able to fool humans for more sentences.

2.2   Text Genre/Style

Generative language models have now been trained and fine-tuned on a great diversity of genres and styles of text, from Reddit posts (Keskar et al., 2019) and short stories (Fan et al., 2018) to Wikipedia (Liu et al., 2018) and news articles (Zellers et al., 2019). Each of these datasets has its own distinct challenges for generation; for example, in the story domain it is acceptable for a generator to make up facts while this would be unacceptable in a Wikipedia article. We are interested in how these differences might impact the ability of humans to detect machine-generated text.

2.3   Reasons Text is Low Quality

A study by van der Lee et al. (2019) found that less than 3% of recent papers on NLG ask for free-text comments when performing human evaluations. And yet, understanding why humans think text is low quality can be very important for diagnosing problems in NLG systems (Reiter and Belz, 2009). Therefore, the RoFT platform collects free-form textual explanations from our annotators on their decisions. Such data, though inevitably noisy, could provide insights into the types of errors that NLG systems introduce, the types of errors humans are sensitive to, and even the types of errors human-written corpora contain (when a rater inadvertently predicts that a human-written sentence is machine-generated).

2.4   Human Factor

The boundary detection task posed by RoFT is an artificial one. We do not expect that real-world uses of machine-generated text would involve such a tidy split of prompt sentences followed by a machine-generated continuation. However, we believe that even an artificial framing such as RoFT's has both the potential to educate the public on what to look for in machine-generated text and give researchers insights into how humans perceive and react to such text. We are particularly interested in how annotators may or may not improve over time and in what ways their respective demographics (for example, paid crowd worker vs. university student) impact their detection skill.

3   System Overview

This section gives an overview of RoFT's design, including the task that annotators are asked to complete and methods for encouraging organic traffic.

3.1 Task Definition

The RoFT annotation task is posed as a game. Users first choose which category they would like to play in (where different categories correspond to different text domains or NLG systems). The "game" then consists of a series of rounds. Each round starts with the user being presented a single sentence that is guaranteed to be human-written. For example, this might be the first sentence of a New York Times article. Afterwards, users may select to display more sentences, one at a time. At each step, they must decide if they believe that the most recent sentence is still written by a human. When the user decides they are confident that a machine has written the most recent sentence (i.e. they have found the "boundary sentence"), the round ends. The user is then asked to provide a natural language explanation of what prompted their decision. In essence, the annotators' goal is to identify the exact sentence where a machine "takes over" and the text is no longer human-written. Figure 2 gives screenshots of the flow of a single round.

3.2 Implementation

The RoFT annotation website is designed to collect data needed to answer a variety of research questions, including those posed in Section 2. In particular, our system stores detailed metadata for each annotation. These include the order in which a user completed annotations, the type of user account associated with each annotation (e.g. paid worker or organic traffic), the NLG system used to produce each generation, and the amount of time each annotation took. The system was developed in Python using the Django Framework and a SQL database. The use of a relational database enables sophisticated queries to be made on the collected annotations for analysis. We plan to make dumps of the database available to other researchers to further promote research into the evaluation of generated text.

3.3 Gamification

Since the cost of collecting human annotations via a crowd platform such as Amazon Mechanical Turk can be prohibitively expensive for large studies, we aimed to build the RoFT website in a manner that would encourage sustained participation without the need for a financial incentive.

Each user has a Profile page (shown in Figure 3) where they can see statistics on the total number of

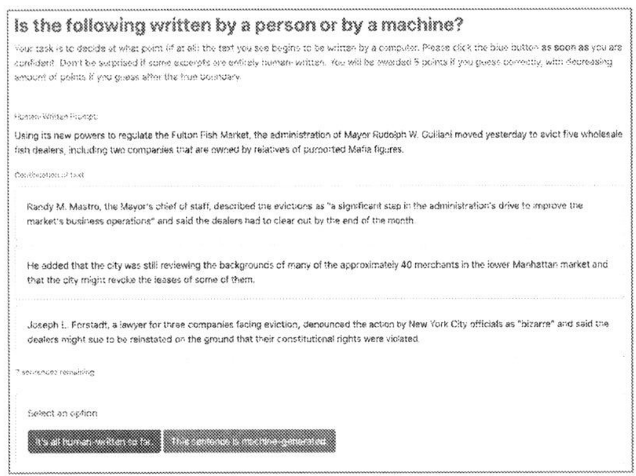

(a) The user is shown an initial sentence and then one sentence of continuation at a time. At each step, the user decides if the latest sentence is human-written or machine-generated and presses the appropriate button.

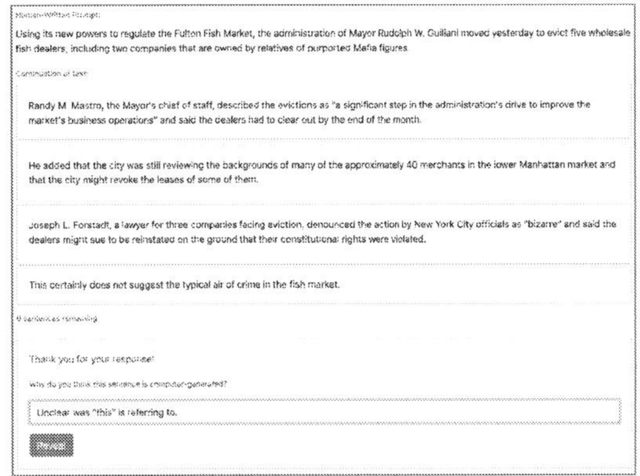

(b) When the user decides that the most recent sentence is machine-generated, they are asked to provide an explanation for their decision.

(c) The true boundary is then revealed. In this case, the user would be alerted that they received 5 points since they guessed the boundary correctly.

Figure 2: The user interface for annotation.

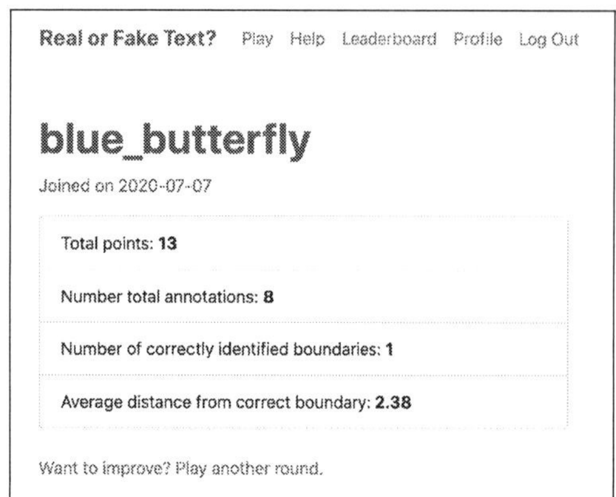

Figure 3: A user's profile page.

annotations they have done, how many points they have earned, and how many questions they have answered perfectly. There is also a leaderboard where users can check how their point count compares to other raters. The leaderboard encourages users to do more annotations, since this is the only way to move up on the rankings.

We received unsolicited compliments from our initial annotators such as "Interesting, fun task" and "Really convincing passages." We intend to add further gamification elements, including leaderboards broken down by text domain, comprehensive statistics on user progress and skill, and the ability to see and up-vote the free-text comments of other users.

3.4 Generations

We ultimately plan to use RoFT to study differences in detection performance across a variety of NLG systems and text domains. The initial version of RoFT includes two complementary categories of text: news and fictional stories. Users have the option to choose which category they would like to annotate.

For the news category, prompts are drawn from the New York Times Annotated Corpus (Sandhaus, 2008) and are truncated to between 1 and 10 sentences long. GROVER (Zellers et al., 2019) is then conditioned on these starting sentences and asked to complete the article. Finally, the outputs from GROVER are truncated so that the sum total number of sentences for each example is 10.

The data on fictional stories was prepared similarly except that the Reddit Writing Prompts dataset (Fan et al., 2018) was used for the prompts, and the GPT-2 XL model (Radford et al., 2019) was used for generation.

Each category contains over 1,500 examples, where for each example the number of human-written context sentences as well as the values of the decoding strategy hyperparameters were chosen randomly. For our initial seeding of data, Nucleus sampling (Holtzman et al., 2019) was used for all decoding, where the p hyperparameter, which controls the diversity of the generated text, was randomly selected to be anywhere from $p = 0$ (argmax) to $p = 1.0$ (full random sampling).

4 Case Study

To show the efficacy of RoFT as an evaluation tool, we present a case study from our initial pilot of over 3000 annotations of generations from the news article domain.

4.1 Data Collection

While our eventual hope is for the RoFT website to have enough organic traffic for useful data to be collected, for the purposes of this study, two hundred Amazon Mechanical Turk workers were paid to complete 10 annotations each on the website. In total, we collected 3244 annotations (7.9% of annotators continued past the minimum of 10 questions they were required to do to get paid). 10% of examples the crowd workers saw were designated attention check questions in which the prompt explicitly stated they should select "human-written" at every step. About 25% of crowd workers failed this check, and after filtering out these annotators, we were left with a total of 1848 high-quality annotations, which we will refer to as the filtered annotation set.

4.2 Inter-Annotator Agreement

There were 768 examples which had at least two crowd workers provide annotations for them (645 of which had at least three annotations provided). This led to 6,115 instances of pairs of annotations on the same examples. Of these, 18.3% predicted the exact same sentence as the boundary, and 28.4%, predicted boundaries at most one sentence apart from each other. When considering only the filtered annotation set, there were 2,064 pairs of annotations. Of these, 18.6% predicted the exact same sentence as the boundary, and 28.3% predicted boundaries at most one sentence apart from each other.

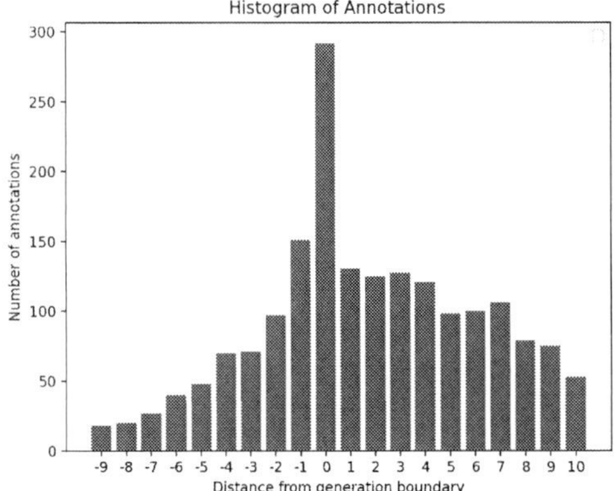

Figure 4: A histogram of the filtered annotation set grouped by the distance (in number of sentences) between the sentence selected by the annotator and the true boundary sentence.

4.3 Evaluation Measures

We consider three methods for evaluating annotator ability.

4.3.1 Accuracy

Among annotators that passed our attention check, 15.8% of the filtered annotations correctly identified the exact boundary between machine and generated text. Additionally, the average annotation from our filtered set was 1.989 sentences after the true boundary. This is consistent with our intuition, namely that current state-of-the-art NLG systems are capable of fooling humans but typically only for one or two sentences.

4.3.2 Distance from Boundary

In Figure 4, we show a histogram of our filtered annotation set grouped by the distance each annotation was away from the true boundary.[1] If annotators are selecting sentences at random, we would expect this distribution to be symmetric about 0. However, the observed distribution is significantly asymmetric, with the left tail (composed of annotators picking human-written sentences) dropping off precipitously while the right tail (composed of machine-generated sentences) decreases more linearly. This asymmetry indicates that our annotators are successfully picking up on clues in the

---

[1] As a note, values closer to zero in our histogram are more likely by construction as there are more opportunities for these distances to be selected. For example, a distance of -9 is only possible if the generation boundary is at the 10th sentence, while a distance of 0 is possible in every configuration. This does not affect our expectation that the distribution be symmetric if annotators are selecting at random.

generated text, and thus the sentence-by-sentence structure of the RoFT experiment is an effective way to evaluate text. These preliminary results bode well for future large-scale use of the tool.

4.3.3 Points Awarded

While accuracy may be a simple and intuitive metric for assessing performance, it is sub-optimal for our purposes as it does not give partial credit for guesses that are after the boundary, despite such guesses being successful identifications of generated text. Average distance (in sentences) from boundary is not sufficient either, as it does not weight all guesses before the boundary equally negatively and thus over-penalizes too-early annotations on examples with late-occurring boundaries.

To combat these issues, we developed a point system to better capture annotator ability. After each annotation, a user is assigned points based on their performance: 5 points for guessing exactly on the boundary and a linearly decreasing number of points for each sentence beyond the boundary. No points are awarded for guesses that appear before the boundary. We use the average points per annotation as our metric for the experiments shown in Figure 5.

4.4 Skill Range of Annotators

There was a significant range in detection ability across the crowd workers. The top 5% of the filtered worker pool earned an average of 3.34 points per annotations while the bottom 5% earned an average of 0.35. Since it is difficult to separate out the influence of inherent skill from that of misaligned incentives (AMT workers were paid for completion, not correctness), more research is necessary to understand differences in annotator ability.

4.5 Impact of Decoding Strategy

During our small-scale case study, we did not see a noticeable correlation between the values of the Nucleus Sampling (Holtzman et al., 2019) hyper-parameter p and the detection accuracy of humans as reported in Figure 5b. This is likely due to the low number of annotations per value of p (n=180) and we hope to run a more comprehensive version of this experiment with more data in the future.

4.6 Impact of Revealing the Boundary

As part of the gamification aspect of the RoFT platform, we reveal the true boundary to our annotators after every annotation they complete. This feature

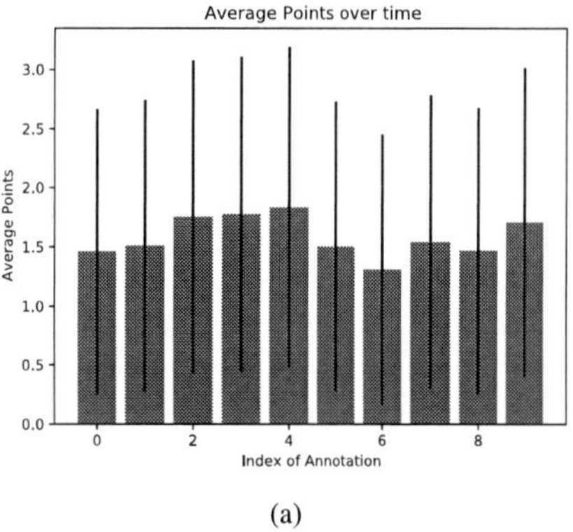

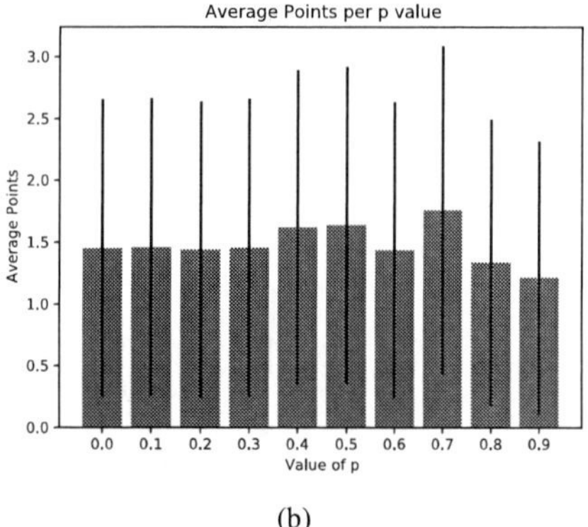

(a)   (b)

Figure 5: In (a) we show the average number of points (Section 4.3) received per annotation in the filtered annotation set grouped by the temporal order in which they were shown to the annotators 0 (first) to 9 (last). In (b) we show average number of points received per item in the filtered annotation for each values of p used for decoding. Error bars are standard deviation. No statistically significant trends were observed in this preliminary study.

adds a level of interactivity to the process and is crucial for ensuring that the RoFT experiment is enjoyable and appeals to the general public. To better understand how this decision affected annotator skill, we analyzed if our annotators got more accurate as they did more annotations. Figure 5a shows that over a session of 10 annotations, annotators exhibit little to no improvement at the annotation task over time. Future studies using the RoFT platform will further investigate if human annotators can be trained to detect generated text over long periods of time and multiple gameplay sessions.

4.7 Free-form Comments

Our proposed annotation system allows annotators to provide a natural language explanation of why they made a particular decision (e.g. classifying a sentence as human-written or machine-generated). Due to minimal oversight, many annotators re-used or copy/pasted their comments across annotations. Filtering for duplicates, we collected over 1200 unique comments, out of around 3000 annotations. Manual inspection shows that many annotations relied on similar clues such as: problems with entailment, formatting (i.e. punctuation), and repetition. These responses can be used to inform future improvements to existing NLG systems and decoding strategies. Additionally, it is possible to use data mining techniques to extract an error taxonomy from the provided natural langauge description of errors.

Sample Annotation
Seems like a conversational statement that doesnt logically follow from a book title reference
not relevant to preceding sentences
I don't think that a human would write about tarot cards in an obituary and it says obituaries plural.
The sentence is too short and simple, sweating computerized.
First time I heard of dinosaur-eating mammals
The sentence is left hanging.
Repeated the second line again and To is written as TO

Table 1: Examples of explanations crowd workers gave for why they thought a sentence was machine-generated.

5 Related Work

Nearly all papers in NLG do some form of human evaluation, usually using Amazon Mechanical Turk (van der Lee et al., 2019). Typically the interfaces for these evaluations are simple web forms. van der Lee et al. (2019) offers a survey of many of these methods. Custom-designed websites for collecting or displaying human evaluations of generated text have become increasingly prominent in the open-ended dialog domain, with ChatEval (Sedoc et al., 2019) and ConvAI (Pavlopoulos et al., 2019) being two examples.

However, RoFT was primarily influenced by other "real or fake" websites that attempt to gamify the detection task, such as `http://www.`

`whichfaceisreal.com/` for generated face images and `https://faketrump.ai/` for generated Tweets. Our task is similar to the one used for human evaluation in Ippolito et al. (2020), except in their task the text shown to raters was either entirely human-written or entirely machine-generated.

The boundary detection task we propose was inspired by the Dialog Breakdown Detection Challenge (Higashinaka et al., 2016), in which the goal is to automatically detect the first system utterance in a conversation between a human and a chatbot system that causes a dialogue breakdown.

6 Conclusion and Future Work

In this work, we have introduced RoFT and have shown how it can be used to collect annotations on how well human raters can tell when an article transitions from being human-written to being machine-generated.

Ultimately, we plan to use RoFT to conduct a large-scale systematic study of the impact of decoding strategy, fine-tuning dataset, prompt genre, and other factors on the detectability of machine-generated text. We also intend to collect and release a large dataset of natural language explanations for why humans think text is machine-generated. We hope that these will provide insights into problems with the human-written text we use as prompts and into the types of errors that NLG systems make.

Such a study will require tens of thousands of human annotations. We hope that by gamifying the annotation process and encouraging organic traffic to the website, we can ultimately bypass the need for crowd workers who, since they are paid by the annotation, are disincentivized from taking the time to provide high quality annotations.

We believe that RoFT provides a powerful tool for understanding the strengths and limitations of a great variety of NLG systems, and we look forward to working with researchers interested in testing out their own model outputs within the RoFT evaluation framework.

Acknowledgements

This research is based upon work supported in part by the DARPA KAIROS Program (contract FA8750-19-2-1004), the DARPA LwLL Program (contract FA8750-19-2-0201), and the IARPA BETTER Program (contract 2019-19051600004). Approved for Public Release, Distribution Unlimited. The views and conclusions contained herein are those of the authors and should not be interpreted as necessarily representing the official policies, either expressed or implied, of DARPA, IARPA, or the U.S. Government. The RoFT website is also supported by a grant from the Google Cloud Platform research credits program.

We thank the members of our lab for their feedback on the design of the RoFT user interface.

References

Angela Fan, Mike Lewis, and Yann Dauphin. 2018. Hierarchical neural story generation. In *Proceedings of the 56th Annual Meeting of the Association for Computational Linguistics (Volume 1: Long Papers)*, pages 889–898.

Ryuichiro Higashinaka, Kotaro Funakoshi, Yuka Kobayashi, and Michimasa Inaba. 2016. The dialogue breakdown detection challenge: Task description, datasets, and evaluation metrics. In *Proceedings of the Tenth International Conference on Language Resources and Evaluation (LREC'16)*, pages 3146–3150.

Ari Holtzman, Jan Buys, Li Du, Maxwell Forbes, and Yejin Choi. 2019. The curious case of neural text degeneration. In *International Conference on Learning Representations*.

Daphne Ippolito, Daniel Duckworth, Chris Callison-Burch, and Douglas Eck. 2020. Automatic detection of generated text is easiest when humans are fooled. In *Proceedings of the 58th Annual Meeting of the Association for Computational Linguistics*, pages 1808–1822.

Nitish Shirish Keskar, Bryan McCann, Lav R Varshney, Caiming Xiong, and Richard Socher. 2019. Ctrl: A conditional transformer language model for controllable generation. *SalesForce Einstein.ai blog*.

Chris van der Lee, Albert Gatt, Emiel van Miltenburg, Sander Wubben, and Emiel Krahmer. 2019. Best practices for the human evaluation of automatically generated text. In *Proceedings of the 12th International Conference on Natural Language Generation*, pages 355–368.

Peter J Liu, Mohammad Saleh, Etienne Pot, Ben Goodrich, Ryan Sepassi, Lukasz Kaiser, and Noam Shazeer. 2018. Generating wikipedia by summarizing long sequences. In *International Conference on Learning Representations*.

John Pavlopoulos, Nithum Thain, Lucas Dixon, and Ion Androutsopoulos. 2019. Convai at semeval-2019 task 6: Offensive language identification and categorization with perspective and bert. In *Proceedings of the 13th International Workshop on Semantic Evaluation*, pages 571–576.

Alec Radford, Jeffrey Wu, Rewon Child, David Luan, Dario Amodei, and Ilya Sutskever. 2019. Language models are unsupervised multitask learners. *OpenAI Blog*, 1(8):9.

Ehud Reiter and Anja Belz. 2009. An investigation into the validity of some metrics for automatically evaluating natural language generation systems. *Computational Linguistics*, 35(4):529–558.

Evan Sandhaus. 2008. The new york times annotated corpus. *Linguistic Data Consortium, Philadelphia*, 6(12):e26752.

João Sedoc, Daphne Ippolito, Arun Kirubarajan, Jai Thirani, Lyle Ungar, and Chris Callison-Burch. 2019. ChatEval: A tool for chatbot evaluation. In *Proceedings of the 2019 Conference of the North American Chapter of the Association for Computational Linguistics (Demonstrations)*, pages 60–65, Minneapolis, Minnesota. Association for Computational Linguistics.

Rowan Zellers, Ari Holtzman, Hannah Rashkin, Yonatan Bisk, Ali Farhadi, Franziska Roesner, and Yejin Choi. 2019. Defending against neural fake news. In *Advances in Neural Information Processing Systems*, pages 9054–9065.

A Data-Centric Framework for Composable NLP Workflows

Zhengzhong Liu[1,2,*], Guanxiong Ding[2], Avinash Bukkittu[2], Mansi Gupta[2], Pengzhi Gao[2], Atif Ahmed[2],
Shikun Zhang[1], Xin Gao[1,2], Swapnil Singhavi[2], Linwei Li[1], Wei Wei[1], Zecong Hu[1], Haoran Shi[1], Xiaodan Liang[3],
Teruko Mitamura[1], Eric P. Xing[1,2], and Zhiting Hu[1,4]

[1]Carnegie Mellon University   [2]Petuum Inc.   [3]Sun Yat-sen University   [4]UC San Diego
[*]`hectorzliu@gmail.com`

Abstract

Empirical natural language processing (NLP) systems in application domains (e.g., healthcare, finance, education) involve interoperation among multiple components, ranging from data ingestion, human annotation, to text retrieval, analysis, generation, and visualization. We establish a unified open-source framework to support fast development of such sophisticated NLP workflows in a composable manner. The framework introduces a uniform data representation to encode heterogeneous results by a wide range of NLP tasks. It offers a large repository of processors for NLP tasks, visualization, and annotation, which can be easily assembled with full interoperability under the unified representation. The highly extensible framework allows plugging in custom processors from external off-the-shelf NLP and deep learning libraries. The whole framework is delivered through two modularized yet integratable open-source projects, namely *Forte*[1] (for workflow infrastructure and NLP function processors) and *Stave*[2] (for user interaction, visualization, and annotation).

1 Introduction

Natural language processing (NLP) techniques are playing an increasingly central role in industrial applications. A real-world NLP system involves a wide range of NLP tasks that interoperate with each other and interact with users to accomplish complex workflows. For example, in an assistive medical system for diagnosis (Figure 4), diverse text *analysis* tasks (e.g., named entity recognition, relation extraction, entity coreference) are performed to extract key information (e.g., symptoms, treatment history) from clinical notes and link to knowledge bases; a medical practitioner could select any extracted entity to *retrieve* similar past cases for reference; text *generation* techniques are used to produce summaries from diverse sources.

To develop domain-specific NLP systems fast, it is highly desirable to have a unified open-source framework that supports: (1) seamless integration and interoperation across NLP functions ranging from text analysis to retrieval to generation; (2) rich user interaction for data visualization and annotation; (3) extensible plug-ins for customized components; and (4) highly reusable components.

A wealth of NLP toolkits exist (§4), such as spaCy (Honnibal and Montani, 2017), DKPro (Eckart de Castilho and Gurevych, 2014), CoreNLP (Manning et al., 2014), for pipelining multiple NLP functions; BRAT (Stenetorp et al., 2012) and YEDDA (Yang et al., 2018) for annotating certain types of data. None of them have addressed all the desiderata uniformly. Combining them for a complete workflow requires non-trivial effort and expertise (e.g., ad-hoc gluing code), posing challenges for maintenance and upgrading.

We introduce a new unified framework to support complex NLP workflows that involve text data ingestion, analysis, retrieval, generation, visualization, and annotation. The framework provides an infrastructure to simply plug in arbitrary NLP functions and offers pre-built and reusable components to build desired workflows. Importantly, the framework is designed to be extensible, allowing users to write custom components (e.g., specialized annotation interfaces) or wrap other existing libraries (e.g., Hu et al., 2019; Wolf et al., 2019) easily.

The framework's design is founded on a data-centric perspective. We design a universal text data representation that can encode diverse input/output formats of various NLP tasks uniformly. Each component (*"processor"*) in the workflow fetches relevant parts of data as inputs, and passes its results to subsequent processors by adding the results to

---

[1]https://github.com/asyml/forte
[2]https://github.com/asyml/stave

Proceedings of the 2020 EMNLP (Systems Demonstrations), pages 197–204
November 16-20, 2020. ©2020 Association for Computational Linguistics

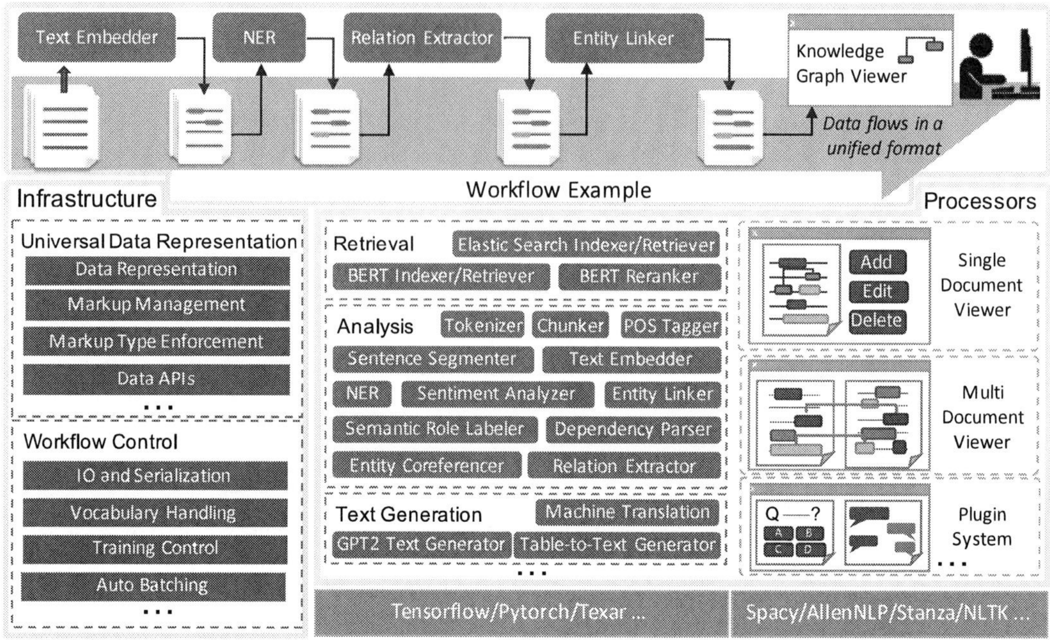

Figure 1: Stack of the data-centric framework for NLP workflows, including workflow *infrastructure*, and *processors* for NLP tasks and interactions (e.g., visualization, annotation). Different processors are composed together with the infrastructure APIs to form an arbitrary complex workflow. The example workflow transforms an unstructured text corpus into a knowledge graph through a series of NLP functions.

the data flow (Figure 1). In this way, different processors are properly decoupled, and each is implemented with a uniform interface without the need of accommodating other processors. Visualization and annotation are also abstracted as standalone components based on the data representation.

We demonstrate two case studies on using the framework to build a sophisticated assistive medical workflow and a neural-symbolic hybrid chatbot.

2 Data-Centric NLP Framework

Figure 1 shows the stack of the framework, consisting of several major parts: **(1)** We first introduce the underlying infrastructure (§2.1), in particular, a universal representation scheme for heterogeneous NLP data. The highly-organized unified representation plays a key role in supporting composable NLP workflows, which differentiates our framework from prominent toolkits such as CoreNLP (Manning et al., 2014), spaCy (Honnibal and Montani, 2017), and AllenNLP (Gardner et al., 2018). We then introduce a range of functionalities that enable the convenient use of the symbolic data/features in neural modeling, which are not available in traditional NLP workflow toolkits such as DKPro (Eckart de Castilho and Gurevych, 2014). **(2)** §2.2 describes how processors for various NLP

tasks can be developed with a uniform interface, and can be simply plugged into a complex workflow. **(3)** finally, the human interaction part offers rich composable processors for visualization, annotation, and other forms of interactions.

2.1 Infrastructure

2.1.1 Universal Data Representation

NLP data primarily consists of two parts: the raw *text source* and the structured *markups* on top of it (see Figure 3 for an example). The markups represent the information overlaid on the text, such as part-of-speech tags, named entity mentions, dependency links, and so forth. NLP tasks are to produce desired text or markups as output, based on vastly different input information and structures,

To enable full interoperation among distinct tasks, we summarize the underlying commonalities between the myriad formats across different NLP tasks, and develop a universal data representation encapsulating information uniformly. The representation scheme defines a small number of *template* data types with high-level abstraction, which can be further extended to encode domain-specific data.

Template data types: We generalize the previous UIMA representation scheme (Götz and Suhre, 2004) to cover the majority of common NLP

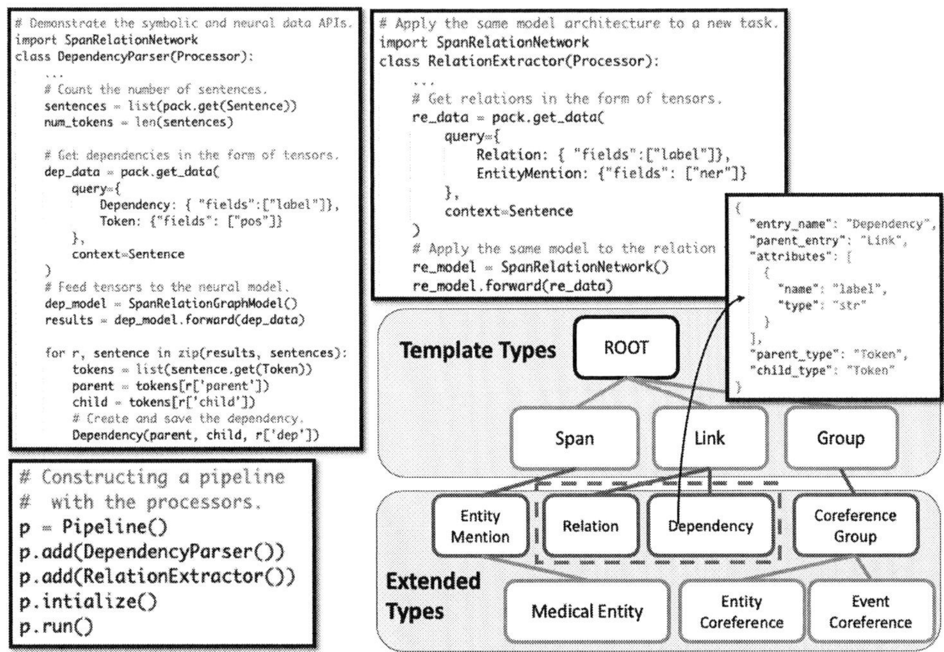

Figure 2: **Top Left**: A dependency parser processor that calls a neural model and save the results; **Top Right**: A relation extractor can use the same model architecture. **Bottom Left**: A pipeline can be constructed by simply adding processors. **Bottom Right**: Example data types offered by the framework or customized by users. `Relation` and `Dependency` both extends `Link`. Definition of `dependency` is done through a simple JSON configuration.

markups. This results in three template data types, each of which contains a couple of attributes.

- `Span` contains two integer attributes, *begin* and *end*, to denote the offsets of a piece of text. This type can mark tokens, entity mentions, and etc.
- `Link` defines a pair of (*parent, child*) which are pointers to other markups, to mark dependency arcs, semantic roles, entity relations, etc.
- `Group` has a *members* attribute, which is a collection of markups. This type can mark coreference clusters, topical clusters, etc.

Extended data types: In order to encode more specific information, each of the template data types can be extended by adding new attributes. For example, the framework offers over 20 extended types for commonly used NLP concepts, such as `Token` and `EntityMention`. Moreover, users can easily add *custom* data types through simple JSON definitions (Figure 2) to fulfill specific needs, such as `MedicalEntity` that extends `EntityMention` with more attributes like patient IDs. Once a new data type is defined, rich data operations (e.g., structured access) as below are automatically enabled for the new type.

Flexible Data Sources: Modern NLP systems face challenges imposed by the volume, veracity and velocity of data. To cope with these, the system is designed with customizable and flexible data sources that embrace technologies such as Indexing (e.g. Elastic Search (Elastic.co)), Databases (e.g. Sqlite), Vector Storage (e.g. Faiss (Johnson et al., 2017)). Users are free to implement flexible "Reader" interface to ingest any source of data.

2.1.2 Facilitation for Neural Modeling

The framework provides extensive functionalities for effortless integration of the above symbolic data representation with tensor-based neural modeling.

Neural representations. All data types are associated with an optional *embedding* attribute to store continuous neural representations. Hence, users can easily access and manipulate the embeddings of arbitrary markups (e.g., entity, relation) extracted from neural models like word2vec (Mikolov et al., 2013) and BERT (Devlin et al., 2019). The system also supports fast embedding indexing and lookup with embedding storage systems such as Faiss (Johnson et al., 2017).

Rich data operations: auto-batching, structured access, etc. Unified data representation enables a rich array of operations to support different data usage, allowing users to access any information in a structured manner. Figure 2 (top left) shows API calls that get all dependency links in a sentence. Utilities such as *auto-batching* and *auto-padding* help aggregates relevant information (e.g., event embeddings) from individual data instances into tensors, which are particularly useful for neural modeling on GPUs.

Neural-symbolic hybrid modeling. Unified data representations and rich data operations make it convenient to support hybrid modeling using both neural and symbolic features. Take retrieval for example, the framework offers retrieval processors (§2.2) that retrieve a coarse-grained candidate set with symbolic features (e.g., TF.IDF) first, and then refine the results with more expensive embedding-based re-ranking (Nogueira and Cho, 2019). Likewise, fast embedding based search is facilitated with the Faiss library (Johnson et al., 2017).

Shared modeling approaches. The uniform input/output representation for NLP tasks makes it easy to share the modeling approaches across diverse tasks. For example, similar to Jiang et al. (2020), all tasks involving the `Span` and `Link` data types as outputs (e.g., dependency parsing, relation extraction, coreference resolution) can potentially use the exact same neural network architecture for modeling. Further with the standardized APIs of our framework, users can spawn models for all such tasks using the same code with minimal edits. Top right of Figure 2 shows an example where the same relation extractor is implemented with dependency parser for a new task, and the only difference lies in accessing different data features.

2.2 Processors

Universal data representation enables a uniform interface to build processors for different NLP tasks. Most notably, *interoperation* across processors supported by the system abstraction allows each processor to interacts with each other via the data flow.

Each processor takes uniformly represented data as inputs and performs arbitrary actions on them. A processor can edit text source (e.g., language generation), add additional markups (e.g., entity detection), or produce side effects (e.g., writing data to disk). Top left of Figure 2 shows the common structure of a processor, that fetches relevant information from the data pack with high-level APIs, performs operations such as neural model inference, writes results back to the data pack and pass them over to subsequent processors. Top right shows the simple API used for plugging processors into the workflow.

A comprehensive repository of pre-built processors. With the standardized concept-level APIs for NLP data management, users can easily develop any desired processors. One can wrap existing models from external libraries by conforming to the simple interfaces. Moreover, we offer a large set of pre-built processors for various NLP tasks, ranging from text retrieval, to analysis and generation. Figure 1 lists a subset of processors.

2.3 Visualization, Annotation, & Interaction

The interfaces for visualization and annotation are implemented as standalone components and designed for different data types.

Single document viewer. We provide a single document interface (Figure 3) that renders the template types. For example, Spans are shown by colored highlights, Links are shown as connectors between the spans. A user can create new spans, add links, create groups, or edit the attributes through intuitive interfaces.

Multi document viewer. *Stave* currently supports a two-document interface. Users can create links across documents. The bottom of Figure 3 shows an example of annotating event coreference. The system is suggesting an event coreference pair and asking for the annotator's decision.

Customization with plugins. While default interfaces support a wide range of tasks, users can create customized interfaces to meet more specific needs. We build a system that can quickly incorporate independently-developed plugins, such as a plugin for answering multiple-choice questions, or a dialogue interface for chat-bots. Some pre-built plugins are showcased in Figure 4. Additionally, the layout can be customized to display specific UI elements, allowing for greater flexibility to use plugins together.

Human-machine collaboration. Universal data representation across all modules not only enhances interoperation between components, but also allows machines and humans to collaborate in a workflow. Human-interactive components can be integrated at any part of the workflow for visualization/reviewing to produce a downstream system that combines the advantages of humans and machines. Machine-assisted annotation can be undertaken straightforwardly: the annotation system simply ingests the data produced by a back-end processor (Figure 3).

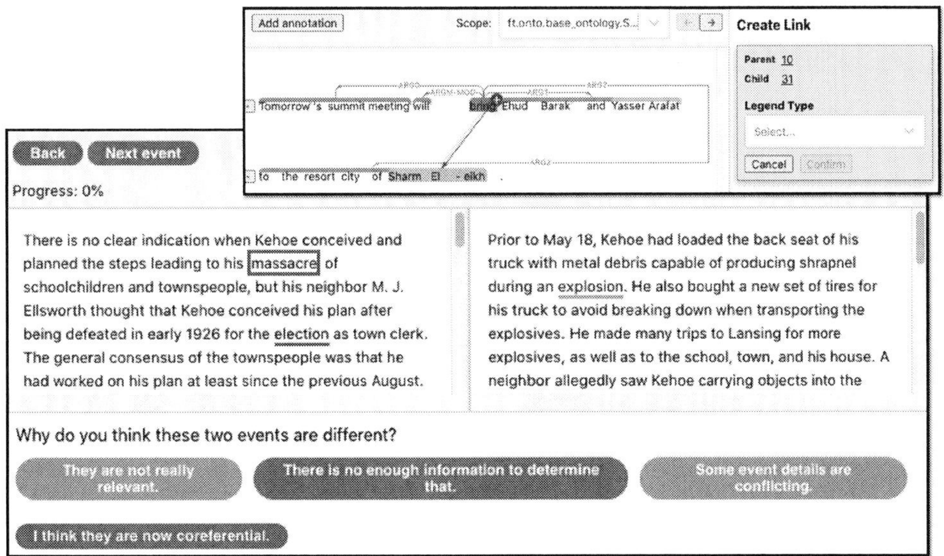

Figure 3: **Top**: Screenshot of the single doc interface shows predicates, entity mentions and semantic role links of one sentence. A new link is being created from "bring" to "Sharm Ei-eikh". **Bottom**: Screenshot of the two document interface for annotating event coreference. The system is suggesting a potential coreference pair. The interfaces are rendered based on the data types. Users can customize the interface to use different UI components.

3 Case Studies

3.1 A Clinical Information Workflow

We demonstrate an information system for clinical diagnosis analysis, retrieval, and user interaction. Figure 4 shows an overview of the system. To build the workflow, we first define domain-specific data types, such as `Clinical Entity Mention`, via JSON config files as shown in Figure 2. We then develop processors for text processing: (1) we create an LSTM-based clinical NER processor (Boag et al., 2015), a Span-Relation model based relation extraction processor (He et al., 2018), and a coreference processor with the End-to-End model (Lee et al., 2017) to extract key information; (2) we build a report generation processor following Li et al. (2019) with extracted mentions and relations; (3) we build a simple keyword based dialogue system for user to interact using natural languages. The whole workflow is implemented with minimal engineering effort. For example, the workflow is assembled with just 20 lines of code; and the IE processors are implemented with around 50 lines of code by reusing libraries and models.

3.2 A ChatBot Workflow

The case study considers the scenario where we have a corpus of movie reviews in English to answer complex queries (e.g., "movies with a positive sentiment starring by a certain actor") by a German user. The iterative workflow consists of a review retrieval processor based on the hybrid symbolic-neural feature modeling (§2.1.2), an NER processor (Gardner et al., 2018) to find actors and movies from the retrieved reviews, a sentiment processor (Hutto and Gilbert, 2014) for sentence polarity, and an English-German translation processor.

4 Related Work

The framework shares some characteristics with UIMA (Götz and Suhre, 2004) backed systems, such as DKPro (Eckart de Castilho and Gurevych, 2014), ClearTK (Bethard et al., 2014) and cTakes (Khalifa and Meystre, 2015). There are NLP toolboxes like NLTK (Bird and Loper, 2016) and AllenNLP (Gardner et al., 2018), GluonNLP (Guo et al., 2019), NLP pipelines like Stanford CoreNLP (Manning et al., 2014), SpaCy (Honnibal and Montani, 2017), and Illinois Curator (Clarke et al., 2012). As in §2.2, our system develops a convenient scaffold and provides a rich set of utilities to reconcile the benefits of symbolic data system, neural modeling, and human interaction, making it suit for building complex workflows.

Compared to open-source text annotation toolkits, such as Protégé Knowtator (Ogren, 2006), BRAT (Stenetorp et al., 2012), Anafora (Chen and Styler, 2013), GATE (Cunningham et al., 2013), WebAnno (Castilho, 2016), and YEDDA (Yang et al., 2018), our system provides a more flexi-

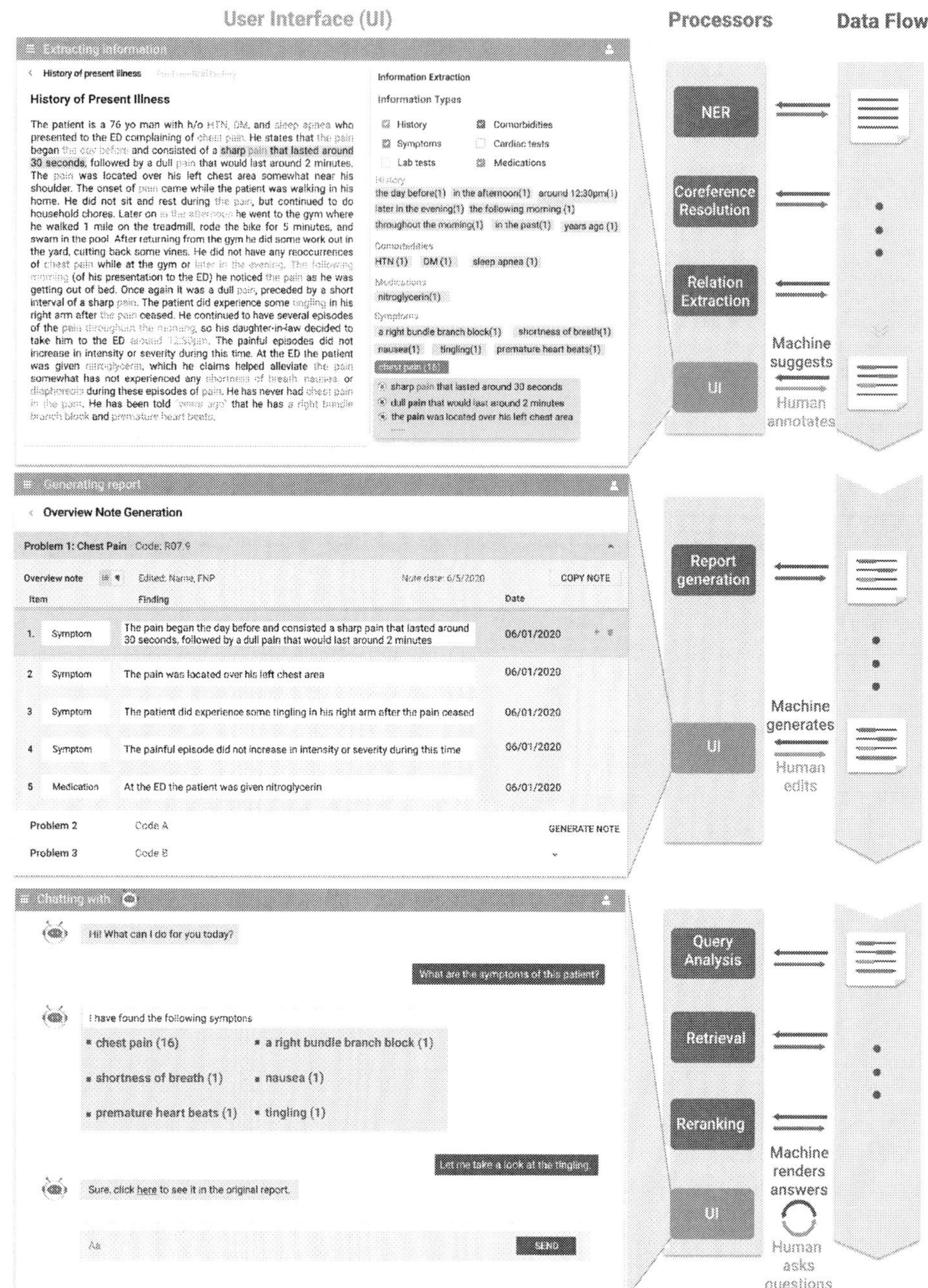

Figure 4: A system for diagnosis analysis and retrieval from clinical notes. The data-centric approach makes it easy to assemble a variety of components and UI elements. Example text was obtained from UNC School of Medicine.

ble experience with customizable plug-ins, extendable data types, and full-fledged NLP support. The Prodigy tool by spaCy is not open-source and supports only pre-defined annotation tasks like NER.

5   Conclusions and Future Work

We present a data-centric framework for building complex NLP workflows with heterogeneous modules. We will continue to improve the framework on other advanced functionalities, such as multitask learning, joint inference, data augmentation, and provide a broader arsenal of processors to help build better NLP solutions and other data science workflows. We also plan to further facilitate workflow development by providing more flexible and robust data management processors.

References

Steven Bethard, Philip Ogren, and Lee Becker. 2014. Cleartk 2.0: Design patterns for machine learning in uima. In *Proceedings of the Ninth International Conference on Language Resources and Evaluation (LREC'14)*, pages 3289–3293, Reykjavik, Iceland. European Language Resources Association (ELRA).

Steven Bird and Edward Loper. 2016. NLTK : The natural language toolkit. In *Proceedings of the ACL-02 Workshop on Effective tools and methodologies for teaching natural language processing and computational linguistics-Volume 1*, March, pages 63–70.

William Boag, Kevin Wacome, Tristan Naumann, and Anna Rumshisky. 2015. CliNER: A Lightweight Tool for Clinical Named Entity Recognition. In *AMIA Joint Summits on Clinical Research Informatics*.

Richard Eckart De Castilho. 2016. A Web-based Tool for the Integrated Annotation of Semantic and Syntactic Structures. In *Proceedings of the Workshop on Language Technology Resources and Tools for Digital Humanities (LT4DH)*, pages 76–84.

Wei-te Chen and Will Styler. 2013. Anafora : A Web-based General Purpose Annotation Tool. In *Proceedings of the NAACL HLT 2013 Demonstration Session*, June, pages 14–19.

James Clarke, Vivek Srikumar, Mark Sammons, and Dan Roth. 2012. An NLP curator (or: How I learned to stop worrying and love NLP pipelines). *Proceedings of the 8th International Conference on Language Resources and Evaluation, LREC 2012*, pages 3276–3283.

Hamish Cunningham, Valentin Tablan, Angus Roberts, and Kalina Bontcheva. 2013. Getting More Out of Biomedical Documents with GATE ' s Full Lifecycle Open Source Text Analytics. *PLOS Computational Biology*, 9(2).

Jacob Devlin, Ming-Wei Chang, Kenton Lee, and Kristina Toutanova. 2019. BERT: Pre-training of deep bidirectional transformers for language understanding. In *Proceedings of the 2019 Conference of the North American Chapter of the Association for Computational Linguistics: Human Language Technologies, Volume 1 (Long and Short Papers)*, pages 4171–4186, Minneapolis, Minnesota. Association for Computational Linguistics.

Richard Eckart de Castilho and Iryna Gurevych. 2014. A broad-coverage collection of portable NLP components for building shareable analysis pipelines. In *Proceedings of the Workshop on Open Infrastructures and Analysis Frameworks for HLT*, pages 1–.

Elastic.co. Elasticsearch.

Matt Gardner, Joel Grus, Mark Neumann, Oyvind Tafjord, Pradeep Dasigi, Nelson F. Liu, Matthew Peters, Michael Schmitz, and Luke Zettlemoyer. 2018. AllenNLP: A Deep Semantic Natural Language Processing Platform. In *Proceedings of Workshop for NLP Open Source Software (NLP-OSS)*, pages 1–6.

T. Götz and O. Suhre. 2004. Design and implementation of the UIMA common analysis system. *IBM Systems Journal*, 43(3):476–789.

Jian Guo, He He, Tong He, Leonard Lausen, Mu Li, Haibin Lin, Xingjian Shi, Chenguang Wang, Junyuan Xie, Sheng Zha, Aston Zhang, Hang Zhang, Zhi Zhang, Zhongyue Zhang, and Shuai Zheng. 2019. GluonCV and GluonNLP: Deep Learning in Computer Vision and Natural Language Processing. Technical report.

Luheng He, Kenton Lee, Omer Levy, and Luke Zettlemoyer. 2018. Jointly Predicting Predicates and Arguments in Neural Semantic Role Labeling. In *ACL 2018*.

Matthew Honnibal and Ines Montani. 2017. spaCy 2: Natural language understanding with Bloom embeddings, convolutional neural networks and incremental parsing.

Zhiting Hu, Haoran Shi, Bowen Tan, Wentao Wang, Zichao Yang, Tiancheng Zhao, Junxian He, Lianhui Qin, Di Wang, et al. 2019. Texar: A modularized, versatile, and extensible toolkit for text generation. In *ACL 2019, System Demonstrations*.

Clayton J. Hutto and Eric Gilbert. 2014. Vader: A parsimonious rule-based model for sentiment analysis of social media text. In *ICWSM*.

Zhengbao Jiang, Wei Xu, Jun Araki, and Graham Neubig. 2020. Generalizing Natural Language Analysis through Span-relation Representations. Technical report.

Jeff Johnson, Matthijs Douze, and Hervé Jégou. 2017. Billion-scale similarity search with gpus. *arXiv preprint arXiv:1702.08734*.

Abdulrahman Khalifa and Stephane Meystre. 2015. Adapting existing natural language processing resources for cardiovascular risk factors identification in clinical notes. *Journal of Biomedical Informatics*, 58S.

Kenton Lee, Luheng He, Mike Lewis, and Luke Zettlemoyer. 2017. End-to-end Neural Coreference Resolution. In *EMNLP 2017*.

Christy Y Li, Xiaodan Liang, Zhiting Hu, and Eric P Xing. 2019. Knowledge-driven Encode, Retrieve, Paraphrase for Medical Image Report Generation. In *AAAI 2019*.

Christopher Manning, Mihai Surdeanu, John Bauer, Jenny Finkel, Steven Bethard, and David McClosky. 2014. The Stanford CoreNLP natural language processing toolkit. In *Proceedings of 52nd Annual Meeting of the Association for Computational Linguistics: System Demonstrations*, pages 55–60, Baltimore, Maryland. Association for Computational Linguistics.

Tomas Mikolov, Kai Chen, Gregory S. Corrado, and Jeffrey Dean. 2013. Efficient estimation of word representations in vector space. *CoRR*, abs/1301.3781.

Rodrigo Nogueira and Kyunghyun Cho. 2019. Passage re-ranking with bert. *ArXiv*, abs/1901.04085.

Philip V Ogren. 2006. Knowtator : A Protégé plug-in for annotated corpus construction. In *Proceedings of the Human Language Technology Conference of the NAACL*, June, pages 273–275.

Pontus Stenetorp, Sampo Pyysalo, and Goran Topi. 2012. BRAT : a Web-based Tool for NLP-Assisted Text Annotation. In *Proceedings of the 13th Conference of the European Chapter of the Association for Computational Linguistics*, pages 102–107.

UNC School of Medicine. History and Physical Examination Examples 5.

Thomas Wolf, Lysandre Debut, Victor Sanh, Julien Chaumond, Clement Delangue, Anthony Moi, Pierric Cistac, Tim Rault, Rémi Louf, Morgan Funtowicz, et al. 2019. Huggingface's transformers: State-of-the-art natural language processing. *ArXiv*, pages arXiv–1910.

Jie Yang, Yue Zhang, Linwei Li, and Xingxuan Li. 2018. YEDDA : A Lightweight Collaborative Text Span Annotation Tool. In *Proceedings of the 56th Annual Meeting of the Association for Computational Linguistics-System Demonstrations*, pages 31–36.

CoRefi: A Crowd Sourcing Suite for Coreference Annotation

Aaron Bornstein[1,2]   **Arie Cattan**[1]   **Ido Dagan**[1]
[1]Computer Science Department, Bar Ilan University, Ramat-Gan, Israel
[2]Microsoft Corporation, Tel-Aviv, Israel
`abornst@microsoft.com` `arie.cattan@gmail.com` `dagan@cs.biu.ac.il`

Abstract

Coreference annotation is an important, yet expensive and time consuming, task, which often involved expert annotators trained on complex decision guidelines. To enable cheaper and more efficient annotation, we present CoREFI, a web-based coreference annotation suite, oriented for crowdsourcing. Beyond the core coreference annotation tool, COREFI provides guided onboarding for the task as well as a novel algorithm for a reviewing phase. COREFI is open source and directly embeds into any website, including popular crowdsourcing platforms.

COREFI Demo: `aka.ms/corefi` Video Tour: `aka.ms/corefivideo` Github Repo: `https://github.com/aribornstein/corefi`

1 Introduction

Coreference resolution is the task of clustering textual expressions (*mentions*) that refer to the same concept in a described scenario. This challenging task has been mostly investigated within a single document scope, seeing great research progress in recent years. The rather under-explored cross-document coreference setting is even more challenging. For example, consider the following sentences originating in two different documents in the standard cross-document coreference dataset ECB+ (Cybulska and Vossen, 2014):

1. *A man suspected of **shooting** three people at an <u>accounting firm</u> where he had worked ...*

2. *A gunman **shot** three people at a suburban <u>Detroit office building</u> Monday morning.*

Recognizing that both sentences refer to the same event ("shooting","shot") at the same location ("accounting firm", "Detroit office") can be very useful for downstream tasks, particularly across

Figure 1: COREFI's end-to-end annotation process

documents, such as multi-document summarization (Falke et al., 2017; Liao et al., 2018) or multi-hop question answering (Dhingra et al., 2018; Wang et al., 2019).

High-quality annotated datasets are valuable to develop efficient models. While Ontonotes (Pradhan et al., 2012) provides a useful dataset for generic single-document coreference resolution, large-scale datasets are lacking for cross-document coreference (Cybulska and Vossen, 2014; Minard et al., 2016; Vossen et al., 2018) or for targeted domains, such as medical (Nguyen et al., 2011). Due to the complexity of the coreference task, existing datasets have been annotated mostly by linguistic experts, incurring high costs and limiting annotation scale.

Aiming to address the cost and scalability issues in coreference annotation, we present COREFI, an embeddable web-component tool suite that supports an end-to-end crowdsourcing process (Figure 1), while providing several contributions over earlier annotation tools (Section 4). COREFI includes an automated onboarding training phase, familiarizing annotators with the tool functionality and the task decision guidelines. Then, actual annotation is performed through a simple-to-use and efficient interface, providing quick keyboard operations. Notably, COREFI provides a reviewing mode, by which an additional annotator reviews and improves the output of an earlier annotation. This mode is enabled by a non-trivial algorithm, that seamlessly integrates reviewing of an earlier

205

Proceedings of the 2020 EMNLP (Systems Demonstrations), pages 205–215
November 16-20, 2020. ©2020 Association for Computational Linguistics

annotation into the progressive construction of the reviewer's annotation.

By open sourcing COREFI, we hope to facilitate the creation of large-scale coreference datasets, especially for the cross-document setting, at modest cost while maintaining quality.

2 The COREFI Annotation Tool

COREFI provides a suite for annotating single and cross-document coreference, designed to embed into crowdsourcing environments. Since coreference annotation is an involved and complex task, we target a *controlled crowdsourcing* setup, as proposed by Roit et al. (2020). This setup consists of selecting designated promising crowd workers, identified in preliminary trap-tasks, and then quickly training them for the target task and testing their performance. This yields a pool of reliable lightly trained annotators, who perform the actual annotation of the dataset.

COREFI supports both the annotator training (onboarding) and annotation production phases, as illustrated in Figure 1. The training phase (Section 2.4) consists of two crowdsourcing tasks, first teaching the tool's functionality and then practicing guided annotation, interactively learning basics of the annotation guidelines. The annotation production phase also consists of two crowdsourcing tasks: first-round coreference annotation, providing a user-friendly interface designed to reduce annotation time (Section 2.2), and a novel reviewing task, in which an additional annotator reviews and improves the initial annotation (Section 2.3).

2.1 Design Choices

Our first major design choice regards the annotation flow. As elaborated in Section 4, two different coreference annotation flows were prominent in prior work. The local pair-based approach aims at annotation simplicity, often motivated by a crowdsourcing setting. Here, an annotator has to decide for a pair of mentions whether they corefer or not, or to proactively find such pairs of corefering mentions. Since coreference is annotated at the level mention pairs, it might require, in the worst case, comparing a mention to all other mentions in the text.

In the cluster-based flow, annotators assign mentions to coreference *clusters*. Here, a mention needs to be compared only against the clusters accumulated so far, or otherwise be defined as start-

ing a new cluster. Indeed, the number of coreference clusters is often substantially lower than the number of mentions, particularly in the cross-document setting, where the same content gets repeated across the multiple texts. For example, in the most popular dataset for cross-document coreference, ECB+ (Cybulska and Vossen, 2014), the number of clusters is about one third of the number of mentions (15122 mentions split into 4965 coreference clusters, including singletons). In COREFI, we adopt the cluster-based approach since we aim at exhaustive coreference annotation across documents, whose complexity would become too high under the pairwise approach. At the same time, we simplify the annotation process and functionality, making it crowdsourceable.

Our second design choice regards detecting referring mentions in text. As elaborated in Section 4, coreference annotation tools, particularly cluster-based (e.g. (Reiter, 2018; Oberle, 2018)), often require annotators to first detect the target mentions before annotating them for coreference. Conversely, recent local pair-based decision tools (Chamberlain et al., 2016; Li et al., 2020) delegate mention extraction to a preprocessing phase, presenting coreference annotators with pre-determined mentions. This simplifies the task and allows annotators to focus their attention on the coreference decisions.

As we target exhaustive crowdsourced coreference annotation, we chose to follow this recent facilitating approach. In addition to the input texts, COREFI takes as input an annotation of the targeted mentions, while optionally allowing annotators to fix this mention annotation. In our tool suite, we followed the approach of Prodigy,[1] where corpus developers may implement their own automated (non-overlapping) mention extraction recipes, or use a separate manual annotation tool for mention annotation, according to their desired mention detection guidelines (which often vary across projects). The resulting mentions can then be fed into COREFI for coreference annotation. We provide an example mention extraction recipe that detects as mentions common nouns, proper nouns, pronouns, and verbs (for event coreference). Such mention detection is consistent with approaches that consider reduced mention spans, mostly pertaining to syntactic heads or named entity spans (O'Gorman et al., 2016).

---

[1] https://prodi.gy/

2.2 Annotation

Figure 2 shows the annotation interface of COREFI.

As initialization, the first candidate mention is automatically assigned to the first coreference cluster, which is placed in the "cluster bank", appearing at the bottom of the screen ((3) in Figure 2). In this bank, each cluster is labeled by the text of its first mention. The annotator is then shown the subsequent mentions, one at a time, with the current mention to assign underlined in purple (2). For each mention, the annotator decides whether to accept it as a valid mention (doing nothing) or to modify its span (easily highlighting the correct span and pressing the 'F' key, for "Fix"). Similarly, the annotator may introduce a new span, missing from the input. To simplify annotation, the tool allows only non-overlapping spans.

The annotator then makes a coreference decision, by assigning the current mention to a new or existing cluster. An existing cluster can be rapidly selected either by selecting it in the cluster bank or by selecting one of its previously-assigned mentions in the text. Once a cluster is selected, it is highlighted in blue along with all its previous text mentions ((3) and (1) in the figure). Rather than assigning mentions to clusters through a slower drag and drop interface (Reiter, 2018; Oberle, 2018) or buttons (Girardi et al., 2014; Aralikatte and Søgaard, 2020), annotation is driven primarily by faster keyboard operations, such as SPACE (assign to an existing cluster) and CTRL+SPACE (new cluster), with quick navigation through arrow keys and mouse clicks.

At any point, the annotator can re-assign a previously assigned mention to another cluster or view any cluster mentions. COREFI supports an unlimited number of documents to be annotated, presented sequentially in a configurable order. Finally, COREFI guarantees exhaustive annotation by allowing task submission only once all candidate mentions are processed.

2.3 Reviewing

To promote annotation quality, annotation projects typically rely on multiple annotations per item. One approach for doing that involves collecting such annotations in parallel and then merging them in some way, such as simple or sophisticated voting (Hovy et al., 2013). Another approach is sequential, where one or more annotations are collected initially, and are then *manually* consolidated by an additional, possibly more reliable, annotator (a "consolidator" or "reviewer") (Roit et al., 2020).

In our case, coreference annotation is addressed as a global clustering task, where an annotator generates a complete clustering configuration for the input text(s). Automatically merging such multiple clustering configurations, where cluster assignments are mutually dependent, might become unreliable. Therefore, in COREFI we follow the sequential manual reviewing approach. To that end, we introduce a novel reviewing task, which receives as input a previously annotated clustering configuration and allows an additional annotator to review and improve it.

The reviewing task follows the same flow of the annotation task, making it trivial to learn for annotators that already experienced with COREFI annotation. At each step, the reviewer is presented with the next mention in the reviewed configuration, and may first decide to modify its span. Next, the reviewer has to decide on cluster assignment for the current mention. The only difference at this point is that the reviewer is presented with candidate cluster assignments which reflect the original annotator assignment (as explained below), displayed just above the cluster bank (Figure 3).

In fact, it is not trivial to reflect the cluster assignment by the original annotator to the reviewer, since that assignment has to be mapped to the current clustering configuration of the reviewer. Ambiguity may arise, resulting in multiple candidate clusters, since an early cluster modification by the reviewer can impact the interpretation of downstream cluster assignments in the original annotation.

To illustrate this issue, consider reviewing a cluster assigned by the original annotator, consisting of three mentions, $\{A, B, C\}$. When presented with the mention A, the reviewer agrees that it starts a new cluster. Then, when reaching B, the reviewer is presented with $\{A\}$ as B's original cluster assignment. Suppose the reviewer disagrees with the annotator that A and B corefer and decides to assign B to a new cluster. Now, when reviewing the mention C, it is no longer clear whether to attribute C's original assignment to $\{A\}$ or $\{B\}$. Hence, the reviewing tool presents both $\{A\}$ and $\{B\}$ as candidate clusters that reflect the original annotator's assignment. The reviewer may then choose either of them, or override the original annotation altogether and make a different assignment. Similar ambiguities arise when the reviewer splits an origi-

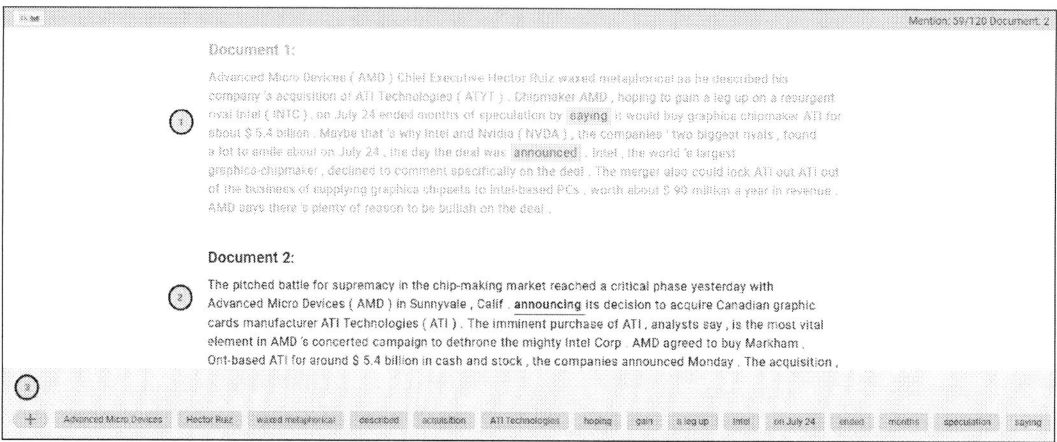

Figure 2: Annotation Interface of COREFI, presenting text and mentions from the ECB+ dataset, used in our pilot study (Section 3). The current mention to assign is underlined in purple (2). The selected cluster is highlighted in blue in the cluster bank (3), along with its mentions in the text (1).

nal mention span and assigns its parts to separate clusters.

To address this challenge, we formulate an algorithm that maps an original cluster assignment to a set of candidate clusters in the current clustering configuration of the reviewer. Generally speaking, the algorithm considers the cluster to which the current mention was assigned in the original annotation, and tracks all earlier token positions in that cluster. These token positions are then mapped back to clusters in the current reviewer's clustering configuration, which become the candidate clusters presented to the reviewer. The algorithm pseudocode is presented in Appendix A, along with a comprehensive example of its application.

2.4 Onboarding

In the proposed controlled crowdsourcing scheme of Roit et al. (2020), annotators were trained in an "offline" manner, reading slides and receiving individual feedback. We propose augmenting this phase with automated training, delivered through two crowdsourcing tasks, described below.

2.4.1 Walk-through Tutorial

During this task, a trainee is walked through the core concepts and functionality of COREFI, such as the "current mention" and the "cluster bank" (Figure 2), and through the annotation operations. These functionalities are presented through a series of intuitive dialogues. To ensure that each feature is correctly understood, the user is instructed to actively perform each operation before continuing to the next (see Appendix B).

2.4.2 Guided Annotation

After acclimating with COREFI's features, users are familiarized with the coreference decision guidelines through a guided annotation task, practicing annotation while receiving automated guiding feedback. If an annotation error is made, the trainee is notified with a pre-prepared custom response, which guides to the correct decision before allowing to proceed. Additionally, following certain decisions, specific important guidelines can be communicated (see Appendix C for examples).

The content of the guided annotation task and the automated responses are easily configurable using a simple JSON configuration schema. This allows tailoring them when applying COREFI for different datasets and annotation guidelines.

Augmenting the controlled crowdsourcing scheme (Roit et al., 2020) with automated training provides key benefits. First, since feedback is automated, the amount of required personalized manual feedback is reduced. Second, annotators benefit from an immediate response for each decision, allowing them to understand their mistakes earlier and improve in real time. We suggest that, for optimal learning of annotation guidelines, these benefits should be coupled with the additional training means of controlled crowdsourcing. These include the provision of guideline slides, for learning and later for reference, and some personalized manual feedback during the training phase.

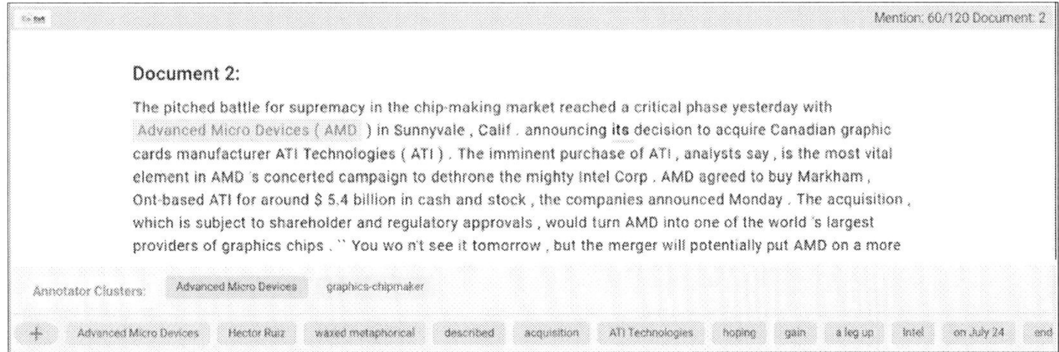

Figure 3: Reviewing interface of COREFI. Candidate clusters found by the reviewing algorithm are shown in purple.

2.5 Implementation Benefits

COREFI was developed using the web component standard and the VUE.JS framework.[2] allowing, it to easily embed into any website, including crowdsourcing platforms. Additionally, COREFI provides output in the standard CoNLL coreference annotation format, enabling training state of the art models and scoring with the official coreference scorer (Pradhan et al., 2014). All COREFI features are easily configurable with HTML encoded JSON and support any UTF-8 encoded language.

3 Pilot Study

To further assess COREFI's effectiveness in a crowdsourcing environment, we performed a small-scale trial on Amazon Mechanical Turk, employing 5 annotators, focusing on the coreference annotation functionality (rather than mention validation). To allow objective assessment of annotation quality, we experimented with replicating coreference annotations from the ECB+ dataset (Cybulska and Vossen, 2014), the commonly used dataset for cross-document coreference over English news articles (Cybulska and Vossen, 2015; Yang et al., 2015; Choubey and Huang, 2017; Kenyon-Dean et al., 2018; Barhom et al., 2019; Cattan et al., 2020). Accordingly, we considered the ECB+ gold mentions as input, requesting crowdworkers to assign them to coreference clusters. Focusing on the controlled crowdsourcing setting, we hired five annotators that were previously selected for annotation by Roit et al. (2020).

On-boarding Annotators were given COREFI's walk-through tutorial and guided annotation tasks,

adapted to the ECB+ guidelines and applied to a part of an ECB+ subtopic (cluster of documents). These two tasks took altogether 11 minutes on average to complete, at a rate of $1.5 a task. Next, workers were asked to annotate an entire ECB+ subtopic (through the actual annotation task). We provided them manual feedback for their mistakes, which consumed 30-40 minutes of researcher time per trained annotator.

Annotation After training, we paid workers $8 to annotate two additional subtopics in full (of about 150 and 200 mentions; in ECB+ only a few sentences are annotated per document, and these were presented for annotation). Each subtopic took 27 minutes on average to annotate, corresponding to an annotation rate of ~400 mentions per hour.

Table 1 presents the performance (F1) of each of the annotators, compared to the ECB+ gold annotations, averaged over the two subtopics. The results are reported using the common evaluation metrics for coreference resolution: **MUC** (Vilain et al., 1995), **B³** (Bagga and Baldwin, 1998), **CEAFe** (Luo, 2005), and **CoNLL** — the average of the three metrics. Considering the decision volume and complexity, as well as the limited training (not providing guideline slides and a single practice round), we find that these results support COREFI's effectiveness for crowdsourcing.[3] As previously mentioned, we expect that annotation quality may be further improved in an actual dataset creation

---

[2]https://vuejs.org/

[3]There are no comparable annotator performance evaluations in the literature. Ontonotes (Pradhan et al., 2012) reports an inter-annotator agreement for experts of 0.87 MUC scores, but these seem to include mention span decisions. The creators of ECB+ (Cybulska and Vossen, 2014) use a different methodology to calculate inter-annotator agreement, not applicable for our setting, reporting a Kappa score of 0.76.

	MUC	B^3	CEAFe	CoNLL
A1	94.0	85.0	77.8	85.6
A2	94.8	91.2	85.4	90.5
A3	95.2	90.2	84.7	90.0
A4	94.8	86.9	76.0	85.9
A5	92.1	82.5	75.7	83.4

Table 1: F1 results of 5 annotators on 2 ECB+ subtopics.

	MUC	B^3	CEAFe	CoNLL
A1	87.0	69.1	62.6	72.9
R1	91.9	80.4	79.8	80.0
R2	88.0	73.4	73.3	78.2
A5	87.0	79.0	62.5	76.2
R1	92.9	87.3	73.0	84.4
R2	90.0	86.2	63.0	79.7

Table 2: F1 results of the reviewing trial.

project, by providing additional guided tasks, annotation guidelines slides, and additional manual feedback.

Reviewing For the reviewing trial, the two best annotators, A2 and A3, were selected as R1 and R2. Two additional annotators (A1 and A5) were each assigned a new unique subtopic, which was then reviewed by both R1 and R2. Table 2 presents the reviewing results, showing consistent improvements after reviewing and assessing the ease of using the reviewing functionality.

4 Related work

As mentioned in Section 2, prior tools for coreference annotation are based on two prominent workflows: pair-based, treating coreference as a pairwise annotation decision, and cluster-based, in which mentions are assigned to clusters. While targeting simplicity, only two pair-based tools supported crowdsourcing annotation, yet they were not applied for producing exhaustively annotated daasets: Phrase Detective (Chamberlain et al., 2016), which was employed in a web-based game setting, and (Li et al., 2020), which was applied in an active learning environment.

Pair-based tools differ in their annotation approaches. In certain tools, such as BRAT (Stenetorp et al., 2012), Glozz (Widlöcher and Mathet, 2012), Analec (Landragin et al., 2012), and MMAX2 (Kopeć, 2014), the annotator first determines mention span boundaries and then links a pair of mentions. Other Pair-based tools (Chamberlain et al., 2016; Li et al., 2020) either provide annotators a single (pre-determined) mention, asking to find a coreferring antecedent, or provide a pair of mentions, asking to judge whether the two corefer. Notably, pair-based tools are less effective for exhaustive coreference annotation, for two reasons. First, they require comparing each mention to all other *mentions*, rather than to already constructed clusters. Second, local pairwise decisions lack awareness of previous cluster assignments, which might hurt annotation quality.

Cluster-based tools, including Cromer (Girardi et al., 2014), Model based annotation tool (Aralikatte and Søgaard, 2020), CorefAnnotator (Reiter, 2018), and SACR (Oberle, 2018), ask annotators to first detect mention spans and then cluster them, thus complicating the overall task without allowing the delegation of mention detection to a preprocessing phase. Such a method does not guarantee exhaustive annotation, since annotators may miss some mentions. With respect to operation efficiency, mentions are often linked to clusters via somewhat slow operations, such as drag-and-drop or selection from a drop-down list, in comparison to the fast keyboard operations in CoRefi.

Notably, to the best of our knowledge, CoRefi is the first cluster-based crowdsourcing tool that provides an end-to-end annotation suite, including automated onboarding tasks and exhaustive reviewing, the latter enabled by our novel reviewing algorithm. Furthermore, it is the first tool that was developed using the WebComponent standard, embeddable in any website.

5 Conclusion

In this paper, we aim to facilitate crowdsourced creation of needed large-scale coreference datasets, in both the within- and the cross-document setting. Our comprehensive end-to-end tool suite, CoRefi, enables high quality and fairly cheap crowdsourcing of exhaustive coreference annotation in various domains and languages. Our experiments demonstrate that CoRefi's automatic onboarding is effective at augmenting Roit et al. (2020)'s controlled crowdsourcing. CoRefi provides the first reviewing algorithm and implementation for cluster-based coreference annotation. Overall, we demonstrated that non-expert annotators can be trained to effectively perform and review coreference annotations, allowing for cost-effective annotation efforts.

Acknowledgments

The work described herein was supported in part by grants from Intel Labs, Facebook, the Israel Science Foundation grant 1951/17, the Israeli Ministry of Science and Technology and the German Research Foundation through the German-Israeli Project Cooperation (DIP, grant DA 1600/1-1).

In addition to the support above, we would like to thank Uri Fried, Ayal Klein, Paul Roit, Amir Cohen, Sharon Oren, Chris Noring, Asaf Amrami, Ori Shapira, Daniela Stepanov, Ori Ernst, Yehudit Meged, Valentina Pyatkin, Moshe Uzan, and Ofer Sabo for their support with architecture, design and crowdsourcing.

References

Rahul Aralikatte and Anders Søgaard. 2020. Model-based annotation of coreference. In *Proceedings of The 12th Language Resources and Evaluation Conference*, pages 74–79, Marseille, France. European Language Resources Association.

Amit Bagga and Breck Baldwin. 1998. Entity-based cross-document coreferencing using the vector space model. In *COLING 1998 Volume 1: The 17th International Conference on Computational Linguistics*.

Shany Barhom, Vered Shwartz, Alon Eirew, Michael Bugert, Nils Reimers, and Ido Dagan. 2019. Revisiting joint modeling of cross-document entity and event coreference resolution. In *Proceedings of the 57th Annual Meeting of the Association for Computational Linguistics*, pages 4179–4189, Florence, Italy. Association for Computational Linguistics.

Arie Cattan, Alon Eirew, Gabriel Stanovsky, Mandar Joshi, and I. Dagan. 2020. Streamlining cross-document coreference resolution: Evaluation and modeling. *ArXiv*, abs/2009.11032.

Jon Chamberlain, Massimo Poesio, and Udo Kruschwitz. 2016. Phrase detectives corpus 1.0 crowdsourced anaphoric coreference. In *Proceedings of the Tenth International Conference on Language Resources and Evaluation (LREC 2016)*, pages 2039–2046, Portorož, Slovenia. European Language Resources Association (ELRA).

Prafulla Kumar Choubey and Ruihong Huang. 2017. Event coreference resolution by iteratively unfolding inter-dependencies among events. In *Proceedings of the 2017 Conference on Empirical Methods in Natural Language Processing*, pages 2124–2133, Copenhagen, Denmark. Association for Computational Linguistics.

Agata Cybulska and Piek Vossen. 2014. Using a sledgehammer to crack a nut? lexical diversity and event coreference resolution. In *Proceedings of the Ninth International Conference on Language Resources and Evaluation (LREC-2014)*, pages 4545–4552, Reykjavik, Iceland. European Languages Resources Association (ELRA).

Agata Cybulska and Piek Vossen. 2015. Translating granularity of event slots into features for event coreference resolution. In *Proceedings of the The 3rd Workshop on EVENTS: Definition, Detection, Coreference, and Representation*, pages 1–10, Denver, Colorado. Association for Computational Linguistics.

Bhuwan Dhingra, Qiao Jin, Zhilin Yang, William Cohen, and Ruslan Salakhutdinov. 2018. Neural models for reasoning over multiple mentions using coreference. In *Proceedings of the 2018 Conference of the North American Chapter of the Association for Computational Linguistics: Human Language Technologies, Volume 2 (Short Papers)*, pages 42–48, New Orleans, Louisiana. Association for Computational Linguistics.

Tobias Falke, Christian M. Meyer, and Iryna Gurevych. 2017. Concept-map-based multi-document summarization using concept coreference resolution and global importance optimization. In *Proceedings of the Eighth International Joint Conference on Natural Language Processing (Volume 1: Long Papers)*, pages 801–811, Taipei, Taiwan. Asian Federation of Natural Language Processing.

Christian Girardi, Manuela Speranza, Rachele Sprugnoli, and Sara Tonelli. 2014. CROMER: a tool for cross-document event and entity coreference. In *Proceedings of the Ninth International Conference on Language Resources and Evaluation (LREC-2014)*, pages 3204–3208, Reykjavik, Iceland. European Languages Resources Association (ELRA).

Dirk Hovy, Taylor Berg-Kirkpatrick, Ashish Vaswani, and Eduard Hovy. 2013. Learning whom to trust with MACE. In *Proceedings of the 2013 Conference of the North American Chapter of the Association for Computational Linguistics: Human Language Technologies*, pages 1120–1130, Atlanta, Georgia. Association for Computational Linguistics.

Kian Kenyon-Dean, Jackie Chi Kit Cheung, and Doina Precup. 2018. Resolving event coreference with supervised representation learning and clustering-oriented regularization. In *Proceedings of the Seventh Joint Conference on Lexical and Computational Semantics*, pages 1–10, New Orleans, Louisiana. Association for Computational Linguistics.

Mateusz Kopeć. 2014. MMAX2 for coreference annotation. In *Proceedings of the Demonstrations at the 14th Conference of the European Chapter of the Association for Computational Linguistics*, pages 93–96, Gothenburg, Sweden. Association for Computational Linguistics.

Frédéric Landragin, Thierry Poibeau, and Bernard Victorri. 2012. ANALEC: a new tool for the dynamic annotation of textual data. In *Proceedings of the Eighth International Conference on Language Resources and Evaluation (LREC-2012)*, pages 357–362, Istanbul, Turkey. European Languages Resources Association (ELRA).

Belinda Z. Li, Gabriel Stanovsky, and Luke Zettlemoyer. 2020. Active learning for coreference resolution using discrete annotation. In *Proceedings of the 58th Annual Meeting of the Association for Computational Linguistics*, pages 8320–8331, Online. Association for Computational Linguistics.

Kexin Liao, Logan Lebanoff, and Fei Liu. 2018. Abstract meaning representation for multi-document summarization. In *Proceedings of the 27th International Conference on Computational Linguistics*, pages 1178–1190, Santa Fe, New Mexico, USA. Association for Computational Linguistics.

Xiaoqiang Luo. 2005. On coreference resolution performance metrics. In *Proceedings of Human Language Technology Conference and Conference on Empirical Methods in Natural Language Processing*, pages 25–32, Vancouver, British Columbia, Canada. Association for Computational Linguistics.

Anne-Lyse Minard, Manuela Speranza, Ruben Urizar, Begoña Altuna, Marieke van Erp, Anneleen Schoen, and Chantal van Son. 2016. MEANTIME, the NewsReader multilingual event and time corpus. In *Proceedings of the Tenth International Conference on Language Resources and Evaluation (LREC 2016)*, pages 4417–4422, Portorož, Slovenia. European Language Resources Association (ELRA).

Ngan Nguyen, Jin-Dong Kim, and Jun'ichi Tsujii. 2011. Overview of BioNLP 2011 protein coreference shared task. In *Proceedings of BioNLP Shared Task 2011 Workshop*, pages 74–82, Portland, Oregon, USA. Association for Computational Linguistics.

Bruno Oberle. 2018. SACR: A drag-and-drop based tool for coreference annotation. In *Proceedings of the Eleventh International Conference on Language Resources and Evaluation (LREC-2018)*, Miyazaki, Japan. European Languages Resources Association (ELRA).

Tim O'Gorman, Kristin Wright-Bettner, and Martha Palmer. 2016. Richer event description: Integrating event coreference with temporal, causal and bridging annotation. In *Proceedings of the 2nd Workshop on Computing News Storylines (CNS 2016)*, pages 47–56, Austin, Texas. Association for Computational Linguistics.

Sameer Pradhan, Xiaoqiang Luo, Marta Recasens, Eduard Hovy, Vincent Ng, and Michael Strube. 2014. Scoring coreference partitions of predicted mentions: A reference implementation. In *Proceedings of the 52nd Annual Meeting of the Association for Computational Linguistics (Volume 2: Short Papers)*, pages 30–35, Baltimore, Maryland. Association for Computational Linguistics.

Sameer Pradhan, Alessandro Moschitti, Nianwen Xue, Olga Uryupina, and Yuchen Zhang. 2012. CoNLL-2012 shared task: Modeling multilingual unrestricted coreference in OntoNotes. In *Joint Conference on EMNLP and CoNLL - Shared Task*, pages 1–40, Jeju Island, Korea. Association for Computational Linguistics.

Nils Reiter. 2018. CorefAnnotator - A New Annotation Tool for Entity References. In *Abstracts of EADH: Data in the Digital Humanities*.

Paul Roit, Ayal Klein, Daniela Stepanov, Jonathan Mamou, Julian Michael, Gabriel Stanovsky, Luke Zettlemoyer, and Ido Dagan. 2020. Controlled crowdsourcing for high-quality QA-SRL annotation. In *Proceedings of the 58th Annual Meeting of the Association for Computational Linguistics*, pages 7008–7013, Online. Association for Computational Linguistics.

Pontus Stenetorp, Sampo Pyysalo, Goran Topić, Tomoko Ohta, Sophia Ananiadou, and Jun'ichi Tsujii. 2012. brat: a web-based tool for NLP-assisted text annotation. In *Proceedings of the Demonstrations at the 13th Conference of the European Chapter of the Association for Computational Linguistics*, pages 102–107, Avignon, France. Association for Computational Linguistics.

Marc Vilain, John Burger, John Aberdeen, Dennis Connolly, and Lynette Hirschman. 1995. A model-theoretic coreference scoring scheme. In *Sixth Message Understanding Conference (MUC-6): Proceedings of a Conference Held in Columbia, Maryland, November 6-8, 1995*.

Piek Vossen, Filip Ilievski, Marten Postma, and Roxane Segers. 2018. Don't annotate, but validate: a data-to-text method for capturing event data. In *Proceedings of the Eleventh International Conference on Language Resources and Evaluation (LREC-2018)*, Miyazaki, Japan. European Languages Resources Association (ELRA).

Haoyu Wang, Mo Yu, Xiaoxiao Guo, Rajarshi Das, Wenhan Xiong, and Tian Gao. 2019. Do multi-hop readers dream of reasoning chains? In *Proceedings of the 2nd Workshop on Machine Reading for Question Answering*, pages 91–97, Hong Kong, China. Association for Computational Linguistics.

Antoine Widlöcher and Yann Mathet. 2012. The glozz platform: A corpus annotation and mining tool. In *Proceedings of the 2012 ACM Symposium on Document Engineering*, DocEng '12, page 171–180, New York, NY, USA. Association for Computing Machinery.

Bishan Yang, Claire Cardie, and Peter Frazier. 2015. A hierarchical distance-dependent Bayesian model for event coreference resolution. *Transactions of the Association for Computational Linguistics*, 3:517–528.

A Reviewing Algorithm

Algorithm 1 implements the mechanism to find potential clusters given the initial annotation and previous reviewing modifications.

Algorithm 1: Reviewing Algorithm

Input: M: Stack of mentions with their
        initial clustering assignment
Output: R: Reviewed Assignment

---
1 $Ant \leftarrow CreateAntecedentMapping(M)$
2 $T2C$: Map of token to cluster ID
3 **while** M *not empty* **do**
4   // Set reviewer span
5     $Sp' \leftarrow \text{ReviewSpan}(M.top())$
6   **while** $M.top().end \leq Sp'.end$ **do**
7       $M.pop()$
8   **end**
9   **if** $M.top().start \leq Sp'.end$ **then**
10      $popSplitPush(M, Sp')$
11   **end**

12   // Set reviewer cluster
13     $C \leftarrow getCandidates(Sp', Ant, T2C)$
14     $cluster \leftarrow selectCluster(C)$
15     $T2C.update(Sp', cluster)$
16     $R.push(Sp', cluster)$
17 **end**

To support span modification, we build two main data structures at the *token* level (lines 1 and 2). Given the original annotation M, we build a static mapping Ant (line 1), where each single token is associated with all tokens from previous mentions that belong to the same coreference cluster. $T2C$ is a growing mapping that will keep track of the reviewer decisions.

After the initialization phase, the reviewer is shown all the annotator mentions in a sequential order. For each presented mention, the reviewer first decides whether to agree or to modify the mention span boundaries (line 5). Future mentions in the stack M that are fully covered by the reviewed span need to be removed (lines 6-8). The reviewer may also split the current mention or partially cover next mentions (line 9-11).

In order to find the potential coreference clusters (line 13), we first use Ant to retrieve the antecedent tokens in the original annotation, for each single token in the reviewed span Sp'. Then, we use the reviewer mapping $T2C$ for each antecedent tokens to identify the possible cluster(s) that will be displayed to the reviewer (Figure 3). Given the coreference decision (assigning to an existing cluster or to a new one) of the reviewer (line 14), we update the reviewer mapping $T2C$ (line 15) and coreference assignments (line 16).

Table 3 illustrates the reviewing decision step by step, given an initial annotation that incorrectly assigned the following gold clustered mentions {{Bank of America, bank, BoA} {American}} into one coreference cluster {Bank of America, American bank, BoA}.

B Tutorial

Figure 4 and 5 demonstrate notifications that explains conceptual aspect of COREFI. Figure 4 explains what the current mention to assign is where as Figure 5 explains what clusters are and how to manage them in the cluster bank. Figure 6 demonstrates a more interactive tutorial prompt. It shows how to make an active coreference decision with the keyboard and encourages the trainee to experiment with in the confines of the tutorial environment to familiarize themselves with the feature.

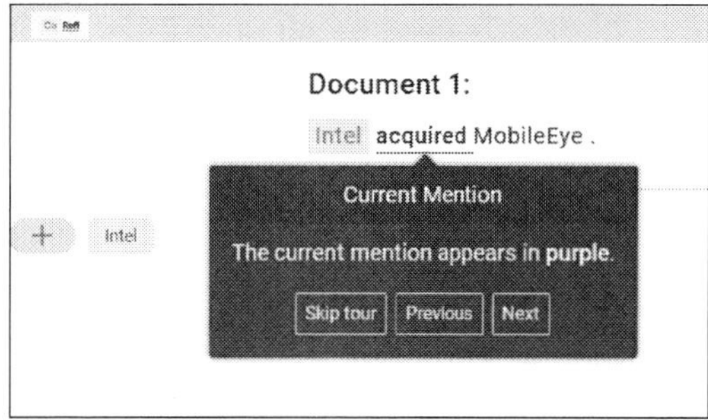

Figure 4: Example of the tutorial explaining the current mention.

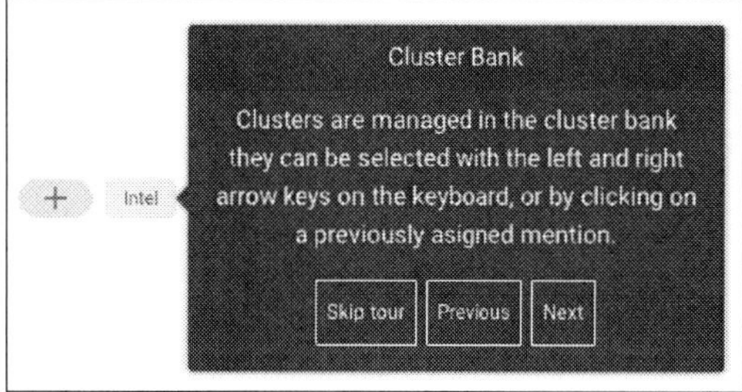

Figure 5: Example of the tutorial explaining the cluster bank.

	Mention Stack	Annotator Candidates	Reviewer Decision	Explanation
1	[**Bank Of America**, American bank, BoA]	{Bank of America}	✓	The reviewer agrees that Bank of America is the start of a new cluster
2	[**American bank**, BoA]	{Bank of America}	Split **American bank** into two mentions	Two mentions are created, **American** and **bank**. The reviewer will next determine the cluster assignment of American.
3	[**American** bank, BoA]	{Bank of America}	Assign **American** to a new cluster	The reviewer is shown {Bank of America} as the candidate cluster since the *token* **American** was assigned with Bank of America by the annotator.
4	[**bank**, BoA]	{Bank of America}, {American}	Assign **bank** to the {Bank of America}	The reviewer is shown both {Bank of America} and {American} as candidate clusters for bank. Now, the reviewer decides to assign bank to the {Bank of America} cluster.
5	[**BoA**]	{{Bank of America, bank}, {American}}	Assign **BoA** to cluster {Bank of America, bank}	The reviewer is shown two candidate clusters {Bank of America, bank} and {American} which correspond to the clusters that include the antecedent tokens of {BoA} initially assigned by the annotator (Bank of America, American bank, BoA).

Table 3: Examples of reviewing assignment, the initial clustering assignment is [(Bank of America, American bank, BoA] and the reviewer modifies into [(Bank of America, bank, BoA), (American)]

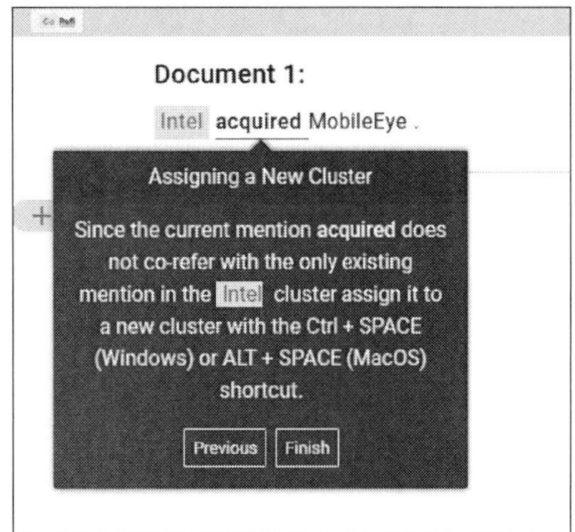

Figure 6: Example of the tutorial explaining the cluster assignment operation.

the coreference guidelines. As the trainee is familiarized with the subtleties of coreference they are less likely to make similar mistakes during annotation of the real dataset.

C Guided Annotation

Figure 7 demonstrates the guided experience of the on-boarding flow of COREFI. In Figure 7, the trainee is learning the nuances of coreference and makes the mistake of attempting to assign the mention name to the same cluster as another mention with the exact same expression. However, in context the name event mention expressed by the current mention does not refer to the selected cluster. The current mention refers to the naming of the Dr. Regina Benjamin as U.S Surgeon General where as the selected cluster refers to the event of naming Dr. Sanjay Gupta to Surgeon General. Since, the correct decision is subtle the user receives a toast informing them that Words can have the same meaning but not corefer. This toast helps to guide the annotator to the correct decision and reinforces

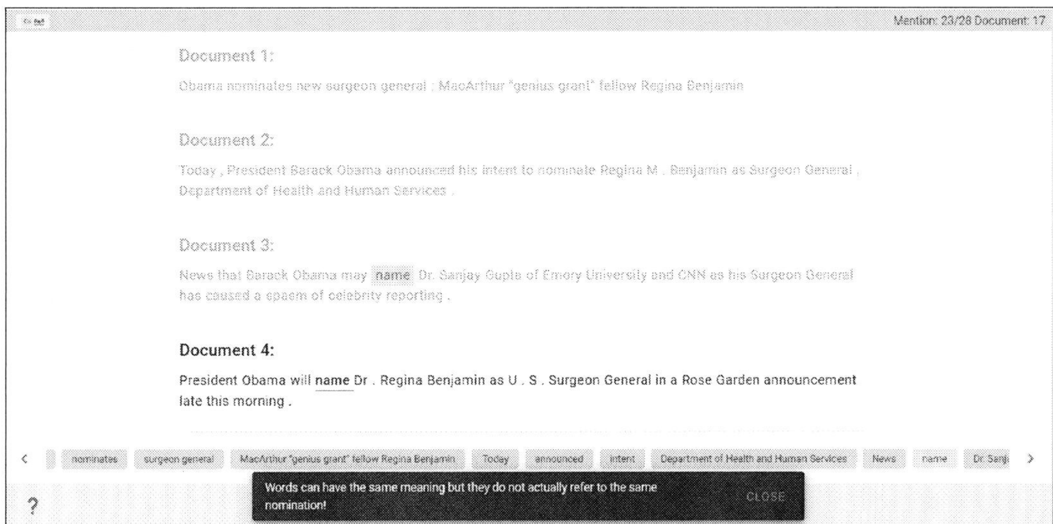

Figure 7: Example of an automatic feedback during the guided annotation.

Langsmith: An Interactive Academic Text Revision System

Takumi Ito[*,1,2] , **Tatsuki Kuribayashi**[*,1,2], **Masatoshi Hidaka**[*,3],
Jun Suzuki[1,4], **and Kentaro Inui**[1,4]
[1]Tohoku University [2]Langsmith Inc. [3]Edge Intelligence Systems Inc. [4]RIKEN
{t-ito, kuribayashi, jun.suzuki, inui}@ecei.tohoku.ac.jp
hidaka@edgeintelligence.jp

Abstract

Despite the current diversity and inclusion
initiatives in the academic community, researchers with a non-native command of English still face significant obstacles when writing papers in English. This paper presents
the *Langsmith* editor, which assists inexperienced, non-native researchers to write English papers, especially in the natural language processing (NLP) field. Our system
can suggest fluent, academic-style sentences
to writers based on their rough, incomplete
phrases or sentences. The system also encourages interaction between human writers
and the computerized revision system. The
experimental results demonstrated that Langsmith helps non-native English-speaker students write papers in English. The system is
available at https://emnlp-demo.editor.
langsmith.co.jp/.

1 Introduction

Currently, diversity and inclusion in the natural
language processing (NLP) community are encouraged. In fact, at the latest NLP conference at the
time of writing[1], papers were submitted from more
than 50 countries. However, one obstacle can limit
this diversity: *The papers must be written in English.* Writing papers in English can be a daunting task, especially for inexperienced, non-native
speakers. These writers often struggle to put their
ideas into words.

To address this problem, we built the *Langsmith*
editor, an assistance system for writing NLP papers
in English.[2] The main feature in Langsmith is a
revision function, which suggests fluent, academic-

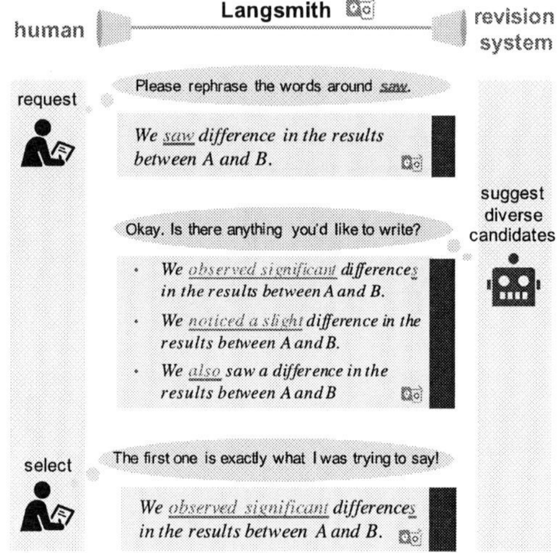

Figure 1: An overview of interactively writing texts
with a revision system.

style sentences based on writers' rough, incomplete drafts.

The drafts might be so rough that it becomes
challenging to understand the user's intended meaning to use as inputs. In addition, several potentially
plausible revisions can exist for the drafts, especially when the input draft is incomplete.

Based on such difficulties, our system provides
two ways for users to customize the revision: the
users can (i) request specific revisions, and (ii) select a suitable revision from diverse candidates (Figure 1). In particular, the request stage allows users
to specify the parts that require intensive revision.

Our experiments demonstrate the effectiveness
of our system. Specifically, students whose first
language is Japanese, which differs greatly from
English, managed to write better drafts when working with Langsmith.

Langsmith has other assistance features as well,
such as text completion with a neural language

---

* The authors contributed equally
[1]The 58th Annual Meeting of the Association for Computational Linguistics
[2]See https://www.youtube.com/channel/
UCjHeZPe0tT6bWxVVvum1bFQ for the screencast.

Proceedings of the 2020 EMNLP (Systems Demonstrations), pages 216–226
November 16-20, 2020. ©2020 Association for Computational Linguistics

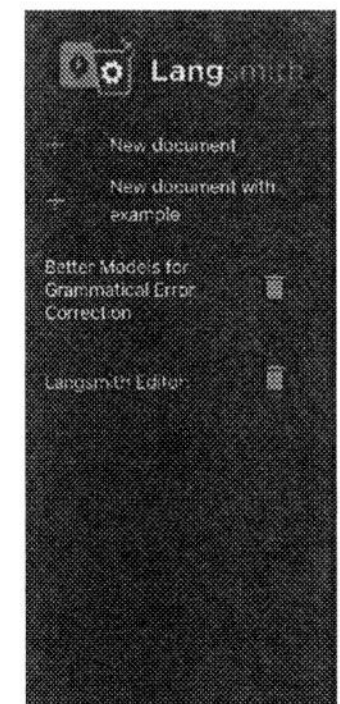

Figure 2: Screenshot of Langsmith. The revision feature suggests various revisions for the input *"Grammar error correction (GEC) () of automatically correcting errors made by a human writer in text."* The characters highlighted in green are added to the original sentence, and the red points indicate tracked deletions.

model. Furthermore, the communication between the server and the web frontend is achieved via a protocol specialized in writing software called the Text Editing Assistance Smartness Protocol for Natural Language (TEASPN) (Hagiwara et al., 2019). We hope that our system will help the NLP community and researchers, especially those lacking a native command of English.[3]

2   Related work

2.1   Natural language processing for academic writing

Academic writing assistance has gained considerable attention in NLP (Wu et al., 2010; Yimam et al., 2020; Lee and Webster, 2012), and several shared tasks have been organized (Dale and Kilgarriff, 2011; Daudaravičius, 2015). These tasks focus on polishing texts in already published articles or documents near completion. In contrast, this study focuses on revising texts in the earlier stages of writing (e.g., first drafts), where inexperienced, non-native authors might even struggle to convey their ideas accurately.

Ito et al. (2019) introduced a dataset and models for revising early-stage drafts, and the 1-to-N nature of the revisions was pointed out. We tackled this difficulty by designing an overall demonstration system, including a user interface.

2.2   Writing assistance tools

Error checkers.   Grammar/spelling checkers are typical writing assistance tools. Some highlight errors (e.g., *Write&Improve*[4]), while others suggest corrections (e.g., *Grammarly*[5], *LanguageTool*[6], *Ginger*[7], and *LinggleWrite*; see Tsai et al. (2020)) for writers.

Langsmith has a revision feature (Ito et al., 2019), as well as a grammar/spelling checker. The revision feature suggests better versions of poor written phrases or sentences in terms of fluency and style, whereas error checkers are typically designed to correct apparent errors only. In addition, Langsmith is specialized for the NLP domain and enables domain-specific revisions, such as correcting technical terms.

Text completion.   Completing a text is another typical feature in writing assistance applications (*WriteAhead*[8], *Write With Transformer*[9], and *Smart Compose*; see Chen, Mia Xu and Lee, Benjamin N. and Bansal, Gagan and Cao, Yuan and Zhang, Shuyuan and Lu, Justin and Tsay, Jackie and Wang, Yinan and Dai, Andrew M. and Chen, Zhifeng and Sohn, Timothy and Wu, Yonghui (2019)). Our system also has a completion feature, which is specialized in academic writing (e.g., completing a text based on a section name).

3   The *Langsmith* editor

3.1   Overview

This section presents Langsmith, a web-based text editor for academic writing assistance (Figure 2). The system has the following three features: (i) text revision, (ii) text completion, and (iii) a gram-

---

[3]This paper was also written using Langsmith.
[4]`writeandimprove.com`
[5]`https://www.grammarly.com`
[6]`https://languagetool.org`
[7]`https://www.gingersoftware.com`
[8]`writeahead.nlpweb.org`
[9]`https://transformer.huggingface.co`

matical/spelling error checker. These features are activated when users select a text span, type a word, or push a special key.

As a case study, this work focuses on paper writing in the NLP domain. Thus, each assistance feature is specialized in the NLP domain. The following sections explain the details of each feature.

3.2 Revision feature

The revision feature, the main feature of Langsmith, suggests better sentences in terms of fluency and style for a given draft sentence (Figure 2). This feature is activated when the user selects a sentence or smaller unit.

Writers sometimes struggle to put their ideas into words. Thus, the input draft for the revision systems can be incomplete, or less informative. Based on such a challenging situation, we examine the REQUEST and SELECT framework to help users discover sentences that better match what the user wanted to write.

REQUEST stage. Langsmith provides two ways for users to request a specific revision, which can prevent unnecessary revisions being provided to the user.

First, users can specify where the system should intensively revise a text.[10] That is, when a part of a sentence is selected, the system intensively rephrases the words around the selected part.[11] Figure 3 demonstrates the change of the revision focus, depending on the selected text span. Note that controlling the revision focus was not explored in the original sentence-level revision task (Ito et al., 2019). This feature is also inspired by Grangier and Auli (2018).

Second, users can insert placeholder symbols, " ( ) ", at specific points in a sentence. The system revises the sentence by replacing the symbol with an appropriate expression regarding its context. The input for the revision in Figure 2 also has the placeholder symbol. Here, for example, the symbol is replaced with "the task." This feature is inspired by Zhu et al. (2019); Donahue et al. (2020); Ito et al. (2019).

SELECT stage. The system provides several revisions (Figure 2). Note that there is typically more

---

[10]The system performs sentence-level revisions. Hence the users are instructed to select the non-sentence-crossing area.

[11]We allow the system to correct the parts outside the selected span because sometimes the revision for a specific part requires another adjustment for the other parts.

(a) Revisions focusing on *This formulation · · · and output.*

(b) Revisions focusing on *promote.*

(c) Revisions focusing on *human–computer interaction.*

Figure 3: The focus of the revision depends on the parts selected by users.

---

than one plausible revision in terms of fluency and style, in contrast to correcting surface-level errors (Napoles et al., 2017).

The diversity of the output revisions is encouraged using diverse beam search (Vijayakumar et al., 2018). In addition, these revisions are ordered by a language model that is fine-tuned for NLP papers. That is, revisions with lower perplexity are listed in the upper part of the suggestion box. Furthermore, the revisions are highlighted in colors, which makes it easier to distinguish the characteristics of each revision.

Implementation. We trained a revision model using LightConv (Wu et al., 2019) implemented in Fairseq (Ott et al., 2019). The revision model generates a sentence based on a given input sentence. The model was trained on a slightly modified version of the synthetic training data used in Ito et al.

218

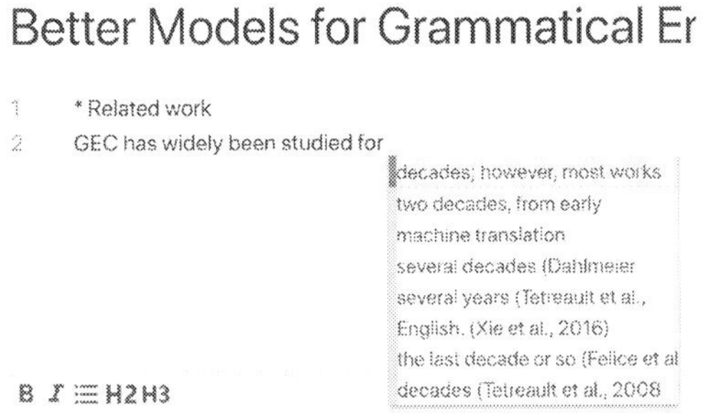

Figure 4: An example of the completion feature. These suggestions are conditioned by the left context, section name (*Related work*) and the paper title (*Better Models for Grammatical Error Correction.*)

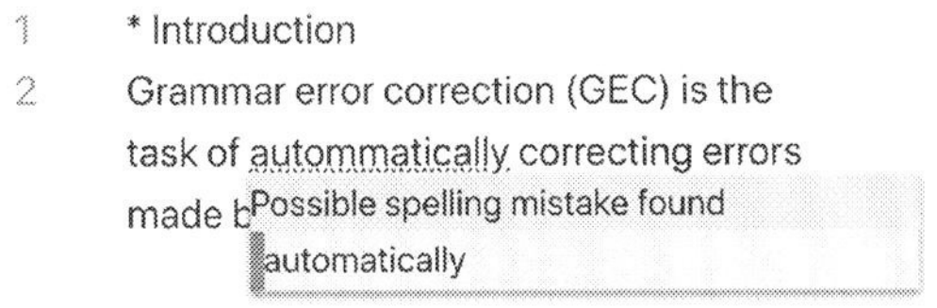

Figure 5: The interface of the error correction feature. Errors are automatically highlighted with a red line. The corrections are suggested when the user hovers over the highlighted words.

(2019). As an example of these modifications, synthetic edit marks were added for a subset of the training data. These marks were attached to a part of the input sentence that has many edits compared to its reference.[12] Thus, the marks can provide a hint for the system to determine where to edit. When using Langsmith, the marks are attached to the span selected by the users. The system is expected to intensively revise the wording in the specified span. Details are in Appendix A.

3.3 Other features

Completion feature. When the user presses the Tab key, the completion feature generates plausible preceding phrases from the cursor point (Figure 4). This feature can consider the paper title and section name as well as the text to the left of the cursor.

We used GPT-2 small (117M) (Radford et al., 2019) fine-tuned on the papers collected from the ACL Anthology[13]. Paper titles and section names were concatenated at the beginning of the corresponding paragraphs in the fine-tuning data. De-

tails are in Appendix B.

Error correction feature. We used Language-Tool,[14] an open-source grammatical/spelling error correction tool. Each time the text changes, this feature is called upon. The detected errors are then automatically highlighted with red lines (Figure 5).The corrections are listed when the user hovers over the highlighted words.

3.4 Protocol

Langsmith was developed based on the TEASPN Software Development Kit (Hagiwara et al., 2019).[15] TEASPN defines a set of APIs for writing software (e.g., text editors) to communicate with servers that implement NLP technologies (e.g., revision model). We extended the protocol to convey title and section information in the completion feature. Since Langsmith is a browser-based tool and frequently communicates with a web server running models, we used WebSocket to achieve smooth communication.

4 Experiments and results

We demonstrate the effectiveness of human–machine interactions in revising drafts implemented in our system. We also check whether the REQUEST stage in the revision feature works adequately.

4.1 On the revised draft quality

Settings. We suppose a situation where a person writes a draft in their native language (non-English language), translates it to English, and then revises it further to create an English-language draft. In order to simulate this situation, we first collected Japanese-language version of the abstract sections from eight Japanese peer-reviewed journals.[16] Then, the abstracts were translated into English with an off-the-shelf translation system[17]. We considered the translated abstracts as first drafts. The task is to revise the first drafts. Expert translators created reference final drafts from the Japanese versions of the drafts.[18] We evaluated the quality of the revised versions by comparing them with the corresponding final drafts.

---

[12]Special symbols are attached at the beginning and the end of the specific subsequence.

[13]https://www.aclweb.org/anthology

[14]https://github.com/languagetool-org/languagetool/releases/tag/v3.2

[15]https://github.com/teaspn/teaspn-sdk

[16]We used the journals accepted at https://www.anlp.jp/en/index.html.

[17]https://translate.google.co.jp

[18]We used https://www.ulatus.com/.

Condition	BLEURT
HUMAN&MACHINE	**-0.45**
HUMAN-ONLY	-0.51
MACHINE-ONLY	-0.51
First drafts	-0.70

Table 1: Comparison of the revision quality. The scores are averaged over the corresponding revisions. Higher scores indicate that the drafts are closer to the final drafts.

Q.	Strongly agree	Slightly agree	Slightly disagree	Strongly disagree
(I)	87.5	12.5	0	0
(II)	50.0	50.0	0	0
(III)	62.5	31.3	6.3	0
(IV)	12.5	50.0	31.3	6.3
(V)	75.0	12.5	6.3	6.3
(VI)	43.8	43.8	12.5	0

Table 2: Results of the user study about (I)-(VI). The scores denote the percentage of the participants who chose the option.

We compared three versions of revised drafts to evaluate the effectiveness of Langsmith:

- one fully and automatically revised by Langsmith (MACHINE-ONLY revision)
- one revised by a human writer without Langsmith (HUMAN-ONLY revision), and
- one revised by a human writer using assistance features in Langsmith (HUMAN&MACHINE revision).

The following paragraphs explain how we obtained the above three versions of the revisions. Appendix C shows the statistics of the drafts.

MACHINE-ONLY revision. We automatically applied the revision feature to the drafts (each sentence) without the REQUEST and Select stages. For each sentence, the revision with the highest generation probability was selected.[19] We created one MACHINE-ONLY revision for each first draft.

HUMAN-ONLY revision. Human writers revise a given first draft. The writers can only access to the error correction feature. This setting simulates the situations that writers typically face.

HUMAN&MACHINE revision. Human writers revise a given first draft with full access to the Langsmith features.

Human writers. We asked 16 undergraduate and master's students at an NLP laboratory to revise the first drafts in terms of fluency and style. The students were Japanese natives, representatives of the inexperienced researchers in a country where the spoken language is considerably different from English. Each participant revised two different first drafts, one with the HUMAN-ONLY setting and the other one with the HUMAN&MACHINE setting.

Half of the participants first revised a draft with the HUMAN-ONLY setting, and then revised another draft with the HUMAN&MACHINE setting; the other half performed the same task in the opposite order. Ultimately, we collected two HUMAN&MACHINE revisions and two HUMAN-ONLY revisions for each first draft.

Comparison and results. We compared the quality of the three versions of the revised drafts: MACHINE-ONLY revision, HUMAN-ONLY revision, and HUMAN&MACHINE revision. We compared the revised drafts with their corresponding final draft using BLEURT (Sellam et al., 2020), the state-of-the-art automatic evaluation metric for natural language generation tasks. Details of the evaluation procedure is shown in Appendix D. Note that the score is not in the range $[0, 1]$, and a higher score means that the revision is closer to the final draft. Table 1 shows that HUMAN&MACHINE revisions were significantly better[20] than MACHINE-ONLY and HUMAN-ONLY revisions. The results suggest the effectiveness of human–machine interaction achieved in Langsmith. Since this experiment was relatively small in scale and only used an automatic evaluation metric, we will conduct a larger-scale experiment with human evaluations in the future.

4.2 User study

After the experiments outlined in Section 4.1, we asked the participants about the usability of Langsmith. The 16 participants were instructed to evaluate the following statements:

(I) Langsmith was more helpful than the Baseline environment for the revision task.

---

[19]The hyperparameters for decoding revisions were the same as the revision feature in Langsmith. Re-ranking with the language model was also employed.

[20]We applied a bootstrap hypothesis test (Koehn, 2004), and the score of HUMAN&MACHINE was significantly higher than the HUMAN-ONLY and MACHINE-ONLY scores ($p < 0.05$).

Feature	percentage
revision	100
completion	31.3
correction	62.5

Table 3: Results of the user study about helpful features. The scores denote the percentage of the participants who chose the feature (multiple choice question).

(II) Comparing the text written by the two environments, the text written with Langsmith was better.

(III) The feature of specifying where to intensively revise was helpful.

(IV) The placeholder feature in the revision feature was helpful.

(V) Providing more than one output from the revision feature was helpful.

(VI) Providing more than one output from the completion feature was helpful.

The participants evaluated the statements (I)-(VI) on a four-point scale: (a) strongly agree, (b) slightly agree, (c) slightly disagree, and (d) strongly disagree. In addition, the participants answered whether each feature was helpful in writing.

Results. Tables 2 and 3 show the results of our user study. From the responses to (I) and (II), we observed that the users were satisfied with the writing experience with Langsmith. The responses to (III), (IV), and (V) support the idea that our RE-QUEST and SELECT stages are helpful. Here, using the place holders was relatively not helpful. The responses to (VI) also suggest that showing several candidates does not bother the users. Table 3 displays the result of whether each feature was helpful in writing. The result indicates that the revision feature was the most useful for creating drafts using the implemented features.

4.3 Sanity check of the REQUEST stage

Finally, we checked the validity of our method to control the revision based on the selected part of the sentence (Figure 3).

Settings. We randomly collected 1,000 sentences from the first drafts created with the translation system. In each sentence with T tokens $x = (w_1, \cdots, w_T)$, we randomly inserted edit marks to specify a certain span $s = (i, j)$ in x ($1 \leq i < j \leq T, 1 \leq j - i \leq 5$). Specifically, special tokens were inserted before w_i and after w_j in x. We denote the input sentence with these edit marks as x^{edit}. We then obtained 10-best outputs of the revision system $(y_1^{\text{edit}}, \cdots, y_{10}^{\text{edit}})$ for each x^{edit}. Here, these output sentences were generated through the diverse beam search with the same settings as the revision feature in Langsmith. We calculated the following score for each input sentence and its revisions:

$$r = |\{y_k^{\text{edit}} \mid x_{i:j} \in \text{ngram}(y_k^{\text{edit}}), 1 \leq k \leq 10\}|$$

where $x_{i:j}$ denotes the subsequence $(w_i, \cdots, w_j)$ in x. The function $\text{ngram}(\cdot)$ returns a set of all the n-grams of a given sequence. A lower r indicates that the subsequence specified with the edit marks are more frequently rephrased.

We also obtained a score r' for each x. r' was calculated using the input without the edit marks x and its 10-best outputs y_k. We compared r and r' for each x.

Results. We observed that r frequently[21] had lower values than r'. That is, a certain subsequence was more rephrased by the revision system when it had the edit marks than when it did not. These results validate our approach of controlling the revision focus, which is implemented in the REQUEST stage of the revision feature.

5 Conclusions

We have presented Langsmith, an academic writing assistance system. Langsmith provides a writing environment, in which human writers use several assistance features to improve the quality of texts. Our experiments suggest that our system is useful for inexperienced, non-native writers in revising English-language papers. We are aware that our experimental settings were not fully well-designed (e.g., we had only Japanese participants, and no human evaluation). We will evaluate Langsmith in more sophisticated settings. We hope that our system contributes to breaking language barriers in the academic community.

Acknowledgement

We are grateful to Ana Brassard for her feedback on English. We also appreciate the participants of our user studies. This work was supported by Grant-in-Aid for JSPS Fellows Grant Number JP20J22697.

---

[21] We conducted the one-side sign test. The difference is significant with $p \leq 0.05$.

References

Chen, Mia Xu and Lee, Benjamin N. and Bansal, Gagan and Cao, Yuan and Zhang, Shuyuan and Lu, Justin and Tsay, Jackie and Wang, Yinan and Dai, Andrew M. and Chen, Zhifeng and Sohn, Timothy and Wu, Yonghui. 2019. Gmail smart compose: Real-time assisted writing. In *Proceedings of the 25th ACM SIGKDD International Conference on Knowledge Discovery & Data Miningg (KDD'19)*, page 2287–2295.

Robert Dale and Adam Kilgarriff. 2011. Helping our own: The HOO 2011 pilot shared task. In *Proceedings of the 13th European Workshop on Natural Language Generation (ENLG 2011)*, pages 242–249.

Vidas Daudaravičius. 2015. Automated evaluation of scientific writing: AESW shared task proposal. In *Proceedings of the Tenth Workshop on Innovative Use of NLP for Building Educational Applications (BEA 2015)*, pages 56–63.

Chris Donahue, Mina Lee, and Percy Liang. 2020. Enabling language models to fill in the blanks. In *Proceedings of the 58th Annual Meeting of the Association for Computational Linguistics (ACL 2020)*, pages 2492–2501. Association for Computational Linguistics.

David Grangier and Michael Auli. 2018. QuickEdit: Editing text & translations by crossing words out. In *Proceedings of the 2018 Conference of the North American Chapter of the Association for Computational Linguistics (NAACL 2018)*, pages 272–282.

Masato Hagiwara, Takumi Ito, Tatsuki Kuribayashi, Jun Suzuki, and Kentaro Inui. 2019. TEASPN: Framework and protocol for integrated writing assistance environments. In *Proceedings of the 2019 Conference on Empirical Methods in Natural Language Processing and the 9th International Joint Conference on Natural Language Processing: System Demonstrations (EMNLP-IJCNLP 2019)*, pages 229–234.

Ari Holtzman, Jan Buys, Li Du, Maxwell Forbes, and Yejin Choi. 2020. The Curious Case of Neural Text Degeneration. In *Proceedings of the 8th International Conference on Learning Representations (ICLR 2020)*.

Takumi Ito, Tatsuki Kuribayashi, Hayato Kobayashi, Ana Brassard, Masato Hagiwara, Jun Suzuki, and Kentaro Inui. 2019. Diamonds in the rough: Generating fluent sentences from early-stage drafts for academic writing assistance. In *Proceedings of the 12th International Conference on Natural Language Generation (INLG 2019)*, pages 40–53.

Philipp Koehn. 2004. Statistical significance tests for machine translation evaluation. In *Proceedings of the 2004 Conference on Empirical Methods in Natural Language Processing (EMNLP 2004)*, pages 388–395.

John Lee and Jonathan Webster. 2012. A corpus of textual revisions in second language writing. In *Proceedings of the 50th Annual Meeting of the Association for Computational Linguistics (ACL 2012)*, pages 248–252.

Courtney Napoles, Keisuke Sakaguchi, and Joel Tetreault. 2017. JFLEG: A fluency corpus and benchmark for grammatical error correction. In *Proceedings of the 15th Conference of the European Chapter of the Association for Computational Linguistics (EACL 2017)*, pages 229–234.

Myle Ott, Sergey Edunov, Alexei Baevski, Angela Fan, Sam Gross, Nathan Ng, David Grangier, and Michael Auli. 2019. fairseq: A fast, extensible toolkit for sequence modeling. In *Proceedings of the 2019 Conference of the North American Chapter of the Association for Computational Linguistics: System Demonstrations (NAACL 2019)*, pages 48–53.

Alec Radford, Jeff Wu, Rewon Child, David Luan, Dario Amodei, and Ilya Sutskever. 2019. Language Models are Unsupervised Multitask Learners.

Thibault Sellam, Dipanjan Das, and Ankur Parikh. 2020. BLEURT: Learning robust metrics for text generation. In *Proceedings of the 58th Annual Meeting of the Association for Computational Linguistics (ACL 2020)*, pages 7881–7892.

Chung-Ting Tsai, Jhih-Jie Chen, Ching-Yu Yang, and Jason S. Chang. 2020. LinggleWrite: a coaching system for essay writing. In *Proceedings of the 58th Annual Meeting of the Association for Computational Linguistics: System Demonstrations (ACL 2020)*, pages 127–133.

Ashwin K. Vijayakumar, Michael Cogswell, Ramprasaath R. Selvaraju, Qing Sun, Stefan Lee, David J. Crandall, and Dhruv Batra. 2018. Diverse Beam Search: Decoding Diverse Solutions from Neural Sequence Models. In *Proceedings of the Thirty-Second AAAI Conference on Artificial Intelligence (AAAI 2018)*, pages 7371–7379.

Thomas Wolf, Lysandre Debut, Victor Sanh, Julien Chaumond, Clement Delangue, Anthony Moi, Pierric Cistac, Tim Rault, R'emi Louf, Morgan Funtowicz, and Jamie Brew. 2019. HuggingFace's Transformers: State-of-the-art Natural Language Processing. *arXiv preprint arXiv:1910.03771*.

Felix Wu, Angela Fan, Alexei Baevski, Yann Dauphin, and Michael Auli. 2019. Pay Less Attention with Lightweight and Dynamic Convolutions. In *Proceedings of the 7th International Conference on Learning Representations (ICLR 2019)*.

Jian-Cheng Wu, Yu-Chia Chang, Teruko Mitamura, and Jason S. Chang. 2010. Automatic Collocation Suggestion in Academic Writing. In *Proceedings of the 48th Annual Meeting of the Association for Computational Linguistics Conference Short Papers (ACL 2010)*, pages 115–119.

Seid Muhie Yimam, Gopalakrishnan Venkatesh, John Lee, and Chris Biemann. 2020. Automatic compilation of resources for academic writing and evaluating with informal word identification and paraphrasing system. In *Proceedings of the 12th Language Resources and Evaluation Conference (LREC 2020)*, pages 5896–5904.

Wanrong Zhu, Zhiting Hu, and Eric Xing. 2019. Text Infilling. *arXiv preprint arXiv:1901.00158*.

A   Details on revision model

Data.   We trained the revision model using the slightly modified version of the synthetic training data introduced in Ito et al. (2019). They created several types of synthetic training data with several noising methods; (i) heuristic noising method, (i) grammatical error generation, (iii) style removal, and (iv) entailed sentence generation. We used the data created by the heuristic noising method, style removal, and the entailed sentence generation for training the revision model. Note that we did not use the data generated by the grammatical error generation because grammatical error correction feature was implemented separately from the revision feature in Langsmith.

We attached the edit marks to the subpart of the training data generated by the style removal method. Let $x_{1:N} = (x_1, x_2, \cdots, x_N)$ and $y_{1:T} = (y_1, y_1, \cdots, y_M)$ be an input sentence with N tokens and its revision with M tokens, respectively. Here x was the synthetic draft sentence generated by the style removal method from y. The training dataset consists of the pairs of (x, y).

For each (x, y), we first determined if each word in x was rewritten compared to y. We assumed that a token $x_i \in x$ was rewritten if a token with the same lemma as x_i was not in $\{y_j | \max(0, i - 3) \leq j \leq \min(M, i + 3)\}$. Here we obtained a sequence $c \in \{0, 1\}^N$, where each element c_i corresponds to whether the token x_i was rewritten or not. If x_i was written in y, c_i is 1; otherwise c_i is 0. Then, we defined a score $r(c)$ for each (x, y) as follows:

$$r(c) = \frac{\sum_{i=1}^{N} c_i}{|c|}$$

where $|\cdot|$ returns the length of the vector. If $r(c) > 0.4$, we did not attach the edit marks.

When $r(c) \leq 0.4$, we obtained a span $s = (a, b)$ for x and c as follows:

$$\underset{(a,b)\in\mathcal{S}}{\arg\max} \quad \sum_{i=a}^{b} c_i' - \sum_{i=0}^{a-1} c_i' - \sum_{i=b+1}^{N+1} c_i'$$

$$\text{where} \quad c_i' = \begin{cases} 10 & (c_i = 1) \\ 0 & (i = 0, N + 1) \\ -1 & (\text{otherwise}) \end{cases}$$

$$\mathcal{S} = \{(a, b) \mid a, b \in 1, \cdots, N, a \leq b\}$$

Based on the obtained $s = (a, b)$, we inserted `<?` before the token x_a, and `?>` after the token x_b. We included the data with special symbols added by such a procedure in the training data.

When the users select a subsequence of a sentence in Langsmith, the edit marks are attached to the input sentence. For example, if the user selects a span "promote" in the sentence "This formulation of the input and output promotes human-computer interaction.", the input to the revision feature is formatted as follows: `This formulation of the input and output <? promotes ?> human-computer interaction.`

Model.   Table 4 shows the hyperparameters of the revision model. In the decoding phase, we used the diverse beam search (Vijayakumar et al., 2018). Beam size is set to 15. The diverse beam group and the diverse beam strength are 15 and 1.0, respectively.

Specifically, we first obtained top-15 hypotheses, and then these hypotheses were re-ranked by the language model. Here, the language model considers 20 tokens in the left context and 20 tokens in the right context beyond the sentence. We excluded the hypotheses with a perplexity greater than 1.3 times the perplexity of the input. We finally showed the top-8 revisions re-ranked to the users. The language model used for re-ranking is the same as the model used for the completion feature (Appendix B).

B   Details on completion model

Data.   We collected 234,830 PDFs of the papers published in ACL Anthology by 2019. We used GROBID[22] for extracting the text information from the PDF files. The training data is formatted as shown in Table 5. The title name is omitted with 20% probability. The order of the sections in the same paper was shuffled.

Model.   We used a pre-trained GPT-2 small (117M). Table 6 shows the hyperparameters for fine-tuning the pre-trained GPT-2. We used an implementation in Transformers (Wolf et al., 2019). We used nucleus sampling (Holtzman et al., 2020) with $p = 0.97$ to generate the texts.

C   Statistics of the drafts

Table 7 shows the statistics of the drafts collected in Section 4. The column "word type" shows the number of types of the tokens used in the drafts.

---

[22]`https://github.com/kermitt2/grobid`

Fairseq model	architecture	lightconv_iwslt_de_en
Optimizer	algorithm	Adam
	learning rate	5e-4
	adam epsilon	1e-08
	adam betas	(0.9, 0.98)
	weight decay	0.0001
	clip norm	0.0
Learning rate scheduler	type	inverse_sqrt
	warmup updates	4000
	warmup init lrarning rate	1e-7
	min learning rate	1e-9
Training	batch size	24,000 tokens
	updates	1,050,530 steps

Table 4: Hyperparameters of the revision feature.

@ Title @

* Section name
Texts in the section
. . .

* Section name
Texts in the section
⟨|endoftext|⟩

@ Title (of another paper) @
. . .

Table 5: The format of the training data for the completion model.

D   Details on the evaluation in Section 4.1

We used BLEURT-Base with 128 max tokens.[23] BLEURT is designed to evaluate the similarity of a given sentence pair. Thus, we first split each draft into sentences, and each sentence in first drafts is aligned with the most similar sentence in the corresponding final draft. Sentence splitting and sentence alignment is achieved by spaCy.[24] Note that the references has been created so that the sentence separation does not change from the original first draft. Finally, we calculate each sentence pair with BLEURT, and averaged the results.

---

[23] https://storage.googleapis.com/bleurt-oss/bleurt-base-128.zip

[24] Sentence similarity is computed using cosine similarity of average word vectors. We used spaCy's en_core_web_lg model.

Model	architecture	gpt2
Optimizer	algorithm	Adam
	learning rate	5e-5
	adam epsilon	1e-8
	adam betas	(0.9, 0.999)
	weight decay	0.0
	clip norm	1.0
Learning rate scheduler	type	linear
	warmup updates	0
	max learning rate	5e-5
	total epochs (just used for scheduling)	100
Training	batch size	262,144 tokens
	updates	138,300 steps

Table 6: Hyperparameters for fine-tuning LMs.

drafts	length	word types
Final drafts (reference)	199 ± 52	108 ± 17
HUMAN&MACHINE	192 ± 40	101 ± 17
HUMAN-ONLY	192 ± 43	100 ± 16
MACHINE-ONLY	199 ± 58	105 ± 22
First drafts	202 ± 56	104 ± 22

Table 7: Statistics of the drafts. The scores are averaged over the drafts. The values following "$\pm$" denote the standard deviation of the scores.

IsOBS: An Information System for Oracle Bone Script

Xu Han*, **Yuzhuo Bai***, **Keyue Qiu***, **Zhiyuan Liu**[†], **Maosong Sun**
State Key Lab on Intelligent Technology and Systems,
Institute for Artificial Intelligence,
Department of Computer Science and Technology, Tsinghua University, Beijing, China
{hanxu17,byz18,qky18}@mails.tsinghua.edu.cn
{liuzy,sms}@mail.tsinghua.edu.cn

Abstract

Oracle bone script (OBS) is the earliest known ancient Chinese writing system and the ancestor of modern Chinese. As the Chinese writing system is the oldest continuously-used system in the world, the study of OBS plays an important role in both linguistic and historical research. In order to utilize advanced machine learning methods to automatically process OBS, we construct an information system for OBS (IsOBS) to symbolize, serialize, and store OBS data at the character-level, based on efficient databases and retrieval modules. Moreover, we also apply few-shot learning methods to build an effective OBS character recognition module, which can recognize a large number of OBS characters (especially those characters with a handful of examples) and make the system easy to use. The demo system of IsOBS can be found from http: //isobs.thunlp.org/. In the future, we will add more OBS data to the system, and hopefully our IsOBS can support further efforts in automatically processing OBS and advance the scientific progress in this field.

1 Introduction

Oracle bone script (OBS) refers to characters carved on animal bones or turtle plastrons. To research OBS is important for both Chinese linguistic and historical research: (1) As shown in Figure 1, OBS is the direct ancestor of modern Chinese and closely related to other languages in East Asia (Xueqin, 2002). Analysis and understanding of OBS is vital for studying the etymology and historical evolution of Chinese as well as other East Asian languages. (2) As shown in Figure 2, on one OBS document carved on one animal bone or turtle plastron, the number of characters ranges from fewer than ten to more than one hundred. Besides,

as OBS is used for divination in ancient China, these documents cover a variety of topics, including war, ceremonial sacrifice, agriculture, as well as births, illnesses, and deaths of royal members (Flad et al., 2008). Therefore, OBS documents constitute the earliest Chinese textual corpora, and to analyze and understand OBS is of great significance to historical research.

Considering that it is often sophisticated and time-consuming to manually process ancient languages, some efforts have been devoted to utilizing machine learning techniques in this field. In order to detect and recognize ancient characters, Anderson and Levoy (2002); Rothacker et al. (2015); Mousavi and Lyashenko (2017); Rahma et al. (2017); Yamauchi et al. (2018) utilize computer vision techniques to visualize Cuneiform tablets and recognize Cuneiform characters, Franken and van Gemert (2013); Nederhof (2015); Iglesias-Franjo and Vilares (2016) apply similar techniques to recognize Egyptian hieroglyphs. For understanding the ancient text, Snyder et al. (2010) first show the feasibility of automatically deciphering a dead language by designing a Bayesian model to match the alphabet with non-parallel data. Then, Berg-Kirkpatrick and Klein (2011) propose a more effective decipherment approach and achieve promising results. Pourdamghani and Knight (2017) adopt a method similar to non-parallel machine translation (Mukherjee et al., 2018; Lample et al., 2018) to decipher related languages, which further inspires Luo et al. (2019) to propose a novel neural approach for automatic decipherment of Ugaritic and Linear B. Doostmohammadi and Nassajian (2019); Bernier-Colborne et al. (2019) explore to learn language models for Cuneiform Text.

These previous efforts have inspired us to apply machine learning methods to the task of processing OBS. However, there are still three main challenges:

---

* indicates equal contribution
[†] Corresponding author

Proceedings of the 2020 EMNLP (Systems Demonstrations), pages 227–233
November 16-20, 2020. ©2020 Association for Computational Linguistics

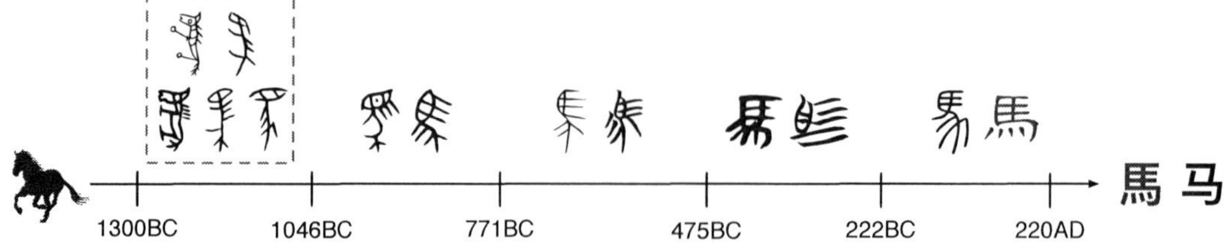

Figure 1: The historical evolution of the character "horse" from OBS to modern Chinese.

Figure 2: An example of an OBS document used in divination.

(1) Different from those ancient Greek and Central Asian scripts, in which letters are mainly used to constitute words and sentences, OBS is hieroglyphic and does not have any delimiter to mark word boundaries. This challenge also exists in modern Chinese scenarios. (2) Although OBS is the origin of modern Chinese, it is quite different from modern Chinese characters. Typically, one OBS character may have different glyphs. Moreover, there are many compound OBS characters corresponding to multiple modern Chinese words. (3) There still lacks an effective and stable system to symbolize and serialize OBS data. Most OBS data is stored in the form of unserialized bone/plastron photos, which cannot support either recognizing characters or understanding text.

The above three challenges make it difficult to use existing machine learning methods for understanding OBS, and the third one is the most crucial. To this end, we construct an information system for OBS (IsOBS) to symbolize and serialize OBS data at the character-level, so that we can utilize machine learning methods to process OBS in the future: (1) We construct an OBS character database, where each character is matched to corresponding modern Chinese character (if it has been deciphered) and incorporates a variety of its glyphs. (2) We construct an OBS document database, which stores more than 5, 000 OBS documents. We also split the images of these documents into character images, and use these character images to construct both the OBS and corresponding modern Chinese character sequences for each document. (3) We also implement a character recognition module for OBS characters based on few-shot learning models, considering there are only a handful of examples for each OBS character. Based on the character recognition module, we construct an information retrieval module for searching in character and document databases.

The databases, character recognition module, and retrieval module of IsOBS provide an effective and efficient approach to symbolize, serialize, and store the data of OBS. We believe IsOBS can serve as a footstone to support further research (especially character recognition and language understranding) on automatically processing OBS in the future.

2 Application Scenarios

As mentioned before, IsOBS is designed for symbolizing, serializing, and storing the OBS data. Hence, the application scenarios of IsOBS mainly focus on constructing databases for both OBS characters and documents, as well as implementing character recognition and retrieval modules for data search.

2.1 Character Database for OBS

In IsOBS, we construct a database to store OBS characters. For each OBS character, both its corresponding modern Chinese character (just for those OBS characters that have been deciphered) and glyph set will be stored. As shown in Figure 3, users can input a modern Chinese character to

228

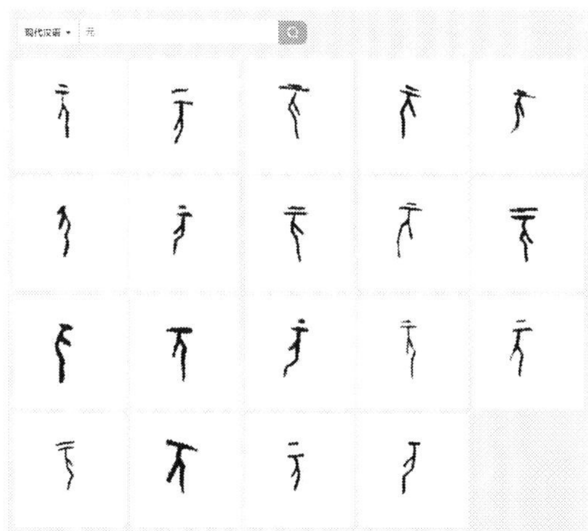

Figure 3: The example of the character database in IsOBS. Users input a modern Chinese character and get its corresponding 19 glyphs.

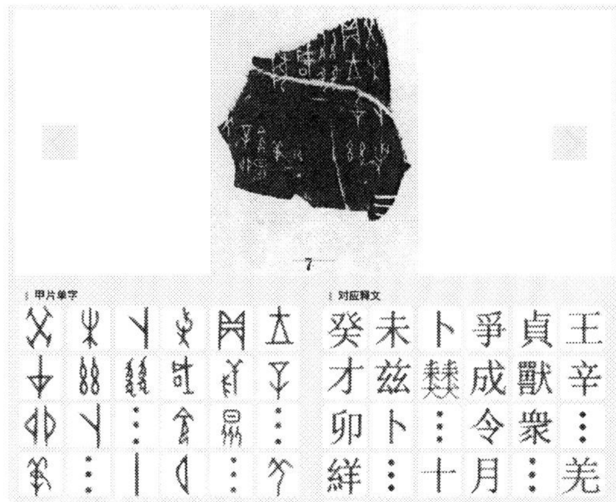

Figure 4: The example of the document database in IsOBS. Users input an identity number and get its corresponding document.

search for all glyphs of its corresponding OBS character. For those OBS characters that have no corresponding modern Chinese characters, we provide interfaces to utilize our character recognition module to search them. We will later introduce this part in more details.

2.2 Document Database for OBS

Besides the character database, we also construct a document database to store OBS documents. As shown in Figure 4, for each document in the document database, we store the image of its original animal bones or turtle plastrons, and both the OBS and modern Chinese character sequences of this document. By querying the specific identity num-

Figure 5: The example of the character recognition module in IsOBS. Users either write by hand or upload a glyph and get possible matches.

ber designated by official collections, users can retrieve the corresponding OBS document from our database. In addition, we also align the character database with the document database, thus when users input one modern Chinese character to retrieve OBS glyphs, the documents mentioning this character can also be retrieved.

2.3 Character Recognition and Information Retrieval Modules

Since OBS characters are hieroglyphs and the character-glyph mappings are quite complex, the character recognition module is thus designed to deal with these complex mappings of input glyph images to their OBS characters. As shown in Figure 5, after we input the handwritten glyph image of the character, the character recognition module returns several latent matching pairs of OBS characters and their corresponding modern Chinese characters. Users can select one matching result for the next search. We also provide other commonly used retrieval methods (e.g. index retrieval), which is helpful for users to quickly find characters and documents in our system to conduct further research.

3 System Framework and Details

In this section, we mainly focus on introducing the overall framework and details of our system, especially introducing how to construct OBS databases and build the character recognition module. The overall framework of IsOBS including all databases and modules is shown in Figure 6.

3.1 OBS Databases

Our databases are constructed from two well-known collections. One is the collection of OBS rubbings and standardized characters compiled by experts in Chinese Academy of Social Sciences (CASS) (Moruo and Houxuan, 1982), and the

Name	Number of Classes	Number of Samples	Description
oracle300	353	11586	Classes with more than 20 examples
oracle600	617	15638	Classes with more than 12 examples
oracle1600	1621	20420	Classes with more than 2 examples

Table 1: The statistics of different dataset with different character sets.

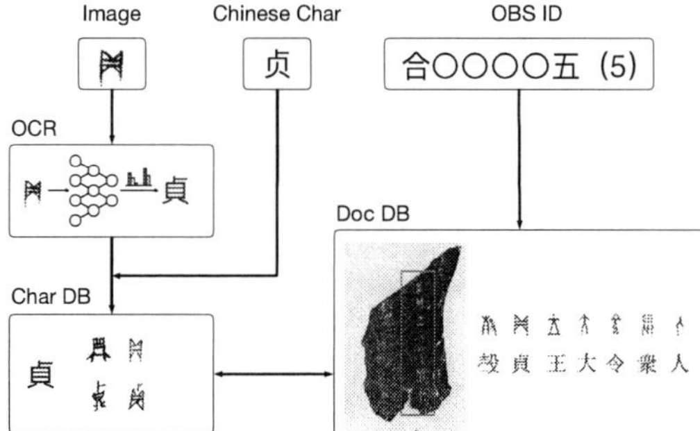

Figure 6: The overall framework of IsOBS including all databases and modules.

other one is the collection of variant written forms (glyphs) of OBS characters with their corresponding modern Chinese characters (Zhao et al., 2009).

For standardized OBS document collection, our databases now contain more than $5,000$ items, each including images of OBS rubbings, corresponding standardized OBS characters and their modern Chinese characters. Previous database platforms have not been able to cut out individual characters, making it difficult to support automatic operations. While our platform can provide finer-grained oracle data in a sequential form, which makes it easier for various electronic systems to conduct operations.

For hand-written OBS character collection, we obtain $22,161$ oracle character examples in $2,342$ classes, from which we create our dataset for training and testing our character recognition module.

3.2 Character Recognition Module

In available OBS character data, each character class usually has just a handful of examples. Due to the scarcity of OBS data, we adopt few-shot learning model for our classifier to capture the patterns from small amounts of data. Specifically, we implement prototypical network (Snell et al., 2017) for classification, which learns a non-linear mapping to embed examples into a feature space where those examples of the same class will cluster around a single prototype representation, as shown

in Figure 7.

The architecture of the prototypical network is shown in Figure 8, and we denote the prototypical network as $f_\phi : \mathbb{R}^D \to \mathbb{R}^M$ for simplicity, where ϕ is the parameters to be learned by training, D and M stand for the dimension of the input data and the dimension of the embedded features respectively.

For each class, the prototype c_i is set as the average of the embeddings of the support set, so the prototype of the class i can be denoted as $c_i = \frac{1}{n_i} \sum_{j=1}^{n_i} f_\phi(x)$, where n_i is the number of samples in the support set of the class.

For each query x, we use f_ϕ to embed the query instance, then compute the distribution of x by the softmax of euclidean distances between $f_\phi(x)$ and the prototypes of each class, in other words,

$$p_\phi(y = i|x) = \frac{\exp(-d(f_\phi(x), c_k))}{\sum_{i'} \exp(-d(f_\phi(x), c_{i'}))}.$$

Aside from prototypical network, we apply other neural networks for comparison, and finally select the most powerful one for our character recognition module. We adopt relation network (Sung et al., 2018), which is also an effective model in the area of few-shot learning, and siamese network (Chopra et al., 2005), for it is also a widely-used model in the area of character classification.

4 Experiment and Evaluation

We evaluate different character recognition models on self-created dataset. The results show that our implementation of prototypical network can achieve stable and competitive results. The datasets and source code can be found from `https://github.com/thunlp/isobs`.

4.1 Dataset

Our newly created dataset is obtained from the collection of hand-written OBS characters mentioned in 3.1. The whole dataset contains $22,161$ character images from $2,342$ classes annotated by experts in OBS character research, each class refers to a unique character and is available on our website.

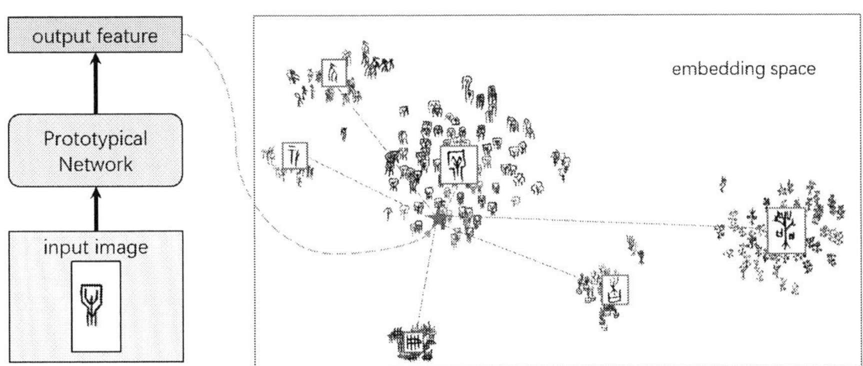

Figure 7: Illustration of prototypical network, with the glyph coordinates in space drawn by t-SNE according to $f_\phi(x)$.

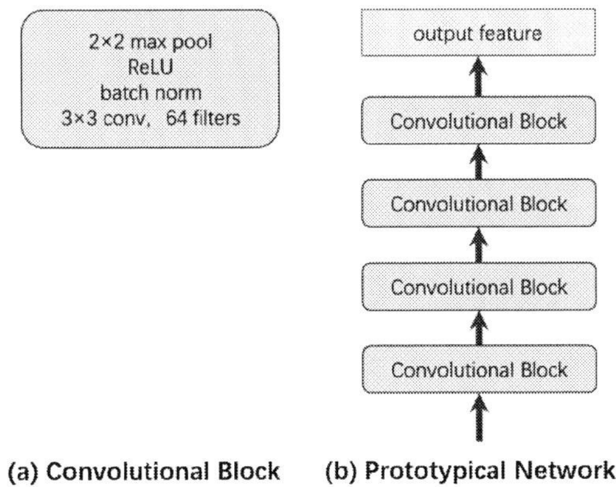

Figure 8: The architecture of prototypical network.

Each image in the dataset is 110 by 200. Considering that both the training and test set should not be empty for each class, our experiment is conducted on part of the dataset, which contains $1,621$ classes and $20,420$ character images. Due to the lack of enough few-shot training data for certain classes, we created three datasets as shown in Table 1. Each dataset is partitioned into training examples and test examples in 3 or 4 to 1 ratio.

4.2   Evaluation Metric

As mentioned above, we use prototypical network to classify OBS characters. For the training part, we use typical few-shot learning method to train the prototypical network. For the evaluation part, as aiming to evaluate the practicability of the model as an OBS character classifier, we score our model by using the top-k accuracy of the whole classification over given dataset, rather than common few-shot learning evaluation. Considering that only the

classes in oracle300 have ample data to do few-shot training, we use the training set of oracle300 to train our model, and perform classification evaluation respectively on oracle300, oracle600 and oracle1600.

4.3   Neural Network Hyper-Parameters

For the few-shot learning models, in each epoch, we train 100 steps. In each step, we randomly select 60 classes for training prototypical network, while the number of selected classes for relation network is 5. For each class, there are 5 randomly chosen support examples and 5 query examples. The learning rate is set to 0.001 at the beginning, and decreases by half for every 20 (for prototypical network) or $100,000$ (for relation network) steps. For siamese network, the learning rate is set to 0.0001, and weight-decay 0.00001.

4.4   Overall Results

Table 2 shows the overall performance of prototypical network on different datasets, and Table 3 shows the performance of different models on oracle600. From these two tables, we can find that:

(1) Prototypical network performs well on both oracle300 and oracle600, with the top-10 accuracy more than 90%.

(2) When generalized to oracle1600, which is larger and consists classes that contains scanty examples, our model still reaches 54.4% accuracy, indicating that our model works in generalized circumstance. As we just train models on oracle300 i.e, most characters in the test sets are not contained in the training set, this is a quite difficult scenario.

(3) Prototypical network notably outperforms

Dataset	hit@1	hit@3	hit@5	hit@10
oracle300	69.4	84.1	88.1	92.3
oracle600	66.0	80.7	85.1	90.0
oracle1600	54.4	69.1	73.8	78.4

Table 2: The result for prototypical network on different dataset (%).

Model	hit@1	hit@5	hit@10
Siamese Network	6.1	16.1	25.2
Relation Network	18.1	45.1	57.7
Prototypical Network	66.0	85.1	90.0

Table 3: The result for prototypical network, relation network, and siamese network on oracle600 (%).

the other two models, which might result from the high-efficiency of few-shot learning on training set with sparse examples and massive classes, as well as the transportability of prototypical network to character classification tasks. Compared to prototypical network, siamese network uses all the training set to train models, which makes it hard to converge; relation network works well on training, but its concatenation and relation modules make it difficult to transfer from few-shot learning to character classification task where the number of examples in each class varies, so the utilization rate of the extra examples is low.

Considering prototypical network outperforms other models, our character recognition module is finally based on prototypical network.

5 Conclusion and Future Work

As to research OBS is important for both Chinese linguistic and historical research, we thus construct an information system for OBS and name the system IsOBS. IsOBS provides an open digitalized platform consisting of the OBS databases, the character recognition module, and the retrieval module. The experimental results further demonstrate that our character recognition module based on few-shot learning models have achieved satisfactory performance on our self-created hand-written OBS character dataset.

In the future, we plan to explore the following directions: (1) to include more OBS document and character data from collection books into our existing databases, (2) to employ generative learning and adversarial algorithms to add more robustness to our model, and (3) to construct a language model for ancient languages. We believe that these three directions will be beneficial for ancient languages research and support further exploration of utilizing machine learning for understanding OBS.

Acknowledgments

This work is supported by the National Key Research and Development Program of China (No. 2018YFB1004503), the National Natural Science Foundation of China (NSFC No. 61732008) and Beijing Academy of Artificial Intelligence (BAAI). Bai and Qiu are supported by Tsinghua University Initiative Scientific Research Program.

References

Sean E. Anderson and Marc Levoy. 2002. Unwrapping and visualizing cuneiform tablets. *IEEE Computer Graphics and Applications*, 22(6):82–88.

Taylor Berg-Kirkpatrick and Dan Klein. 2011. Simple effective decipherment via combinatorial optimization. In *Proceedings of EMNLP*, pages 313–321.

Gabriel Bernier-Colborne, Cyril Goutte, and Serge Léger. 2019. Improving cuneiform language identification with bert. In *Proceedings of VarDial*, pages 17–25.

Sumit Chopra, Raia Hadsell, and Yann LeCun. 2005. Learning a similarity metric discriminatively, with application to face verification. In *Proceedings of CVPR*, pages 539–546.

Ehsan Doostmohammadi and Minoo Nassajian. 2019. Investigating machine learning methods for language and dialect identification of cuneiform texts. *Proceedings of NAACL-HLT*, pages 188–193.

Rowan K Flad, Sarah Allan, Rod Campbell, Xingcan Chen, Lothar von Falkenhausen, Hui Fang, Magnus Fiskesjö, Zhichun Jing, David N Keightley, Evangelos Kyriakidis, et al. 2008. Divination and power: a multiregional view of the development of oracle bone divination in early china. *Current Anthropology*, 49(3):403–437.

Morris Franken and Jan C van Gemert. 2013. Automatic egyptian hieroglyph recognition by retrieving images as texts. In *Proceedings of MM*, pages 765–768.

Estíbaliz Iglesias-Franjo and Jesús Vilares. 2016. Searching four-millennia-old documents: A text retrieval system for egyptologists. In *Proceedings of LaTeCH*, pages 22–31.

Guillaume Lample, Alexis Conneau, Ludovic Denoyer, and Marc'Aurelio Ranzato. 2018. Unsupervised machine translation using monolingual corpora only. In *Proceedings of ICLR*.

Jiaming Luo, Yuan Cao, and Regina Barzilay. 2019. Neural decipherment via minimum-cost flow: From ugaritic to linear b. In *Proceedings of ACL*, pages 3146–3155.

Guo Moruo and Hu Houxuan. 1982. *The collection of Oracle Bone scripts.*

Seyed Muhammad Hossein Mousavi and Vyacheslav Lyashenko. 2017. Extracting old persian cuneiform font out of noisy images (handwritten or inscription). In *Proceedings of MVIP*, pages 241–246.

Tanmoy Mukherjee, Makoto Yamada, and Timothy Hospedales. 2018. Learning unsupervised word translations without adversaries. In *Proceedings of EMNLP*, pages 627–632.

Mark-Jan Nederhof. 2015. Ocr of handwritten transcriptions of ancient egyptian hieroglyphic text. *Altertumswissenschaften in a Digital Age: Egyptology, Papyrology and beyond, Leipzig.*

Nima Pourdamghani and Kevin Knight. 2017. Deciphering related languages. In *Proceedings of EMNLP*, pages 2513–2518.

Abdul Monem S Rahma, Ali Adel Saeid, and Muhsen J Abdul Hussien. 2017. Recognize assyrian cuneiform characters by virtual dataset. In *Proceedings of ICTA*, pages 1–7.

Leonard Rothacker, Denis Fisseler, Gerfrid GW Müller, Frank Weichert, and Gernot A Fink. 2015. Retrieving cuneiform structures in a segmentation-free word spotting framework. In *Proceedings of HIP*, pages 129–136.

Jake Snell, Kevin Swersky, and Richard Zemel. 2017. Prototypical networks for few-shot learning. In *Proceedings of NIPS*, pages 4077–4087.

Benjamin Snyder, Regina Barzilay, and Kevin Knight. 2010. A statistical model for lost language decipherment. In *Proceedings of ACL*, pages 1048–1057.

Flood Sung, Yongxin Yang, Li Zhang, Tao Xiang, Philip HS Torr, and Timothy M Hospedales. 2018. Learning to compare: Relation network for few-shot learning. In *Proceedings of CVPR*, pages 1199–1208.

Li Xueqin. 2002. The xia-shang-zhou chronology project: methodology and results. *East Asian Archaeology*, 4(1):321–333.

Kenji Yamauchi, Hajime Yamamoto, and Wakaha Mori. 2018. Building a handwritten cuneiform character imageset. In *Proceedings of LREC 2018.*

Liu Zhao, Hong Biao, and Zhang Xinjun. 2009. *The new collection of Oracle Bone scripts.*